S0-BUH-165

AR
ANNUAL REVIEW OF
SOCIOLOGY

ANNUAL REVIEW OF SOCIOLOGY

VOLUME 18, 1992

JUDITH BLAKE, *Editor*
University of California, Los Angeles

JOHN HAGAN, *Associate Editor*
University of Toronto

ANNUAL REVIEWS INC. 4139 EL CAMINO WAY. P. O. BOX 10139. PALO ALTO, CALIFORNIA 94303-0897

AR ANNUAL REVIEWS INC.
Palo Alto, California, USA

International Standard Serial Number: 0360–0572
International Standard Book Number: 0–8243–2218-5
Library of Congress Catalog Card Number: 75-648500

♾ The paper used in this publication meets the minimum requirements of American National Standard for Information Sciences—Permanence of Paper for Printed Library Materials, ANSI Z39.48-1984.

Typesetting by Kachina Typesetting Inc., Tempe, Arizona; John Olson, President; Janis Hoffman, Typesetting Coordinator; and by the Annual Reviews Inc. Editorial Staff

PRINTED AND BOUND IN THE UNITED STATES OF AMERICA

PREFACE

With this volume, we continue our new-found tradition of a prefatory chapter by a distinguished senior sociologist. In a personal account of his intellectual and career history, Professor Hawley tell us much not only about himself but about the field. For example, the six-person department at Michigan where he earned his doctorate assuredly gave little hint of what was to come at that institution! His chapter also highlights a point found in numerous personal essays by senior sociologists—only limited information was available to help in their choice of sociology as a field. We trust that one function of the *Annual Review of Sociology* is to provide students who are making career decisions with a rapid survey of the scope and depth of sociological research and analysis.

The essays in this volume reflect the increasingly comparative nature of sociology, whether international or historical. They also provide cumulative evidence of the discipline's empirical contribution to major policy issues—population aging, homelessness, crime and deviance, fertility in the Third World. As our readers consider the essays presented here, we wish to emphasize that *Annual Review* articles differ from standard sociology articles. There must be a literature for us to review. Not infrequently, our desire to do an important *Annual Review* essay founders on the lack of research on the topic. For the literature that enables us to move ahead, we depend on our colleagues' energy and creativity.

The primary purpose of the *Annual Review of Sociology* continues to be to provide authoritative surveys of recent important sociological theory and research in specialized fields (or of recent literature from other disciplines that is important for the development of a speciality within sociology). Authors are asked to provide not annotated bibliographies but critical assessments of current work in the field surveyed. The most useful chapters both summarize past contributions and identify future directions that appear promising.

We continue our practice of identifying 12 broad categories that provide a general framework within which the review chapters can be housed. These categories serve as a heuristic device rather than a rigid structure; some topics fit into more than one category. Within this loose framework, the specific topics for review change each year.

(*Continued*)

Finally, this volume is the first in many years that will not benefit from the energy and talent of Dick Scott throughout the production process. Whether as a member of the Editorial Committee (Vols. 8–12), or as Editor (Vols. 13–17) Professor Scott's contribution has been notable. We have greatly missed it during this past year and pledge our best efforts to keep the *Review* at the level of excellence that he, and Ralph Turner before him, established.

The Editors

Annual Review of Sociology
Volume 18 (1992)

CONTENTS

(Continued)

RELATED ARTICLES FROM OTHER *ANNUAL REVIEWS*

From the *Annual Review of Anthropology*, Volume 21 (1992)

Mobility and Sedentism, R. L. Kelly
Origins and Spread of Pastoralism in Africa, A. Smith
Quantitative Methods in Archaeology, A. Ammerman
Infant Feeding Practices and Child Development, K. A. Dettwyler and C. Fishman
Sexuality and Social Relationships in Primates, B. Smuts
Language and Gender, S. McConnell-Ginet and P. Eckert
"Culture" in Studies of Cultures and Cultural Studies, D. Rajasingham

From the *Annual Review of Psychology*, Volume 43 (1992)

Common-Sense Psychology and Scientific Psychology, H. H. Kelley
Human Emotions: Function and Dysfunction, K. Oatley and J. M. Jenkins
Training and Development in Work Organizations, S. Tannenbaum and G. Yukl
Personality: Structure and Assessment, J. S. Wiggins, A. L. Pincus

From the *Annual Review of Public Health*, Volume 13 (1992)

HIV Infection and AIDS in Children, T. C. Quinn, A. Ruff, and J. Modlin
Worksite Drug Testing, D. C. Walsh, L. Elinson, and L. Gostin

ANNUAL REVIEWS INC. is a nonprofit scientific publisher established to promote the advancement of the sciences. Beginning in 1932 with the *Annual Review of Biochemistry,* the Company has pursued as its principal function the publication of high quality, reasonably priced *Annual Review* volumes. The volumes are organized by Editors and Editorial Committees who invite qualified authors to contribute critical articles reviewing significant developments within each major discipline. The Editor-in-Chief invites those interested in serving as future Editorial Committee members to communicate directly with him. Annual Reviews Inc. is administered by a Board of Directors, whose members serve without compensation.

ANNUAL REVIEWS OF
Anthropology
Astronomy and Astrophysics
Biochemistry
Biophysics and Biomolecular Structure
Cell Biology
Computer Science
Earth and Planetary Sciences
Ecology and Systematics
Energy and the Environment
Entomology
Fluid Mechanics
Genetics
Immunology
Materials Science
Medicine
Microbiology
Neuroscience
Nuclear and Particle Science
Nutrition
Pharmacology and Toxicology
Physical Chemistry
Physiology
Phytopathology
Plant Physiology and Plant Molecular Biology
Psychology
Public Health
Sociology

SPECIAL PUBLICATIONS

Excitement and Fascination of Science, Vols. 1, 2, and 3

Intelligence and Affectivity, by Jean Piaget

For the convenience of readers, a detachable order form/envelope is bound into the back of this volume.

Amos H. Hawley

Annu. Rev. Sociol. 1992. 18:1–14

THE LOGIC OF MACROSOCIOLOGY

*Amos H. Hawley**

Professor *emeritus*, University of North Carolina, Chapel Hill, North Carolina 27514

KEY WORDS: macrosociology, human ecology, social organization

---

A Biographical Note

Amos H. Hawley received his AB degree from the University of Cincinnati in 1936, and his PhD from the University of Michigan in 1941. He taught at the University of Michigan from 1941 to 1966, serving as chair of the department from 1951 to 1961. During that period he also served at various times as demographic advisor to the government of the Philippines, the Netherland Antilles, Thailand, and Malaysia. From 1966 to 1976 he was a professor of sociology at the University of North Carolina, and Kenan Professor there from 1971 to 1976. Professor Hawley is a Fellow of the American Academy of Arts and Sciences; he was president of the Population Association of America in 1971 and of the American Sociological Association in 1978. He holds a Litt. D. from the University of Cincinnati and has been the recipient of the Lynd Award from the Urban and Community Sociological Section of the ASA and of the Award for Human Ecology Contributions from Cornell University. Professor Hawley is the author of 150 papers and books.

INTRODUCTION

It will come as no surprise to anyone who has read my work to be told that I am committed to a macro view of social phenomena.[1] I'll not try to explain

*I am indebted to Everett Wilson, W. Richard Scott, John Kasarda, and Steven Appold for helpful comments in the preparation of this paper.

0360-0572/92/0815–0001$02.00

that predilection as I have very little faith in introspections of that sort. Rather I will try to trace briefly the history of my intellectual bias and then turn to a defense of that position. In this I shall regard the macro view as embodied in the concept of organization, and I shall use that concept in the broadest sense to include all forms of organization from the simplest to the most complex.

My introduction to sociology was quite fortuitous. I had returned to school at the University of Cincinnati after a three-year, Depression-induced absence, with the intention of studying English literature. Soon I began to hear enthusiastic comments about lectures being given on an intriguing subject matter by an exceptional teacher. The professor was James A. Quinn and the subject was introductory sociology. A friend persuaded me to visit the class a time or two. That I did and I found the materials and their presentation as fascinating as my friend had promised. The text was *An Introduction to the Science of Sociology,* by R. E. Park and E. W. Burgess (1921). The choice was understandable for Quinn had been a student of Park at the University of Chicago. Sociology was for me a new and exciting way of thinking about the world around me. I had not been aware of the possibility that everyday experiences could be dissected, analyzed, and shown to possess systematic properties. After staying with the introductory course as an auditor to the end of the semester, I elected to major in sociology.

It was not long before I came across C. H. Cooley's *Social Organization* (1929), and soon thereafter G. H. Mead's *Mind, Self and Society* (1934). The two volumes opened a new vista for me with their compelling arguments that so intrinsic and private a matter as one's conception of self is a product of social interaction. Thus I was predisposed very early to regard the group as the fundamental unit of collective life; only later did I come to appreciate the full implication of that position. Given the importance of interaction it seemed to me that psychology should have something to contribute to an understanding of that process. So I decided to minor in that field. But after ten or twelve course hours in psychology I found I had learned nothing useful about collective life.

At this late date I cannot say how long I would have stayed with sociology had I not discovered human ecology. For that, too, I am indebted to James Quinn. The further I had read into the literature of sociology (as of the late 1930s) the more it impressed me as a classificatory enterprise embellished here and there with philosophical speculations. By contrast, the macroscopic yet earthy point of view of human ecology, free of all psychological baggage, appealed to me greatly. Its lucid propositions, its convincing demonstration of patterns in collective life, and the seeming beauty of the analogy with the

[1]My use of "macro" is very similar to that of Smelser (1988) in that it denotes the use of organizations and networks of organizations, as opposed to psychological properties of individuals, as units of analysis.

biotic community, all derivable with a minimum of postulates about human nature, won me completely as a student and a proponent. Whatever vague notions I might have had at the outset about what to do with an undergraduate concentration in sociology crystallized in my senior year in a decision to pursue the subject in graduate school with a view toward becoming a professional sociologist. Applications for admission to the University of Chicago and the University of Michigan brought modest inducements. I opted for the latter because I had become much impressed with the writings of R. D. McKenzie, then chairman of the department at Michigan.

Graduate study at Michigan was not all I had hoped it would be. The department was small and weak. Of the six full-time staff members only two, R. C. Angell and McKenzie, provided any intellectual challenge for the student. After my first productive year with McKenzie, however, he began to show symptoms of what proved to be a degenerative disease. His activities were progressively curtailed. Midway in what was my fifth semester, McKenzie became too ill to continue. I was drafted to assume his teaching assignments—a large undergraduate course in human ecology and a graduate course in population. The experience for me was traumatic; for the students it must have been depressing. At any rate I continued teaching two courses through each of the next three semesters while working on a dissertation at odd hours. By May of 1940 I had a final draft of a dissertation in hand. Before that month was out, however, McKenzie succumbed. My dissertation committee had to be reconstituted, and a final oral was held near the end of the summer. I was then appointed an instructor in the department. Prior to that I was persuaded by Mrs. McKenzie and a vice president of the Ronald Press to finish a book on human ecology which McKenzie had contracted to do for that Press. But McKenzie's files held no part of a manuscript, only fragmentary notes and many transcribed excerpts from the publications of other authors. It was clear that I would have to proceed on my own while trying to represent McKenzie's ideas as faithfully as possible. The prospect was intimidating. Somehow I managed to finish a manuscript for the book in 1948. Two years later it was published under the title *Human Ecology: A Theory of Community Structure*.

During my graduate years and later as I worked on the human ecology manuscript, I became increasingly disenchanted with the then received conception of human ecology. The prevailing preoccupation with spatial distributions, which had attracted me at first, seemed to me a theoretical cul-de-sac. My readings of the works of bioecologists such as Elton (1927), Wheeler (1928), Braun-Blanquet (1932), Allee (1938), and others taught me that the important contribution to be gained from the analogy drawn from bioecology had been overlooked, namely, that adaptation to environment is a collective phenomenon. It is accomplished, that is, only through organization. Not only was the field thus opened to fascinating theoretical explorations, human ecology was placed squarely in the purview of sociology. Spatial analysis thus receded to a place of secondary concern as attention shifted to the study of change, structure, and functioning of the social system in an environmental context. That context comprises not only the biophysical realm but equally importantly the surrounding socio-economic-political matrix. To a considerable extent this interest is shared with sociology. Indeed, human ecology and sociology have converged more than a little.[2] A macrolevel treatment of organization and society is no longer, if it ever was, a monopoly of human ecology (cf Blau 1977, Lenski & Lenski 1987). Human ecology takes its place as one of several paradigms in the inclusive field of sociology.

AN ALTERNATIVE VIEW

A commonly used starting point in thoughts about the social system is that of an aggregate of individuals who establish interrelations, thereby forming an organized group. The group is then thought to be able to relate itself to other groups to create complex groups. In the progress from a simple aggregate to an organized group to a network of organized groups, one or more emergent properties are thought to appear. These, presumably, are relationships. Relationships are emergent because they are not inherent in the individual; they cannot be known by an examination of the individual organism. This seems to be a fair representation of how sociologists have viewed the ontogeny of societal organization. I also have held that view. I have said that human ecology is a study of how populations organize to adapt to given environments. Now I believe that such a statement, appealing as it is to common sense, puts the cart before the horse.

A more tenable assumption is that organization has precedence over the individual. All evidence points to the fact that there is no individual life—whether it be cell, organ, or organism—apart from an organization (von Bertalanffy 1952:12–14, Weiss 1971, Coleman 1971). The seemingly intangible character of organization and the obvious substantial quality of the human individual are both misleading. The comparison invites a misplacement of abstraction. The separate individual is an analytical fiction, though a very useful one. Analysis is a tactic we employ to understand what is a whole. It is used, however, always with a loss of information. To view individuals simply as biological organisms is to lose sight of the accumulation of behavior patterns they have acquired; to regard persons as independent actors is to reckon without the manifold organizational involvements in which their

[2]Namboodiri has argued persuasively that ecological-demography constitutes the core of sociology (1988).

behavior patterns are embedded. A reductionist argument, though methodologically defensible, has no theoretical support.[3]

This raises the question of what credence can be attached to the individual as a unique contributor to organization, whether as leader, scholar, inventor, or through whatever special abilities may be manifested. That there is a dualism in social situations cannot be denied. Max Weber (Gerth & Mills 1946: 253 ff) phrased it as charisma versus discipline. The prototype of discipline is bureaucracy. If these poles are ideal types, in the sense that they hold true only when all relevant variables are constant, perhaps we can substitute the variable quality of individual ability and initiative for the one, and a more adaptive concept of organization for the other. Giddens thinks of actor and organization (structure) as comprising a recursive system (1984: p. 5). Yet for all of the individual's irritability and capacity, he or she can only act in patterns and with information provided by or through organization. "No man is an island entire of itself;" said John Donne, "every man is a piece of the continent, a part of the main" (59:108). And that thought has been echoed in the works of numerous poets and novelists. But it has been left to the sociologist to explicate the foundations of that elemental principle. The difficulty with explanation in such matters lies in determining the extent to which the influences of peripheral organizations enter into the behaviors of individuals in any given organization.

It is to be noted in passing that erratic, undisciplined, and riotous action occurs where organization has been rendered ineffective. Cataclysmic events or permanent or temporary ostracisms can destroy an entire role structure or simply exclude an individual from such a structure. The consequence is a regression to extraorganizational and random behaviors. It is also possible, of course, that an organization can be so rigid as to stifle all degrees of freedom and flexibility.

In view of the argument thus far, how is one to understand the prevailing preoccupation with individuals which holds them to be prime movers in all things social? That belief is of fairly recent origin, for it was not always so. In the tribal kinship residence system, the individual is entirely possessed by the group; there is little individual life apart from a particular group and very few degrees of freedom of activity within it. The most severe penalty for transgressions of group ways is ostracism. Historically, however, dominance by a

[3]A reductionist fallacy identifies an object with its elements. Such instances, say Cohen & Nagel (1934: 383), are found in an argument that sees "scientific books as nothing but words, animate or inanimate nature as nothing but atoms, lines as nothing but points, and society as nothing but individuals, instead of holding books, nature, lines and society to be constituted by words, atoms, points and individuals, respectively, connected in certain ways." (See also Webster 1973).

single group over the individual eventually yielded to a multiplication of group influences as organizations became more numerous and complex. Boulding (1968) has said that an organizational revolution occurred in mid-nineteen century. But I believe that the process of so-called individuation began much earlier than that. Von Martin (1944) finds the beginnings in the Renaissance during which urban organization grew at the expense of feudalism.[4] Since then, of course, organizations have increased geometrically.

No one organization in the modern world can be sovereign over individual life. Instead the contemporary individual may be thought of as a locus formed at the intersection of numerous organizational ambits. In his comments on this fact Simmel confined his remarks to so-called voluntary organizations (1953). But it is also true that all other kinds of organizations intersect on individuals. Autonomy is an illusion resting on the individual's liberty to choose among organizations in which to participate. One may shop at one store or another, join or not join a club, affiliate with one church or another, or even elect the government under which to live. But the decision to participate is not an option; it is made for the person. "In the entire course of social evolution," declared Durkheim, "there has not been a single time when individuals determined by careful deliberation whether or not they would enter into the collective life or into one collective life rather than another (1958)."[5]

Nothing that has been said should be construed to mean that organization is independent of personnel or population. People of various kinds and numbers are required to staff the functional positions of organizations. But the requirement is for people of defined categories rather than for people with personal identities. Population is by way of being a necessary condition. The sufficient condition lies in the interaction of organization, population, and environment.

Given the primacy of organization the issue of emergence disappears. The disappearance is due not to an antithesis between reductionism and emergence, but to the fact that both rest on an incorrect supposition, namely, the independence of the individual. Nor does the multiplication of relations among organizations and the complexity compounded thereby revive the emergence question at a higher level.[6] What happens with added complexity is the appearance of new functions, actually subdivisions of pre-existing functions, and an elaboration of the relational network linking new to older

[4]Sir Henry Maine stated the transition in more general terms as change from status to contract. He found the uses of contract well advanced in ancient Roman law (1917).

[5]Coleman contends that a defect of a macrolevel position is that it assumes the existence of a social system as a starting point (1986, p. 1322). The same objection applies to a micro level position. In either case some unit must be assumed.

[6]On this point I differ radically from Devereaux who contends that every change in organizations is an occasion of emergence. (1940)

functions. But neither functional subdivisions nor the added relations are new qualities, as the emergence concept requires. They are rather repetitions and extensions of what is already in being.

The assumption of organization primacy and the macrolevel approach it implies should not be confused with philosophical holism. The latter argument holds that a phenomenon, and especially a social phenomenon, is to be viewed as the "totality of all the properties or aspects of a thing, and especially of all the relations holding between its constituent parts" (Popper 1957, p. 76). It follows from the holist position that wholes can only be known in their wholeness, and not through analysis of unit parts. Because it does not allow abstraction, the holist method must be that of intuition. None of this is acceptable in a macrolevel treatment of social phenomena. This position rather acknowledges the necessity for dissection and analysis of selected aspects of a whole, as is done in all scientific investigation. The constituent parts are functions or roles, relations and categories of individuals. Other abstractions, such as personalities and their components, are left to microlevel approaches. There is nothing in the discipline of sociology that I have been able to discover which enables one to identify, to say nothing of measuring, motives, values, or other internal attributes of individuals (cf Mayhew 1980).

The primacy assumption raises the nettlesome question of where or how organization originated, a familiar chicken-or-egg dilemma. To be caught up in an infinite regress promises no answer. It is enough to acknowledge: no organization, no survival. Born with no clothes, tools, or foreknowledge of any kind, the human infant is utterly dependent on others from the beginning, and it is a dependence from which he or she is never freed. The initial dependence occurs in a parent-child relationship, the most primitive form of organization, one which may owe its existence to selection. From that simple form, organizations multiplied and diversified. What the sequence might have been is unknown, for we have no natural history of organization. The sweeping homogeneity-to-heterogeneity of Spencer (1921), the equally general mechanical-to-organic solidarity of Simpson (1933), or the more elaborate classificatory schemes of anthropological evolutionists (e.g. Goldschmidt 1959) are of no great help. They describe large-scale social systems without filling in the details represented by small units of organization. A developmental or evolutionary concept should apply to organizations of all sizes. At the risk of oversimplification, it may be argued that all organizations change, whether toward expansion or contraction, with the assimilation of inputs from other organizations. Inputs in the form of techniques or ideas are in effect behavior patterns which had their prior existence as organizational components. Their assimilation in a receiving organization necessitates rearrangements of relations and other structural elements in that organization, and those alterations usually have cumulative potential. Tracing the path of organization formation and development one encounters an immediate difficulty in the marked differences among organizations. That circumstance makes a taxonomy imperative. A simple yet useful classification is composed of corporate and categoric types. Perhaps, in describing these organizational modes, I will be forgiven for repeating what I have said on more than one previous occasion (Hawley 1986, pp. 73 ff).

The corporate form of organization is composed of complementing differences or specializations. The family is the simplest and doubtless the earliest manifestation of such a unit. Its division of labor, though rudimentary, contains a principle of organization which lends itself to extensive elaboration and increases of scale. A progression from farm household to craftsman and mercantile shops to large-scale enterprise is accompanied by refinements of specialization from industry to skill to task. The multiplication of specializations orders them in transitive sequences extending through several levels of simplification. As functions increase arithmetically, relations increase geometrically.[7] Thus complexity tends to grow logistically, approaching an asymptote at which internal communication costs approximate net gains from organization. As that point on a growth curve nears, either growth ceases or a centrifugal tendency develops. In the latter case the outcome appears, on the one hand, as a departmentalization within the organization or, on the other hand, as an establishment of new units or organizations.

The categoric type of organization, adopted by units that make similar demands on environment, is the simplest of all forms of organization. It proliferates in the internal networks of corporate units. Differentiation of experiences and interests are to the differentiation of functions as woof is to warp. Such units occur as mutual aid gatherings, clubs, labor and professional associations, and social classes. They wax in the presence of a threat and wane in its absence. Where the challenge to a common interest is recurrent or continuous, the unit acquires some degree of permanence. To attain that state, however, a staff of administrators must appear, for that is not, as in the corporate unit, an intrinsic element of categoric organization. It then becomes possible to develop controls on competition for the resource on which all depend. But the administrative staff needed to mount a set of controls on

[7]James Coleman (1971, pp. 66-73) measures growth by increases in the number of links in the chains of functions from the point of origin of a material or item of information to the final consumer.

Organization ecologists have used an evolution model in studies of births and deaths of organizations in systemic environments. Competition among organizations for limited resource space results in the selection of the most fitted (e.g. Carroll 1988). To note that those studies do not reveal how organizations advance from conception to maturity does not in any way denigrate the value of that work.

competition presupposes a large membership. Increases in size bring other changes in the categoric unit. With size comes heterogeneity, for adherents have many and diverse organizational attachments. Thus the initial commonality tends to become more abstract and more vulnerable to discord. In fact one or more subdivisions of the common interest can find enough supporters to form one or more subunits within the larger unit. What may begin as a single splinter group tends to pursue an accelerating course as unit formations follow one another until the whole resembles a polyp of cells. The Reformation, as a case in point, gave rise to numerous Protestant sects; likewise, polities are often rendered into a number of partisan groups, and professional associations becomes hosts to many divisions and sections. Where on a size continuum subdivisions are most likely to occur has not been determined. Perhaps it is not until an administrative cadre is put in place, which usually lags well behind size increases, that potential subunits find a favorable environment. They can then claim their respective identities while continuing to receive administrative services. In short, it seems that a categoric type of organization can advance the incidence of organization by spawning reproductions of itself, for it too is subject to a centrifugal tendency.

Despite these differences, a kind of similarity exists among all organizations. As units, both corporate and categoric, accumulate within a network of interrelations, they tend toward structural isomorphism. That follows from two exigencies to which all are subject. First, every organization must have within its composition a function which relates it to its environment--both biophysical and ecumenic[8] environments in cases of inclusive organizations, and systemic environments where limited or specialized organizations are concerned. Second, all units of organization included in a network of interrelations must be able to participate in the flow of communications.

The first is responsible for the inescapable hierarchical arrangement of functions. Even in the most rudimentary organization, as found in temporary assemblages for mutual aid, some one function appears to define the task, set the cadence, and otherwise give direction to the environmental exchange. In more complex organizations a king, a president, or an entrepreneur stands at the head of a set of functional linkages. And every step of removal from the chief or key function in a descending chain of functions is a further step toward indirectness of relation to environment and a further diminution of the share of power in the system.[9] There is also a demographic as well as a

[8]I use ecumenic as a convenient way to refer to the total socio-cultural-economic-political universe from which influences affecting any given organization originate.

[9]This conception of the roots of inequality in a population stands in contrast to Parson's (1940, p. 843) explanation in terms of differential evaluation, and Dahrendorf's (1970, pp. 14–15) account based on the presence of norms to which sanctions are attached. In my view both of these suggestions pertain to derivative factors, that is, valuation follows power and norms are expressive of power.

functional stratification in the hierarchy. The simpler the role the larger the number of units engaged.

The second circumstance contributing to isomorphism is the mere fact of being enmeshed in a system of interrelations. Every unit so involved must be able to interact effectively with other units in the network. Thus all units tend to acquire organizational components that enable them to participate in communication flows. All become subject to financial and legal accountability. Accordingly all avail themselves of accounting, legal, personnel, and communication services. Where the units of organization attain large size, they can include appropriate specialists in their work forces. Large businesses, industries, educational institutions, churches, and charitable agencies converge upon a common form. The standardizing effects of communication are reinforced further by competition. Units competing for the same clientele or resource arrange their organizations to accommodate to the circumstances attending the clientele or resource on which all depend. They adopt similar technologies and employ similar specialists.

Relations between organizations parallel those within organizations. That is, some organizations are connected through their complementary differences, i.e. symbiotically, others on the basis of their similarities. Illustrative of the first is the essential operating structure of an urban community. It consists in a set of more or less specialized units of organization, constituting a network of exchange relations. Lesser networks within the larger one are represented, for example, by the social service sector, by the legal establishment, and by industrial complexes, each composed of several specialized functional agencies. On the other hand, linkages form among units engaged in similar activities such as associations of merchants, of manufacturers, of fraternal lodges, and of educational institutions. These coalescences are addressed to the control of competition and to coaction as lobbies for particular legislation or other advantages.

Networks and associations are mutually advantageous to their members. But mutuality does not necessarily mean equality. "It is a basic property of nature. . .," said Margalef, "that any exchange between two systems of differing information content does not result in a partition or equalizing of the information, but increases the differences. The system with more accumulated information becomes still richer from the exchange" (1968, pp. 16–17). The relations of parts suppliers to a manufacturing firm, of local to national governments, of individual chapters to the central office of an interregional association would seem to be of the order described by Margalef. The relations in these examples seem to correspond to those between specialist and generalist organizations as discussed by Hannan & Freeman (1977). Generalist organizations are more strategically located in an information and energy network and therefore are in command of greater resources.

A correlation of organizational complexity and population size has been suggested in one or two prior references. To be more specific, in organized populations of comparable size and technological sophistication equal amounts of diversity or specialization are to be expected. Although the number of small and large units of organization may vary as between populations, the total volume of organization tends toward parity. Stated differently, the person-hours devoted to retailing, transportation, communication, professional services, and other specialized activities approach an equivalent number regardless of the different scales of units. There is a circularity here which should be acknowledged inasmuch as a unitary population is defined by the scope of its inclusive organization. And technology and organization are so intimately connected that they can be regarded as different aspects of the same thing. Yet there is something to be gained from making explicit what might otherwise be overlooked.

In opposing organization and individual as I have been doing in this discussion, one should be prepared to speak to the question of whether an organization is capable of acting as a unit. Charles Tilly raised that issue some time ago in a paper titled "Do Communities Act?" (1973) His answer confirmed an affirmative opinion expressed earlier by Homans (1950, p. 319). Certain conditions, however, are required, said Tilly. Those are (i) there is homogeneity with reference to the main divisions of power; (ii) costs of communication rise rapidly with distance; and (iii) control over land is valued but uncertain. The conception of community to which these conditions pertain refers to what is commonly recognized as a neighborhood association, a localized residence group mobilized to oppose some form of undesirable encroachment, in other words, a categoric group. As is well known, however, the neighborhood association seldom lasts beyond the removal of a given threat. All organizations founded on some particular homogeneity demonstrate a capacity for unified action as long as a threat to a common interest lasts. They lose that ability more often than not when the challenge is no longer present. What Tilly neglected to include in his statement of requirements for unitary action is a division of labor, transitory though it may be, especially a centralization of coordinating responsibility together with some supporting functions.[10]

The corporate organization also acts as a unit. it produces a more complicated product or service than individuals acting separately can accomplish, and it can do so repeatedly and continuously. No one who has experienced a

[10]The Townsend movement is an interesting case of an organization which emerged in the 1930s to promote the common needs of older people. But with the passage of social security legislation it lost its reason for being. Its administrative staff then sought to convert the organization to an enterprise for door-to-door sales. The rapid decline of membership spelled failure for that effort (Messenger 1955).

philharmonic orchestra performing a Beethoven symphony can doubt the capacity for unit behavior. In contrast to the organization based on homogeneity which can only produce energy additively, the corporate unit generates energy multiplicatively as its organization takes form. Its formation is accompanied by negative entropy or, stated in the parlance of economics, there are economies of scale. That is due in part to its ability to employ highly capitalized technologies. And that, in turn, is supported by the relative permanence of corporate organization. Its longevity over-reaches that of its personnel; individuals come and go, but the structure remains in place. In affording continuity through time, organization makes history possible. Not only is time economized, it is extended.

Organizational economies have the further effect of producing substitutes for population. Increased output per worker means fewer workers per unit of product. That can translate eventually into reductions in the proportion of a population engaged in the labor force. Thus population size tends to lose its relevance as an indicator of economic potential, for smaller numbers can produce equivalent products.[11] The matter is complicated, moreover, by the tendencies of organizations to extend their scopes beyond the boundaries of governmental jurisdictions. The demographic basis of industrial organization, for example, has shifted historically from a local to an urban, a regional, a national, and finally to an international population. Consequently the relation of a politically bounded population to the producing sector of its economy has become exceedingly difficult to measure. Measurement requires a determination of the contribution of a local labor force to the gross product of the international economy.

I have spoken of organization growth as a progression on a logistic curve, running its course as it nears an asymptote formed at the point where inputs and outputs are equal. Improvements of organization cause the asymptote to shift farther away from the point of origin. There are occasions, however, in which the asymptote is moved toward the starting point, that is, organizations sometimes decline. While growth rests on an excess of inputs over outputs (revenues over costs), decline occurs when the ratio is reversed, when outputs exceed inputs. That can come about through an exhaustion of resources, a depletion of population below labor power needs, technological changes occurring elsewhere which render a given organization obsolete, or over-expansion that leads to administrative costs in excess of returns from production.[12] How much decline will occur depends on the amount of discrepancy between input and output and the level of inputs. Where the disparity is small the decline is apt to be short-lived. But where the discrepancy is large

[11]It may be noted, too, that with technological advances brought about by organization development, longevity increases constitute substitutes for births, for fewer births are needed to produce a given number of person-years of life.

[12]The consequences of over-expansion are not found only in political units. Wilson (1985) has

the decline tends to be extensive. And should the inputs from resource reserves be too small, it may be impossible to arrest decline. Barring that contingency, decline will cease when the input-output balance is restored. An equilibrium, however, is unlikely to be more than temporary.[13]

CONCLUSION

Now it is reasonable to ask: What is the utility of a macrolevel view of social phenomena? My answer is that in most respects it makes good sociological sense. The origins of virtually all societal problems are traceable to organizational malfunction or nonfunction. Crime, poverty, pollution, and political disorder are to be understood in such terms, the tendency to attribute such events to motives or meannesses in persons notwithstanding. Although it may be expedient in some instances to hold individuals accountable, as in the applications of laws, that is usually in default of a means for holding organizations responsible. The despot, the exploiter, the racial discriminator, the insurrectionist is invariably the spokesman for an organization. There is thus a justification for allowing an analytical position to serve as a guideline in policy formation.

There is also a potential disutility in the macrolevel point of view. It can encourage an uncritical application of a general principle to policy issues. It can lend support to what Popper calls "the totalitarian intuition" (1957, p. 97). Policies designed to impose a rigid order on society and thereby eliminate individual freedom can be rationalized on such a basis. But well short of that extreme are many political decisions that override individual considerations, some benign, others malignant. Among the first are such practices as graduated taxation, compulsory education, and eminent domain. On the other hand, legally sanctioned racial discrimination and institutionalized absolutism of whatever kind are malignant from the standpoint of both the individual and the body politic. Perhaps the best protection against misapplication of the macrolevel perspective is the maintenance of social system openness. That calls for unrestricted freedom of discourse within and between polities. For then frequent challenges and incursions from without and a resulting competition among organizations may prevent any organization from gaining dominance in affairs outside its immediate responsibility.

described in perceptive detail a similar outcome in an academic institution. Centrifugal forces already at work in the professionalization of faculty qualifications lost their unifying counterpoise as a result of a reckless creation of multiple campuses coupled with unwise admission policies and neglect of the central mission of the institution. The result was a decline of a once distinguished educational institution to a fraction of its former size and a corresponding attrition in its quality.

[13]Gordon Childe's studies of ancient empires (1946, p. 267) led him to the conclusion that there was no middle position between growth and decline; when one ceases the other begins.

Literature Cited

Allee, W. C. 1938. *The Social Life of Animals*. New York: W. W. Norton

Blau, P. 1977. A macrosociological theory of social structure. *Am. J. Sociol.* 83:26–54

Boulding, K. 1968. *The Organizational Revolution: A Study in the Ethics of Economic Organization*. Chicago: Triangle

Braun-Blanquet, J. 1932. *Plant Sociology*. (Trans. G. D. Fuller, H. S. Conrad). New York: Macmillan

Carroll, G. R. ed. 1988. *Ecological Models of Organization*. Cambridge, Mass: Ballenger

Childe, G. 1946. *What Happened in History*. New York: Pelican

Cohen, M. R., Nagel, E. eds. 1934. *An Introduction to Logic and Scientific Method*. New York: Harcourt, Brace

Coleman, J. S. 1971. Social systems. In *Hierarchically Organized Systems in Theory and Practice,* ed. by P. A. Weiss New York: Hafner

Coleman, J. S. 1986. Social theory, social research and a theory of action. *Am. J. Sociol.* 91:1309–35

Cooley, C. H. 1929. *Social Organization*. New York: Scribners

Dahrendorf, R. 1970. On the origin of inequality among men. In *The Logic of Social Hierarchies,* ed. by E. 0. Laumann, P. M. Siegel, R. Hodge, pp. 3–30. Chicago: Markham

Devereaux. G. 1940. Conceptual scheme for society. *Am. J. Sociol.* 45:687–706

Donne, J. 1959. *Devotions, upon Emergent Occasions XVII*. Ann Arbor, Mich: Univ. Mich. Press

Durkheim, E. 1938. *The Rules of Sociological Method,* Transl. S. A. Solovay, J. C. Mueller. Glencoe, Ill: Free Press. 8th ed.

Elton, C. 1927. *Animal Ecology*. New York: Macmillan

Gerth, H., Mills, C. W. eds. 1946. *From Max Weber: Essays in Sociology*. New York: Oxford

Giddens, A. 1984. *The Constitution of Society*. Berkeley, Calif: Univ. Calif. Press

Goldschmidt, W. 1959. *Man's Way: A Preface to an Understanding of Human Society*. New York: Holt, Rinehart & Winston

Hannan, M. T., Freeman, J. 1977. The population ecology of organizations. *Am. J. Sociol.* 82:929–64

Hawley, A. H. 1986. *Human Ecology: A Theoretical Essay*. Chicago: Univ. Chicago Press

Homans, G. C. 1950. *The Human Group*. New York: Harcourt, Brace

Lenski, G., Lenski, J. 1987. *Human Societies: An Introduction to Macrosociology*. New York: McGraw-Hill. 5th ed.

Maine, H. 1917. *Ancient Law*. London: Everyman

Margalef, R. 1968. *Perspectives in Ecological Theory*. Chicago: Univ. Chicago Press

Mayhew, B. H. 1980. Structuralism versus individualism: Part I. Shadow-boxing in the dark. *Soc. Forces* 59:335–75

Mead, G. H. 1934. *Mind, Self and Society*. Chicago: Univ. Chicago Press

Messenger, S. 1955. Organizational transformation: a study of a declining social movement. *Am. Sociol. Rev.* 20:3–10

Namboodiri, K. 1988. Ecological demography: its place in sociology. *Am. Sociol. Rev.* 53:619–33

Parsons, T. 1940. An analytical approach to the theory of stratification. *Am. J. Sociol.* 45:841–62

Popper, K. R. 1957. *The Poverty of Historicism*. New York: Harpers

Simmel, G. 1955. Conflict. The Web of Group Affiliation. Transl. K. Wolf, R. Bendix. Glencoe, Ill: Free Press

Simpson, G. 1933. *Emile Durkheim on the Division of Labor in Society*. New York: Macmillan

Smelser, N. J. 1988. Social structure. In *Handbook of Sociology,* ed. N. J. Smelser, pp. 9–19. Beverly Hills, Calif: Sage

Spencer, H. 1921. *The Principles of Sociology,* Vol. 1. New York: Appleton-Century-Crofts

Tilly, C. 1973. Do communities act? *Sociol. Enquiry* 43:200–9

von Bertalanffy, L. 1952. *Problems of Life*. New York: Harpers

von Martin, A. 1944. *Sociology of the Renaissance*. London: Kegan Paul

Webster, M. 1973. Psychological functionalism, methodological individualism and large scale problems. *Am. Sociol. Rev.* 43:258–73

Weiss, P. A. 1971. Some basic principles of hierarchic systems. In *Hierarchically Organized Systems in Theory and Practice,* ed. by P. A. Weiss, pp. 1–44. New York: Hafner

Wheeler, W. M. 1928. *The Social Insects*. New York: Harcourt, Brace

Wilson, E. K. 1985. What counts in the death or transformation of an organization. *Soc. Forces* 64:259–79

Annu. Rev. Sociol. 1992. 18:15–38

SOCIAL STRESS: THEORY AND RESEARCH

Carol S. Aneshensel

Department of Community Health Sciences, School of Public Health, University of California, Los Angeles, California 90024-1772

KEY WORDS: stress-reactivity, social support, coping, mental health

Abstract

This chapter differentiates the stressful consequences of social organization from the stressful antecedents of psychological disorder. The pivotal distinction concerns whether the occurrence of stressors is viewed as socially determined, or as independent of social placement. Recent research is evaluated concerning both the social distribution of stress and social variation in response to stress. Two particularly productive areas of inquiry are also reviewed: self-efficacy as a mediator between social position and stress; and the intersection of macro- and micro-stress processes in economic and occupational spheres, with emphasis upon gender stratification. This review concludes that the occurrence of systemic stressors is not necessarily an indication of a social system run amok but may reflect instead the system functioning precisely as it is supposed to function.

INTRODUCTION

Stress research typically is viewed as a subspecialty within medical sociology, a perspective that obscures commonalities with more traditional sociological areas of inquiry, especially social stratification. This situation has arisen, at least in part, because stress researchers have adopted ways of organizing

0360-0572/92/0815-0015$02.00

theory and research more relevant to medicine than sociology. For example, stress research tends to be concerned less with the origins of stressful life experience than with the consequences of such experiences for outcomes of illness, especially psychological disorder (Pearlin 1989). Matters of structure, organizations, roles, and other social constructs often are superimposed upon such disease-oriented models.

A pivotal distinction between sociological and clinical orientations is whether stressors are conceptualized as socially patterned or as independent of location in the social system. In crude analytic terms, whether stressors are treated as intervening or independent variables. I use these analytic labels to distinguish models of the stressful consequences of social organization from models of the social antecedents of psychological disorder (Aneshensel et al 1991).

This essay clarifies how social organization matters to the origins and consequences of stressful life experience. First, an overview of the current status of the field is presented as a framework for examining selected issues in stress research. The next two sections contrast twin themes concerning the social distribution of stress versus social variation in response to stress. Two particularly productive areas of inquiry are then reviewed: self-efficacy as a mediator between social position and stress; and the intersection of macro- and micro-stress processes in the economic and occupational spheres, with emphasis upon gender stratification. This review advances the perspective that stress is an inevitable consequence of social organization.

OVERVIEW

Conceptualizations of stress usually emphasize the following elements: a state of arousal resulting either from the presence of socioenvironmental demands that tax the ordinary adaptive capacity of the individual or from the absence of the means to attain sought-after ends (Lazarus 1966, Pearlin 1983, Menaghan 1983). External circumstances that challenge or obstruct are labeled stressors; stress refers to internal arousal. Thus, stress is not an inherent attribute of external conditions, but emanates from discrepancies between those conditions and characteristics of the individual—his or her needs, values, perceptions, resources, and skills. In an analogy to engineering physics, Smith (1987) maintained that stress should be assessed not merely as load, but as load relative to the supporting surface.

Socioenvironmental conditions differ in the capacity to evoke stress, however; some conditions threaten virtually everyone, whereas others are uniformly navigated with ease. This principle is illustrated by the various strategies developed to weight life events according to the average amount of readjustment required (e.g. Dohrenwend et al 1978). Events differ from one another in average ratings, due to characteristics of the event, and ratings of a single event differ across raters, due to characteristics of the rater. The presence of both inter-event and intra-event variation mirrors the interplay of person and environment.

Stress research continues to emphasize one particular type of stressor, life-event change. This emphasis has persisted despite long-standing, cogent criticism that enduring problems of ordinary social life have been neglected, a theme elaborated below. B.S. Dohrenwend and associates (1978) defined life-event stressors as objective occurrences of sufficient magnitude to change the usual activities of most persons. The initial conceptualization of any change as stress-provoking has given way to agreement that undesirable events are most psychologically distressing; other dimensions such as whether events can be controlled or predicted are of secondary importance (Ross & Mirowsky 1979, Thoits 1983).

The deleterious health effects of life change are of consistently modest magnitude; few who encounter life events suffer ill health as a result. Kessler and associates (1985) described several strategies used to address an assumed problem of measurement-error attenuation: specifying especially stress-provoking events, assessing duration and recency of exposure, and specifying context. Improved measures, however, have not increased noticeably the association between events and psychological distress (Thoits 1983). Consequently, attention has shifted to social psychological factors regulating the impact of stress (Kessler et al 1985).

Most prominent is the concept of social support. Definitions of support abound, but most include whether a person's basic social needs—affection, esteem, approval, belonging, identity and security—are satisfied through interaction with others (Cobb 1976, Thoits 1982). House & Kahn (1985) have identified three distinct dimensions: integration, the existence of relations; networks, their structure; and support systems, their socioemotional, instrumental, informational, and appraisal dimensions.

Social support, especially socioemotional support, is related inversely to diverse forms of psychological disorder, physical morbidity, and mortality (e.g. Turner 1981, Aneshensel & Stone 1982, Turner 1983, Kessler & McLeod 1985, Wethington & Kessler 1986, House et al 1988, Moen et al 1989, Ross & Mirowsky 1989). Longitudinal studies demonstrate reciprocal relationships: causal influence goes from support to mental health and vice versa (Turner 1981, Aneshensel & Huba 1984). A major emphasis concerns whether social support acts as a stress-buffer, ameliorating the deleterious effects of stress (Dean & Lin 1977). In reviewing this contradictory literature, Kessler & McLeod (1985) concluded that the mental health impact of stress is buffered by emotional and perceived social support, but not by membership in social networks.

Research concerning the nature and effectiveness of coping also has proliferated over the past decade. Folkman & Lazarus (1980) defined coping as cognitive and behavioral efforts made to master, tolerate, or reduce external and internal demands and conflicts. Coping behavior differs from coping resources, that is, from preexisting assets such as self-esteem called upon when stress does arise. Functions of coping include avoiding or eliminating the stressor, containing the proliferation of secondary stressors, altering the meaning of the situation, and managing states of arousal (Pearlin & Schooler 1978, Pearlin & Aneshensel 1986). Folkman & Lazarus (1980) categorized coping as problem-focused versus emotion-focused.

Coping and social support are functionally isomorphic concepts. For example, Thoits (1984) conceptualized social support as coping assistance. Coping refers to actions taken in one's own behalf, whereas support refers to actions undertaken by another person. Coping and social support perform parallel functions, influencing the occurrence and impact of stressful life experience (Pearlin & Aneshensel 1986).

THE SOCIAL DISTRIBUTION OF STRESS

Conceptual Issues

A core issue is whether distributions of stressors vary across social strata as a result of some causal link between social location and stressors. Sociological interest in stress was fueled by findings of an inverse relationship between mental disorder and social class. Proponents of early social causation perspectives reasoned that low-status social groups showed high rates of disorder because members of these groups disproportionally encountered difficult, harsh, or traumatic life conditions. Elevated rates of disorder also were attributed to restricted group access to social, economic, or personal resources—assets used to combat difficult life circumstances (e.g. Dohrenwend & Dohrenwend 1969). The major alternatives are social drift and social selection hypotheses: psychological disorder produces downward social mobility or selection out of social roles. With the possible exception of severe disorders such as schizophrenia, the empirical evidence supports the hypothesis of social causation (Mechanic 1972, Liem & Liem 1978, Wheaton 1978, Eaton 1986, Fox 1990).

The structural perspective on social causation understands stress both as a consequence of location in the social system and as a determinant of some outcome, most typically psychological distress. The focal relationships are between social position and psychological distress; stressful life experience is but one pathway linking structure to emotional well-being. This research agenda emphasizes specification of these pathways, including the conditions under which relationships occur. Also, these relationships may be universal or apply to only some subgroups of the population. In sum, location in the social system influences the probability of encountering stressors, which in turn increase the probability of becoming emotionally distressed; these relationships may occur only among some groups, or only under certain conditions.

When stress is conceptualized as an independent variable, however, the focal relationships are between stress and psychological distress. Social attributes are controlled to eliminate spurious relationships between stress and health. This approach assumes that social attributes do not directly or indirectly cause psychological distress (cf Rosenberg 1968). For example, covariation may reflect common causation. In this approach, the oft-unrecognized assumption is that variation in the distribution of stressors across social strata is happenstance.

Life Events

Do distributions of stressors vary meaningfully across strata? The response to this query depends quite simply upon how stressors are conceptualized and operationalized. Dohrenwend & Dohrenwend (1969) proposed that social class differences in rates of life-event change generate corresponding class differences in rates of psychological impairment. They found instead class differences in the psychological impact of similar levels of life change. B.S. Dohrenwend (1970, 1973, 1977, 1978) found that group differences in events are limited to select categories of events and specific social attributes. Many recent inquiries have adopted Kessler's (1979a) technique for decomposing group differences in distress into components due to differential exposure to stress, differential vulnerability to stress, both, or neither. In an early application, Kessler (1979b) concluded that differential exposure contributes little to social class, gender, and marital status differences, except in the case of nonwhites compared to whites. Two recent reviews have concluded that social group differences in overall exposure to life change are minimal (Thoits 1987, Kessler et al 1985).

The most critical issue concerning the validity of these conclusions is whether events have been selected properly from the universe of all possible events. Life-event checklists have suffered from a number of methodological deficiencies enumerated comprehensively elsewhere (e.g. Dohrenwend et al 1978, Thoits 1983). For present purposes, the most important concern is whether event inventories represent adequately the entire spectrum of life events, given that no finite measure can count all possible events (Tausig 1982). Dohrenwend and associates (1978) stated this problem as defining the "population" of events from which a "sample" of events is selected. Events should be selected with probabilities proportional to a meaningful criterion. In practice, events usually are selected in an arbitrary manner.

The pool of selected events may disproportionally represent events more likely to occur to some social groups than others. This problem is analogous to bias in academic ability tests: content validity is suspect unless the pool of test items constitutes a representative sample of the performance domain shared in common by various subgroups of the population (American Psychological Association 1974). Thoits (1983) reviewed the content validity of event inventories and concluded that the universe of events has not been sampled uniformly. Specifically, events occurring to young adults have been oversampled, while those occurring to women, minorities, and the poor have been undersampled. Golding and associates (1991) found that conclusions about ethnic variation in exposure are contingent primarily upon which events are counted. The strategy used to select events predetermines the observed social distribution. This conclusion applies to counts of all events or specific types of events, e.g. social network events. Consequently, the arbitrary "sampling" of events impinges substantially upon inferences regarding differences among social groups in exposure to life events.

Chronic Stressors

Life-event change illuminates only one tiny corner of the universe of social stressors; omitted are problematic life circumstances that recur or persist. According to Pearlin (1975a, 1983, 1989), the major precursors of distress are more likely to occur in the conflicts and frustrations experienced by ordinary people doing ordinary things than in exotic, ephemeral, or once-in-a-lifetime events. Liem & Liem (1978) criticized conclusions about social class for failing to consider the chronicity of stressors among lower social classes, such as lengthy unemployment among working-class men. Reliance upon the deceptively simple measurement strategy of event inventories has been described as a methodological expedient: chronic stressors are more difficult to assess because such problems often are subjective in nature (Eckenrode 1984, Kessler et al 1985, Pearlin 1989).

Nonetheless, a considerable accumulation of evidence links persistent and recurrent stressors to psychological distress, physical morbidity, and mortality (Liem & Liem 1978, Pearlin et al 1981, Wheaton 1983, Ross & Huber 1985, House et al 1986). Also, life events produce persistent elevations in psychological distress only when the events themselves are persistent or recurrent (Aneshensel 1985, Lin & Ensel 1984, Norris & Murrell 1987). According to Avison & Turner (1988), chronic strains, event-related stressors, and time-ambiguous events all contribute independently to depressive symptomatology, but chronic strains are most potent. The relative impact of stressors may vary across the life course, however, with chronic stress most important among the elderly, and acute stress most important at younger ages (Turner & Noh 1988).

Several distinct sources of chronic stress have been identified. Wheaton (1983) delineated the following: barriers in the achievement of life goals; inequity in the form of inadequate rewards relative to invested effort or qualifications; excessive or inadequate environmental demand; frustration of role expectations; and resource deprivation. Chronic stressors also include difficulties associated with participation in institutionalized roles (Pearlin 1983); enduring interpersonal difficulties (Avison & Turner 1988); status inconsistency, goal-striving stress, and life-style incongruity (Dressler 1988); disjunction of economic goals and educational means (Farnworth & Lieber 1989); social and economic hardship including poverty, crime, violence, overcrowding, and noise (Pearlin & Lieberman 1979, Eckenrode 1984), homelessness (La Gory et al 1990), and chronic physical disability (Turner & Noh 1988).

Role occupancy is a necessary but not sufficient condition of role strain. Instead, stress arises as a consequence of the experiences entailed in the enactment of a role. For example, Pearlin (1975a) argued that men and women may occupy the same role, such as worker, but be exposed to different constraints and imperatives as a consequence of gender stratification. The dimensions of ongoing role strain include difficulty in satisfying role demands, interpersonal conflict with others in the role set, incompatible demands across roles, role captivity, gains or losses of roles, and restructuring of continuing roles (Pearlin 1983). Women, the young, and those of low socioeconomic status encounter the most severe role strains (Pearlin & Lieberman 1979).

Economic strains—particularly potent contributors to psychological distress—bear an obvious relationship to structure via dependency upon income. Ross & Huber (1985) found that family income is not the sole determinant of economic hardship among married couples. Being young, having young children, and having little education increase economic strains, as does being nonwhite, at least among husbands. Poverty and lack of education have a synergistic effect on economic hardship, especially among women: compared to the better educated, the poorly educated need more money to fend off economic hardship.

Inconsistency of social standing can be a structural source of stress in itself. Dressler (1988) distinguished three forms of inconsistency involving disparate dimensions of status: status inconsistency (discrepancy between occupation and income), goal-striving stress (discrepancy between aspirations and achievements), and life-style incongruity (consumption patterns and cosmopolitan behaviors inconsistent with social class). The latter is the best predictor of depression among southern blacks, although there are life-course differences: the effects of life-style incongruity and goal-striving stress are most pronounced among young persons, while status inconsistency has a greater effect among older persons. Dressler maintained that any social group with limited access to socially valued goals will seek social status through conspicuous consumption: life-style incongruity arises whenever upward mobility is prevented.

Pearlin (1975b) demonstrated that status inconsistency among spouses is problematic only for those who value upward social mobility. People to whom status advancement is important and who have married mates of lower social status origins are apt to experience disruptions of reciprocity, expressiveness, affection, and value sharing within the marital exchange. Neither status heterogamy by itself nor status striving by itself produces marital stress; rather, it is the confluence of these two conditions. The effects of status inequality persist over lengthy marriages, even among those who have experienced mobility after marriage.

Duration Versus Structure

The categorization of stressors as chronic or acute is artificial, often inaccurate, and generally counterproductive. The distinction refers solely to the duration of exposure to the stressor, not to the length of its effect (Wheaton 1983). Duration of exposure is more often assumed than assessed: numerous events are not "eventful" at all, but unfold over long periods of time (Avison & Turner 1988). Also, life events tend to be stable over time, reflecting ongoing social, economic, and psychological determinants (Aneshensel & Frerichs 1982, Norris & Murrell 1987, Turner & Noh 1988, McFarlane et al 1983). Moreover, acute and chronic stressors often are related. Pearlin and associates (1981), for example, found that ongoing difficulties in social role enactment are both a product of eventful change and a pathway through which events damage emotional well-being. Similarly, Eckenrode (1984) found events alter patterns of daily living.

Acute events and chronic strains have come to stand as proxies for several attributes of stressors other than duration, and it is these other attributes that warrant attention. Acute stressors usually are equated with objective, discrete events that are not the result of the individual's psychological functioning. Chronic stressors, in contrast, are seen as subjective, influenced by emotional functioning, and lacking a clear origin in time (Kessler et al 1985).

The pivotal issue concerns the treatment of occurrences partially or wholly the responsibility of the person affected. These occurrences usually are excluded from event inventories for purposes of measurement purity. This set of events, however, overlaps substantially with the set of socially caused events. This exclusionary strategy, therefore, has had the unintended consequence of removing the concept of stress from social structure and processes (Wheaton 1990, Aneshensel et al 1991). The very nature of most chronic stressors as on-going social, economic, and personal circumstances usually means that the individual is an active participant in the origin or maintenance of the problem. The inclusion of such circumstances introduces possible measurement contamination by other constructs, such as psychological disorder. The expedient solution of restricting measures of stress to fateful events appears methodologically rigorous, but sacrifices many of the most theoretically meaningful social elements within the universe of stress.

This universe encompasses a spectrum of causal possibilities ranging from random misfortune through systemic adversity. This universe is cross-cut by the duration of exposure dimension, but both acute and chronic stressors may be random or systemic. Descriptions of the social distribution of stress remain equivocal because random and systemic stressors have been merged indiscriminately. The core task, I submit, is to identify those types of stressors that arise as a consequence of social organization.

SOCIAL VARIATION IN RESPONSE TO STRESS

Group Differences in Vulnerability

The failure of life events to account for group differences in psychological distress, the exposure hypothesis, focused attention on stress-reactivity, the vulnerability hypothesis (Kessler et al 1985). Kessler's (1979a) analytic technique ignited interest in intergroup variation in vulnerability. Mixed results have been reported for gender, race, social class, and marital status (e.g. Myers et al 1975, Pearlin & Johnson 1977, Kessler 1979b, Kessler & Essex 1982, Wheaton 1982, Kessler & McLeod 1984, Kessler & Neighbors 1986, Neff 1985, Newmann 1986, Thoits 1987, Turner & Avison 1989, Turner & Noh 1983, McLeod & Kessler 1990). Vulnerability typically is operationalized, in essence, as group differences in the coefficient for psychological distress regressed upon a stressor. Equating differential vulnerability with differences in the impact of stress upon a single outcome is problematic because the effects of stress are nonspecific (Aneshensel et al 1991). The central difficulty with vulnerability research is not the restricted range of stressors considered, as in the previous section, but rather the restricted range of outcomes.

In an influential study, Kessler & McLeod (1984) reported a female preponderance of psychological distress resulting from a greater exposure and vulnerability of women to social network events, often referred to as the "high cost of caring." Turner & Avison (1989) replicated these findings for chronically disabled adults, but rejected the conclusion that women generally are less capable of dealing with stress because events occurring to oneself are more depressive to men than women. Newmann (1986) found that chronic stressors do not have a greater depressive impact on women than men. She maintained that the relative impact of life events on women has been overestimated because important risk factors for women have been omitted from analysis.

Kessler & Neighbors (1986) found a negative interaction between race and class: racial differences in psychological distress are most pronounced at the lowest socioeconomic levels. Alternatively, poverty is more damaging to blacks than whites. Stress-by-race interactions, however, were not examined. In a separate analysis restricted to whites, McLeod & Kessler (1990) found that socioeconomic status is associated negatively with the distressing effects of life events, a class vulnerability spanning different components of socioeconomic status and several life crises. In contrast, Neff (1985) found no significant interactions of stress with class, race, or race-class combinations with regard to psychological distress.

Thus, group variation in stress-reactivity is itself variable. Several conditions contribute to these inconsistencies.

Conditions Influencing Vulnerability

The type of stressor considered is critical to the assessment of differential vulnerability. For example, some studies have demonstrated a greater depressive impact among women than men for social network events, but others have found a greater depressive impact among men than women for other stressors, including negative controllable events (Thoits 1987), occupational strain (Pearlin 1975a), and events to oneself (Turner & Avison 1989). Stress-reactivity also may depend upon constellations of social statuses, a possibility receiving scant attention. An exception is the finding of Turner & Avison (1989) that gender differences in vulnerability are contingent upon employment status.

Vulnerability effects are quite sensitive to the type of outcome examined as well. Dohrenwend & Dohrenwend (1976) discredited theories arguing that women are under greater stress and hence more prone to psychiatric disorder because the female preponderance of disorder is limited to select types of disorder. Aneshensel and colleagues (1991) extended this argument to explanations invoking differential vulnerability. The impact of stress was compared for outcomes of affective or anxiety disorder, substance abuse or dependence, and any psychiatric disorder. Gender differences in stress-reactivity were found to be disorder-specific, not indicative of global differences in stress-reactivity. Bias in estimates of stress-reactivity result from implicitly treating a single disorder as a proxy for all disorder, or indeed for all possible stress outcomes.

For example, some social groups may be more prone to stress-induced physical illness than to psychological distress (Lin & Ensel 1989). Yet Thoits (1983) concluded that total change is most important in the etiology of physical disorder, not undesirable change as in the etiology of psychological disorder. Similar sensitivity is demonstrated for the stress-buffering role of moderate alcohol consumption, which emerges only with regard to somatic symptoms and not to affective symptoms (Neff 1984).

An overlooked factor in differential vulnerability is the interaction of acute and chronic stressors. This potential is demonstrated by findings that chronic stress (neighborhood overcrowding) exacerbates cardiovascular reactivity to a challenging task and lengthens recovery time (Fleming et al 1987). According to Eaton (1978), life events have the greatest depressive impact among persons who have not previously experienced similar stressors. Also, Wheaton (1982) suggested that extensive exposure may provide immunity. In his engineering analogy, Smith (1987) described how the elastic limit of a metal can be increased by the successive application of escalating strains, until the fracture point of the material is reached. Social processes are unlikely to mirror material physics, but the interactive effects of stressors over time merit further investigation. Prior social circumstances, especially the presence of role-related stress, determine whether life transitions (such as divorce) are even experienced as stressful, or function instead as stress-relief (Wheaton 1990).

The Influence of Social Support and Coping

Group differences in average stress-reactivity often are equated implicitly with deficits in coping resources without direct assessment of coping deficits, or more importantly, whether coping deficits account for group differences in average regression coefficients. Vulnerability interaction terms, however, merely stand as proxies for other, unspecified attributes. These interaction terms should be accounted for analytically by the direct modeling of the factors regulating vulnerability. This analytic strategy is analogous to explaining mean differences in psychological distress through the specification of other attributes that differ among groups, generate psychological distress, and thereby produce group differences in distress.

One notable exception is the work by Menaghan regarding the interaction of social placement and coping in three social roles: marriage, parenthood, and occupation (Menaghan 1982, 1983, Menaghan & Merves 1984). This research revealed that neither lower social status nor female gender is associated consistently with less adaptive coping efforts. Groups differ in their behavioral responses to stress, but these differences do not reflect the consistent selection of effective or ineffective strategies. Thoits reported similar negative findings for coping resources including mastery, self-esteem, structural supports, and support from a confidant (Thoits 1982, 1984, 1987). The effects of certain stressful events are exacerbated by deficits in coping resources, but this intensification does not account consistently for differences between social groups in responsiveness to negative life events.

A closely related issue concerns the functional meaning of stress-buffering. According to Wheaton (1985), stress-buffering occurs when a resource reduces the harmful effect of exposure to stress. Many researchers equate buffering exclusively with a conditional relationship: the psychological effect of stress varies inversely with the resource. Wheaton (1985) identified an additional model of buffering and three illusory buffering models on the basis of the relationship between resources and stress. In stress-suppression models, stress exposure mobilizes a resource, which then alleviates distress. Stress is "buffered" because indirect effects via the resource are oppositional to direct effects: the total causal effect is reduced. In the first illusory buffering model, stress depletes the resource. The direct causal effect of stress is reduced, but the total causal effect of stress is unchanged, albeit explicated. Second, stress-deterrent models portray resources as causally antecedent to stress: resources reduce exposure to stress, not its impact. In the third illusory buffering model, stress and resources have separate and opposite effects but are completely independent of one another. Resources counterbalance the stressor, but do not buffer stress because support operates even in the absence of stress.

In this context, stress-buffering can be seen as a necessary component of effective coping behavior, given that coping behavior is elicited by the occurrence of a stressor. On the other hand, coping resources such as social support may be unchanged by exposure to stress, or they may be depleted or enhanced. Stress and social support exert mutual causal effects, but the precise nature of these effects is complex (Aneshensel & Frerichs 1982, Aneshensel & Huba 1984, Lin etal 1985). For example, life events often alter social support, even when the event itself is not a loss of support (Atkinson et al 1986). Evidence concerning the extent to which social support influences the occurrence of stress is equivocal (e.g. McFarlane et al 1983, Mitchell & Moos 1984, Norris & Murrell 1987).

Coping techniques are situation-specific with regard to both use and effectiveness, i.e. contingent upon the nature of the problem confronted. Strategies successful with one problem may not be used with another, or if used, may exacerbate the situation (Pearlin & Schooler 1978, Menaghan 1983, Pearlin 1989, Mattlin et al 1990). Folkman & Lazarus (1980), for example, found that the context and appraisal of the event are the most potent determinants of coping behavior. According to Pearlin & Schooler (1978), those who are under the greatest strain, the poor and less educated, utilize the least effective coping repertoires.

Menaghan (1983) has observed that conclusions about coping effectiveness are determined by the choice of the criteria for evaluating effectiveness. The criteria she specified are isomorphic to the functions of coping: reduction in the presenting problems, avoidance of distress, and maintenance of sense of self (Pearlin & Schooler 1978). Menaghan and her colleagues have concluded that coping efforts are more effective in reducing or containing distress than in avoiding or eliminating problematic conditions, at least for problems in work, marriage, and parenthood (Menaghan 1982, 1983, Menaghan & Merves

1984). For example, the coping strategies most often used in response to marital problems—selective ignoring and becoming resigned—intensify distress and have no impact on future marital problems. In contrast, negotiation and optimism decrease subsequent problems but are under-utilized by those with the most severe initial problems (Menaghan 1982).

Menaghan & Merves (1984) demonstrated that individual coping efforts are less important determinants of subsequent role problems than are structural constraints. For occupations, these constraints are job prestige, full-time employment, youth, and negative job changes. In parenting, family composition emerges as the key influence. In marriage, duration is most salient. They attributed these patterns to life-course variations in role demands and to societal stratification of resources.

In summary, while group differences in the average psychological impact of stress have been described, these differences do not necessarily equate with generalized group differences in responsiveness to stress. Coping deficits often are invoked post hoc to account for group variation in stress-responsiveness, but direct assessment of coping resources and behaviors does not account consistently for differential vulnerability. These kinds of results prompted Thoits (1987) to conclude that stress-reactivity is highly specific in nature—unique to certain kinds of events experienced by particular social groups. I concur but add that vulnerability effects also are unique to select outcomes.

SOCIAL CLASS, SELF-EFFICACY, AND STRESS

Class and Efficacy

Perhaps the most thoroughly developed linkage between social standing and stress is the concept of self-efficacy, a cognitive orientation attributing outcomes such as success and failure to personal attributes, such as ability and effort. As noted by Mirowsky & Ross (1984), the concepts of self-efficacy, mastery, internal locus of control, personal control, perceived control of the environment, and instrumentalism are virtually synonymous, and are opposite in meaning to fatalism, external locus of control, powerlessness, and learned helplessness. They described these orientations as socially transmitted conceptions of reality arising from exigencies of life that are not uniformly distributed within or across societies.

Although self-efficacy is a personal characteristic, the emergence of this cognitive orientation is connected to social stratification. Mastery varies inversely with socioeconomic status (Pearlin & Radabaugh 1976, Thoits 1987, Ross & Mirowsky 1989; Mirowsky & Ross 1990a). Pearlin & Radabaugh (1976) credited mastery to class-based opportunities and achievements, while Ross & Mirowsky (1989) ascribed powerlessness to such lower social class conditions as the inability to achieve one's ends, inadequate resources and opportunities, restricted alternatives, and jobs that limit autonomy. The elements of a lower-class orientation include rigidity and fatalism, authoritarian conservatism, personal rigidity, mistrust, external conformity, fatalism, and an emphasis on rules and organization (Kohn 1972, Wheaton 1983).

If social placement influences self-concept, then the self-concept of members of minority groups should reflect their disadvantaged social status, but in fact blacks have a relatively high sense of self-esteem. Hughes & Demo (1989) analyzed this seeming paradox by distinguishing the determinants of a belief in one's own value (esteem) from a sense of competence and personal control (efficacy) for adult American blacks. Personal efficacy is strongly affected by location in the stratification system, but social placement has at best a weak and indirect relationship to self-esteem: education enhances efficacy, which in turn elevates self-esteem. According to Hughes & Demo, self-efficacy is affected more than self-concept by inequality in the macrosocial system.

Efficacy and Stress Processes

Mastery is inversely related to psychological distress and ameliorates the psychological impact of stress. For example, Kaplan and associates (1983) found that attitudes of self-derogation moderate the impact of life events on psychological distress assessed ten years later. Kaplan and associates also related self-derogation to the subsequent occurrence of life-events, suggesting that coping deficits fail to prevent stress. Wheaton (1980) found that fatalism mediates the relationship between socioeconomic status and psychological distress: low-status persons are fatalistic and hence distressed.

Self-efficacy affects psychological distress via its impact on coping behavior. According to Wheaton (1980), fatalism undermines persistence and effort. In contrast, coping ability is diminished by inflexibility rather than fatalism (Wheaton 1983). Seeman and colleagues (1988) found that mastery encourages social learning and flexibility, which make effective, instrumental behavior more likely, and escape behavior such as problem drinking less likely. Active, problem-focused coping is most likely to occur among persons who feel a sense of subjective control (Thoits 1987, Ross & Mirowsky 1989). Exposure to stress, however, may wear away self-efficacy (Seeman et al 1988). For example, Pearlin and colleagues (1981) found stressful life experience becomes psychologically distressing to the extent that self-concept is eroded.

The Situational Context of Efficacy

The efficacy of coping behavior is situation-specific, as described previously, suggesting that a belief in personal control may be counterproductive at times, especially when stressors cannot in fact be controlled. Wheaton (1980) maintained that a continuing emphasis on external attributions is pervasively harmful, even though such attributions may be beneficial in some specific circumstances. Such attributions make the goals of social action seem less attainable, undermining motivation. Thoits (1987) advanced a related argument: a sense of control should lessen the psychological impact of even fateful events by encouraging active problem-solving in the aftermath. Mirowsky & Ross (1990b) found that depression is associated with feeling control over good and bad outcomes; no measurable benefit accrues by claiming responsibility for good outcomes and denying responsibility for bad ones, as predicted by defense theory. Thus, the impact of personal efficacy spans various types of stressful encounters, not merely those that could be prevented or reversed by personal skill or effort.

According to Mirowsky & Ross (1990a), the relationship between psychological distress and personal control depends upon whether a sense of control is derived from one's social standing. They found no limits to the psychological benefits of greater control when control is based on social status. There are diminishing returns to control, however, when control is not based on status. Also, there is no single optimum level of control: instead, the optimum increases as social status increases. These findings do not support the notion that fatalism decreases distress among low-status persons, the so-called "consolation prize" theory.

The findings of Hughes & Demo (1989) illuminate the dynamics surrounding causal attributions for success and failure among blacks. Attributing low achievement to racial discrimination as opposed to individual failure is irrelevant to personal self-esteem and personal efficacy. The interaction of social class and attributions on self-esteem is nonsignificant as well. These investigators concluded that social class is not central to self-esteem among blacks, not even among those who believe achievement is due to individual effort.

The problem of considering solitary outcomes in stress research is demonstrated by Wheaton's (1983) findings that fatalism and inflexibility exacerbate the impact of stress on depressive and schizophrenia-like symptoms, but not symptoms of anxiety. In general, schizophrenic symptoms are less affected by stress-related factors than are symptoms of depression and anxiety. Similarly, Mirowsky & Ross (1984) found that a belief in external control is related to depression, but not to anxiety. They conclude that external beliefs may have undesirable consequences in some domains but are not inherently pathological or pathogenic.

The limits of mastery are demonstrated by a recent study of the homeless. La Gory and co-workers (1990) found psychological resourcefulness has a much stronger impact on distress than any objective condition, including social support, life events, health, environmental use, sex or age. Nonetheless, mastery is insufficient to compensate for the harmful effects of homelessness, nor does mastery mediate the damaging effects of impoverished life circumstances.

ECONOMIC CHANGE, UNEMPLOYMENT, AND WORK-RELATED STRESS

The pervasive influence of socioenvironmental factors upon individual stress processes is revealed perhaps most graphically with regard to the economic and occupational spheres. Economic stress plays a major role connecting social class with psychological impairment. Yet, these individual-level relationships are embedded within macrolevel economic dynamics.

Macroeconomic Change and Individual Stress

The cumulative work of Dooley & Catalano provides persuasive evidence that macrolevel economic processes influence individual-level stress processes. Their theoretical model includes several direct linkages: environmental economic change produces individually experienced life-event change, life events produce symptoms of psychological disorder, and symptoms create a demand for services (Dooley & Catalano 1980). For example, economic contractions generate undesirable job and financial events, which in turn increase illness and injury (Catalano & Dooley 1983) and the use of mental health services (Dooley & Catalano 1984), at least among those of middle socioeconomic status. Persons working in industries with contracting employment opportunities are more likely to seek help than those working in stable or expanding industries; these relationships are independent of person-centered characteristics, such as symptomatology (Catalano et al 1986). Gortmaker and colleagues (1982) found that the relationship between stress and the utilization of health services may be most pronounced in the absence of illness. Associations among economic change, stressors, and mood may be specific to metropolitan areas (Dooley et al 1981), but relationships between economic change and admissions to mental health facilities appear comparable across areas (Catalano et al 1981).

Catalano and colleagues (1986) offered a striking illustration of the problems inherent in equating the impact of stress with a single outcome. They found that desirable job events are related positively to considering seeking help, albeit not to actual help-seeking. This finding runs counter to the widely held belief that only undesirable events are stressful, a belief based almost exclusively upon findings pertaining to psychological distress; the earlier notion, however, is supported, that change per se is stressful.

Unemployment and Work-Related Stress

One essential link between macrolevel economic change and individual stress processes is the occurrence of unemployment and other work-related events. Unemployment exerts a substantial negative effect on emotional functioning and physical health status (Kessler et al 1987, 1989). Job disruptions are psychologically distressing, at least in part because these changes generate personal economic strain (Pearlinet al 1981). The psychological impact of involuntary job loss is exacerbated by a lack of socioemotional support (Gore 1978). Poorly educated blacks are most adversely affected psychologically by unemployment, a differential not accounted for by socioeconomic considerations (Hamilton et al 1990). In contrast, Ensminger & Celentano (1990) found that unemployment distresses men and women similarly. Their findings are important because they considered the factors most likely to contribute to gender differences: family circumstances, worries about children and family, and centrality of the work role.

Unemployment is stressful and exerts deleterious effects upon well-being, but being employed is not always beneficial. Perceived occupational stress is related to various physical and psychological disorders (House et al 1979), and chronic job pressures are related to increased mortality (House et al 1986). These associations are not due to a simple tension reduction model of substance use (Mensch & Kandel 1988, Cooper 1990).

As with unemployment, social support exerts some ameliorative effect upon job stress. LaRocco and associates (1980) found job-related stress is buffered more pervasively by support from coworkers than support from supervisors or family. An overlooked finding is that buffering is confined to the impact of job-related stress on mental and physical health. Buffering does not occur for the relationship between job-stress and job-related strains. Conclusions regarding whether the impact of support is contingent upon the level of job stress therefore depend upon the criteria used to operationalize the impact of stress.

The coping behaviors of individuals bear little relationship to the development of occupational stress. Menaghan & Merves (1984) found that occupational distress is increased by efforts to restrict expectations and decreased by use of optimistic comparisons. These coping efforts do not affect subsequent occupational problems, however, nor were these problems affected by the other two coping behaviors examined—direct action and selective ignoring. Characteristics of work life, however, did influence the evolution of problems, including occupational prestige, full-time employment, and income. These investigators inferred that occupational problems embedded in structural conditions often are impervious to the coping actions of individual workers (cf Mechanic 1974).

Gender Stratification and Work-Related Stress

The intersection of occupational, family, and gender roles continues to generate a substantial body of stress-related research. Work concerning the impact of employment per se on women's well-being has yielded equivocal results, although an overall beneficial impact of employment seems likely (e.g. Aneshensel et al 1981, Gore & Mangione 1983, Krause & Markides 1985, Rosenfeld 1989). Kandel and associates (1985) found that the aggregate benefit of complex role configurations results from opposing processes: certain role constellations exacerbate stress experienced in other roles, while other constellations have the reverse impact. The impact of work and homemaker roles is not universally positive or negative, but depends upon role-related experiences (Pearlin 1975a, Aneshensel 1986).

Any gender comparison of work-related stress must consider the gender stratification of the occupational system (Aneshensel & Pearlin 1987). Lennon (1987) noted that such stratification means women and men typically encounter work environments imposing different demands and constraints, conditions with disparate mental health consequences. She found a lack of substantive complexity is detrimental to both men and women, but emerges as sex-typical types of disorder: women respond with demoralization, whereas men react with drinking. Loscocco & Spitze (1990) focused upon gender differences in how work is structured, noting that women and men seldom work together in the same job. They described a "gender model" which predicts that gender moderates the relationship between aspects of the job and well-being. They found instead that women and men are influenced similarly by factors indicative of job-stress—job demands, job deprivations and rewards, and the physical and social work environment—findings supporting a "job model" of gender and work.

Ross & Mirowsky (1988) asserted that stress among employed mothers is generated by temporary disjunctures in the internal organization of family roles and the integration of the family with other institutions. Specifically, they reasoned that one facet of family roles has changed (employment of mothers), but other family roles (e.g. husband's participation in childcare) and the family's links to other institutions (e.g. formal childcare) have not kept pace. Thus, difficulty obtaining childcare and lack of paternal participation in childcare generate stress and emotional distress among employed wives, but not fathers. Ross & Mirowsky (1988) attributed these conditions to macrolevel economic and demographic trends (e.g. increased demand for female labor).

In sum, unemployment and work-related stress are harmful to both genders, although the manner in which stress is manifested by women and men may differ. Working outside of the home or working as a homemaker both may generate stress for women, contingent upon experiences within these roles and the social, economic, and historical context within which these roles are enacted.

CONCLUSIONS

Chance adversity intrudes on the lives of most persons, but stress also arises as a predictable outcome of ordinary social organization. The psychiatric view of disorder as abnormal generates an implicit assumption that the social antecedents of disorder also are abnormal. This orientation contrasts sharply with Merton's (1938) theoretical account of anomie and nonconforming behavior: social orders permitting normal emotional functioning also generate circumstances in which emotional disorder constitutes a normal or predictable response. The occurrence of social stress, therefore, can be seen as an inevitable consequence of social organization.

Only some systemic sources of stress stem from the failure of the social system to function as it should, stressors that could be eliminated. The occurrence of systemic stressors is not necessarily an indication of a social system run amok but may reflect instead the system functioning precisely as it is supposed to function. For example, a capitalist free-enterprise system inevitably produces business failure and unemployment; the sole questions are which industries falter and what occupations encounter contracting employment opportunities. The imperatives associated with maintenance of the social system inevitably create tension between the individual and the collectivity. These systemic sources of tension can be shifted from one location in the system to another but cannot be eliminated entirely. Thus, stressful life circumstances and their emotional consequences may be and often are experienced by perfectly ordinary people integrated into the normative structures of society.

Systemic conditions of tension are more prevalent among some social groups than others, largely as a consequence of inequality in the distributive system (Pearlin 1989). At an individual level, stress can be understood in terms of a person's unique characteristics, experiences, and history. Group differences in exposure to stress, by contrast, point inexorably toward social structural origins. Two major pathways linking structure with stress are exclusion from full participation in the social system and participation that fails to provide the expected returns. Individuals occupy social roles, especially major social roles, to satisfy needs and attain goals; often these needs are essential to the survival or self-actualization of the individual and entail important life goals. Violation of role proscriptions, by the individual or by other members of the role set, renders social interactions unreliable. Likewise, exclusion from role occupancy and institutional participation, voluntary or involuntary, means social interactions occur outside of the normative system and are therefore likely to be unreliable. The lack of reliable social interaction jeopardizes need-satisfaction, goal-attainment, and the effective functioning of the social system.

These points are illustrated quite clearly with regard to marriage. First, the unmarried generally encounter more chronic stressors than do the married, including greater social isolation (Pearlin & Johnson 1977). Some married couples experience marked marital discord, of course, often as a consequence of the failure of one or both partners to adhere to normative standards for how a spouse qua spouse is supposed to act (Pearlin 1983, Aneshensel 1986). Indeed, marital stress emerges as an inevitable aspect of marriage. Mirowsky (1985) found shared decision-making power is psychologically beneficial for both spouses: complete domination and total subservience generate more depression for both spouses. The critical finding, however, is that no one level of shared power minimizes depression for both partners. Husbands and wives cannot both maximize their psychological well-being: the husband, the wife, or both spouses necessarily experience a suboptimal level of well-being. The typical power distribution favors husbands more often than wives. The power distribution within a given marriage, however, varies as a function of the social location of the couple. Nonetheless, the married are less psychologically distressed on average than the unmarried.

Stress has demonstrated adverse effects upon psychological and physical health, but these outcomes capture only part of the cost associated with social stress. When discrete health outcomes are investigated, many of those damaged by stress are counted as undamaged because they manifest stress-reactions as other outcomes (Aneshensel et al 1991). The total social, psychological, and economic costs of stress have not yet been assessed, therefore, because only some manifestations have been counted. These costs may well include outcomes of relevance to areas of sociological interest other than medical sociology, including crime and delinquency, diminished educational and occupational achievement, lost productivity, and downward social mobility.

Acknowledgments

Preparation of this review was supported in part by grants from the National Institute of Mental Health (RO 1 MH42816 and RO1 MH40831). I wish to thank Vicki Ebin for her precise abstracts of a voluminous amount of bibliographic material and Gloria Krauss for her editorial improvements. My interpretation of this body of literature benefitted from discussions with fellow participants in the Consortium for Research Involving Stress Processes, funded by the W.T. Grant Foundation.

Literature Cited

Am. Psychol. Assoc., Am. Educ. Res. Assoc., Natl. Counc. Measurement Educ. 1974. *Standards for Educational and Psychological Tests*. Washington, DC: Am. Psychol. Assoc.

Aneshensel, C. S. 1985. The natural history of depressive symptoms: Implications for psychiatric epidemiology. *Res. Commun. Ment. Health* 5:45–75

Aneshensel, C. S. 1986. Marital and employment role-strain, social support, and depression among adult women. In *Stress, Social Support, and Women*, ed. S. E. Hobfoll, pp. 99–114. New York: Hemisphere

Aneshensel, C. S., Frerichs, R. R. 1982. Stress, support, and depression: A longitudinal causal model. *J. Commun. Psychol.* 10:363–76

Aneshensel, C. S., Frerichs, R. R., Clark, V. A. 1981. Family roles and sex differences in depression. *J. Health Soc. Behav.* 22(4): 379–93

Aneshensel, C. S., Huba, G. J. 1984. An integrative causal model of the antecedents and consequences of depression over one year. *Res. Commun. Ment. Health* 4:35–72

Aneshensel, C. S., Pearlin, L. I. 1987. Structural contexts of sex differences in stress. In *Gender and Stress*, ed. R. C. Barnett, L. Biener, G. K. Baruch, pp. 75–95. New York: Free

Aneshensel, C. S., Rutter, C. M., Lachenbruch, P. A. 1991. Social structure, stress, and mental health: Competing conceptual and analytic models. *Am. Sociol. Rev.* 56: 166–78

Aneshensel, C. S., Stone, J. D. 1982. Stress and depression: A test of the buffering model of social support. *Arch. Gen. Psychiatry* 39:1392–96

Atkinson, T., Liem, R., Liem, J. H. 1986. The social costs of unemployment: Implications for social support. *J. Health Soc. Behav.* 27(4):317–31

Avison, W. R., Turner, R. J. 1988. Stressful life events and depressive symptoms: Disaggregating the effects of acute stressors and chronic strains. *J. Health Soc. Behav.* 29(3):253–64

Catalano, R., Dooley, D. 1983. Health effects of economic instability: A test of economic stress hypothesis. *J. Health Soc. Behav.* 24(1):46–60

Catalano, R., Dooley, D., Jackson, R. 1981. Economic predictors of admissions to mental health facilities in a nonmetropolitan community. *J. Health Soc. Behav.* 22(3): 284–97

Catalano, R., Rook, K., Dooley, D. 1986. Labor markets and help-seeking: A test of the employment security hypothesis. *J. Health Soc. Behav.* 27(3):277–87

Cobb, S. 1976. Social support as a moderator of life stress. *Psychosom. Med.* 38(5):300–14

Cohen, S., Syme, S. L., ed. 1985. *Social Support and Health*. Orlando, Fla: Academic

Cooper, M. L., Russell, M., Frone, M. R. 1990. Work stress and alcohol effects: A test of stress-induced drinking. *J. Health Soc. Behav.* 31(3):260–76

Dean, A., Lin, N. 1977. The stress-buffering role of social support: Problems and prospects for systematic investigation. *J. Nerv. Ment. Dis.* 165(6):403–17

Dohrenwend, B. P., Dohrenwend, B. S. 1969. *Social Status and Psychological Disorder: A Causal Inquiry*. New York: Wiley-Intersci.

Dohrenwend, B. P., Dohrenwend, B. S. 1976. Sex differences and psychiatric disorders. *Am. J. Sociol.* 81(6):1447–54

Dohrenwend, B. S. 1970. Social class and stressful events. In *Psychiatric Epidemiology: Proc. Int. Symp., Aberdeen Univ. 22–25 July 1969*, ed. E. H. Hare, J. K. Wing, pp. 313–19. London: Oxford Univ. Press

Dohrenwend, B. S. 1973. Social status and stressful life events. *J. Pers. Soc. Psychol.* 28(2):225–35

Dohrenwend, B. S. 1977. Anticipation and control of stressful life events: An exploratory analysis. In *The Origins and Course of Psychopathology: Methods of Longitudinal Research*, ed. J. S. Strauss, H. M. Babigian, M. Roff, pp. 135–86. New York: Plenum

Dohrenwend, B. S. 1978. Social status and responsibility for stressful life events. In *Stress and Anxiety*, ed. C. D. Spielberger, I. G. Sarason, 5:25–42. Washington, DC: Hemisphere

Dohrenwend, B. S., Krasnoff, L., Askenasy, A. R., Dohrenwend, B. P. 1978. Exemplification of a method for scaling life events: The PERI Life Events Scale. *J. Health Soc. Behav.* 19(2):205–29

Dooley, D., Catalano, R. 1980. Economic change as a cause of behavioral disorder. *Psychol. Bull.* 87(3):450–68

Dooley, D., Catalano, R. 1984. Why the economy predicts help-seeking: A test of competing explanations. *J. Health Soc. Behav.* 25(2):160–76

Dooley, D., Catalano, R., Jackson, R., Brownell, A. 1981. Economic, life, and symptom changes in a nonmetropolitan community. *J. Health Soc. Behav.* 22(2):144–54

Dressler, W. W. 1988. Social consistency and psychological distress. *J. Health Soc. Behav.* 29(1):79–91

Eaton, W. W. 1978. Life events, social supports, and psychiatric symptoms: A reanalysis of the New Haven data. *J. Health Soc. Behav.* 19(2):230–34

Eaton, W. W. 1986. *The Sociology of Mental Disorders*. New York: Praeger. 2nd ed

Eckenrode, J. 1984. Impact of chronic and acute stressors on daily reports of mood. *J. Pers. Soc. Psychol.* 46(4):907–18

Ensminger, M. E., Celentano, D. D. 1990. Gender differences in the effect of unemployment on psychological distress. *Soc. Sci. Med.* 30(4):469–77

Farnworth, M., Leiber, M. J. 1989. Strain theory revisited: Economic goals, educational means, and delinquency. *Am. Sociol. Rev.* 54(2):263–74

Fleming, I., Baum, A., Davidson, L. M., Rectanus, E., McArdle, S. 1987. Chronic stress as a factor in physiologic reactivity to challenge. *Health Psychol.* 6(3):221–37

Folkman, S., Lazarus, R. S. 1980. An analysis of coping in a middle-aged community sample. *J. Health Soc. Behav.* 21(3):219–39

Fox, J. W. 1990. Social class, mental illness, and social mobility: The social selection-drift hypothesis for serious mental illness. *J. Health Soc. Behav.* 31(4):344–53

Golding, J. M., Potts, M. K., Aneshensel, C. S. 1991. Stress exposure among Mexican Americans and non-Hispanic whites. *J. Commun. Psychol.* 19(1):37–59

Gore, S. 1978. The effect of social support in moderating the health consequences of unemployment. *J. Health Soc. Behav.* 19(2): 157–65

Gore, S., Mangione, T. W. 1983. Social roles, sex roles and psychological distress: Additive and interactive models of sex differences. *J. Health Soc. Behav.* 24(4):300–12

Gortmaker, S. L., Eckenrode, J., Gore, S. 1982. Stress and the utilization of health services: A time series and cross-sectional analysis. *J. Health Soc. Behav.* 23(1):25–38

Hamilton, V. L., Broman, C. L., Hoffman, W. S., Renner, D. S. 1990. Hard times and vulnerable people: Initial effects of plant closing on autoworkers' mental health. *J. Health Soc. Behav.* 31(2):123–40

House, J. S., Kahn, R. L. 1985. Measures and concepts of social support. See Cohen & Syme 1985, pp. 83–108

House, J. S., Landis, K. R., Umberson, D. 1988. Social relationships and health. *Science* 241:540–45

House, J. S., Strecher, V., Metzner, H. L., Robbins, C. A. 1986. Occupational stress and health among men and women in the Tecumseh community health study. *J. Health Soc. Behav.* 27(1):62–77

House, J. S., McMichael, A. J., Wells, J. A., Kaplan, B. H., Landerman, L. R. 1979. Occupational stress and health among factory workers. *J. Health Soc. Behav.* 20(2):139–60

Hughes, M., Demo, D. H. 1989. Self-perceptions of Black Americans: Self-esteem and personal efficacy. *Am. J. Sociol.* 95(1):132–59

Kandel, D. B., Davies, M., Raveis, V. H. 1985. The stressfulness of daily social roles for women: Marital, occupational and household roles. *J. Health Soc. Behav.* 26(1):64–78

Kaplan, H. B., ed. 1983. *Psychosocial Stress: Trends in Theory and Research*. New York: Academic

Kaplan, H. B., Robbins, C., Martin, S. S. 1983. Antecedents of psychological distress in young adults: self-rejection, deprivation of social support, and life events. *J. Health Soc. Behav.* 24(3):230–44

Kessler, R. C. 1979a. A strategy for studying differential vulnerability to the psychological consequences of stress. *J. Health Soc. Behav.* 20(2):100–8

Kessler, R. C. 1979b. Stress, social status, and psychological distress.*J. Health Soc. Behav.* 20(3):259–72

Kessler, R. C., Essex, M. 1982. Marital status and depression: The importance of coping resources. *Soc. Forces* 61(2):484–507

Kessler, R. C., House, J. S., Turner, J. B. 1987. Unemployment and health in a community sample. *J. Health Soc. Behav.* 28(1):51–59

Kessler, R. C., McLeod, J. D. 1984. Sex differences in vulnerability to undesirable life events. *Am. Sociol. Rev.* 49(5):620–31

Kessler, R. C., McLeod, J. D. 1985. Social support and mental health in community samples. See Cohen & Syme 1985, pp. 219–40

Kessler, R. C., Neighbors, H. W. 1986. A new perspective on the relationships among race, social class, and psychological distress. *J. Health Soc. Behav.* 27(2):107–15

Kessler, R. C., Price, R. H., Wortman, C. B. 1985. Social factors in psychopathology: Stress, social support, and coping processes. *Annu. Rev. Psychol.* 36:531–72

Kessler, R. C., Turner, J. B., House, J. S. 1989. Unemployment, reemployment, and emotional functioning in a community sample. *Am. Sociol. Rev.* 54(4):648–57

Kohn, M. L. 1972. Class, family, and schizophrenia: A reformulation. *Soc. Forces* 50:295–313

Krause, N., Markides, K. S. 1985. Employment and psychological well-being in Mexican American women. *J. Health Soc. Behav.* 26(1):15–26

La Gory, M., Ritchey, F. J., Mullis, J. 1990. Depression among the homeless. *J. Health Soc. Behav.* 31(1):87–101

LaRocco, J. M., House, J. S., French, J. R.

P. Jr. 1980. Social support, occupational stress, and health. *J. Health Soc. Behav.* 21(3):202–18
Lazarus, R. S. 1966. *Psychological Stress and the Coping Process*. New York: McGraw-Hill
Lennon, M. C. 1987. Sex differences in distress: The impact of gender and work roles. *J. Health Soc. Behav.* 28(3):290–305
Liem, R., Liem, J. 1978. Social class and mental illness reconsidered: The role of economic stress and social support. *J. Health Soc. Behav.* 19(2):139–56
Lin, N., Ensel, W. M. 1984. Depression-mobility and its social etiology: The role of life events and social support. *J. Health Soc. Behav.* 25(2):176–88
Lin, N., Ensel, W. M. 1989. Life stress and health: Stressors and resources. *Am. Sociol. Rev.* 54(3):382–99
Lin, N., Woelfel, M. W., Light, S. C. 1985. The buffering effect of social support subsequent to an important life event. *J. Health Soc. Behav.* 26(3):247–63
Loscocco, K. A., Spitze, G. 1990. Working conditions, social support, and the well-being of female and male factory workers. *J. Health Soc. Behav.* 31(4):313–27
Mattlin, J. A., Wethington, E., Kessler, R. C. 1990. Situational determinants of coping and coping effectiveness. *J. Health Soc. Behav.* 31(1):103–22
McFarlane, A. H., Norman, G. R., Streiner, D. L., Roy, R. G. 1983. The process of social stress: Stable, reciprocal, and mediating relationships. *J. Health Soc. Behav.* 24(2):160–73
McLeod, J. D., Kessler, R. C. 1990. Socioeconomic status differences in vulnerability to undesirable life events. *J. Health Soc. Behav.* 31(2):162–72
Mechanic, D. 1972. Social class and schizophrenia: Some requirements for a plausible theory of social influence. *Soc. Forces* 50:305–13
Mechanic, D. 1974. Social structure and personal adaptation: Some neglected dimensions. In *Coping and Adaptation*, ed. E. V. Coehlo, D. A. Hamburg, J. E. Adans, pp. 32–44. New York: Basic
Menaghan, E. G. 1982. Measuring coping effectiveness: A panel analysis of marital problems and coping efforts. *J. Health Soc. Behav.* 23(3):220–34
Menaghan, E. G. 1983. Individual coping efforts: Moderators of the relationship between life stress and mental health outcomes. See Kaplan 1983, pp. 157–91
Menaghan, E. G., Merves, E. S. 1984. Coping with occupational problems: The limits of individual efforts. *J. Health Soc. Behav.* 25(4):406–23
Mensch, B. S., Kandel, D. B. 1988. Do job conditions influence the use of drugs? *J. Health Soc. Behav.* 29(2):169–84
Merton, R. K. 1938. Social structure and anomie. *Am. Sociol. Rev.* 3:672–82
Mirowsky, J. 1985. Depression and marital power: An equity model. *Am. J. Sociol.* 91(3):557–92
Mirowsky, J., Ross, C. E. 1984. Mexican culture and its emotional contradictions. *J. Health Soc. Behav.* 25(1):2–13
Mirowsky, J., Ross, C. E. 1990a. The consolation-prize theory of alienation. *Am. J. Sociol.* 95(6):1505–35
Mirowsky, J., Ross, C. E. 1990b. Control or defense? Depression and the sense of control over good and bad outcomes. *J. Health Soc. Behav.* 31(1):71–86
Mitchell, R. E., Moos, R. H. 1984. Deficiencies in social support among depressed patients: Antecedents or consequences of stress? *J. Health Soc. Behav.* 25(4):438–52
Moen, P., Dempster-McClain, D., Williams, R. M. Jr. 1989. Social integration and longevity: An event history analysis of women's roles and resilience. *Am. Sociol. Rev.* 54(4):635–47
Myers, J. K., Lindenthal, J. J., Pepper, M. P. 1975. Life events, social integration and psychiatric symptomatology. *J. Health Soc. Behav.* 16(4):421–27
Neff, J. A. 1985. Race and vulnerability to stress: An examination of differential vulnerability. *J. Pers. Soc. Psychol.* 49(2): 481–91
Neff, J. A. 1984. The stress-buffering role of alcohol consumption: The importance of symptom dimension. *J. Hum. Stress* Spring:35–42
Newmann, J. P. 1986. Gender, life strains, and depression. *J. Health Soc. Behav.* 27(2):161–78
Norris, F. H., Murrell, S. A. 1987. Transitory impact of life-event stress on psychological symptoms in older adults. *J. Health Soc. Behav.* 28(2):197–211
Pearlin, L. I. 1975a. Sex roles and depression. In *Life-Span Developmental Psychology: Normative Life Crises*, ed. N. Datan, L. Ginsberg, pp. 191–207. New York: Academic
Pearlin, L. I. 1975b. Status inequality and stress in marriage. *Am. Sociol. Rev.* 40: 344–57
Pearlin, L. I. 1983. Role strains and personal stress. See Kaplan 1983, pp. 3–32
Pearlin, L. I. 1989. The sociological study of stress. *J. Health Soc. Behav.* 30(3):241–56
Pearlin, L. I., Aneshensel, C. S. 1986. Coping and social supports: Their functions and applications. In *Applications of Social Science to Clinical Medicine and Health Policy*, ed. L. H. Aiken, D. Mechanic, pp.

417–37. New Brunswick, NJ: Rutgers Univ. Press

Pearlin, L. I., Johnson, J. S. 1977. Marital status, life-strains and depression. *Am. Sociol. Rev.* 42:704–15

Pearlin, L. I., Lieberman, M. A. 1979. Social sources of emotional distress. *Res. Commun. Ment. Health* 1:217–48

Pearlin, L. I., Menaghan, E. G., Lieberman, M. A., Mullan, J. T. 1981. The stress process. *J. Health Soc. Behav.* 22(4):337–56

Pearlin, L. I., Radabaugh, C. W. 1976. Economic strains and the coping functions of alcohol. *Am. J. Sociol.* 82(3):652–63

Pearlin, L. I., Schooler, C. 1978. The structure of coping. *J. Health Soc. Behav.* 19(1):2–21

Rosenberg, M. 1968. *The Logic of Survey Analysis*. New York: Basic

Rosenfield, S. 1989. The effects of women's employment: Personal control and sex differences in mental health. *J. Health Soc. Behav.* 30(1):77–91

Ross, C. E., Huber, J. 1985. Hardship and depression. *J. Health Soc. Behav.* 26(4): 312–27

Ross, C. E., Mirowsky, J. 1979. A comparison of life-event weighting schemes: Change, undesirability, and effect-proportional indices. *J. Health Soc. Behav.* 20(2):166–77

Ross, C. E., Mirowsky, J. 1988. Child care and emotional adjustment to wives' employment. *J. Health Soc. Behav.* 29(2):127–38

Ross, C. E., Mirowsky, J. 1989. Explaining the social patterns of depression: Control and problem solving—or support and talking? *J. Health Soc. Behav.* 30(2):206–19

Seeman, M., Seeman, A. Z., Budros, A. 1988. Powerlessness, work, and community: A longitudinal study of alienation and alcohol use. *J. Health Soc. Behav.* 29(3):185–98

Smith, W. K. 1987. The stress analogy. *Schizophr. Bull.* 13(2):215–20

Tausig, M. 1982. Measuring life events. *J. Health Soc. Behav.* 23:52–64

Thoits, P. A. 1982. Life stress, social support, and psychological vulnerability: Epidemiological considerations. *J. Commun. Psychol.* 10:341–62

Thoits, P. A. 1983. Dimensions of life events that influence psychological distress: An evaluation and synthesis of the literature. See Kaplan 1983, pp. 33–103

Thoits, P. A. 1984. Explaining distributions of psychological vulnerability: Lack of social support in the face of life stress. *Soc. Forces* 63(2):453–81

Thoits, P. A. 1987. Gender and marital status differences in control and distress: Common stress versus unique stress explanations. *J. Health Soc. Behav.* 28(1):7–22

Turner, R. J. 1981. Social support as a contingency in psychological well-being. *J. Health Soc. Behav.* 22(4):357–67

Turner, R. J. 1983. Direct, indirect, and moderating effects of social support on psychological distress and associated conditions. See Kaplan 1983, pp. 105–55

Turner, R. J., Avison, W. R. 1989. Gender and depression: Assessing exposure and vulnerability to life events in a chronically strained population. *J. Nerv. Ment. Dis.* 177(8):443–55

Turner, R. J., Noh, S. 1983. Class and psychological vulnerability among women: The significance of social support and personal control. *J. Health Soc. Behav.* 24(1):2–15

Turner, R. J., Noh, S. 1988. Physical disability and depression: A longitudinal analysis. *J. Health Soc. Behav.* 29(1):23–37

Wethington, E., Kessler, R. C. 1986. Perceived support, received support, and adjustment to stressful life events. *J. Health Soc. Behav.* 27(1):78–89

Wheaton, B. 1978. The sociogenesis of psychological disorder: Reexamining the causal issues with longitudinal data. *Am. Sociol. Rev.* 43:383–403

Wheaton, B. 1980. The sociogenesis of psychological disorder: An attributional theory. *J. Health Soc. Behav.* 21(2):100–24

Wheaton, B. 1982. A comparison of the moderating effects of personal coping resources on the impact of exposure to stress in two groups. *J. Commun. Psychol.* 10:293–311

Wheaton, B. 1983. Stress, personal coping resources, and psychiatric symptoms: An investigation of interactive models. *J. Health Soc. Behav.* 24(3):208–29

Wheaton, B. 1985. Models for the stress-buffering functions of coping resources. *J. Health Soc. Behav.* 26(4):352–64

Wheaton, B. 1990. Life transitions, role histories, and mental health. *Am. Sociol. Rev.* 55:209–23

Annu. Rev. Sociol. 1992. 18:39–61

JOB MOBILITY AND CAREER PROCESSES

Rachel A. Rosenfeld

Department of Sociology, University of North Carolina, Chapel Hill, North Carolina 27599

KEY WORDS: employment histories, occupations, dynamic models, life course, labor markets

Abstract

Renewed interest in the movement of people between jobs highlights the roles of time and opportunity structures in career development. Vacancy-driven models provide the background for many conceptions of the opportunity structure, with recent work on labor markets and economic segmentation contributing characterization of particular structures. Individuals' job-relevant resources, constraints, and contacts interact with structural characteristics to create careers. Careers take place over time, but different aspects of time (e.g. time in the firm versus time in the labor force) have different implications for mobility. Future work in this area needs to develop better understanding of the mechanisms by which job mobility occurs and leads to different kinds of careers.

INTRODUCTION

Much of the research on social mobility has focused on intergenerational mobility, investigating the extent to which social inequality is reproduced across generations. While this line of research continues to be important, the last couple of decades have seen renewed interest in intragenerational mobility and work histories.

0360–0572/92/0815–0039$2.00

In the 1940s and 1950s, a few researchers had analyzed work histories (e.g. Blumen et al 1955, Form & Miller 1949, Lipset & Bendix 1952, Palmer 1954, Parnes 1954, Reynolds 1951). Then, as part of studying the process of intergenerational mobility, Blau & Duncan (1967) paid attention to mobility from the first job to one held at a given date. This approach, however, ignored the timing of career development and the nature of underlying job shifts. In the 1970s and 1980s, sociological interest in labor market structures and the life course, an increase in data sets including complete or partial work histories, advances in mobility modeling, and the availability of software with which to estimate such models spurred analysis of actual job shifting and career processes. This research of the last 15 to 20 years is reviewed here. In particular, I concentrate on studies using job histories to see what factors affect an individual's job mobility and its outcomes. This type of work has great potential to add to our understanding both of individuals' career development over their lives and of the nature and effects of career opportunity structures.

JOB SHIFTING AND CAREERS

In job-shift research, the basic unit of analysis is a job or pair of jobs adjacent in a work history. A job is a particular kind of work with a particular employer. A person holds a job for a given time, then leaves for a different or similar job, with the same or a different employer, or moves out of employment. In some cases, of course, the researcher will not see the end of a particular job because it is not completed at the time of observation. With information on the timing of jobs, one can investigate not just the occurrence but also the rates of job changing: Given that a person is in a particular state (a job or type of job), how fast does the person leave that state for another? (For introductions to event history methods used to study rates, see Allison 1984, Mayer & Tuma 1990b, Petersen 1991, Tuma & Hannan 1984.)

Here, a *career* is defined as a sequence of jobs (Spilerman 1977). Job shifts are thus the building blocks of individuals' careers. At the same time, use of the term *career* has overtones of some sort of progress or at least coherence to the jobs a person holds over the work life (Wilensky 1960). Those using job shifts to outline career structures are usually looking for patterns in job histories, although "random" careers are empirically possible. Among other things, significant increases in job rewards are assumed to take place by changing positions, rather than within a given job (Sørensen 1974:45, Tuma 1985; although see results of Bartel 1980, Borjas 1981, and Hannan et al 1990). Much of the research looks at job shifts that yield gains in some job outcome, compares shifts in different directions, or interprets job shifts as though they were upward. What constitutes a "job shift" or "promotion" is not always clear. Due to space constraints, however, I do not discuss such measurement issues here.

Whether and when a person changes jobs depends on the nature of the opportunity structure facing an individual. Workers' job-relevant resources and other characteristics may determine where they enter a given job structure as well as how fast they move within and out of it. Chances for mobility can change over time, as individuals, organizations, and the larger social and economic structure change. As the discussion to follow shows, to understand career processes fully, one needs to consider all these factors (the opportunity structure, individuals' resources and characteristics, and time), as well as the specific ways in which particular workers come to find out about or be chosen for new jobs (Granovetter 1986, Halaby 1988, Skvoretz 1984b, Sørensen 1974, 1975, 1977, 1979, Stolzenberg 1988, Tuma 1976, 1985). The rest of the review is organized around these components.

EFFECTS OF OPPORTUNITY STRUCTURES AND RESOURCES ON MOBILITY

Structure can have many different meanings in terms of theoretical content and empirical operationalization. There are various ways of locating and describing opportunity structures within which careers take place: by tracing them inductively through observed job shifts, using observed shifts to estimate formal models of mobility and opportunity, or employing preexisting typologies and gradings either directly or indirectly. The type of mobility detected within a given structure will depend on how the links between jobs are classified: by particular job title, groupings of job titles, occupation, industry, occupational sex type, economic sector, firm, relative income or status, and so on (Althauser & Kalleberg 1990, Breiger 1990a). Further, it is difficult to separate consideration of workers' characteristics from those of structural effects. In some of the literature, workers' characteristics such as race and sex identify separate opportunity regimes (Skvoretz 1984b, Sørensen 1975, 1979), while in many other cases hypotheses are about the interaction between opportunity structures and workers' resources.

Vacancy-Driven Models

VACANCY CHAINS Much of the research on job mobility draws on insights from vacancy chain models (White 1970). Such models use data on job shifts to discover the underlying opportunity structure by analyzing the movement of job vacancies, which move opposite from individuals. The basic assumptions of these models are that mobility depends on the availability of empty positions and that the filling of jobs is interdependent. One person's move to a new job or out of a job system creates an opening to be filled. A person from within the system going to that job leaves his or her previous job vacant and so on. A person entering a system to take a job ends a chain of vacancies. While jobs may be created or destroyed, they exist independently of particular incumbents.

Researchers have estimated vacancy models for the clergy (White 1970), mental hospital superintendents (Abbott 1990), and collegiate football (Smith & Abbott 1983) and basketball (Smith 1983) coaches. Comparisons among occupations and among strata of positions within a given occupation tell where mobility opportunities are greater, as measured by longer vacancy chains. (See Chase 1991 and Stewman 1986 for more details on these models and their applications.) The timing of moves is not a concern in such models, although Abbott (1990) explored historical change in mental hospital superintendency vacancy chains.

From the perspective of the individual, when job moves are interdependent in this way, "the patterning of a career may reflect nothing more than the cumulative effect of inclusion in a number of vacancy chains during the course of that career" (Smith & Abbott 1983:1163). This is one justification for including previous position (or job history) in models of individuals' mobility. To my knowledge, however, no one has explicitly included measures derived from analysis of vacancy chains to predict individuals' career development. (See White 1970, chapter 12, for an attempt to link particular men's careers with vacancy chains.)

LABOR DEMAND MODELS AND VENTURI TUBES Stewman and his collaborators (Stewman 1975, Konda & Stewman 1980, Stewman & Konda 1983, Stewman & Yeh 1991; see also Stewman 1986, 1988) have extended Markov process vacancy chain models to study organizational promotion rather than the links between specific vacancies. They see promotion probabilities as dependent not only on vacancy creation per se, but also on the distribution and source of vacancies (exits, new jobs), the number and nature of competitors for a higher job, and managerial decisions about who should fill vacant positions.

Personnel records showed that a number of organizations were shaped as pyramids, with declining numbers of jobs at progressively higher grades (Stewman & Konda 1983, Stewman 1986, Stewman & Yeh 1991). Multiple grade ratios (MGRs), calculated from the relative sizes of adjacent grade levels and vacancies' arrivals at a level, indicate career chances at different organizational levels. Stacking the MGRs across levels yields Venturi tubes which show the shape of promotion opportunities for the job structure. With the exception of the military and school administration, the Venturi tubes did not look like pyramids. Rather, career opportunities opened up at intermediate levels.

Stewman & Konda (1983) used individuals' seniority to trace through the implications of models for people's careers, but could do this only by partitioning their sample rather than estimating models for individuals' movement. DiPrete & Soule (1988) included job ladder–specific MGRs to predict job mobility of white collar US federal employees, while in a study of blue collar employees in a large West German engineering firm, Brüderl et al (1991b) used grade levels' yearly promotion rates as the measure of mobility opportunity at different levels. In both cases, level-specific opportunity had direct effects that increased individuals' promotion rates and also modified the effects of other variables. Effects of work experience tended to be overestimated without consideration of mobility opportunity, while in some cases sex, race, or nationality effects were underestimated. Brüderl et al also found that a set of dummies for hierarchical level worked well as a proxy for the more direct measure of varying opportunity.

VACANCY COMPETITION MODEL Sørensen (1977) develops a vacancy competition model that also begins with the idea that vacancies create opportunities for mobility. He assumes that job rewards, which are attached to jobs, are exponentially distributed, an assumption generating a pyramid-shaped reward structure. The general proportions of the pyramid are stable over time. The higher one's job rewards, the fewer jobs still higher. The shape parameter, governing how broad or pointed the structure is, indicates how many jobs exist that are better than those at a particular level. Opportunity for mobility is determined by the shape parameter and by a parameter measuring the rate at which higher jobs become vacant, which is constant across levels. Thus, opportunity is the same at each level (in contrast with Stewman & Konda's 1983 organizational results).

Individuals enter the opportunity system with a given set of resources (with relative resources being more important than absolute levels; Sørensen 1979, Tuma 1976). To create the greatest contrast between this model and human capital theories, Sørensen (1977) assumes resources do not change with time in the system—or at least that changes in resources have no necessary relationship to the opening of vacancies and mobility (Sørensen 1979). These resources determine the best possible job a person can fill. At least some people will enter below their optimum level, if there is not a vacancy there. The longer they are in the system, the more time they will have had to take advantage of vacancies and the smaller the gap will be between their potential and their current rewards. Estimation of individual-level models of job shifting or attainment change yields estimates of the opportunity parameters (Sørensen 1979, Sørensen & Tuma 1981; see also Brüderl 1992, Nielsen & Rosenfeld 1981).

On the basis of this model, resources would be expected to have positive effects on upward mobility, with job rewards and time having negative effects. And such effects are usually observed. But given that time negatively indicates the discrepancy between rewards and resources and that opportunity is independent of level, one would not expect both time and current rewards to be significant (Allmendinger 1989a, Blossfeld 1986, Brüderl et al 1991b, Sørensen & Tuma 1981). In some cases, however, they are. For example, in the US Office of the Comptroller of the Currency, the greater the distance to move up from the entry position (measured by the number of strata above this level), the greater upward wage mobility. But length of service also had a significant negative effect (Skvoretz 1984a).

Skvoretz (1984b) shows that Sørensen's vacancy competition model can be considered a constrained version of Stewman & Konda's (1983) model of organizational opportunity and goes on to extend these models. He argues that vacancy-driven opportunities can vary over historical time (as Stewman & Konda allow), over position (again as Stewman & Konda allow), but also over types of resources (which is not explicit in either model). When promotion rates vary over historical time, but not levels and resources, then an effect of time in the system might simply indicate the history of promotions available, not necessarily a constant exposure to chances to move up. Different opportunity systems may have different mechanisms by which characteristics such as position, resources, and experience are related to opportunity.

ALTERNATIVES TO VACANCY-DRIVEN MOBILITY Vacancy models contain the most fully developed theories of how job shifts, especially upward ones, develop careers. As seen, they have implications for interpreting models of individuals' job changing. Other theories, such as human capital theory, can account for the pattern of job attainment over time, but not as well for job mobility (Tuma 1985). But not all mobility is vacancy driven. Jobs are not always independent of particular incumbents; moves are not always interdependent and conditioned on a vacancy being present. Other sources of mobility need to be considered.

Workers may create jobs or have jobs created around them. A good example is the move into self-employment, excluded from much job-shifting research. While in some cases there is a vacancy to fill (e.g. an established or new practice or store), in many other cases the newly self-employed calls the job into being (Harrison 1988). Rates of movement into self-employment do not depend on resources and current position as do other types of moves (Hachen 1990) and are explained by variables not usually included in mobility studies, such as religion (though see Halaby 1982), and self-employment history (Carroll & Mosakowski 1987).

Within organizations, there can be accrual mobility, where an employee whose responsibilities and knowledge go beyond what is normally expected in the job has a new, formerly nonexistent position formed around him or her (Miner & Estler 1985). This may be more likely to happen when an organization or its environment is changing. Such mobility does not usually create a vacancy for someone else. Further, jobs can be created for new as well as continuing employees.

In other cases, promotion is noncompetitive. Rather, after a certain time with the organization (or showing a certain level of competence), one moves up in grade without there needing to be a vacancy there (Spilerman 1986). This is the case, for example, with rank advancement in most US universities (Clark 1987). Unions also tend to emphasize seniority-based rewards (Baron 1984, Granovetter 1986). Stewman & Yeh (1991) recognize seniority mobility and model it along with vacancy-driven mobility.

In one large firm, Rosenbaum (1984, 1990) discovered relatively low persistence of specific jobs over time. Harrison (1988) argues this is true for the national labor market as well, that jobs do not have stable identities, such that one can follow specific vacancies. He develops an opportunity flow model in which job creation and abolition are treated as processes that help generate demand "in the form of individually indistinguishable but denumerable occupational opportunities" (p. 8).

Labor Market Segmentation

The early literature on labor market segmentation (Kalleberg & Sørensen 1979) was concerned about labor mobility and workers' careers. Most of the sociological work using this literature, however, has analyzed the impact of various labor market and economic characteristics on job rewards at a given time. But those studying job shifting draw on these theories for insights into how opportunity structures affect mobility, as well as using patterns of job mobility to validate segmentation typologies. Consideration of vacancy-driven mobility models crosscuts use of labor market and economic segmentation concepts. In some cases, labor market divisions are seen as locating types of vacancies, vacancy chains, or vacancy-influenced promotion structures. In other cases, they are used to suggest where vacancy models are more likely to be applicable.

INTERNAL LABOR MARKETS Many people who have studied how careers are built by job shifting have organized their examination of structural effects around the concept of the internal labor market. In an internal labor market, workers are assumed to enter at specific entry ports and carry out their careers thereafter at least partly protected from competition with those outside the market. Usually an internal labor market is also defined as one offering a career ladder and chances for promotion. Researchers often identify internal labor markets as jobs or sets of jobs within a firm, especially within large firms, although they can operate within occupations even across firms (Althauser 1989a).

A related distinction is between "open" or "flexible" employment structures and "closed" or "inflexible" ones (Sørensen & Tuma 1981, Tuma 1985). In "closed," "inflexible" structures, the employer cannot easily adjust wages to an individual's productivity, so job shifts are the main mechanism by which wage increases come about. Further, the employer relinquishes some control over terminating the employment relationship. Internal labor markets are one way in which workers are motivated in a closed employment structure.

If internal labor markets offer greater mobility opportunities, then one should see more upward movement, less downward movement, and less movement out of such markets (Carroll & Mayer 1984, 1986, Hachen 1990, Tuma 1985). Indeed, among US men, the rate of downward wage mobility within firms and in closed employment relationships is very small (Sandefur 1981a, Sørensen & Tuma 1981, Tuma 1985). German life history data showed that being in a larger organization slowed all job shifts, but increased within-firm moves and slowed moves out of the firm. At the same time, it had no effect on upward moves within a firm (Carroll & Mayer 1986), perhaps because more detailed specification of the internal labor market was needed, a point discussed below.

A number of researchers have contrasted mobility processes within and out of internal labor markets. Sørensen & Tuma (1981) and Tuma (1985) argue that vacancy competition is more likely when there is a "closed" or "inflexible" employment relationship, such that one should see results consistent with predictions of vacancy competition for moves within such markets. In particular, time in the labor force should significantly decrease the rate of job mobility, especially upward mobility, only in open markets. Hachen (1990), Sørensen & Tuma (1981), and Tuma (1985) all find some, though not entirely consistent, support for this. (See also DiPrete & Krecker 1991.)

Employers have different information about current as compared with potential employees (Rosenbaum 1979, Tuma 1976). Easily observed markers such as education, race, or sex may therefore be more important for mobility across firms, while less easily observed or transferred resources and skills are more important for moves up within a firm or internal market. Further, when workers make decisions about whether to leave an employer, they may use more easily observed job rewards, such as prestige and wages, as the basis for comparison, such that these would exert stronger negative effects on moves across than within firms (Sandefur 1981b, Tuma 1985). Again, while there is some support for these ideas, results are mixed (Felmlee 1982, Hachen 1990, Sandefur 1981a,b, Sørensen & Tuma 1981, Tuma 1985).

Use of firm or occupational records allows more detailed analysis of actual internal labor markets; it also reduces problems of recall for within-firm job changes. In a large US insurance company that had a preference for promoting from within, exits were lower from higher grades and from positions with higher promotion opportunities (Petersen et al 1989, Petersen & Spilerman 1990). While such structural effects were stronger on exits for career reasons, they were similar for exits for personal reasons, suggesting even these decisions can be responsive to career incentives. (See also Felmlee 1984a.) Over all regular grades, promotion declined with grade. Education did affect promotions, though no clear pattern emerged of its having a stronger effect on exits. (Rosenbaum 1984, Spilerman & Lunde 1991, and Wise 1975 also show how different educational credentials and performance influence promotions.) Further, Spilerman & Lunde (1991) found that, contrary to Sørensen's (1977) model, promotion chances were higher when the match between credentials and job demands was good. Effects of firm and job tenure suggested that firm-specific human capital helped retain an employee and job-specific human capital led to promotion.

At the same time, it is not enough simply to use grade level. A given firm may have *sets* of job ladders and internal labor markets (Althauser 1989b, DiPrete 1989, DiPrete & Krecker 1991, DiPrete & Soule 1986, 1988, Spilerman & Petersen 1989). A given job ladder may cover only a certain range of salary grades. To move up farther, the employee needs to change job ladders. Or employees may change ladders in ways that do not lead to upward mobility (DiPrete & Krecker 1991). In the insurance firm Spilerman & Petersen (1989) studied, promotion (a move up in salary grade) did not depend on a vacancy's being present. A move to another job ladder, however, did. They show that promotion was less likely at salary grades that tended to be job ladder ceilings. The company's posting and bidding policy, which encouraged transfers to other job categories, seemed to reduce those firm exits due to approaching a promotion ceiling. DiPrete & Soule (1988) had similar results.

What influences advancement in grade on a given ladder may differ from what leads to a change of ladders or set of ladders, often in ways similar to predictions about within- as compared with between-firm shifts. Because of credential requirements and screening on an easily observed characteristic, formal education seems more important in movement across ladders than in promotion on a ladder (DiPrete & Krecker 1991, DiPrete & Soule 1988). There is a negative relationship between opportunity on a given job ladder and a tier shift. In addition, those at higher grades are more likely to shift ladders, while those with more seniority are less likely to (DiPrete & Soule 1988). Further, investigation of movement between as well as on job ladders clarifies how race and sex differences in mobility occur (Halaby 1982, Sandefur 1981a, Skvoretz 1984a). In the federal civil service, once women reached upper administrative and professional levels, they advanced at the same rate as men. But they had trouble reaching these levels. On the other hand, controlling for sex, nonwhites, while entering at lower levels, had promotion rates within and across tiers similar to those of whites (DiPrete 1989).

There can be different paths to a given job—with different implications for further mobility—and a given job can lead to a number of different further opportunities (Gaertner 1980, Macdonald 1987, Rosenbaum 1979, 1984, 1990, Spenner et al 1982, Spilerman 1977). Althauser (1989b, Althauser & Kalleberg 1990), with data on a number of companies, used transitions between jobs to find the linkages up and between ladders that form career pathways. Characteristics of the career line and a job's location on it affected the rate of job shifting: The closer a job, on average, to the end of the career lines of which it was a part, the slower a job shift (Althauser 1989b, Althauser & Kalleberg 1990).

Althauser (1989b:179) argues that the key characteristic of an internal labor market is that "there occurs a progressive development of skill or knowledge and a corresponding, regular advancement from less to more responsible and demanding tasks and positions composed of such tasks." This implies that, within an internal labor market, the longer the time on a particular job, the more likely advancement (see also White & Althauser 1984). He uses this implication (along with demographic and locational characteristics of paths) to specify the subset of career lines likely to be true internal labor markets.

OCCUPATIONAL LABOR MARKETS AND ECONOMIC SECTORS Differences among types of firms, industries, and occupations in their job rewards, career ladders, and employment relationships should affect the job shifts underlying careers. Predominantly male occupations, for example, have been characterized as offering higher rewards and greater promotion opportunities than predominantly female occupations. In at least one study, however, occupations with a higher proportion of women were those with faster rates of upward authority moves (Hachen 1990). After the fact, Hachen speculates that predominantly female occupations involve more intensive supervision and thus have more layers of lower-level authority through which to move. To the extent that better jobs retain workers, one might predict lower turnover, although Waite & Berryman (1986) suggest that those in an atypical occupation are more likely to leave because of mismatch with the job and lack of acceptance. They failed to find effects of sex composition on women's probability of changing jobs—and discovered men were less likely to change jobs if they were in a typically female occupation, perhaps because these men have (or think they have) greater chances for promotion in these jobs.

Carroll & Mayer (1986) characterized occupations by class characteristics roughly along the lines of Wright (1978). They expected—and found—classes with more organizational authority to be more stable, with slower rates of job mobility. White-collar employees moved more slowly downwards in wages as compared with blue-collar workers, even though there were no collar-color differences in rates of upward and lateral moves. Further, class variables had much stronger effects for across-firm than within-firm mobility, with no effect on upward mobility within firms. (See also Mayer & Carroll 1987.)

Those who see the economy as segmented along firm and industry lines have described the core as offering higher rewards, more job security, and greater career opportunities (in closed employment relationships), while the periphery includes more unstable, low-reward, dead-end jobs. Being in the monopoly sector slows between-employer moves and increases the rate of within-employer moves. It has no effect, however, on involuntary moves and a negative effect on the rate of upward authority moves (Hachen 1990; see also D'Amico & Brown 1982). With a more refined industrial typology (Stinchcombe 1979; see also Hachen 1988b), Carroll & Mayer (1986; Mayer & Carroll 1987) showed not only that industrial sectors affected the various kinds of job mobility, but also that the magnitude of organizational size and class effects varied across sectors.

A problem with these studies of labor market segmentation is that they do not look at people's destinations when they leave a firm. Labor market segmentation theories postulate that one way in which these structures affect careers is by limiting job mobility across segments, especially later in the work life and especially when this would involve movement to a "higher" segment. Moves across segment boundaries do occur, however. When they change jobs, people change sex-type of occupation (Jacobs 1989, Rosenfeld 1983, 1984, Rosenfeld & Spenner forthcoming), economic sector (D'Amico & Brown 1982, Rosenfeld 1983), type of firm (Rosenfeld & Jones 1986), social class (Mayer & Carroll 1990), and occupation—even within firms (DiPrete 1990, DiPrete & Krecker 1991, Stier & Grusky 1990).

If these boundaries are meaningful for an understanding of careers, then we would expect to see patterns in such movement as well as effects of individuals' resources and other characteristics on sector shifts. (See also Lipset & Bendix 1952, Palmer 1954, Reynolds 1951.) Flows across labor market boundaries do seem stronger in some directions than others. In Germany, the professional and higher service class had a rate of class changing about 90% lower than that for farm workers (Mayer & Carroll 1990). At least for US men over 20, those who were mobile were less likely to move from the periphery to the core and more likely to make intrasector shifts as they got older (D'Amico & Brown 1982, Rosenfeld 1983; see also Tolbert 1982.) And the likelihood of upward wage mobility increased with moves out of the competitive sector and decreased with moves into it (Rosenfeld 1983).

People are more likely to move from a sex-atypical to sex-typical occupation than in the reverse direction (Jacobs 1989, Rosenfeld 1983, 1984, Rosenfeld & Spenner, forthcoming). Finding little that explained the likelihood of moves among occupations with different sex types, Jacobs (1989) developed the image of a revolving door for sex-type mobility. A sample of young Washington State women provided more information on jobs and background than Jacobs had. Their rates of movement between and within male and female occupations were consistent with differences in careers between sex-type sectors. While moves set in sex-typical occupations seemed to be more part of "real" than random careers, especially for professionals, only for moves between typically male occupations did the pattern of effects associated with "closed" employment systems (positive effect of resources, negative effect of rewards, no effect of time) appear. Further, higher aspirations and stronger early work commitment kept a woman in or drew her to predominately male occupations (Rosenfeld & Spenner, forthcoming). Thus the analysis of boundary crossing, combined with a closer look at types of shifts from various segments, indicates that occupational category and industry type influence how job shifts affect labor market rewards over time. At the same time, one needs to look more closely at job contexts (including within-firm labor markets) to see how occupational and job characteristics affect career development (Baron 1990, Rosenfeld & Spenner, forthcoming).

NATIONAL MARKETS Still another level of labor market and institutional structure that can affect how job shifts shape careers is the national one (Mayer & Schoepflin 1989). To my knowledge, Allmendinger (1989a) provides the only cross-national comparison of the job mobility process using job history data rather than information on jobs at given times or career points (Kalleberg 1988). She finds that Norwegians & Americans (both white and black) have a greater average number of jobs than do West Germans. But West Germans have a greater proportion of all jobs that are moves up in status, suggesting that their work trajectories are more structured. Net of individual characteristics, macroeconomic variables account for differences within Europe in overall job-shifting rates, but not for the European/US differences. The macroeconomic variables account for all the between-country variance in rates of upward mobility.

The *process* of job shifting and upward mobility differs across countries. Macroeconomic conditions, for example, matter more for US than European upward prestige mobility. In countries with more stratified and standardized educational systems (Norway & Germany), educational credentials affect job shifting and upward mobility, while in the United States, years of education are what counts. (See also Allmendinger 1989b.) Further, in terms of patterns of significance of labor force experience, origin status, and resources, the European, but not American, results are consistent with predictions of Sørensen's (1977) vacancy competition model.

TIME

In addition to a focus on opportunity structures, most of the sociological research on job shifting has an interest in how time affects career processes, as was seen in the discussion above. A number of different clocks run during an individual's work life, however, and life-cycle stage can be important as well. Further, labor markets are not invariant over time. Organizations change over time along with the legal, social, and economic regional or national context (Grandjean 1981, Osterman 1984b).

Time in the Individual's Work Life

LABOR FORCE EXPERIENCE The general expectation, and usual result, is that voluntary job shifts decline with time in the labor force. For Sørensen (1977) this reflects a declining discrepancy between current and potential positions. Others emphasize that over time workers learn more about the labor market and their place in it (with consequent better fit between themselves and their jobs), develop skills particular to a given job or employer, accumulate greater investments with an employer (pensions, etc; Bartel 1982), and have a shorter time over which to enjoy any benefits from a new job.

"Time in the labor force" is measured as time since leaving school, actual labor force experience, and cumulative employment. In data on white men, Tuma (1985) did not find results differed when using years since leaving school versus length of work experience. For groups with more or longer periods of nonemployment, however, the exact measurement of labor force or employment experience could affect results, although Hachen (1988a) did not find evidence of this. Further, work experience is usually measured from last exit from schooling. In both the United States and Norway (although not in Germany), there is a transition period, when many people combine employment and school, simultaneously or sequentially. The nature of this transition period affects later job mobility (Allmendinger 1989a,b; see also Hogan & Astone 1986).

FIRM-SPECIFIC SENIORITY One might further specify the opportunity structure to which a person has been exposed or in which a person has human capital and other investments. Many explanations of the effect of labor market experience hold with greater force for tenure with a given employer. Petersen & Spilerman (1990) show that departure for career reasons declined rapidly with seniority, while quits for family reasons were less influenced by years with the firm. Further, even controlling for job position, seniority had some negative effect on promotion rates. In a public utilities firm, managers' rate of movement across job titles also declined with length of service (Halaby 1982).

DURATION DEPENDENCE The effect of time spent in a particular state has perhaps been considered more than any other timing variable. Again, the general expectation (and common finding) is that duration dependence is negative. The longer a person is on a given job, the arguments go, the better the job match (Flinn 1986), the greater the nontransferable skill and knowledge (and perhaps particular rewards) (Tuma 1976), the fewer outside job contacts (Granovetter 1986), and the greater "cumulative inertia" (Sørensen & Tuma 1981). Further, unobserved differences in the propensity to change states show up as negative duration dependence, although in practice it is difficult empirically or even substantively to distinguish effects of unobserved heterogeneity from those of duration dependence (Blossfeld & Hamerle 1990, Congdon 1985, Galler & Poetter 1990, Hutchison 1988, Tuma & Hannan 1984).

There are, however, arguments for positive duration dependence. Over time, a worker might become increasingly dissatisfied with an initially unsatisfactory job or increasingly feel the rewards do not match her or his resources, especially those acquired on the job (Congdon 1985, Sørensen & Tuma 1981). Sørensen & Tuma (1981:82) reason that "In upward moves, positive and negative duration dependence are likely to be confounded, while in downward moves the mechanisms that produce negative duration dependence should prevail" and present results consistent with this. Hachen (1990), however, does not find this pattern, and Congdon (1985), with data on Irish occupational mobility, reports positive duration dependence for both upward and downward moves, which becomes stronger with controls for unobserved heterogeneity.

Althauser (1989b, Althauser & Kalleberg 1990, White & Althauser 1984) posits that on-the-job learning is what drives mobility within internal labor markets. Duration dependence measures increasing skill and knowledge and is therefore expected to be positive within these markets. He uses positive duration dependence to verify that a given set of jobs does constitute a firm internal labor market.

Arguments that duration dependence can be both positive and negative imply that it might be nonmonotonic. Allowing for this, Petersen & Spilerman (1990) see that the probability of a promotion first increased, then decreased with time in grade. In contrast with firm exits, where duration effects were weak or nonsignificant, "the process of promotion follows a renewal process, where the relevant clock is time since last promotion…" (p. 94). On the other hand, while young men in their first jobs showed negative duration dependence, young women's quits declined across time in the job, then increased, perhaps because they were increasingly likely to leave to start families (Donohue 1988).

There may also be lagged dependence effects: those who are promoted early (relative to their entry cohorts) could be those who have been identified as fast-trackers or stars and who will be promoted faster at later stages of their careers (Rosenbaum 1979, 1984, 1990, Stewman & Konda 1983). Although one might expect hypotheses about tournament mobility to apply more to higher level white-collar workers, Brüderl et al (1991a) find that among German blue-collar workers, the faster the first promotion, the faster later ones.

AGE Age is highly collinear with labor force experience (Felmlee 1984b, Tuma 1985) and correlates as well with other measures of job experience. Within a job, of course, age, labor force experience, and duration all vary together, making it difficult to separate their effects (Petersen 1986). Age is sometimes used as a proxy for other time measures (e.g. Felmlee 1982, 1984a,b, Sørensen 1974, Tuma 1976), and in analyses of job shifts generally, its effect is often insignificant or weak when other time measures are included (Kandel & Yamaguchi 1987, Tuma 1976).

There is the possibility, however, of real age norms in organizations: after a certain age (say, 40), a person might be considered "too old" for certain promotions (Rosenbaum 1979, 1984, Stewman 1988). Petersen & Spilerman (1990) discovered that the age when a person enters a job grade has a negative effect on promotion similar to that of firm seniority, although it has a smaller effect on quits. Even beyond such age barriers, those who enter a system at relatively young ages or are promoted when younger may be perceived as those who are especially able and likely to achieve still more. Managers who joined a California utilities firm at older ages had slower rates of job shifts (Halaby 1982). In Great Britain, those who first became Members of Parliament when they were younger, especially in their 30s, had higher rates of movement to higher positions (Macdonald 1987). Male academic psychologists who received their doctorates at an earlier age moved faster between schools (which often led to an increase in rank or institutional prestige) (Rosenfeld & Jones 1986). Age may have a different meaning for women. Insignificant age effects for women (Donohue 1988, Halaby 1982, Rosenfeld & Jones 1986) perhaps indicate that while older women suffer the same mobility disadvantages as older men, they are also perceived as more desirable employees because they are considered less likely to leave an organization to take care of family responsibilities than are younger women.

Life Cycle Effects

Given the identification of recent job mobility research as part of life course research (Mayer & Tuma 1990b), it is surprising that life course concepts are not more visible in this literature. There is not enough explicit attention to stages of a work life. Entering the work force is often a process rather than an event, as Allmendinger (1989a,b) demonstrates. Timing of job shifts early in the work life might differ from timing later. In contrast with many others, Felmlee (1982) reports positive age effects on the rate of voluntary job shifts, greater for moves within than between employers. Her data were on relatively young women, 19–29 at the end of the data collection period, an age range within which employers might look on somewhat older ages as a sign of maturity, as well as being past initial childbearing. Similarly, for Hispanic men Tuma (1976) finds positive effects of age on job shifting to about age 22 and then virtually no effect.

Despite the general finding that the rate of job shifting slows with age or labor force experience, some people have found that first jobs are longer than others. Shavit et al (1990) speculate that this is true for Israeli men because they are reluctant to leave their jobs when faced with impending military service, while Mayer & Carroll (1990:39) hypothesize that in Germany, first jobs may be jobs "held after three-year apprenticeships and often in the same firm. Therefore they are less likely to show the characteristics of a job-search period." An alternative explanation is that people fail to report shorter early jobs. But with personnel records of a large bank, Althauser (1989b) also found longer waiting times for first jobs, one explanation for which would be that these tended to be positions in which training and selection took place. Spenner et al (1990) link the segmented nature of the British education system to variation in how long people hold their first jobs; more research along these lines is needed. In discussions of how opportunities are structured, the level at which one enters a system is discussed as indicating potential for advancement. Yet there is relatively little research on how this level—or career trajectory up to a given job—affects later outcomes (Rosenbaum 1979, 1984, 1990).

At older ages, people move toward retirement. Again, this can be a process rather than an event. Ruhm (1990) distinguishes between career jobs and bridge jobs as people move out of the labor force, but we know relatively little about how job changing ends a work career (see, for example, Bartel & Borjas 1977, Beck 1986).

There is also neglect of how other life domains and the life courses of other family members affect the work career. As is true for attainment and work research more generally, analysis of women's job shifting includes more explicit attention to family factors. In Felmlee's analyses (1982, 1984b), marriage, especially to a husband with a higher income, decreased job mobility, while having young children made it more likely that a woman moved from full-time to part-time employment. Women with more family responsibilities moved more slowly from jobs they thought of as just ways to get money to jobs they considered parts of careers (Rosenfeld & Spenner 1988). The only family effect on rate of shifting across sex-type boundaries

Rosenfeld & Spenner (forthcoming) discovered was unexpected: women with young children moved faster to predominately male occupations, perhaps because of income needs.

Organizational, National, and Legal Change

While organizational change can take the form of restructuring jobs and employment relationships (DiPrete 1989, 1991, Kanter 1984, Pfeffer & Baron 1988, Stewman & Konda 1983), job-shifting research that considers organizational change usually measures it by changing size. In general, expansion leads to greater mobility opportunity but can affect different groups differently (Baron 1984). In the Office of the Comptroller of the Currency, women were more sensitive to changes in the size of the workforce than men, benefitting from growth, but also suffering more from decline (Skvoretz 1984a). In a German firm, among blue-collar workers, men seemed more affected by economic change than women, while the advantage of citizens over noncitizens increased during periods of contraction (Brüderl et al 1991b).

Secular and cyclical economic conditions at the regional or national level can affect mobility chances, in part through effects on organizational size, but also through changing the distribution of opportunity between firms (DiPrete 1991, Hachen 1988b). Allmendinger's (1989a) work illustrated how national differences in economic conditions and their effects led to differences in job-shifting rates across countries. Blossfeld (1986) shows that in Germany, those who took their first jobs when the country had become more modernized and when labor market conditions were better entered at higher levels. They moved up more slowly but were also protected from downward moves. After labor market entry, during periods of economic development or cyclical upturns, mobility increased. Sørensen & Blossfeld (1989) further suggest that cohort differences in career trajectories represent expansion of economic sectors which provided better chances for upward mobility.

Legal changes can also alter mobility chances both in general and for specific groups (Abbott & Smith 1984). In the United States in the 1960s and 1970s, equal employment opportunity and affirmative action legislation was enacted to increase opportunity for women and racial/ethnic minority groups. This legislation led to upward mobility programs in the federal civil service that, among other things, restructured career paths. These changes increased mobility rates. Because a large proportion of employees were women and nonwhites, this increase benefitted these groups. There was no evidence, however, that "minority" group members had an advantage over men or whites in getting promotions from lower level positions (DiPrete 1989, DiPrete & Soule 1986).

LINKING MECHANISMS

Halaby (1988:9) argues that "Sociological models of voluntary job mobility have little to say about worker action and information as mechanisms of change in achievement." Sørensen (1975:460–61) discusses the job-shifting process as one in which "job opportunities become known to the individual and create impulses to leave a job," but does not develop this line of thought. Halaby (1988) and Stolzenberg (1988) build frameworks that include components similar to those in models Tuma (1976) and Sørensen (1977) outline: a worker's current rewards, resources, and perceptions of the opportunity structure. But they emphasize the cognitive processes by which workers are motivated to search for information about other jobs and then evaluate them relative to the ones they currently hold. Only if, as a result of this process, the worker believes there are relative gains to be made will he or she voluntarily change jobs.

The line of research that has most directly concentrated on the mechanisms by which mobile workers learn about jobs is that on methods of job search. The general expectation, and usual result, is that use of personal networks leads to better jobs and better job matches (Campbell & Rosenfeld 1985, Granovetter 1974). Ways of finding a new job and the importance and availability of contacts are not independent of the nature of the opportunity structure, but depend on the size, bureaucratization, markets, and hierarchical structure of an organization (Lin 1990, Marsden & Campbell 1990).

The individual worker, of course, is not the only actor in the job-shifting process. Employers and managers are involved as well (Baron 1984, Granovetter 1986, Stewman 1988). Much job-shift analysis is based on voluntary job shifts, but recognizes that the processes and outcomes of involuntary shifts are different (Hachen 1990, Sørensen 1974, Sørensen & Fuerst 1978). Even in voluntary shifts, employers' hiring and promotion criteria—and their implementation of them—are important. Unions and professional associations (as well as legal regulations) can help shape these hiring and promotion policies. Further, decisions about job changes often involve family considerations, as well. In general, then, there is a need to specify the mechanisms and processes by which individuals come to be matched with given jobs across their job histories, with more attention to how people are "embedded" in social relationships (Granovetter 1986).

CONCLUSIONS

Research on job shifting highlights the influence of structure and time on career development. Many conceptions of the opportunity structure incorporate elements of vacancy models, but there are alternative ways in which mobility is created. With information on a given organization, it is possible to detail career paths and opportunity structures as well as the nature of managerial decision making about promotions, but the cost is that it is difficult to follow careers that move away from a particular employer. When we use information from general samples, we lose detail about the particular mobility regimes. What we need is not a proliferation of "structural" variables to include in models of job shifts, but a better understanding of the dimensions and mechanisms that define "opportunity structures" (Baron 1984, Sørensen 1986) and affect different kinds of job mobility. Many of the approaches discussed in this review see structure as interacting with resources, but here too there is a need for better specification of which types of resources are important for mobility in different settings and why. (For an example of an approach focusing on workers' personality traits, see Silver & Spilerman 1990.)

Many dimensions of time affect career development: some are viewed as proxies for different types of resources, others are taken as indicating the workings of "structure." Perhaps one reason why there are contradictory results about the effect of time in the labor force (taken as a test of vacancy competition models) is that important aspects of career timing are usually excluded from a given piece of research. Petersen & Spilerman (1990) do perhaps the best job of keeping track of the different individual clocks. As well, the life course framework alerts us to consider what is happening in other life domains. Further, changes over time in the economic, legal, and cultural context indicate changing demand for workers.

There is a need to continue to examine complete work histories. A problem with much of the work on job shifts is that one loses sight of the complete career line. Petersen's (1988) linking of discrete job shifts with continuous outcomes helps connect study of the underlying job shifts with the resulting career trajectory in terms of labor market rewards such as earnings (Hannan et al 1990, Rosenfeld & Nielsen 1984). Abbott & Hrycak's (1990) use of optimal matching to find "typical" career lines brings us back to earlier concerns with finding patterns in sequences of positions (e.g. Form & Miller 1949, Palmer 1954, Spilerman 1977).

We now have the methodology to deal with the dynamic development of careers, and we at least know what kinds of data we need. Ahead is the challenge of developing a deeper conceptual and theoretical understanding of work histories and careers.

ACKNOWLEDGMENTS

This research was supported in part by a grant from the Institute for Research in Social Science and the resources of the Carolina Population Center. I am grateful to Daishiro Nomiya and Mark Van Buren for bibliographic assistance, to Lynn Igoe for editorial suggestions, and to Robert Althauser, Peter Blau, David Hachen, François Nielsen, Kim Lane Scheppele, Aage Sørensen, and Seymour Spilerman for very useful comments.

Literature Cited

Abbott, A. 1990. Vacancy models for historical data. See Breiger 1990b, pp. 80–102

Abbott, A., Hrycak, A. 1990. Measuring resemblance in sequence data: An optimal matching analysis of musicians' careers. *Am. J. Sociol.* 96:144–85

Abbott, A., Smith, D. R. 1984. Governmental constraints and labor market mobility. Turnover among college athletic personnel. *Work Occup.* 11:29–53

Allison, P. D. 1984. *Event History Analysis. Regression for Longitudinal Event Data.* Beverly Hills, Calif: Sage

Allmendinger, J. 1989a. *Career Mobility Dynamics: A Comparative Analysis of the United States, Norway, and West Germany. Studien und Berichte 49.* Berlin: Max-Planck-Inst. Bildungsforschung

Allmendinger, J. 1989b. Educational systems and labor market outcomes. *Eur. Sociol. Rev.* 5:231–50

Althauser, R. P. 1989a. Internal labor markets. *Annu. Rev. Sociol.* 15:143–61

Althauser, R. P. 1989b. Job histories, career lines and firm internal labor markets. *Res. Soc. Strat. Mobil.* 8:177–200

Althauser, R. P., Kalleberg, A. L. 1990. Identifying career lines and internal labor markets within firms: A study in the interrelationships of theory and methods. See Breiger 1990b, pp. 308–56

Baron, J. N. 1984. Organizational perspectives on stratification. *Annu. Rev. Sociol.* 10:37–69

Baron, J. N. 1990. Are the doors revolving or still locked shut? *Contemp. Sociol.* 19:347–49

Bartel, A. P. 1980. Earnings growth on the job and between jobs. *Econ. Inquiry* 18:123–37

Bartel, A. P. 1982. Wages, nonwage job characteristics, and labor mobility. *Indust. Labor Relat. Rev.* 35:578–89

Bartel, A. P., Borjas, G. J. 1977. Middle-age job mobility: Its determinants and consequences. In *Men in the Pre-Retirement Years,* ed. S. L. Wolfbein, pp. 39–97. Philadelphia: Temple Univ.

Beck, S. H. 1986. Mobility from preretirement to postretirement job. *Sociol. Q.* 27: 515–31

Blau, P. M., Duncan, O. D. 1967. *The American Occupational Structure.* New York: Wiley

Blossfeld, H-P. 1986. Career opportunities in the Federal Republic of Germany: A dynamic approach to the study of life-course, cohort, and period effects. *Eur. Sociol. Rev.* 2:208–25

Blossfeld, H-P., Hamerle, A. 1990. Unobserved heterogeneity in hazard rate models: A test and an illustration from a study of career mobility. See Mayer & Tuma 1990a, pp. 241–52

Blumen, I., Kogan, M., McCarthy, P. J. 1955. *The Industrial Mobility of Labor as a Probability Process. Cornell Studies in Industrial and Labor Relations,* Vol. 6. Ithaca, NY: Cornell Univ.

Borjas, G. J. 1981. Job mobility and earnings over the life cycle. *Indust. Labor Relat. Rev.* 34:365–76

Breiger, R. L. 1990a. Introduction: On the structural analysis of social mobility. See Breiger 1990b, pp. 1–23

Breiger, R. L., ed. 1990b. *Social Mobility and Social Structure.* Cambridge: Cambridge Univ. Press

Brüderl, J. 1992. Dynamic models and inequality research: A reexamination of the Sørensen model. *Sociol. Methods Res.* 21:In press

Brüderl, J., Diekmann, A., Preisendörfer, P. 1991a. Patterns of intraorganizational mobility: Tournament models, path dependency, and early promotion effects. *Soc. Sci. Res.* 20:197–216

Brüderl, J., Preisendörfer, P., Ziegler, R. 1991b. *Upward mobility in organizations: The effects of hierarchy and opportunity structure.* Unpublished ms. Inst. Sociol., Univ. Munich

Campbell, K. E., Rosenfeld, R. A. 1985. Job search and job mobility: Sex and race differences. *Res. Sociol. Work.* 3:147–74

Carroll, G. R., Mayer, K. U. 1984. Organizational effects in the wage attainment process. *Soc. Sci. J.* 21:5–22

Carroll, G. R., Mayer, K. U. 1986. Job-shift patterns in the Federal Republic of Germany: The effects of social class, industrial sector, and organizational size. *Am. Sociol. Rev.* 51:323–41

Carroll, G. R., Mosakowski, E. 1987. The career dynamics of self-employment. *Admin. Sci. Q.* 32:570–89

Chase, I. D. 1991. Vacancy chains. *Annu. Rev. Sociol.* 17:133–54

Clark, B. R. 1987. *The Academic Life: Small*

Worlds, Different Worlds. Princeton, NJ: Carnegie Found. Advancement Teaching
Congdon, P. 1985. Heterogeneity and timing effects in occupational mobility: A general model. *Oxford Bull. Econ. Stat.* 47:347–69
D'Amico, R., Brown, T. 1982. Patterns of labor mobility in a dual economy: The case of semiskilled and unskilled workers. *Soc. Sci. Res.* 11:153–75
DiPrete, T. A. 1989. *The Bureaucratic Labor Market: The Case of the Federal Civil Service*. New York: Plenum
DiPrete, T. A. 1990. Adding covariates to loglinear models for the study of social mobility. *Am. Sociol. Rev.* 55:757–73
DiPrete, T. A. 1991. *Industrial restructuring, organizational labor markets, and the mobility response of American workers in the 1980s*. Unpublished ms. Dept. Sociol., Duke Univ.
DiPrete, T. A., Krecker, M. L. 1991. Occupational linkages and job mobility within and across organizations. *Res. Soc. Strat. Mobil.* 10:91–131
DiPrete, T. A., Soule, W. T. 1986. The organization of career lines: Equal employment opportunity and status advancement in a federal bureaucracy. *Am. Sociol. Rev.* 51:295–309
DiPrete, T. A., Soule, W. T. 1988. Gender and promotion in segmented job ladder systems. *Am. Sociol. Rev.* 53:26–40
Donohue, J. J. III. 1988. Determinants of job turnover of young men and women in the United States: A hazard rate analysis. *Res. Polit. Econ.* 6:257–301
Felmlee, D. H. 1982. Women's job mobility processes within and between employers. *Am. Sociol. Rev.* 47:142–51
Felmlee, D. H. 1984a. A dynamic analysis of women's employment exits. *Demography* 21:171–83
Felmlee, D. H. 1984b. The dynamics of women's job mobility. *Work Occup.* 11:259–81
Flinn, C. J. 1986. Wages and job mobility of young workers. *J. Polit. Econ.* 94:S88–110
Form, W. H., Miller, D. C. 1949. Occupational career pattern as a sociological instrument. *Am. J. Sociol.* 54:317–29
Gaertner, K. N. 1980. The structure of organizational careers. *Sociol. Educ.* 53:7–20
Galler, H. P., Poetter, U. 1990. Unobserved heterogeneity in models of unemployment duration. See Mayer & Tuma 1990a, pp. 226–40
Grandjean, B. D. 1981. History and career in a bureaucratic labor market. *Am. J. Sociol.* 86:1057–92
Granovetter, M. 1974. *Getting a Job*. Cambridge, Mass: Harvard Univ. Press
Granovetter, M. 1986. Labor mobility, internal markets, and job matching: A comparison of the sociological and economic approaches. *Res. Soc. Strat. Mobil.* 5:3–39
Hachen, D. S. Jr. 1988a. Gender differences in job mobility rates in the United States. *Soc. Sci. Res.* 17:93–116
Hachen, D. S. Jr. 1988b. Industrial labor markets and job mobility rates. *Res. Soc. Strat. Mobil.* 7:35–68
Hachen, D. S. Jr. 1990. Three models of job mobility in labor markets. *Work Occup.* 17:320–54
Halaby, C. N. 1982. Job-shift differences between men and women in the workplace. *Soc. Sci. Res.* 11:1–29
Halaby, C. N. 1988. Action and information in the job mobility process: The search decision. *Am. Sociol. Rev.* 53:9–25
Hannan, M. T., Schömann, K., Blossfeld, H-P. 1990. Sex and sector differences in the dynamics of wage growth in the Federal Republic of Germany. *Am. Sociol. Rev.* 55:694–713
Harrison, R. J. 1988. Opportunity models: Adapting vacancy models to national occupational structures. *Res. Soc. Strat. Mobil.* 7:3–33
Hogan, D. P., Astone, N. M. 1986. The transition to adulthood. *Annu. Rev. Sociol.* 12:109–30
Hutchison, D. 1988. Event history and survival analysis in the social sciences. II: Advanced applications and recent developments. *Qual. Quant.* 22:255–78
Jacobs, J. A. 1989. *Revolving Doors: Sex Segregation and Women's Careers*. Stanford, Calif: Stanford Univ. Press
Kalleberg, A. L. 1988. Comparative perspectives on work structures and inequality. *Annu. Rev. Sociol.* 14:203–25
Kalleberg, A. L., Sørensen, A. B. 1979. The sociology of labor markets. *Annu. Rev. Sociol.* 5:351–79
Kandel, D. B., Yamaguchi, K. 1987. Job mobility and drug use: An event history analysis. *Am. J. Sociol.* 92:836–78
Kanter, R. M. 1984. Variations in managerial career structures in high-technology firms: The impact of organizational characteristics on internal labor market patterns. See Osterman 1984a, pp. 109–31
Konda, S. L., Stewman, S. 1980. An opportunity labor demand model and Markovian labor supply models: Comparative tests in an organization. *Am. Sociol. Rev.* 45:276–301
Lin, N. 1990. Social resources and social mobility: A structural theory of status attainment. See Breiger 1990b, pp. 247–71
Lipset, S. M., Bendix, R. 1952. Social mobility and occupational career patterns: II. Social mobility. *Am. J. Sociol.* 57:494–504
Macdonald, S. E. 1987. *Political ambition and attainment: A dynamic analysis of par-*

liamentary careers. PhD thesis. Univ. Mich., Ann Arbor

Marsden, P. M., Campbell, K. E. 1990. Recruitment and selection processes: The organizational side of job searches. See Breiger 1990b, pp. 59–79

Mayer, K. U., Carroll, G. R. 1987. Jobs and classes: Structural constraints on career mobility. *Eur. Sociol. Rev*. 3:14–38

Mayer, K. U., Carroll, G. R. 1990. Jobs and classes: Structural constraints on career mobility. See Mayer & Tuma 1990a, pp. 23–52

Mayer, K. U., Schoepflin, U. 1989. The state and the life course. *Annu. Rev. Sociol*. 15:187–209

Mayer, K. U., Tuma, N. B., eds. 1990a. *Event History Analysis in Life Course Research*. Madison, Wisc: Univ. Wisc. Press

Mayer, K. U., Tuma, N. B. 1990b. Life course research and event history analysis: An overview. See Mayer & Tuma 1990a, pp. 3–20

Miner, A. S., Estler, S. E. 1985. Accrual mobility: Job mobility in higher education through responsibility accrual. *J. Higher Educ*. 56:121–43

Nielsen, F., Rosenfeld, R. A. 1981. Substantive interpretations of differential equation models. *Am. Sociol. Rev*. 46:159–74

Osterman, P., ed. 1984a. *Internal Labor Markets*. Cambridge, Mass: MIT Press

Osterman, P. 1984b. Introduction: The nature and importance of internal labor markets. See Osterman 1984a, pp. 1–22

Palmer, G. L. 1954. *Labor Mobility in Six Cities: A Report on the Survey of Patterns and Factors in Labor Mobility 1940–50*. New York: Soc. Sci. Res. Council

Parnes, H. S. 1954. *Research on Labor Mobility: An Appraisal of Research Findings in the United States. Bull. No. 65*. New York: Soc. Sci. Res. Council

Petersen, T. 1986. Estimating fully parametric hazard rate models with time-dependent covariates. *Sociol. Methods Res*. 14:219–46

Petersen, T. 1988. Analyzing change over time in a continuous dependent variable: Specification and estimation of continuous state space hazard rate models. *Sociol. Method*. 18:137–64

Petersen, T. 1991. The statistical analysis of event histories. *Sociol. Methods Res*. 19: 270–323

Petersen, T., Spilerman, S. 1990. Job quits from an internal labor market. See Mayer & Tuma 1990a, pp. 69–95

Petersen, T., Spilerman, S., Dahl, S-A. 1989. The structure of employment terminations among clerical employees in a large bureaucracy. *Acta Sociol*. 32:319–38

Pfeffer, J., Baron, J. N. 1988. Taking the workers back out: Recent trends in the structuring of employment. *Res. Organ. Behav*. 10:257–303

Reynolds, L. G. 1951. *The Structure of Labor Markets: Wages and Labor Mobility in Theory and Practice*. New York: Harper

Rosenbaum, J. E. 1979. Tournament mobility: Career patterns in a corporation. *Admin. Sci. Q*. 24:220–41

Rosenbaum, J. E. 1984. *Career Mobility in a Corporate Hierarchy*. New York: Academic

Rosenbaum, J. E. 1990. Structural models of organizational careers: A critical review and new directions. See Breiger 1990b, pp. 272–307

Rosenfeld, R. A. 1983. Sex segregation and sectors: An analysis of gender differences in returns from employer changes. *Am. Sociol. Rev*. 48:637–55

Rosenfeld, R. A. 1984. Job changing and occupational sex segregation: Sex and race comparisons. In *Sex Segregation in the Workplace: Trends, Explanations, Remedies,* ed. B. F. Reskin, pp. 56–86. Washington, DC: Natl. Acad. Sci. Press

Rosenfeld, R. A., Jones, J. A. 1986. Institutional mobility among academics: The case of psychologists. *Sociol. Educ*. 59: 212–26

Rosenfeld, R. A., Nielsen, F. 1984. Inequality and careers: A dynamic model of socioeconomic achievement. *Sociol. Methods Res*. 12:279–321

Rosenfeld, R. A., Spenner, K. I. 1988. Women's work and women's careers: A dynamic analysis of work identity in the early life course. In *Social Structures and Human Lives,* ed. M. W. Riley, 1:285–305. Newbury Park, Calif: Sage

Rosenfeld, R. A., Spenner, K. I. 1992. Occupational sex segregation and careers. *Work Occup*. In press

Ruhm, C. J. 1990. Career jobs, bridge employment, and retirements. In *Bridges to Retirement: Older Workers in a Changing Labor Market,* ed. P. B. Doeringer, pp. 92–107. Ithaca, NY: ILR

Sandefur, G. D. 1981a. Black/white differences in job shift behavior: A dynamic analysis. *Sociol. Q*. 22:565–79

Sandefur, G. D. 1981b. Organizational boundaries and upward job shifts. *Soc. Sci. Res*. 10:67–82

Shavit, Y., Matras, J., Featherman, D. L. 1990. Job shifts in the career beginnings of Israeli men. See Mayer & Tuma 1990a, pp. 53–68

Silver, C. B., Spilerman, S. 1990. Psychoanalytic perspectives on occupational choice and attainment. *Res. Soc. Strat. Mobil*. 9:181–214

Skvoretz, J. 1984a. Career mobility as a Poisson process. *Soc. Sci. Res*. 13:198–220

Skvoretz, J. 1984b. The logic of opportunity and mobility. *Soc. Forces* 63:72–97

Smith, D. R. 1983. Mobility in professional occupational-internal markets: Stratification, segmentation and vacancy chains. *Am. Sociol. Rev.* 48:289–305

Smith, D. R., Abbott, A. 1983. A labor market perspective on the mobility of college football coaches. *Soc. Forces* 61:1147–67

Sørensen, A. B. 1974. A model for occupational careers. *Am. J. Sociol.* 80:44–57

Sørensen, A. B. 1975. The structure of intragenerational mobility. *Am. Sociol. Rev.* 40:456–71

Sørensen, A. B. 1977. The structure of inequality and the process of attainment. *Am. Sociol. Rev.* 42:965–78

Sørensen, A. B. 1979. A model and a metric for the analysis of the intragenerational status attainment process. *Am. J. Sociol.* 85:361–84

Sørensen, A. B. 1986. Theory and methodology in social stratification. In *Sociology from Crisis to Science?* Vol. 1. *The Sociology of Structure and Action,* ed. U. Himmelstrand, pp. 69–95. Beverly Hills, Calif: Sage

Sørensen, A. B., Blossfeld, H-P. 1989. Socioeconomic opportunities in Germany in the post-war period. *Res. Soc. Strat. Mobil.* 8:85–106

Sørensen, A. B., Fuerst, S. 1978. Black-white differences in the occurrence of job shifts. *Sociol. Soc. Res.* 62:537–57

Sørensen, A. B., Tuma, N. B. 1981. Labor market structures and job mobility. *Res. Soc. Strat. Mobil.* 1:67–94

Spenner, K. I., Kerckhoff, A. C., Glass, T. A. 1990. Open and closed education and work systems in Great Britain. *Eur. Sociol. Rev.* 6:215–35

Spenner, K. I., Otto, L. B., Call, V. R. A. 1982. *Career Lines and Careers.* Lexington, Mass: Lexington Books

Spilerman, S. 1977. Careers, labor market structure, and socioeconomic achievement. *Am. J. Sociol.* 83:551–93

Spilerman, S. 1986. Organizational rules and the features of work careers. *Res. Soc. Strat. Mobil.* 5:41–102

Spilerman, S., Lunde, T. 1991. Features of educational attainment and job promotion prospects. *Am. J. Sociol.* 97:689–720

Spilerman, S., Petersen, T. 1989. *Organizational structure, determinants of promotion, and gender differences in attainment.* Unpublished ms. Dep. Sociol., Columbia Univ.

Stewman, S. 1975. Two Markov models of open system occupational mobility: Underlying conceptualizations and empirical tests. *Am. Sociol. Rev.* 40:298–321

Stewman, S. 1986. Demographic models of internal labor markets. *Admin. Sci. Q.* 31:212–47

Stewman, S. 1988. Organizational demography. *Annu. Rev. Sociol.* 14:173–202

Stewman, S., Konda, S. L. 1983. Careers and organizational labor markets: Demographic models of organizational behavior. *Am. J. Sociol.* 88:637–85

Stewman, S., Yeh, K. S. 1991. Structural pathways and switching mechanisms for individual careers. *Res. Soc. Strat. Mobil.* 10:133–68

Stier, H., Grusky, D. B. 1990. An overlapping persistence model of career mobility. *Am. Sociol. Rev.* 55:736–56

Stinchcombe, A. L. 1979. Social mobility in industrial labor markets. *Acta Sociol.* 22:217–45

Stolzenberg, R. M. 1988. Job quits in theoretical and empirical perspective. *Res. Soc. Strat. Mobil.* 7:99–131

Tolbert, C. M. II. 1982. Industrial segmentation and men's career mobility. *Am. Sociol. Rev.* 47:457–77

Tuma, N. B. 1976. Rewards, resources, and the rate of mobility: A nonstationary multivariate stochastic model. *Am. Sociol. Rev.* 41:338–60

Tuma, N. B. 1985. Effects of labor market structure on job shift patterns. In *Longitudinal Analysis of Labor Market Data,* ed. J. J. Heckman. B. Singer, pp. 327–63. Cambridge: Cambridge Univ. Press

Tuma, N. B., Hannan, M. T. 1984. *Social Dynamics: Models and Methods.* Orlando, Fla: Academic

Waite, L. J., Berryman, S. E. 1986. Job stability among young women: A comparison of traditional and nontraditional occupations. *Am. J. Sociol.* 92:568–95

White, H. C. 1970. *Chains of Opportunity: System Models of Mobility in Organizations.* Cambridge, Mass: Harvard Univ. Press

White, R. W., Althauser, R. P. 1984. Internal labor markets, promotions, and worker skill: An indirect test of skill ILMs. *Soc. Sci. Res.* 13:373–92

Wilensky, H. L. 1960. Work, careers, and integration. *Int. Soc. Sci. J.* 12:543–60

Wise, D. A. 1975. Personal attributes, job performance, and probability of promotion. *Econometrica* 43:913–31

Wright, E. O. 1978. *Class, Crisis, and the State.* London: NLB

Annu. Rev. Sociol. 1992. 18:63–84

CRIME AND DEVIANCE IN THE LIFE COURSE

Robert J. Sampson

Department of Sociology, University of Chicago, Chicago, Illinois 60637

John H. Laub

College of Criminal Justice, Northeastern University, Boston, Massachusetts 02115, and Murray Research Center, Radcliffe College, Cambridge, Massachusetts 02138

KEY WORDS: antisocial behavior, longitudinal analysis, life-course dynamics, stability and change, age and crime

---

Abstract

Criminological research has emphasized the strong relationship between age and crime, with involvement in most crimes peaking in adolescence and then declining. However, there is also evidence of the early onset of delinquency and of the stability of criminal and deviant behavior over the life course. In this essay we reconcile these findings by synthesizing and integrating longitudinal research on childhood antisocial behavior, adolescent delinquency, and adult crime with theory and research on the life course. Consistent with a life-course perspective, we focus on continuities and discontinuities in deviant behavior over time and on the social influences of age-graded transitions and salient life events. Furthermore, we critically assess the implications of stability and change for longitudinal research. We conclude with an emerging research agenda for studying the relationship of crime and deviance with a broad range of social phenomena (e.g. occupational attainment, opportunity structures, marital attachment) over the life course.

0732–0582/92/0410–0084$02.00

INTRODUCTION

Accepted wisdom holds that crime is committed disproportionately by adolescents. According to data from the United States and other industrialized countries, property and violent crime rise rapidly in the teenage years to a peak at about ages 16 and 18, respectively, with a decline thereafter until old age (Hirschi & Gottfredson 1983, Farrington 1986, Flanagan & Maguire 1990). The overrepresentation of youth in crime has been demonstrated using multiple sources of measurement—whether official arrest reports (Federal Bureau of Investigation 1990), self-reports of offending (Rowe & Tittle 1977), or victim reports of the ages of offenders (Hindelang 1981). It is thus generally accepted that, in the aggregate, age-specific crime rates peak in the late teenage years and then decline with age.

The age-crime curve has had a profound impact on the organization and content of sociological studies of crime by channeling research to a focus on adolescents. As a result sociological criminology has traditionally neglected the theoretical significance of childhood characteristics and the link between early childhood behaviors and later adult outcomes (see Robins 1966, Caspi et al 1989, McCord 1979, Farrington 1989, Gottfredson & Hirschi 1990, Loeber & LeBlanc 1990, Sampson & Laub 1990). Although criminal behavior does peak in the teenage years, evidence reviewed below indicates an early onset of delinquency as well as continuity of criminal behavior over the life course. By concentrating on the teenage years, sociological perspectives on crime have thus failed to address the life-span implications of childhood behavior.

At the same time, criminologists have not devoted much attention to the other end of the spectrum—desistance from crime and the transitions from criminal to noncriminal behavior in adulthood (Cusson & Pinsonneault 1986, Shover 1985, Gartner & Piliavin 1988). As Rutter (1988a: 3) argues, we know little about "escape from the risk process" and whether predictors of desistance are unique or simply the opposite of criminogenic factors. Therefore, not only has the early life course been neglected, but so has the relevance of social transitions in young adulthood and the factors explaining desistance from crime as people age.

In this paper we confront these issues by bringing both childhood and adulthood back into the criminological picture of age and crime. To accomplish this goal we synthesize and integrate the research literature on the life course and crime. As described below, the life-course perspective highlights continuities and discontinuities in behavior over time and the social influences of age-graded transitions and life events. Hence, the life course is concerned not only with early childhood experiences but also with salient events and socialization in adulthood. To the extent that the adult life course does explain variation in adult crime unaccounted for by childhood development, change must be considered part of the explanatory framework in criminology, along with the stability of early individual differences.

The life-course perspective also bears on recent controversies that have embroiled criminology. While all agree that the issue of age and crime is important, conflicting views have emerged on the implications of age for the study of crime and deviance. Hirschi & Gottfredson (1983) argue that the age-crime curve is invariant over different times, places, crime types, and demographic subgroups. Moreover, they believe that age has a direct effect on crime that cannot be explained by social factors, that the causes of crime are the same at every age, and hence that longitudinal research is not needed to study the causes of crime (see also Gottfredson & Hirschi 1987, 1988, 1990). By contrast, Farrington (1986) argues that the age-crime curve reflects variations in prevalence rather than incidence and that incidence does not vary consistently with age. He also presents evidence to suggest that the relation between age and crime varies over time and by offense type, location, and gender. Blumstein & Cohen (1979) argue further that individual crime rates are constant during a criminal career, implying that arrest rates do not always decrease with age for all offenders (see also Blumstein et al 1988).

Accordingly, even fundamental "facts" about the age-crime relationship and their implications for research design are subject to much debate. This predicament provides yet another motivation to link the study of age and crime to the life-course perspective. Indeed, the data on age and crime lend themselves naturally to a concern with how criminal behavior changes as individuals pass through different stages of the life course. By integrating knowledge on crime with age-graded transitions in the life course, our review attempts to shed further light on the age-crime debate.

This paper is organized in the following manner. Before assessing the criminological literature directly, we first highlight major ideas in life-course research and theory. In subsequent sections we then examine the research on continuity (stability) and discontinuities (change) in crime over the life course. In the final sections, we outline a research agenda on age and crime that stems from a reconceptualization of stability and change.

THE LIFE COURSE PERSPECTIVE

The life course has been defined as "pathways through the age differentiated life span," where age differentiation "is manifested in expectations and options that impinge on decision processes and the course of events that give shape to life stages, transitions, and turning points" (Elder 1985: 17). Similarly, Caspi et al (1990: 15) conceive of the life course as a "sequence of culturally defined age-graded roles and social transitions that are enacted over time." Age-graded transitions are embedded in social institutions and are subject to historical change (Elder 1975, 1991).

Two central concepts underlie the analysis of life-course dynamics. A trajectory is a pathway or line of development over the life span such as worklife, marriage, parenthood, self-esteem, and criminal behavior. Trajectories refer to long-term patterns and sequences of behavior. Transitions are marked by specific life events (e.g. first job or first marriage) that are embedded in trajectories and evolve over shorter time spans—"changes in state that are more or less abrupt" (Elder 1985: 31–32). Some transitions are age-graded and some are not; hence, what is often assumed to be important is the normative timing and sequencing of changes in roles, statuses, or other socially defined positions along some consensual dimension (Jessor et al 1991). For example, Hogan (1980) emphasizes the duration of time (spells) between a change in state and the ordering of events, such as first job or first marriage, on occupational status and earnings in adulthood. Caspi et al (1990: 25) argue that delays in social transitions (e.g. being "off-time") produce conflicting obligations that enhance later difficulties (see also Rindfuss et al 1987). As a result, life-course analyses are often characterized by a focus on the duration, timing, and ordering of major life events and their consequences for later social development.

The interlocking nature of trajectories and transitions may generate turning points or a change in the life course (Elder 1985: 32). Adaptation to life events is crucial because the same event or transition followed by different adaptations can lead to different trajectories (Elder 1985: 35). The long-term view embodied by the life-course focus on trajectories implies a strong connection between childhood events and experiences in adulthood. However, the simultaneous shorter-term view also implies that transitions or turning points can modify life trajectories—they can "redirect paths." Social institutions and triggering life events that may modify trajectories include school, work, the military, marriage, and parenthood (see e.g. Elder 1986, Rutter et al 1990, Sampson & Laub 1990).

In addition to the study of trajectories of change and the continuity between childhood behavior and later adulthood outcomes, the life-course framework encompasses at least three other themes: (i) a concern with the social meanings of age throughout the life course, (ii) intergenerational transmission of social patterns, and (iii) the effects of macrolevel events (e.g. Great Depression, World War II) and structural location (e.g. class and gender) on individual life histories (see Elder 1974, 1985). As Elder (1991) notes, a major objective of the study of the life course is to link social history and social structure to the unfolding of human lives. To address these themes individual lives are studied through time, with particular attention devoted to aging, cohort effects, historical context, and the social influence of age-graded transitions. Naturally, prospective longitudinal research designs form the heart of life-course research.

Of all the themes emphasized in life-course research, the extent of stability and change in both behavior and personality attributes over time is perhaps the most complex. Stability versus change in behavior is also one of the most hotly debated and controversial issues in the social sciences (Brim & Kagan 1980a, Dannefer 1984, Baltes & Nesselroade 1984). Given its pivotal role we thus turn to an assessment of the research literature as it bears on stability and change in criminal behavior. Although personality development is obviously an important topic (see Block 1971, Caspi 1987), space considerations demand that we focus primarily on behavior. As we shall see, the research literature contains evidence for both continuity and change in deviant behavior over the life course.

STABILITY OF CRIME AND DEVIANCE

Unlike sociological criminology, the field of developmental psychology has long been concerned with the continuity of maladaptive behaviors (Brim & Kagan 1980a, Caspi & Bem 1990). As such, a large portion of the longitudinal evidence on stability comes from psychologists and others who study "antisocial behavior" generally, where the legal concept of crime may or may not be a component. An example is the study of aggression in psychology (Olweus 1979). In exploring this research tradition, our purpose is to highlight the extent to which deviant childhood behaviors have important ramifications, whether criminal or noncriminal, in later adult life.

Our point of departure is the widely reported claim that individual differences in antisocial behavior are stable across the life course (Olweus 1979, Caspi et al 1987, Loeber 1982, Robins 1966, Huesmann et al 1984, Gottfredson & Hirschi 1990, Jessor et al 1977, 1991). The stability of crime and antisocial behavior over time is often defined as homotypic continuity, which refers to the continuity of similar behaviors or phenotypic attributes over time (Caspi & Bem 1990: 553). For example, in an influential study of the aggressiveness of 600 subjects, their parents, and their children over a 22-year period, Huesmann et al (1984) found that early aggressiveness predicted later aggression and criminal violence. They concluded that "aggression can be viewed as a persistent trait that. . . possesses substantial cross-situational constancy" (1984: 1120). An earlier study by Robins (1966) also found a high level of stability in crime and aggression over time.

More generally, Olweus's (1979) comprehensive review of over 16 studies on aggressive behavior revealed "substantial" stability—the correlation between early aggressive behavior and later criminality averaged .68 for the studies reviewed (1979: 854–55). Loeber (1982) completed a similar review of the extant literature in many disciplines and concluded that a "consensus" has been reached in favor of the stability hypothesis: "children who initially display high rates of antisocial behavior are more likely to persist in this behavior than children who initially show lower rates of antisocial behavior" (1982: 1433). Recent empirical studies documenting stability in criminal and deviant behavior across time include West & Farrington (1977), Wolfgang et al (1987), Shannon (1988), Elliott et al (1985), and Jessor et al (1991).

Although more comprehensive, these findings are not new. Over 50 years ago the Gluecks found that virtually all of the 510 reformatory inmates in their study of criminal careers "had experience in serious antisocial conduct" (Glueck & Glueck 1930: 142). Their data also confirmed "the early genesis of antisocial careers" (1930: 143). In addition, the Gluecks' follow-up of 1000 males originally studied in *Unraveling Juvenile Delinquency* (1950) revealed remarkable continuities. As they argued in *Delinquents and Non-Delinquents in Perspective:* "while the majority of boys originally included in the nondelinquent control group continued, down the years, to remain essentially law-abiding, the greatest majority of those originally included in the delinquent group continued to commit all sorts of crimes in the 17–25 age-span" (1968: 170). Findings regarding behavioral or homotypic continuity are thus supported by a rich body of empirical research that spans several decades (for more extensive discussion see Robins 1966, 1978, West & Farrington 1977, Gottfredson & Hirschi 1990). In fact, much as the Gluecks reported earlier, Robins (1978) summarized results from her studies of four male cohorts by stating that "adult antisocial behavior virtually requires childhood antisocial behavior" (1978: 611).

Perhaps more intriguing, the linkage between childhood misbehavior and adult outcomes is found across life domains that go well beyond the legal concept of crime. This phenomenon is usually defined as heterotypic continuity—continuity of an inferred genotypic attribute presumed to underlie diverse phenotypic behaviors (Caspi & Bem 1990: 553). For instance, a specific behavior in childhood might not be predictive of the exact same behavior in later adulthood but might still be associated with behaviors that are conceptually consistent with that earlier behavior (Caspi & Moffitt 1991: 4). Although not always criminal per se, adult behaviors falling in this category might include excessive drinking, traffic violations, marital conflict or abuse, and harsh discipline of children. Gottfredson & Hirschi (1990: 91) invoke a similar idea when they refer to adult behaviors "analogous" to crime such as accidents, smoking, and sexual promiscuity.

Evidence for the behavioral coherence implied by heterotypic continuity is found in the Huesmann et al (1984) study, where they report that aggression in childhood was related not just to adult crime but to spouse abuse, drunk driving, moving violations, and severe punishment of offspring. Other studies reporting a similar coalescence of deviant and criminal acts over time include West & Farrington (1977), Robins (1966), and Jessor et al (1991). It is interesting that the findings of heterotypic continuity generated largely by psychologists are quite consistent with criminological research, showing little or no specialization in crime as people age (Wolfgang et al 1972, Blumstein et al 1986, Elliott et al 1989, Osgood et al 1988).

Invoking another dimension of heterotypic continuity, Caspi (1987) has argued that personality characteristics in childhood (e.g. ill tempered behavior) will not only appear across time but will be manifested in a number of diverse situations. Specifically, Caspi (1987: 1211) found that the tendency toward explosive, undercontrolled behavior in childhood was recreated over time, especially in problems with subordination (e.g. in education, military, and work settings) and in situations that required negotiating interpersonal conflicts (e.g. marriage and parenting). For example, children who display temper tantrums in childhood are more likely to abort their involvement with education, which in turn is related to a wide range of adult outcomes such as unemployment, job instability, and low income. In *Deviant Children Grown Up,* Lee Robins also found strong relations between childhood antisocial behavior and adult employment status, occupational status, job stability, income, and mobility (1966: 95–102). Robins went so far as to conclude that "antisocial behavior [in childhood] predicts class status more efficiently than class status predicts antisocial behavior" (1966: 305). In a similar vein, Sampson & Laub's (1990) reanalysis of longitudinal data from the Gluecks' archives found that childhood antisocial behavior strongly predicted not just adult criminality but outcomes as diverse as joblessness, divorce, welfare dependence, and educational failure— independent of childhood economic status and IQ.

Implications for Social Theories of Crime

There is ample evidence that antisocial behavior is relatively stable across stages of the life course, regardless of traditional sociological variables like stratification. As Caspi & Moffitt (1991: 2) conclude, robust continuities in antisocial behavior have been revealed over the past 50 years in different nations (e.g. Canada, England, Finland, New Zealand, Sweden, and the United States,) and with multiple methods of assessment (e.g. official records, teacher ratings, parent reports, and peer nominations of aggressive behavior). These replications across time and space yield an impressive generalization that is rare in the social sciences.

Antisocial behavior in childhood also predicts a wide range of troublesome adult outcomes, supporting Hagan & Palloni's (1988) observation that delinquent and criminal events "are linked into life trajectories of broader significance, whether those trajectories are criminal or noncriminal in form"

(1988: 90, see also Hagan 1991). Because most research by criminologists has focused either on the teenage years or adult behavior limited to crime, this idea has not been well integrated into the criminological literature.

As a result of this dual neglect, sociological approaches to crime have been vulnerable to attack for not coming to grips with the implications of behavioral stability. Not surprisingly, developmental psychologists have long seized on stability to argue for the primacy of early childhood and the irrelevance of the adult life course. But even recent social theories of crime take much the same tack, denying that adult life-course transitions can have any real effect on adult criminal behavior. For example, Gottfredson & Hirschi (1990: 238) argue that ordinary life events (e.g. jobs, getting married, becoming a parent) have little effect on criminal behavior because crime rates decline with age "whether or not these events occur." They go on to argue that the life-course assumption that such events are important neglects its own evidence on the stability of personal characteristics (1990: 237, see also Gottfredson & Hirschi 1987). And, since crime emerges early in the life course, traditional sociological variables (e.g. peers, labor market, marriage) are again presumed impotent. The reasoning is that since crime emerges before sociological variables appear, the latter cannot be important, even in modifying known trajectories.

A dominant viewpoint in criminology is therefore that stability in crime over the life course is generated by population heterogeneity in an underlying criminal propensity that is established early in life and remains stable over time (Wilson & Herrnstein 1985, Gottfredson & Hirschi 1990, Nagin & Paternoster 1991). Precisely because individual differences in the predisposition to commit crime emerge early and are stable, childhood and adult crime will be positively correlated. The hypothesized causes of early propensity cover a number of factors, including lack of self control (Gottfredson & Hirschi 1990), parental criminality (Farrington et al 1975), impulsivity (Wilson & Herrnstein 1985), and even heredity (Rowe & Osgood 1984). Although primarily methodological in nature, the heterogeneity argument has import for theoretical understanding, implying that the correlation between past and future delinquency is not causal. Rather, the correlation is spurious because of the heterogeneity of the population in its propensity to crime.

It is clear that traditional approaches to stability leave little room for the relevance of sociological theories of age-graded transitions. As it turns out, however, whether the glass of stability appears half empty or half full seems to result at least as much from theoretical predilections as from empirical reality. Moreover, not only are there important discontinuities in crime that need to be explained, a reconsideration of the evidence suggests that stability itself may be explained by sociological influences over the life course. To assess these alternative conceptions we first review the evidence on change, followed by a revisionist look at the explanation of stability.

CHANGE AND THE ADULT LIFE COURSE

In an important paper Dannefer (1984) sharply critiques existing models of adult development, drawn primarily from the fields of biology and psychology, for their exclusive "ontogenetic" focus and their failure to recognize the "profoundly interactive nature of self-society relations" and the "variability of social environments" (1984: 100). He further argues that "the contributions of sociological research and theory provide the basis for understanding human development as socially organized and socially produced, not only by what happens in early life, but also by the effects of social structure, social interaction, and their effects on life chances throughout the life course" (1984:106). Is there evidence in the criminological literature to support Dannefer's (1984) general observations regarding change over the life course and the importance of social structure and interaction?

We begin to answer this question with a seeming paradox — while studies reviewed earlier do show that antisocial behavior in children is one of the best predictors of antisocial behavior in adults, "most antisocial children do not become antisocial as adults" (Gove 1985: 123). Robins (1978) found identical results in her review of four longitudinal studies, stating that most antisocial children do not become antisocial adults (1978: 611). A follow-up of the Cambridge-Somerville Youth study found that "a majority of adult criminals had no history as juvenile delinquents" (McCord 1980: 158). Cline (1980: 665) states that although there is "more constancy than change … there is sufficient change in all the data to preclude simple conclusions concerning criminal career progressions." He concludes that there is far more heterogeneity in criminal behavior than previous work has suggested, and that many juvenile offenders do not become career offenders (Cline 1980: 669–70). Loeber & LeBlanc make a similar point: "Against the backdrop of continuity, studies also show large within-individual changes in offending, a point understressed by Gottfredson & Hirschi" (1990: 390).

Caspi & Moffitt's (1991) review reaches a similar conclusion when they discover large variations in the stability of antisocial behavior over time. In particular, antisocial behavior appears to be highly stable and consistent only in a relatively small number of males whose behavior problems are quite extreme. Loeber's (1982) review also found that extremes in antisocial conduct were linked to the magnitude of stability. Moffitt (1991) builds on this information to argue that stability is a trait among those she terms "life-course persistent" delinquents. In other words, whereas change is the norm for most adolescents, stability characterizes those at the tail of the antisocial-conduct distribution. This conceptualization points to the dangers of relying on measures of central tendency that mask divergent subgroups.

Moffitt's (1991) review further suggests that social factors may work to modify childhood trajectories for the majority of youth who are not "life-course persistent." In support of this idea recent criminological research suggests that salient life events influence behavior and modify trajectories—a key thesis of the life course model. A follow-up of 200 Borstal boys found that marriage led to "increasing social stability" (Gibbens 1984: 61). Knight et al (1977) discovered that while marriage did not reduce criminality, it reduced antisocial behavior such as drinking and drug use (see also Osborn & West 1979, West 1982, Rand 1987). Osborn (1980) examined the effect of leaving London on delinquency and found that subjects who moved had a lower risk of reoffending when compared with a similar group who stayed in London (see also West 1982). Rand (1987) found mixed results of going into the armed forces on later offending, but for some subgroups criminal behavior declined after serving in the military. And, there is some evidence that episodes of unemployment lead to higher crime rates (Farrington et al 1986).

In the context of personality characteristics, Caspi (1987) found that although the tendency toward explosive, under-controlled behavior in childhood was evident in adulthood, "invariant action patterns did not emerge across the age-graded life course" (1987: 1211). Similarly, using a prospective longitudinal design to study poverty, Long & Vaillant (1984) found both discontinuity and continuity across three generations of subjects. The transmission of "underclass" or dependent life styles was not inevitable or even very likely, refuting the hypothesis that the chances of escape from poverty are minimal. "The transmission of disorganization and alienation that seems inevitable when a disadvantaged cohort is studied retrospectively appears to be the exception rather than the norm in a prospective study that locates the successes as well as the failures" (Long & Vaillant 1984: 344).

This is an important methodological point that applies to the stability of crime. Looking back over the careers of adult criminals exaggerates the prevalence of stability. Looking forward from youth reveals the successes and failures, including antisocial adolescents who go on to be normal functioning adults. This is the paradox noted earlier—adult criminality seems to be always preceded by childhood misconduct, but most conduct-disordered children do not become antisocial or criminal adults (Robins 1978).

Two recent studies of crime support a dual concern with stability and change, using a prospective approach to life histories. First, Rutter et al (1990) analyzed follow-up data from two groups of youth. One was a sample of youth institutionalized in group homes because of family dysfunctions (e.g. parental criminality, abuse, desertion). The other was a quasi-random sample of the population of noninstitutionalized individuals of the same age living in inner-city London. Both groups were thus similar in composition but varied on childhood adversity. Consistent with the stability literature, Rutter et al (1990) found that the high-risk institutionalized youth went on to experience a diversity of troublesome outcomes in adulthood, including crime. By comparison, the control group was relatively well adjusted in later life.

Yet Rutter et al (1990) found in both groups considerable heterogeneity in outcomes that was associated with later adult experiences. In particular, marital support in early adult life provided a protective mechanism that inhibited deviance. Positive school experience among females was another factor that promoted desistance from crime, especially indirectly through its effect on planning and stable marriage choices. These results maintained despite controls for numerous measures of childhood deviance (1990: 152), leading Rutter et al to rule out individual self-selection bias as an explanation (cf Nagin & Paternoster 1991). As they concluded: "the data showed substantial heterogeneity in outcomes, indicating the need to account for major discontinuities as well as continuities in development. In that connection marital support from a nondeviant spouse stood out as a factor associated with a powerful protective effect" (1990: 152). Adult transitions in the life course can thus "modify the effect of adversities experienced in childhood" (Rutter et al 1990: 152). They also pointed out a key reason why change is possible—because the chain of stability "relied on multiple links, each one dependent on the presence of some particular set of features, there were many opportunities for the chain of adversity to be broken" (Rutter et al 1990: 137).

In a second study along similar lines, Sampson & Laub (1990) theorized that social ties to the adult institutions of informal social control (e.g. family, community, work) influence criminal behavior over the life course despite delinquent and antisocial background. Their organizing principle derived from the central idea of social control theory—crime and deviance result when an individual's bond to society is weak or broken. Their theoretical model focused on the transition to adulthood and, in turn, the new role demands from higher education, full-time employment, military service, and marriage. Unlike much life-course research, however, Sampson & Laub (1990) emphasized the quality or strength of social ties more than the occurrence or timing of discrete life events (cf Hogan 1978, Loeber & LeBlanc 1990: 430–32). For example, while Gottfredson & Hirschi (1990: 140–41) argue that marriage per se does not increase social control, a strong attachment to one's spouse and close emotional ties increase the social bond between individuals and, all else equal, should lead to a reduction in criminal behavior (cf Shover 1985: 94). Similarly, employment alone does not increase social control. It is employment coupled with job stability, job commitment, and ties to work that should increase social control and, all else equal, lead to a reduction in criminal behavior. It was thus the social capital in the institutional relationship that was hypothesized to dictate the salience of informal social control at the individual level.

Sampson & Laub's theory of informal social control found support in an analysis of the natural histories of two groups of boys that differed dramatically in childhood antisocial behavior. More specifically, they reexamined the life histories originally gathered by Glueck & Glueck (1968) of 500 delinquents and 500 control subjects matched on age, IQ, SES, and ethnicity and followed from ages 14 to 32. Consistent with the Gluecks' earlier reports, the results showed marked differences in adolescent delinquency that were relatively stable over the life course. For example, as adults the former delinquents were much more likely to be arrested and report excessive drinking compared with the control-group men (1990: 615).

Consistent with a theory of adult development and informal social control, however, Sampson & Laub (1990: 616–24) found that job stability and marital attachment in adulthood were significantly related to changes in adult crime—the stronger the adult ties to work and family, the less crime and deviance among both delinquents and controls. The results were consistent over a wide variety of outcome measures, control variables for childhood antisocial behavior, and analytical techniques, and the effect estimates were largely invariant across the two groups that varied on childhood delinquency. Hence, much like Rutter et al (1990), the Sampson & Laub study suggests that social ties embedded in adult transitions (e.g. marital attachment, job stability) explain variations in crime unaccounted for by childhood deviance.

RETHINKING STABILITY AND CHANGE

Taken as a whole, the foregoing review suggests that conclusions about the inevitability of antisocial continuities have either been overstated or misinterpreted. In terms of the former, stability coefficients are far from perfect and leave considerable room for the emergence of discontinuities. In retrospect, criminologists should have been forewarned about making sweeping generalizations of stability in light of the lengthy history of prediction that shows childhood variables to be quite modest prognostic devices. Known as the false positive problem, childhood prediction scales invariably result in the substantial over-prediction of future criminality (Loeber & Stouthamer-Loeber 1987, Farrington & Tarling 1985). Likewise, prediction attempts often fail to identify accurately those who will become criminal even though past behavior suggests otherwise (false negatives).

In probably the best recent study on this topic, White et al (1990: 521) document that, consistent with past research, "early antisocial behavior is the best predictor of later antisocial behavior." Nevertheless, their data clearly show the limitations of relying only on childhood information to understand behavior over time. As White et al (1990: 521) argue, a high false positive rate precludes the use of early antisocial behavior alone as a predictor of later crime. They go on to note the general inaccuracy of specific predictions and how the heterogeneous nature of delinquency in later adolescence (and by implication, adulthood) thwarts accurate prediction.

The prediction literature again reinforces the need to look at both stability and change, and hence the futility of either/or conceptions of human development. Namely, while there is longitudinal consistency, research has established large variations in later adolescent and adult criminal behavior that are not simply accounted for by childhood propensities. Furthermore, these changes in adult criminality appear to be structured by social transitions and adult life events in the life course (Rutter et al 1990, Sampson & Laub 1990), underscoring the utility of a life-course perspective.

Equally important, however, is the fact that the conception of stability traditionally used in criminology is quite narrow and has been frequently misinterpreted. Rank-order correlations and other measures of stability refer to the consistency of between-individual differences over time and consequently rely on an aggregate picture of relative standing. As Huesmann et al (1984) note, what remains stable over time is the aggressiveness of an individual relative to the population (1984: 1131). Stability coefficients do not measure the consistency or heterogeneity of individual behaviors over time (i.e. individual change). Consider Gottfredson & Hirschi's (1990) argument that "If there is continuity over the life course in criminal activity, it is unnecessary to follow people over time" (1990: 230). The continuity to which they refer is relative stability, which does not mean that individuals remain constant in their behavior over time. In conjunction with a conceptualization of the adult life course as a probabilistic linkage or chain of events and transitions (Rutter et al 1990), it becomes clearer how change is possible—if not likely—despite the stability of relative rank orderings. The following sections elaborate on the implications for the study of crime of a revised conceptualization of both change and stability.

Assessing Individual Change

A promising direction for future research is the analysis of individual pathways of crime and deviance. That is, rather than relying on stability coefficients or aggregate age-crime curves, an alternative conception of change is to map individual trajectories embedded in the life course. One approach entails grouping subjects according to their individual patterns of change. In his study *Lives Through Time,* Block (1971) compared "changers and nonchangers" with respect to personality. He then developed a more detailed typology that permitted an assessment of personality change over time. Similarly, Crouter & McHale (1990) recently developed a three-fold typology of parental monitoring whereby children were grouped by important individual differences in development. Block (1971) and Crouter & McHale (1990: 20–21) argue that such individual trajectories are the best way to assess developmental change and its antecedents, concomitants, and consequences.

A similar strategy is to use growth curves that measure the direction and amount of systematic change in behavior over multiple time points (Jessor et al 1991, Rogosa 1988, Rogosa et al 1982). Like criminology, longitudinal research in the behavioral sciences at large has focused almost exclusively on the consistency of individual differences over time rather than the consistency of individual behavior. But as Rogosa (1988: 172) argues, research questions about growth and development "center on the systematic change in an attribute over time, and thus the individual growth curves are the natural foundation for modeling the longitudinal data." Similarly, Caspi & Bem (1990: 569) argue that when the term "change" appears in the literature, it frequently refers to the absence of continuity. Caspi & Bem call for the development of theory to begin to account for "systematic" change as opposed to the mere absence of continuity. Accounting for developmental trajectories in crime and deviance will help to distinguish between true systematic change fostered by life transitions and the absence of continuity.

Focusing on growth curves and systematic change parallels Farrington's (1988) argument that criminology has neglected the study of changes within individuals in favor of between-individual analyses. As one example, it is quite common to study whether unemployed persons have higher crime rates than the employed. It is rare that we investigate whether an individual moving from employment to a state of unemployment increases criminal activities, a methodology where each person acts as his or her own control (Farrington 1988: 180). Only by studying both individual change trajectories and between-individual differences in stability are we likely to resolve some of the current controversies on age and crime. This seems especially true with respect to Gottfredson & Hirschi's claim that the causes of crime are the same at each age, a claim rooted in prior between-individual analyses (1990: 123–144).

In short, the conceptualization, measurement, and analysis of change have not had the same attention as stability. Given this imbalance, a focus on change ought to take center stage in future research, alongside stability. This orientation recognizes that the two concepts are not mutually exclusive as is often thought (Jessor 1983). To the contrary, intra-individual change and inter-individual differences in intra-individual change are both concerns of developmental study and are uniquely reserved to research that is longitudinal in design and that undertakes repeated measurements and analysis of the same individuals over time (Jessor et al 1991 VII–1). Rather than being irreconcilable, continuity and change "are best seen as two aspects of a single dialectical process in which even major transformations of individuality emerge consequentially from the interaction of prior characteristics and circumstances" (Jessor et al 1991: VII-2).

Explaining Continuity

Perhaps ironically, even the stability of individual differences in crime over time is amenable to a sociological life-course perspective. This point is often overlooked because the mere empirical documentation of stability has begged the important theoretical question of why continuity exists. In particular, given the negative consequences that much antisocial behavior generates, why should it persist? Is "early propensity" the only conceptual tool we need to understand stability over time? Efforts to understand the structural and interactional processes underlying stability over the life course have been given rather short shrift, primarily because research on stability and continuities in deviant behavior has stopped at the point of prediction. Recent thinking has attempted to move beyond mere prediction in an effort to address issues of explanation.

One explanation consistent with a life-course perspective is that the relationship of past to future crime is generated by state dependence. This hypothesis implies that committing a crime has a genuine behavioral influence on the probability of committing future crimes. In other words, crime itself—whether directly or indirectly—causally modifies the future probability of engaging in crime (Nagin & Paternoster 1991: 166). In this regard Caspi (1987) has argued that antisocial children replicate their antisocial behavior in a variety of adult realms in large part because of the differing reactions that antisocial behavior brings forth. Maladaptive behaviors are "found in interactional styles that are sustained both by the progressive accumulation of their own consequences (cumulative continuity) and by evoking maintaining responses from others during reciprocal social interaction (interactional continuity)" (Caspi et al 1987: 313, emphasis added). As an example of the latter, interactional continuity might be sustained when the child with temper tantrums provokes angry and hostile reactions in parents and teachers, which in turn feed back to trigger further antisocial behavior by the child.

Extending the idea of cumulative continuity, Moffitt (1991) argues that social reactions to delinquency generate negative consequences that further diminish life chances. Official labeling, incarceration, school failure, and other negative life events associated with delinquency may lead to the "closing of doors" as far as opportunities go. Official mechanisms of delinquency control may thus interfere with successful adult development through the cumulative continuity of lost opportunity, above and beyond that generated by early propensity to antisocial conduct and what Caspi et al (1987) refer to as interactional continuity.

The notion of cumulative continuity is consistent with the original contentions of labeling theory that reactions to primary deviance may create problems of adjustment that foster additional crime in the form of secondary deviance (Lemert 1951). A good example is the negative effects of arrest and incarceration on future employment chances (Bondeson 1989). Here the connection between official childhood misbehavior and adult outcomes may be accounted for in large part by the structural disadvantages and diminished life chances accorded institutionalized and stigmatized youth. Institutionalization may also weaken informal social bonds to school, friends, and family, in turn enhancing the risk of future crime (see e.g. Wheeler 1961). The stigma of conviction may even extend across generations, explaining the effects of parental conviction on sons' delinquency regardless of family background and early propensity to crime (Hagan & Palloni 1990).

Clearly, then, the idea that official labels, incarceration experiences, and rejection by institutions of informal social control are criminogenic is a classic state-dependence interpretation of the link between past and future crime. Parenthetically, it should be noted that state dependence effects do not have to be positive. Deterrence theory suggests that reactions by the criminal justice system (e.g. arrest, imprisonment) have a deterrent effect on future offending (Nagin & Paternoster 1991). Either way, the essential point according to the state dependence argument is that the relationship between past and future crime is causal in nature.

As noted earlier, traditional accounts of continuity rest on population heterogeneity in an underlying propensity for crime that is established early in life and remains stable over time (see Nagin & Paternoster 1991). From this alternative viewpoint the diverse outcomes correlated with childhood antisocial behavior are all expressions of the same underlying trait. However, population heterogeneity is still consistent with the life-course framework because the changing manifestations of the same construct over time are structured by social opportunities to commit crime, differential reactions by the criminal justice system, and constraints imposed by aging (Shover 1985: 77–125, Gottfredson & Hirschi 1990: 177–178). The observed stability in crime and deviance may even be underestimated by the failure to conceptualize life-course transitions in social opportunities. For example, in asking whether crime declines with age, we do not know whether adults are disproportionately involved in crimes typically not counted in official statistics, especially white collar offenses (see Braithwaite 1989: 46). It is conceivable that while street crime declines with age, white collar offending and other "hidden" deviance (family violence, alcohol abuse) take up the slack (see also Moffitt 1991). This concern highlights the need to link age and crime with the life-course framework by explicating how age-graded transitions (e.g. work and family careers) create both opportunities for crime and differential probabilities of detection and labeling by official agents of social control.

It is fair to say, then, that even if individual propensity remains relatively constant, explanations of continuity across the life course require that we account for the structure of social opportunities and the differing labels attached to behaviors as people age. Moreover, it is also important to recognize that ecological constancy (e.g. community constraints) and continuities in the interpersonal environment may underlie individual-level stability. Indeed, behavioral patterns may show stability simply because the contextual environment remains stable. Although further discussion of environmental stability is beyond the scope of our review, the key point is that behavioral stability does not necessarily imply causal forces operating solely at the level of the individual. Therefore, whether derived from heterogeneity among individuals in an early propensity that manifests itself differently across time, state dependence fostered by social reactions to crime and interactional styles, or constancy in ecological context, the fact remains that explanations of stability are inextricably tied to a sociological perspective on the life-course.

FURTHER RESEARCH NEEDS

Advances in knowledge on crime and delinquency over the life course require not only rethinking what we mean by stability and change, but a fresh infusion of data we can use to address key limitations of past research. The first step is to counterbalance the dominance in criminological research of cross-sectional designs, and, to a lesser extent, short-term panel studies. Indeed, there have been surprisingly few longitudinal data sets that prospectively follow individuals over extended periods of the life course (see also Farrington 1979, Blumstein et al 1986, Tonry et al 1991). Combined with the tendency of researchers to analyze longitudinal data cross-sectionally, it is understandable that information gleaned from the typical panel study in criminology often simply reaffirms the results of cross-sectional research. But, rather than dismissing longitudinal research as Gottfredson & Hirschi (1987 1990) advocate, we believe a more productive strategy is to collect or analyze longitudinal data in ways that permit proper inferences on individual trajectories of stability and change (Rutter 1988a, Rogosa 1988). Note that the need for fresh data does not necessarily imply new and potentially expensive data (cf Tonry et al 1991), for there are excellent data archives capable of sustaining research on the life course in different historical and macrolevel contexts (see e.g. Elder 1974, McCord 1979, Vaillant 1983, Caspi et al 1987, Featherman et al 1984, Elliott et al 1989, Sampson & Laub 1990).

Second, longitudinal studies of crime have often failed to measure the timing and sequencing of changes in salient life events over the life course. In fact, longitudinal data sets in criminology frequently focus on unchanging demographic characteristics that have little bearing on theories of the life course (see Tonry et al 1991, Blumstein et al 1986). To establish influences on individual development one must account not only for background factors but the changing nature of important life events (e.g. work, family, and military ties), especially during the late adolescence to young adulthood transition. Quantitative measurement of the timing, duration, and ordering of life transitions has the further advantage of permitting substantive applications of event-history analyses (see Featherman & Lerner 1985), growth curve trajectories (Rogosa et al 1982), and recent methods for detecting resemblance in career sequence data (Abbott & Hyrack 1990).

A third limitation of prior research in criminology is the narrow focus on legally defined categories of crime. As we have documented, one of the staples of developmental research is the heterotypic continuity of antisocial behaviors. Consequently there is a need to measure a wide spectrum of behaviors both legal and illegal that are relevant to the study of crime. This strategy permits addressing the question of whether there are individuals for whom antisocial behavior, regardless of the actual sphere in which the activity occurs, does not decline with age (e.g. absenteeism at work as an adult might be conceptualized as the theoretical equivalent of truancy in childhood). Other life-domains ripe for inquiry include occupational mobility, educational attainment, poverty, physical health, mental health, and homelessness, especially as they interact with class of origin. For example, Hagan's (1991) recent research suggests that the effect of adolescent deviance on adult stratification outcomes is contingent on social class background (see also Jessor et al 1991). More generally, we need to broaden our conceptualization to investigate the impact of childhood delinquency and structural location on a wide range of non-crime outcomes that nonetheless have significance for adult development.

A fourth and related limitation is that explanations of the age-crime curve have focused mostly on official accounts of crime. Reliance on arrest data may exaggerate age differences and stability—the former because of differential recording by age and the latter because official reaction may "close doors" in ways that reinforce tendencies to later crime. One interpretation of continuity offered above relied on state dependence, whereby official labeling in adolescence mortgages the future in terms of employment, marriage, and other social bonds, in turn leading to increased criminality as an adult. The continuity between official juvenile crime and adult outcomes may thus reflect much more than simple propensities in childhood (Hagan & Palloni 1990). Societal reactions to crime may also interact with age (Gartner & Piliavin 1988: 302, Shover 1985). Research should thus examine the extent to which labeling, particularly formal labeling by the criminal justice system, affects life-course development relating to crime and non-crime outcomes.

Fifth, the research questions demand that data collection efforts include qualitative as well as quantitative data on variables and persons (Magnusson & Bergman 1990, Cairns 1986). Qualitative data derived from systematic open-ended questions or narrative life histories can help uncover underlying social processes of stability and change. They can also help to confirm the results derived from quantitative analyses. Using prospective natural histories, we further need to identify subjective transitions in the life course independently of behavioral transitions in understanding desistance from crime (Gartner & Piliavin 1988: 302). For example, Sampson & Laub (1990) and Rutter et al (1990) provide evidence that the assumption of social roles and the subsequent effects of informal social controls around these roles may help account for the age-crime relation. Qualitative data would be especially useful here because social transitions (e.g. marriage, parenthood, work) probably do not have the same meaning for everyone (Rutter 1989: 20). Our point is not that one approach is better than the other; rather, both are needed to understand development in the life course.

Finally, in implementing all the above strategies we need research that better "unpacks" the meaning of age. Rutter (1989) argues that in order to understand age changes in behavior, chronological age must be broken down into its component parts. Without this separation, "age is devoid of meaning" (1989: 3). According to Rutter (1989), from a developmental perspective age reflects at least four components: cognitive level, biological maturity, duration of experiences, and types of experiences. Separating these and other components of age (e.g. biological vs chronological age) surely will help to resolve conflicts over the direct and indirect effects of age on crime.

CONCLUSION

The traditional hostility among sociologists toward research establishing early childhood differences in delinquency and antisocial behavior that remain stable over time is unwarranted. Not only can stability be studied sociologically, its flip side is change, and the latter appears to be systematically structured by adult bonds to social institutions. The unique advantage of a sociological perspective on the life course is that it brings the formative period of childhood back into the picture yet recognizes that individuals can change through interaction with key social institutions as they age. With improvements in measurement and conceptualization, the prospects appear bright for future research to uncover the interlocking trajectories of crime, deviance, and human development.

Acknowledgments

We would like to thank Avshalom Caspi, John Hagan, Richard Jessor, and Temi Moffitt for their helpful comments on an earlier draft.

Literature Cited

Abbott, A., Hrycak, A. 1990. Measuring resemblance in sequence data: An optimal matching analysis of musicians' careers. *Am. J. Sociol.* 96:144–85

Baltes, P., Nesselroade, J. 1984. Paradigm lost and paradigm regained: Critique of Dannefer's portrayal of life-span developmental psychology. *Am. Sociol. Rev.* 49:841–46

Block, J. 1971. *Lives Through Time*. Berkeley: Bancroft

Blumstein, A., Cohen, J. 1979. Estimation of individual crime rates from arrest records. *J. Crim. Law Criminol.* 70:561–85

Blumstein, A., Cohen, J., Roth, J., Visher, C., eds. 1986. *Criminal Careers and "Career Criminals"*. Washington, DC: Natl. Acad. Sci.

Blumstein, A., Cohen, J., Farrington, D. 1988. Criminal career research: Its value for criminology. *Criminology* 26:1–35

Bondeson, U. 1989. *Prisoners in Prison Societies*. New Brunswick: Transaction

Braithwaite, J. 1989. *Crime, Shame, and*

Reintegration. Cambridge: Cambridge Univ. Press

Brim, O., Kagan, J. 1980a. Constancy and change: A view of the issues. See Brim & Kagan 1980b, pp. 1–25

Brim, O., Kagan, J., eds. 1980b. *Constancy and Change in Human Development*. Cambridge: Harvard Univ. Press

Cairns, R. B. 1986. Phenomena lost: Issues in the study of development. In *The Individual Subject and Scientific Psychology,* ed. J. Valsiner, pp. 97–111. New York: Plenum

Caspi, A. 1987. Personality in the life course. *J. Pers. Soc. Psychol.* 53:1203–13

Caspi, A. Elder, G. H. Jr., Bem, D. 1987. Moving against the world: Life- course patterns of explosive children. *Dev. Psychol.* 23:308–13

Caspi, A., Bem, D., Elder, G. H. Jr. 1989. Continuities and consequences of interactional styles across the life course. *J. Pers.* 57:375–406

Caspi, A., Bem, D. 1990. Personality continuity and change across the life course. In *Handbook of Personality: Theory and Research,* ed. L. A. Pervin, pp. 549–75. New York: Guilford

Caspi, A., Elder, G. H. Jr., Herbener, E. 1990. Childhood personality and the prediction of life-course patterns. See Robins & Rutter 1990, pp. 13–35

Caspi, A., Moffitt, T. 1991. The continuity of maladaptive behavior:From description to understanding in the study of antisocial behavior. In *Manual of Developmental Psychopathology,* ed. D. Cicchetti, D. Cohen. New York: Wiley. In press

Cline, H. F. 1980. Criminal behavior over the life span. See Brim & Kagan 1980b, pp. 641–74

Crouter, A., McHale, S. 1990. Family processes in single- and dual-earner contexts: Themes from the Penn State Family Relationships Project. *Conf. Paper, Bridging Levels of Analysis in the Study of Women's Lives Across Three Longitudinal Data Sets,* Woods Hole, Mass.

Cusson, M., Pinsonneault, P. 1986. The decision to give up crime. In *The Reasoning Criminal: Rational Choice Perspectives of Offending,* ed. D. B. Cornish, R. V. Clarke, pp. 72–82. New York: Springer-Verlag

Dannefer, D. 1984. Adult development and social theory: a paradigmatic reappraisal. *Am. Sociol. Rev.* 49:100–6

Elder, G. H. Jr. 1974. *Children of the Great Depression*. Chicago: Univ. Chicago Press

Elder, G. H. Jr. 1975. Age differentiation and the life course. *Annu. Rev. Sociol.* 1:165–90

Elder, G. H. Jr. 1985. Perspectives on the life course. In *Life Course Dynamics,* ed. G. H. Elder Jr., pp. 23–49. Ithaca: Cornell Univ. Press

Elder, G. H. Jr. 1986. Military times and turning points in men's lives. *Dev. Psychol.* 22:233–45

Elder, G. H. Jr. 1991. The life course. In *The Encyclopedia of Sociology,* ed. E. F. Borgatta, M. L. Borgatta. In press

Elliott, D., Huizinga, D., Ageton, S. 1985. *Explaining Delinquency and Drug Use*. Beverly Hills: Sage

Elliott, D., Huizinga, D., Menard, S. 1989. *Multiple Problem Youth: Delinquency, Substance Use, and Mental Health Problems*. New York: Springer-Verlag

Farrington, D. 1979. Longitudinal research on crime and delinquency. In *Crime and Justice,* ed. N. Morris, M. Tonry, 1:289–348. Chicago: Univ. Chicago Press

Farrington, D. 1986. Age and crime. In *Crime and Justice,* ed. N. Morris, M. Tonry, 7:189–250. Chicago: Univ. Chicago Press

Farrington, D. 1988. Studying changes within individuals: The causes of offending. See Rutter 1988b, pp. 158–83

Farrington, D. 1989. Later adult life outcomes of offenders and nonoffenders. In *Children at Risk: Assessment, Longitudinal Research, and Intervention,* ed. M. Brambring, F. Losel, H. Skowronek, pp. 220–44. New York: Walter de Gruyter

Farrington, D., Gallagher, B., Morley, L., Ledger, R. J. St., West, D. 1986. Unemployment, school leaving, and crime. *Br. J. Criminol.* 26:335–56

Farrington, D., Gundry, G., West, D. 1975. The familial transmission of criminality. *Med. Sci. Law* 15:177–86

Farrington, D., Tarling, R., eds. 1985. *Prediction in Criminology*. Albany: State Univ. NY Press

Featherman, D., Hogan, D., Sorenson, A. 1984. Entry in adulthood: Profiles of young men in the 1950s. In *Life-Span Development and Behavior,* ed. P. Baltes, O. Brim Jr., 6:160–203. Orlando: Academic Press

Featherman, D., Lerner, R. 1985. Ontogenesis and sociogenesis: Problematics for theory and research about development and socialization across the lifespan. *Am. Sociol. Rev.* 50:659–76

Federal Bureau of Investigation. 1990. *Age-Specific Arrest Rates and Race-Specific Arrest Rates For Selected Offenses*. Washington, DC: US Dep. Justice

Flanagan, T., Maguire, K., eds. 1990. *Sourcebook of Criminal Justice Statistics - 1989*. Washington, DC: US Govt. Print. Off.

Gartner, R., Piliavin, I. 1988. The aging offender and the aged offender. In *Life-Span Development and Behavior,* ed. P. B.

Baltes, D. L. Featherman, R. M. Lerner, 9:287–315. Hillside, NJ: Erlbaum
Gibbens, T. C. N. 1984. Borstal boys after 25 years. *Br. J. Criminol.* 24:49–62
Glueck, S., Glueck, E. 1930. *500 Criminal Careers*. New York: Knopf
Glueck, S., Glueck, E. 1950. *Unraveling Juvenile Delinquency*. New York: Commonwealth Fund
Glueck, S., Glueck, E. 1968. *Delinquents and Nondelinquents in Perspective*. Cambridge: Harvard Univ. Press
Gottfredson, M., Hirschi, T. 1987. The methodological adequacy of longitudinal research on crime. *Criminology* 25:581–614
Gottfredson, M., Hirschi, T. 1988. Science, public policy, and the career paradigm. *Criminology* 26:37–55
Gottfredson, M., Hirschi, T. 1990. *A General Theory of Crime*. Stanford: Stanford Univ. Press
Gove, W. R. 1985. The effect of age and gender on deviant behavior: A biopsychosocial perspective. In *Gender and the Life Course,* ed. A. S. Rossi, pp. 115–44. New York: Aldine
Hagan, J. 1991. Destiny and drift: Subcultural preferences, status attainments, and the risks and rewards of youth. *Am. Sociol. Rev.* 56:567–82
Hagan, J., Palloni, A. 1988. Crimes as social events in the life course: Reconceiving a criminological controversy. *Criminology* 26:87–100
Hagan, J., Palloni, A. 1990. The social reproduction of a criminal class in working-class London, circa 1950–1980. *Am. J. Sociol.* 96:265–99
Hindelang, M. J. 1981. Variations in sex-race-age-specific incidence rates of offending. *Am. Sociol. Rev.* 46:461–74
Hirschi, T., Gottfredson, M. 1983. Age and the explanation of crime. *Am. J. Sociol.* 89:552–84
Hogan, D. P. 1978. The variable order of events in the life course. *Am. Sociol. Rev.* 43:573–86
Hogan, D. P. 1980. The transition to adulthood as a career contingency. *Am. Sociol. Rev.* 45:261–76
Huesmann, L. R., Eron, L. D., Lefkowitz, M. M. 1984. Stability of aggression over time and generations. *Dev. Psychol.* 20:1120–34
Jessor, R. 1983. The stability of change: psychosocial development from adolescence to young adulthood. In *Human Development: An Interactional Perspective,* ed. D. Magnusson. New York: Academic
Jessor, R., Donovan, J., Costa, F. 1991. *Beyond Adolescence: Problem Behavior and Young Adult Development*. Cambridge: Cambridge Univ. Press.
Jessor, R., Jessor, S. L. 1977. *Problem Behavior and Psychosocial Development: A Longitudinal Study of Youth*. New York: Academic
Knight, B. J., Osborn, S. G., West, D. 1977. Early marriage and criminal tendency in males. *Br. J. Criminol.* 17:348–60
Lemert, E. 1951. *Social Pathology*. New York: McGraw-Hill
Loeber, R. 1982. The stability of antisocial child behavior: A review. *Child Dev.* 53:1431–46
Loeber, R., Stouthamer-Loeber, M. 1987. Prediction. In *Handbook of Juvenile Delinquency,* ed. H. C. Quay, pp. 325–82. New York: Wiley
Loeber, R., LeBlanc, M. 1990. Toward a developmental criminology. In *Crime and Justice,* ed. M. Tonry, N. Morris, 12:375–437. Chicago: Univ. Chicago Press
Long, J., Vaillant, G. H. 1984. Natural history of male psychological health, XI: Escape from the underclass. *Am. J. Psychol.* 141:341–46
Magnusson, D., Bergman, L. 1990. A pattern approach to the study of pathways from childhood to adulthood. See Robins & Rutter 1990, pp. 101–15
McCord, J. 1979. Some child-rearing antecedents of criminal behavior in adult men. *J. Pers. Soc. Psychol.* 37:1477–86
McCord, J. 1980. Patterns of deviance. In *Human Functioning in Longitudinal Perspective,* ed. S. B. Sells, R. Crandall, M. Roff, J. S. Strauss, W. Pollin, pp. 157–65. Baltimore: Williams & Wilkins
Moffitt, T. E. 1991. *Life-course persistent and adolescence limited antisocial behavior: A developmental taxonomy*. Univ. Wisc., Madison. Unpublished manuscript
Nagin, D., Paternoster, R. 1991. On the relationship of past and future participation in delinquency. *Criminology* 29:163–90
Olweus, D. 1979. Stability of aggressive reaction patterns in males: A review. *Psychol. Bull.* 86:852–75
Osborn, S. G. 1980. Moving home, leaving London, and delinquent trends. *Br. J. Criminol.* 20:54–61
Osborn, S. G., West, D. 1979. Marriage and delinquency: A postscript. *Br. J. Criminol.* 18:254–56
Osgood, D. W., Johnston, L. D., O'Malley, P. M., Bachman, J. G. 1988. The generality of deviance in late adolescence and early adulthood. *Am. Sociol. Rev.* 53:81–93
Rand, A. 1987. Transitional life events and desistance from delinquency and crime. See Wolfgang et al 1987, pp. 134–62
Rindfuss, R., Swicegood, C. G., Rosenfeld, R. 1987. Disorder in the life course: How

common and does it matter? *Am. Sociol. Rev*. 52:785–801

Robins, L. 1966. *Deviant Children Grown Up*. Baltimore: Williams & Wilkins

Robins, L. 1978. Sturdy childhood predictors of adult antisocial behavior: Replications from longitudinal studies. *Psychol. Med.* 8:611–22

Robins, L., Rutter, M., eds. 1990. *Straight and Devious Pathways from Childhood to Adulthood*. Cambridge: Cambridge Univ. Press

Rogosa, D. 1988. Myths of longitudinal research. In *Methodological Issues in Aging Research*, ed. K. W. Schaie, R. T. Campbell, W. Meredith, S. C. Rawlings, pp. 171–209. New York: Springer

Rogosa, D., Brandt, D., Zimowski, M. 1982. A growth curve approach to the measurement of change. *Psychol. Bull.* 92:726–48

Rowe, D., Osgood, D. W. 1984. Heredity and sociological theories of delinquency: A reconsideration. *Am. Sociol. Rev*. 49:526–40

Rowe, A., Tittle, C. 1977. Life cycle changes and criminal propensity. *Sociol. Q*. 18:223–36

Rutter, M. 1988a. Longitudinal data in the study of causal processes: Some uses and some pitfalls. See Rutter 1988b, pp. 1–28

Rutter, M., ed. 1988b. *Studies of Psychosocial Risk: The Power of Longitudinal Data*. Cambridge: Cambridge Univ. Press

Rutter, M. 1989. Age as an ambiguous variable in developmental research: Some epidemiological considerations from developmental psychopathology. *Int. J. Behav. Dev*. 12:1–34

Rutter, M., Quinton, D., Hill, J. 1990. Adult outcomes of institution-reared children: Males and females compared. See Robins & Rutter 1990, pp. 135–57

Sampson, R. J., Laub, J. H. 1990. Crime and deviance over the life course:The salience of adult social bonds. *Am. Sociol. Rev*. 55: 609–27

Shannon, L. 1988. *Criminal Career Continuity: Its Social Context*. New York: Human Sci.

Shover, N. 1985. *Aging Criminals*. Beverly Hills: Sage

Tonry, M., Ohlin, L. E., Farrington, D. P. 1991. *Human Development and Criminal Behavior: New Ways of Advancing Knowledge*. New York: Springer-Verlag

Vaillant, G. E. 1983. *The Natural History of Alcoholism*. Cambridge: Harvard Univ. Press

West, D. 1982. *Delinquency: Its Roots, Careers, and Prospects*. London: Heinemann

West, D., Farrington, D. 1977. *The Delinquent Way of Life*. London: Heinemann

Wheeler, S. 1961. Socialization in correctional communities. *Am. Sociol. Rev*. 26:697–712

White, J., Moffitt, T., Earls, F., Robins, L., Silva, P. 1990. How early can we tell?: Predictors of childhood conduct disorder and adolescent delinquency. *Criminology* 28:507–33

Wilson, J. Q., Herrnstein, R. 1985. *Crime and Human Nature*. New York: Simon & Schuster

Wolfgang, M., Figlio, R., Sellin, T. 1972. *Delinquency in a Birth Cohort*. Chicago: Univ. Chicago Press

Wolfgang, M., Thornberry, T., Figlio, R., eds. 1987. *From Boy to Man: From Delinquency to Crime*. Chicago: Univ. Chicago Press

Annu. Rev. Sociol. 1992. 18:85–108

CHANGING FERTILITY PATTERNS AND POLICIES IN THE THIRD WORLD

Geoffrey McNicoll
Research School of Social Sciences, Australian National University, Canberra, Australia

KEY WORDS: population, demography, birth control, economic development, social policy

Abstract

Average fertility in the third world has fallen from 6 children per woman in the 1960s to about 4 in the 1980s. Global population growth, however, is still adding nearly a billion people a decade—a process that has large, mostly adverse, welfare implications. Fertility trends in the main third world regions and in selected countries are described. Differences in social and political organization, economic conditions, cultural orientations, and policy directions yield distinctive paths of fertility decline. Explanations of them exhibit the range and variety of theories of social change in general. Matters of contention include the appropriate scope of an economic calculus in fertility decision-making and the relative significance of "structural" and "cultural" content in characterizing the decision environment and its sources of change. Much fertility research has been concerned with issues in technical demography such as birth interval dynamics or, in the case of policy, with the operational problems of family planning programs. A redressing of this imbalance is needed, making for a less microanalytic theoretical stance and greater attention to the public choice dimensions of fertility policy.

INTRODUCTION

The coherence of the "third world," never great, has been progressively diminishing in demographic as well as political and economic terms over

0360-0572/92/0815-0085$02.00

several decades. The countries that constituted this group[1] had almost uniformly high fertility in the 1950s and 1960s, with a population-weighted average total fertility rate (TFR) of about 6.[2] (The total fertility rate, or total fertility, is the average number of births a woman would have over her life at prevailing rates of childbearing—i.e. roughly, average family size before mortality.) By the late 1980s the total fertility rate had dropped to just below 4. The differing trends in five major third world regions are shown on the left side of Figure 1.

The declines depicted, notably the halving of family size in East and Southeast Asia, are among the major social changes of our time. Explaining them, moreover, is of interest not just as social history writ large: Hanging over human societies, and likely to affect the world's political, economic, and ecological well-being, are the potential consequences of continued vast increases in human numbers. Global population growth is now adding nearly a billion people a decade. The total passed three billion in 1960, four billion in 1975, five billion in 1987, and on present expectations will reach six billion in 1998 and seven billion in 2008. The momentum of this growth—the structural implication of the lag between birth and reproduction—will carry even a low-fertility world to 11 billion before leveling or falling back, and if fertility drops more slowly, the peak will be much higher. The nature of the feedbacks that relate population growth consequences to its determinants—whether located in the economics of family life, in the cultural orientations or political organization of societies, in the physical and biological systems within which we are placed (and of which we are part), or in the policy responses that are elicited—will govern how the end-game of human population growth is played, and its outcomes.

These are big themes. Indeed, it could be argued that there are few issues where social theory should more urgently and rigorously be applied, where research on the nature of past experience and the efficacy of contemporary policy action would be more consequential. But social scientists aside from

[1]Taken here as coinciding with the United Nations's "less developed regions": Africa, Asia excluding Japan, Latin America, Melanesia, Micronesia, and Polynesia. The break up of the "second world" and the progression of a number of Asian countries to first-world income levels are eroding what value remains in the categorization other than as an indication of initial (say, 1950s) conditions.

[2]This and most subsequent population estimates not otherwise attributed are taken from the latest volume of the United Nations's biennial series of population estimates and projections (United Nations 1991), the standard source for country-level and regional demographic data in a systematic comparative format. The annual *Demographic Yearbook,* compiled by the United Nations Statistical Office, has a somewhat different provenance, hewing closely to census materials provided by national statistical agencies. The World Bank also publishes population projections by country and region—a single series rather than the United Nations's three variants and rashly extending to 2150 rather than 2025 (Bulatao et al 1990). These roughly coincide with the United Nations's medium series for the period of overlap.

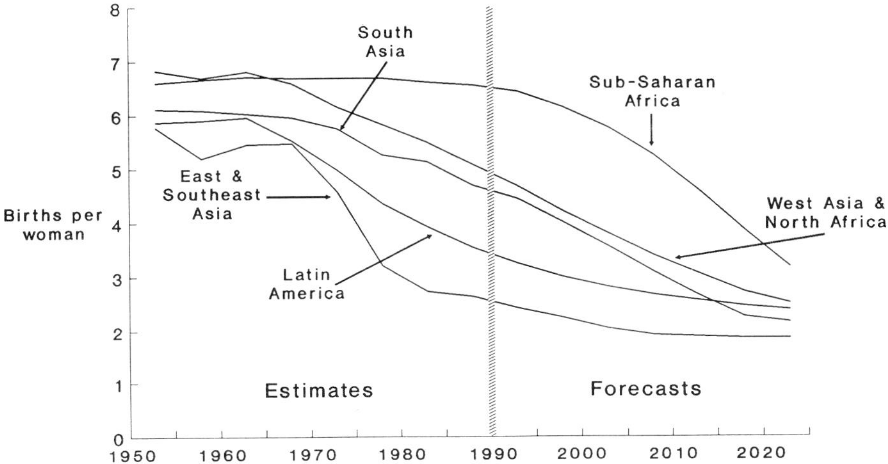

Figure 1. Total fertility rates of major third-world regions: estimates (1950–1985) and projections (1990–2025). Source of data: United Nations (1991).

demographers have evinced only modest research interest. For sociologists, fertility, if it is granted to be more than a background noise against which social change takes place, tends to be incidental to an interest in gender and family. For many economists, fertility is a simple exercise in consumer choice, not even under conditions of serious market failure. Worries about the aggregate scale of population, from this standpoint, are redolent of a pre-technological, agrarian view of the world. For social scientists of all stripes, fertility tends to be seen as a quasimedical subject and antinatalist policy as a component of public health policy—to do with clinics and nurses and the distribution of contraceptives.

There is, of course, an extensive demographic literature on the determinants of third world fertility and on fertility policy, as the citations here attest. But much of the research effort skirts the larger issues of social change that one might have expected to be centrally relevant. Demography's strong empirical bent is usually reckoned an advantage—speaking whereof we know; when it comes to garnering and transferring lessons of experience, however, it turns out that the numbers have settled much less than has been supposed.

FERTILITY DECOMPOSED

Fertility, simple in outcome, is a complex and drawn-out process in the making—features that require attention in any sociological treatment. Human physiology imposes a natural stage-ordering that can illuminate how various social and behavioral factors influence the timing and number of births. The dependency of the probability of a birth on a woman's age and number of preceding births brings to fertility analysis an important life-cycle or cohort perspective (a *cohort* being a group of people linked by some specified common circumstance in their past—such as being born in the same period). And fertility, whether the outcome of a deliberate decision or of inadvertence, also raises issues of foresight, preference, and trade-offs among competing desires. Fertility patterns and internal dynamics can be displayed in different ways by drawing on these several perspectives.

The value for analyzing fertility change of separating out the determinants of marriage, conception, and fetal mortality was established in a classic paper by Davis & Blake (1956). These are fertility's intermediate or proximate determinants—the biological and behavioral factors through which and only through which fertility can change. Using a variant of the Davis-Blake framework, Bongaarts (1978) developed a computable model of the proximate determinants. (See also Bongaarts & Potter 1983. A cruder decomposition, quantifying the separate effects of marriage and fertility within marriage, was devised for use with thinner historical data by Coale 1967.) The Bongaarts model decomposes the difference between the actual number of births the average woman has (i.e. the total fertility rate) and the notional maximum number of births possible in an average reproductive life (estimated to be about 15) into components attributable to the more important proximate factors. For fertility differences among populations, these factors are marriage—or some looser equivalent, the levels of contraceptive use and induced abortion, the effect of breastfeeding (which inhibits ovulation), and the extent of sexual abstinence after birth.

Transparent, analytically simple, and relatively undemanding of data, this model has exerted a powerful influence on fertility analysis. The clarity it brings to monitoring fertility change is illustrated in Figure 2, showing the proximate components of Thailand's fertility decline over two decades. It can reveal when apparently constant fertility is covering significant underlying change—such as an increasing use of contraception that is offset by a shortening duration of breastfeeding. Less happy results among some users have been inattention to the extent of interdependence among the proximate determinants, overreadiness to use them to impute or deny intentionality (the breastfeeding/abstinence intersection is particularly subject to contention), and, more generally, a tendency to confine explanation to this limited calculus.

A more elaborate proximate determinants model specified at the individual rather than population level is presented in Hobcraft & Little (1984). At the cost of complexity, their approach uses more of the information available in fertility surveys and can feed directly into regression analyses cast at the household level. Menken (1987) assesses the merits of the different

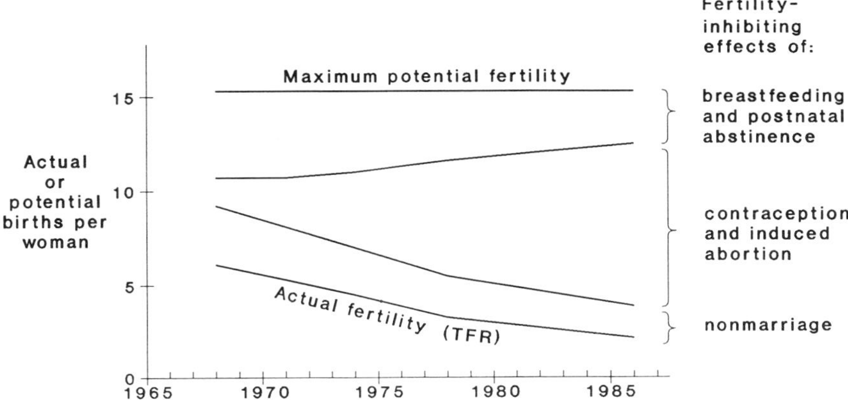

Figure 2. Decomposition of the difference between maximum potential fertility and the actual total fertility rate (TFR), Thailand, 1968-1986. Source of data: Knodel et al (1987), 1987 Thailand DHS.

approaches. Proximate determinants analysis (mainly the Bongaarts-variety) is applied in numerous analyses of World Fertility Survey data, notably Casterline et al (1984) and United Nations (1987).

A different but equally important perspective on fertility draws on the concept of parity progression, introduced by Ryder and Henry in the 1950s. (*Parity* here means the number of children a woman has borne.) The parity progression ratio for a particular cohort of women is the proportion who, having reached that parity, go on to have one or more subsequent births. If the ratio for progression from parity i to $i + 1$ is denoted a_i, then the total fertility rate for the cohort can be expressed in terms of parity progression ratios by $a_0 + a_0a_1 + a_0a_1a_2 + \ldots$ (Ryder 1986a). Fertility dynamics can be analyzed in terms of parity progression ratios and birth interval distributions in a manner analogous to the conventional analysis in terms of age-specific fertility rates (Feeney 1983). The approach has particular application to assessment of fertility control programs (Feeney & Yu 1987).

A third decomposition of fertility, more problematic than proximate determinants or parity progression analysis, is into "wanted" and "unwanted" components. This partitioning is based on survey responses on family size preferences, adjusted for exposure to risk of conception (Westoff 1981, Lightbourne 1987). Drawing on 48 national fertility surveys from third world countries in the 1970s and 1980s, Bongaarts (1990) estimates an average "wanted TFR" of 3.8 compared to an actual TFR of 5.0. Attitudinal data, however, are hard to interpret—especially when fertility is changing. The hypothetical situations enquired about can be at best very loosely specified;

nothing like an economic demand curve can be imputed from the responses (compare the problem of interpreting likely responses to a market survey enquiring about "wanted automobiles"). Notwithstanding, measures of unwanted fertility—and of analogous kinds of splits into "planned-unplanned" or "intended-unintended" births—are stock in trade of family planning programs.

DATA COLLECTION

Demography has always been distinctive among the social sciences for its profusion of data—lambasted by one critic for "pathological numeracy." On fertility, decennial censuses remain a major data source except in the most statistically backward countries. Registration systems, once seen as virtually a hallmark of civil society, routinely try to record births and deaths, although rarely with much success in most third world countries. Household sample surveys, in contrast, have been signally successful, vastly adding to the stock of demographic information.

Numerous surveys of fertility levels and patterns and of contraceptive knowledge, attitudes, and practice (KAP surveys) were taken in the 1960s, intended to support the establishment of family planning programs and to monitor expected program achievements in cutting fertility. A considerably greater ambition on the demographic side lay behind the establishment of the World Fertility Survey (WFS) in 1972 under the auspices of the International Statistical Institute, with US & United Nations funding. This massive data gathering enterprise—described by two leading participants as "the largest social survey ever undertaken" and "one of the more bizarre products of the realization that something had to be done to curb rapid population growth" (Cleland & Hobcraft 1985:1)—conducted comparable national sample surveys of ever-married, reproductive-age women in 61 countries from 1974 to 1984. It is a major source of what we know about recent fertility patterns and proximate determinants in the third world—especially in sub-Saharan Africa, where demographic data had been rudimentary. The analyses it spawned dominated demographic journals and PhD theses in the 1980s. Despite being a series of one-time surveys, the detailed pregnancy histories it collected from all respondents gave it temporal depth. The WFS program also contributed significantly to analytic methods, particularly in the field of event-history analysis (Hobcraft & Murphy 1986). Comprehensive accounts of WFS operations and findings are presented in Cleland & Hobcraft (1985) and Cleland & Scott (1987). With equal vigor but at a somewhat more pedestrian level and with more austere funding, the WFS's work has been continued in the Demographic and Health Surveys (DHS) program based in the United States.

The contribution of these surveys to understanding the determinants of fertility is controversial. Critics argue that they illuminate little beyond the fringe of proximate determinants—although that itself can be seen as a considerable accomplishment. The heavy store put on data comparability has worked against experimentation and creativity (except in areas of technical demographic measurement), so that the unusual privilege demographers have had among social scientists of being able to design their own research instruments has tended to be wasted. In line with time-honored practice in demographic enquiries, the surveys establish fertility differentials by a few standard socioeconomic characteristics (household structure, rural or urban residence, occupation, years of education, and such like) and these can be linked to fertility-related behavior more precisely than before, but influences on fertility at deeper levels of socioeconomic and cultural systems remain obscure. For critical comment on the WFS program—rightly accepted as the best of the demographic survey enterprises in the third world—see Demeny (1980), Miró (1980), Blake (1983), and Ryder (1986b).

Finally, fertility data can also come from intensive examination of small populations, by piecing together existing records (as through "family reconstitution"), or, in real time, from "demographic laboratories" and quasi-anthropological fieldwork. Family reconstitution is mainly of interest for historical demography; its most spectacular accomplishment is the 300-year series of fertility and marriage rates constructed for England from parish baptism and marriage records (Wrigley & Schofield 1981). Demographic laboratories—longitudinal studies of vital events and their covariates—are highly labor intensive and, not surprisingly, very few in number. The largest and by far the most effective is the field research station in the subdistrict of Matlab, Bangladesh, run by the International Centre for Diarrhoeal Disease Research, Bangladesh. Matlab data have supported a wide variety of demographic investigations, and the site has also been used for statistical trials of specific designs of antinatalist programs (Phillips et al 1982). Less quantitative, but no less ambitious in seeking insight, anthropological methods are increasingly being adapted to fertility research (Caldwell et al 1988a). Fieldwork is typically measured in months rather than the one or two years standard in anthropology proper and often involves a team rather than a lone investigator. While not without its own problems of preconception, the approach promises escape from the analytical and interpretive ruts that have bedeviled fertility survey research.

PATTERNS OF FERTILITY TRANSITION

The secular fertility decline of the now industrialized countries, in which fertility has fallen from somewhere in the range of 4–7 children per woman to below 3, is conveniently described as the fertility transition. In most of

Europe and in North America and Australia, the decisive part of this decline was in the period 1880–1930; in Japan and the lagging parts of Europe, it was in the first half of this century. In the newly industrialized third world countries—the so-called NICs—the transition has been a phenomenon of the last three decades. Elsewhere in the third world the decline is still in train or, in some places, yet to begin.

The historical record of fertility declines in the West and Japan is a major source for understanding third world fertility behavior and the forces acting upon it, and for forming expectations about its future course. The principal generalization drawn from this record associates fertility and mortality declines with each other and with the multifarious changes entailed in "modernization." As an offshoot of modernization theory, this demographic transition theory has shared in the castigation now routinely accorded the former. Yet, at least in general terms, many of the associations are quite well substantiated—though allowing ample scope for dispute over emphasis. Declines in fertility are linked in some degree to economic growth (Figure 3 shows the modern cross-sectional picture) and the transformation it has

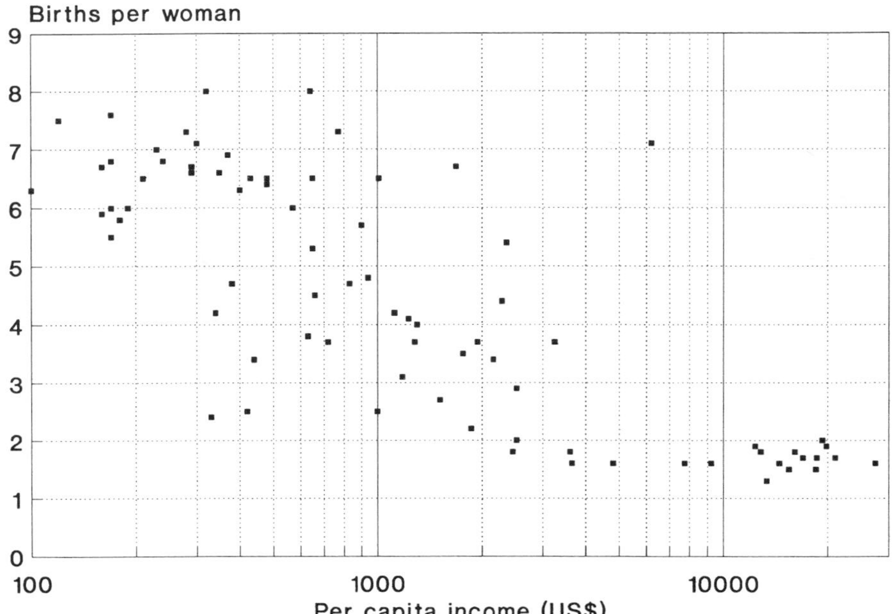

Figure 3. Total fertility rate by per capita income, 1988, for countries of 5 million population and above. (Outliers: upper-right, Saudi Arabia; lower-left, China and Sri Lanka.) Source of data: World Bank (1990).

wrought in the household economy (Lindert 1980); to "social development"—principally, wider access to education and improvements in women's relative status in the family and economy (Caldwell 1980); and to major cultural changes such as secularization and the supplanting of local by national frames of reference and loci of sanctions (Lesthaeghe 1983, Watkins 1991). The criticisms have come from the fact that apparent exceptions, sometimes striking ones, can be found to many such links—though this presumably should be a stimulus to theoretical refinement rather than cause for dismissal. One such controversy that has particular resonance in present-day policy debate, the problem of characterizing the pretransition fertility regime, is reviewed below.

In the contemporary world, there are evident additional factors bearing on fertility transition. Most prominently, there is the existence of the low-fertility industrialized countries as sources of technology, centers of power in the international economy, and object lessons of modern, consumerist lifestyles and patterns of social organization—inescapable models, for good and ill, confronted daily. Amid the assorted cultural baggage that has been transferred is the imperative (and the apparatus) of development planning, a minor part of which is concerned with explicit efforts by governments to induce lower fertility.

A literature survey on third world fertility written two decades ago would have largely concerned itself with differential fertility (by income, occupation, religion, etc)—then a still active research field, the results from which it was assumed would bear on how new behavior patterns would percolate through a society. But the rapid fertility declines of recent decades have tended to cut across such divisions, even where some of the relativities have been maintained. Social structure and culture are of course implicated, but in a society-specific institutional context. Hence the attention to regional and country detail below.

A Regional Overview

The regional trends in fertility summarized in Figure 1 can be briefly glossed as follows.

In *Latin America,* fertility has fallen by about 40% since the 1960s. A few countries have changed little (Bolivia, Guatemala, Honduras, Nicaragua, El Salvador, Haiti), but the three largest outside the southern cone, Brazil, Mexico, and Colombia, have shared in the decline. (Third world more by geographic accident than by history, Argentina has had relatively low fertility for decades.) Strenuous government efforts to promote birth control occurred in Colombia and, belatedly, in Mexico; none occurred—indeed, there was government opposition until 1978—in Brazil. Explanations for the declines have largely been couched in terms of household survival strategies, seen as specific by class in these highly differentiated societies. A separate corpus of demographic research takes more the family planner's view: social change as program-generated. If there is no family planning program as such, the activities of health practitioners may have been a rough functional equivalent: this has been argued in both Brazil and Mexico (Alba & Potter 1986).

East and Southeast Asia, with a few exceptions (Burma, Indochina, lately the Philippines), has been the stellar performer in the third world economic stakes over the last several decades. Its leaders, Taiwan and South Korea, have been the exemplars of "growth with equity," rapid economic advance without the extremes of inequality that once had been assumed a necessary accompaniment. Several Southeast Asian economies have sought to follow that model. China's economic path, of course, has been radically different, but under the Dengist reforms of the 1980s its divergence has lessened considerably (Greenhalgh 1989). Demographic transition in the region is also far advanced, with problems of rapid population aging now taking the place of high fertility on the agenda of social policy concerns. Candidates for explanation of fertility decline have included strong-minded government (and in China, direct political pressures), rising incomes, efficient family planning programs, and "neo-Confucian culture"—although the last can hardly apply to most of Southeast Asia.

South Asian fertility decline for the most part has been detectable but sluggish, a demographic version of what an Indian economist has referred to as the Hindu rate of change. Fertility averaged 6 children per woman in the 1950s and 1960s; it was a little below 5 in the 1980s. The region is of course far from homogeneous. Across a broad northern swathe—Pakistan, Bangladesh, and some of the largest Indian states: Rajasthan, Uttar Pradesh, Madhya Pradesh, Bihar—fertility has fallen only slightly if at all. In many other Indian states and in Sri Lanka appreciable and even large declines have occurred: total fertility is 2.6 in Sri Lanka, about 3 in Kerala, and below 4 in Punjab. For India, the state-wise demographic explicanda over 1961–1981 are marshalled and disciplined by Bhat et al (1984), but another 160 million persons have been added since 1981. Dyson & Moore (1983) trace north-south differences in fertility (and child mortality) in the subcontinent to the broad cultural distinction between (northern) Aryan and (southern) Dravidian areas that are reflected in kinship systems and levels of female autonomy. Overlaying such factors would be differences in economic performance (Punjab doing well, Kerala poorly) and in governmental effectiveness.

West Asia and North Africa still has high to very high fertility—reaching a TFR of 8 in Yemen. Only Turkey, Cyprus, Israel, Lebanon, and Tunisia have shown substantial declines; Egypt is perennially assumed to be in the early stages of transition. In aggregate, as Figure 1 shows, the region is following a "South Asian" path. Research on fertility determinants has largely been confined to modelling the effects of conventional socioeconomic factors and efforts to measure family planning program influence in the few countries where significant programs have been operating (chiefly, Turkey, Egypt, and Tunisia).

Sub-Saharan Africa, finally, is the region with least indication of fertility decline. It passed Europe's population (about 500 million—excluding USSR) in the late 1980s, with an annual number of births about four times that of Europe. United Nations projections show its 1990 population doubling by 2013, trebling by 2025. Total fertility for the region is estimated to have been roughly constant in the range 6–7 since the 1950s, though in earlier decades it must have been considerably lower than this. In a few countries it has exceeded 8. A notable downward trend is apparent in South Africa and, recently, in Botswana, Zimbabwe, and Kenya—the latter now often taken as presaging wider change. However, the timing of the declines built into the United Nations projections on the right side of Figure 1, while by no means impossible, is necessarily highly speculative.

There is little consensus on fertility determinants in sub-Saharan Africa beyond the proximate factors set out in Bongaarts et al (1984). For the World Bank, the region is a sort of backward Asia: Fertility transition will be brought about by the familiar combination of socioeconomic development and family planning programs. Economic growth has suffered under ill-advised statist policies but will revive with the shift toward the more deregulated, outward-looking strategies long advocated by the Bank; progress in extending education, health services, and family planning programs will work to speed up the fertility change (World Bank 1986). Other analysts find more that is exceptional about the region. Caldwell & Caldwell (1987) emphasize belief systems that convey a horror of childlessness, reinforcing the tangible returns parents receive from children. Family systems that work against a single household economy and make for gender-specific interests in high fertility are discussed in Fapohunda (1988) and Frank & McNicoll (1987). A variety of cultural and institutional perspectives on African fertility and its proximate components are gathered in three significant edited volumes: Page & Lesthaeghe (1981), Lesthaeghe (1989), and Ebigbola & van de Walle (1987).

Any investigation of the nature of an "African" path to low fertility must now take into account the implications of the AIDS epidemic. In the most-affected countries, beyond the direct effects in reversing a steady if slow improvement in health and mortality, are potentially profound repercussions for the economy and social relations, both in turn impinging on fertility. In the already large literature on AIDS in Africa, little research attention has thus far been given to fertility. (A relevant review article, on "sexual networks," is Caldwell et al 1989.)

Canonical Cases

Certain countries, because of the pace or distinctive pattern of their fertility decline, their perceived exemplary value to others, the intensity of research scrutiny accorded them, or sheer demographic weight, have become canonical for students of fertility transition. Those noted in this category here are China, India, Bangladesh, Thailand, Indonesia, and Brazil (together over 60% of the third world population).

China's modern demographic history is in its own way as extraordinary as its political history. The dominating events are the disastrous famine of 1958–1961 associated with the development policy known as the Great Leap Forward and the plummeting of fertility under the stringent antinatalist policy of the 1970s. The famine caused an estimated 27–30 million deaths above normal levels (Ashton et al 1984) and some 25 million fewer births (Peng 1987). Total fertility, which had averaged about 6 before and after the famine, fell to 4.0 in 1960 and 3.3 in 1961—reflected in the East Asian trend line in Figure 1. (See Banister 1987 on China's demographic statistics.) The birth planning campaign that began in 1971, following a series of policy switches in the preceding two decades (Chen & Kols 1982), mobilized both the highly effective health system and the formidable apparatus of state and Party authority. By 1980, the TFR was 2.2. The economic reforms that demolished collectivized agriculture put renewed upward pressure on fertility in the early 1980s, though this was countered by a radical effort, especially in the cities, to institute a one-child per family rule. Luther et al (1990) show the initially strong effect of the latter policy on progression from parity 1 to 2, and subsequent relaxation. Total fertility has risen slightly since the mid-1980s, to about 2.5 children per woman.

Disentangling what is Chinese, what is communist, and what is generic about China's fertility decline is a complex problem on which the comparison with Taiwan provides critical evidence. A major essay in comparative analysis on this subject is Greenhalgh (1988), which traces out distinctive paths of fertility transition in rural China, urban China, and Taiwan as characterized by differently evolving economic and political institutions. The salience of benefit-cost considerations in decision making by families across the Chinese cultural area is stressed; Confucianism as explanation gets short shrift—as does the effect of government roles in the supply of contraceptive services. For different perspectives on China's fertility decline see Birdsall & Jamison (1983), Whyte & Parish (1984), Wolf (1986), and Peng (1989).

On *India*, there is a large demographic literature but one that, on fertility, concentrates on proximate determinants and the family planning program (see Singh et al 1989 for a representative collection). India experienced a brief but drastic departure from its "soft-state" bureaucratic tradition in family planning during the Emergency of 1975–1976, when official exasperation with poor performance was converted into a single-minded pursuit of results. Sterilizations were trebled (to some 8 million in 1976), with widespread reports of coercion (Gwatkin 1979) and longstanding damage to the program in the following years. Still one of the best interpretive studies of India's fertility in context over the longer term is Cassen (1978), a minutely detailed work that defies synopsis. Notable also is the report by Caldwell et al (1988b) on an intensive investigation of demographic change in rural Karnataka, employing a variety of quasi-anthropological techniques. The authors portray a complex series of changes in family economics and power relations, on balance reducing the demand for children by parents.

Bangladesh, largely because of the continual stream of Matlab data, has been the object of much demographic research. The overall fertility regime is discussed by Arthur & McNicoll (1978) and Cain et al (1979), and its implications for policy by Demeny (1975). The regime depicted is one in which the costs of high fertility can in effect be transferred to disadvantaged groups—notably women and the poor—and to some extent forward in time. The position, of course, is not static: the combination of sheer economic exigency and even slim opportunities for economic mobility can make for shifts in fertility preferences; institutional forms change; and cultural orientations respond to new information flows. (On what has been termed "poverty-led" transition, a concept sometimes applied to Bangladesh but originally developed with reference to Kerala, see Basu 1986.) Matlab research gives a moderately optimistic view of the prospects for fertility decline—and for the family planning program role in it (Phillips et al 1988). Some of this research, for example, suggests that intensive outreach programs may be able to elude patriarchal opposition to birth control (Simmons et al 1988).

Thailand and *Indonesia* (like Taiwan earlier) are cases of major fertility decline where government family planning program efforts are often held up as exemplary. The Thai fertility decline and its proximate components are summarized in Figure 2. Knodel et al (1987) give a four-stranded explanation: rapid and fundamental social change that has raised the economic burden of large families; a cultural setting conducive to acceptance of birth control; a preexisting latent demand for means of fertility regulation (inferred from focus-group discussions with older people); and the efforts of the government's family planning program to increase the awareness and use of modern contraceptive methods. The weight accorded the family planning program, however, is not buttressed by exploration of the relevant counterfactual: that is, the likely course of Thai fertility under the vibrant economic growth and rampant Western and Japanese cultural influences that have been experienced, in the absence of that progam. In Indonesia, successes in the early years of antinatalist policy (after 1967, following the pronatalism of the Sukarno government) probably owed much to the administrative muscle of a militarized local government under the so-called New Order, promoting family planning program goals unopposed from the political left. As the economy picked up from near-collapse and booming oil revenues allowed a massive expansion of education and the health system, consumer demand for fertility control took over as the driving force. For analyses of the case, varying in emphasis, see Freedman et al (1981), McNicoll & Singarimbun (1983), and Hugo et al (1987).

Brazil can be seen as canonical for Latin America, though the English-language literature on the case is sparse. Total fertility was about 6 children per woman in the 1960s, near 3 in the mid-1980s. The proximate determinants and some major socioeconomic covariates are set out by Merrick & Berquó (1983). The fertility decline has occurred across economic strata and in rural as well as urban areas. Wood & Carvalho (1988) trace the fairly similar fertility outcomes to several quite distinct processes: rural proletarianization (a shift from tenant farmer and sharecropper, to whom children were a benefit, to independent and often part-time wage laborer, to whom they were not); worsening economic conditions for the urban poor; and rising consumption aspirations for the more affluent. (Mortality outcomes among these groups are predictably unequal.) Family planning, qua program, played at most a slight role.

EXPLANATIONS AND INTERPRETATIONS

The experience reviewed above clearly suggests different patterns of fertility transition. Low fertility is an ultimately necessary counterpart to low mortality, but differences in social and political organization, economic conditions, cultural orientations, and policy directions will be reflected in distinctive paths to that end. Moreover, fertility decline is as an element of broader social change, so explanations of it will potentially encounter all the problems of social change theory. The subject of fertility transition is likely to remain beset by controversy.

Pretransition Fertility and the Onset of Decline

One such controversy concerns the nature of the pretransition fertility regime. How much if any deliberate regulation of fertility was taking place in a society prior to the onset of secular fertility decline is investigated in historical fertility studies such as Princeton's European Fertility Project (Coale & Watkins 1986). There are modern policy issues at stake. Under a pretransition regime of no deliberate regulation, fertility decline can be interpreted simply as a response to an externally supplied innovation. The efforts of modern family planning programs to promote contraceptive practice find a close historical analogue. If, on the other hand, fertility decline was less a shift from natural to controlled childbearing than an adaptive response to perceived changes in parental interests vis à vis marriage and children, and in the institutional and cultural surrounds within which those interests are defined, then the policy lessons would point toward measures that seek to modify that decision environment (Carlsson 1966).

The European Fertility Project has been taken as supporting the former view (Coale 1973, Knodel & van de Walle 1979, Watkins 1987)—sometimes termed the "Princeton view." Pretransition fertility is seen as being under social rather than individual control, exercised chiefly by customary rules limiting marriage. Fertility regulation within marriage is a behavioral innovation—the result, firstly, of the bringing of fertility decision making within the "calculus of conscious choice" and, secondly, in the spread of knowledge of contraception (particularly, coitus interruptus). Motivation to limit births within marriage, by implication, already existed in latent form: significant numbers of births were unwanted, especially by their mothers. For the contemporary third world, a very similar interpretation of cross-national WFS data is argued by Cleland (1985) and Cleland & Wilson (1987): fertility transition is tied to ideational change—not change in ideas to do with children and their benefits and costs but in ideas concerning acceptability and means of reproductive control.

The opposing view of pretransition fertility can also find some support. It would seem, for example, to be more consistent with some recent work in economic and social history that has pushed the origins of individualism well back into the premodern era. Direct historical evidence on the prevalence of birth control practice is very sparse, though this may reflect public inadmissibility of the practice, or cultural transmission confined to networks of women, rather than zero prevalence. (In a significant study based on Mormon data, Bean et al 1990, however, find indications of widespread recourse to birth control on the American frontier in the nineteenth century.) Even in the contemporary third world the prevalence of so-called folk methods of contraception is poorly documented—this is an unsatisfactory aspect of fertility surveys like the WFS. Effectiveness is a partly separate issue: many have followed Himes (1936) in dismissing folk methods as ineffective; a few, like Riddle (1991), demur. Moreover, individual-level ineffectiveness does not preclude appreciable aggregate demographic effect.

The intention to limit or space births on the part of one or both partners can be assumed to lie behind practice of terminal abstinence, contraception, and abortion. It may also govern the duration of postnatal abstinence (often coinciding with the period of breastfeeding) and even, to some extent, the timing of marriage. A further complication in detecting intentionality in reproductive behavior is that actions to limit family size may precede marriage and extend beyond birth. Marriage itself may be used instrumentally;

outmigration or fostering-out of children may be options; and neglect or abandonment of infants may be practiced. (On these issues, see Davis 1963, Blake 1985, Shorter 1975, Scrimshaw 1978.) The expectation that nowadays such complications can be avoided by simply asking people about their past or present childbearing plans, though it has spawned a significant subindustry in interpreting the standard repertoire of survey questions, has not been borne out.

The problem of intention is thoroughly muddied in the literature by its identification with a narrower debate over the prevalence of "natural" fertility—a term used to denote fertility uninfluenced by parity-dependent efforts at regulation. To the extent that deliberateness is reflected in departures from a "natural" sequence of birth intervals (that is, a sequence generated by biological effects such as the onset of secondary sterility), it is possible to infer the degree of fertility regulation by the shape of the age-schedule of marital fertility rates (Coale & Trussell 1974, Ewbank 1989). This procedure is quite widely used, although the validity of the inference is disputable. Blake (1985) sets out a number of objections to reading intentions from birth rate schedules; Hobcraft (1985) finds empirical evidence from the WFS against the parity-specific nature of controlled fertility behavior.

Theories of Fertility Decline

The shift away from a general theory of demographic transition to more situation-specific analysis has been accompanied by a divergence of theoretical perspectives. Among matters of contention are the appropriate scope of an economic calculus in fertility decision making and the relative salience of "structural" and "cultural" content in characterizing the decision environment and its sources of change. (For earlier reviews, see Freedman 1979 and Jones 1982.)

Microeconomics offers fertility theory the concept of a household production function, in which the incomes and time of household members are combined to produce the array of commodities (which can include "child services") that yield utility and, over time, welfare. Economic growth and the consequent rising value of human time lead to substitution effects in the household favoring fewer and "higher-quality" children—that is, children embodying larger investments in health and education. (See Becker 1976, Schultz 1981.) Setting the Beckerian household within a straightforward neoclassical economy, secular fertility decline can be depicted as a response to changing factor prices and changing opportunities and opportunity costs in the labor market (Nerlove 1974, Schultz 1985). Leibenstein (1975) substitutes some greater sociological content for neoclassical economic rigor by admitting less than fully maximizing behavior by parent/consumers and effects of social mobility on preferences. Application to fertility of the "new institutional economics," a potentially promising path, is as yet barely begun (see, however, Ben-Porath 1980, Arthur 1982).

A simple benefit-cost model of fertility decision making lies at the kernel of two influential interpretations of fertility decline: those of Easterlin and Caldwell. In the model of Easterlin (1978; see also Easterlin & Crimmins 1985), the economic calculus cuts in when fertility decisions become conscious and the demand for children falls below "supply"—making the model consistent with the natural fertility hypothesis and taking some account of biological constraints. Caldwell's (1982) view of fertility transition centers on changes in the family—in particular, the process he calls "emotional nucleation," entailing a strengthened conjugal bond and newfound obligations by parents toward their children. In a series of interrelated papers thick with field observation, he argues that fertility falls in response to a reversal in the direction of net lifetime transfers between parents and children. In the perception of parents, a child, rather than being an economic asset, becomes a substantial burden—a change Caldwell associates with the shift away from familial production, the spread of modern schooling, and "Western" cultural influence. Empirical specification of the model, however, has proven difficult. (For criticism of the thesis from various angles, see Thadani 1978, Cain 1982, and Schultz 1983.)

Convergence of, say, South Asian or African family structure to a conjugal nuclear form was once seen as an inevitable accompaniment of urban industrialization. The case no longer seems strong; indeed, there is increasing evidence of the persistence and resilience of family forms in the course of development (Hajnal 1982). Fertility may still fall, but within family systems that adapt idiosyncratically to evolving circumstance (see Greenhalgh 1988 on the Chinese case).

The implicit intergenerational contract of Caldwell's transition theory has evident ties to fertility but plausibly is only a part of the institutional and cultural setting that governs a demographic regime. Changes in that setting may bring different elements of it into apposition with fertility, altering the nature of decision trade-offs. An a priori ranking of the salience of such elements constricts the interpretation of particular cases. For more general statements on the institutional and cultural determinants of fertility by authors who are far from reaching consensus among themselves, see Davis & Blake (1956) (pioneering in this context as well as for its treatment of proximate determinants), and more recently, Cain 1983, Greenhalgh 1990, Kreager 1986, Lesthaeghe & Surkyn 1988, McNicoll 1978, 1980, Potter 1983, and R. Smith 1986. Formal confrontation with the empirical record in this research tradition is not well developed; H. Smith (1989) has pertinent remarks on the problems and agenda.

Contrasting stances on the determinants of fertility decline frequently echo broader debates on social change theory and epistemology that by their nature will not soon be resolved, indeed are perhaps unresolvable. Among such debates (some clearly overlapping) are those on the program of methodological individualism, the value of economic modes of analysis beyond narrowly "economic" domains of behavior, the explanatory role of "culture" in one or other of its conceptions, the relative worth of moral economy and political economy perspectives, "soft" determinism and historical contingency, the "embeddedness" of behavior in networks of social relations, the nature of the implicit model of the person—from "oversocialized" to anarchic individualist, and so on. Often the fertility literature displays scant awareness of the larger issues in play.

There are other debates in social change where fertility research arguably should be engaged but is not, notwithstanding vigorous dispute in the larger field. Sociobiology is a case in point: the biology of reproduction is treated with sophistication, the putative biology of reproductive behavior is not. (See, however, Turke 1989.) Another instance, perhaps more notable, is feminism. Seccombe (1983:24) remarks on the near absence of feminist perspectives and debates in the mainstream demographic journals: "One would never guess, reading these journals, that childbearing was a sex-specific and gender differentiated process."

Fertility Policy: Effort and Efficacy

Fertility policy in the third world has come to mean family planning programs. Early questioning of this linkage on the grounds of the likely ineffectiveness of such programs in comparison to measures directed at influencing parental demand for children (Davis 1967, Hauser 1967), or of the irrelevance of both policy and program to the entire fertility transition of the West and Japan, was powerless against a burgeoning international movement, able to point to modern contraception as the means by which fertility was declining and to its own programs as a principal source of the supplies or services employed. (See Demeny 1988 and Hodgson 1983, 1988 on the intellectual and political history of the issue, and Berelson et al 1990 on some of the arguments.) The oddity, a priori, of associating fertility policy with health—and of giving effect to policy through a government program reaching into the most intimate of family behaviors—is no longer remarked upon.

Yet the efficacy of family planning programs is by no means well resolved. Elaborate multivariate statistical studies seek to measure the effect of family planning program "effort" over and above socioeconomic determinants of fertility (Lapham & Mauldin 1984, Birdsall 1985, Lapham & Simmons 1987, Entwistle 1989). Critics, however, dispute the model specification—suggesting, for example, that "effective" programs are largely a response to a service demand that would otherwise be catered to through private channels (Demeny 1979, Hernandez 1984). "Program effort" would thus be contaminated, reflecting in part fertility determinants not captured by the socioeconomic measures included. Differing statistical models estimated on cross-national data yield estimates of the contribution of programs to fertility change ranging from 40% (Boulier 1985) to 3–10% (Hernandez 1984). Direct experimental research that might be able to narrow this range is difficult to mount and understandably concentrates on trying to devise new, potentially more effective program interventions rather than modelling actual government activities, warts and all (Phillips et al 1982).

Since fertility is declining in most of the third world, the heat of this argument has abated. It remains, however, a critical issue in Africa. Many (including the international agencies) would see the apparently successful family planning programs of Thailand and Indonesia as models for emulation by African countries (Caldwell & Caldwell 1989)—although equally relevant might be the experience of Pakistan, with decades of program effort to zero effect. Other dimensions of family planning programs—their sensitivity to cultural context and the quality of services provided—remain of interest (Warwick 1982). A brief country-by-country summary of official policy positions and actions is compiled in United Nations (1987–1990).

The niche that once was occupied by policies or proposals for policies "beyond family planning" now seems virtually empty, albeit partly for the reason that far-from-garden-variety programs can still keep the name. Monetary incentives for sterilization are widely used in South Asia as an inherent program component. Even China's policy, wielding political as well as monetary disincentives to gain compliance, sometimes passes as a family planning program. (The ethical issues raised by such additions to the basic functions of information provision and service delivery are treated by Berelson & Lieberson 1979.) Other mooted directions of policy—efforts to mobilize informal networks or groups of women whose interests might be served by lower fertility, manipulation of the benefits and costs of children, reform of marriage- and family-law, and such like—tend to be seen as marginal accretions to the mainline effort. The blinkering of population policy may have avoided some excesses; more certainly it has led to many missed opportunities.

FUTURES FOR FERTILITY AND FERTILITY RESEARCH

The right- hand side of Figure 1 sketches the medium-variant United Nations expectations for trends in third world fertility. This is a surprise-free future in which the transition now in train will be smoothly completed, and Africa, the laggard, will follow only a decade or two behind the average. In the World Bank projections, replacement fertility is attained around 2030 in East & Southeast Asia and Latin America, 2055 in South Asia and West Asia/North Africa, and 2060 in sub-Saharan Africa.

Surprises have to be large indeed to impinge on demographic change at this level. The Chinese famine of 1958–1961 did so; the AIDS epidemic (not yet factored in) is likely to do so in Africa, and perhaps elsewhere. Yet such disasters have ecological and social-organizational roots of a kind that are potential sources of other disruptions in coming decades.

What of the scope for more marginal and perhaps policy-based changes in the demographic future? Under alternative scenarios of third world development within a "normal" range, fertility declines could be faster or slower than suggested. The United Nations's low and high variant projections for the world in 2025, reflecting marginal judgments of that sort, are 7.6 and 9.4 billion—a range equivalent to one third of the present world population.

Research on third world fertility should thus remain high on the social science agenda. Much of what has been settled in the field is technical demography: birth interval dynamics, relations between fertility and its proximate determinants, and such like. Most research on fertility determinants takes a firmly microanalytic stance, fueled by the mass of household survey data produced since the 1960s. (See the exhaustive review of studies by Bulatao & Lee 1983.) Ryder (1983) argues strongly for a redressing of that balance—for more research where "the unit of analysis is not the individual act but the normative instruction." If subservience to a normative setting is rejected as the vice of oversocialization, research efforts should be directed at identifying the microfoundations of such settings (the program traced out on a broader canvas by Hechter 1983), or at their social historical origins and cultural dynamics (the program for a "political economy of fertility" sketched by Greenhalgh 1990).

On fertility policy, there has been a comparable imbalance in research attention: in this case, toward the operational problems of family planning programs. (For the exhaustive review see Lapham & Simmons 1987.) Seen from the middle of fertility transition the foreshortened perspective of the physician or clinic worker in the frontlines of the contraceptive revolution comes to dominate: policy is logistics. But the sociologist, like the historian, will no doubt find deeper forces at work: in retrospect the programs may appear to have been mostly tinkering—and the focus on them preemptive of other lines of policy thinking. A research agenda that would place fertility policy more appropriately as an issue of public choice, albeit concerning an inaccessible and culturally central domain of life, is implicit in Demeny (1986, 1988). Social scientists may yet gain a right to claim, when the fertility transition is over, that they had more than a marginal part in it.

ACKNOWLEDGMENTS

I appreciate comments on a draft of this review from Paul Demeny, Susan Greenhalgh, and Susan Watkins.

Literature Cited

Alba, F., Potter, J. E. 1986. Population and development in Mexico since 1940: an interpretation. *Popul. Dev. Rev.* 12:47–75

Arthur, W. B. 1982. Review of G. S. Becker, A Treatise on the Family. *Popul. Dev. Rev.* 8:393–97

Arthur, W. B., McNicoll, G. 1978. An analytical survey of population and development in Bangladesh. *Popul. Dev. Rev.* 4: 23–80

Ashton, B., Hill, K., Piazza, A., Zeitz, R. 1984. Famine in China, 1958–61. *Popul. Dev. Rev.* 10:613–45

Banister, J. 1987. *China's Changing Population*. Stanford: Stanford Univ. Press

Basu, A. M. 1986. Birth control by assetless workers in Kerala: the possibility of a poverty-induced fertility transition. *Dev. Change* 17:265–82

Bean, L. L., Mineau, G. P., Anderton, D. L. 1990. *Fertility Change on the American Frontier: Adaptation and Innovation*. Berkeley: Univ. Calif. Press

Becker, G. S. 1976. *The Economic Approach to Human Behavior*. Chicago: Univ. Chicago Press

Ben-Porath, Y. 1980. The F-connection: families, friends, and firms and the organization of exchange. *Popul. Dev. Rev.* 6:1–30

Berelson, B., Jejeebhoy, S., Kelley, A. C., McNicoll, G. 1990. The great debate on population policy revisited. *Int. Fam. Plan. Perspect.* 16:126–50

Berelson, B., Lieberson, J. 1979. Government efforts to influence fertility: the ethical issues. *Popul. Dev. Rev.* 4:581–613

Bhat, P. N. M., Preston, S., Dyson, T. 1984. *Vital Rates in India 1961–81*. Washington, DC: Natl. Acad. Sci.

Birdsall, N., ed. 1985. *The Effects of Family Planning Programs on Fertility in the Developing World*. Work. Pap. No. 677. Washington, DC: World Bank

Birdsall, N., Jamison, D. T. 1983. Income and other factors influencing fertility in China. *Popul. Dev. Rev.* 9:651–75

Blake, J. 1983. Review of World Fertility Survey Conference 1980: Record of Proceedings. *Popul. Dev. Rev.* 9:153–56

Blake, J. 1985. The fertility transition: continuity or discontinuity with the past? In *Int. Popul. Conf., Florence, 1985,* 4: 393–405. Liège: Int. Union Sci. Study Popul.

Bongaarts, J. 1978. A framework for analyzing the proximate determinants of fertility. *Popul. Dev. Rev.* 4:105–32

Bongaarts, J. 1990. The measurement of wanted fertility. *Popul. Dev. Rev.* 16:487–506

Bongaarts, J., Frank, O., Lesthaeghe, R. 1984. The proximate determinants of fertility in sub-Saharan Africa. *Popul. Dev. Rev.* 10:511–37

Bongaarts, J., Potter, R. G. 1983. *Fertility, Biology, and Behavior: An Analysis of the Proximate Determinants*. New York: Academic

Boulier, B. L. 1985. Family planning programs and contraceptive availability. Their effects on contraceptive use and fertility. See Birdsall 1985, pp. 41–115

Bulatao, R. A., Bos, E., Stephens, P. W., Vu, M. T. 1990. *World Population Projections. 1989–1990 Edition: Short- and Long-Term Estimates*. Baltimore: Johns Hopkins Univ. Press

Bulatao, R. A., Lee, R. D., eds. 1983. *Determinants of Fertility in Developing Countries,* Vols. 1, 2. New York: Academic

Cain, M. 1982. Perspectives on family and fertility in developing countries. *Popul. Stud.* 36:159–75

Cain, M. 1983. Fertility as an adjustment to risk. *Popul. Dev. Rev.* 9:688–702

Cain, M., Khanam, S. R., Nahar, S. 1979. Class, patriarchy, and women's work in Bangladesh. *Popul. Dev. Rev.* 5:405–38

Caldwell, J. C. 1980. Mass education as a determinant of the timing of fertility decline. *Popul. Dev. Rev.* 6:225–55

Caldwell, J. C. 1982. *Theory of Fertility Decline*. London: Academic

Caldwell, J. C., Caldwell, P. 1987. The cultural context of high fertility in sub-Saharan Africa. *Popul. Dev. Rev.* 13:409–37

Caldwell, J. C., Caldwell, P. 1989. Is the Asian family planning program model suited to Africa? *Stud. Fam. Plan.* 19:19–28

Caldwell, J. C., Caldwell, P., Quiggan, P. 1989. The social context of AIDS in sub-Saharan Africa. *Popul. Dev. Rev.* 15:185–234

Caldwell, J. C., Hill, A. G., Hull, V. J., eds.

1988a. *Micro-Approaches to Demographic Research*. London: Kegan Paul
Caldwell, J. C., Reddy, P. H., Caldwell, P. 1988b. *The Causes of Demographic Change: Experimental Research in South India*. Madison, Wisc: Univ. Wisc. Press
Carlsson, G. 1966. The decline of fertility: innovation or adjustment process. *Popul. Stud.* 20:149–74
Cassen, R. H. 1978.*India: Population, Economy, Society*. New York: Holmes & Meier
Casterline, J. B., Singh, S., Cleland, J. G., Ashurst, H. 1984. *The Proximate Determinants of Fertility*. WFS Comp. Stud. No. 39. Voorburg, Netherlands: Int. Stat. Inst.
Chen, P., Kols, A. 1982. Population and birth planning in the People's Republic of China. *Popul. Rep. Ser. J.* No. 25
Cleland, J. 1985. Marital fertility decline in developing countries: theories and the evidence. See Cleland & Hobcraft 1985, pp. 223–52
Cleland, J., Hobcraft, J., eds. 1985. *Reproductive Change in Developing Countries: Insights from the World Fertility Survey*. Oxford: Oxford Univ. Press
Cleland, J., Scott, C., eds. 1987. *The World Fertility Survey: An Assessment*. Oxford: Oxford Univ. Press
Cleland, J., Wilson, C. 1987. Demand theories of the fertility transition: an iconoclastic view. *Popul. Stud.* 41:5–30
Coale, A. J. 1967. Factors associated with the development of low fertility: an historic summary. In *Proc. World Popul. Conf., 1965*, 2:205–9. New York: United Nations
Coale, A. J. 1973. The demographic transition reconsidered. In *Int. Popul. Conf., Liège, 1973*, 1:53–71. Liège: Int. Union Sci. Study Popul.
Coale, A. J., Trussell, T. J. 1974. Model fertility schedules: variations in the age structure of childbearing in human populations. *Popul. Index* 40:185–258
Coale, A. J., Watkins, S. C., eds. 1986. *The Decline of Fertility in Europe*. Princeton, NJ: Princeton Univ. Press
Davis, K. 1963. The theory of change and response in modern demographic history. *Popul. Index* 29:345–66
Davis, K. 1967. Population policy: will current programs succeed? *Science* 158:730–39
Davis, K., Blake, J. 1956. Social structure and fertility: an analytic framework. *Econ. Dev. Cult. Change* 4:211–35
Demeny, P. 1975. Observations on population policy and population program in Bangladesh. *Popul. Dev. Rev.* 1:307–21
Demeny, P. 1979. On the end of the population explosion. *Popul. Dev. Rev.* 5:141–62
Demeny, P. 1980. [Discussion] In *World Fertility Survey Conf. 1980: Record of Proceedings*, 1:137–44. Voorburg, Netherlands: Int. Stat. Inst.
Demeny, P. 1986. Population and the invisible hand. *Demography* 23:473–87
Demeny, P. 1988. Social science and population policy. *Popul. Dev. Rev.* 14:451–79
Dyson, T., Moore, M. 1983. On kinship structure, female autonomy, and demographic behavior in India. *Popul. Dev. Rev.* 9:35–60
Easterlin, R. A. 1978. The economics and sociology of fertility: a synthesis. In *Historical Studies of Changing Fertility*, ed. C. Tilly, pp. 57–113. Princeton, NJ: Princeton Univ. Press
Easterlin, R. A., Crimmins, E. M. 1985. *The Fertility Revolution: a Supply-Demand Analysis*. Chicago: Univ. Chicago Press
Ebigbola, J. A., van de Walle, E., eds. 1987. *The Cultural Roots of African Fertility Regimes*. Proc. Ife Conf. Philadelphia: Popul. Stud. Cent. Univ. Penn.
Entwisle, B. 1989. Measuring components of family planning program effort. *Demography* 26:53–76
Ewbank, D. C. 1989. Estimating birth stopping and spacing behavior. *Demography* 26:473–83
Fapohunda, E. R. 1988. The non-pooling household: a challenge to economic theory. In *A Home Divided: Women and Income in the Third World*, ed. D. H. Dwyer, J. Bruce, pp. 143–54. Stanford: Stanford Univ. Press
Feeney, G. 1983. Population dynamics based on birth intervals and parity progression. *Popul. Stud.* 37:75–89
Feeney, G., Yu, J. 1987. Period parity progression measures of fertility in China. *Popul. Stud.* 41:77–102
Frank, O., McNicoll, G. 1987. An interpretation of fertility and population policy in Kenya. *Popul. Dev. Rev.* 13:209–43
Freedman, R. 1979. Theories of fertility decline: a reappraisal. *Soc. Forces* 58:1–17
Freedman, R., Khoo, S. E., Supraptilah, B. 1981. Use of modern contraceptives in Indonesia: a challenge to the conventional wisdom. *Int. Fam. Plan. Perspect.* 7:3–15
Greenhalgh, S. 1988. Fertility as mobility: Sinic transitions. *Popul. Dev. Rev.* 14:629–74
Greenhalgh, S. 1989. Land reform and family entrepreneurship in East Asia. *Popul. Dev. Rev.* 15(Suppl.):77–118
Greenhalgh, S. 1990. Toward a political economy of fertility: anthropological contributions. *Popul. Dev. Rev.* 16:85–106
Gwatkin, D. R. 1979. Political will and family planning: the implications of India's Emergency experience. *Popul. Dev. Rev.* 5:29–59

Hajnal, J. 1982. Two kinds of preindustrial household formation system. *Popul. Dev. Rev.* 8:449–94

Hauser, P. M. 1967. Family planning and population programs. *Demography* 4:397–414

Hechter, M., ed. 1983. *Microfoundations of Macrosociology*. Philadelphia: Temple Univ. Press

Hernandez, D. J. 1984. *Success or Failure? Family Planning Programs in the Third World*. Westport, Conn: Greenwood

Himes, N. E. 1936. (1970). *Medical History of Contraception*. New York: Shocken

Hobcraft, J. 1985. Family-building patterns. See Cleland & Hobcraft 1985, pp. 64–86

Hobcraft, J., Little, R. J. A. 1984. Fertility exposure analysis: a new method for assessing the contribution of proximate determinants to fertility differentials. *Popul. Stud.* 38:21–45

Hobcraft, J., Murphy, M. 1986. Demographic event history analysis: a selective review. *Popul. Index* 52:3–27

Hodgson, D. 1983. Demography as social science and policy science. *Popul. Dev. Rev.* 9:1–34

Hodgson, D. 1988. Orthodoxy and revisionism in American demography. *Popul. Dev. Rev.* 14:541–69

Hugo, G. J., Hull, T. H., Hull, V. J., Jones, G. W. 1987. *The Demographic Dimension in Indonesian Development*. Singapore: Oxford Univ. Press

Jones, G. W. 1982. Fertility determinants: sociological and economic theories. In *International Encyclopedia of Population*, 1:279–86. New York: Free

Knodel, J., Chamratrithirong, A., Debavalya, N. 1987. *Thailand's Reproductive Revolution: Rapid Fertility Decline in a Third-World Setting*. Madison, Wisc: Univ. Wisc. Press

Knodel, J., van de Walle, E. 1979. Lessons from the past: policy implications of historical fertility studies. *Popul. Dev. Rev.* 5:217–45

Kreager, P. 1986. Demographic regimes as cultural systems. In *The State of Population Theory: Forward from Malthus*, ed. D. Coleman, R. Schofield, pp. 131–55. Oxford: Blackwell

Lapham, R. J., Mauldin, W. P. 1984. Family planning program effort and birth rate decline in developing countries. *Int. Fam. Plan. Perspect.* 10:109–18

Lapham, R. J., Simmons, G. B., eds. 1987. *Organizing for Effective Family Planning Programs*. Washington, DC: Natl. Acad. Sci.

Leibenstein, H. 1975. The economic theory of fertility decline. *Q. J. Econ.* 89:1–31

Lesthaeghe, R. 1983. A century of demographic and cultural change in Western Europe: an exploration of underlying dimensions. *Popul. Dev. Rev.* 9:411–35

Lesthaeghe, R., Surkyn, J. 1988. Cultural dynamics and economic theories of fertility change. *Popul. Dev. Rev.* 14:1–45

Lesthaeghe, R., ed. 1989. *Reproduction and Social Organization in Sub-Saharan Africa*. Berkeley: Univ. Calif. Press

Lightbourne, R. E. 1987. Reproductive preferences and behaviour. See Cleland & Scott 1987, pp. 838–61

Lindert, P. H. 1980. Child costs and economic development. In *Population and Economic Change in Developing Countries*, ed. R. A. Easterlin, pp. 5–69. Chicago: Univ. Chicago Press

Luther, N. Y., Feeney, G., Zhang, W. 1990. One-child families or a baby boom? Evidence from China's one-per-hundred survey. *Popul. Stud.* 44:341–57

McNicoll, G. 1978. Population and development: outlines for a structuralist approach. *J. Dev. Stud.* 14:79–99

McNicoll, G. 1980. Institutional determinants of fertility change. *Popul. Dev. Rev.* 6:441–62

McNicoll, G., Singarimbun, M. 1983. *Fertility Decline in Indonesia: Analysis and Interpretation*. Washington, DC: Natl. Acad. Sci.

Menken, J. 1987. Proximate determinants of fertility and mortality: a review of recent findings. *Sociol. Forum* 2:697–717

Merrick, T. W., Berquó, E. 1983. *The Determinants of Brazil's Recent Rapid Decline in Fertility*. Washington, DC: Natl. Acad. Sci.

Miró, C. 1980. The potential of the WFS to clarify the socio-economic determinants of fertility in developing countries. In *World Fertility Survey Conf. 1980: Record of Proceedings*, 1:337–51. Voorburg, Netherlands: Int. Stat. Inst.

Nerlove, M. 1974. Household and economy: toward a new theory of population and economic growth. *J. Polit. Econ.* 82 (Suppl.):200–18

Page, H. J., Lesthaeghe, J. 1981. *Child-spacing in Tropical Africa: Traditions and Change*. London: Academic

Peng, X. 1987. Demographic consequences of the Great Leap Forward in China's provinces. *Popul. Dev. Rev.* 13:639–70

Peng, X. 1989. Major determinants of China's fertility transition. *China Q.* March:1–37

Phillips, J. F., Simmons, R., Koenig, M. A., Chakraborty, J. 1988. Determinants of reproductive change in a traditional society: evidence from Matlab, Bangladesh. *Stud. Fam. Plan.* 19:313–34

Phillips, J. F., Stinson, W. S., Bhatia, S.,

Rahman, M., Chakraborty, J. 1982. The demographic impact of the Family Planning Health Services Project in Matlab, Bangladesh. *Stud. Fam. Plan.* 13:131–40
Potter, J. E. 1983. Effects of societal and community institutions on fertility. See Bulatao & Lee 1983, 2:627–65
Riddle, J. M. 1991. Oral contraceptives and early-term abortifacients during classical antiquity and the Middle Ages. *Past Present* 132:3–32
Ryder, N. B. 1983. Fertility and family structure. *Popul. Bull. United Nations* 15:15–34
Ryder, N. B. 1986a. Observations on the history of cohort fertility in the United States. *Popul. Dev. Rev.* 12:617–43
Ryder, N. B. 1986b. Review of J. Cleland and J. Hobcraft. *Reproductive change in developing countries. Popul. Dev. Rev.* 12: 341–49
Schultz, T. P. 1981. *Economics of Population.* Reading, Mass: Addison-Wesley
Schultz, T. P. 1983. Review of J. C. Caldwell, *Theory of Fertility Decline. Popul. Dev. Rev.*9:161–68
Schultz, T. P. 1985. Changing world prices, women's wages, and the fertility transition: Sweden, 1860–1910. *J. Polit. Econ.* 93: 1126–54
Scrimshaw, S. C. M. 1978. Infant mortality and behavior in the regulation of family size. *Popul. Dev. Rev.* 4:383–403
Seccombe, W. 1983. Marxism and demography. *New Left Rev.* 137:22–47
Shorter, E. 1975. *The Making of the Modern Family.* New York: Basic
Simmons, R., Baqee, L., Koenig, M. A., Phillips, J. F. 1988. Beyond supply: the importance of female family planning workers in rural Bangladesh. *Stud. Fam. Plan.* 19:29–38
Singh, S. N., Premi, M. K., Bhatia, P. S., Bose, A., eds. 1989. *Population Transition in India,* Vols. 1, 2. New Delhi: B. R.
Smith, H. L. 1989. Integrating theory and research on the institutional determinants of fertility. *Demography* 26:171–84
Smith, R. M. 1986. Transfer incomes, risk and security: the roles of the family and the collectivity in recent theories of fertility change. In *The State of Population Theory: Forward from Malthus,* ed. D. Coleman, R. Schofield, pp. 188–211. Oxford: Blackwell
Thadani, V. N. 1978. The logic of sentiment: the family and social change. *Popul. Dev. Rev.* 4:457–99
Turke, P. W. 1989. Evolution and the demand for children. *Popul. Dev. Rev.* 15:61–90
United Nations. 1987. *Fertility Behaviour in the Context of Development: Evidence from the World Fertility Survey. Popul. Stud. No. 100.* New York: UN
United Nations. 1987–1990. *World Population Policies,* Vols. 1, 2, 3. *Popul. Stud. No. 102.* New York: UN
United Nations. 1991. *World Population Prospects 1990. Popul. Stud. No. 120.* New York: UN
Warwick, D. P. 1982. *Bitter Pills: Population Policies and Their Implementation in Eight Developing Countries.* Cambridge: Cambridge Univ. Press
Watkins, S. C. 1987. The fertility transition: Europe and the third world compared. *Sociol. Forum* 2:645–73
Watkins, S. C. 1991. *From Provinces into Nations: The Demographic Integration of Western Europe, 1870–1960.* Princeton, NJ: Princeton Univ. Press
Westoff, C. F. 1981. Unwanted fertility in six developing countries. *Int. Fam. Plan. Perspect.* 7:43–52
Whyte, M. K., Parish, W. C. 1984. *Urban Life in Contemporary China.* Chicago: Univ. Chicago Press
Wolf, A. P. 1986. The preeminent role of government intervention in China's family revolution. *Popul. Dev. Rev.* 12:101–16
Wood, C. H., Carvalho, J. A. M. 1988. *The Demography of Inequality in Brazil.* Cambridge: Cambridge Univ. Press
World Bank. 1986. *Population Growth and Policies in Sub-Saharan Africa.* Washington, DC: World Bank
World Bank. 1990. *World Development Report 1990.* New York: Oxford Univ. Press
Wrigley, E. A., Schofield, R. S. 1981. *The Population History of England, 1541–1871: A Reconstruction.* London: Arnold

Annu. Rev. Sociol. 1992. 18:109–27

TWO APPROACHES TO SOCIAL STRUCTURE: Exchange Theory and Network Analysis

K. S. Cook and J. M. Whitmeyer

Department of Sociology, University of Washington, Seattle, Washington 98195

KEY WORDS: social exchange, exchange networks, power, social networks

---

Abstract

Much convergence exists between exchange theory and network approaches to social structure. Starting with the work of Emerson, exchange theory increasingly has considered social structure explicitly, as both product and constraint. Exchange theory and network analysis both conceptualize social structure as a configuration of social relations and positions, i. e. as a set of actors diversely linked into networks. Exchange theory and most work in network analysis are based on similar conceptions of the actor. Where exchange theory and network analysis differ is in their view of the links between positions. Exchange theory stresses the exchange aspects of all ties and contends that the appropriate network in any analysis is one that contains all relevant exchange relations. Network analysis tends to be more catholic about the nature of the links.

INTRODUCTION

Social structure is one of the central concepts in sociological analysis. It is also at the core of many of the most influential theories within the field of sociology. Durkheim, Parsons, Levi-Strauss, Marx, Weber, Merton, Coser,

0360-0572/92/0815-0109$02.00

Blau, Coleman, and many others have developed conceptions of social structure in their attempts to provide explanatory frameworks that encompass both human behavior and institutional persistence and change. Our task here is to begin to specify how two different literatures within sociology can be brought together in the analysis of social structure and structural forms. These two traditions are exchange theory and network approaches to structure. To accomplish this task we provide a brief statement of historical context, placing this chapter in the relevant stream of work that has been conducted on the topic of social structure. This statement is followed by reviews of the commonalities and differences in the approaches to structure taken by exchange theorists and network analysts. We conclude with comments about future developments linking these two traditions.

A fairly comprehensive treatment of the different approaches to social structure can be found in the volume edited by Peter Blau (1975). Various conceptions of social structure are presented by authors that include Bierstedt, Blau, Bottomore, Coleman, Coser, Goode, Homans, Lenski, Lipset, Merton, Parsons, and Wallace. Blau identifies three major approaches to social structure: (i) social structure as a configuration of social relations and positions, (ii) social structure as the substratum that underlies all of social life and history, and (iii) social structure as a "multidimensional space of the differentiated social positions of the people in a society or other collectivity" (Blau 1975:14).

The approach to social structure adopted by exchange theorists (including Blau 1964) and a majority of the network analysts is the first alternative, the configurational approach. We focus primarily upon this general approach to social structure. We omit from our discussion the structuralism characteristic of Levi-Strauss (though this is mentioned, by Ekeh 1974, as a distinct tradition within exchange theory) and subsequent developments along this line. What Blau refers to as the multidimensional approach is characteristic of his more recent work (e.g. Blau 1977). In the next section we first review the treatment of social structure by exchange theorists and then move to network approaches.

SOCIAL STRUCTURE: AN EXCHANGE PERSPECTIVE

Exchange theorists advance a basic image of social structure as a configuration of social relations among actors (both individual and corporate), where the relations involve the exchange of valued items (which can be material, informational, symbolic, etc). Exchange theory increasingly has involved explicit consideration of social structure, as both product and constraint, typically in the form of networks of social relations. We will comment on the similarities and differences in the perspectives on social structure of three of the principal exchange theorists in historical progression.

Homans' View of Social Structure

Homans' (1961, 1964) primary purpose was the study of the "subinstitutional" or "elementary" forms of behavior. Homans developed a theory of social behavior based primarily upon behavioral principles of analysis. He took as the domain of his explanatory framework (1961:3), "the actual social behavior of individuals in direct contact with one another." He refers to this behavior as elementary and clearly distinguishes it from behavior that can be defined as obedience to the norms of a society (including role-related behavior). Role-conforming behavior was institutionalized behavior, thus actual behavior was defined by Homans as subinstitutional.

For Homans, social structures emerge from elementary forms of behavior and change over time in response to changes in this behavior by aggregates. (He does not address in any detail the complex interplay between microlevel processes and aggregate level outcomes.) He argued that the similar behavior of enough people can alter existing social structures and institutions and even, under some conditions, replace them. "Sometimes the great rebellions and revolutions, cracking the institutional crust, bring out elementary social behavior hot and straight from the fissures" (Homans 1961:398). His analysis of social behavior endures as a classic in sociology precisely because his vision of the underpinnings of social structure and institutional forms is straightforward and is linked so clearly to the actions of individuals (i.e. to their responses to rewarding and punishing circumstances).

Though the focus of Homans' theoretical framework was the relations between actors in direct contact with one another, he did acknowledge the structural importance of indirect exchange relations. An example is the social relation between employees of the same employer, who are related indirectly in second-order exchange relations through their common link to the same employer. In this sense the basic format for exchange network analysis existed in the earliest formulations.

Blau's Early View of Social Structure

While Homans' work is distinctly microsociological in character, Blau's (1964) major treatise on exchange and power is an explicit statement of the micro-macro linkage problem, before micro-macro issues became a fashionable topic in sociology in the 1980s (e.g. Alexander et al 1987, Collins 1981, Cook 1991, Huber 1991, etc). Blau's focus was the development of a theory of social structure and institutions based upon a sound microfoundation, a theory of social exchange. Two major features differentiate Blau's work from that of Homans. First, Blau did not base his theory of exchange upon behavioral principles; instead he introduced aspects of micro-economic reasoning into his analysis of distinctly social exchange (see Heath 1976). Second, recognizing that social structures have emergent properties, he extended the theory beyond subinstitutional phenomena.

Blau discusses processes like group formation, cohesion, social integration, opposition, conflict, and dissolution in terms of principles of social exchange. In his view various forms of social association generated by exchange processes over time come to constitute quite complex social structures (and substructures). The coordination of action in large collectivities is made possible by common values in the social system which mediate the necessary indirect exchanges. Thus Blau's theory moves far beyond direct contact between individual actors, incorporating complex indirect exchange processes. Structural change in both small and large social structures is analyzed in terms of social forces like differentiation, integration, organization, and opposition. Blau and, subsequently, Emerson (1972a,b) both made power processes central to their analysis of the emergence of social structures and structural change.

Emerson's Exchange Network Theory and Related Developments

Of the three major theorists, Homans was the most psychological in focus and thus in many respects the most microsociological. Blau focused attention on the more macro level, emphasizing microprocesses primarily as a foundation for building a more complex theory of emergent processes in social structures and institutional change. Emerson developed a behavioral model of individual action but emphasized the shift to a more macro level of analysis through the incorporation of collective actors and networks into his formulation. As Turner (1986:304) puts it, Emerson's approach "removes much of the vagueness surrounding Homans' and Blau's conceptualizations of social structures as 'institutional piles' and 'organized collectives'. Social structure in network analysis has a more precise definition as patterns of connections among actors in networks of exchange relations."

In his seminal work on exchange theory Emerson (1972ab) produced a well-developed formulation based upon behavioral principles (similar to those found in Homans' work). He embedded his general power/dependence principle (1962, 1964) in the context of an exchange theoretical framework which took as its psychological base, behavioral principles of reinforcement, satiation, extinction, etc. Part II (1972b) of this work takes social structure as the central subject matter and includes rudimentary theoretical statements regarding mechanisms of structural change (see Cook 1987:216–7 for a description of the model of social structure developed in Part II).

Emerson (1972a:41) noted two major shortcomings with Homans' behavioral formulation. First, it had no real conception of society except as an aggregation of individual behavior. In this sense its conception of social structure was too rudimentary. Second, it treated as "given" the social context surrounding "behaving persons," that is, the social structures and structural changes that sociologists seek to comprehend.

An actor in Emerson's theory is conceived as a "point where many exchange relations connect" (1972b:57). The actor can be a person, a corporate group (or collective actor), or a role-occupant. This conception of "actor" makes the theory applicable at different levels of analysis, and the theory has been applied to relations between individuals, organizations, and even nation-states. The primary focus is upon exchange relations as the building blocks for more complex social structures called exchange networks or corporate groups (involving intragroup exchanges). As Emerson (1972b:60) notes, "the concept of an exchange relation, and the principles which surround it, provide a basis for studying the formation and change of social structures as enduring relations among specified actors, with the exchange relations as the structural unit."

Exchange networks are viewed as connected sets of exchange relations. An early, important advance was the distinction between positive and negative exchange connections. If an actor's exchange in one relation is positively related to the actor's exchange in another relation, the relations are positively connected; if the relationship is negative, they are negatively connected[1] (for further discussion see Emerson 1972b). A primary focus of the subsequent theoretical and empirical work (e.g. Cook 1987) has been on specification of the principles of exchange and power that apply to different kinds of network structures (which Emerson referred to as "structural prototypes," such as monopoly structures, stratified networks, circles, and chains). In particular, attention has been focused on the relationship between types of exchange connections and the distribution of power and dependence among actors in various network structures (e.g. Cook & Emerson 1978, Cook et al 1983, etc). Structural change is viewed in the theory as a consequence of various social processes (e.g. coalition formation) in exchange networks and within corporate groups initiated, in part, because of a power imbalance either within the exchange relation (relational power imbalance) or within the exchange network structure (structural power imbalance) (see Gillmore 1987, Cook & Gillmore 1984, Cook & Emerson 1978, Emerson 1981, Molm 1989, Cook 1990, etc).

In conclusion, exchange network theory, initiated with Emerson's work (e.g. 1972a,b and subsequent work) and continuing in that of others (e.g. Cook 1977, Cook & Emerson 1978, Willer & Anderson 1981, Markovsky et al 1988, etc), has attempted to fuse perspectives previously considered incompatible (see Blau 1975, Merton 1975), incorporating both psychological factors and social constraints in terms of alternatives and opportunity struc-

[1]The actual definitions (Emerson 1972b:70) are: a negative connection is one in which an increase in "the frequency or 'magnitude'" of one exchange in which an actor is involved "produces or implies a decrease" in a second such exchange. A positive connection is one in which an increase in one exchange in which an actor is involved "produces or stimulates" an increase in a second such exchange.

tures. This is, in our view, the major accomplishment of recent developments in exchange theory (referred to as either structural versions of exchange theory or exchange network theory). It is this more recent version of exchange theory which is most compatible with the fundamental view of social structure embedded in much of the work in network analysis. We now turn to an explicit consideration of the relationship between exchange theory and network analysis, beginning with an overview of what network analysis is.

LINKING EXCHANGE AND NETWORK APPROACHES

What is Network Analysis?

In discussing the potential for linking these two traditions of work in sociology we must begin with one key difference. Exchange theory is really the name of a class of theories all of which have much in common (e.g. the theories of Homans, Blau, Emerson, Thibaut & Kelley, Coleman etc). Exchange theory can be seen as an approach to interaction and structure based on two principles: (i) The actor can be modeled as motivated by interests or rewards/punishments—i.e. all behavior can be seen as so motivated; (ii) most interaction consists of the exchange of valued (though not necessarily material) items. Network analysis, on the other hand, has been less theoretically and more empirically driven (see Wellman 1983). Network analysis is rooted in the empirical observation that patterns of interaction of many actors can be looked at as networks.

A narrow conception of network analysis exists, which considers it a type of "structural" analysis. "Network analysts. . . try to describe [regular network patterns] and use their descriptions to learn how network structures constrain social behavior and social change" (Wellman 1983:157). This version of network analysis contends, in agreement with the "structuralist" position in Sociology (e.g. Blau 1977, Mayhew 1980), that all important social phenomena can be explained primarily, if not completely, by social structure. The network version of this position is professed by, for example, Berkowitz (1982), Wellman (1983), Skvoretz (1990), and, to some extent, Burt (1982b).

For three reasons, we take a broader view of network analysis. First, many network-related studies do not fit with the more narrow conception of the structuralist approach, such as studies of the creation and/or maintenance of networks (e.g. Galaskiewicz 1982, Mizruchi & Stearns 1988), or with studies that investigate the influence of non network factors on network characteristics (e.g. Feld 1981, Fischer 1982, Laumann & Marsden 1982). We wanted to include these. Second, by excluding consideration of the individual actor, the narrow structuralist approach excludes linkage of network analysis with exchange theory. We consider such a linkage to be both natural and potentially fruitful. Third, some network structuralists are less strictly structuralist in practice than in principle (e.g. Burt 1982b).

Numerous reviews of network analysis exist (e.g. Mitchell 1974, Berkowitz 1982 ch. 1, Wellman 1983, Marsden 1990), so the history we present here is brief. The contemporary area of network analysis has been formed through a cross-fertilization of work from several different disciplines, with different empirical and even theoretical aims. We can identify at least three sources for network analysis: empirical work in social anthropology (e.g. Bott 1957, Mitchell 1969, Kapferer 1972), the practice of sociometry (e.g. Moreno 1951), and more abstract mathematical models and theory such as biased net theory (Rapoport 1957) and graph theory (e.g. Harary et al 1965). As is evident in this review, the diversity of origins continues in the present diversity of subjects of empirical research and structural interests (e.g. network structure as an independent or dependent variable).

The development of network analytic tools and techniques proceeded rapidly, beginning in the early 1970s, among anthropologists and sociologists. Debate among the early network analysts focused not only on the appropriate measures of important concepts and methods of data collection (e.g. observation, diaries, surveys), but also on whether or not there was anything to be called "network theory." To some extent, this debate continues. Positions on the issue range from that of Barnes (quoted in Mitchell 1974:282): "there is no such thing as a theory of social networks," to that of Burt (1982b) who formulated a structural theory of action to provide theoretical underpinning for network conceptions of structure.

According to Marsden (1990:453), much network analysis "can be viewed as part of a research program to develop social structural measures." These measures can then be utilized by various theorists in their efforts to include in their theories and empirical research measures of social structural concepts (e.g. range, centrality, and density of actors' social networks—see Marsden 1990 for a comprehensive review). For example, network analysis has been combined with functional analysis and role theory. Recently, proposals have been made to combine it with expectation states theory (Fararo & Skvoretz 1986) and with Giddens' structuration theory (Haines 1988).

From the beginning some network analysts used exchange theory to provide the theoretical basis for the analysis of the social interactions they represented in network terms (e.g. Kapferer 1972, Whitten & Wolfe 1974, etc). Various authors (e.g. Turner 1986, 1987, Collins 1988, etc) have commented on the potential for linking exchange and network approaches to social structure. Collins (1988:412), for example, remarks about the "growing awareness of the connection between networks and market or exchange theories... two conceptions of how individuals link together into a larger social structure." In an influential review piece, Mitchell (1974) argued that transactional theories (including exchange theory) formed a natural alliance with network concepts. Kapferer (1972) even proposed exchange theory as "the most suitable basis for network analysis" (quoted in Mitchell 1974:282).

We agree with Kapferer. However, since exchange theory and network analysis are different types of entities, it is difficult to talk about integrating them without clarifying the specific ways in which they are compatible or incompatible as perspectives. One obvious but relatively unimportant difference is in how these approaches are practiced—how hypotheses are tested, how the data are gathered and analyzed, etc. More critical for the issue of linkage between them are compatibilities and incompatibilities in (*a*) their views of action, i.e. the models of the actor underlying each approach, and (*b*) their views of structure. We discuss each of these topics, along with some prescriptions regarding future developments that might integrate aspects of these two traditions in ways quite fruitful for sociologists.

The Individual-Level Model

No two theoretical approaches are compatible, nor can they be linked effectively, if they have fundamentally different models of the individual actor. We believe that most work in network analysis is at least compatible with the exchange theory premise of the actor as motivated by interest or reward/punishment. However, that which is not compatible cannot be linked with exchange theory. For example, Haines (1988) advocates basing network analysis in Giddens's "conception of agency"—an alternative individual-level model incompatible with that of exchange theory. Similarly, Fararo & Skvoretz (1986) suggest basing network analysis in expectation states theory. This work may be compatible with exchange theory, but only if the individual level models of expectation states theory and exchange theory are compatible, which seems dubious (see, e.g., Berger et al 1972b).

Burt (1982b) claims to have a different model of the actor, but this is an overstatement. Exchange theory analysis holds (i) for any model of the actor wherein the actor pursues interests whatever they may be, and (ii) where at least some of the interests are satisfied through social interaction. Exchange theory makes no commitment to the origin of those interests, although some individual exchange theorists do have their preferred supplementary, more microlevel models on this point. These may conflict with Burt's model which says that an actor's interests stem from the actor's network position. However, Burt's model is fully compatible with the most basic principles of exchange theory. Namely, Burt's actors do have interests, some of which they do pursue and obtain through social interaction.

Biased-net theorists (e.g. Fararo & Skvoretz 1987, Skvoretz 1990) claim that no individual-level model is necessary, a position which echoes the views of other non network structuralists such as Mayhew (1980) and Blau (1977).

Biased-net theory describes and even seeks to explain (see Skvoretz 1990) network structure as global or regional deviations from randomness (or "biases"), possibly in a number of different dimensions. Contrary to the stated claim that no model of the actor is necessary, this theory implies and indeed requires a certain model of the actor. Namely, actors must exhibit these biases, and apart from the biases there can be no other deviation of actors' behavior from randomness large and widespread enough to distort the picture of the network. This model of the actor clearly is different from that of exchange theory and makes these two approaches incompatible.[2]

One assumption concerning the model of the actor is critical to much work in network analysis and exchange theory. This is the assumption that the same model of the actor can be used for organizations (or perhaps specific types of organizations such as corporations) and for individual humans. This assumption is widespread among network analysts whose actors are organizations (e.g. Laumann et al 1985, Mizruchi 1989, 1990ab), and widespread among exchange theorists (e.g. Emerson 1972b, Markovsky et al 1988) and indeed some other theorists in sociology (e.g. Berger et al 1989).

Yet both a priori considerations and empirical evidence call the assumption into question (see Caputo 1989, Stinchcombe 1989). Social organizations are made up of entities with their own interests and capable of acting autonomously; human beings are not. For example, in his analysis of the creation of institutions by corporate donor and nonprofit donee organizations to reduce the transaction costs of donations, Galaskiewicz (1982) must make use of the differences of interests within organizations.

The issue of the validity of the organizational actor is related to the extensive debate (cf Mizruchi & Schwartz 1987) between the resource dependence and the social class positions over the purpose of intercorporate ties in the form of interlocking directorates. The resource dependence position (Perucci & Pilisuk 1970, Pfeffer 1972, 1987, Pfeffer & Salancik 1978, Berkowitz et al 1978/1979, Burt et al 1980, Burt 1983, Mizruchi 1989, 1990a,b) argues that intercorporate ties are created for the purpose of maximizing corporate profit through lessening corporate dependence, and that they are effective at this. This perspective is strongly related to the exchange theory perspective, with the actors involved being organizational actors (Berger et al 1989). The class position (Zeitlin 1974, Domhoff 1975, Soref 1976, Useem 1978, 1979, 1984, Bonacich & Domhoff 1981, Gogel & Koenig 1981, Palmer 1983, Palmer et al 1986, Bearden & Mintz 1987, Soref & Zeitlin 1987, Johnsen & Mintz 1989) argues that intercorporate ties are created as a result of human individuals (or families) pursuing their own class interests. This position is

[2]Some biases may generate structure which resembles that generated by exchange processes. However, our concern here is with differences in the underlying models of the actor.

also compatible with exchange theory if it is accepted that elite individuals' personal interests are congruent with their class interests. Most versions of the class perspective fit this formulation. The elite network may be seen as an example of a social circle, a type of social structure which Emerson (1972b) explains in exchange terms. Here, however, the actors are human individuals.

There is some empirical evidence for each position. The centrality of financial institutions in intercorporate networks, for example, has been well established (Mariolis 1975, Sonquist & Koenig 1975, Mintz & Schwartz 1981, Mizruchi 1982, Stokman et al 1984). Mizruchi (1989, 1990b) has shown that intercorporate network positions, especially the existence of indirect links through financial institutions, predict similarity of political behavior (contributions to PACs). On the other hand, Bearden & Mintz (1987) found that while banks were indeed central in the intercorporate network, bankers as individuals were not prominent in linking roles. Johnsen & Mintz (1989) looked at the director network, the "dual" (see Breiger 1974, Berkowitz 1982) of the intercorporate network, and found social ties generally to be causally prior to intercorporate links between individuals. Studies have found a low rate of reconstitution of directorate ties that are accidentally broken (Koenig et al 1979, Palmer 1983, Palmer et al 1986).

As a comment on both positions we may add Galaskiewicz's (1989) points, in his presentation of unresolved questions concerning interorganizational networks at the metropolitan level, that (*a*) ties created for one reason may be used for another (p. 82); and (*b*) creating ties for some purpose does not mean necessarily that they will be effective (p. 86). Similarly, we may note that it is possible that interlocking directorate ties are created according to individual human interests, yet other organizational behavior is best explained by the dependence of organizational actors. This issue is not yet resolved.

The View of Structure

We can distinguish two general conceptions of structure in network analysis. The more common view conceives of structure as a pattern of particular ties between actors, where variation in the network in the existence or strength of ties is meaningful and consequential. The other conceives of structure as a general deviation from random ties for particular groups, or perhaps the entire network. In other words, the first view sees structure as a composition of particular ties, the second sees structure as a general perhaps multidimensional deviation from randomness. The second view is the biased net perspective (e.g. Rapoport 1957, Fararo & Skvoretz 1987). The first view is taken by virtually all other network analysts and is also that of exchange theorists (Collins 1988).

Thus the general view of structure of most network analysts and exchange theorists is the same. Where differences exist is in their views of the details of structure—the ties. These differences constitute the greatest challenge to compatibility and linkage between the two approaches. In brief, fitting their theoretical base, exchange theorists assume that ties consist of the exchange of valued items. Fitting their more empirical starting point, network analysts are frequently more catholic about the content of ties (Marsden 1990). However, there is much variation in the treatment of content, between network analysts and even within the work of individual scholars. Frequently, this depends on the aspect of the structure-action relationship being investigated. Therefore, we look at some of the network analysis literature to examine the compatibility of the exchange theory stance with various treatments of tie content.

Virtually all studies that undertake to show the effects of action on structure clearly take ties to consist of exchange. That is, studies that look at the construction or maintenance of networks (e.g. Verbrugge 1979, Wellman 1979, Burt 1982a, Feld 1981, 1982, 1984, Galaskiewicz 1982, Palmer et al 1986, Suitor 1987, Mizruchi & Stearns 1988, Barley 1990, S. L. Feld & J. J. Suitor, unpublished paper,[3] N. P. Hummon, unpublished paper[4]) or which analyze the effect of variation in personal characteristics or the interests of actors on variation in network characteristics (e.g. Fischer 1982, Laumann & Marsden 1982, K. E. Campbell & B. A. Lee, unpublished papers[5]) specify the ties in their networks explicitly or implicitly as exchange ties. Thus, they are entirely compatible with exchange theory. The reasoning behind Granovetter's various arguments (Granovetter 1973, 1983) concerning the creation and effects of strong and weak ties is in accord with exchange theory principles. For example, stronger ties mean more secure access to resources; thus those with fewer personal resources are more likely to rely on strong ties (Granovetter 1983).

A few studies undertake to show the effect of structure not, or not only, on action but on affect (e.g. Fischer 1982, Marsden 1983). These studies too take an exchange view of ties. For example, Fischer (1982) finds that network density is positively related to feeling better for low-income respondents, but negatively related for high-income respondents. For an explanation he suggests that low-income people are better off with dense cliques because, unlike high-income people, they lack the material and social resources to manage dispersed networks (p. 150).

[3]S. L. Feld, J. J. Suitor, *Mothers and best friends: alternative sources of social support for young married women in seven western countries*. Paper pres. at X Sunbelt Social Network Conf., 1990, San Diego, Calif.

[4]N. P. Hummon, *Organizational structures and network processes: an exploration of exchange processes*. Paper pres. at X Sunbelt Int. Social Network Conf., 1990, San Diego, Calif.

[5]K. E. Campbell, B. A. Lee, *Personal networks in urban neighborhoods: description and variation, 1991*. B. A. Lee, K. E. Campbell, *Neighbor networks of blacks and whites,* Paper pres. at ASA Annu. Meet., 1990, Washington, DC

The difficulties arise with some studies that examine the effect of structure on action, or in some cases, on other aspects of structure. The exchange theory position concerning this relationship is that the relevant network is one that consists of all relevant and important ties due to exchange (i.e. of valued items) and only those ties. Granovetter (1985) has called for acknowledging the close embeddedness of behavior in networks of interpersonal relations. Since interpersonal relations are virtually always exchange relations, the exchange theory position is completely in agreement with his argument.

The exchange theory position is compatible with many network analysis studies (e.g. Marsden 1983, 1987, Coleman 1988, Ridley & Avery 1979). However, according to this position, many other studies are too permissive. They include certain types of ties without theoretical justification (i.e. specification in exchange terms); they leave out important types of ties and important actors. They also fail to pay enough attention to the interplay between interests and the items being exchanged and to the differing effects of complementary, common, and opposing interests. Thus they fail to perceive the structural implications of these few-actor interactional complexities. As examples, we consider the widely used concept of the directionality of ties as well as some recent work on centrality.

The directionality of ties frequently is an important factor in network analyses. For example, Knoke & Burt (1983) define prestige to be a measure of the degree to which an actor is the object of connections. However, whenever a relation consists of exchange, any purported directionality comes from specifying only one side of the exchange. In such a case, apparent directionality is due to the incomplete specification of content and is a spurious factor. For example, Knoke & Burt (1983; see also Burt 1987) measure the prestige of physicians in terms of being solicited for advice. But this is an exchange: the solicitation is exchanged for advice (Blau 1955, Homans 1961). The connection could just as easily be specified with the opposite directionality, i.e. being the object of advice-giving. Thus, prestige stems not from directionality but from the content of the exchange relations and the asymmetry involved.

Centrality generally is taken to mean "network position-conferred advantage." In the network analytic literature, more attention has been given to its specification and measurement than to any other issue (e.g. Bonacich 1972, 1987, Freeman 1979, Knoke & Burt 1983, Marsden 1982, 1983, 1987, Mizruchi et al 1986, Stephenson & Zelen 1989, Friedkin 1991). Recently some new measures have been devised specifically for centrality in communication networks in which exchange is ignored (Stephenson & Zelen 1989, D. L. Kincaid, unpublished paper,[6] Friedkin 1991). Exchange theory

[6]D. L. Kincaid, *Communication network dynamics: cohesion, centrality, and cultural evolution,* 1990

claims that interactions, and by extension the effects of network structure on action and structure, occur only due to the exchange value of the items transferred (which may be material, symbolic, informational, etc).[7] Therefore, when the exchange relations in the network are obscured, the causal processes involved in centrality will be likewise hidden. When the exchange relations are excluded, the results are likely to be spurious if not in error.

Not all studies involving communication networks are at odds with exchange theory. The effect of network structure in Bonacich (1990), for example, is explained as the effect of network position on the expected relative gain from communicating versus not communicating. Network structure is shown to affect the likelihood of an actor communicating in the kind of "communication dilemma" situations studied by Bonacich. In Laumann & Knoke (1989; see also Galaskiewicz 1979, Knoke 1983) ties in the communication networks persist due to the actors' dependence on the information and the similarities in the actors' interests.

Exchange theory, however, suggests an alternative to be tested against explanations in terms of communication networks which ignore exchange processes. First, all exchange links relevant to the behavior which is the dependent variable should be included in the analysis (see Galaskiewicz 1989). For example, Kincaid (see footnote 6) presents a network of communication concerning family planning for a Korean village (from Rogers & Kincaid 1981). Are there exchange links to people with interests in the behaviors in question that are not represented in the communication network? If so, it is likely that exchange theory would make different calculations of centrality and perhaps even different predictions concerning its effects.

Second, ties should be considered in terms of the valued items exchanged. According to exchange theory, the very existence of a tie or link, including a communication tie, suggests the existence of interested exchange between two parties. The content of the communications may be influential, but even so the communication must be considered in the context of an exchange of valued items, whether these are the communications themselves (i.e. in terms of informational or symbolic value) or other items.

For example, for the measures of centrality he proposes for "social influence networks," Friedkin (1991) provides a theoretical basis in the form of coefficients meant to represent one actor's influence on another. For an exchange theorist, however, this is insufficient, because the interactional process goes unspecified. If the influence does not occur through exchange processes in the given network, exchange theory suggests that relevant exchange processes are being ignored and that the effects of the given influence

[7]Exchange theory does acknowledge the effect of previously existing ties, that is, of ongoing exchange relationships.

channels are possibly spurious. If the influence does correspond to exchange processes, collapsing these into coefficients obscures the most interesting effects of structure. Thus exchange theory suggests that analysis in light of the exchange processes necessarily occurring (e.g. in terms of the interdependencies among the actors) should be more revealing of both the effects of structure and the underlying power and influence processes.

Exchange theorists have made (and experimentally demonstrated) at least one important discovery which has had some influence in network analysis. This is the difference between positively and negatively connected exchange networks and their implications for network-conferred advantage (see Emerson 1972b, Cook et al 1983, Yamagishi et al 1988). We refer to this structural property as "polarity."[8] One reason types of connections or polarity is important is that for many networks, the distribution of power and influence may depend on the polarity of the network (Cook et al 1983). Thus, Bonacich (1987) modified his earlier (1972) measure of centrality so that it would apply not just to positively connected networks but to negatively connected networks as well (see also Marsden 1987; P. Kappelhoff, unpublished paper[9]).

The theoretical reasoning behind the concept of polarity in exchange network theory can contribute to a solution of the debate between structural equivalence (roughly, having equivalent ties to the same other actors—from Lorrain & White 1971) and cohesion (roughly, being closely tied to each other) as explanations of the similarity of actors' behavior (e.g. Friedkin 1984, Burt 1987, Erickson 1988, Mizruchi 1989, 1990a, Galaskiewicz & Burt 1991). Cohesion is bound into the very concept of structural equivalence (Borgatti & Everett 1992). Thus, it is impossible to distinguish structurally between two-step (indirect) cohesion and structural equivalence (M. S. Mizruchi, unpublished paper[10]). Burt (1987) recognizes this but makes it clear that at the heart of the debate is a dispute over the process causing behavioral similarity. Cohesion operates as an infectious process; structural equivalence operates as a noninfectious process, perhaps through imitation.[10]

Exchange theory suggests that the two processes are theoretically compatible and possible, even within the same network, and that which process is likely to be dominant is itself affected by a structural property, namely, polarity. In a positively connected network, it is probable that cohesion processes will be stronger. The common interests of the indirectly connected

[8]We introduce a new term here as a shorthand for types of connections and/or degrees of connectivity. The term can apply either to entire networks (e.g. all relations are negatively connected) or to subnetworks (e.g. some relations are negative and some are positive as in a "mixed" network. See Yamagishi et al 1988.)

[9]P. Kappelhoff, *Power in exchange systems: a new look at the Coleman-model of collective action,* 1990

[10]M. S. Mizruchi, *Cohesion, equivalence, and similarity of behavior: a theoretical and empirical assessment,* 1990.

actors make it likely that infectious processes will lead to similar behaviors (see Laumann & Knoke 1989). In a negatively connected network, however, these infectious processes are not likely, and it is probable that structural equivalence processes will be more dominant (see Mizruchi 1990a).

To sum up, network analysis differs importantly from exchange theory in two ways. First, some network analysts claim to use a different individual-level model, or to use none. However, with the notable exception of biased-net theory, the individual-level models of exchange theorists and network analysts are fundamentally compatible, if not identical. Second, and most critically, network analysts and exchange theorists tend to view certain aspects of structure differently. Their views of what structure is and the relation between action and structure are highly similar. However, they frequently differ in their view of the nature of the ties that make up networks. For exchange theorists, network ties consist of exchange relations of valued items, and what matters causally is the exchange value (i.e. due to actors' interests) of the items exchanged. Many network theorists are much more catholic, and allow a variety of types of ties independently of any exchange of valued items. There is no theoretical specification in network analysis of the content of the tie or social relationship represented as a link between actors or a line between nodes in a network. Exchange theory suggests ways of constructing alternative, perhaps superior, explanations of events within networks and of network effects than do some of the more atheoretical versions of network analysis. Whether the network analysis or the exchange theory position is a more fruitful approach can only be resolved through future empirical and theoretical work.

CONCLUSION

In the past fifteen years there has been a kind of convergence among some of the approaches to social structure in sociology. Two generally compatible approaches are exchange theory and network analysis. As Collins (1988:412) points out, "These models picture individual actors as both free and constrained. Human beings have the capacity to create or negotiate whatever they can at any moment in time. But they always act in a structured situation, so that the consequences and conditions of their creativity and negotiation are nevertheless patterned by larger relationships beyond their control." Moreover, as we have argued in this review, exchange theory and network analysis have similar conceptions of both action and structure. It is true that some network analysts have downplayed any consideration of the individual actor, and some exchange theorists have undertheorized social structure. Nevertheless, the images of structure and action Collins presents have become fused and are both reflected in recent developments in exchange network theory and in much work in network analysis.

It is a measure of the progress achieved that earlier statements regarding what is central to structural analysis in sociology clearly viewed these alternatives as incompatible (e.g. Blau 1975, Stinchcombe 1975). Nevertheless, further theoretical refinements will be required to flesh out the underdeveloped features of this emerging general model of social structure and action (see Hechter 1991).

In conclusion it is important to reiterate a point often lost in debates about the relative merits of particular theoretical approaches: no single perspective or approach (network analysis and exchange theory included) can explain all social and cultural phenomena (see, e.g. Merton 1975). Even the marriage of network and exchange approaches would not be able to lay claim to the role of "grand theory" in sociology. Nevertheless, the convergence of these two approaches does have the potential to be broader in scope and more powerful in explanatory terms than either approach alone. For this to happen, however, more work needs to be done clarifying points of useful articulation as well as areas of conflict or mutual exclusivity. Our review chapter is an attempt to initiate this task.

ACKNOWLEDGMENTS

The authors' names have been listed alphabetically. We acknowledge an earlier grant from the National Science Foundation (SES8519319), to K. S. Cook, M. R. Gillmore, and T. Yamagishi, for support of the development of exchange network theory.

Literature Cited

Alexander, J. C., Giesen, B., Munch, R., Smelser, N. J., eds. 1987. *The Micro-Macro Link*. Berkeley: Univ. Calif. Press

Barley, S. R. 1990. The alignment of technology and structure through roles and networks. *Admin. Sci. Q.* 35:61–103

Bearden, J., Mintz, B. 1987. The structure of class cohesion: the corporate network and its dual. See Mizruchi & Schwartz 1987, pp. 187–207

Berger, J., Eyre, D. P., Zelditch, M. 1989. Theoretical structures and the micro/macro problem. In *Sociological Theories in Progress: New Formulations*, ed. J. Berger, M. Zelditch, B. Anderson, pp. 11–32. Newbury Park, Calif: Sage

Berger, J., Zelditch, M., Anderson, B., eds. 1972a. *Sociological Theories in Progress*, Vol. 2. Boston: Houghton Mifflin

Berger, J., Zelditch, M., Anderson, B., Cohen, B. P. 1972b. Structural aspects of distributive justice: a status value formulation. See Berger et al 1972a, pp. 119–46

Berkowitz, S. D. 1982. *An Introduction to Structural Analysis*. Toronto: Butterworths

Berkowitz, S. D., Carrington, P. J., Kotowitz, Y., Waverman, L. 1978/1979. The determination of enterprise groupings through combined ownership and directorship ties. *Soc. Networks* 1:75–83

Blau, P. M. 1964. *Exchange and Power in Social Life*. New York: Wiley

Blau, P. M., ed. 1975. *Approaches to the Study of Social Structure*. New York: Free

Blau, P. M. 1977. *Inequality and Heterogeneity*. New York: Free

Bonacich, P. 1972. Technique for analyzing overlapping memberships. In *Sociological Methodology 1972*, ed. H. L. Costner, pp. 176–85. San Francisco: Jossey-Bass

Bonacich, P. 1987. Power and centrality: a family of measures. *Am. J. Sociol.* 92: 1170–82

Bonacich, P. 1990. Communication dilemmas in social networks: an experimental study. *Am. Sociol. Rev.* 55:448–59

Bonacich, P., Domhoff, G. W. 1981. Latent

classes and group membership. *Soc. Networks* 3:175–96

Borgatti, S. P., Everett, M. G. 1992. Notions of position in social network analysis. In *Sociological Methodology 1992,* ed. P. V. Marsden. Washington, DC: Am. Sociol. Assoc. In press

Bott, E. 1957. *Family and Social Network: Roles, Norms, and External Relationships in Ordinary Urban Families.* London: Tavistock

Breiger, R. L. 1974. The duality of persons and groups. *Soc. Forces* 53:181–90

Burt, R. S. 1982a. A note on cooptation and definitions of constraint. See Marsden & Lin 1982, pp. 219–33

Burt, R. S. 1982b. *Toward a Structural Theory of Action.* New York: Academic

Burt, R. S. 1983. *Corporate Profits and Cooptation: Networks of Market Constraints and Directorate Ties in the American Economy.* New York: Academic

Burt, R. S. 1987. Social contagion and innovation: cohesion versus structural equivalence. *Am. J. Sociol.* 92:1287–335

Burt, R. S., Christman, K. P., Kilburn, H. C. Jr. 1980. Testing a structural theory of corporate cooptation: interorganizational directorate ties as a strategy for avoiding market constraints on profits. *Am. Sociol. Rev.* 45:821–41

Caputo, D. A. 1989. Network perspectives and policy analysis: a skeptical view. See Perrucci & Potter 1989, pp. 111–17

Coleman, J. S. 1988. Free riders and zealots: the role of social networks. *Sociol. Theory* 6:52–57

Collins, R. 1981. On the microfoundations of macrosociology. *Am. J. Sociol.* 86:984–1014

Collins, R. 1988. *Theoretical Sociology.* San Diego: Harcourt Brace Jovanovich

Cook, K. S. 1977. Exchange and power in networks of interorganizational relations. *Sociol. Q.* 18:62–82

Cook, K. S., ed. 1987. *Social Exchange Theory.* Newbury Park, Calif: Sage

Cook, K. S. 1990. Linking actors and structures: an exchange network perspective. In *Structures of Power and Constraint,* ed. C. Calhoun, M. W. Meyer, W. R. Scott. Cambridge: Cambridge Univ. Press

Cook, K. S. 1991. The microfoundations of social structure. See Huber 1991, pp. 29–45

Cook, K. S., Emerson, R. M. 1978. Power, equity, and commitment in exchange networks. *Am. Sociol. Rev.* 43:721–30

Cook, K. S., Emerson, R. M., Gillmore, M. R., Yamagishi, T. 1983. The distribution of power in exchange networks: theory and experimental results. *Am. J. Sociol.* 89: 275–305

Cook, K. S., Gillmore, M. R. 1984. Power, dependence, and coalitions. In *Advances in Group Processes,* ed. E. Lawler, 1:27–58. Greenwich, Conn: JAI

Domhoff, G. W. 1975. Social clubs, policy planning groups, and corporations: a network study of ruling class cohesiveness. *Insurgent Sociol.* 5:173–84

Ekeh, P. P. 1974. *Social Exchange Theory: The Two Traditions.* Cambridge, Mass: Harvard Univ. Press

Emerson, R. M. 1962. Power-dependence relations. *Am. Sociol. Rev.* 27:31–40

Emerson, R. M. 1964. Power-dependence relations: two experiments. *Sociometry* 27:282–98

Emerson, R. M. 1972a. Exchange theory, part I: a psychological basis for social exchange. See Berger et al 1972a, pp. 38–57

Emerson, R. M. 1972b. Exchange theory, part II: exchange rules and networks. See Berger et al 1972a, pp. 58–87

Emerson, R. M. 1981. Social exchange theory. In *Social Psychology: Sociological Perspectives,* ed. M. Rosenberg, R. Turner, pp. 30–65. New York: Academic

Erickson, B. H. 1988. The relational basis of attitudes. In *Social Structures: A Network Approach,* ed. B. Wellman, S. D. Berkowitz, pp. 99–121. Cambridge: Cambridge Univ. Press

Fararo, T. J., Skvoretz, J. 1986. E-state structuralism: a theoretical method. *Am. Sociol. Rev.* 51:591–602

Fararo, T. J., Skvoretz, J. 1987. Unification research programs: integrating two structural theories. *Am. J. Sociol.* 92:1183–1209

Feld, S. L. 1981. The focused organization of social ties. *Am. J. Sociol.* 86:1015–35

Feld, S. L. 1982. Social structural determinants of similarity among associates. *Am. Sociol. Rev.* 47:797–801

Feld, S. L. 1984. The structured use of personal associates. *Soc. Forces* 62:640–52

Fischer, C. S. 1982. *To Dwell Among Friends: Personal Networks in Town and City.* Chicago: Univ. Chicago Press

Freeman, L. C. 1979. Centrality in social networks: conceptual clarification. *Soc. Networks* 1:215–39

Friedkin, N. E. 1984. Structural cohesion and equivalence explanations of social homogeneity. *Sociol. Methods Res.* 12:235–61

Friedkin, N. E. 1991. Theoretical foundations for centrality measures. *Am. J. Sociol.* 96:1478–504

Galaskiewicz, J. 1979. *Exchange Networks and Community Politics.* Beverly Hills, Calif: Sage

Galaskiewicz, J. 1982. Modes of resource allocation: corporate contributions to nonprofit organizations. See Marsden & Lin 1982, pp. 235–53

Galaskiewicz, J. 1989. Interorganizational networks mobilizing action at the metropolitan level. See Perrucci & Potter 1989, pp. 81–96

Galaskiewicz, J., Burt, R. S. 1991. Interorganization contagion and corporate philanthropy. *Admin. Sci. Q.* 36:88–105

Gillmore, M. R. 1987. Implications of general versus restricted exchange. See Cook 1987, pp. 170–89

Gogel, R., Koenig, T. 1981. Commercial banks, interlocking directorates and economic power: an analysis of the primary metals industry. *Soc. Probl.* 29:117–28

Granovetter, M. 1973. The strength of weak ties. *Am. J. Sociol.* 78:1360–80

Granovetter, M. 1983. The strength of weak ties: a network theory revisited. *Sociol. Theory* 1:201–33

Granovetter, M. 1985. Economic action and social structure: the problem of embeddedness. *Am. J. Sociol.* 91:481–510

Haines, V. A. 1988. Social network analysis, structuration theory and the holism-individualism debate. *Soc. Networks* 10: 157–82

Harary, F., Norman, R. Z., Cartwright, D. 1965. *Structural Models: An Introduction to the Theory of Directed Graphs*. New York: Wiley

Heath, A. 1976. *Rational Choice and Social Exchange: A Critique of Exchange Theory*. Cambridge: Cambridge Univ. Press

Hechter, M. 1991. From exchange to structure. See Huber 1991, pp. 46–50

Homans, G. C. 1961. *Social Behavior: Its Elementary Forms*. New York: Harcourt Brace

Homans, G. C. 1964. Bringing men back in. *Am. Sociol. Rev.* 29:809–18

Huber, J., ed. 1991. *Macro-Micro Linkages in Sociology*. Newbury Park, Calif: Sage

Johnsen, E., Mintz, B. 1989. Organizational versus class components of director networks. See Perrucci & Potter 1989, pp. 57–80

Kapferer, B. 1972. *Strategy and Transaction in an African Factory*. Manchester, Eng: Manchester Univ. Press

Knoke, D. 1983. Organization sponsorship and influence reputation of social influence associations. *Soc. Forces* 61:1065–87

Knoke, D., Burt, R. S. 1983. Prominence. In *Applied Network Analysis: A Methodological Introduction,* ed. R. S. Burt, M. J. Minor, pp. 195–222. Beverly Hills: Sage

Koenig, T., Gogel, R., Sonquist, J. 1979. Models of the significance of interlocking corporate directorates. *Am. J. Econ. Soc.* 38:173–83

Laumann, E. O., Knoke, D. 1989. Policy networks of the organizational state: collective action in the national energy and health domains. See Perrucci & Potter 1989, pp. 17–55

Laumann, E. O., Knoke, D., Kim, Y-H. 1985. An organizational approach to policy formation: a comparative study of energy and health domains. *Am. Rev. Sociol.* 50:1–19

Laumann, E. O., Marsden, P. V. 1982. Microstructural analysis in interorganizational systems. *Soc. Networks* 4:329–48

Lorrain, F., White, H. C. 1971. Structural equivalence of individuals in social networks. *J. Math. Sociol.* 1:49–80

Mariolis, P. 1975. Interlocking directorates and the control of corporations. *Soc. Sci. Q.* 56:425–39

Markovsky, B., Willer, D., Patton, T. 1988. Power relations in exchange networks. *Am. Sociol. Rev.* 53:220–36

Marsden, P. V. 1982. Brokerage behavior in restricted exchange networks. See Marsden & Lin 1982, pp. 201–18

Marsden, P. V. 1983. Restricted access in networks and models of power. *Am. J. Sociol.* 88:686–717

Marsden, P. V. 1987. Elements of interactor dependence. See Cook 1987, pp. 130–48

Marsden, P. V. 1990. Network data and measurement. *Annu. Rev. Sociol.* 16:435–63

Mayhew, B. H. 1980. Structuralism versus individualism: Part I, shadowboxing in the dark. *Soc. Forces* 59:335–75

Merton, R. K. 1975. Structural analysis in sociology. See Blau 1975, pp. 21–52

Mintz, B., Schwartz, M. 1981. The structure of intercorporate unity in American business. *Soc. Probl.* 29:87–103

Mitchell, J. C., ed. 1969. *Social Networks in Urban Situations: Analyses of Personal Relationships in Central African Towns*. Manchester, Eng: Manchester Univ. Press

Mitchell, J. C. 1974. Social networks. *Annu. Rev. Anthropol.* 3:279–99

Mizruchi, M. S. 1982. *The American Corporate Network: 1904–74*. Beverly Hills: Sage

Mizruchi, M. S. 1989. Similarity of political behavior among large American corporations. *Am. J. Sociol.* 95:401–24

Mizruchi, M. S. 1990a. Cohesion, equivalence, and similarity of behavior: an approach to the study of corporate political power. *Sociol. Theory* 8:16–32

Mizruchi, M. S. 1990b. Determinants of political opposition among large American corporations. *Soc. Forces* 68:1065–88

Mizruchi, M. S., Mariolis, P., Schwartz, M., Mintz, B. 1986. Techniques for disaggregating centrality scores in social networks. In *Sociological Methodology 1986,* ed. N. B. Tuma, pp. 26–48. Washington, DC: Am. Sociol. Assoc.

Mizruchi, M. S., Schwartz, M., eds. 1987.

Intercorporate Relations:The Structural Analysis of Business. Cambridge: Cambridge Univ. Press

Mizruchi, M. S., Stearns, L. B. 1988. A longitudinal study of the formation of interlocking directorates. *Admin. Sci. Q.* 33:194–210

Molm, L. D. 1989. Punishment power: a balancing process in power-dependence relations. *Am. J. Sociol.* 94:1392–418

Moreno, J. L. 1951. *Sociometry, Experimental Method and Science of Society*. Beacon, NY: Beacon House

Palmer, D. 1983. Broken ties: interlocking directorates and intercorporate coordination. *Admin. Sci. Q.* 28:40–55

Palmer, D., Friedland, R., Singh, J. V. 1986. The ties that bind: organizational and class bases of stability in a corporate interlock network. *Am. Sociol. Rev.* 51:781–96

Perrucci, R., Pilisuk, M. 1970. Leaders and ruling elites: the interorganizational bases of community power. *Am. Sociol. Rev.* 35: 1040–57

Pfeffer, J. 1972. Size and composition of corporate boards of directors. *Admin. Sci. Q.* 17:218–28

Pfeffer, J. 1987. A resource dependence perspective on intercorporate relations. See Mizruchi & Schwartz 1987, pp. 25–55

Pfeffer, J., Salancik, G. R. 1978. *The External Control of Organizations: A Resource Dependence Perspective*. New York: Harper & Row

Rapoport, A. 1957. A contribution to the theory of random and biased nets. *Bull. Math. Biophys.* 19:257- 71

Ridley, C. A., Avery, A. W. 1979. Social network influence on the dyadic relationship. In *Social Exchange in Developing Relationships,* pp. 223–46. New York: Academic

Rogers, E. M., Kincaid, D. L. 1981. *Communication Networks: Toward a New Paradigm for Research*. New York: Free

Skvoretz, J. 1990. Biased net theory: approximations, simulations, and observations. *Soc. Networks* 12:1–22

Sonquist, J. A., Koenig, T. 1975. Interlocking directorates in the top US corporations: a graph theory approach. *Insurgent Sociol.* 5:196–230

Soref, M. 1976. Social class and division of labor within the corporate elite. *Sociol. Q.* 17:360–68

Soref, M., Zeitlin, M. 1987. Finance capital and the internal structure of the capitalist class in the United States. See Mizruchi & Schwartz 1987, pp. 56–84

Stephenson, K., Zelen, M. 1989. Rethinking centrality: Methods and examples. *Soc. Networks* 11:1–7

Stinchcombe, A. L. 1975. Merton's theory of social structure. In *The Idea of Social Structure,* ed. L. A. Coser. New York: Harcourt Brace Jovanovich

Stinchcombe, A. L. 1989. An outsider's view of network analyses of power. See R. Perrucci & Potter 1989, pp. 119–33

Stokman, F., Ziegler, R., Scott, J. 1984. *Networks of Corporate Power: An Analysis of Ten Countries*. Oxford: Polity

Suitor, J. J. 1987. Friendship networks in transitions: married mothers return to school. *J. Soc. Personal Relat.* 4:445–61

Turner, J. 1986. *The Structure of Sociological Theory*. Homewood, Ill: Dorsey

Turner, J. 1987. Social exchange theory: future directions. See Cook 1987, pp. 223–38

Useem, M. 1978. The inner group of the American capitalist class. *Soc. Probl.* 25:225–40

Useem, M. 1979. The social organization of the American business elite. *Am. Sociol. Rev.* 44:553–71

Useem, M. 1984. *The Inner Circle*. New York: Oxford Univ. Press

Verbrugge, L. M. 1979. Multiplexity in adult friendships. *Soc. Forces* 57:1286–1309

Wellman, B. 1979. The community question: the intimate networks of East Yorkers. *Am. J. Sociol.* 84:1201–31

Wellman, B. 1983. Network analysis: some basic principles. *Sociol. Theory* 1:155–200

Whitten, N. E., Wolfe, A. W. 1973. Network analysis. In *The Handbook of Social and Cultural Anthropology,* ed. J. J. Honigman, pp. 717–46. Chicago: Rand McNally

Willer, D., Anderson, B., eds. 1981. *Networks, Exchange and Coercion: The Elementary Theory and Its Applications*. New York: Elsevier

Yamagishi, T., Gillmore, M. R., Cook, K. S. 1988. Network connections and the distribution of power in exchange networks. *Am. J. Sociol.* 93:833–51

Zeitlin, M. 1974. Corporate ownership and control: the large corporation and the capitalist class. *Am. J. Sociol.* 79:1073–1119

Annu. Rev. Sociol. 1992. 18:129–60

SOCIAL SCIENCE RESEARCH AND CONTEMPORARY STUDIES OF HOMELESSNESS

*Anne B. Shlay**

Institute for Policy Studies, The Johns Hopkins University, Baltimore, Maryland 21218

Peter H. Rossi

Department of Sociology, University of Massachusetts, Amherst, Massachusetts 01003

KEY WORDS: housing, poverty, policy, welfare, employment

Abstract

This review takes stock of contemporary social science research on homelessness. Research on homelessness in the 1980s has been prompted by the increased numbers and visibility of homeless persons including men, women, and families, as well as young people without families. Most empirical research employs a working definition of homelessness as the condition of those people who are without a permanent place to live. However, a wide range in perspectives differ over what homelessness is. In part, this reflects recognition of some the dynamics of homelessness that include intermittent movement in and out of homeless situations. But it also reflects changes in social values over what constitutes adequate housing. Research shows that the population of homeless persons is diverse, although most homeless persons are young and single. Many have severe chronic problems including mental illness, alcoholism, physical disabilities, and poor health. A significant number have criminal histories. Many were raised in foster care situations. All

0732–0582/92/0410–0129$02.00

suffer from economic deprivation, and many have experienced long-term unemployment. Considerable disagreement exists over the number of homeless persons, in part because the scarcity of resources to address this problem politicizes the debate. There is also strong disagreement over the root causes of homelessness.

Debate over the causes of homelessness is caught up in whether the focus of research should be on structural forces that permit homelessness to occur or the immediate reasons why people become homeless. Research now suggests that the extreme situation of homelessness may be more accurately portrayed as the result of the convergence of many factors that drive this phenomenon, including housing market dynamics, housing and welfare policy, economic restructuring and the labor market, and personal disabilities. Policies designed to ameliorate homelessness have been inadequate to stem the tidal forces that produce such severe destitution, and this trend is likely to continue. Future important directions include addressing the role of employment and social ties in producing homelessness, comparing the economic and social situation of homeless and non-homeless persons, evaluating programs designed to aid homeless persons, and developing international comparisons of homelessness.

Introduction

The forecasting scorecard of social scientists arguably has recorded more failures than successes. Notable among recent forecasting failures are the claims in the 1950s and 1960s that homelessness in America was about to disappear (Bogue 1963). Rather than disappearing into history, homelessness surged strongly in the 1980s. Currently (1991) public opinion regards homelessness as one of the country's most pressing social problems.

In addition to the set of classical issues that plagues other research areas, social science research on homelessness manifests a high level of politicization. The critical issues facing research on contemporary homelessness include defining what is meant by homelessness, describing the characteristics and composition of the homeless population, assessing the macrostructural and microlevel causes of homelessness, counting the homeless, and evaluating public and private attempts to address problems of homelessness as well as attempts to prevent it. Each of these issues presents both technical and political aspects. Researching homelessness is not for those who would avoid controversy.

The "New" Research on Homelessness

In studying homelessness, social researchers today can look back to a long and rich history. Most of the earlier investigations of homelessness focused on "hobohemia" (also known as skid row) where concentrations of single room occupancy hotels (SROs), boarding houses, inexpensive eating places, and spot labor employment agencies attracted casual and transient laborers in zones of transition (Anderson 1923, Zorbaugh 1929, Sutherland & Locke 1936, Park & Burgess 1967).

It is important to note that these homeless men were technically not without housing; they had addresses and places in which to sleep. Social researchers called them homeless because they were adult males who lived outside normal family life. Having a place to live with family made a house into a home. Without a place and a family to live with, a man was homeless.

After World War II, skid row populations declined as demand for transient labor decreased (Lee 1980, Bahr 1967). Findings that homelessness was on the decline helped to justify urban renewal efforts in city after city (Bogue 1963, Bahr & Caplow 1973). Urban renewal programs and housing market forces led to the demolition of most of the cheap skid row hotels (Miller 1982, Hoch & Slayton 1989).

For more than a decade, homelessness was not a popular research topic. In the early 1980s, a convergence of several macrosocial changes brought the issue of homelessness back into the public eye and put it back on the social research agenda (Elliott & Krivo 1991). Most important of all, homelessness began to increase and to spill out of the diminished skid rows.

Not only were there more homeless people, but they were more visible throughout our urban centers (Rossi 1989a). Skid rows, shrinking in size with urban renewal and the expansion of downtown, could no longer provide shelter for the majority of homeless persons (Bahr 1967). Decriminalization of public drunkenness and vagrancy in the 1970s as well as redefinitions of loitering and other public "nuisances" also gave more visibility to the homeless as people who previously would have been put in jail and who, therefore, sheltered temporarily, were less in the public view (Beard 1987, Rossi 1989b, Interagency Committee on Homelessness 1990).

Finally, public notice of the homeless became inevitable, with the demand that localities develop programs to tackle this problem (Hopper & Hamberg 1984, Baxter & Hopper 1981, 1982). Scarce or now absent skid row missions and flophouses were no longer viable options. The emergence of women and children as the "new homeless" particularly attracted attention (Birch 1985a, Stoner 1983, Bachrach 1984b, Bassuk & Rubin 1987, Kozol 1988, US General Accounting Office 1989, Wolch & Akita 1989, Kryder-Coe et al 1991). Increased visibility of, increased expenditures for, and growth in numbers of the homeless forced the issue of homelessness ever higher on the public agenda.

The Politics of Social Research on Homelessness

As with other public policy areas, much of the research on homelessness postdates proposed policies. Accordingly, research tends to be judged by the fit between findings and existing policies and programs. Researchers who emphasize the structural causes of homelessness accuse others of "blaming the victim" by emphasizing the problems of individuals (Milburn & Watts 1986, Snow et al 1985, Hoch 1986, Hoch & Slayton 1989, Swanstrom 1989). Those who emphasize the precipitant causes of homelessness criticize structural investigations for ignoring the special needs of homeless people in professing that the "homeless are just like you and me, but unlucky!" (Stern 1984, Wright 1988a).

Counting the homeless is especially political. Advocates believe that there is a "need" to show startlingly large numbers of homeless people, particularly of the most "worthy homeless," women and children who are neither mentally ill, nor with drug or alcohol problems or criminal histories (Wright 1988a, Rossi 1987).

Causal analyses also are not exempt from scrutiny (Holden 1986a). For example, to advocate for more federal expenditures for low-income housing seems to require support for a causal relationship between homelessness and the absence of federal support for low-income housing (Carlinger 1987, Huttman 1988, Huttman 1990, Swanstrom 1989). Although analyses that stress high unemployment rates as causes of homelessness are not rejected, they receive far less favorable attention than those that stress housing issues.

What Is Homelessness?

Studies in the 1950s and 1960s of skid row residents (the "old homeless") often defined homelessness in terms of personal ties and relationships to the broader society; homelessness was not seen primarily as a housing problem (Bahr 1973, Bahr & Garrett, 1976). Contemporary definitions of homelessness are more directly linked to the housing situations of persons. Yet within that general tendency there is much disagreement on detail. Certainly those who have no shelter at all are included by all as homeless as well as those who have to resort to "emergency shelters" for housing. But some extend the term to include people who have some shelter, including persons doubled up with relatives or friends, in hospitals, prisons, or jails, or even renting a room in single room–occupancy hotels (Fischer & Breakey 1986, Hope & Young 1988).

The various definitions each support a different view of the magnitude of the problem of homelessness. Advocates for the homeless favor more inclusive definitions, whereas more conservative commentators stress narrower ones (Kondratas 1986). The debate over the definition of homelessness also reflects changes in social values concerning what constitute adequate housing situations (Shlay 1985a,b). The post–World War II improvements in housing conditions have enlarged social expectations about how people "should" be housed. This has led some to define homelessness even more broadly to include people who are "badly" housed, in units falling far short of acceptable quality.

Importantly, the wide range in perspectives over what homelessness is reflects recognition of some of its dynamics. Researchers have shown that for many homelessness is intermittent (Rossi et al 1986). At any point in time, those who are then precariously housed may have been homeless in the past and may become homeless in the future. The line between being homeless and being domiciled is a fuzzy boundary, often and easily crossed.

Who is Homeless?

Determining the characteristics of homeless persons is important for understanding the dynamics of homelessness, for developing mechanisms that can prevent homelessness, for deciding what types of help and support homeless persons require, as well as for assessing who is at risk of homelessness. Research has focused largely on measuring the age, sex, family status, race and ethnicity, economic and labor market status, and personal vulnerabilities of homeless people.

One might expect that studying the characteristics of homeless persons, although difficult, would be free of debate. However, studying who is homeless has also created divisions within the field. There are two main issues over which disagreement has arisen. The first is whether the research findings support a view of the homeless as a diverse or homogeneous population. The second issue is whether the findings indicate individual vulnerabilities or institutional failures.

HOMELESS PEOPLE: A DIVERSE OR HOMOGENEOUS GROUP

The concern over whether homeless people are diverse or homogeneous is not a debate over numbers but over interpretation of the numbers, one fueled in part by the competition for scarce resources to ameliorate problems of homelessness.

The "old homeless" were fairly homogeneous—largely white, male, single, and beyond middle age (Swanstrom 1989, Hoch & Slayton 1989, Cohen & Sokolovsky 1989). Using the old homeless as a standard, many observers believe the contemporary homeless to be a diverse group, pointing to the increased presence of women, children, and families among the homeless as well as increased diversity in race and ethnicity.

Those who assert the homogeneity of the homeless compare them with the general adult population. In that comparison, the homeless are much more heavily composed of the extremely poor, males, single persons, and young adults than are the general population. These findings support the contention that the homeless are a largely homogeneous population.

As in most of the controversies about homelessness, the roots of the different positions lie in political issues. Those who stress the diversity of the homeless are also those who want to emphasize that the homeless are not too different from the homed and that homelessness is an event that can occur to all Americans. In contrast, the supporters of the homogeneity theory stress the view that homelessness has its roots in the distinctive characteristics of the homeless.

CHARACTERISTICS AND COMPOSITION OF THE HOMELESS: A META-ANALYSIS

There is no single authoritative study of the homeless of the 1980s. Instead, there are many studies: At least 60 local and national primary data collection investigations of the characteristics and composition of the population of homeless persons were conducted from 1981 to 1988. Although these studies do not focus on any uniform set of measures, they collectively provide sufficient information across any single indicator to begin to identify central tendencies. Despite the diversity of locale and method, the studies converge on a fairly clear demographic and social portrait.

To use these studies, we compute averages across 60 empirical studies. Each separate research study is a case, and each study's finding is a data point in this "meta-analysis." Combining information from 60 case studies is a cost-effective way to estimate the characteristics of homeless persons for the United States as a whole. (The *Appendix* contains a complete list of all of the studies used.)

The studies are quite diverse in methodology. Sixty percent are based on interviews with samples of shelter residents only. The remainder were based on interviews with shelter residents and people living on the streets. Sample sizes among these investigations ranged from 35 to 7578 persons. One study was based entirely on men from a men's shelter. Another study was based entirely on women from a women's shelter. Therefore, some of the variation in the characteristics of homeless persons (e.g. by gender) among these studies is, in part, an artifact of the variation in sampling designs. The data base for this research is the entire set of studies. Our focus is on breadth rather than quality.

THE DEMOGRAPHY OF HOMELESSNESS We summarize in Table 1 the gender, age, racial, and family characteristics of homeless persons as shown in the 60 studies. The average study found that approximately three quarters of homeless persons were male, with those studies conducted in the early 1980s no different in this respect than those conducted later. Clearly the 1980s homeless were predominantly male.

In the average study, almost all were unmarried. Yet unlike the former skid row residents, these homeless persons tended to be young, and very few homeless persons were elderly.

Table 1 Racial and demographic characteristics of homeless people (Source: Sixty local and national empirical studies of homeless persons. See Appendix.)

	Mean (standard deviation)	Range	Number of studies
Percent male	74% (25)	0–100%	60
Percent unmarried	87% (10)	60–100%	41
Median age	36.97 (4.33)	29–53	36
Mean age	36.51 (2.68)	31–43	35
Percent < 30 years old	35% (15)	15–100%	32
Percent > 60 years old	7% (4)	1–19%	39
Percent black	44% (23)	6–90%	52
Percent Hispanic	12% (7)	1–31%	37
Percent American Indian	6% (6)	0–23%	19

On the average, the studies found over 40% of the homeless persons were black. The large standard deviation around this central tendency is explained in part by regional differences; in the northern regions the homeless were more likely to be black than in the western or southern regions of the United States. The studies found fewer homeless persons who were Hispanic or American Indian.

The finding that the majority of homeless persons are single, young men (both black and white) runs counter to the assertions of two national studies conducted in the late 1980s that were not included in this data base because they were not based on direct enumerations of homeless populations. A study of homelessness in 26 cities conducted by the US Conference of Mayors, which asked mayors (and their staffs) to provide estimates, reported that only 49% of the homeless were single men, with the remaining 51% composed of women and children (Reyes & Waxman 1987). According to this report, one third of the urban homeless were families with children.

The second study, a Department of Housing and Urban Development (HUD) national survey of shelters for homeless persons in 1988, is based on interviews with managers of a national sample of shelters and providers of housing vouchers. HUD found that shelter capacity for homeless families had increased dramatically; between 1984 and 1988 the proportion of shelter beds reserved for homeless families grew from 21% to 40%. By 1988, 36% of US shelters for homeless people served primarily homeless families (US Department of Housing and Urban Development 1989).

There is no way to reconcile the findings from direct enumerations with those of the latter two studies except to refer to their procedures. In part, the differences are due to the fact that few homeless families have been found living on the streets, with virtually all homeless families found in shelters. But in large part, the differences we believe are due to the fact that the estimates of experts are unconstrained by direct enumeration and therefore tend to exaggerate both the size of the homeless population and the numbers of those homeless who attract more sympathy. For both reasons, these two national studies probably overestimate homeless families.

THE ECONOMIC STATUS OF HOMELESS PERSONS It is the economic status of homeless persons that put them outside the housing market, as is shown in Table 2. The vast majority of these homeless persons were unemployed (mean = 81%), and unemployment rates of 75% or more were found among the homeless in three quarters of these investigations. Furthermore, the studies that measured duration have shown that unemployment is often very long-term (Rossi 1989a, Burt & Cohen 1990). Rossi (1989a) found that the duration of unemployment was longer than that of homelessness, indicating that homeless people were unemployed for a lengthy period before losing their housing.

It is no surprise that the homeless in these studies were extremely poor. On average, the yearly incomes of homeless persons would be about $1236–

Table 2 Economic characteristics of homeless persons (Source: Sixty local and national empirical studies of homeless persons. See Appendix.)

	Mean (standard deviation)	Range	Number of studies
Mean monthly income	$174.00 (96.17)	$25–$337	15
Median monthly income	$103.57 (110.02)	$0–$400	14
Percent unemployed	81% (15)	25–100%	42
Percent receiving general assistance	20% (12)	4–55%	26
Percent receiving SSI	10% (7)	2–38%	31
Percent receiving AFDC	8% (7)	1–25%	15

$2088 annually. One fifth to one fourth reported no income at all over the month preceding interviews. Even those studies finding the highest average annual income levels (from $4000 to $4800) reported income levels that were inadequate to rent a market-rate apartment while also paying for daily necessities such as food, clothes, and health care.

Although almost all homeless are in principle eligible for some sort of income benefits from public sources because of their poverty, such aid was not a major income source for homeless persons. Only 20% received General Assistance (GA) and even fewer people (10%) received Supplemental Security Income (SSI). Only two studies reported that at least half of their samples received GA benefits.

Despite the growing presence of many homeless families who are primarily single parent, female-headed households with children, an extremely small number of homeless persons (8%) received Aid to Families with Dependent Children (AFDC). Of course, only adults providing direct custodial care for children are eligible for AFDC payments, and most homeless people were not eligible because they were single males without children. Accordingly, those studies reporting the highest percentages of homeless persons receiving AFDC (20% and 25%, respectively) also found higher percentages of homeless women (37% and 38%, respectively). Possibly once families are qualified to receive AFDC they become able to acquire a place to live although low AFDC benefits are cited as one of the causes of families becoming homeless (Rossi 1989a, Wolf 1991, Newman & Schnare 1988).

DISABILITY PREVALENCE RATES AMONG THE HOMELESS Research on disabilities of homeless persons is often charged with blaming individuals for their homeless situation, because it focuses on the characteristics of persons rather than on the economic system, housing market, or social structure. The rebuttal is that most social structural faults have their consequences for individuals and are reflected in their disabilities.

Table 3 shows some of the major personal vulnerabilities of homeless persons, as discovered in the meta-analysis. The mental health status and history of homeless persons has received substantial attention. At issue is the extent of mental illness among the population of homeless persons and the roles of deinstitutionalization and noninstitutionalization as factors in the growth of homelessness. Wide variation in estimates of the prevalence of mental illness are shown because there is neither a universally accepted definition of mental illness nor a common method for measuring mental illness (Bachrach 1984a, Fischer & Breakey 1986, Wright 1988b).

Method, in part, explains the wide variance in estimates. Psychiatrists, psychologists, and others using standard diagnostic interview schedules found higher rates of mental illness (Bassuk et al 1984, Institute of Medicine 1988)

Table 3 Personal vulnerabilities of homeless persons (Source: Sixty local and national empirical studies of homeless persons. See Appendix.)

	Mean (standard deviation)	Range	Number of studies
% ever in psychiatric hospital	24% (16)	10–100%	40
% ever with detox experience	29% (15)	4–76%	22
% ever with prison experience (felony)	18% (13)	4–49%	20
% ever with jail experience (misdemeanor)	32% (18)	11–82%	18
% ever with either jail or prison experience or both	41% (18)	8–82%	26
% disabled	25% (18)	3–63%	18
% in bad health	38% (11)	19–66%	20
% with current mental illness	33% (23)	4–100%	22
% with alcohol addiction	27% (15)	3–71%	27
% with no friends	36% (22)	2–87%	14
% with no kin in contact	31% (9)	12–50%	18

than did researchers who relied on the judgments of observers without such professional skills (Snow et al 1985, Wright 1988b).

One study reporting that at most 10% of its sample of homeless persons were mentally ill suggested that at issue was the "medicalization of the problem of homelessness" (Snow et al 1985). Yet others have argued that the majority of homeless persons are mentally ill with severe chronic illnesses such as schizophrenia or manic depression as well as major personality disorders (Bassuk 1984, Fischer et al 1986). And still others, alarmed that even 20%–30% of homeless persons may be chronically mentally ill, consider homelessness in large part to be a mental health issue (Farr et al 1986).

At the same time, some consensus is beginning to emerge that about 30% of the homeless suffer from some form of mental illness (Wright & Weber 1987, Wright 1988b). The numbers in Table 3 support this conclusion, suggesting that on average, one quarter to one third of the population of homeless persons has a serious mental health problem. This also means that most homeless people are not mentally ill.

It has been reported that mental illness and drug and alcohol abuse often accompany one another (Institute of Medicine 1988, Milburn 1990). Research on the Robert Wood Johnson Health Care for the Homeless demonstration projects in 16 cities reported that approximately 40% of the people in the study considered mentally ill were also substance abusers (Wright & Weber 1987). A study of Los Angeles's homeless population reported a similar finding (Farr et al 1986). Other studies include substance abuse as a dimension of mental illness (Fischer et al 1986).

Table 3 shows that alcohol and drug abuse characterize a significant proportion of the population of homeless persons. On average, 29% of these homeless persons had been admitted to a detoxification facility to be treated for drug or alcohol abuse. An equivalent number of homeless people (27%) were addicted to alcohol. Only three studies reported rates of alcohol addiction under 10%.

Although very few homeless persons received SSI (a program providing cash assistance to the non-aged with severe health problems), many homeless persons were characterized as disabled. Table 3 shows that an average of one quarter of the population of homeless persons were disabled; these were mainly measured as self reports. Almost half of the studies included in this analysis reported disability rates of 15–30% of their samples of homeless persons, a finding corroborated by the Robert Wood Johnson Health Care for the Homeless research that found that 31% had at least one chronic physical disorder (Wright & Weber 1987).

Even more homeless people reported themselves to be in poor health (Wright 1987, Wright et al 1987). Cause and effect are clearly entangled here: Being homeless may lead to illness, and poor health may precipitate homelessness. Table 3 shows that an average of 38% of the population of homeless persons reported themselves to be in bad health. Unlike other estimates of the personal vulnerabilities of homeless persons, the variance around this estimate is small.

It is no surprise that the homeless often go without food and eat poorly when they do. A national study of users of soup kitchens and shelters found that the average homeless person ate less than two meals per day and frequently did not eat for entire days (Cohen & Burt 1990). Although it was found that soup kitchens and shelters provide nutritious meals, they do not provide all the meals eaten by the homeless, with the consequence that their total food intake is nutritionally deficient.

A substantial proportion of the population of homeless persons have been incarcerated, either in prison or in jail. Table 3 shows that on average 18% of the population of homeless persons had served time in prison after being convicted of a felony, and about one third of the population of homeless persons had been jailed on misdemeanor charges. An average of 41% of the population of homeless persons experienced some form of incarceration within the criminal justice system. Research suggests that homeless persons are more likely to be picked up by the police and put in jail because of bizarre behavior or because they seem likely to be dangerous either to others or to themselves (Lamb 1984). Homeless mentally ill persons were also believed to be incarcerated more because deinstitutionalization of the mentally ill has eliminated noncriminal institutional alternatives (Dear & Wolch 1987). This research suggests that the high rate of incarceration may reflect not the misdemeanor behavior of homeless persons but rather the criminal justice system's treatment of homeless persons.

The high rate of felony convictions and prison experiences, however, indicates that many of the homeless have committed crimes serious enough to warrant prison terms of a year or more, a characteristic that cannot be simply the "criminalization" of mentally ill persons. Of those studies that examined the prevalence of prison experiences among homeless persons, almost half reported such for 10%–25% of their samples. This may indicate that criminal history, the experience of prison, and the status of being an ex-convict play a role in the dynamics of homelessness (Piliavin et al 1990).

Research studies consistently show that the homeless lack strong ties to social networks. Table 3 shows that on average, 36% reported having no friends, with 31% reporting virtually no contact with family members. Homeless persons' social networks are significantly smaller than the social networks of non-homeless poor people (Sosin et al 1988). This means that the possibility for social and economic support offered by adult friends or family members does not exist for very significant portions of the homeless, including homeless families.

An important finding is that homeless persons are more likely to have been raised in a foster care situation (Sosin et al, 1988). Because children so raised often have no ties with their kin, family members are not available for aid and support when help is needed. Moreover, these children may not be fully prepared for the labor market (Piliavin et al 1990).

Hoch & Slayton (1989) suggest that homeless persons experience "community." Studying the social networks of a sample of Chicago's SRO residents, they found that only 15% of this sample reported having no close personal relationship and argued that social disaffiliation is not characteristic of the "new homeless." Of course, this study deals with persons who are usually considered homed and are clearly more integrated than the Chicago homeless found in shelters and on the streets (Rossi 1989a).

Determining whether homeless persons are socially isolated appears to depend on whether emphasis is attached to the number of social ties or the virtual absence of social ties. For example, a study of a sample of Bowery skid row residents reported that these homeless men experienced more isolation than other groups of men but that they did not experience "total isolation" (Cohen & Sokolovsky 1989). Another study of homeless persons in Chicago found that homeless people had less contact with domiciled friends and families than did other poor people, but that they did have a social network comprised of other homeless people (Sosin et al 1988).

Poverty and other characteristics that coincide with homelessness are considered to create a pool of children at risk of incurring serious mental, developmental, and behavioral problems (Institute of Medicine 1988). Some research points to very severe consequences of homelessness for children, but it does not distinguish the impact of homelessness per se from the overall experience of poverty that all homeless children have (Bassuk & Rubin 1987). Research that compares the social, behavioral, and psychological characteristics of homeless children to those of domiciled poor children shows less dramatic effects (Molnar et al 1991). This research suggests that homelessness increases the problems of poor children, although the manifest effects of poverty on these children are already enormous (Schorr 1988).

DURATION OF HOMELESSNESS A central question in studying homelessness is whether being homeless is a temporary, transitional, or episodic condition lasting a relatively short period of time, or whether it is a permanent and chronic problem (Freeman & Hall 1987, Rossi 1989a, Burt & Cohen 1990). Measuring the duration of homelessness is confounded by the seeming intermittent character of the experience; people who are homeless over the long-term often find places to live from time to time. It is generally agreed that to measure the amount of time spent homeless requires asking when people last resided in a permanent housing situation or when people first became homeless (Freeman & Hall 1987, Burt & Cohen 1990).

Yet even this approach tends to underestimate the duration of homelessness and overestimate the number of short-term homeless persons because the information is collected at a point when the homeless experience is still ongoing. The steady growth in the number of homeless persons throughout the 1980s may also lead to overestimations of the numbers of short-term homeless persons because more people entered into homeless situations. The assumption that homeless persons are intercepted in the middle of a homeless episode has led some to double their homeless duration estimates (Freeman & Hall 1987, Rossi 1989a).

Our meta-analysis found that the average time spent homeless was just under two years; all but two studies reported that the average time spent homeless was greater than 14 months. At the same time, these studies reported that the majority of their samples were homeless for less than six months.

It is now understood that the numbers reflect the considerable variation in duration, and hence that there are no meaningful central tendencies in the distribution (Rossi 1989a, Burt & Cohen 1990). The large numbers of people who have been homeless for long periods of time and the continual entrance of newcomers into situations of homelessness have led some to conclude that regardless of the seeming episodic nature of homelessness, it is a permanent and long-term part of the US metropolitan landscape (Lang 1989, Sosin et al 1990).

How Many Homeless People?

Considerable disagreement exists over how many homeless persons there are in particular localities or in the nation. National estimates of the number of homeless persons range from 250,000 to 3,000,000 people, and local estimates also show a wide range. Estimates are derived in a variety of ways, some amounting to sheer guesses and others using more credible approaches.

The difficulties that beset estimation are inherent in the nature of homelessness. Modern censuses and sample surveys are based almost exclusively on enumerations of persons living in "dwelling units." Obviously, by definition, the homeless cannot be reached in that way, especially those who live outdoors, in vehicles, in abandoned buildings, or in public places such as bus stations. Homeless persons staying in shelters can be enumerated as living in "congregate quarters," but there is no easy way to reach and enumerate those who do not.

A variety of approaches have been developed using direct and indirect methods (Holden 1986b). There have been no attempts to conduct a direct count of the entire universe of homeless persons in the United States. All existing counts have been conducted at the local level, primarily in cities. Although the 1990 Census made a special effort to enumerate all persons living in shelters, only a partial count was made of homeless persons outside of shelters. Accordingly the 1990 Census results, when available, can only be a lower bound.

Estimates of the number of homeless people have been constructed by surveying presumably knowledgeable key informants, asking for their "expert" judgments about the numbers of homeless in their localities (Hombs & Snyder 1982, US Department of Housing and Urban Development 1984, Reyes & Waxman 1987). Local estimates of the number of homeless persons vary according to the knowledge base of key informants, key informants' definition of homelessness, and consistency in defining a local place (Appelbaum 1990, Rossi 1989a, Cowan et al 1988).

Research using key informants has produced the extreme high values in the range of national estimates of homelessness (Hombs & Snyder 1982, US Department of Housing and Urban Development, 1984). Critics of a controversial 1984 study by HUD (US Department of Housing & Urban Development 1984) argue that faulty methods produced unrealistically low estimates of the number of homeless persons (US General Accounting Office 1985). Yet critics of a 1982 study conducted by the advocacy organization Center for Creative Non-Violence (Hombs & Snyder 1982) also agreed that the high estimates of the number of homeless people found in this study were not based on any systematic method whatsoever (Kondratas 1986, Freeman & Hall 1987, Rossi 1989a). Clearly, the guesses of key informants do not converge on credible estimates.

The number of homeless persons has been extrapolated through the use of street-to-shelter ratios. In one controversial study, a sample of homeless persons in New York City food kitchen lines were asked the proportion of time spent living on the street and in shelters (Freeman & Hall 1987). Taking the average time spent on the street relative to time spent in shelters, an estimate of the number of homeless street people was extrapolated from direct counts of shelter residents, using an assumption that the street-to-shelter ratios were uniform across cities (and equal to New York City ratios). This study has been criticized (Rossi 1989a) for presuming that the street-to-shelter ratio in New York City applied to all other cities (Appelbaum 1990). Indeed, from place to place, a wide range of street-to-shelter ratios has been reported (Wiegard 1985).

In a few localities direct counts of the homeless have been attempted. In some localities, researchers have counted homeless (appearing) persons in public places (Robinson 1985, Wiegard 1985, Goldstein et al 1989, Lee 1989, Ryan et al 1989, LaGory et al 1989). More thorough surveys include interviewing people in public places to ask whether they were homeless: In Nashville, where the more thorough approach was used, counts have been undertaken for several years; these reveal a remarkable stability in the size of the population of homeless persons (Wiegard 1985, Lee 1989). Most such counts have been undertaken only in parts of the localities studied, usually the areas known to be frequented by homeless persons.

The most credible estimates have been based on modifications to the conventional area probability sampling designs. The first study to employ a probability sampling design to study homeless people living in shelters and on the street was conducted in Chicago by NORC (Rossi et al 1986, Rossi et al 1987, Rossi 1989a). Two sample designs were used; one addressed to the homeless living in shelters and the other to homeless living outside shelters and conventional dwelling units. The shelter survey yielded a probability sample of shelters and systematic samples of persons living in the selected shelters. The "street survey" was based on thorough searches of non-dwelling unit places—sidewalks and alleys, vacant lots, abandoned buildings, parked vehicles, hallways, basements and roofs, etc—in a probability sample of

Chicago census blocks stratified according to expert estimates of the density of homeless persons on each block. The street survey was undertaken in the dead of the night. Persons living in shelters and on the streets were interviewed both to determine their housing status and to collect basic demographic and epidemiological data.

Properly combined, the surveys provide a statistically sound basis for estimating the total homeless population of Chicago. The approach used by Rossi and NORC is not specific to Chicago and can be generalized to the national scene. Unfortunately, it is very expensive because the searches of samples of blocks are labor-intensive.

Although the Chicago homeless research is considered to be the most rigorous study of homelessness to date, it has been sharply criticized, for sending off-duty, plainclothes policemen to accompany interviewers (homeless people are harassed by police), for identifying homeless persons by asking them if they are homeless (homeless people are ashamed of being homeless), for failing to enumerate the "hidden homeless" (the hidden homeless, by hiding, cannot be counted), and for not including the homeless among residents of jails, prisons, and public hospitals as part of the homeless population (Cowan et al 1988, Freeman & Hall 1987, Appelbaum 1990). A large part of the attack on this research appears to be a reaction to its "low" count—2300, constituting less than 15% of Chicago advocates' estimate of homeless persons (Rossi 1987).

Since Rossi's 1985–1986 study, probability sampling designs have been used to estimate the homeless populations of Los Angeles (Hamilton, Rabinowitz & Alschuler, Inc. 1988) and Washington DC (Michael et al 1990). Up to this point, no national probability based studies have been undertaken.

Although enumerations of all the homeless in the nation have not yet been undertaken, there are enumerations of significant portions of the nation's homeless. National studies of the homeless in shelters or those using other services have been undertaken. One source relied on for the 1984 HUD national estimates was derived from a sample survey of shelters in metropolitan areas which obtained data on shelter capacities and occupancies (HUD 1984). A more recent study undertaken by the Urban Institute was based on 1987 samples of homeless persons residing in shelters or using food kitchens in 20 cities; these samples were selected to serve as representative of cities over 100,000 (Burt & Cohen 1989). Using information obtained from homeless users of food kitchens to estimate the number of homeless who are not shelter users and extrapolating to the nation, Burt & Cohen arrive at an estimate of 600,000 homeless in the nation in 1987. Note that this estimate is based on making a number of assumptions about the non-sheltered homeless that may be faulty.

Counting the number of homeless persons is confounded by the many meanings of homelessness. Most empirical investigations measure the amount of literal homelessness. Therefore, the research obtains lower numbers of homeless persons than expected by the advocates of more inclusive definitions of homelessness.

Recent research has attempted to expand the scope of homeless research by attempting to estimate the population of persons at high risk of becoming homeless, proceeding on the assumption that the high risk population consists of extremely poor single persons. Using the *Current Population Survey,* Rossi has shown that domiciled extremely poor persons are much more numerous than the homeless, about 5.7 million people (Rossi 1989b).

Why Homelessness?

As might be expected, there is strong disagreement over the root causes of the current presence and continual growth of homelessness across the United States. A major issue is whether homelessness stems from housing shortages, acute poverty, physical and emotional disabilities, joblessness, economic structural change, capitalism, changes in family structure, or a niggardly welfare state (Wolch & Akita 1989, Lang 1989, Rossi, 1989a, Wright 1989, US General Accounting Office 1985), or some combination of such factors.

Reports on the causes of homelessness often contain a list of factors that produce it (Wright 1989, Goldstein et al 1989, Smith 1985). But the extreme situation of homelessness may be more accurately portrayed as the result of the convergence of the many factors that drive this phenomenon (Rossi 1989a). Each factor in itself is insufficient to cause large and increasing numbers of homeless persons. But these factors may interact to multiply the effects of each to the extent that it becomes impossible for many people to acquire and maintain permanent housing. In this vein, the roots of homelessness are found in analyzing the US political economy (Belcher & Singer 1988, Lang 1989). Homelessness may be driven by a convergence of political, social, and economic forces that include housing market dynamics, economic restructuring, deindustrialization and labor market changes, welfare and income maintenance policy, and policy to support vulnerable, disabled groups (Wolch et al 1988, Wolch & Akita 1989, Rossi 1989a, Wright & Lam 1986).

Yet acknowledging the multitude of forces involved emphasizes the substantial gaps in current knowledge about the causes of homelessness. While many people become homeless, others under the same apparent conditions do not. There is virtually no empirically supported theory about the conditions that lead in and out of homelessness; this lack arises in part because of the absence of a theoretically driven research agenda. At issue are the incidence of and conditions associated with entering and escaping from homelessness, whether homelessness is a chronic or brief phenomena, the consequences of becoming homeless, and the conditions that prevent homelessness either from reoccurring or occurring at all. Addressing these issues requires a longitudinal design that compares the characteristics and life experiences of homeless and domiciled individuals and families.

Moreover, it has been argued that cross-sectional or single-point-in-time research strategies provide misleading information because they tend to overrepresent the characteristics of persons with longer episodes of homelessness (Sosin et al 1990). One of the only longitudinal studies of homelessness, while based on a limited sample, found that homelessness was best viewed not as either long-term or brief but as extreme residential instability, suggesting that understanding homelessness requires research that focuses on people on and off the street (Sosin et al 1990).

Importantly, longitudinal research on homelessness would be able to disentangle the influence of personal vulnerabilities from those of "events" on homelessness and to determine the policies and structural dimensions most responsible for homelessness as well as those that make its occurrence less likely. Longitudinal research on homelessness is important not only because it follows the same people but because it can account for the time-dependent nature of homelessness.

HOUSING MARKET DYNAMICS AND HOUSING POLICY

Metropolitan areas are currently experiencing an acute shortage of low-income housing (Wright & Lam 1986, Swanstrom 1989, Hoch & Slayton 1989). Therefore, homelessness is partly the result of an array of forces operating on the urban land and housing markets that have worked to reduce the supply of affordable housing. These forces include those that have bid up the price of housing as well as those that have led to the destruction and demolition of low-income housing.

Downtown revitalization and gentrification have increased the price of central city housing, displaced residents of formerly lower-income neighborhoods, and decimated the single-room-occupancy housing stock (Wright & Lam 1986, Hartman & Zigas, 1991a, Swanstrom 1989, Hoch & Slayton 1989, Ringheim 1990, Hartman & Zigas 1991b). Indeed, there is evidence that homelessness increases with economic growth which raises local property values (Logan & Molotch 1987, Freeman & Hall 1987). The benefits of economic growth do not "trickle down" to low-income persons; rather, poor people are harmed in this historical period by the fallouts of economic growth.

An opposing conservative perspective has been advanced by Tucker (1990) whose research has claimed that rent control is implicated in homelessness by making low-rent housing unprofitable. Yet later research using Tucker's data found that rent control did not have an independent effect on homelessness when city housing and employment characteristics are taken into account (Appelbaum et al 1991).

The negative impacts of central city growth and changes upon the poor have been intensified by suburbs' and cities' use of zoning and other land-use policies to exclude low-income housing and non-nuclear families from their communities (Shlay & Rossi, 1981, Hartman & Zigas 1991a, Ritzdorf 1984, Witkin 1981). In addition, housing codes embodying mainstream conceptions of housing quality help to set the stage for homelessness by rendering the construction of new low-income housing impossible without large subsidies (Freeman & Hall 1987).

These changes in urban structure and form bring federal cutbacks in housing programs to center stage. At the precise period where the need for housing subsidies was increasing, the amount of public subsidy was sharply reduced. The number of new households serviced each year declined throughout the 1980s (Hartman & Zigas 1991b). At the same time, middle class homeowners retained their indirect housing subsidy through their ability to deduct interest payments from their taxable income.

ECONOMIC RESTRUCTURING AND THE LABOR MARKET

Because of economic restructuring, the loss of manufacturing employment, the rising skill level demanded in new jobs that pay well, and the increasing number of low wage jobs in the service sector, the metropolitan employment base is increasingly unable to provide jobs that pay enough to permit people with few skills to acquire and maintain tenure in permanent housing. Unemployment and long-term joblessness are cited as major reasons for homelessness (Rossi 1989a). Although the proportion of persons below the poverty level has not increased by very much, these structural changes have concentrated poverty among the minority populations in urban areas. Large numbers of these populations have essentially no income for housing (Ellwood & Summers 1986).

Homelessness also stems from the reduced income levels of households and families (Rossi 1989b). Declining real incomes of households may not automatically lead to these low-income households becoming homeless. However, the poverty of such households may prevent them from aiding more destitute friends and kin. Many would-be homeless people live in households maintained by others, especially close kin such as parents and siblings; this is why they are termed the "hidden homeless" (Rossi 1989a, Milhaly 1991).

WELFARE AND INCOME MAINTENANCE POLICY

The reductions in federal appropriations for employment and training programs, income maintenance assistance, and food stamps that accompanied the Reagan and Bush presidencies meant that fewer people in need could be assisted when the need for assistance was dramatically increasing and that the funds made available were less. Even if funding levels had been maintained at their pre-1980 levels, the available resources would have been unable to ameliorate problems of homelessness effectively because the real value of these benefits had been so severely eroded by inflation (Ellwood & Summers 1986).

While the need for job training increased, funding for employment and training programs decreased (Bassi & Ashenfelter, 1986, Wolch & Akita 1989). A reduced supply of low-income housing combined with low AFDC benefits is one major reason why homeless families with children have emerged on the urban scene (Wolf 1991). Welfare assistance, through providing a shelter allowance, may also be considered a form of housing assistance. However, these allowances only cover a fraction of the actual cost of housing (Newman & Schnare 1988). For single persons, lower General Assistance benefits (which vary dramatically among states) do not provide sufficient resources to rent an apartment or even a room (Rossi 1989a). More generous SSI benefits which average less than $350 per month are still inadequate to pay for daily necessities and housing in most urban centers (Newman & Schnare 1988). The large gap between household income levels and local rent levels is considered to be a structural force that creates a population at risk of homelessness (Ringheim 1989, Ringheim 1990, Elliott & Krivo 1991).

THE ROLE OF DISABILITIES IN CREATING PERSONAL VULNERABILITIES

Although many homeless people suffer from disabilities resulting from drug and alcohol abuse, mental and physical illness, and criminal convictions, these vulnerabilities may not be the ultimate causes of their homelessness (Redburn & Buss, 1986, Rossi & Wright 1987). One view is that personal vulnerabilities indirectly affect homelessness by interfering with people's abilities to participate in the labor market and to maintain stable and secure relationships with friends and family (Rossi 1989a). Chronic disabilities may promote economic destitution through the lack of economic and social support that accompanies being chronically disabled.

Patterns of causation may also vary among subgroups. Homelessness for women (and for homeless families) is often preceded by domestic violence (Sidel 1986). The enlarged role of domestic violence in forcing a homeless situation may not indicate that domestic violence is increasing but rather suggest that women experiencing abuse and battering have more options to leave oppressive family situations, as is demonstrated by the increased number of shelters for battered women.

Programs and Policies to Address Homelessness

Although research consistently supports the necessity of long-term solutions to homelessness, most of the programs and policies in place deal with homelessness in the short-term, as emergency situations (Redburn & Buss 1986, Buss 1990). The largest line items under the McKinney Act in 1989 (the most important federal legislation to aid homeless persons) were for emergency shelter and assistance. The smallest appropriations went to job training, adult literacy, and alcohol and drug treatment (Schwartz & Glascock 1989).

A three-tiered approach to providing housing for the homeless has been recommended (Baxter et al 1982, Mayer & Shuster 1985). The first tier is composed of emergency shelters, including those that provide overnight housing and those that provide shelter during the daytime (e.g. drop-in centers) (Sosin et al 1988).

This approach is criticized because it is a temporary solution, often of poor quality, providing an unsafe environment frequently avoided by homeless persons (Huttman 1988, Rossi 1989a). Indeed, the 1988 HUD shelter survey reported an occupancy rate of 66% (US Department of Housing and Urban Development 1989).

The second tier, transitional housing, is currently attracting more public and private funding (Heskin 1987). This approach allows stays of longer durations than emergency housing, usually from six months to one year, and typically provides an array of support services (or connections to services) that include drug treatment, medical care, job training, education and child care for homeless families (Shlay 1986, Bach & Steinhagen 1987, Bassuk 1988, Schwartz & Glascock 1989). The goal is to aid homeless people in making the transition to permanent housing.

No research has systematically examined the impact of transitional housing on the lives of homeless persons. Despite the absence of research, transitional housing programs are criticized for potentially reinstitutionalizing homeless persons and creating "service dependent ghettos" (Dear & Wolch 1987, Hoch & Slayton 1989). Yet the short-term tenancy of transition housing residents, the large need for intense service delivery, and the current status of programs to address homelessness raise questions about the validity of these concerns.

The third tier consists of permanent housing for homeless people. With virtual unanimity, almost all commentators call for more low-cost housing to redress homelessness (Wright & Lam, 1986, Rossi 1989a). Yet providing permanent housing has prompted the least amount of activity (Hartman & Zigas 1991b, Stegman 1991). Homelessness is treated largely as a short-term housing problem because developing long-term, low-income housing is confounded by the decreased availability of construction and rent subsidies, large building acquisition and rehabilitation costs, the high costs of developing new low-income housing and high interest rates. Moreover, very deep subsidies are needed because most homeless persons cannot afford to pay any rent at all (Rossi 1989a).

Since the low-income housing stock for poor single persons has mostly been single-room-occupancy hotels (SROs), efforts are increasing to preserve this housing, to halt demolition, and to fight gentrification forces (Kasinitz 1984, Mostoller 1985, Hoch & Slayton 1989). Although SRO rents are lower than conventional apartment rents, they remain too high for many homeless people and subsidies are therefore required (Rossi 1989a).

The McKinney Act provides for housing vouchers to subsidize the homeless in existing housing. Critics argue that housing vouchers (demand-side housing subsidies) are inadequate because of the small supply of affordable housing units in which the vouchers could be used (Swanstrom 1989).

Existing subsidized housing also appears not to be the answer. Waiting lists for all subsidized housing programs are extremely long, indicating that they cannot alter the immediate condition of homelessness in the short-term unless subsidies are targeted to homeless persons. In addition, most housing assistance does not aid the majority of homeless persons who are young and single because the vast majority of aid goes either to elderly persons or to families with children (Hartman & Zigas 1991b).

Another approach to homelessness is to provide social services to the homeless. As with housing assistance, the major target of social services is homeless families. Combining services and housing, The Robert Wood Johnson Foundation with the Department of Housing and Urban Development has taken the lead in developing demonstration programs that coordinate public and private resources for addressing the needs of homeless mentally ill persons and homeless families with children.

With the not surprising discovery that homeless people suffered from a multitude of physical problems, providing health care for homeless persons became a focus of national attention. In 1985, the Robert Wood Johnson Foundation and Pew Memorial Trust jointly funded nineteen cities for four years to establish clinics to coordinate and provide health care for homeless persons. An evaluation of this demonstration project showed that it was feasible to provide health care systems accessible to homeless persons (Wright 1987, Wright et al 1987, Wright & Weber 1987). It is likely that this success in private initiative was directly responsible for the health care provisions contained in the McKinney Act (Institute of Medicine 1988).

The food and nutritional needs of homeless persons have also received increasing national attention, generating support from both public and private sources (Cooper 1987). Providing free food has led to the development of a national organizational infrastructure that obtains food from suppliers and distributes it to local food banks who then supply food to local service providers. Soup kitchens and food pantries, primarily operated by religious organizations and other nonprofit organizations, are available to any person in need. Indeed, there is evidence that the free food available from food kitchens enables many precariously housed persons to put most of their income into housing, thereby preventing or postponing homelessness (Sosin et al 1988, Burt & Cohen 1989). This suggests that without free food, the number of homeless people might even be larger.

The recognition that existing efforts to aid homeless persons are inadequate has fostered a wide range of policy recommendations for preventing homelessness. These include recommendations to revise US social welfare policy (Rossi 1989a), expand the availability of job training programs (Redburn & Buss 1986), and enlarge public and private support for increasing the availability of low-income housing (Swanstrom 1989, Hartman & Zigas 1991b). It has also been suggested that homeless persons organize themselves into unions that can advocate on their own behalf (Cress 1990).

Recommendations include short- and long-term measures. Suggested short-term measures are those that intervene in the proximate causes of homelessness. These include increasing individual access to existing services and augmenting support for emergency shelters (Baxter & Hopper 1981, Baxter & Hopper 1982, Baxter et al 1982).

Long-term measures deal more directly with those factors that obstruct the production of affordable housing and those that produce acute poverty. In addition to increasing subsidies, suggested housing initiatives include developing non-conventional housing (e.g. shared housing), initiating new tenure forms (e.g. community land trusts), altering prevailing zoning codes, encouraging new forms of housing production (e.g. manufactured housing), enacting housing market restrictions (e.g. anti-speculation laws) and increasing housing credit availability (Birch 1985b, Hartman & Stone 1986, Lang 1989, van Vliet 1989). It has also been suggested that the United States adopt the third world's ongoing housing production method of self-help where unemployed homeless residents construct their own homes; others argue that squatting in vacant housing would remedy some homelessness (Burns 1987, Borgos 1986).

Short-term measures suggested to improve the US welfare system include increasing welfare benefits (i.e. AFDC, GA, and SSI), joint coordination of housing and welfare subsidies, an expansion of eligibility for assistance to include families with dependent adults, public sector intervention in the labor market (e.g. public sector employment) and national economic planning (Belcher & Singer 1988, Newman & Schnare 1988, Rossi 1988).

Long-term measures to alter the conditions that produce homelessness are by definition designed to alleviate problems accompanying acute poverty and an inadequate supply of low-cost housing. Reducing the prevalence of homelessness is not equivalent to eliminating poverty although policy designed to benefit homeless persons would also provide positive benefits for non-homeless poor persons from whose ranks the population of homeless persons is recruited (Rossi 1989b, Hartman & Zigas, 1991a).

Homelessness: A US or Worldwide Phenomenon?

Homelessness is not new to third world cities. Rapid urbanization, urban primacy and now the introduction of "mega-cities" have led to large numbers of homeless persons in developing countries who cannot be absorbed by already severely strained labor and housing markets (Rondinelli 1983, Chase-Dunn, 1985). Indeed, US research on homelessness has a parochial quality because it does not take into account either worldwide homelessness nor third world innovations in addressing this problem (e.g. self-help) (Burns 1987).

Yet there are important differences between US and third world homelessness. Third world homeless persons are recent migrants to cities; in the US homeless persons tend to be long-term residents (Burt & Cohen 1990). Moveover, third world homelessness is a product, in part, of rapid urban growth while increasing US homelessness has been accompanied by central city population decline.

A stronger parallel exists between US and European homelessness (Friedrichs 1988). Increasing numbers of homeless persons have been reported in several European countries such as France and Great Britain. Speculation on the causes of European homelessness mirror US findings—economic restructuring, a decline in the low-income housing stock, unemployment, and cutbacks in welfare spending (Lang 1989, Ferrand-Bechmann 1988, Murie & Forrest 1988). In addition, British and French homeless are also dominated numerically by men who are rapidly being joined by women and children (Murie & Forrest 1988). These similarities suggest that US homelessness is not unique but is a product of economic and political forces found in many modern market economies (Adams 1986). If homelessness is a phenomenon driven by the current politics governing market economics, it may develop in eastern European countries that are dismantling their socialist economies and embracing market principles.

Future Roles and Directions for Social Science Research

Until now the role of social research has mainly been to document the social characteristics of homeless persons and to monitor the size of the homeless population. It is now time to explore more the precipitant and structural underpinnings of homelessness, and to outline the role of policy in fostering or preventing a homeless situation. Consensus appears to be growing that contemporary homelessness is not temporary but will be with us for some time. Social research will need to play an even more important role in developing our knowledge base concerning this tragedy. Social research must maintain its commitment to the methodological rigor that this complex problem deserves despite the pressures of social movements and political forces to come up with a variety of "right" answers.

Many aspects of homelessness require more attention by the social research community. Homelessness is a multidimensional problem, and the different facets of this problem are not well understood. While research has been more attentive to homelessness as a housing or mental health problem, less concern has been placed on other important aspects of this problem. One of these is the role of employment (Sosin et al 1988, Rossi 1988, Elliott & Krivo 1991). Research needs to address the dynamics of homelessness in terms of labor market participation, joblessness, structural change, and the stabilization of the economy. This is particularly important in understanding the homelessness of young single men. Clearly longitudinal studies of the paths taken and events encountered on the way to homelessness and back to the domiciled condition are called for.

A second important issue is the role of social ties in homelessness. This is not to equate homelessness with social disaffiliation but to examine explicitly the place of family and friendship networks in the process of becoming and staying homeless. A promising direction in this vein is the recent focus on the foster care experiences of homeless persons (Piliavin et al 1990). Here again, longitudinal studies are needed to determine how primal kinship ties deteriorate under adversity and what social relations sustain them.

To aid in the development of remedies to homelessness, research needs to continue to compare the economic and social situations of homeless persons to non-homeless persons. Social science research has a central role to play in determining the strengths and weaknesses of various strategies to address homelessness, particularly those programs that offer the possibility of moving homeless persons off the streets, into the labor market, into permanent housing, and, ultimately, into the social and economic mainstream. Programs are in place, but they do not appear to have clear objectives nor have they generated hard estimates of their effectiveness. Good social science evaluations are called for.

Important lessons may be garnered from international comparisons of homelessness. It would be useful to understand the relationship between homelessness and variations in characteristics of countries including housing, economic and welfare policy, types of economies (e.g. market versus socialist), community culture, standard of living, and quality of life. We believe significant variation occurs among countries in homelessness: For policy purposes as well for the understanding of structural causes, we need to know the sources of these variations.

ACKNOWLEDGMENTS

We thank Michael Bell, Marta Elliott, John Hagan, and two anonymous reviewers for helpful comments, Sam Bedinger for computer assistance, Jean Biddinger for her prodigious application of Word Perfect, and Lester Salamon and Sandra Newman for their enthusiasm for this work.

Appendix of Studies on Which This Review is Based

Baker, S. G., Snow, D. A. 1989. Homelessness in Texas: Estimates of population size and demographic composition. In *Homelessness in the United States: State Surveys*, J. A. Momeni, pp. 205–17. Westport, Conn: Greenwood

Baumann, D. J., Grisby, C., Beavais, C., Schultz, D. F. 1986. *The Austin Homeless*. Austin: Univ. Texas Press

Brown, C., McFarlane, S., Parardes, R., Stark, L. 1983. *The Homeless of Phoenix: Who Are They and What Should Be Done (Summer Study)*. Phoenix: Phoenix South Community Health Cent.

Brown, C., McFarlane, S., Parardes, R., Stark, L. 1983. *The Homeless of Phoenix: Who Are They and What Should Be Done (Winter Study)*. Phoenix: Phoenix South Community Health Cent.

Brown, C., McFarlane, S., Parardes, R., Stark, L. 1983c. *The Homeless of Phoenix: Who Are They and What Should Be Done (Census)*. Phoenix: Phoenix South Community Health Cent.

Burt, M. R., Cohen, B. E. 1988. *Feeding the Homeless: Does the Prepared Meals Provision Help?* Urban Inst. Rep. Prepared for Food & Nutrit. Serv: US Dep. Agric.

Chaiklin, H. 1985a. *Report on the Homeless: Needs of Soup Kitchen*. Baltimore: Univ. Md.

Chaiklin, H. 1985b. *Report on the Homeless: The Service Needs of Shelter Care Residents*. Baltimore: Univ. Md.

Chicago Coalition for the Homelessness. 1983. *When You Don't Have Anything: A Street Survey of Homeless People in Chicago*. Chicago: Chicago Coalition for the Homeless

Crystal, S. 1982. *New Arrivals: First Time Shelter Clients*. New York: Hum. Resources Admin.

Crystal, S., Goldstein, M. 1984a. *Correlates of Shelter Utilization: One Day Study (Fort Washington Armory)*. New York: Hum. Resources Admin.

Crystal, S., Goldstein, M. 1984b. *Correlates of Shelter Utilization: One Day Study (Greenpoint Shelter)*. New York: Hum. Resources Admin.

Crystal, S., Goldstein, M. 1984c. *Correlates of Shelter Utilization: One Day Study (Women's Shelter Annex)*. New York: Hum. Resources Admin.

Crystal, S., Goldstein, M. 1984d. *Correlates of Shelter Utilization: One Day Study (Men in Shelters)*. New York: Human Resources Admin.

Crystal, S., Goldstein, M. 1984e. *Correlates of Shelter Utilization: One Day Study (Women in Shelters)*. New York: Hum. Resources Admin.

Crystal, S., Goldstein, M. 1982. *Chronic and Situational Dependency: Long Term Residents in a Shelter for Men*. New York: Hum. Resources Admin.

Crystal, S., Ladner, S., Towber, R. nd. *Multiple Impairment Patterns in the Mentally Ill Homeless*. New York: Hum. Resources Admin.

Dockett, K. 1989. *Street Homeless People in the District of Columbia: Characteristics and Service Needs*. Washington, DC: Univ. District of Columbia

Farr, R. K., Koegel, P., Burnham, A. 1986. *A Study of Homelessness and Mental Illness in the Skid Row Area of Los Angeles*. Los Angeles County: Dep. Public Health

Fischer, P. J., Shapiro, S., Breakey, W. R., Anthony, J. C., Kramer, M. 1984. *Mental health and social characteristics of the homeless: A survey of Mission users*. Presented at Am. Public Health Assoc., Johns Hopkins Univ. Sch. Public Health

Freeman, R. B., Hall, B. 1987. Permanent homelessness in America? Popul. Res. Policy Rev. 6:3–27

Hamilton, Rabinowitz, & Alshuler, Inc. 1986.

The 1986 L.A. Skid Row Demographic Survey. Los Angeles: Hamilton Rabinowitz & Alshuler, Inc.

Institute for Research on Poverty. 1987. Tracking the homeless. In *Focus*. Madison: Univ. Wisc. Inst. Res. Poverty

James, F. 1988. *Numbers and Characteristics of the Homeless: A Preliminary Application in Colorado of a New Methodology*. Denver: Univ. Colo. Press

LaGory, M., Ritchey, F. J., Mullis, J. 1987a. *The Homeless of Alabama (Phase 1 & 2) 1987*. Birmingham: Univ. Ala., Dep. Sociol.

LaGory, M., Ritchey, F. J., Mullins, J. 1987b. *The Homeless of Alabama (Phase 3)*. Birmingham: Univ. Ala. Dep. Soc.

Lee, B. A. 1988a. *Homelessness in Tennessee (Chattanooga)*. Nashville, Tenn: Vanderbilt Univ. Dep. Sociol.

Lee, B. A. 1988b. *Homelessness in Tennessee (Knoxville)*. Nashville, Tenn: Vanderbilt Univ. Dep. Sociol.

Lee, B. A. 1988c. *Homelessness in Tennessee (Memphis)*. Nashville, Tenn: Vanderbilt Univ. Dep. Sociol.

Lee, B. A. 1988d. *Homelessness in Tennessee (Nashville)*. Nashville, Tenn: Vanderbilt Univ. Dep. Sociol.

Maurin, J., Russell, L. 1989. Homelessness in Utah. In *Homeslessness in the United States: State Surveys*, J. A. Momeni. Westport, Conn: Greenwood

Morse, G., Shields, N. M., Hanneke, C. R., Calsyn, R. J., Burger, G. K., Nelson, B. 1985. *Homeless People in St. Louis: A Mental Health Program Evaluation*. St. Louis, Mo: Dep. Mental Health

Mowbray, C. T., Johnson, S., Solarz, A. 1987. *Homelessness in a State Hospital Population*. Detroit: Hospital & Community Psychiatry

Mowbray, C. T., Solarz, A., Combs, M., Johnson, S. 1986. Mental health and homelessness in Detroit. *Psychosocial Rehab. J.*

Mulkern, V. 1984. *Homeless Needs Assessment Study: Findings and Recommendations*. Cambridge, Mass: Hum. Serv. Res. Inst.

Multnomah County Oregon. 1985. *The Homeless 1984*. Multnomah County, Ore: Hum. Serv., Soc. Serv. Div.

Owen, G., Mattessich, R., Williams, T. 1987. *Results of the Twin City Survey of Emergency Shelter Residents*. Minneapolis, Minn: Wilder Res. Cent.

Philadelphia Health Management Corp. 1985. *Homelessness in Philadelphia (Interviews)*. Philadelphia, Penn: Philadelphia Health Mgmt. Corp.

Philadelphia Health Management Corp. 1985. *Homelessness in Philadelphia: People, Needs and Services (Admissions)*. Philadelphia, Penn: Philadelphia Health Manage. Corp.

Providence Center for Counseling and Psychiatric Services. 1987. *Delivering Mental Health Services to the Homeless: A Survey of the Service Needs of the Homeless*. Providence, RI: Providence Ctr. Counsel. Psychiatr. Serv.

Rafferty, Y. 1991. Developmental and educational consequences of homelessness on children and youth. In *Homeless Children and Youth: A New American Dilemma*, ed. J. H. Kryder-Coe, L. M. Salamon, J. M. Molnar, pp. 105–39. New Brunswick, NJ: Transaction

Robinson, F. G. 1985. *Homeless People in the Nation's Capital*. Washington, DC: Univ. of the District of Columbia, Cent. Appl. Res. & Urban Policy

Ropers, R. 1988. *The Invisible Homeless: A New Urban Ecology (Single Resident Occupancy Study)*. New York: Insight

Ropers, R. 1985. *The Rise of the Urban Homeless*. Los Angeles: Public Affairs Rep., Univ. Calif., Berkeley

Ropers, R., Robertson, M. 1984. *The Inner City Homeless of LA: An Empirical Assessment*. Los Angeles: UCLA Sch. Public Health

Rossi, P. H., Fisher, G. A., Willis, G. 1986. *The Condition of the Homeless of Chicago, 1986*. Amherst, Mass. and Chicago: Soc. Demogr. Res. Inst., NORC, Univ. Mass.

Roth, D., Bean, J., Lust, N., Saveneau, T. 1985. *Homelessness in Ohio: A Study of People in Need*. Columbus, Ohio: Ohio Dep. Mental Health

Schutt, R. K. 1988. *Health Problems and Service Needs Among Boston's Homeless*. Presented at Symp. on Homelessness and Extreme Poverty, AAAS Annu. Meet., Boston, Univ. Mass.

Schutt, R. K., Garrett, G R. 1986. *Homeless in Boston 1985: The View from Long Island*. Boston: Univ. Mass., Dep. Sociol.

Schutt, R. K., Garrett, G. R. 1985. *A Report on the Homeless: New Guests at the Long Island Shelter*. Boston: Univ. Mass. Dep. Sociol.

Shaffer, D., Caton, C. W. 1984. *Runaway and Homeless Youth in New York City*. New York: Columbia Univ. Coll. Physicians & Surgeons

Snow, D. A., Baker, S. G., Anderson, L., Martin, M. 1986. The myth of pervasive mental illness among the homeless. *Soc. Probl.* 33:407–23

Solarz, A. 1985. *Social Support Among the Homeless*. Detroit: Mich. State Univ. Dep. Psychol.

Solarz, A., Bogat, G. A. 1986. *An Examination of Criminal Behavior Among the Home-*

less. Detroit: Mich. State Univ. Dep. Psychol.
Sosin, M. R., Colson P., Grossman, S. 1988. *Homelessness in Chicago: Poverty and Pathology, Social Institutions, and Social Change*. Chicago: Chicago Community Trust
Struening, E. L. 1987. *A Study of Residents of the New York City Shelter System*. New York: NY City Dep. Mental Health
Vernez, G., Burnam, M. A., McGlynn, E., Trude, S., Mittman, B. 1987a. *Review of California's Program for the Homeless Mentally Disabled (SMD)*. Santa Monica: Rand
Vernez, G., Burnam, M.A., McGlynn, E., Trude, S., Mittman, B. 1987b. *Review of California's Program for the Homeless Mentally Disabled (Non-SMD)*. Santa Monica: Rand
Woods, W., Burdell, E. 1987. *Homelessness in Cincinnati*. Cincinnati, Ohio: Appl. Info. Res.
Wright, J. D., Weber, E. 1987. *Homelessness and Health*. New York: McGraw-Hill

Literature Cited

Adams, C. T. 1986. Homelessness in the post-industrial city. *Urban Affairs Q*. 21:527–49
Anderson, N. 1923. *The Hobo: The Sociology of Homeless Men*. Chicago: Univ. Chicago Press
Appelbaum, R. P. 1990. Counting the homeless. See Momeni 1990, pp. 1–16
Appelbaum, R. P., Dolny, M., Dreier, P., Gilderbloom, J. 1991. *Scapegoating Rent Control: Masking the Causes of Homelessness. J. Am. Plan. Assoc*. 57:153–64
Bach, V., Steinhagen, R. 1987. *Alternatives to the Welfare Hotel: Using Emergency Assistance to Provide Decent Transitional Shelter for Homeless Families*. New York: Community Serv. Soc.
Bachrach, L. L. 1984a. Interpreting research on the homeless mentally ill: some caveats. *Hosp. Community Psychiatry* 35:914–17
Bachrach, L. L. 1984b. *The Homeless Mentally Ill and Mental Health Services: An Analytical Review of the Literature*. Washington, DC: US Dep. Health Hum. Serv.
Bahr, H. M. 1967. The gradual disappearance of skid row. *Soc. Probl*. 15:41–45
Bahr, H. M. 1973. *Skid Row: An Introduction to Disaffiliation*. New York: Oxford Univ. Press
Bahr, H. M., Caplow, T. 1973. *Old Men Drunk and Sober*. New York: New York Univ. Press
Bahr, H. M., Garrett, G. R. 1976. *Women Alone: The Disaffiliation of Urban Females*. Lexington, Mass: Lexington Books
Bassi, L. J., Ashenfelter, O. 1986. The effect of direct job creation and training programs on low-skilled workers. In *Fighting Poverty: What Works and What Doesn't*, ed. S. H. Danziger, D. H. Weinberg, pp. 133–51. Cambridge, Mass: Harvard Univ. Press
Bassuk, E. L. 1984. The homeless problem. *Sci. Am*. 251:40–45
Bassuk, E. L. 1988. Redefining transitional housing for homeless families. *Yale Law Policy Rev*. 6:49–67
Bassuk, E. L., Rubin, L., Laurist, A. 1984. Is homelessness a mental health problem? *Am. J. Psychiatr*. 141:1546–50
Bassuk, E. L., Rubin, L. 1987. Homeless children: A neglected population. *Am. J. Orthopsychiatr*. 5:1–9
Baxter, E., Hopper, K. 1981. *Private Lives, Public Spaces: Homeless Adults on the Streets of NYC*. New York: Community Serv. Soc. NY, Inst. Soc. Welfare Res.
Baxter, E., Hopper, K. 1982. The new mendicancy: homeless in New York City. *Am. J. Orthopsychiatr*. 52:395
Baxter, E., Hopper, K., Cox, S., Klein, L. 1982. *One Year Later: The Homeless Poor in New York City, 1982*. New York : Community Serv. Soc.
Beard, R., ed. 1987. *On Being Homeless: Historical Perspectives*. New York: Mus. City of New York
Belcher, J. R., Singer, J. 1988. Homelessness: A cost of capitalism. *Soc. Policy* 18:44–48
Bingham, R. D., Green, R. E., White, R. E., eds. 1987. *The Homeless in Contemporary Society*.Beverly Hills, Calif: Sage
Birch, E. L. 1985a. The unsheltered woman: definition and needs. See Birch, pp. 21–46
Birch, E. L. 1985b. *The Unsheltered Woman: Women and Housing in the 80s*. New Brunswick, NJ: Cent. Urban Policy Res.
Bogue, D. J. 1963. *Skid Row in American Cities*. Chicago: Univ. Chicago
Borgos, S. 1986. Low-income homeownership and the ACORN squatters campaign. In *Critical Perspectives on Housing,* ed. R. G. Bratt, C. Hartman, A. Meyerson, pp. 428–46. Philadelphia, Penn:Temple Univ. Press
Burns, L. E. 1987. Third world solutions to the homelessness problem. See Bingham et al 1987, pp. 231–48
Burt, M. R., Cohen, B. E. 1989. *America's Homeless: Numbers, Characteristics, and Programs that Serve Them, Urban Institute Report 89-3*. Washington, DC: Urban Inst.
Burt, M. R., Cohen, B. E. 1990. A sociodemographic profile of the service-

using homeless: findings from a national survey. See Momeni 1990, pp. 17–38
Buss, T. F. 1990. Public policies for reducing homelessness in America. See Momeni 1990, pp. 153–64
Carlinger, M. S. 1987. Homelessness: a housing problem. See Bingham et al 1987, pp. 119–30
Chase-Dunn, C. 1985. The coming of urban primacy in Latin America. *Compar. Urban Res.* 11:14–31
Cohen, B. E., Burt, M.R. 1990. Food sources and intake of homeless persons. See Momeni 1990, pp. 39–60
Cohen, C. I., Sokolovsky, J. 1989. *Old Men of the Bowery: Strategies for Survival Among the Homeless*. New York: Guilford
Cooper, M. A. 1987. The role of religious and nonprofit organizations in combatting homelessness. See Bingham et al 1987, pp. 130–49
Cowan, C. D., Breakey, W. R., Fischer, P. J. 1988. The methodology of counting the homeless. In *Committee on Health Care for Homeless People, Homelessness, Health and Human Needs,* pp. 169–82. Washington, DC: Natl. Acad. Press
Cress, D. M. 1990. *Look out world, the meek are getting ready: implications of mobilization among the homeless*. Presented at Annu. Meet. Am. Sociol. Assoc., August, Washington, DC
Dear, M. J., Wolch, J. R. 1987. *Landscapes of Despair: From Deinstitutionalization to Homelessness*. Princeton, NJ: Princeton Univ. Press
Elliott, M. E., Krivo, L. J. 1991. Structural determinants of homelessness in the United States. *Soc. Probl.* 38:113–31
Ellwood, D. T., Summers, L. H. 1986. Poverty in America: Is welfare the answer or the problem. In *Fighting Poverty: What Works and What Doesn't,* ed. S. H. Danziger, D. H. Weinberg, pp. 78–105. Cambridge, Mass: Harvard Univ. Press
Farr, R. K., Koegel, P., Burnam, M. A. 1986. *A Study of Homelessness and Mental Illness in the Skid Row Area of Los Angeles*. Los Angeles: County of Los Angeles Dep. Public Health
Ferrand-Bechmann, D. 1988. Homelessness in France: Public and private policies. See Friedrichs 1988, pp. 147–56
Fischer, P. J., Breakey, W. R. 1986. Homelessness and mental health: An overview. *Int. J. Mental Health* 14:6–41
Fischer, P. J., Shapiro, S., Breakey, W. R., Anthony, J. C., Kramer, M. 1986. Mental health and social characteristics of the homeless: A survey of mission users. *Am. J. Public Health* 76:519–24
Freeman R. B., Hall B. 1987. Permanent homelessness in America? *Popul. Res. Policy Rev.* 6:3–27
Friedrichs, J. 1988. *Affordable Housing and the Homeless*. New York: Walter de Gruyter
Goldstein, I., Bartelt, D., Ryan, P. 1989. *Homelessness in Philadelphia: Roots, Realities and Resolutions*. Philadelphia, Penn: Coalition on Homelessness in Philadelphia
Hamilton, Rabinowitz & Alschuler, Inc. 1988. *The Changing Face of Misery: Los Angeles' Skid Row Area in Transition: Housing and Social Services Needs of Central City East*. Los Angeles: Community Redev. Agency
Hartman, C., Stone, M. E. 1986. A socialist housing alternative for the United States. In *Critical Perspectives on Housing,* ed. R.G. Bratt, C. Hartman, A. Meyerson, pp. 484–513. Philadelphia, Penn: Temple Univ. Press
Hartman, C., Zigas, B. 1991a. What is wrong with the housing market. See Kryder-Coe et al 1991, pp. 175–93
Hartman, C., Zigas, B. 1991b. What is wrong with our housing programs. See Kryder-Coe et al 1991, pp. 197–224
Heskin, A. D. 1987. Los Angeles: Innovative local approaches. In *The Homeless in Contemporary Society,* ed. R. Bingham, R. E. Green, S. B. White, pp. 170–184. Beverly Hills: Sage
Hoch, C. J. 1986. Homeless in the United States. *Housing Stud.* 1:228–40
Hoch, C. J., Slayton, R. 1989. *New Homeless and Old: Community and the Skid Row Hotel*. Philadelphia: Temple Univ. Press
Holden C. 1986a. Homelessness: Experts differ on root causes. *Science* 237:569–70
Holden, C. 1986b. Counting the homeless. *Science* 234:281–82
Hombs, M. E., Snyder, M. 1982. *Homelessness In America: A Forced March to Nowhere*. Washington, DC: Community for Creative Non-Violence
Hope M., Young J. 1988. *The Faces of Homelessness*. Lexington, Mass: D.C. Heath Company
Hopper K., Hamberg, J. 1984. *The Making of America's Homeless: From Skid Row to New Poor*. New York: Commun. Serv. Soc.
Huttman, E. 1990. Homelessness as a long term housing problem in America. See Momeni 1990, pp. 81–94
Huttman, E. 1988. Homelessness as a housing problem in an inner city in the United States. See Friedrichs 1988
Interagency Committee on Homelessness. 1990. Draft of 1990 Report. Washington, DC

Institute of Medicine. 1988. *Homelessness, Health and Human Needs*. Washington, DC: Natl Acad. Press

Kasinitz, P. 1984. Gentrification and homelessness: The single room occupant and the inner city revival. *Urban Soc. Change Rev.* 17:9–14

Kondratas, S. A. 1986. A strategy for helping America's homeless. In *Housing the Homeless,* ed. J. Erickson, C. Wilhelm, pp.144–49. New Brunswick, NJ: Cent. Urban Policy Res.

Kozol, J. 1988. *Rachel and her Children: Homeless Families in America*. New York: Crown

Kryder-Coe, J. H., Salamon, L. M., Molnar, J. M. 1991. *Homeless Children and Youth: A New American Dilemma*. New Brunswick, NJ: Transaction

La Gory, M., Ritchey, F. J., O'Donoghue, R., Mullis, J. 1989. Homelessness in Alabama: A variety of people and experiences. See Momeni 1989, pp. 1–20

Lamb, H. R. 1984. Alternatives to hospitals. In *The Chronic Mental Patient: Five Years Later,* ed. J. A. Talbott, pp. 215–32. Orlando, Fla: Grune & Stratton

Lang, M. H. 1989. *Homelessness Amid Affluence: Structure and Paradox in the American Political Economy*. New York: Praeger

Lee, B. A. 1980. Disappearance of skid row: some ecological evidence. *Urban Affairs Q.* 16:81–107

Lee, B. A. 1989. Stability and change in an urban homeless population. *Demography* 26:323–34

Logan, J. R., Molotch, H. L. 1987. *Urban Fortunes: The Political Economy of Place*. Berkeley, Calif: Univ. Calif. Press

Mayer, R., Shuster, T. 1985. *Developing Shelter Models for the Homeless: 3 Program Design Options*. New York: Community Serv. Soc. NY

Michael, D., Lachan, R., Thornbury, J. S. 1990. *Handouts for the DC-MADS Homeless and Transient Population Study*. Research Triangle Park, NC: Res. Triangle Inst.

Milburn, N. G. 1990. Drug abuse among homeless people. See Momeni 1990, pp. 61–80

Milburn, N. G., Watts, R. J. 1986. Methodological issues in research on the homeless and the homeless mentally ill. *Int. J. Mental Health* 14:42–60

Milhaly, L. 1991. Beyond the numbers: homeless families with children. See Kryder-Coeet al 1991, pp. 11–32

Miller, R. J. 1982. *The Demolition of Skid Row*. Lexington, Mass: Lexington, Books

Molnar, J., Rath, W. R., Klein, T. P., Lowe, C., Hartmann, A. H. 1991. *Ill Fares the Land: The Consequences of Homelessness and Chronic Poverty for Children and Families in New York City*. New York: Bank Street Coll. Educ.

Momeni, J. A. 1989. *Homelessness in the United States: State Surveys*. Westport, Conn: Greenwood

Momeni, J. A. 1990. *Homelessness in the United States: Data and Issues*. Westport, Conn: Greenwood

Mostoller, M. 1985. A single room: housing for the low-income person. See Birch, 1985b, pp. 191–216

Murie, A., Forrest, R. 1988. The new homeless in Britain. See Friedrichs 1988, pp. 129–46.

Newman, S. J., Schnare, A.B. 1988. *Subsidizing Shelter: The Relationship Between Welfare and Housing Assistance*. Washington, DC: Urban Inst. Press

Park, R. E., Burgess, E. W. 1967. *The City*. Chicago: Univ. Chicago Press

Patton, L. T. 1988. The rural homeless. In *Committee on Health Care for Homeless People, Homelessness, Health and Human Needs,* pp. 183–217. Washington, DC: Natl. Acad. Press

Piliavin, I., Sosin, M., Westerfelt, H., Matsueda, R. 1990. Conditions contributing to chronic homelessness: An exploratory study. Submitted

Redburn, F. S., Buss, T. 1986. *Responding to America's Homeless: Public Policy Alternatives*. New York: Praeger

Reyes, L. M., Waxman, L. 1987. *The Continuing Growth of Hunger, Homelessness and Poverty in America's Cities*. Washington, DC: US Conf. Mayors

Ringheim, K. 1990. *The structural determinants of homelessness: A study of 8 cities*. Presented at Annu. Meet. Am. Sociol. Assoc. August, Washington, DC

Ringheim, K. 1989. *Estimating a Population at Risk of Homelessness: The Roles of Income and Rental Housing Stock in Two Metropolitan Areas. Research Report No. 89–139* Ann Arbor, Mich:Popul. Stud. Ctr., Univ. Mich.

Ritzdorf, M. 1984. Strategies for reducing community fears of group homes in American municipalities. *Housing Soc.* 11:2

Robinson, F. G. 1985. *Homeless People in the Nation's Capital*. Washington, DC: Ctr. Appl. Res. Urban Policy, Univ. District of Columbia

Rondinelli, D. A. 1983. *Secondary Cities in Developing Countries: Policies for Diffusing Urbanization*. Beverly Hills, Calif: Sage

Rossi, P. H. 1989a. *Down and Out In America: The Origins of Homelessness*. Chicago: Univ. Chicago Press

Rossi, P. H. 1989b. *Homelessness in Amer-*

ica: Selected Topics. Amherst, Mass: Soc. Demogr. Res. Inst.

Rossi, P. H. 1988. Minorities and homelessness. In *Divided Opportunities: Minorities, Poverty and Social Policy*, ed. G. D. Sandefur, M. Tienda, pp. 87–115. New York: Plenum

Rossi, P.H. 1987. No good applied research goes unpunished. *Soc. Sci. Mod. Soc.* 25:73–80

Rossi, P. H., Fisher, G.A., Willis, G. 1986. *The Condition of the Homeless of Chicago*. Amherst, Mass: Soc. Demogr. Res. Inst.

Rossi, P. H., Wright, J. D. 1987. The determinants of homelessness. *Health Affairs* 6:19–32

Rossi, P. H., Wright, J. D., Fisher, G. S., Willis, G. 1987. The urban homeless: estimating composition and size. *Science* 235:1336–41

Ryan, P., Goldstein, I., Bartelt, D. 1989. *Homelessness in Pennsylvania: How Can This Be?* Philadelphia, Penn: Coalition on Homelessness in Penn.

Schorr, L. B., Schorr, D. 1988. *Within Our Reach: Breaking the Cycle of Disadvantage*. New York: Anchor

Schwartz, D. C., Glascock, J. H. 1989. *Combatting Homelessness: A Resource Book*. New Brunswick, NJ: Am. Affordable Housing Inst.

Shlay, A. B. 1986. Women, space and community: A feminist agenda. *Urban Resources* 3:1–4

Shlay, A. B. 1985a. Castles in the sky: Measuring housing and neighborhood ideology. *Environ. Behav.* 17:593–626

Shlay, A. B. 1985b. Taking apart the American dream: The influence of income and family composition on residential evaluations. *Urban Stud.* 23:253–70

Shlay, A. B., Rossi, P.H. 1981. Not In that neighborhood: Estimating net effects of zoning. *Am. Sociol. Rev.* 46:703–19

Sidel, R. 1986. *Women and Children Last: The Plight of Poor Women in Affluent America*. New York: Viking Penguin

Smith, N. 1985. Homelessness: Not one problem, but many. *J. Inst. Socioecon. Stud.* 10:53–67

Snow, D. A., Baker, S. G., Anderson, L., Martin, M. 1985. The myth of pervasive mental illness among the homeless. *Soc. Prob.* 33:407–23

Sosin, M. R., Colson, P., Grossman, S. 1988. *Homelessness in Chicago: Poverty and Pathology, Social Institutions and Social Change*. Chicago: Chicago Community Trust

Sosin, M. R., Piliavin, I., Westerfelt, H. 1990. Toward a a longitudinal analysis of homelessness. *J. Soc. Issues* 46:157–74

Stegman, M. A. 1991. Remedies for homelessness: An analysis of potential housing policy and program responses. See Kryder-Coe et al 1991, pp. 225–70

Stern, M. 1984. The emergence of the homeless as a public problem. *Soc. Serv. Rev.* 58:291–301

Stoner, M. 1983. The plight of homeless women. *Soc. Serv. Rev.* December:565–81

Sutherland, E. H., Locke, H. J. 1936. *Twenty Thousand Homeless Men*. Chicago: Lippincott

Swanstrom, T. 1989. No room at the inn: Housing policy and the homeless. *J. Urban Contemp. Law* 35:81–108

Tucker, W. 1990. *The Excluded Americans: Homelessness and Housing Policies*. Washington, DC: Regnery Gateway

US Dep. Housing & Urban Dev. 1989. *A Report on the 1988 National Survey of Shelters for the Homeless*. Washington, DC: US Off. Policy Dev. Res.

US Dep. Housing & Urban Dev. 1984. *A Report to the Secretary on the Homeless and Emergency Shelters*. Washington, DC: US Dep. Housing & Urban Dev. Off. Policy Dev. Res.

US General Accounting Office. 1989. *Children and Youths: About 68,000 Homeless and 186,000 in Shared Housing at Any Given Time*. Washington, DC: US Gen. Account. Off.

US General Accounting Office. 1985. *Homelessness: A Complex Problem and the Federal Response*. Washington, DC: US Gen. Account. Off.

van Vliet, W. 1989. Growth restrictions and affordable housing: dwellings versus people. See Friedrichs 1989, pp. 13–26

Wiegard, R. B. 1985. Counting the homeless. *Am. Demogr.* 7:34–37

Witkin, G. 1981. But not in my neighborhood. *Planning* 47:23–26

Wolch, J. R., Akita, A. 1989. The federal response to homelessness and its implications for American cities. *Urban Geogr.* 10:62–85

Wolch, J. R., Dear, M., Akita, A. 1988. Explaining homelessness. *J. Am. Plan. Assoc.* 54:443–53

Wolf, L. A. 1991. The welfare system's response to homelessness. See Kryder-Coe et al 1991, pp. 271–84

Wright, J. D. 1987. The national health care for the homeless program. See Bingham et al 1987, pp. 150–70

Wright, J.D. 1988a. The worthy and unworthy homeless. *Society* 25:64–69

Wright, J. D. 1988b. The mentally ill homeless: What is myth and what is fact? *Soc. Probl.* 35:182–91

Wright, J. D. 1989. *Address Unknown: Homelessness in Contemporary America*. Hawthorne, NY: Aldine de Gruyter

Wright, J. D., Lam, J. 1986. The low income housing supply and the problem of homelessness. *Soc. Policy* Fall

Wright, J. D., Rossi, P. H., Knight, J. W., Weber-Burdin, E., Tessler, R.C., et al. 1987. Homelessness and health: The effects of life style on physical well-being among homeless people in NYC. *Res. Soc. Probl. Public Policy* 4:(Spring)

Wright, J. D., Weber, E. 1987 *Homelessness and Health*. New York: McGraw Hill

Wright, J.D., Weber-Burdin, E., Knight, J., Lam, J. 1987. *The National Health Care for the Homeless Program: The First Year*. Amherst, Mass: Soc. Demogr. Res. Inst.

Zorbaugh, H. 1929. *The Gold Coast and the Slum*. Chicago: Univ. Chicago Press

Annu. Rev. Sociol. 1992. 18:161–85

GLOBAL STRUCTURES AND POLITICAL PROCESSES IN THE STUDY OF DOMESTIC POLITICAL CONFLICT

J. Craig Jenkins and Kurt Schock

Department of Sociology, The Ohio State University, Columbus, Ohio 43210

KEY WORDS: political violence, social conflict, political instability, revolution/rebellion, social movements

---

Abstract

The comparative study of domestic political conflict has experienced a paradigm shift with the replacement of theories emphasizing deprivation and system imbalance with theories of the political and structural sources of protest and rebellion. This review summarizes criticisms of the earlier theories, arguing that these have been subsumed by newer theories that focus on the relationships between political processes, the state, the capitalist world economy, the inter-state system and the origins and dynamics of social protest and political rebellion. We outline two useful approaches: a *political process* theory that emphasizes the impact of internal political institutions and processes, such as political exclusion, indigenous organization, and political opportunity structures; and theories of *global structures* that focus on the external or international processes of incorporation into the capitalist world economy, the social effects of foreign capital penetration, and political dependence on core states. Finally we examine the possibilities for constructing a synthetic theory of political conflict by treating these theories alternately in an

0732–0582/92/0410–0161$02.00

additive fashion or through specifying indirect effects. Problems of measurement and methodology are discussed, especially the importance of developing dynamic models of political conflict.

INTRODUCTION

In the past two decades, the comparative study of domestic political conflict has experienced a paradigm shift, with the rise of perspectives emphasizing the political and structural origins of social protest and political rebellion. Resource mobilization theory, rational choice models of collective action, political process theory, state-centric analyses of social revolutions, dependency, and world system interpretations of Third World rebellions have become the primary center of attention. At the same time, an older tradition of research guided by relative deprivation and system integration theories of grievances has reached an impasse; it lacks a coherent theoretical rationale that solves significant puzzles, it produces significant negative results, and its most interesting findings are better explained by these alternative approaches.

This review traces this shift of perspectives and recent comparative research on the sources of domestic political conflict. By domestic political conflict, we mean noninstitutionalized coercive or threatening interactions between citizens and states. Following Tilly's (1984) conception of national social movements as sustained interactions between challengers and states, we treat social movements insofar as they engage in sustained collective action. We distinguish two types of noninstitutionalized collective actions by citizens: social protests aimed at limited issues such as changing the policies of authorities or particular personnel; and rebellions dealing with fundamental issues such as who governs and what is the structure of authority. As Gurr (1989: 103) has argued, the former are generally nonviolent and may include legal means of action while the latter, because of their direct challenge to authorities, are disruptive and often entail violence. Because state repression is highly interactive with protest and rebellion, we treat it insofar as it is tied up with the broader conflict processes generated by challenges.

Past reviews have emphasized the clash between the grievance (or Deprived Actor) theories and resource mobilization (or Rational Actor) perspectives, looking for a series of critical tests that will resolve the dispute between these rival approaches (Eckstein 1980, Zimmermann 1980, Ramirez 1981, Lichbach 1989). We follow in this tradition insofar as we argue that the grievance theories have major logical and empirical shortcomings, and that their most interesting findings are better explained by the new political and structural approaches. However, we go beyond this traditional debate by examining the possible integration of the political process and global structural arguments. These perspectives share common assumptions about the inherency of conflict and the centrality of power in shaping domestic conflicts. They might therefore be seen as complementary perspectives, the political process theories dealing with the internal political processes within states that create challenges, while the global structure theories account for the external or global structures that create these internal structures and processes. Alternatively it might be that these are rival perspectives with quite different arguments about the nature of social protest and rebellion. The central question of this review, then, is, the feasibility of synthesizing these two approaches. Before embarking, however, we need to look briefly at what is to be explained.

HOW TO STUDY DOMESTIC CONFLICT: PROBLEMS OF MEASUREMENT AND METHOD

The conceptual distinction between protest and rebellion is essential for testing theories about the global distribution and characteristics of domestic conflict. It also has a strong basis in cross-national evidence about domestic conflict. Beginning with early exploratory factor analyses (Rummel 1966, Tanter 1965) through more recent validations (Banks 1972, Hibbs 1973), this distinction has held up. Under various labels (e.g. "turmoil," "protest"), the incidences of demonstrations, riots, boycotts, and political strikes have clustered together in particular countries and times, while armed attacks, attempted coups, assassinations, and political deaths ("internal war," "subversion," "rebellion") have found a common ground.

Recent analyses have drawn heavily on standardized data sets, especially *The World Handbook of Political and Social Indicators* (Taylor & Jodice 1983). These data are readily accessible and, treated with caution, produce reliable evidence about the global distribution and characteristics of domestic conflict. There are, however, significant limitations. The severe intercoder reliability problems with riots, for example, render this a questionable indicator. There are also questions of source reliability (i.e. newspaper-derived content analysis of events), which are probably more significant in earlier years and in Third World countries. For highly visible events such as successful coups and political deaths, these data appear to be sufficiently reliable (Snyder 1978, Jackman & Boyd 1979). Armed attacks, however, are probably underreported relative to political deaths, thereby favoring the latter as an index of rebellion (Weede 1981). Similarly, estimates of the incidence, size, and characteristics of protest demonstrations and governmental sanctions are less reliable. A preferable solution would be to use structural equation techniques to construct measures of underlying latent variables (Bollen 1989). This would build off the older tradition of factor analysis (e. g. Rummel 1966) and allow analysts to make explicit assumptions about the nature of errors in statistical models.

A major problem with past work has been the use of the sum of political deaths as an index of rebellion. Despite the fact that controls for target, actor, and issue have been available in the *World Handbook* data since 1968, most analysts have continued to use total deaths, failing to distinguish challenger from state-inflicted violence and thereby confusing rebellion with state repression (for a notable exception, see Boswell & Dixon 1990). Insofar as these correlate significantly (personal analyses), this may not be a major problem, but we really do not know the implications of this problem. The collective action tradition of analysis pioneered by Charles Tilly has been a major corrective in this respect, forcing analysts to clarify their units of analysis and the interaction of states with challengers over time.

Many studies have also dealt with the incidence of events rather than their features and have failed to normalize for population. If one is seeking to capture the intensity of protest or rebellion, the size and duration (or volume) of collective action is a more useful measure than simple incidence (Gurr & Duvall 1973, Shorter & Tilly 1974). Failing to normalize for population leaves one open to the possibility that the simple hazard of collective action is the major explanation. There are also statistical problems with highly skewed samples, especially with death estimates, that can be best dealt with by logging and establishing ceilings when appropriate. Cross-national analysts have also failed to check for influential outliers despite the availability of convenient outlier diagnostics (Bollen & Jackman 1985), leaving the stability of their inferences unclear.

There have also been significant methodological problems. Past work has largely been guided by cross-sectional methods, typically aggregated national attribute measures with a time lag between independent and dependent variables. Frequently these studies have adopted lagged panel designs (i. e. regression analysis in which an earlier panel of the dependent measure is introduced as a control variable in predicting a lagged panel of the dependent measure). This does not, however, actually tap temporal processes. It is also based on a less complete equation relative to change-score based designs (Hannan 1976). As well, it limits the focus to explaining the difference between conflicts in an earlier period and a later period. By regressing an earlier panel of the dependent measure against a later panel, the focus is effectively shifted from the global distribution of conflict to the shift (including error in meaurement) across panels. Finally, these aggregate measures largely fail to capture the subjective side of collective action, especially the intentions of challengers and the culture of social protest movements.

An alternative is the comparative-historical analysis of particular protests and groups, such as Walton's (1984) analysis of *Reluctant Rebels* or the national case studies of working class movements, assembled by Katznelson (1986). These provide a firm grounding in the specifics of particular protests and the institutional contexts in which struggles are carried out. They present, however, a major dilemma in terms of the trade-off between specificity and generality. Their richness can also be a barrier to generalization, identifying so many factors that it is difficult to specify those that are the most central and that are generalizable across cases. There is also a tendency to assume a deterministic notion of causation as opposed to a probabilistic one and to assume that single cases refute general theories.

A third alternative has been the collective action tradition pioneered by Charles Tilly and his collaborators. By combining social history methods with the quantitative analysis of trends in the collective action of specific groups or populations, this approach has the major virtue of capturing the goals of actors, the forms of contention, and their interactions with authorities over time with quantitative rigor. However, it shares the comparative-historical limitation of being able to deal simultaneously with only two or three settings. It also entails major costs in terms of collecting new data.

A fourth alternative which is yet to be fully explored is the use time-sensitive techniques, such as times-series analysis and event history methods, on conventional cross-national data. Aside from a few notable cases (e.g. Kowalewski 1991), these techniques have primarily been applied to single contexts (see Olzak 1989). With the increasing availability of longer time-series with cross-national data, these techniques for testing dynamic models will eventually become a major focus. Before these methodological innovations can catch hold, however, we need a firmer sense of the available theories.

SYSTEM INTEGRATION THEORIES: RELATIVE DEPRIVATION, SYSTEM IMBALANCES, AND UPROOTING

The dominant approaches in the past have been guided by a social integration assumption that societies and social units are normally integrated systems tied together by a common framework of values and sentiments. Political conflict is seen as "contingent" in the sense that the fundamental human disposition is assumed to be toward "peace," with social integration the norm (Eckstein 1980). Contingencies that create intense grievances or "strains" must occur to block this disposition before aggressive actions occur. Rapid, massive, and uneven social changes are typically identified as the source of these blockages, creating intense grievances that set off conflicts. Aggressive action is seen as affective rather than rationally calculated, and a close association between political aggression and individual deviance such as crime and suicide is typically assumed. Those who are the most deprived or frustrated, either in absolute terms or relative to their expectations, are the most likely to participate in political conflicts.

There have been three distinct formulations: an aggregate social psychological version centered on "just deserts" or relative deprivation (Olson 1963, Feierabend & Feierabend 1966, Davies 1969, Gurr 1970), a system imbalance thesis centering on the relationship between social mobilization and political institutionalization (Deutsch 1966, Huntington 1968), and a social uprooting hypothesis (Kornhauser 1959, Olson 1963, Eisenstadt 1966). Since the last approach has been thoroughly discredited on both logical and empirical grounds (Halebsky 1976, Zimmermann 1980:178–83, Rule 1988:91–118), we do not discuss it here.

Relative Deprivation

The relative deprivation hypothesis has received the most attention and has frequently been incorporated into the other formulations. The central idea is that the discrepancy between people's value capabilities and their value expectations (or "just deserts") creates frustrations that are "the necessary precondition for civil strife of any kind" (Gurr 1970: 596). This discrepancy has been traced to three major factors: (i) the J-curve of short-term drops in satisfactions (Davies 1969, Gurr 1970, Hibbs 1976), (ii) the strains of modernization stemming from a rising ratio of "want formation" to "want satisfaction" (Olson 1963, Feierabend & Feierabend 1966, Huntington 1968), and (iii) economic inequalities which either directly create envy and thereby frustrations (Russett 1964), expose people to the standards of others and thereby create grievances (Nagel 1974), or, if persistent and combined with slow growth or differential advancement, create discontents (Hirschman 1973). In the most sophisticated formulation, Gurr (1970) qualifies the effects of relative deprivation by including two additional steps: the politicization of that discontent based on the availability of normative and utilitarian justifications for violence, and its actualization in violent attacks on political targets as determined by the balance of coercion between regimes and dissidents.

Gurr (1968, 1969, 1970) and his collaborators (Gurr & Duvall 1973, Gurr & Lichbach 1979, 1986) have generated a series of cross-national analyses showing that short-term economic deprivations (or "stress"), as indicated by changing exports, inflation, and GNP growth, and persisting deprivations (or "strain"), as indicated by economic and political discrimination and potential separatism, have contributed to the intensity of conflict. These studies, however, have been faulted for a number of problems, the most important being: (i) the indirect measurement of deprivation based on objective circumstances such as declining exports or GNP, without demonstrating an actual gap between the subjective standards of "just deserts" and value abilities, (ii) possible ecological fallacies from using aggregate measures of both independent and dependent variables, especially when the theory specifies an individual level of analysis, (iii) the psychological reductionism stemming from attempting to explain collective action in terms of individual attitudes, (iv) the treatment of institutionalized political antagonisms, labelled "economic and political discrimination," as longstanding relative deprivation when they might be better conceptualized as political exclusion, and (v) the consistently stronger predictive power of political variables, such as the balance of coercion and political discrimination, over short-term relative deprivation (Hibbs 1973, Tilly 1975, Zimmermann 1983:62–72, Rule 1988:211–12). Of these, the last is ultimately the most condemning for it undercuts the central contention that relative deprivation is fundamental.

A second "strains of modernization" approach has similar problems. The Feierabends and their collaborators (Feierabend & Feierabend 1966, 1972, Feierabend et al 1969, 1970, also Huntington 1968) argued that increasing social mobilization (literacy, media exposure, education) combined with slow economic growth (caloric in-take, physicians, telephones) created a rising ratio of "want formation" to "want satisfactions." Political conflict, then, should have a curvilinear relationship to economic development, i.e. should be greater among mid-developed countries. They found, however, a linear negative relation, which has been borne out by subsequent research (Hardy 1979, Weede 1981). Their work also has the same problems with indirect measurement and ecological fallacies. Their index of instability was based on expert panel judgments rather than event analysis, which tapped the intensity but not the extent of conflicts (Synder 1976). They were also unprepared for one of their most interesting findings, a curvilinear effect of regime coercion, that indicated the centrality of political processes. Nor has Olson's (1963) argument about rapid growth been supported. Rapid growth is either irrelevant or gives rise to less conflict, while negative or stagnant growth is positively related (Zimmermann 1980:179–80, Muller & Weede 1990), suggesting absolute deprivation.

Several studies of the 1960s urban riots addressed the measurement gap by examining individuals, but the studies generally produced weak or negative results and typically focused on protest potential rather than actual behavior (McPhail 1971, Muller 1980). The most definitive research has been the work by Muller and his collaborators (Grofman & Muller 1973, Muller 1979, Muller & Jukam 1983) which used individual data to capture relative standards and actual participation. Muller, however, concluded that an alternative "expectations-value-norms" approach is more useful; this is one in which relative deprivation is a weak indirect factor, and the politicization of discontent in terms of regime legitimacy and utilitarian calculations are the central determinants.

A third focus involves the "economic inequality–political conflict nexus" (Lichbach 1989). Four versions of this "nexus" have drawn on relative deprivation ideas: (i) a simple linear model based on the greater envy of the poor and the greediness of the rich (Russett 1964, Sigelman & Simpson 1977, Park 1986, Muller & Seligson 1987), (ii) a curvilinear effect (or inverted V-curve) based on the psychological tendency to define standards based on those who are similarly positioned, thereby creating the greatest grievances at mid-levels of inequality (Nagel 1974), (iii) a positively accelerated effect based on the idea that inequality is a necessary but not sufficient condition for the mobilization of discontent and therefore shows only at higher levels (Muller 1985), and (iv) Hirschman's (1973) "tunnel effect" thesis that inequality is bearable so long as all are advancing at the same rate but, if advancement is slow and inequality persistent, it creates grievances. This last has been specified as a V-curve, i.e. that relative deprivation is greater at the higher and lower levels of inequality. It can also be specified in terms of a simple time lag between inequality and grievances and the combination of slow growth, blocked mobility, and persistent inequality.

The first proposition has received stronger support from studies using the top 20% share of personal and household income inequality (Park 1986, Muller & Seligson 1987) than from studies using Gini coefficients (Sigelman & Simpson 1977, Park 1986). Because the Gini coefficients better index the linear model and the top 20% share taps what Midlarsky (1988) has called "patterned inequality" (i.e. a bifurcated distribution of a small number of large holders and a large number of small holders), this is weak support. Hardy (1979) and Weede (1981, 1987) found that the amount of wealth to be distributed (or average income) eliminated the significance of income inequality, suggesting absolute deprivation. Others have found positive results using Gini indices of landholding inequality among less developed countries (Russett 1964, Tanter & Midlarsky 1967), which Muller & Seligson (1987) found to be relevant insofar as it explained income inequality.

The inverted V-curve hypothesis has not received support. Nagel (1974) found negative results for landholding inequality, and Sigelman & Simpson (1977) found negative effects for personal income inequality. As for the positively accelerated model, Muller (1985) found that a polynominal of the top 20% household income shares worked. This result, however, depended on controlling for violence in the prior panel and excluding two influential outliers, Panama & Zimbabwe (Weede 1986, Muller 1986). Moreover, the stronger predictors were political opportunity structures as based on governmental sanctions and an inverted U-curve of institutionalized political and civil rights.

Finally, Hirschman's (1973) "tunnel effect" thesis has been supported insofar as time lags between inequality and rebellion have worked better. But the positive V-curve was not supported by the work of Sigelman & Simpson (1977). The mobility and slow growth hypotheses have not been evaluated directly, but at best, they can be interpreted without necessarily referring to relative deprivation.

These studies have major measurement and conceptual problems. The samples have ranged from a handful of less developed countries to a maximum of 62 countries. Because of data limitations, the less developed countries have been underrepresented. Since several theories (e.g. Russett 1964) are formulated in terms of these, this is a major limitation. Ultimately, the dispute between the average-income and the inequality propositions can be resolved only with larger samples. Communist states also have been frequently excluded. There are in addition comparability problems such as adjusting personal income to capture the more relevant household income. The negative studies (e.g. Nagel 1974, Hardy 1979, Weede 1981) have used short time-frames (typically five-year panels) to measure rebellion. Inequality might take time to create grievances, requiring longer intervals and multiple panels (e.g. Muller 1985). Finally, relative deprivation theories have failed to address the arguments that inequalities directly create grievances (Paige 1975, Midlarsky 1988).

The logical and empirical status of relative deprivation theory is seriously in doubt. While the idea is intuitively appealing that some sense of injustice is a necessary aspect of rebellion (Moore 1978), it does not follow that this sense of injustice must be produced prior to collective action. Nor does it appear to be independent of the political processes and economic inequalities central to the alternative "contingency" or political process and global structures theories. Korpi (1974) has argued that a narrowing balance of power simultaneously creates relative deprivation among subordinates while also increasing the likelihood of successful rebellion. Similarly, McAdam (1982) has argued that political opportunities create a cognitive liberation which produces grievances while simultaneously creating mobilization. Relative deprivation can also be treated as a reward dimension for a rational actor model (Muller & Weede 1990). The class polarization thesis argues that bifurcated inequalities create alienation and thereby challenges (Paige 1975, Midlarsky 1988). In other words, relative deprivation may well be dispensable. At the minimum, if relative deprivation is critical, then it should be measured as directly as possible and shown to be independent of the political and structural processes that create conflicts.

System Imbalances

The system imbalance approach is inseparable from the system integration assumption. The underlying idea is that of a social system with a set of distinct subsystems that are structurally incompatible or "imbalanced." While several have quarreled with the empirical measurement of imbalances, the equilibrium assumption is an axiom rather than a testable hypothesis. As such, its importance lies in whether it can generate testable hypotheses that receive support. The major hypotheses have been posed in terms of the strains of modernization such as rapid urbanization and industrialization, or an imbalance of urbanization, educational growth, or media exposure with industrialization. None of these hypotheses, however, have received support (Hibbs 1973, Zimmermann 1983:105–108).

Attention has centered on Huntington's (1968) theory of a political participation crisis. Specifying a complex model in which social mobilization contributes (along with slow economic development and limited mobility opportunities) to political participation, the central idea is that political demands have outrun the capacities of the political system (which are assumed to change slowly), thereby spilling over into noninstitutionalized political action.

The theory centers attention on mobilization and the political incorporation of new groups. It has major conceptual and measurement problems, however. First, social mobilization is presented as unidimensional and holistic, although empirical studies have found it to be multidimensional and group-specific (Sigelman 1979). Institutionalization fares little better. Defined as the "adaptability, complexity, autonomy and coherence" of governmental institutions, the major indicators are actually measures of instability (e.g. the ratio of contested to total elite successions, the incidence of overt alienation). Finally, institutionalization has been found to reduce conflict, but the institutionalization/mobilization gap has not (Sigelman 1979, Sanders 1981). This, of course, can be interpreted as support for political opportunity arguments.

POLITICAL PROCESS THEORIES: RESOURCE MOBILIZATION, POLITICAL OPPORTUNITIES, AND WEAK REGIMES

The political process theories assume that conflicts are "inherent" in that actors are self-interested power maximizers who resort to conflicts when political circumstances are favorable (Eckstein 1980). By synthesizing rational actor models along with class conflict and political institution theories, these analysts have argued that collective action stems from political struggles over the entry of new groups and is determined by the mobilization of contenders and the structure of political opportunities.

In comparative analyses, the central arguments have revolved around Tilly's (1978) polity model. Polities are organized around a division between members with routine low-cost access and challengers who are excluded. Regimes are institutionalized rules that define who can claim "what, when and how." Members have a vested interest in keeping outsiders excluded, not only because of any direct conflicts but also because the entry of new groups raises the possibility of an alteration of regime rules and thereby the bases of their access. Challengers, by contrast, have an interest in altering rules to gain access and, under favorable opportunities, use unruliness to do so.

Political Exclusion

Excluded groups resort to unruliness because of their lack of access (Piven & Cloward 1977, Tilly 1978). The division between members and outsiders is a qualitative break with members resorting to unruliness only if threatened with a loss of access or a general realignment. The strongest support for this comes from Shorter & Tilly's (1974) analysis of French strikes and studies of the 1960s protest movements in the United States (McAdam 1982, Jenkins 1985). Similarly, protest and violence tend to form waves or cycles which cluster around generalized contentions over the entry of new groups, and violence tends to peak after regime realignments (Tilly et al 1975, Jenkins & Brents 1989, Tarrow 1989).

Some have argued, however, that political access is not a qualitative variable and that challenging groups may lack fixed political interests (Rule 1988: 193). While there is no single test for polity membership, one of strongest pieces of support comes from the consistent cross-national finding that separatist potential (mainly ethnically based) and political and economic discrimination determine the intensity of rebellions (Gurr 1968, Gurr & Duvall 1973, Gurr & Lichbach 1979, Boswell & Dixon 1990).

At the extreme of open regimes, the boundary may be fuzzy, but no regime is completely open. Historical studies have also found recurrent patterns of claims and forms of collective action, indicating persistence in the groups and interests at stake. There has been little research on member unruliness but, if the white supremacist response to the civil rights movement is typical (McAdam 1982:142–45), insider groups respond to threats to their claims with disruptive tactics. In this vein, Grant & Wallace (1991) show that weak polity members such as labor unions resort to violence once legal means of protest have been exhausted.

Interests, Resources, and Indigenous Organization

Some versions of resource mobilization theory have adopted the "extreme" position that grievances are a necessary but not sufficient condition for mobilization (McCarthy & Zald 1977). A more sophisticated approach has treated interests as structurally fixed and then allowed short-term events to alter the calculation of rewards. Paige (1975) argues that a zero-sum conflict stemming from agricultural production based on land and unskilled labor creates rebellion. Economic subsistence crises stimulate peasant rebellions (Scott 1976, Eckstein 1989). Short-term deprivations produced by sudden and dramatic impositions that can be blamed on external powers or exploitative elites then provoke mobilization, as Walton & Ragin (1990) found for austerity protests against IMF sanctions.

Challenges have to be mobilized, and mobilization rests on resources and organization. The autonomy and cohesion of peasant villages contributes to peasant mobilization (Wolf 1969, Skocpol 1979, Jenkins 1982). Urbanization has been linked to austerity protests (Walton 1989, Walton & Ragin 1990) and ethnic mobilization (Olzak & Nagel 1986). Similarly, rural-urban labor migration and the maintenance of interpersonal interregional ties has helped create rural-urban political coalitions in Third World rebellions (Walton 1984). Unionization and Communist Party membership have contributed to protest and rebellion (Hibbs 1973:130–31, Gurr & Lichbach 1979). Yet we know little about the organizational bases of protest, especially outside of Western democracies.

Organizers are also critical. Migdal (1974:232) argued that classical peasant revolts were spontaneously based on cohesive villages while contemporary peasant movements were organized by revolutionary leaders. What creates large numbers of organizers and allows them to develop institutionalized alliances with excluded groups? We have only a few promising ideas. Oberschall (1973:120–33) argued that segmental societies with sharp ethnic cleavages create pools of potential leaders as well as ethnic solidarities which can be mobilized. Concentrations of underemployed middle-class aspirants are often identified as a source of revolutionary leadership (Rejai 1980). Peripheral regions outside of state control provide "free zones" for revolutionary organizing (Wolf 1969, Goodwin & Skocpol 1989). Organizing strategies that emphasize tangible collective goods such as land redistribution, predictable marketing, and collective defense build institutionalized exchanges between organizers and peasant villages (Migdal 1974). Yet, overall, we have little comparative knowledge of the sources of leadership and the organizing strategies that mobilize large-scale challenges.

The Structure of Political Opportunities

The thesis of an inverted U-curve relationship between political opportunities and collective action has received considerable support. Initially advanced by Eisinger (1973) to explain black urban protest in terms of forms of city government, the basic logic is that in closed systems opportunities are restricted and challengers suppressed; in open systems, extensive opportunities eliminate the need for noninstitutionalized actions. Mixed systems with moderate opportunities, then, are most likely to experience unruliness. Similarly, the process of opening up opportunities encourages protests which, if confronted with repression, lead to rebellion. Tarrow (1988: 429–30) has distinguished five types of opportunities: institutional opportunities, the stability of coalitions and alignments, elite divisions and/or tolerance for protest, the presence of support groups and allies, and the policy-making capacities of states.

The inverted U-curve hypothesis has received consistent support from studies of institutionalized civil and political rights (labelled "regime repressiveness") (Muller 1985, Muller & Seligson 1987, Boswell & Dixon 1990, Muller & Weede 1990). The civil rights hypothesis captures the ability to mobilize independent of governmental controls, while the political rights hypothesis taps formal access to the state (and conversely exclusion) (Gastil 1989). Some have argued, however, that the Gastil indices tap capitalist property rights and commercial freedoms instead of political rights (Hartman & Hsiao 1988). While the scorings of several countries are questionable, the indices are strongly related to Bollen's (1983) democratization index (Bollen, personal communication) and, in the absence of better measures should continue to be used.

A second support is from Gurr's (1989:113–15) analysis of regimes. Distinguishing three types of regimes (democratic, autocratic, and elitist/neopatrimonial), the intensity of protest and rebellion is greatest in elitist systems, lower in democracies, and lowest in autocratic (bureaucratic-authoritarian and communist) states. Institutional opportunities also determine the form of collective action; democracies experience protests because of their openness, while autocracies and elitist regimes confront rebellions because of their relative closure.

A third base of evidence involves state repression. State repression raises the costs of collective action, but it also incites groups to challenge authorities. It can then be posed in either linear terms or as an inverted U-curve with the greater rebellion at midlevels of repression. Hibbs (1973:180–82) found a simultaneous linear relationship between the imposition of governmental sanctions and the incidence of protest and rebellion. Others have supported the inverted U-curve model (Gurr 19780, Lichbach & Gurr 1981, Muller & Weede 1990). Likewise, several have found support for the thesis that erratic and indiscriminate repression creates more intense rebellion (Zimmerman 1980:196–97, Lichbach 1987). Finally, the idea can be posed as a temporal process with extreme repression temporarily suppressing challenges but undermining the legitimacy of regimes, leading to revolutionary challengers once controls are relaxed (e.g. Iran and Nicaragua [Dix 1984]).

Several have argued that elite divisions and instability create opportunities for challengers, thereby spurring protests and rebellions (Piven & Cloward 1977, Skocpol 1979). Defining elites as those who occupy the command posts of the state, one can extend Tilly's (1978:213–15) ideas about divided governments in revolutionary situations to elite sponsorship of challengers. In liberal democratic regimes, closely fought electoral competition encouraged a center/left government to support the labor movement during the 1930s (Jenkins & Brents 1989) and the civil rights and farm worker movements in the 1960s (McAdam 1982, Jenkins 1985). Similarly, Kimmel (1988) has argued that elite divisions stemming from the fiscal crises of absolutist states explain the formation of revolutionary coalitions between the landowning nobility and political outsiders. Or divisions can simply weaken the repressive capacities of states, thereby opening the way for rebellions (Skocpol 1979). Divisions within the military and between military rulers and the upper classes in Latin American bureaucratic-authoritarian regimes have created member-challenger coalitions (Stepan 1985).

The idea that elite instability creates rebellion has received little cross-national attention. Coups have been treated as a result of rebellion. Yet, if elite cohesion and consensus on a formula for rule are conceived as independent factors, then elite instability might generate rebellion. McGowan (1975) found that elite instability in sub-Saharan Africa produced rebellion but not vice versa. In an analysis of a global sample, Schock (1990) found a simultaneous relationship between elite instability and political violence.

Elite instability is especially important in neopatrimonial regimes, such as those of the Shah of Iran, Samoza in Nicaragua, and Ferdinand Marcos in the Phillipines (Eisenstadt 1978, Goldstone 1986, Goodwin & Skocpol 1989). Power in these regimes is personally manipulated by dictatorial rulers, who, in contrast to bureaucratic-authoritarian regimes and communist states, block the formation of stable group or corporate prerogatives. Thus, the regimes fail to develop mass incorporating institutions, thereby alienating elite and middle class groups. They also tend to create corrupt and ineffective administrations which undermine state repressive capacities, produce erratic repression, and alienate foreign sponsors whose financial and political backing are critical bases of support.

The support group thesis extends this argument to polity members. Polity members who perceive major gains from bringing in new groups often act as sponsors. Liberal churches and labor unions were significant sponsors for the civil rights, farm worker, and women's movements during the 1960s (Freeman 1975, Morris 1984, Jenkins 1985). Similarly, the Catholic Church has become a direct sponsor of urban, labor, and broader democratization movements, using its claims to sacred authority to challenge autocratic regimes in Latin America, Spain, and Poland (Johnston & Figa 1988, Levine & Mainwaring 1989).

Finally, policy-making structures may determine opportunities. Kitschelt (1986) distinguishes between "input" structures that create opportunities for mobilization and moderate strategies and "output" structures that determine movement success. Comparing environmental movements in Western democracies, he argues that open input structures create strong, assimilative movements while strong output structures create major policy innovations.

Similarly, Gelb (1990) has applied this argument to the diverse experiences of feminist movements in Sweden, the United States, and Britain.

Some have argued that these political process theories lack a clear picture of the structural bases of power and conflict. The relationship between the upper classes and the state is not analyzed. Nor are states and their international contexts incorporated. This work has also centered on the Western democracies, providing a potentially biased basis for generalization. A healthy corrective, then, is to look at recent thinking about global structures and their impact on states and domestic conflicts, especially as they bear on Third World states.

GLOBAL STRUCTURES OF CONFLICT: DEPENDENCY, WORLD SYSTEM, AND GLOBAL HEGEMONY THEORIES

Dependency and world system theories are primarily analyses of the historical spread of capitalism and its structural effects on Third World countries. They also advance a distinctive analysis about the sources of domestic conflict in terms of the disruptive effects of capitalist incorporation and the class polarization created by economic and political dependency. They have been criticized for not granting sufficient independence to political factors and for overemphasizing international forces in explaining Third World social structures. We therefore highlight the points at which these global structural approaches can be supplemented by the internally oriented arguments of the political process theories and by analysis of inter-state political relations.

The central idea is that of a qualitative divergence between the wealthy and powerful *core* states that were early centers of capitalist development and the impoverished and weak *peripheral* states that were colonized and incorporated into the world economy by these states. This is both an historical argument and a thesis about contemporary global inequality. The core benefits from international trade and investment, experiencing sufficient economic growth and use of advanced labor controls to regulate class conflict, while the periphery experiences class polarization because of the coercive labor controls and the social distortions produced by economic dependence and external domination. Political institutions reflect this global division of labor; strong democratic states are typical of the core while weak authoritarian and elitist states typically are in the periphery. A set of *semiperipheral* states are also identified that have experienced significant externally linked industrialization, combining forms of labor control and developing larger if not stronger states (Wallerstein 1979, Evans 1979). While there is some dispute about whether rebellion is greater in the periphery or the semiperiphery, both are more polarized and thereby rebellious than the core.

Capitalist Incorporation: Terms and Timing

The thesis that incorporation into the capitalist world economy sets off rebellions has been applied historically to the peasant wars and revolutionary contests of the sixteenth through the nineteenth centuries and to contemporary rebellions in the Third World. Two theses have been advanced: resistance against capitalist intrusion by peasants and indigenous peoples to the transformation of land rights, commercialization and the imposition of coercive labor (Wolf 1969, Wallerstein 1974, 1989, Scott 1976, Walton 1984), and class polarization stemming from contemporary economic and political dependence (Paige 1975, Timberlake & Williams 1987, Walton & Ragin 1990, Boswell & Dixon 1990).

The intrusion argument centers on the disruption created by the historical growth of production for the international market. Capitalist incorporation entailed the commercialization of land, the imposition of coercive labor such as slavery and the hacienda, and the elimination of independent subsistence means among peasants and indigenous peoples. Closely connected to these was the development of colonialism and mercantilist policies designed to consolidate the dominance of core states over their peripheral regions. These impositions threatened the traditional autonomy and subsistence claims of these populations, provoking rebellion.

The polarization thesis has been applied to contemporary rebellions. Third World societies are characterized by patterned inequality, which is rooted in colonial heritage and persisting dependence on foreign capital and trade. Economic dependence creates the social distortions of widening inequality, slow economic growth and a stagnant quality of life, tertiarization of the labor force, and overurbanization. It also increases the mobilization potential of the lower classes and creates upper class and elite divisions while simultaneously weakening the legitimacy of the state and its ability to control oppositions through exclusionary and repressive means.

Dependence, Distorted Development and Class Polarization

The simplest version of the polarization thesis centers on export agriculture. Paige (1975) argues that the development of export enclaves and the decline of imperialist controls has created the seed bed for revolutionary nationalism. Advancing a theory of agrarian class conflict, he argues that export agriculture entails a zero-sum conflict between landowners and workers which creates rebellion. If the lower class lacks cohesion (i.e. hacienda system), it engages in erratic revolt, if cohesive (i.e. migratory labor estates and plantations), sustained revolutionary nationalism emerges. This thesis has been criticized as class reductionist (Skocpol 1982, Jenkins 1983), but it does include a theory of mobilization based on class structures and of opportunities based on decolonization. The problem is that it assumes a constant relation among these factors rather than demonstrating it.

A more complex version centers on persisting colonial trade patterns and the "associated-dependent development" created by transnational corporate investments and debt. Export dependency stemming from the export of unprocessed primary products, commodity concentration, and limited numbers of trade partners creates slower growth and a lower quality of life (Delacroix & Ragin 1981, Dixon 1984, Jaffee 1985). It also contributes to increased inequality, especially where tied to a bifurcated landholding system (Rubinson 1976, Bornschier & Ballmer-Cao 1979). Because of its connections to foreign investments in large-scale agriculture, export dependence displaces smallholders and subsistence producers and typically provides fewer employment opportunities, thereby producing overurbanization (Bradshaw 1987).

Industrialization based on foreign investment and loans has similar effects. Transnational investments create capital-intensive production that employs small numbers of high-paid workers, thereby creating inequality and absorbing less labor. Investments in agriculture and extractive industry displace smallholders and subsistence producers, forcing them into the informal sector and tertiary employment (Evans & Timberlake 1980, Timberlake & Kentor 1983, London 1987). Foreign investment creates slower growth, reduced quality of life (including higher infant mortality), increased inequality and thereby provokes domestic rebellion (Bornschier & Chase-Dunn 1985, Williams & Timberlake, 1984, London & Williams 1988, Wimberly 1990, Robinson & London 1991). Finally, foreign indebtedness generally reduces growth and quality of life (Sell & Kunitz 1987), except in capital-starved Africa where it has short-term positive effects (Bradshaw & Wahl 1991). Its effects on inequality are unclear, but insofar as debt is linked to transnational investments and strong states, it should create greater asset concentration.

These distortions simultaneously create greater hardship and mobilization potential, thereby producing class polarization. Landholding and income inequality are sources of Third World rebellion (Timberlake & Williams 1987, Boswell & Dixon 1990). Rapid urbanization and overurbanization create greater mobilization potential, facilitating the formation of unions, churches, and neighborhood groups which mobilize protests and rebellions (Eckstein 1989, Walton & Ragin 1990).

Exclusionary, Semi-Repressive, and Divided Regimes

Does dependence also create the political opportunities for rebellion in terms of exclusionary, semi-repressive regimes with a divided upper class and elite? Several have argued that dependence weakens the state in terms of its penetration of the domestic economy, undermines its legitimacy, and reduces its international autonomy (Wallerstein 1974). It creates a political division between a comprador bourgeoisie committed to strengthening dependency and a national bourgeoisie supporting "closed door" national development (Walton 1984, Boswell 1985). This split prevents the formation of a hegemonic bloc that effectively addresses economic problems, such as the debt crisis (Walton 1989). It also creates neopatrimonial elitist regimes which lack incorporating institutions and rely on erratic repression to control oppositions. This pattern would seem to make a peripheral state more volatile.

A second view is that transnational investments and debt require a strong state and that, by creating a triple alliance between transnational capital, state managers, and a national bourgeoisie, they reinforce the growth and potential autonomy of the state (Evans 1979). Bureaucratic-authoritarian regimes with their stronger fiscal capacities and centralized structures are less vulnerable to upper class and elite divisions and have sufficient repressive means to control oppositions. They also have sufficient international autonomy to claim greater legitimacy. At the same time, however, centralized power and accepted responsibility for economic development make the state a highly visible target for blame, e.g. the austerity measures adopted in response to the debt crisis (Walton & Ragin 1990). State growth also creates a potential middle-class opposition among government workers. Exclusionary policies against labor unions politicize labor conflict, thereby creating a rebellious clash with the skilled workers of the larger enterprises. Finally, these states also temper their exclusionary policies by promoting corporatist unions, neighborhood associations, and political clubs, thereby placing them in the middle range of institutional opportunities. These features seem to make the semiperiphery more volatile.

These ideas have received some support from cross-national analyses. A central debate has been whether economic dependence *directly* provokes rebellion or works *indirectly* through distorting internal social structures. Timberlake & Williams (1984) found moderate negative effects of transnational penetration on institutional opportunities (labelled "exclusion") and thereby indirectly on governmental repression. They did not, however, examine the inverted U-curve opportunity models. They also found that inequality creates repression via reducing opportunities (Williams & Timberlake 1984). And they showed that the semiperiphery and periphery were more prone to rebellion (Timberlake & Williams 1987). Bradshaw (1985) found that transnational penetration created state growth in sub-Saharan Africa, thereby creating protest, but that inequality was not independently significant. Similarly, London & Robinson (1989) found that transnational investment created rebellion directly but inequality did not. Boswell & Dixon (1990), however, found support for the distortion thesis with transnational penetration, export agriculture and semiperipheral position reducing economic growth and increasing inequality and thereby indirectly producing rebellion. Finally, Robinson & London (1991) reversed their earlier conclusions, finding support for both direct and indirect (via inequality) effects of foreign investment.

These studies, however, have only begun to examine the effects of economic dependence. We know little about the distribution of assets in urban areas, nor do we know much about urban mobilization processes. Elite divisions have been largely neglected. Significantly, no one has devised a set of comparative measures of political exclusion that is distinct from institutional opportunities.

Finally, a major gap in our knowledge is the role of ethnic nationalism, which frequently creates polarization more powerful than class inequality. While several have emphasized the importance of nationalist mobilization in anticolonial revolts, this does not account for the incidence of ethnically based conflicts. Ethnic conflicts are a major source of violence in the Middle East, Africa, and Asia (von der Mehdan 1973: 17), but we have little comparative work on the sources of these conflicts. Many are commmunal attacks on other groups, partially stemming from colonial tensions but also from political and economic competition in the postcolonial states (Olzak & Nagel 1986). Others are more organized challenges, such as secessionist movements and bids for regional autonomy. To date, these have not been as systematically studied if only because of the difficulty of data collection and comparative analysis.

Political Dependence and Global Hegemony

A final contention has centered on the autonomy and significance of political dependence. Skocpol (1979) has argued that the inter-state system is autonomous of the world capitalist economy, creating regime crises and foreign interventions that lead to revolutionary situations. Similarly, international relations theorists (Gilpin 1987, Keohane 1984) have advanced global hegemony theories positing that stability in the capitalist world economy depends on the existence of a hegemonic state which provides an international currency and opens markets, and secondly, that such hegemony is inherently self-limiting, giving rise to long wave cycles of stability in international regimes. In terms of predicting rebellion, these theories offer several useful ideas. First, foreign military interventions (including war losses) have frequently stimulated domestic challlenges by weakening repressive capacities, intensifying domestic tensions and the sponsorship of domestic insurgencies (Small & Singer 1982). Second, the likelihood of core state intervention against peripheral revolts is increased by instability in the inter-state system as well as by stagnation in the world economy (Kowalewski 1991). A final idea pertains to the political dependence of Third World states on foreign providers of armaments. Boswell & Dixon (1990) found that the greater the vulnerability of Third World states based on arms supply concentration, the greater the likelihood of rebellion. While these aspects of political dependence are generally associated with economic dependence, they represent a distinctive factor in Third World rebellions and reinforce the idea that inter-state political relations are autonomous from global economic structures.

CONCLUSION: A SYNTHETIC THEORY OF CONFLICT

We have argued that the traditional system integration approaches have reached an impasse, lacking a coherent theoretical rationale and a unique set of empirical puzzles that they can successfully address. Its most interesting findings—the effects of inequality, short-term deprivations, separatist potential, struggles over political incorporation and state strength—can be better explained by alternative power struggle approaches that integrate the political process and global structures theories. These approaches share the assumption that conflict is inherent and that power structures are the central determinants of domestic conflicts. Their explanatory focus, however, has been quite different. The political process theories have emphasized the internal or domestic political processes that give rise to collective action and state repression, while the global approaches have dealt with external or international forces that shape domestic social structures and political institutions. The political theories have been used to account for the domestication of political contention in the Western democracies, while the latter have generally dealt with Third World rebellion and revolutionary transformations.

Several have argued that these theories, then, should be treated as complementary. Some have argued for this integration on conceptual grounds (Kick 1980, Walton 1984, Eckstein 1989) while others have relied on cross-national quantitative analyses (Walton & Ragin 1990, Boswell & Dixon 1990, Robinson & London 1991). Such a synthesis might be seen as addressing the weaknesses of these theories while it builds on their strengths. The political process approaches have lacked a clear conception of the state and its relationship to dominant classes and to the international environment. Their strength has been in accounting for collective action in terms of the mobilization of specific groups and the changing structure of political opportunities. The global structure theories have been criticized for their reductionist tendencies. These theorists have relied on structural explanations in terms of world capitalism and international hegemony but lacked a conception of political agency. Their strong suit has been explaining class polarization in the Third World or the vulnerability of weaker states to the world powers.

The best strategy for constructing such a synthesis is to assume that the state is potentially autonomous in the sense that it is an independent force in political struggles and that political choices are structurally constrained but not determined by the global economy and inter-state system. Some have argued for an additive synthesis in which political and global explanations are treated simultaneously as explanations of domestic conflict (Walton & Ragin 1990). Others have assumed that global structures work indirectly through domestic institutions and processes, thereby determining conflicts (Boswell & Dixon 1990, Robinson & London 1991). The evidence favors the latter point of view. Moreover, this strategy offers the promise of leaving the question open to further research, thereby encouraging researchers to clarify the interaction between global structures and domestic processes.

A longstanding tension has existed between comparative case methods, frequently used to support political process arguments, and cross-national methods, which have typically been used to support global structure arguments. This, however, is a product of our limited evidence and imagination in devising new analyses, not of the methods themselves. There is no logical reason why global structures cannot be brought into comparative-historical analyses (e.g. Walton 1984) or that political processes cannot be captured with cross-national methods (e.g. Aflatooni & Allen 1991). We need stronger evidence from comparative historical studies about how the constraints of the global economy and the inter-state system constrain domestic structures and processes. We also need better indicators of political processes, such as elite divisions and regime types, and a serious treatment of temporal processes such as political opportunities and protest cycles in cross-national studies.

A huge empirical gap currently limits our understanding of ethnic antagonisms. These constitute a major source of domestic protests and rebellions throughout the world. While class explanations help clarify these antagonisms in colonial and postcolonial settings, they are not sufficient. Ethnic stratification not only interfaces with class inequality in complex ways but may well be inherently more polarizing than economic antagonisms. This is a topic that deserves major attention.

The significance of global politics and its relationship with the capitalist world economy is likely to remain an open and complex question. States are independent actors with their own institutional heritages, mobilization capacities, and strategies. At the same time, they are buffeted by the winds of international economic change and shaped by the rivalries and alliances in the inter-state system. Rather than attempting to resolve this conceptual tension by metatheoretical assertion, we favor an eclectic approach that leaves open for investigation the extent to which state institutions, inter-state rivalries, and foreign military interventions that produce Third World rebellions can be explained by global economic as opposed to political structures. We seem to have developed a clearer theoretical sense of how to explain domestic conflicts. Now we need to get on with the hard work of actually analyzing the processes that generate protest and rebellion.

ACKNOWLEDGMENTS

We benefitted greatly by the comments of York Bradshaw, Mark Lichbach, Peter Evans, and Chuck Tilly, as well as by the financial support of the National Science Foundation SES-9113820.

Literature Cited

Aflatooni, A., Allen, M. P. 1991. Government sanctions and collective political protest in periphery and semiperiphery states. *J. Polit. Milit. Sociol.* 19:1–28

Banks, A. S. 1972. Patterns of domestic conflict: 1919–39 and 1946–66. *J. Confl. Resolut.* 16:41–50

Bollen, K. A. 1983. World system position, dependence, and democracy: the cross-national evidence. *Am. Sociol. Rev.* 48:468–79

Bollen, K. A. 1989. *Structural Equations with Latent Variables*. New York: Wiley

Bollen, K. A., Jackman, R. W. 1985. Regression diagnostics. *Sociol. Methods Res.* 13:510–42

Bornschier, V., Ballmer-Cao, T. 1979. Income inequality: a cross-national study of the relationships between MNC-penetration, dimensions of the power structure and income distribution. *Am. Sociol. Rev.* 44:487–506

Bornschier, V., Chase-Dunn, C. 1985. *Transnational Corporations and Underdevelopment*. New York: Praeger

Boswell, T. E. 1985. The utility of world-system theory for explaining social revolutions: a comparison of Skocpol and Lenin. *Calif. Soc.* 8:19–37

Boswell, T., Dixon, W. J. 1990. Dependency and rebellion: a cross-national analysis. *Am. Sociol. Rev.* 55:540–59

Bradshaw, Y. W. 1985. Dependent development in black Africa: a cross-national study. *Am. Sociol. Rev.* 50:195–207

Bradshaw, Y. W. 1987. Urbanization and underdevelopment: a global study of modernization, urban bias and economic dependency. *Am. Sociol. Rev.* 52:224–39

Bradshaw, Y. W., Wahl, A. 1991. Foreign debt expansion, the International Monetary Fund and regional variation in Third World poverty. *Int. Stud. Q.* 35:251–72

Davies, J. C. 1969. The J-curve of rising and declining satisfactions as a cause of some great revolutions and a contained rebellion. See Graham & Gurr 1969, pp. 690–730

Delacroix, J., Ragin, C. 1981. Structural blockage. *Am. J. Soc.* 86:1311–47

Deutsch, K. 1966. *The Nerves of Government*. New York: Free Press

Dix, R. H. 1984. Why revolutions succeed and fail. *Polity* 26:423–46

Dixon, W. J. 1984. Trade concentration, economic growth and the provision of basic human needs. *Soc. Sci. Q.* 65:761–74

Eckstein, H. 1980. Theoretical approaches to explaining collective political violence. See Gurr 1980, pp. 135–66

Eckstein, S., ed. 1989. *Power and Popular Protest*. Berkeley: Univ. Calif. Press

Eisenstadt, S. N. 1966. *Modernization*. Englewood Cliffs: Prentice-Hall

Eisenstadt, S. N. 1978. *Revolutions and the Transformation of Societies*. New York: Free Press

Eisinger, P. 1973. The conditions of protest behavior in American cities. *Am. Polit. Sci. Rev.* 67:11–28

Evans, P. 1979. *Dependent Development*. Princeton: Princeton Univ. Press

Evans, P., Timberlake, M. 1980. Dependence, inequality, and the growth of the tertiary: a comparative analysis of less developed countries. *Am. Sociol. Rev.* 45:531–52

Feiereabend, I. K., Feierabend, R. L. 1966. Aggressive behaviors within polities, 1948–1962: a cross-national study. *J. Confl. Resolut.* 10:249–71

Feierabend, I. K., Feierabend, R. L., Nesvold, B. A. 1969. Social change and political violence: cross-national patterns. See Graham & Gurr 1969, pp. 632–87

Feierabend, I. K., Nesvold, B. A., Feierabend, R. L. 1970. Political coerciveness and turmoil. *Law Soc. Rev.* 5:93–118

Feierabend, I. K., Feierabend, R. L. 1972. Systemic conditions of political aggression: an application of frustration-agression theory. See Feierabend et al 1972, pp. 136–83

Feierabend, I. K., Feierabend, R. L., Gurr, T. R., eds. 1972. *Anger, Violence, and Politics*. Englewood Cliffs: Prentice-Hall

Freeman, J. 1975. *The Politics of Women's Liberation*. New York: McKay

Gastil, R. D. 1989. *Freedom in the World*. New York: Freedom House

Gelb, J. 1990. Feminism and political action. In *Challenging the Political Order*, ed. R. J. Dalton, M. Kuechler, pp. 137–54. New York: Oxford Univ. Press

Gilpin, R. 1987. *The Political Economy of International Relations*. Princeton, NJ: Princeton Univ. Press

Goldstone, J. 1986. Revolutions and Superpowers. In *Superpowers and Revolutions*, ed. J. R. Adelman, pp. 38–48. New York: Praeger

Goodwin, J., Skocpol, T. 1989. Explaining revolutions in the contemporary third world. *Polit. Soc.* 17:489–509

Graham, H. D., Gurr, T. R., eds. 1969. *Violence in America*. New York: Praeger

Grant, D. S., Wallace, M. 1991. Why do strikes turn violent? *Am. J. Sociol.* 96:1117–50

Grofman, B. N., Muller, E. N. 1973. The strange case of relative gratification and potential for political violence: the V-curve hypothesis. *Am. Polit. Sci. Rev.* 57:514–39

Gurr, T. R. 1968. A causal model of civil strife: a comparative analysis using new indices. *Am. Polit. Sci. Rev.* 62:1104–24

Gurr, T. R. 1969. A comparative study of civil strife. See Graham & Gurr 1969, pp. 572–632

Gurr, T. R. 1970. *Why Men Rebel*. Princeton: Princeton Univ. Press

Gurr, T. R., ed. 1980. *Handbook of Political Conflict*. New York: Free Press

Gurr, T. R. 1989. Protest and rebellion in the 1960s: the United States in world perspective. In *Violence in America,* ed. T. R. Gurr, 2:101–30. Newbury Park: Sage

Gurr, T. R., Duvall, R. D. 1973. Civil conflict in the 1960s: a reciprocal theoretical system with parameter estimates. *Comp. Polit. Stud.* 6:135–69

Gurr, T. R., Lichbach, M. I. 1979. A forecasting model for political conflict within nations. In *To Auger Well,* ed. J. D. Singer, M. D. Wallace, pp. 153–93. Beverly Hills: Sage

Gurr, T. R., Lichbach, M. I. 1986. Forecasting internal conflict: a competitive evaluation of empirical theories. *Comp. Polit. Stud.* 19:3–36

Halebsky, S. 1976. *Mass Society and Political Conflict*. Cambridge: Cambridge Univ. Press

Hannan, M. T. 1976. Issues in panel analysis of national development. In *National Development and the World System,* ed. M. T. Hannan, J. Mayer, pp. 17–33. Univ. Chicago.

Hardy, M. A. 1979. Economic growth, distributional inequality, and political conflict in industrial societies. *J. Polit. Milit. Soc.* 7:209–27

Hartman, J., Hsiao, W. 1988. Inequality and violence: issues of theory and measurement in Muller. *Am. Sociol. Rev.* 53:794–99

Hibbs, D. 1973. *Mass Political Violence*. New York: Wiley

Hibbs, D. A. Jr. 1976. Industrial conflict in advanced industrial societies. *Am. Polit. Sci. Rev.* 70:1033–58

Hirschman, A. 0. 1973. The changing tolerance for income inequality in the course of economic development. *Q. J. Econ.* 87:544–66

Huntington, S. 1968. *Political Order in Changing Societies*. New Haven: Yale Univ. Press

Jackman, R. W., Boyd, W. A. 1979. Multiple sources in the collection of data on political conflict. *Am. J. Polit. Sci.* 23:434–58

Jaffe, D. 1985. Export dependence and economic growth: a reformulation and respecification. *Soc. Forces* 64:102–18

Jenkins, J. C. 1983. Why do peasants rebel? Structural and historical theories of modern peasant rebellions. *Am. J. Soc.* 88:487–514

Jenkins, J. C. 1985. *The Politics of Insurgency*. New York: Columbia Univ. Press

Jenkins, J. C., Brents, B. 1989. Social protest, hegemonic competition and social reform. *Am. Sociol. Rev.* 54:891–910

Johnston, H., Figa, J. 1988. The church and political opposition: comparative perspectives on mobilization against authoritarian regimes. *J. Sci. Stud. Relig.* 7:32–47

Katznelson, I. 1986. *Working Class Formation*. Princeton, NJ: Princeton Univ.Press

Keohane, R. 1984. *After Hegemony*. Princeton, NJ: Princeton Univ. Press

Kick, E. L. 1980. World system properties and mass political conflict within nations: theoretical framework. *J. Polit. Milit. Soc.* 8:175–90

Kimmel, M. S. 1988. *Absolutism and its Discontents*. New Brunswick: Transaction

Kitschelt, H. 1986. Political opportunity structures and political protest: anti-nuclear movements in four democracies. *Br. J. Polit. Sci.* 16:57–85

Kornhauser, W. 1959. *The Politics of Mass Society*. New York: Free Press

Korpi, W. 1974. Conflict, power, and relative deprivation. *Am. Polit. Sci. Rev.* 68:1569–78

Kowalewski, D. 1991. Core intervention and periphery revolution, 1821–1985. *Am. J. Sociol.* 97:70–95

Levine, D. H., Mainwaring, S. 1989. Religion and popular protest in Latin America: contrasting experiences. See Eckstein 1989, pp. 203–40

Lichbach, M. I. 1987. Deterrence or escalation? The puzzle of aggregate studies of repression and dissent. *J. Confl. Resolut.* 31:266–97

Lichbach, M. I. 1989. An evaluation of "Does economic inequality breed political conflict?". *Stud. World Polit.* 41:431–70

London, B. 1987. Structural determinants of third world urban change: an ecological and political economic analysis. *Am. Sociol. Rev.* 52:28–43

London, B., Williams, K. 1988. Multinational corporate penetration, protest, and basic needs provision in non-core nations: a cross-national analysis. *Soc. Forces* 66: 747–73

London, B., Robinson, T. D. 1989. The effect of international dependence on income inequality and political violence. *Am. Sociol. Rev.* 54:305–7

McAdam, D. 1982. *Political Process and the Development of Black Insurgency, 1930–1970*. Chicago: Univ. Chicago Press

McCarthy, J. D., Zald, M. N. 1977. Resource mobilization and social movements: a partial theory. *Am. J. Soc.* 82:1212–41

McGowan, P. 1975. Predicting instability in tropical Africa. In *Quantitative Analysis in*

Foreign Policy and Forecasting, ed. M. K. O'Leary, W. D. Coplin, pp. 35–78. New York: Praeger

McPhail, C. 1971. Civil disorder participation: a critical examination of recent research. *Am. Sociol. Rev.* 36:1058–73

Midlarsky, M. I. 1988. Rulers and ruled: patterned inequality and the onset of mass political conflict. *Am. Polit. Sci. Rev.* 82:429–509

Migdal, J. S. 1974. *Peasants, Politics, and Revolution.* Princeton, NJ: Princeton Univ. Press

Moore, B. 1978. *Injustice.* New York: Sharpe

Morris, A. 1984. *The Origins of the Civil Rights Movement.* New York: Free Press

Muller, E. N. 1979. *Aggressive Political Participation.* Princeton: Princeton Univ. Press

Muller, E. N. 1980. The psychology of political protest and violence. See Gurr 1980, pp. 69–99

Muller, E. N. 1985. Income inequality, regime repressiveness, and political violence. *Am. Sociol. Rev.* 51:47–61

Muller, E. N. 1986. Income inequality and political violence: the effect of influential cases. *Am. Sociol. Rev.* 51:441–45

Muller, E. N., Jukam, T. 0. 1983. Discontent and aggressive political behavior *Br. J. Polit. Sci.* 13:159–79

Muller, E. N., Seligson, M. A. 1987. Inequality and insurgency. *Am. Polit. Sci. Rev.* 81:425–51

Muller, E. N., Weede, E. 1990. Cross-national variation in political violence: a rational actor approach. *J. Confl. Resolut.* 34:624–51

Nagel, J. 1974. Inequality and discontent: a non-linear hypothesis. *World Polit.* 26:453–72

Oberschall, A. 1973. *Social Conflict and Social Movements.* Englewood Cliffs: Prentice-Hall

Olson, M. Jr. 1963. Rapid growth as a destabilizing force. *J. Econ. Hist.* 23:529–52

Olzak, S., Nagel, J. 1986. *Competitive Ethnic Relations.* New York: Academic

Olzak, S. 1989. Analysis of events in the study of collective action. *Annu. Rev. Sociol.* 15:119–41

Paige, J. 1975. *Agrarian Revolutions.* New York: Free Press

Park, K. H. 1986. Reexamination of the linkage between income inequality and political violence. *J. Polit. Milit. Soc.* 14:185–97

Piven, F. F., Cloward, R. A. 1977. *Poor People's Movements.* New York: Pantheon

Ramirez, F. 0. 1981. Comparative social movements. *Int. J. Comp. Soc.* 22:3–21

Rejai, M. 1980. Theory and research in the study of revolutionary personnel. See Gurr 1980, pp. 100–31

Robinson, T. D., London, B. 1991. Dependency, inequality, and political violence. *J. Polit. Milit. Sociol.* 19:119–56

Rubinson, R. 1976. The world-economy and the distribution of income within states: a cross-national study. *Am. Sociol. Rev.* 41:638–59

Rule, J. B. 1988. *Theories of Civil Violence.* Berkeley: Univ. Calif. Press

Rummel, R. J. 1966. Dimensions of conflict behavior within nations, 1946–59. *J. Confl. Resolut.* 10:65–73

Russett, B. M. 1964. Inequality and instability: the relation of land tenure to politics. *World Polit.* 16:442–54

Sanders, D. 1981. *Patterns of Political Instability.* New York: Macmillan

Schock, K. 1990. *Resource mobilization and world system/dependency theories of political violence: an integrated cross-national analysis.* MA thesis. Ohio State Univ., Columbus

Scott, J. C. 1976. *The Moral Economy of the Peasant.* New Haven: Yale Univ. Press

Sell, R. W., Kunitz, S. J. 1986. The debt crisis and the end of an era in mortality decline. *Stud. Comp. Int. Dev.* 21:3–30

Shorter, E., Tilly, C. 1974. *Strikes in France.* New York: Cambridge Univ. Press

Sigelman, L. 1979. Understanding political instability: an evaluation of the mobilization-institutionalization approach. *Comp. Polit. Stud.* 12:205–28

Sigelman, L., Simpson, M. 1977. A cross-national test of the linkage between economic inequality and political violence. *J. Confl. Resolut.* 21:105–28

Skocpol, T. 1979. *States and Social Revolutions.* New York: Cambridge Univ. Press

Skocpol, T. 1982. What makes peasants revolutionary? In *Power and Protest in the Countryside,* ed. R. P. Weller, S. E. Guggenheim, pp. 157–79. Durham: Duke Univ. Press

Small, M., Singer, J. D. 1982. *Resort to Arms.* Beverly Hills: Sage

Snyder, D. 1976. Theoretical and methodological problems in the analysis of governmental coercion and collective violence. *J. Polit. Milit. Soc.* 4:277–93

Snyder, D. 1978. Collective violence. *J. Confl. Resolut.* 22:499–534

Snyder, D., Kick, E. L. 1979. Structural position in the world system and economic growth, 1955–1970. *Am. J. Soc.* 84:1096–26

Stepan, A. 1985. State power and the strength of civil society in the southern cone of Latin America. In *Bringing the State Back In,* ed.

P. Evans, D. Rueschemeyer, T. Skocpol, pp. 317–43. New York: Cambridge Univ. Press

Tanter, R. 1965. Dimensions of conflict behavior within and between nations, 1958–60. *J. Confl. Resolut.* 10:41–64

Tanter, R., Midlarsky, M. 1967. A theory of revolutions. *J. Confl. Resolut.* 11:264–80

Tarrow, S. 1988. National politics and collective action: recent theory and research in Western Europe and the United States. *Annu. Rev. Sociol.* 14:421–40

Tarrow, S. 1989. *Democracy and Disorder*. New York: Cambridge Univ. Press

Taylor, C. L., Jodice, D. A. 1983. *World Handbook of Political and Social Indicators*. New Haven: Yale Univ. Press. 3rd ed.

Tilly, C. 1975. Revolutions and collective violence. In *Handbook of Political Science*, ed. F. I. Greenstein, N. W. Polsby, 3:483–555. Reading: Addison-Wesley

Tilly, C. 1978. *From Mobilization to Revolution*. Reading: Addison-Wesley

Tilly, C. 1984. Social movements and national politics. In *Statemaking and Social Movements*, ed. C. Bright, S. Harding, pp. 297–317. Ann Arbor: Univ. Michigan Press

Tilly, C., Tilly, L., Tilly, R. 1975. *The Rebellious Century, 1830–1930*. Cambridge: Harvard Univ. Press

Timberlake, M., Kentor, J. 1983. Economic dependence, overurbanization, and economic growth: a study of less developed countries. *Sociol. Q.* 24:489–507

Timberlake, M., Williams, K. R. 1984. Dependence, political exclusion and government repression: some cross-national evidence. *Am. Sociol. Rev.* 49:141–46

Timberlake, M., Williams, K. R. 1987. Structural position in the world system, inequality, and political violence. *J. Polit. Milit. Soc.* 15:1–15

von der Mehden, F. R. 1973. *Comparative Political Violence*. Englewood Cliffs: Prentice-Hall

Wallerstein, I. 1974. *The Modern World System*, Vol. 1. New York: Academic Press

Wallerstein, I. 1979. *The Capitalist World Economy*. New York: Cambridge Univ. Press

Wallerstein, I. 1989. *The Modern World System*, Vol. 3. San Diego: Academic Press

Walton, J. 1984. *Reluctant Rebels*. New York: Columbia Univ. Press

Walton, J. 1989. Debt, protest, and the state in Latin America. See Eckstein 1989, pp. 299–328

Walton, J., Ragin, C. 1990. Global and national sources of political protest: third world responses to the debt crisis. *Am. Sociol. Rev.* 55:876–90

Weede, E. 1981. Income inequality, average income, and domestic violence. *J. Confl. Resolut.* 25:639–54

Weede, E. 1986. Income inequality and political violence reconsidered. *Am. Sociol. Rev.* 51:438–41

Weede, E. 1987. Some new evidence on correlates of political violence. *Eur. Sociol. Rev.* 3:97–108

Williams, K. R., Timberlake, M. 1984. Structural inequality, conflict, and control: a cross-national test of the threat hypothesis. *Soc. Forces* 63:414–31

Wimberly, D. W. 1990. Investment dependence and Third World mortality. *Am. Sociol. Rev.* 55:75–91

Wolf, E. 1969. *Peasant Wars of the Twentieth Century*. New York: Harper & Row

Zimmermann, E. 1980. Macro-comparative research on political protest. See Gurr 1980, pp. 167–237

Zimmermann, E. 1983. *Political Violence, Crises, and Revolutions*. Cambridge: Schenkman

Annu. Rev. Sociol. 1992. 18:187–208

CONTEMPORARY RESEARCH ON SOCIAL DEMOCRACY

Gosta Esping-Andersen and Kees van Kersbergen

European University Institute, Firenze, Italy

KEY WORDS: welfare state, economic performance, neocorporatism, full employment

Abstract

This review examines the comparative, empirical literature that concerns the impact of social democracy on welfare state development and on economic performance. The theoretical basis of this research lies in reformist social democratic ideology which, in turn, is given substantial empirical confirmation in the sense that the balance of political power influences outcomes. The case against traditional modernization theory and other critiques is found to be strong, especially when the social democratic effect combines strong left parties with trade unions. The credibility of the social democratic model is particularly strong if we consider its consistent validation in cross-sectional as well as time-series analyses. It is, however, doubtful whether the "social democratic" thesis is applicable outside the framework of the advanced industrial democracies.

INTRODUCTION

Social democracy has a double meaning, at once denoting a political movement and its purported achievements. This review, however, addresses only studies on the effects of social democratic labor movements, not those on how the movements themselves evolved. This restriction seems warranted in light

0360-0572/92/0815-0187$02.00

of the rich literature that has emerged on the consequences of social democracy in the past decade.[1]

What, then, is to be explained? To a social democrat, the answer would be, simply, progress toward the democratic socialist society.

This may sound unscientific, but even a cursory reading of the scholarly literature reveals its indebtedness to social democracy's theoretical understanding of itself. Here we have a body of research that takes its key hypotheses from its own object of investigation. We cannot avoid a brief excursion into the legacy of social democratic thought because it lingers on as the theoretical ghost of almost all contemporary research.

The origins of the social democratic model are usually attributed to Eduard Bernstein (1969, originally 1898), but its modern formulation emerged in the flourishing debate on the limits and possibilities of reformism between the wars, a debate dominated by the Austro-German-Swedish social democrats, such as Max Adler (1933), Otto Bauer (1919), Eduard Heiman (1929), Ernst Jungen (1931), Karl Renner (1953), and Ernst Wigforss (1941). The renewed debate after World War II was dominated by British and Swedish thinkers such as C.A.R. Crosland (1956) and Gunnar Myrdal (1960, 1970).

In the spirit of Eduard Bernstein, social democratic theory concerned itself more with strategy than with the end-result. it came to view welfare state and full employment policies (social and economic citizenship) as doubly necessary; they were the preconditions for labor movement power and were, concommitantly, the building-blocks of socialism. Strong social rights, backed by employment guarantees, would strengthen the working classes, nurture solidarity, lessen the prerogatives of capital, and thus weaken the force of the market system. As Heiman (1929) put it, capitalism will recede as the frontiers of the "social idea" move forward. Reforms help realize the " social democratic image of society" (Castles 1978). In contrast to the apocalyptic strategy of marxist-leninism, social democratic theory believed that the socialist transformation could best be accelerated by nurturing (while modifying) an efficient capitalist economy. As a consequence, social democrats stress a "productivistic" strategy. Against liberal orthodoxy, they claim a

[1]Several works review the comparative research on the social bases of social democratic movements, for example, Bartolini (1983), Esping-Andersen (1985a), Paterson & Thomas (1977, 1988), Przeworski (1985), and Przeworski & Sprague (1986). The literature on individual cases is, of course, enormous and linguistically heterogeneous. Our review emphasizes the English-language literature and includes studies published in other languages only when their importance necessitates it. One of the authors of this review faced the delicate problem of having to review much of his own work. To minimize awkwardness, his research was reviewed by Kees van Kersbergen. For helpful comments on earlier drafts of this article we would like to thank Frank Castles, Alexander Hicks, Peter Lange, and John Stephens, all of whom happen to be chief protagonists in the saga to follow.

positive-sum relationship between equality and efficiency; indeed, optimal economic efficiency must rely on social rights and equality (for a recent account, see Johansson 1982).

Contemporary research has obviously shied away from defining the dependent variable as "socialism". Yet, the social democratic claim that certain policies or reforms have proto-socialist qualities is occasionally assumed to be valid. Authors such as Stephens (1979) and Stephens & Stephens (1982) imply that the achievements of the most successful social democracies, e.g. Sweden, constitute embryonic socialism. Most studies, however, are more pragmatically interested in establishing whether the parliamentary socialist strategy can produce outcomes that are fundamentally different.

Following social democratic theory's own emphasis on welfare state development and full employment, research on "social democratization" usually focuses either on welfare state characteristics (its size, egalitarianism, comprehensiveness, and the quality of social rights), or on economic performance (full employment and economic growth). The core argument that social democracy is capable of transforming the equality-efficiency trade-off into a positive-sum game has been examined more sporadically. Most studies fall essentially into two distinct groups: studies of welfare state outcomes, and research on economic performance.

The principal independent variable, social democracy as a movement, is usually defined according to one of three criteria. One, exemplified by Paterson & Thomas (1977), defines inclusion in formalistic terms such as official party label or membership in the 2nd International. The second approach is to identify social democratic movements in terms of a set of substantive political goals or strategic choices: a commitment to socialism via parliamentary reformism (Castles 1978, Stephens,1979, Esping-Andersen 1985a, Przeworski 1985, and Przeworksi & Sprague, 1986) or, as is the case in Paterson & Thomas (1988), in terms of the pursuit of Keynesean full employment welfare state policies.

The vast majority, however, adopt a third, essentially heuristic approach. The problem of definition may be dodged in cases where the study concentrates on specific social democratic experiences such as those of Castles (1978), Esping-Andersen (1985a), Higgins & Apple (1981), Korpi (1978), Pontusson (1988), or Schmidt (1982). The most common heuristic approach is found in the multi-nation "correlational" design where social democratic movements are simply equated with whatever locally constitutes the "left"—see Alt (1985), Cameron (1984), Esping-Andersen (1985b, 1990), Garrett & Lange (1986), Griffin et al (1989), Hewitt (1977), Hibbs (1977), Hicks (1988), Hicks et al (1989), Korpi (1983, 1989), Lange & Garrett (1985, 1987), Schmidt (1983), Stephens (1979), Swank & Hicks (1985), and Whiteley (1983).

SOCIAL DEMOCRACY AND THE WELFARE STATE

The debate on the social democratization of capitalism has naturally centered on equality, either in terms of the distributive end-result, or in terms of the institutional commitments of welfare states, such as universalism, solidarity, the generosity of social rights, and their capacity to "de-commodify" workers (Esping-Andersen 1990, Western 1989).

The first generation of research was primarily a debate with the once dominant "logic of industrialism" thesis as represented by Wilensky & Lebeaux (1958), Cutright (1965), and Pryor (1968), but increasingly also with the "median voter" view of democratic polities as represented in particular by Jackman (1975 1986). Hence, the objective was two-fold: to demonstrate that politics matter and that the party composition of the polity makes a decisive difference. Hewitt (1977) was one of the first to explicitly examine the capacity of social democratic labor movements to affect redistribution in both these senses.

The causal effect of social democracy on welfare state outcomes was subsequently corroborated by a large number of studies that employed a variety of research designs. In the comparative case-study approach, some studies emphasized the Scandinavian experience in particular, primarily because of the seemingly close association between social democratic dominance and advanced welfare states (Castles 1978, Korpi 1978, Esping-Andersen & Korpi 1986, Esping-Andersen 1985a). Others sought to identify the social democratic effect via matched comparisons between "failed" and "successful" cases, such as Higgins & Apple's (1981) and Pontusson's (1988) British-Swedish contrast, Esping-Andersen & Korpi's (1984) or Scharpf's (1984) comparison of Austria, Germany and Sweden, and Hage et al's (1989) four-nation comparison. By comparing nations in which the welfare state outcomes seemed to diverge despite social democratic movements of similar strength, these studies served to identify more concretely the conditions under which social democratic movements are capable of introducing change. Three key conclusions emerge from these studies. Castles (1978) emphasized the weakness of the right as a basic precondition; Stephens (1979) and Higgins & Apple (1981) were among the first to suggest that the political efficacy of social democracy is contingent on trade union strength or cohesion; and Castles (1978) as well as Esping-Andersen (1985a) held that the social democratic model could only be pursued effectively through political coalition building (especially with the agrarians).

The dominant approach has been to test the social democratic thesis on the basis of 16–20 advanced nations (Hewitt 1977, Korpi 1983, Stephens 1979, Swank & Hicks 1984 1985, Esping-Andersen 1985b) . Most analyses are cross-sectional, but (pooled-) time series analyses have become common in recent years (Alvarez et-al. 1991, Griffin et al 1989, Hicks, et.al 1989, Korpi 1989). Using a variety of different measures of both social democratic strength, and of policy outcomes (from social spending and redistribution to various institutional characteristics), most of these studies had in common a theory of working class mobilization of political power, that is, the social democratization of capitalist societies depends on the degree to which the balance of political power favors labor; in most cases, the political parties were identified as the chief causal agents.

The power resources argument has been most fully developed by Korpi (1983) but has been subject to several amendments. Apart from the emphasis on the relative weakness and fragmentation of the right (Castles,1978 1985), and on the decisiveness of political class alliances (Esping-Andersen 1985a,b) mentioned above, there is an emerging consensus in the literature that the policy efficacy of left parties depends on the extent to which they can count on strong trade unionism (Stephens 1979) and, especially, on a centralized, neocorporatist industrial relations system (Cameron 1984, Schmidt 1983, Scharpf 1984, 1987, Hicks et al 1989).

As Shalev (1983) has pointed out, many of these studies assume the social democratic welfare state to be a leap in the direction of socialism or, indeed, an early image of the future "good society." Several authors have challenged this kind of embryonic socialism assumption. Tilton's (1990) analysis of Swedish social democratic ideology argues that its dominant values have their roots in a radical-liberal commitment to freedom of choice rather than to socialism. Baldwin (1990) rejects the causal link between social democracy and solidaristic social policies since, in his analysis, their mainsprings are not necessarily in the working classes. Similarly, Heclo & Madsen (1986) and Therborn (1989) argue that the principles of solidarity and equality that characterize Swedish social democracy have less to do with socialism than with the Swedish historical tradition. Thus, it may very well be Swedish history, and not social democracy, that constitutes the root cause of reform. The implication is that the Swedish model is inapplicable elsewhere, so that even if Sweden did arrive at socialism, it is doubtful that the next candidate in terms of labor movement power mobilization ever would approximate Swedish-style achievements.

In the debate with the functionalist "logic of industrialism" thesis (and its marxist equivalent), the explanatory power of left parties cum trade union strength seemed to hold up against standard demographic and modernization variables, such as age structure and GDP per capita. Yet, the results depend very much on differences in variable measurement and methodological design. Left-power explanations tend to be spurious when controlling for age structure when the outcome is measured as social expenditure ratios (Pampel & Williamson 1989, Esping-Andersen 1990) because such a large share of spending is age-dependent. As Griffin et al (1986) show, cross-sectional and time-series models may tell different stories. Aside from such methodological issues (to be discussed at the end of this article), the recent literature has mainly been preoccupied with a reexamination of what is to be explained and of how social democracy may be decisive.

The one-to-one relationship between labor movement power and welfare outcomes has been challenged in different ways. In one group we find those who emphasize the decisiveness of neocorporatist solutions to global economic dependency. Cameron (1978, 1984) suggests that the association between strong social democracy and welfare states is linked to a country's position in the international economy. Specifically he argues that the vulnerability that small, open economies face favors the expansion of the public economy so as to reduce uncertainty via social guarantees, full employment, and more active government management of the economy. As elaborated more fully in the work of Katzenstein (1985), the real causal chain would appear to be that small open nations develop democratic corporatist structures as a way to enhance domestic consensus, facilitate economic adjustments, and maintain international competitiveness. While democratic corporatism is promoted by the presence of strong social democratic labor movements, Katzenstein (1985) points to Switzerland and the Netherlands to suggest that they may not constitute a necessary condition. At this point it becomes increasingly difficult to separate the neocorporatist argument from the social democratic thesis.

Cameron's argument has often been mistakenly interpreted as a rejection of the social democratic thesis: the explanatory power attached to "openness" seems to suggest that the effect of social democracy is spurious. However, the gist of his thesis (see especially Cameron 1984) was more deeply historical, suggesting that the openness of an economy favors certain structural features in societies which, in turn, enhance the power of labor. Since small, open economies tend to be industrially concentrated, they also tend to develop strong and unified interest organizations. The capacity to forge broad consensus and to mobilize power is further helped by the homogeneity and concentration of the labor force. The possible interactive effect of international and national factors in the production of welfare outcomes needs to be explored more fully.

The importance of neocorporatist arrangements for social democratic success has been stressed in the studies of Schmidt (1983), Keman (1988), and Hicks et al (1989). They suggest that social democracy is most likely to promote (and defend) welfare statism successfully if its parliamentary power is matched by strong consensus-building mechanisms in both the polity and economy. These studies also suggest that neocorporatist intermediation comes to play an especially important role in maintaining welfare policies during economic crises periods: the distributive battles that erupt when growth declines are better managed with "all-encompassing" interest organizations. Studying income distribution, Hicks & Swank (1984) and Muller (1989) suggest that the strength of left parties (and economic openness) influences redistribution directly, while trade unionization and centralization have decisive indirect effects. There appears to be a growing consensus that parties or unions alone have little effect, that successful social democratization, so to speak, requires a configuration of strong left parties in government backed by an encompassing and centralized trade union movement. As we shall discover, this explanatory model gains empirical support in the economic performance literature.

A second important reconsideration began with the undeniable fact that early welfare state reforms rarely, if ever, were initiated by the socialists, and that several countries (e.g. the Netherlands) pursue equality and welfare statism without the advocacy of a strong labor movement (see, for example, Castles, 1978, 1985, Stephens 1979, Skocpol & Amenta 1986, and Wilensky, 1981). This suggested the need to elaborate the political process of welfare state construction. The most influential answer came from those who showed that christian democracy (or Catholicism) constitutes a functional equivalent or alternative to social democracy, a point raised early on by Stephens (1979). Schmidt (1980, 1982) suggests that the two movements can be functionally equivalent, at least during periods of economic prosperity, and Wilensky (1981) argues that the two overlap considerably in ideological terms, and that Catholicism indeed constitutes a more important determinant of welfare statism than does left power. In a recent study, van Kersbergen (1991) challenges both of these interpretations, arguing instead for a competition model: christian democratic regimes are most likely to boost welfare state programs and spending when they face intense electoral challenge from the left. However, both Esping-Andersen (1990) and van Kersbergen (1991) suggest that christian democracy and social democracy result in fundamentally different kinds of welfare states. Most importantly, christian democracy is reluctant to expand collective social services and does not demonstrate the kind of full employment commitment integral to the social democratic model.

The explanatory power of social democracy also has been questioned in terms of the historical roots of welfare state reforms. Based on a study of France, Britain, Germany, the Netherlands, and the United States, De Swaan (1988) puts forward what might be termed an elite-conflict explanation, arguing that welfare states developed through conflicts and compromises struck between elites in response to their understanding of underlying social problems and needs. Moreover, the catalyst for change was not so much the rising working classes as the declining veto power of the traditional petit bourgeoisies. De Swaan's argument provides indirectly some support for the kind of state-centered accounts found in Heclo (1974), in Heclo and Madsen (1986), and in Weir et al (1988), and also in the interactive model of Hage et al (1989), where the efficacy of left power depends on state structure and state responses. De Swaan's critique loses some of its bite, however, because he fails to consider key social democratic cases, Scandinavia in particular. The inclusion of the Scandinavian countries in a broader European comparison is, in contrast, what makes Baldwin's (1990) rejection of the social democratic thesis so much more challenging. Trying to trace the origins of key welfare state characteristics, such as universalism and solidarity, Baldwin shows that what we typically attribute to the social democratic movements should, instead, be traced to the efforts of diverse "risk classes" to secure themselves. In his account, the historical role of the social democratic movements is essentially a spurious one; indeed, Baldwin goes so far as to argue that the agrarians were the real root cause of the Scandinavian model.

It may be that Baldwin exaggerates the role of the agrarians, and he certainly downplays the impact of social democratic movements in key junctures of Scandinavian social reform. Yet, the real value of his study lies in unravelling the contents of the "black box" that is, in effect, substituted for a serious analysis of how demands are transformed into party politics. Baldwin challenges adherents of the social democratic model to rethink the relationship between class and politics. Is it possible that social democratic movements represent "risk-class" alliances rather than working classes?

Aside from much greater attention to the historical process by which social democratic power translates into outcomes, the recent literature has begun rethinking what precisely the theory should explain. The choice of many (especially early) studies to gauge welfare state achievements in terms of social expenditures was defended in pragmatic terms (spending data were reliable and easy to collect), and substantively (they should reflect "effort" or the scope of the social wage). Yet the spending variable has been criticized for its loose correspondence to the theoretical issues of social democratization (Esping-Andersen, 1990). In particular, aggregate spending ratios fail to distinguish the characteristic effects of social democracy from those of other political forces such as christian democracy.

The choice of a variable that measures income inequality and redistribution appears immediately to gain face validity to the extent that equality is the traditional socialist goal. Since the early study by Hewitt (1977), there is considerable evidence in favor of a social democratic effect on income distribution (Bjorn 1979, Stephens 1979, van Arnhem et al 1982, Hicks & Swank 1984, Swank & Hicks 1985, Muller 1989, Hage et al 1989). Still, income distribution is for several reasons a problematic variable. On technical grounds, aggregate data available until the recent arrival of the Luxembourg Income Study (see Smeeding et al 1990, and Mitchell 1990) are not truly comparable. On theoretical grounds, income redistribution is problematic to the extent that the kinds of universalistic and generous welfare programs associated with successful social democratic politics may lose their redistributive effect because they increasingly favor the middle classes (Le Grand 1982, Goodin & Le Grand 1987, Esping-Andersen 1990). Ringen (1987) argues that large welfare states will generate greater equality, but this may be true only of transfers. With the rising importance of collective services, any firm conclusion must await more research on non-cash income distribution.

There is some evidence to suggest that the social democratic effect is more evident when measured against institutional characteristics of welfare states. This is the case in Myles' (1984) study of pension systems, in Korpi's (1989) study of sickness insurance, and in Esping-Andersen's (1990) study of welfare state attributes such as universalism, the public-private mix, the importance of means tests, and active labor market policies. Yet as research has moved in the direction of studying the institutional properties of welfare states, it has also been forced away from the kind of linear "more or less" social democratization conception that has dominated the literature. Instead, following Titmuss (1974) and Furniss & Tilton (1977), recent studies emphasize distinct types of welfare states clusters, among which the "social democratic" type constitutes but one (Castles & Mitchell 1990, Esping-Andersen 1990, van Kersbergen 1991). As Castles & Mitchell (1990) argue, the identification of a core social democratic type of welfare state may be too Eurocentric. Their study suggests that the means-tested, residual type of welfare state found in Australia should be considered as the result of a coherent social democratic strategy once we take into account labors success in establishing guaranteed employment and wage growth (see also Castles 1985).

The rethinking of the causal link between labor movement power and welfare state outcomes in recent studies has considerably improved our capacity to distinguish cause from consequence. In a sense, current research seems to be heading toward two conclusions, both of which harbor considerable risk. First, in comparison to the heydays of consensus around the linear, highly Swedocentric, social democratic model, the current emphasis on the specification and individualization of cases threatens to paralyze the search for generalizations. Second, there is a growing tendency to argue that social democratic movements produce nothing that other movements (say, christian democracy) or institutional arrangements (neocorporatism) cannot produce. This is, at least, the case within the welfare state expenditure literature.

SOCIAL DEMOCRACY AND THE ECONOMY

Welfare state and full employment growth policies are unified in the social democratic model. Most research, however, has examined them separately. Within social democratic theory the coupling was expressed in a variety of ways. At the most abstract level, the decision to shelve the socialization question led to a reordering of the strategic reform sequence. The classical doctrine that assumed that collective ownership was the necessary first step was turned on its head, and the full employment welfare state was viewed as the necessary precursor to "economic democratization." The idea sprang from the tactical need to disassociate social democracy from the politically suicidal socialization question, but also from a unique understanding of the possibilities of politics and the dynamics of capitalism: First, a democratically owned economy presumes an educated and resourceful citizenry—hence the welfare state and social citizenship. Second, its introduction requires broad consensus that is better attained once the social democratic image of society is firmly institutionalized. Third, because of the inevitable tendency toward "organized capitalism," economic socialization is inherent, but what is required is political steering so as to nurture the positive and arrest the negative aspects of economic modernization. In sum, it was assumed that a democratic economy would evolve via a full employment growth strategy that was backed by an egalitarian welfare state apparatus. It was furthermore assumed that the capitalist economy could be effectively steered by political means to produce desirable outcomes. Clearly, the social democrats put their faith in Keynesean-type economic management, a certain degree of planning, and above all, in the possibilities for a positive-sum relationship between equality and efficiency (Crosland 1956, Myrdal 1960, 1970, Martin 1975, 1981).

The major null-hypothesis to the social democratic theory finds its articulation both in the analysis of Kalecki (1943) and in standard neoclassical economic thought. Kalecki believed that sustained full employment would be impossible because of its effects on wages and inflation. Neoclassical theory emphasizes the negative efficiency consequences of a full employment welfare state economy in terms of inflation, slow growth, impaired competitiveness, and productivity (Okun 1975, Lindbeck 1981, Balassa 1984).

Contemporary research on the economic performance of social democracy is nested in this controversy and falls logically into two main categories. In the first, we find studies whose primary concern is full employment: as Scharpf (1984:267) puts it, "Is social democracy capable of decoupling employment from the development of a capitalist economy?" In the second category we group studies that more or less explicitly address the efficiency trade-off problem; as such, their major concern is economic growth performance.

Social Democracy and Full Employment

Much of the literature from the golden age of full employment in the 1960s seemed to suggest that the new tools of economic management would satisfactorily resolve the full employment problem (an illustrative example is

Shonfield 1965). The issue reemerged with the divergence in national employment performance that followed the 1973 oil-shock. Hibbs (1977) pioneered the debate with his now classical study of social democratic parties and macroeconomic policy. Defining policy options in terms of the Phillips-curve trade-off, his study showed a significant left-party effect on full employment and a corresponding conservative party inclination to favor price stability.

Hibbs's study raised two critical issues that have preoccupied subsequent research. If, as Hibbs's findings suggest, sustained full employment is associated with social democratic governance, how do we explain the performance of conservative regimes such as Switzerland or Japan? And why are some strong social democracies, like Denmark, unable to assure full employment? The second issue has to do with the "black box" problem: What are the mechanisms and conditions by which left parties can maintain full employment? Shifting from Hibbs's sole focus on parties, recent research emphasizes the importance of neocorporatist institutions.

Inspired by simultaneous research which indicated that strike rates and industrial unrest were significantly lower in nations where the organizational power of labor was high (Hibbs 1978, Korpi & Shalev 1980), many authors argued that the social democrats' ability to maintain full employment was a function of their links to the trade union movement. Of particular importance was the capacity for political exchange, according to which a powerful, unified, and centralized trade union movement could impose effective wage restraint in return for desired macroeconomic outcomes (Crouch 1985, Goldthorpe 1984a, Lange, 1984, Lehner 1988, Lembruch 1984). The crucial effect of left parties and neocorporatist interest concertation for full employment was demonstrated by Alt (1985), Cameron (1984), Hicks (1988), Hicks & Patterson (1989), Keman (1984), Lehner (1988), Schmidt (1983, 1985, 1987, 1988), and Scharpf (1984 1987). A major puzzle remained, namely why some countries with very weak unions and left parties also were capable of full employment. One answer is offered by Schmidt (1985 1988) and Therborn (1986) who suggest the existence of a rival conservative road to full employment. This path is characterized by either politically induced labor supply reduction (Switzerland averted unemployment by exporting large numbers of foreign workers and by discouraging female participation), or by wage accomodation from workers restrained by their weak organizational resources (as in the United States). Another answer follows Mancur Olson's (1982) theory and posits a "hump-shaped" relationship, according to which full employment is best secured when the left is either extremely weak or strong (see, in particular, Hicks & Patterson 1989, and Alvarez et al 1991). This model is discussed below.

Schmidt and Therborn make usefully problematic in their work the meaning of full employment. Most studies have used standardized OECD unemployment figures, but these fail to reveal whether lower unemployment rates are attained through labor supply reductions. Hence, the capacity of some countries to combine full employment with maximum participation (as in Sweden) must count for more than when it is coupled to low and, perhaps, declining participation.

Recent research similarly stresses the need to analyze the contents and strategic diversity of full employment policies (Martin 1975, 1981, Scharpf 1984, 1987, Therborn 1986, Esping-Andersen 1990). Of particular interest are the links between welfare state and employment policies. It is evident that some nations have tried to solve unemployment problems with social transfer programs (early retirement especially) while others have stressed active labor market policies and job expansion in welfare state services. The national differences in this scenario coincide with those found in welfare state research (Esping-Andersen 1990).

If, as so much research has shown, full employment is a function of an interaction between parties and unionism, we would expect to find nations distributed along a "hump-shaped" curve: the worst-off countries would be those in which strong unions support weak left parties or vice versa, because in these cases either the party cannot count on union discipline, or the unions will not trust government to deliver acceptable quid pro quos. This pattern also finds support in recent economic research (Calmfors & Driffill 1988).

Oddly enough, these results seem to confirm the validity of two otherwise distant theses. First, there is clear evidence in favor of a power resource mobilization theory (Korpi 1983). Second, the conditions for full employment that emerge in this literature parallel Olson's (1982) theory of why economies rise and decline: if the objective is full employment, labor is best served either by all power or by none.

A fairly strong consensus has now formed around the interactive model, although it has been subject to various amendments. With reference to the initial adoption of Keynesean policy, state-centered theory has suggested that government bureaucracies played a more central role than the left parties (Weir & Skocpol 1985). It has also been held that the actors of real importance in neocorporatist concertation intermediation are the employers' federations rather than labor (Swenson 1989). The latter argument constitutes an interesting parallel to Castles' (1978) emphasis on the strength and unity of the political right. Virtually all these studies address the social democrats' ability to maintain full employment in the adversity of the post-1973 era. And, despite conceptual finetuning or variable additions, a basic consensus has emerged around the interactive left-neocorporatism model of explanation. Precisely by having focused on a period of prolonged economic crisis, the systematic finding that social democracy matters seems to suggest that it may be possible to decouple employment from the logic of capitalist economies, at least to a degree. In other words, there is evidence to suggest that full employment welfare states do not necessarily engender the kinds of negative trade-offs suggested by Kalecki's scenario or by neoclassical economic theory. The final answer to this question depends, of course, on social democracy's ability to sustain growth.

Social Democracy and Economic Growth

Most studies of social democracy's employment performance have dealt only tangentially, if at all, with the associated efficiency issue. In turn, research on social democracy's growth performance hardly ever studies employment performance as an endogenous variable. The basic question in the literature on growth is whether welfare state size affects growth negatively. A few studies examine the left-party effect directly.

The claim that a social democratic strategy will impair economic performance is made with reference to a complex of negative effects. On one hand, neoclassical economics has stressed the negative work-incentives of high taxes and generous welfare benefits (for an overview, see Danziger et al 1981 and Lindbeck 1981). While this is normally argued in terms of microeconomic behavior, a significant negative incentive effect should translate into suboptimal aggregate productivity and thus long-term growth performance. On the other hand, it is held that too much public expenditure (and a full employment wage push) depresses savings and investment rates, raises inflation, and harms international competitiveness (Okun 1975, Balassa 1984). Public choice economists come to similar conclusions but see the ultimate culprit in the rent-seeking goals of institutional actors (Olson 1982, Mueller 1983). In any case, if the proposed effects are to be meaningfully negative they should be evident in long-term growth rates; this is also how the empirical literature approaches the question.

The neoclassical claim that welfare states harm growth was hardly, if ever, tested rigorously. Certainly, neither Lindbeck (1981) nor Balassa (1984) provided much hard evidence for their generalizations. And the public choice economists (such as Choi 1983) who sought to test the theory of institutional sclerosis employed proxy variables for sclerosis (age of a nation or years of democracy) that assumed a fair amount of faith. [2] Have the sociologists, then, produced solid empirical support for a social democratic thesis?

The evidence in favor of a direct social democratic political effect on

[2]Persson & Tabellini (1991) test two econometric models, one with a long historical time-series, another for the postwar period. Both demonstrate that inequality has a negative impact on economic growth rates.

growth is mixed. Whiteley's (1983) study suggests a weak positive effect of left parties in government, but his model suffers from heteroscedasticity problems and suggests that the main impact is on employment. Schmidt's (1983) study uses a composite economic performance variable and is thus not entirely comparable, but the results indicate that the social democratic party effect disappears while the same kind of concertation/neocorporatism effect found for employment also is significant for growth. The studies by Lange & Garrett (1985, 1987), Garrett & Lange (1986), and Alvarez et al (1991) give additional support for a neocorporatism effect. And, also these studies indicate a "hump-shaped" pattern of growth as the result of an interaction between strong social democratic parties and trade-union centralization. Parallel to the case of full employment, the worst performance occurs when either of the two branches of the labor movement is weak. Jackman (1987) has sought to refute these findings by reference to a lack of model robustness: If Norway (with its oil) is omitted, the positive effect of political partisanship disappears. Garrett & Lange (1986) retested the original model without Norway and concluded that, although weakened, the model remained convincing. Their claim was given further support by Hicks (1988), Hicks & Patterson (1989), and Alvarez et al (1991).

The social democratic thesis receives additional, albeit also inconsistent, indirect support from research on the growth effects of welfare state expenditures. Both Korpi (1985) and Friedland & Sanders (1985) claim that, if anything, welfare states have a positive effect on growth rates. However, like Jackman earlier, Saunders (1985 1986) also casts some doubt on the robustness of this finding and suggests that we need to disaggregate expenditure categories. This is what makes the Friedland-Sanders study particularly interesting, because it differentiates the growth impact by expenditure types, and suggests that social transfers have a positive effect on growth (presumably the Keynesean demand effect), while collective services and transfers to business have negative growth consequences. In a later study, Castles & Dowrick (1990) find no evidence of a negative relationship between social expenditures and economic performance.

Very few studies have tested the impact of left party cum union and welfare state expenditure variables simultaneously. Lane & Ersson (1987), seeking to test Olson's thesis of institutional sclerosis, conclude that social democratic governments have a negative but statistically nonsignificant effect on growth. On this issue, by far the most sophisticated studies are Hicks (1988) and Alvarez et al(1991). Both show effects of left parties and neocorporatism consistent with those of Lange and Garrett. Of greater interest is Hicks' (1988) observation that government redistribution has a depressing effect on economic growth which, however, is offset by the presence of a strong left cum trade union system. The implication is that the equality-efficiency trade-off can be overridden if encompassing unions can moderate their wage claims. This view echoes Geiger & Geiger's (1978) highly original study on the long-term capacity to manage the equality-efficiency issue. These authors suggest that, up to a certain point, growth and efficiency are aided by redistributive welfare programs, but when egalitarianism reaches a certain level, the positive effect turns negative. This is their diagnosis of why the celebrated Swedish model began to decay in the late 1970s.

The literature on social democracy and economic performance shares with its welfare state equivalent the basic methodological problems that go with inherent overdetermination: too many variables with too few cases. Still, the accumulated research over the 1980s shows a certain consistency of results that gains added credibility by its interdisciplinary (including sociologists, political scientists, and economists) character. In the concluding part of this review, we examine methodological issues and discuss major substantive challenges in this literature.

METHODOLOGICAL PROBLEMS

The linear (ordinary least squares—OLS) model has been favored in the quantitative literature, especially in cross-sectional studies. This may have caused unanticipated theoretical distortions since it assumes a linear model of social democracy. The gist of Shalev's (1983) "swedocentrism" critique was that, with Sweden always scoring highest, such models implicitly suggest that Swedish-level social democratic power will produce Swedish-level welfare states, full employment, or growth. Hence, the linear model has an inbuilt tendency to confirm the social democratic theory. Suppose there is a threshold below which social democratic power mobilization has no effect at all? Or, as Schmidt (1983) has argued, what if the causal connection changes from one period to the next?

Overdetermination is a constant problem in this research field. To a degree, more sophisticated statistical techniques have helped overcome this problem. Pooled-time series analyses are now common (Korpi 1989, Castles & Dowrick 1990, Alvarez et al 1991), but the promise of increasing observations is sometimes offset by restricted variance over time. This is less of a problem in the economic-effects literature, but it remains an important barrier to research on the welfare state: long-term data on social policies are difficult to find, while there is little change in social programs from year to year.

Recent literature has begun to use econometric diagnostic tests to compensate for over determination (e.g. Castles & Dowrick 1990 and van Kersbergen 1991). In fact, small samples have the advantage that in-depth scrutiny of the residuals is feasible. Hence, linearity violations or structural breaks can offer opportunities for fine-tuning hypothesis.

Technical issues aside, over-determination may be less problematic than normally assumed. When so many studies, regardless of design (case-approach or correlational), variable operationalization or measurement, converge on a similar explanatory account, their credibility seems more secure.

Another positive methodological trend involves the growing interplay between correlational and in-depth analyses of cases. The former (an example is van Kersbergen 1991) test and retest new propositions emanating from the latter; the latter (an example is Baldwin 1990) open black boxes and question the validity of the former. But, as we noted earlier, the same trend is jeopardized by the individualization of cases. So that, as each case of social democracy is (rightly) shown unique, and as the linear world view is dismissed, generalization becomes difficult.

THEORETICAL ISSUES

The literature seems to be converging around a common model. Simply put, social democratic parties are more capable of altering the distribution system and maintaining growth with full employment when they are linked to powerful and centralized trade union movements. They do not necessarily escape from trade-offs between equality and efficiency, but they do succeed in shifting distributional pressures from the market to the state. Hence, the labor movement trades market wages for a social wage and, by doing so, reaps the benefits of full employment and strong social citizenship. In contrast, a worst case scenario occurs when either the union movement or the party is weak.

If this represents the real accomplishments of social democracy, the literature may have raised more questions than it has answered. For one, these gains arise also in countries with neither strong unionism nor parties, although the evidence clearly indicates a substantially better welfare state in the cases dominated by social democracy. Hence, if one can assume that the chief interest of wage earners is to protect themselves from market dependency, empirical research suggests that a strong social democracy is their best guarantee.

A second, more worrisome problem is the close association of the social democratic model with the Scandinavian countries. In terms of the welfare state and full employment performance, the presence of a "social democratic regime" is limited to the Nordic nations; there exist other cases of strong left parties cum unions (Austria, for example), but their welfare states are neither universalistic nor egalitarian, and their full employment performance is based on labor supply reduction. The theoretical consequences are substantial. First, our conclusions pertain to a small geographical enclave and our theory of social democracy might therefore be a theory of Scandinavia (on this point, see also Castles & Merrill 1989). Put differently, we cannot distinguish nation-effects from the effects of social democracy. Second, as much of the literature demonstrates, we are comparing clusters of nations with qualitatively different political economies, not a distribution along a neat axis. The social democratic model may therefore be invalid if its generalizations assume that similar left party cum trade unionism will bring similar results outside Scandinavia.

The social democratic thesis gains strength from the fact that it is based on welfare state and economic performance after the 1973 economic crisis. Yet, as a growing literature argues, this is the very same period in which occurred a rapid erosion of the institutional and organizational framework that made social democracy possible in the first place. From very different perspectives, Boyer (ed) (1988), Goldthorpe (1984a), Lash & Urry (1987) and Offe (1985) all suggest that "organized capitalism," and thus the social democratic model, is being undone by the demands of flexibility and the pressures toward differentiation inherent in the new postindustrial or post-Fordist economy. In a rather similar vein, Esping-Andersen (1987) argues that institutional accommodation to full employment is unsustainable as long as the public sector remains the principal channel of distributional conflicts. As its capacity to absorb trade-offs is exhausted, social democracy's capacity to maintain a full employment welfare state will erode. Due to mobility of capital in the new global economy, it is also dubious whether the small open country status that once facilitated neocorporatist concertation will guarantee similar benefits in the future. As suggested by Mjoset (1986) and Pontusson (1987), one way to interpret these arguments is that the social democratic model was historically specific. It may have constituted but one among several ways of politically and institutionally regulating the fordist capitalist order. Since social democracy's strength lay in its mobilization of the industrial working class masses, it is an open question whether it will have any capacity for power in a postindustrial society.

The last decade has produced an evident decay of social democratic movements, especially in countries where they achieved near-hegemony. The widely cited "collapse" of the Swedish model can be regarded as consistent with the end-of-organized-capitalism argument. Still, as social democracy erodes in Northern Europe, it seems to flourish in the South, notably in France, Greece, and Spain. Does this indicate a new era for social democracy? The question is difficult to answer because research on the new Mediterranean socialism has just begun. That it may not constitute a parallel to old-fashioned northern social democracy is indicated by evidence that Greek PASOK socialism is largely clientelistic, and that the French and Spanish parties are only vaguely parties of the working class; their strength seems to derive very much from personal leadership (Merkel 1989, Paterson & Thomas 1988).

The Mitterand regime has certainly promoted social democratic-style welfare and full employment policies, but then the French socialists entirely lack the crucial link to a unified, all-encompassing trade union movement. Indeed, France's failure to secure full employment actually confirms the argument of the "consensual social democratic thesis." Spanish socialism comes closer to the Scandinavian model with its capacity for neocorporatist deals, but here also the union movement is weak and in decline. In addition, the Spanish version of neocorporatist concertation is not comparable in terms of outcomes because its main objective was to restructure the economy and bring Spain into the EEC (Perez-Diaz 1986). In fact, Spain suffers from Europe's highest unemployment rate. Virtually all accounts of Southern European social democracy agree on the lack of major progress in the direction of "social democratization"; many suggest that it is not comparable at all with the traditional, established social democratic movements. [3] Social democracy's decay in the North is therefore unlikely to be compensated by a surge in either southern nor eastern Europe. Hence, the issue of whether social democracy will produce a transition from capitalism to socialism may soon lose its relevance. A more timely question is whether a transition from socialism to capitalism is possible under the aegis of christian democracy or neoliberalism?

[3]For an overview of Southern European social democracy, see Giner (1984) and Gallagher & Williams (1989). On the Spanish case, see Perez-Diaz (1986, 1990) and Merkel (1989); Estivill and Hoz (1990) provide an overview of the industrial relations side of the issue. On France, see Cameron (1988), Bell & Criddle (1984), Hall (1985), Kesselman (1982), Ross & Jenson (1983), and Ross et al (1987).

Literature Cited

Adler, M. 1933. Wandlung der Arbeiterklasse. *Der Kampf* 26:367–82

Alt, J. 1985. Political parties, world demand and unemployment: Domestic and international sources of economic activity. *Am. Polit. Sci. Rev.* 79:1016–40

Alvarez, R. M., Garret, G., Lange, P. 1991. Government partisanship, labor organization, and macroeconomic performance. *Am. Polit. Sci. Rev.* 85:539–56

Balassa, B. 1984. The economic consequences of social policies in the industrialized countries. *Weltwirtschaftlisches Arch.* 120:213–27

Baldwin, P. 1990. *The Politics of Social Solidarity. Class Bases of the European Welfare State 1875–1975*. Cambridge: Cambridge Univ. Press

Bartolini, S. 1983. The membership of mass parties: the social democratic experience. In *Western European Party System,*, ed. H. Daalder, P. Mair. London: Sage

Bauer, 0. 1919. *Der Weg zum Sozialismus*. Vienna:Volksbuchhandlung

Bell, D., Criddle, B. 1984. *The French Socialist Party Resurgence and Victory*. Oxford: Oxford Univ. Press

Bernstein, E. 1969. (1898). *Evolutionary Socialism*. New York: Schocken

Bjorn, L. 1979. Labor parties, economic growth, and redistribution in five capitalist countries. *Comp. Soc. Res.* 2:93–128

Boyer, R., ed 1988. *The Search for Labour Market Flexibility* Oxford: Oxford Univ. Press

Calmfors, L., Driffill, J. 1988. Bargaining structure, corporatism and macroeconomic performance. *Econ. Policy* 6:14–61

Cameron, D. R. 1978. The expansion of the public economy: A comparative analysis. *Am. Polit. Sci. Rev.* 72:1243–61

Cameron, D. R. 1984. Social democracy, corporatism, labor quiescence and the representation of economic interests in advanced capitalist society. In *Order and Conflict in Contemporary Capitalism*, ed. J. H. Goldthorpe, pp. 143–78. Oxford: Oxford Univ. Press

Cameron, D. R. 1988. The colors of a rose: on the ambiguous record of French socialism. *Ctr. Eur. Stud. Work. Pap.* Cambridge, Mass: Harvard Univ.

Castles, F. G. 1978. *The Social Democratic Image of Society: A Study of the Achievements and the Origins of Scandanavian Social Democracy in Comparative Perspective*. London: Routledge & Kegan Paul

Castles, F. G. 1985. *The Working Class and Welfare: Reflections on the Political Development of the Welfare State in Australia and New Zealand, 1890–1980*. London: Allen & Unwin

Castles, F. G. 1989. Social protection by other means. Australia's strategy of coping with external vulnerability. In *The Comparative History of Public Policy,* ed. F. G. Castles. Oxford: Oxford Univ. Press

Castles, F., Merrill, V. 1989. Towards a general model of public policy outcomes. *J. Theor. Polit.* 1:177–212

Castles, F. G., Dowrick, S. 1990. The impact of government spending levels on medium-term economic growth in the OECD, 1960–85. *J. Theor. Polit.* 2:173–204

Castles, F. G., Mitchell, D. 1990. Three worlds of welfare capitalism or four? *Public Policy Prog. Discuss. Pap. 21* Canberra: Aust. Natl. Univ.

Choi, K. 1983. A statistical test of Olson's model. In *The Political Economy of Growth,* ed. D. Mueller, pp. 57–78. New Haven: Yale Univ. Press

Crosland, C. A. R. 1956. *The Future of Socialism*. London: Cape

Crouch, C. 1985. Conditions for trade union wage restraint. In *The Politics of Inflation and Economic Stagnation,* ed. L. Lindberg, C. S. Maier, pp. 105–39. Washington, DC: Brookings Inst.

Cutright, P. 1965. Political structure, economic development and national social security programs. *Am. J. Sociol.* 60:539–55

Danziger, S., Haveman, R., Plotnik, R. 1981. How income transfer programs affect work, savings, and the income distribution. *J. Econ. Lit.* 19:975–1028

De Swaan, A. 1988. *In Care of the State. Health Care, Education and Welfare in Europe and the USA in the Modern Era*. Cambridge, UK: Polity

Esping-Andersen, G. 1985a. *Politics Against Markets. The Social Democratic Road to Power*. Princeton, NJ: Princeton Univ. Press

Esping-Andersen, G. 1985b. Power and distributional regimes. *Polit. Soc.* 14:223–56

Esping-Andersen, G. 1987. Institutional accommodation to full employment: a comparison of policy regimes. In *Coping with the Economic Crisis,* ed. H. Keman, H. Paloheimo, P. F. Whiteley, pp. 83–110. London: Sage

Esping-Andersen, G. 1990. *The Three Worlds of Welfare Capitalism*. Cambridge, UK: Polity/Princeton, NJ: Princeton Univ. Press

Esping-Andersen, G., Korpi, W. 1984. Social policy as class politics in postwar capitalism: Scandinavia, Austria and Germany. See Goldthorpe 1984, pp. 179–208

Esping-Andersen, G., Korpi, W. 1986. From poor relief to institutional welfare states: the development of Scandinavian social policy. In *The Scandinavian Model: Welfare States and Welfare Research,* ed. R. Erikson et al, pp. 39–74. Armonk, NY: Sharpe

Estivill, J., Hoz, J. M. 1990. Transition and crisis: the complexity of Spanish industrial relations. In *European Industrial Relations: The Challenge of Flexibility,* ed. G. Baglioni, C. Crouch. London: Sage

Friedland, R., Sanders, J. 1985. The public economy and economic growth in Western market economies. *Am. Sociol. Rev.* 50:421–37

Furniss, N., Tilton, T. 1977. *The Case for the Welfare State: From Social Security to Social Equality*. Bloomington: Ind. Univ. Press

Gallagher, T., Williams, A. P., eds. 1989. *Southern European Socialism in Government*. Manchester: Manchester Univ. Press

Garrett, G., Lange, P. 1986. Performance in a hostile world: economic growth in capitalist democracies, 1974–1982. *World Polit.* 38:517–45

Geiger, T., Geiger, F. 1978. *Welfare and Efficiency*. Washington, DC: Natl. Plan. Comm.

Giner, S. 1984. Southern European socialism in transition. In *The New Mediterranean Democracies,* ed. G. Pridham, pp. 138–57. London: Sage

Goldthorpe, J. 1984a. The end of convergence: corporatist and dualist tendencies in modern Western societies. See Goldthorpe 1984b, pp. 315–43

Goldthorpe, J., ed. 1984b. *Order and Conflict in Contemporary Capitalism*. Oxford: Clarendon

Goodin, R. E., Le Grand, J. 1987. *Not Only the Poor: The Middle Classes and the Welfare State*. London: Allen & Unwin

Griffin, L. J., Walters, P. B., O'Connell, P.

J., Moor, E. 1986. Methodological innovations in the analysis of welfare-state development: pooling cross-sections and time series. In *Futures for the Welfare State*, ed. N. Furniss. Bloomington: Ind. Univ. Press

Griffin, L. J., O'Connell, P. J., McCammon, H. J. 1989. National variation in the context of struggle: postwar class conflict and market distribution in the capitalist democracies. *Can. Rev. Sociol. Anthropol.* 26:37–68

Hage, J., Hanneman, R., Gargan, E. T. 1989. *State Responsiveness and State Activism. An Examination of the Social Forces and State Strategies that Explain the Rise in Social Expenditure in Britain, France, Germany and Italy, 1870–1968*. London: Unwin Hyman

Hall, P. 1985. Socialism in one country: Mitterand and the struggle to define a new economic policy in France. In *Socialism, the State and Public Policy in France*, ed. P. Cerny, M. Schain, pp. 81–107. London: Methuen

Heclo, H. 1974. *Modern Social Policies in Britain and Sweden*. New Haven: Yale Univ. Press

Heclo, H., Madsen, H. J. 1986. *Policy and Politics in Sweden*. Philadelphia: Temple Univ. Press

Heiman, E. 1929. *Soziale Theorie des Kapitalismus*. Tubingen: Mohr. Reprinted 1980, Frankfurt: Suhrkamp

Hewitt, C. 1977. The effect of political democracy and social democracy on equality in industrial societies: a cross-national comparison. *Am. Sociol. Rev.* 42:450–64

Hibbs, D. 1977. Political parties and macroeconomic policy. *Am. Polit. Sci. Rev.* 71:1467–87

Hibbs, D. 1978. On the political economy of long-run trends in strike activity. *Br. J. Polit. Sci.* 8:153–76

Hicks, A. 1988. Social democratic corporatism and economic growth. *J. Polit.* 50:677–704

Hicks, A., Swank, D. 1984. On the political economy of welfare expansion. *Comp. Polit. Stud.* 17:81–119

Hicks, A., Patterson, X. 1989. On the robustness of the left corporatist model of economic growth. *J. Polit.* 51:662–75

Hicks, A., Swank, D., Ambuhl, M. 1989. Welfare expansion revisited: policy routines and their mediation by party, class and crisis, 1957–1982. *Eur. J. Polit. Res.* 17:401–30

Higgins, W., Apple, N. 1981. *Class Mobilization and Economic Policy: Struggles over Full Employment in Britain and Sweden*. Stockholm: Arbetslivcentrum

Jackman, R. W. 1975. *Politics and Social Equality: A Comparative Analysis*. New York: Wiley

Jackman, R. W. 1986. Elections and the democratic class struggle. *World Polit.* 39:123–46

Jackman, R. W. 1987. The politics of economic growth in the industrial democracies, 1974–1980: Leftist strength or Northsea oil? *J. Polit.* 49:242–56

Johansson, S. 1982. When is the time ripe? *Polit. Power Soc. Theory* 3:113–44

Jungen, E. 1931. *Socialpolitik och Socialism*. Stockholm: Tiden

Kalecki, M. 1943. Political aspects of full employment. *Polit. Q.* 14:322–31

Katzenstein, P. J. 1985. *Small States in World Markets:Industrial Policy in Europe*. Ithaca, NY: Cornell Univ. Press

Keman, H. 1984. Politics, policies and consequences: a cross-national analysis of public policy-formation in advanced capitalist democracies, 1967–1981. *Eur. J. Polit. Res.* 12:147–70

Keman, H. 1988. *The Development Toward Surplus Welfare: Social Democratic Politics and Policies in Advanced Capitalist Democracies (1965–1984)*. Amsterdam: CT Press

Kesselman, M. 1982. Prospects for democratic socialism in advanced capitalism. *Polit. Soc.* 11:397–438

Korpi, W. 1978. *The Working Class in Welfare Capitalism: Work, Unions and Politics in Sweden.*. London: Routledge & Kegan Paul

Korpi, W. 1983. *The Democratic Class Struggle*. London: Routledge & Kegan Paul

Korpi, W. 1985. Economic growth and the welfare state: leaky bucket or irrigation system? *Eur. Sociol. Rev.* 1:97–118

Korpi, W. 1989. Power, politics, and state autonomy in the development of social citizenship: social rights during sickness in eighteen OECD countries since 1930. *Am. Sociol. Rev.* 54:309–28

Korpi, W., Shalev, M. 1980. Strikes, power and politics in the Western nations, 1900–1976. *Polit. Power Soc. Theory* 1:301–34

Lane, J. E., Ersson, S. 1987. Politics and economic growth. *Scand. Polit. Stud.* 10:19–34

Lange, P. 1984. Unions, workers and wage regulation: the rational bases of consent. See Goldthorpe 1984, pp. 98–123

Lange, P., Garrett, G. 1985. The politics of growth: strategic interaction and economic performance in the advanced industrial democracies, 1974–1980. *J. Polit.* 47:792–827

Lange, P., Garrett, G. 1987. The politics of growth reconsidered. *J. Polit.* 49:257–74

Le Grand, J. 1982. *The Strategy of Equality*. London: Allen & Unwin

Lehner, F. 1988. The political economy of distributive conflict. In *Managing Mixed Economies,* ed. F. Castles, F. Lehner, M. G. Schmidt, pp. 54–96. Berlin: de Gruyter

Lembruch, G. 1984. Concertation and the structure of corporatist networks. See Goldthorpe 1984b, pp. 60–80

Lindbeck, A. 1981. *Work Disincentives in the Welfare State*. Vienna, Manz: Nationalokonomische Gesellschaft Lectures

Martin, A. 1975. Is democratic control of capitalist economies possible? In *Stress and Contradiction in Modern Capitalism,* ed. L. Lindberg et al, pp. 13–56. Lexington, Mass: Heath

Martin, A. 1981. Economic stagnation and social stalemate in Sweden. In *Monetary Policy, Selective Credit Policy, and Industrial Policy in France, Britain, West Germany and Sweden*. US Congr. Joint Econ. Comm. Washington, DC: US Congress

Merkel, W. 1989. Sozialdemokratische Politik in einer post-keynesianischen Ara? *Politische Vierteljahresschrift* 30:629–54

Mitchell, D. 1990. *Income transfer systems: a comparative study using microdata*. PhD thesis. Australian Natl. Univ. Canberra

Mjoset, L. 1986. *Norden Dagen Derpaa*. Oslo: Universitetsforlaget

Mueller, D., ed. 1983. *The Political Economy of Growth*. New Haven: Yale Univ. Press

Muller, E. N. 1989. Distribution of income in advanced capitalist states: political parties, labour unions, and the international economy. *Eur. J. Polit. Res.* 17:367– 400

Myles, J. 1984. *Old Age in the Welfare State*. Boston: Little, Brown

Myrdal, G. 1960. *Beyond the Welfare State*. New Haven: Yale Univ. Press

Myrdal, G. 1970. *The Challenge of World Poverty*. New York: Pantheon

Offe, C. 1985. *Disorganized Capitalism*. Cambridge, Mass: MIT Press

Okun, A. 1975. *Equality and Efficiency: The Big Trade-Off*. Washington, DC: Brookings Inst.

Olson, M. 1982. *The Rise and Decline of Nations*. New Haven: Yale Univ. Press

Pampel, F. C., Williamson, J. B. 1989. *Age, Class, Politics, and the Welfare State*. Cambridge, UK: Cambridge Univ. Press

Paterson, W., Thomas, A. 1977. *Social Democratic Parties in Western Europe*. London: Croom Helm

Paterson, W., Thomas, A. 1988. *The Future of Social Democracy*. Oxford: Clarendon

Perez-Diaz, V. 1986. Economic policies and social pacts in Spain during the transition. *Eur. Sociol. Rev.* 2:1–19

Perez-Diaz, V. 1990. Governability and the scale of governance: meso-governments in Spain. *Juan March Inst. Work. Pap. No. 6*, Madrid

Persson, T., Tabellini, G. 1991. Is inequality harmful for growth? Theory and evidence. *NBER Work. Pap. No. 3599*

Pontusson, J. 1988. *Swedish Social Democracy and British Labour: Essays on the Nature and Conditions of Social Democratic Hegemony*. Ithaca: Cornell Univ. Western Soc. Pap.

Pryor, F. L. 1968. *Public Expenditure in Communist and Capitalist Countries*. London: Allen & Unwin

Przeworski, A. 1985. *Capitalism and Social Democracy*. Cambridge: Cambridge Univ. Press

Przeworski, A., Sprague, J. 1986. *Paper Stones*. Chicago: Univ. Chicago Press

Renner, K. 1953. *Wandlungen der Modernen Gesellschaft*. Vienna: Wiener Volksbuchhandlung

Ringen, S. 1987. *The Possibility of Politics. A Study in the Political Economy of the Welfare State*. Oxford: Clarendon

Ross, G., Hoffman, S., Malzacher, S., eds. 1987. *The Mitterand Experiment*. Cambridge, Mass: Harvard Univ. Press

Ross, G., Jenson, J. 1983. French socialism in crisis. *Stud. Polit. Econ.* 11:71–104

Saunders, P. 1985. Public expenditures and economic performance in OECD countries. *J. Public Policy* 5:1–21

Saunders, P. 1986. What can we learn from international comparisons of public sector size and economic performance? *Eur. Sociol. Rev.* 2:52–60

Scharpf, F. 1984. Economic and institutional constraints of full employment strategies: Sweden, Austria and Germany, 1973–1982. See Goldthorpe 1984, pp. 257–90

Scharpf, F. 1987. *Sozialdemokratische Krisenpolitik in Europa*. Frankfurt: Campus Verlag

Schmidt, M. G. 1980. *CDU und SPD an der Regierung. Ein Vergleich ihrer Politik in den Länder*. Frankfurt/New York: Campus

Schmidt, M. G. 1982. *Wohlfaliftsstaatliche Politik unter bürgerlichen und sozialdemokratischen Regierungen*. Frankfurt/New York: Campus

Schmidt, M. G. 1983. The welfare state and the economy in periods of economic crisis. *Eur. J. Polit. Res.* 11:1–26

Schmidt, M. G. 1985. *Der Schweizerische Weg zur Vollbeschaftigung*. Frankfurt: Campus Verlag

Schmidt, M. G. 1987. The politics of full employment in western democracies. *Ann. Am. Acad.* 492:171–81

Schmidt, M. G. 1988. The politics of labour

market policy: structural and political determinants of rates of unemployment in industrial nations. In *Managing Mixed Economies,* ed. F. Castles, F. Lehner, M. Schmidt, pp. 4–53. Berlin: de Gruyter

Shalev, M. 1983. The social democratic model and beyond: two generations of comparative research on the welfare state. *Comp. Soc. Res.* 6:315–51

Shonfield, A. 1965. *Modern Capitalism.* Oxford: Oxford Univ. Press

Skocpol, T., Amenta, E. 1986. States and social policies. *Annu. Rev. Sociol.* 12:131–57

Smeeding, T. M., O'Higgins, M., Rainwater, L. 1990. *Poverty, Inequality and Income Distribution in Comparative Perspective. The Luxembourg Income Study (LIS).* New York: Harvester & Wheatsheaf

Stephens, E. H., Stephens, J. D. 1982. The labor movement, political power and workers' participation in Western Europe. *Polit. Power Soc. Theory* 3:215–50

Stephens, J. D. 1979. *The Transition from Capitalism to Socialism.* London: Macmillan

Swank, D. H., Hicks, A. 1984. On the political economy of welfare expansion: a comparative analysis of 18 advanced capitalist democracies, 1960–1971. *Comp. Polit. Stud.* 17:81–119

Swank, D. H., Hicks, A. 1985. The determinants and redistributive impacts of state welfare spending in the advanced capitalist democracies, 1960–1980. In *Political Economy in Western Democracies,* ed. N. J. Vig, S. E. Schier, pp. 115–39. New York: Holmes & Meier

Swenson, P. 1989. *Fair Shares. Unions, Pay, and Politics in Sweden and West Germany.* Ithaca: Cornell Univ. Press

Therborn, G. 1986. *Why Some People Are More Unemployed than Others:The Strange Paradox of Growth and Unemployment.* London: Verso

Therborn, G. 1987. Welfare states and capitalist markets. *Acta Sociol.* 30:237–54

Therborn, G. 1989. Nation och Klass, tur och skicklighet: Vagar till standig (?) makt. In *Socialdemokratins Samhalle,* ed. K. Misgeld, pp. 342–68. Stockholm: Tiden

Tilton, T. 1990. *The Political Theory of Swedish Social Democracy. Through the Welfare State to Socialism.* Oxford: Clarendon

Titmuss, R. D. 1974. *Social Policy: An Introduction.* London: Allen & Unwin

van Arnhem, J., Corina, M., Schotsman, G. 1982. Do parties affect the distribution of income? In *The Impact of Parties,,* ed. F. Castles, pp. 283–364. London: Sage

van Kersbergen, K. 1991. *Social capitalism: A study of christian democracy and the postwar settlement of the welfare state.* PhD thesis. European Univ. Inst., Firenze, Italy

Weir, M., Skocpol, T. 1985. State structures and the possibilities for 'Keynesian' responses to the Great Depression in Sweden, Britain and the United States. See Evans et al 1985, pp. 107–63

Weir, M., Orloff, A. S., Skocpol, T. 1988. *The Politics of Social Policy in the United States.* Princeton, NJ: Princeton Univ. Press

Western, B. 1989. Decommodification and the transformation of capitalism: welfare state development in seventeen OECD countries. *Austr. NZ J. Sociol.* 25:200–21

Whiteley, P. 1983. The political economy of economic growth. *Eur. J. Polit. Res.* 11:197–213

Wigforss, E. 1941. *Fraan Klasskamp till Samverkan.* Stockholm: Tiden

Wilensky, H. L., Lebeaux, C. N. 1958. *Industrial Society and Social Welfare.* New York: Sage

Wilensky. H. L. 1981. Leftism, Catholicism, and democratic corporatism: the role of political parties in recent welfare state development. In *The Development of Welfare States in Europe and America,* ed. P. Flora, A. J. Heidenheimer, pp. 345–82. New Brunswick: Transaction

Annu. Rev. Sociol. 1992 18:209–32

MEDICALIZATION AND SOCIAL CONTROL

Peter Conrad

Department of Sociology, Brandeis University, Waltham, Massachusetts 02254–9110

KEY WORDS: medical social control, medical profession, demedicalization, medical model, deviance

Abstract

This essay examines the major conceptual issues concerning medicalization and social control, emphasizing studies published on the topic since 1980. Several issues are considered: the emergence, definition, contexts, process, degree, range, consequences, critiques, and future of medicalization and demedicalization. Also discussed are the relation of medicalization and social control, the effect of changes in the medical profession and organization on medicalization, and dilemmas and lacunae in medicalization research.

INTRODUCTION

Medicalization describes a process by which nonmedical problems become defined and treated as medical problems, usually in terms of illnesses or disorders. This article reviews the work of sociologists, anthropologists, historians, physicians, and others who have written about medicalization. While I briefly discuss some of the seminal writings on the topic, the emphasis here is on work published after 1980, because a compilation of earlier writings is available elsewhere (see Conrad & Schneider 1980a).

0360-0572/92/0815-0209$02.00

THE EMERGENCE OF MEDICALIZATION

During the 1970s the term medicalization crept into the social scientific literature. While it literally means "to make medical," it has come to have wider and more subtle meanings. The term has been used more often in the context of a critique of medicalization (or overmedicalization) than as a neutral term simply describing that something has become medical.

Critics of the widening realm of psychiatry were the first to call attention to medicalization, although they did not call it that (e.g. Szasz 1963). Pitts (1968), Freidson (1970) and Zola (1972) presented the initial examinations of medicalization and medical social control. They took their inspiration from sources as different as Parsons (1951) and labeling theory. Parsons was probably the first to conceptualize medicine as an institution of social control, especially the way in which the "sick role" could conditionally legitimate that deviance termed illness. Freidson and Zola based their conceptions, in part, on the emergent social constructionism embedded in the then current labeling or societal reaction perspective.

A number of "case studies" of the medicalization of deviance were published in the 1970s: Conrad (1975) on hyperactivity in children, Scull (1975) on mental illness, Pfohl (1977) on child abuse, and Schneider (1978) on alcoholism as a disease. Other studies analyzed changes from nonmedical to medical definitions and treatments, although they did not necessarily use a medicalization framework (e.g. Foucault 1965, Gusfield 1967, Wertz & Wertz 1989). Illich (1976) used the conception "the medicalization of life" in his influential critique of medicine. Thus, by the time Conrad & Schneider (1980a) wrote *Deviance and Medicalization: From Badness to Sickness,* there was already a substantial literature to build upon.

Medicalization and Definitions

Although much has been written about medicalization, the definition has not always been clearly articulated. Most agree that medicalization pertains to the process and outcome of human problems entering the jurisdiction of the medical profession, but there are differences in the way they see the process. One of the most straightforward definitions is presented by Zola (1983:295): Medicalization is a "process whereby more and more of everyday life has come under medical dominion, influence and supervision." In an early statement, Conrad (1975:12) sees it as "defining behavior as a medical problem or illness and mandating or licensing the medical profession to provide some type of treatment for it." While these definitions are serviceable they both make the assumption that the problem must move into the jurisdiction of the medical profession; in certain instances, however, the medical profession is only marginally involved or even uninvolved (e.g. alcoholism). This has led to some confusion about what constitutes demedicalization.

The key to medicalization is the definitional issue. Medicalization consists of defining a problem in medical terms, using medical language to describe a problem, adopting a medical framework to understand a problem, or using a medical intervention to "treat" it. This is a sociocultural process that may or may not involve the medical profession, lead to medical social control or medical treatment, or be the result of intentional expansion by the medical profession. Medicalization occurs when a medical frame or definition has been applied to understand or manage a problem; this is as true for epilepsy as for "gender dysphoria" (transexualism). The interest in medicalization has predominantly focused on previously nonmedical problems that have been medicalized (and, often, thought to be inappropriately medicalized), but actually medicalization must include all problems that come to be defined in medical terms.

While the definitional issue remains central, a broader conceptual frame helps clarify the meaning of medicalization (Conrad & Schneider 1980b). Medicalization can occur on at least three distinct levels: the conceptual, the institutional, and the interactional levels. On the conceptual level a medical vocabulary (or model) is used to "order" or define the problem at hand; few medical professionals need be involved, and medical treatments are not necessarily applied. On the institutional level, organizations may adopt a medical approach to treating a particular problem in which the organization specializes. Physicians may function as gatekeepers for benefits that are only legitimate in organizations that adopt a medical definition and approach to a problem, but where the everyday routine work is accomplished by nonmedical personnel. On the interactional level, physicians are most directly involved. Medicalization occurs here as part of doctor-patient interaction, when a physician defines a problem as medical (i.e. gives a medical diagnosis) or treats a "social" problem with a medical form of treatment (e.g. prescribing tranquilizer drugs for an unhappy family life). Thus it becomes clearer that medicalization is a broad definitional process, which may or may not directly include physicians and their treatments (although it often does). Subcultures, groups, or individuals may vary in their readiness to apply, accept, or reject medicalized definitions (Cornwell 1984).

There have been general and specific critiques of medicalization. The general critiques argue that the medicalization case has been overstated and that there are considerable constraints to medicalization (Fox 1977, Strong 1979). The specific critiques focus more directly on the conceptual validity of the case studies (Woolgar & Pawluch 1985, Bury 1986). The theoretical frame underlying these cases of medicalization is a type of social constructionism (cf Spector & Kitsuse 1977, Schneider 1985), although this is not explicitly noted in all the writings. Put simply, this perspective presents reality and knowledge as "socially constructed," shaped by its human constructors, and brackets the assumption that there is any a priori reality "out there" to be discovered. These medicalization studies document the historical "discovery" of a medical problem, with attention to who said what, when, and with what consequences. This requires examining the professional literature, events, and claims-making activities (cf Spector & Kitsuse 1977). It is worth noting that some studies do not argue that a medical diagnosis is merely a social construction, but rather analyze how the problem came into the medical domain.

Bury's (1986) critique is the most relevant to medicalization studies. He contends that since social constructionism assumes the relativity of all knowledge, constructionism itself is affected by the same forces as scientific knowledge. It is not an independent "judge" (as analysts seem to assume); so on what basis can we differentiate a "discovery" from an "invention?" Bury further contends this has led analysts to exaggerate the extent of medicalization in contemporary society. In a response, Nicholson & McLaughlin (1987:118) make the important point that displaying the social and contextual nature of knowledge—e.g. how medical categories emerge—does not necessarily mean the knowledge is false. It is important to distinguish between the sociological investigation of how knowledge is developed and sustained, and how the knowledge is to be evaluated. King (1987), however, aligns himself more with Bury. Using transexualism as an example, he argues that the notion of the "invention" of transexualism as gender dyspohoria is no more credible than alternative (i.e. standard medical) interpretations. But he also notes that depicting the cultural production of knowledge doesn't necessarily undermine it. While Bury's critique should caution researchers about the limits of constructionism, this in itself does not compromise its usefulness for sociological studies. The bottom line is that medicalization analysts create new understandings about social processes involved in the construction of medical knowledge, which may or may not lead to evaluation of the process of that (biomedical) category or knowledge. While it is true that most medicalization analysts seem to imply overmedicalization, this evaluation is not inherent in the perspective.

Occasionally medicalization analyses are criticized for positing a social model to replace the medical model (Whalen & Henker 1977). This is a spurious criticism; it is the critics who focus on the issue of causation. Nearly all medicalization analyses bracket the question of causation of the particular behavior or condition and focus instead on how the problem came to be designated as a medical one. Medicalization researchers are much more interested in the etiology of definitions than the etiology of the behavior or condition (Conrad 1977). Indeed, this may reflect a weakness in medicalization research; analysts have offered or examined few viable alternatives to medicalized approaches to problems like alcoholism (Roman 1980b).

Medicalization has occurred for both deviant behavior and "natural life processes." Examples of medicalized deviance include: madness, alcoholism, homosexuality, opiate addiction, hyperactivity and learning disabilities in children, eating problems from overeating (obesity) to undereating (anorexia), child abuse, compulsive gambling, infertility, and transexualism, among others. Natural life processes that have become medicalized include sexuality, childbirth, child development, menstrual discomfort (PMS), menopause, aging, and death. While the specific origins and consequences of each of these arenas of medicalization may differ, many of the issues are similar.

CONTEXTS OF MEDICALIZATION

Analysts have long pointed to social factors that have encouraged or abetted medicalization: the diminution of religion, an abiding faith in science, rationality, and progress, the increased prestige and power of the medical profession, the American penchant for individual and technological solutions to problems, and a general humanitarian trend in western societies. While factors like these do not explain increasing medicalization over the past century, they have provided the context. Sociologists have examined two important contextual aspects affecting medicalization: secularization and the changing status of the medical profession.

Secularization

Numerous writers have suggested that medicine has "nudged aside" (Zola 1972) or "replaced" (Turner 1984, 1987) religion as the dominant moral ideology and social control institution in modern societies. Many conditions have become transformed from sin to crime to sickness. In Weberian terms, this is of a piece with the rationalization of society (Turner 1984). The argument is that secularization leads to medicalization.

There is some recent evidence to support this, largely in the writings of social historians (see also Clarke 1984). Brumberg (1988:7) sees anorexia as a type of secularized salvation:

> From the vantage point of the historian, anorexia nervosa appears to be a secular addiction to a new kind of perfectionism, one that links personal salvation to the achievement of an external body configuration rather than an internal spiritual state.

Although physicians had little to do with it, social responses to suicide were secularized in the eighteenth century due to a general loss in confidence in diabolical powers; according to MacDonald (1989), suicide was more or less medicalized by default. Homosexuality was medicalized in part in response to harsh religious and criminal sanctions; if it was hereditary, then the deviant behavior was not a voluntary act (Conrad & Schneider 1980a:181–85, but also see Greenberg 1988:406–11). Infertility used to be in the realm of the gods, as evidenced by fertility votives found the world over, but now it is firmly within the jurisdiction of medicine (Rothman 1989, Greil 1991).

It is often assumed that religious groups by definition resist secularization and medicalization, since these may erode theological turf. In a recent article, Bull (1990) questions this line of reasoning. He uses the case of Seventh Day Adventists, who have developed a rather substantial medical presence. He argues that this group "promotes secularization through their implacable opposition to the public role of religion" (p. 255) and that it also "operates a dynamic and effective instrument for extending and defending medical regulation of society" (p. 256) through their health regulations and doctrines. Thus Adventists encourage both secularization and medicalization, rather than being affected by it.

In fact, medicalization may have a rather ambivalent relation to marginal religious groups. On the one hand, medicalization has been used to oppose and neutralize cults, particularly in the name of treating "brainwashed" members (Robbins & Anthony 1982). On the other hand, some healing cults among the poor and marginal classes have embraced the medical view. The symbols of some traditional Latin American healing cults fuse the power of religious healing and modern medicine by basing their beliefs and worship on the imagery of particular doctors as medical saints (Low 1988).

While it is true that medicine is in important ways nudging aside religion as our moral touchstone, the interface of medicine and religion is more complex than a simple secularization thesis would suggest.

The Medical Profession, Pediatrics and Medicalization

Although "medical imperialism" cannot be deemed the central explanation for medicalization (Zola 1972, Conrad & Schneider, 1980b), the organization and structure of the medical profession has an important impact. Professional dominance and monopolization have certainly had a significant role in giving medicine the jurisdiction over virtually anything to which the label "health" or "illness" could be attached (Freidson 1970:251). As we note later, the impact of the enormous changes in the organization of medicine in the last two decades on medicalization is an area in need of study, as well as is the reciprocal effects of medicalization on the profession (Schneider & Conrad 1980).

While it is difficult to predict future changes, a well researched historical example can provide insight.

In a provocative paper, Pawluch (1983) shows how in a changing social environment pediatricians were able to adapt their orientations to maintain their practices. In the context of an improved standard of living, public health measures, and preventive vaccinations, there were fewer sick children for pediatricians to treat. Pawluch argues that pediatricians weathered this professional crisis by changing the focus of their practices, first by becoming "baby feeders," and recently by including children's troublesome behavior in their domain. The new "behavioral pediatrics" enabled pediatricians to maintain and enhance their medical dominance by expanding their medical territory. This led to the medicalization of a variety of psychosocial problems of children.

Halpern (1990), in an important article, contests some of Pawluch's interpretation. She argues that routinization of work, rather than market decline, preceded behavioral pediatrics. To the recently trained academic specialists, general outpatient care seemed "unappealingly routine" (Halpern 1990:30). The "new pediatrics" was a vehicle for academic generalists to secure a place in medical schools dominated by subspecialists and to make their own training and routine clinical work more stimulating. She argues that understimulated specialists in search of professional standing rather than underused clinical practitioners took the lead in medicalization. While the data cannot be conclusive, based on a review of studies, Halpren suggests that pediatricians do not seem to have increased their treatment of psychosocial disorders in recent decades. She further suggests that physicians need not treat the medicalized disorders themselves, but can become the managers of medical care, while auxiliaries and extenders provide treatments in a medical frame. Put another way, Halpern suggests that medicalization in pediatrics occurred more on the conceptual and institutional levels than on the interactional level of patient treatment (cf Conrad & Schneider 1980b).

Whether Halpern's "routinization hypothesis" or Pawluch's "market hypothesis" is more nearly correct, or some combination of both as Halpern (1990:35) seems to indicate, it is clear that medicalization is in part a by-product of intraprofessional issues that underlie the growth of behavioral pediatrics. The cases of hyperactivity (Conrad 1975, 1976) and learning disabilities (Carrier 1983, Erchak & Rosenfeld 1989) are examples of the increased medicalization of childhood behavioral problems.

MEDICAL SOCIAL CONTROL

Social control is a central and important concept in sociology. Most societies develop therapeutic styles of social control (Horwitz 1991), especially when individualism is highly valued. Durkheim (1893/1933) differentiated between repressive and restitutive controls, seeing the latter as more characteristic of complex societies. The social control aspect of medicine was conceptualized initially by Parsons (1951), when he depicted illness as deviance and medicine and the "sick role" as the appropriate mechanism of social control. Early analysts (Pitts 1968, Zola 1972) indicated that medical social control would likely replace other forms of control; while this has not occurred, it can be argued that medical social control has continued to expand (see below, The Range of Medicalization). While numerous definitions of medical social control have been offered (Pitts 1968, Zola 1972, Conrad 1979, O'Neill 1986), in terms of medicalization "the greatest social control power comes from having the authority to define certain behaviors, persons and things" (Conrad & Schneider 1980a:8). Thus, in general, the key issue remains definitional—the power to have a particular set of (medical) definitions realized in both spirit and practice.

This is not to say that medical social control is not implemented by the medical profession (it generally is), or that it is not abetted by powerful forms of medical technology (it often is). It is to say that without medicalization in a definitional sense, medical social control loses its legitimacy and is more difficult to accomplish. The development of a technique of medical social control (e.g. a pharmaceutical intervention) may precede the medicalization of a problem, but for implementation some type of medical definition is necessary (e.g. Conrad 1975). More typically, however, medicalization precedes medical social control.

In the context of medicalizing deviance, Conrad (1979) distinguished three types of medical social control: medical ideology, collaboration, and technology. Simply stated, medical ideology imposes a medical model primarily because of accrued social and ideological benefits; in medical collaboration doctors assist (usually in an organizational context) as information providers, gatekeepers, institutional agents, and technicians; medical technology suggests the use for social control of medical technological means, especially drugs, surgery, and genetic or other types of screening. While these are overlapping categories, they do allow us to characterize types of medical social control. Perhaps the most common form is still "medical excusing" (Halleck 1971), ranging from doctor's notes for missing school to disability benefits, to eligibility to the insanity defense.

To these categories we can add a fourth—medical surveillance. Based on the work of Foucault (1973, 1977), this form of medical social control suggests that certain conditions or behaviors become perceived through a "medical gaze" and that physicians may legitimately lay claim to all activities concerning the condition. Perhaps the classic example of this is childbirth, which, despite all the birthing innovations of the last two decades (Wertz & Wertz 1989), remains firmly under medical surveillance. Indeed, the medical surveillance of obstetrics has now expanded to include prenatal lifestyles, infertility, and postnatal interaction with babies (Arney 1982).

Some significant developments have occurred in medical social control over the past decade. In terms of ideological control, PMS (premenstrual syndrome) has emerged as an explanation of a variety of types of female deviance (Riessman 1983). In terms of collaboration, many work organizations have implemented Employee Assistance Programs (EAPs) (Roman 1980a, Sonnenstuhl 1986) and worksite screenings for drugs (Walsh et al 1992) and AIDS, both strategies for medical detection (identification), and in the case of EAPS, medical intervention. Forms of medical technological control which have been recently examined by social scientists include penile implants for male sexual dysfunction (Teifer 1986), hormonal and surgical treatments for transsexualism (Billings & Urban 1992), genetic screening (Hubbard & Henifin 1985), and chemical executions in implementing the death penalty (Haines 1989). Beyond the childbirth example, analysts have examined the extension of medical surveillance to the body (Armstrong 1983, Turner 1984), mental illness and homelessness (Snow et al 1986), and to a certain extent, lifestyle (Conrad & Walsh 1992; but see discussion in The Range of Medicalization section).

Medical collaboration and technology can have deadly outcomes. The most disturbing (and horrifying) case of medical control is the German physicians' genocidal collaborations with the Nazis, including formulating and carrying out the eradication of the "genetically defective" (Lifton 1986, Proctor 1988). These also included the medical technological interventions in concentration camp killings which were couched as medical operations (Lifton, 1986). Fortunately, most forms of medical social control are not so diabolical or lethal, but the case of the Nazi doctor exemplifies the extreme, destructive use of medical social control.

In a very different context, Bosk (1985) examines the profession's social control of itself—in terms of self-regulation and control of deviance—and finds the profession to be tolerant and forgiving of its own, as opposed to its less tolerant treatment of lay population deviance. This has been manifested recently by the emergence of the notion of "impaired physicians" as a medicalized explanation for physician deviance (Stimson 1985, T. Johnson 1988). The impaired physician concept is largely based upon the extant medicalization of substance abuse, and it allows the medical profession to "take charge of a significant amount of physician deviance, and to keep it away from the control of licensing and disciplinary bodies" (Stimson 1986:161). Thus the profession uses medicalized social control to reinforce its claims for self-regulation.

One needs to be cautious in making claims about the actual functioning of medicalized social control. While EAPs certainly appear to be a strategy for controlling deviant work performance, studies suggest that most employees using EAPs are self-referrals rather than supervisor referrals (Sonnenstuhl 1982, 1986), raising the question of whether these can be classified as a means of corporate social control.

Although analysts have written about medical social control for over four decades, very few studies have compared medical social control to other forms of control or have examined the growth of medical control in the context of changing social control. Such comparative studies would need either historical or cross-sectional data and in all likelihood would require some type of quantification. Two studies meet these criteria. Pastor (1978) studied transportation and admission to detoxification units. He compared medical and legal approaches to public drunkenness and found that 77% of medical rescue unit contacts ended up officially processed, compared to only 14% of police contacts. He concludes that "once mobilized, medicine is a more active, committed form of control than law" (Pastor 1978:382). Melick & associates (1979), using comparative historical arrest rate data covering nearly 40 years, found the number of males with police records admitted to psychiatric facilities has steadily and consistently increased. Melick et al argue that this represents a change in societal response to deviance—from criminal to medical—but they maintain that this shift was not ideological, occurring rather out of administrative necessity (crowded prisons and available mental hospital beds). While these studies support a medicalization hypothesis, we need more such studies to better understand how different forms of social control are used and under what conditions.

Social control, however, is rarely an either/or situation. As several researchers have pointed out, changes in social control may be cyclical and are subject to change (Conrad & Schneider, 1980a). Peyrot (1984) aptly reminds us that new clinical perspectives cannot be expected to fully supplement earlier modes of social control; for example, drug addiction remains within the purview of the criminal justice system despite medicalization (see also Johnson & Waletzko 1991). Thus it is not surprising that we find medical-legal hybrids in areas like addiction, drinking-driving, and gambling.

THE PROCESS OF MEDICALIZATION

Conrad & Schneider (1980a:261–77) presented a five-stage sequential model of the medicalization of deviance based on the comparison of several historical cases. While analysts have used this model to examine compulsive gambling (Rosencrance 1985), premenstrual syndrome (Bell 1987a), and learning disabilities (Erchak & Rosenfeld 1989), there has been little evaluation or development of this conceptual model. Peyrot's (1984) reframing of the stages and cycles of drug abuse is one of the few published critiques. Perhaps the model is inappropriate for other cases or is too general to be useful; still, it is unclear why the model has been ignored rather than criticized or modified. This is not to say that analysts have ignored the process of medicalization. If there is a theme to the issues raised in the discussion, it centers on the degree to which physicians and the medical profession are active in the medicalization process. Physicians were involved as claims-makers with hyperactivity (Conrad 1975), child abuse (Pfohl 1977), aging (Estes & Binney 1989), menopause (McCrea 1983, Bell 1987b, 1990), PMS (Riessman 1983, Bell 1987a), and the emergence of behavioral pediatrics (Pawluch 1983, Halpern 1990). Medical claims-making usually takes the form of writing in professional journals, official professional reports, activities in speciality organizations, and developing special clinics or services.

There are also cases where generally physicians are uninvolved or their initial involvement is minimal; the most obvious cases are in substance abuse—alcoholism (Schneider 1978), opiate addiction (Conrad & Schneider 1980a) and EAPs (Roman 1980a, Sonnenstuhl, 1986). At least two reported cases exist of active medical resistance to medicalization. Haines (1989) suggests the medical profession resists medical involvement in lethal injections for criminal executions, a process perceived as a threat to their professional interests. Kurz (1987) reports that there is resistance among medical emergency department (ED) personnel to the medicalization of woman battering . Some resistance to medicalization on the interactional or doctor-patient level is not surprising in situations like the ED or in busy practices where only limited medical resources are available (cf Strong 1979).

Organized lay interests frequently play a significant role in medicalization (Conrad & Schneider 1980a). Scott (1990), for example, suggests in the case of post traumatic stress disorder (PTSD) that a small group of Vietnam veterans consciously and deliberately worked along with psychiatrists to create such a diagnosis and to have it institutionalized in DSM-III. Sexual addiction, which received considerable mass media publicity, while having advocates, has never been legitimated in DSM-III or in any other "official" source (Levine & Troiden 1988). Similar lay claims-making can be seen in the cases of alcoholism (Schneider 1978) and EAPs (Trice & Bayer 1984), as well as in various challenges to medicalization described below (see section on Demedicalization).

Several authors have pointed out that patients sometimes are actively involved in medicalization. There is evidence for this from historical studies of childbirth (Wertz & Wertz 1989), homosexuality (Greenberg 1988, Hansen 1989), and more recently for PMS (Riessman 1983). It is clear that patients are not necessarily passive and can be active participants in the process of medicalization (cf Gabe & Calnan 1989).

Taken together these studies support the contention that medicalization is an interactive process and not simply the result of "medical imperialism" as well as that the medical profession can take a variety of roles and positions in the process (cf Strong 1979, Conrad & Schneider 1980b). Over the past 15 years a goodly number of cases of medicalization have accumulated in the social science literature. Detailed secondary analysis could further specify the process of medicalization. It is worth noting that few analysts have yet examined the cultural and structural factors underlying medicalization (for significant exceptions see Roman 1988, Roman & Blum 1991, Estes & Binney 1989, Binney et al 1990).

DEGREES OF MEDICALIZATION

In most cases medicalization is not complete; some instances of a condition may not be medicalized, competing definitions may exist, or remnants of previous definition cloud the picture. Therefore rather than seeing medicalization as an either/or situation, it makes sense to view it in terms of degrees. Some conditions are almost fully medicalized (e.g. death, childbirth), others are partly medicalized (e.g. opiate addiction, menopause), and still others are minimally medicalized (e.g. sexual addiction, spouse abuse).

We do not yet have a good understanding of which factors affect the degrees of medicalization. Certainly the support of the medical profession, availability of interventions or treatments, existence of competing definitions, coverage by medical insurance, and the presence of groups challenging the medical definition, are all likely to be significant factors.

Two examples can highlight some of the issues. While the claim has been made that battering or spouse abuse is a medical problem (Goodstein & Page 1981), evidence suggests that it is only minimally medicalized (Kurz 1987). This is particularly interesting because child abuse has been more completely medicalized (Pfohl 1977). In this case, issues of competing definitions, "ownership" (Gusfield 1981 and lack of medical support seem to be factors. The dominant definition of spouse abuse is not medical but feminist; the feminist movement championed the problem and its "treatment" (battered women's shelters) and thus can be said to "own" the problem (see Tierney 1982, Wharton 1987). As a second example, general agreement exists that menopause has been medicalized on a conceptual level (MacPherson 1981, Bell 1990). Data from a cross-sectional patient survey in Canada suggest, however, that it has not been medicalized to any great extent, and the use of hormone treatments for "symptoms" is relatively low (Kaufert & Gilbert 1986). Thus medicalization may be uneven; on the doctor-patient (interactional) level, menopause does not seem highly medicalized, while on a conceptual level it certainly is.

The existence of competing definitions may affect the degree of medicalization. When competing definitions are represented by strong interest groups, as with drug addiction, it is less likely for problems to be fully medicalized. While occasionally sociologists champion competing definitions (e.g. Galliher & Tyree 1985), more often sociologists present an analysis or critique without explicit alternatives. Despite some claims to the contrary (e.g. Strong 1979), sociologists tend not to be competitors to medicalized conceptions (Roman 1980b). As is discussed below, politicized challenges to medicalized concepts can affect the degrees the medicalization as well.

There is another dimension to the degree of medicalization: how expansive is the medical category? While some categories are narrow and circumscribed, others can expand and incorporate a variety of other problems. Hyperactivity initially applied only to overactive, impulsive, and distractible children (especially boys); however, now as attentional deficit disorder (ADD) it has become more inclusive. The diagnosis has expanded to include more teenagers, adults, and hypoactive girls (Wender 1987). Despite, or perhaps because of, evidence that ADD is an inadequately specified category (Rubinstein & Brown 1984), labeling and treatment seem to be increasing. One study found a consistent doubling of the rate of treatment for ADD children every four to seven years, so that 6% of all public elementary school students were receiving stimulant medications in 1987 (Safer & Krager, 1988). The rates rose faster in secondary than elementary schools.

Another interesting case is Alzheimer's Disease (AD). Although some analysts don't use a medicalization frame (Gubrium 1986, Fox 1989), that which was historically termed senility is now a broader and more inclusive category (Halpert 1983). AD was once an obscure disorder; it is now considered among the top five causes of death in the United States. Fox (1989) suggests that the key issue in the change in conceptualization of AD was the removal of "age" as a criterion, thus ending the distinction between AD and senile dementia. This dramatically increased the potential cases of AD, by including cases of senile dementia above 60 years old. Cognitive decline now became defined as a result of a specific disease rather than an inevitable aspect of aging. Some have suggested that expanding the definition of AD has shrunk the range of what is deemed to constitute normal aging (Robertson 1990), as well as resulted in a failure to recognize the extent to which cognitive decline can be socially produced (Lyman 1989).

A final example of category expansion is alcoholism. In recent years family members of alcoholics have been partly medicalized as enablers, codependents, and "adult children of alcoholics" (Lichtenstein 1988). Worksite programs have also expanded from "industrial alcoholism programs" to Employee Assistance Programs, and EAPs now are broadened into emotional health programs that include substance abuse, smoking, family problems and work dilemmas in their purview (Sonnenstuhl 1986, Conrad & Walsh 1992). In part this may result from a "murkiness" in the disease concept (Roman & Blum 1991), which allows for a certain malleability and expansiveness.

THE RANGE OF MEDICALIZATION

Publications in the 1980s enumerated the medicalization of numerous forms of deviance and natural life processes. Studies in the past decade have particularly examined the breadth of the medicalization of women's lives: battering, gender deviance, obesity, anorexia and bulimia, and a host of reproductive issues including childbirth, birth control, infertility, abortion, menopause and PMS. As Riessman (1983) notes, for a variety of complex reasons, women may be more vulnerable to medicalization than men. In any case, it is abundantly clear that women's natural life processes (especially concerning reproduction) are much more likely to be medicalized than men's, and that gender is an important factor in understanding medicalization.

In addition to studies of the medicalization of women's lives, considerable research on the medicalization of aging and alcoholism has been published. Estes & Binney (1989) have examined both the conceptual and policy (practice) aspects of the medicalization of aging. They note how more and more aspects of aging have come into medical jurisdiction and how the medical frame has become dominant in aging research, funding, and studies, especially as related to the National Institute of Aging. Estes & Binney point to the important role of Medicare in medicalizing problems of the elderly; because physicians are the only ones authorized to certify the need for care, increased services are seen in a medical frame. This point is illustrated by the medical shaping of Home Health Agencies (Binney et al 1990). Several authors (Binney et al 1990, Azzarto 1986) take the medicalization of elderly services as a measure of the medicalization of aging. When we include the previously discussed studies of menopause and Alzheimer's Disease, our knowledge base on the medicalization of aging broadens and deepens. Zola (1991) has recently argued that the issues of aging and disability are converging; as most people age they will develop disabilities, and barring death, most people with disabilities will age. Given the changing American demographic patterns into the twenty-first century, and the continuing insurance coverage only for "medical" problems, it seems likely that the medicalization of aging will persist and expand. And since a majority of the elderly are women, it is likely aging and gender issues will continue to converge.

The medicalization of deviant drinking and alcohol use has long been a topic of sociological interest (Gusfield 1967, Schneider 1978, Levine 1978). The emphasis of those studies has been on the impact of prohibition and repeal, the emergence of Alcoholic's Anonymous, and the development of the disease concept. Work has continued along these lines (e.g. Denzin 1987), especially questioning the scientific validity of the disease concept (Fingarette 1988). But much of the medicalization-oriented writing in the last decade has focused on specific issues like EAPs and to a lesser extent, the expansion of the concept of alcoholism (Peele 1989). Some new areas may be on the horizon. Roman & Blum (1991:780) suggest that the "health warning labels" on alcohol products "increase perceived risk associated with alcoholism consumption." They may affect public conceptions of alcoholism by making the drinker more responsible for his or her health problems. This may reinvigorate the moral elements of the moral-medical balance in the definition of alcoholism. It is likely, however, that the disease concept will continue to dominate thinking about alcoholism, with the success of Alcoholics Anonymous and the continued organizational supports for the disease concept, especially in terms of third party reimbursement for treatment of alcoholism, workplace EAPS, and encouragement from the alcohol beverage industry (Roman 1988, Peele 1989).

A key aspect of medicalization refers to the emergence of medical definitions for previously nonmedical problems. Thus when social or behavioral activities are deemed medical risks for well-established biomedical conditions, as is becoming common, we cannot say that it is a case of medicalization. There is some confusion around this, especially in terms of the recent concerns with health and fitness (e.g. Crawford 1980). In the 1980s "health promotion" and "wellness" activities were touted as increasing individual health and reducing risk of disease. For example, not smoking, low cholesterol diets, and exercising regularly could reduce the risk of heart disease. Although health promotion may create a "new health morality" (Becker 1986), based on individual responsibility for health (and lifestyle change), it does not constitute a new medicalization of exercise or diet. While the process is similar to medicalization in that it fuses behavioral and medical concerns, it may be better conceptualized as "healthicization." With medicalization, medical definitions and treatments are offered for previous social problems or natural events; with healthicization, behavioral and social definitions are advanced for previously biomedically defined events (e.g. heart disease). Medicalization proposes biomedical causes and interventions; healthicization proposes lifestyle and behavioral causes and interventions. One turns the moral into the medical, the other turns health into the moral. (Conrad 1987)

CONSEQUENCES OF MEDICALIZATION

Although medical interventions typically are judged by how efficacious they are, the social consequences of medicalization occur regardless of medical efficacy. They are independent from the validity of medical definitions or diagnoses or the effectiveness of medical regimens.

Numerous analysts have described consequences of medicalization. Conrad & Schneider (1980a:245–52) separate the consequences into the "brighter" and "darker" sides. Like most sociologists, they emphasize the darker side: assumption of medical moral neutrality, domination by experts, individualization of social problems, depoliticization of behavior, dislocation of responsibility, using powerful medical technologies, and "the exclusion of evil." The criticism of medicalization fundamentally rests on the sociological concern with how the medical model decontextualizes social problems, and collaterally, puts them under medical control. This process individualizes what might be otherwise seen as collective social problems.

These issues have been reflected and developed in subsequent writings. For example, Carrier (1983:952) argues how learning disability theory "misrecognizes and thus masks the effects of social practices and hierarchy." This has been noted for other problems as well (Lyman 1989, Riessman 1983). Medicalized conceptions of battering can lead to therapy and distract from a focus on patriarchal values and social inequality (Tierney 1982). Medical control may also affect public opinion and social policy. Rosenberg (1988, p. 26) suggests that policymakers have a penchant for medical solutions because they are "less elusive than the economic and political measures which are its natural counterparts." In a highly stratified society, medicalization may have implications for social justice (Gallagher & Ferrante 1987, Light 1989).

A few cases of medicalization bring up different issues. Post traumatic stress disorder is an instance where the cause of the disorder was shifted from the particularities of an individual's background to the nature of war itself; it is "normal" to be traumatized by the horrors of war (Scott 1990). Also of interest is the example of medical organizing against nuclear war. By depicting the devastation from nuclear war as "the last epidemic," Physicians for Social Responsibility and later the American Medical Association turned a political issue into a medical one. This was a very successful strategy for claims-making and organizing, and allowed physicians to make political statements in the name of health. To a degree both of these examples decontextualized the issue (war), but with different consequences than those in medicalizing deviance. One of the main differences here was that the issue turned on the effects of war, more than on war itself. In general, sociologists remain skeptical about medicalization, although ambivalent in the recognition of certain gains and losses (Riessman 1983).

DEMEDICALIZATION

Medicalization is a two-way process. Demedicalization refers to a problem that no longer retains its medical definition. In the late nineteenth century, masturbation was considered a disease and was the object of many medical interventions (Engelhardt 1974). By the twentieth century it was no longer defined as a medical problem nor was it the subject of medical treatment. Some analysts have suggested that the use of medical auxiliaries (e.g. midwives or physician assistants) instead of doctors represents demedicalization (Fox 1977, Strong 1979). This, however, confuses demedicalization with deprofessionalization. Demedicalization does not occur until a problem is no longer defined in medical terms and medical treatments are no longer deemed to be appropriate solutions. Demedicalization could be said to have taken place, for example, if childbirth were defined as a family event with lay attendants, if chronic drunkenness were reconstituted as an educational problem, or if menopause reverted to a natural life event, inappropriate for any medical intervention.

Childbirth in the United States has been medicalized for more than a century. The medical monopoly of childbirth is more recent (Wertz & Wertz 1989). In the last 15 years, the childbirth, feminist, and consumer movements have challenged medicine's monopoly of birthing. This has given rise to "natural childbirth," birthing rooms, nurse-midwives, and a host of other reforms, but it has not resulted in the demedicalization of childbirth. Childbirth is still defined as a medical event, and medical personnel still attend it. In the context of American society, even lay midwifery may not mean complete demedicalization. In Arizona licensed lay midwives have been pressured toward a more medical model of childbirth, especially through licensing and legal accountability in a medically dominated environment (Weitz & Sullivan 1985).

The classic example of demedicalization in American society is homosexuality. In response to the protest and picketing of the gay liberation movement (with some sympathetic psychiatric allies), in 1973 the American Psychiatric Association officially voted to no longer define (i.e. include in DSM-III) homosexuality as an illness. This represented at least a symbolic demedicalization (Conrad & Schneider 1980a, Bayer 1981). Here politicization of medicalization created an overt conflict which resulted in the demedicalization. Although some argue that lesbianism has yet to be demedicalized (Stevens & Hall 1991), it seems evident that today homosexuality is at least as often considered a lifestyle as an illness. As several observers note (e.g. Murray & Payne 1985), the onset of the AIDS epidemic has led to a partial remedicalization of homosexuality, albeit in a different form.

There are two other examples of demedicalization worth noting. The Independent Living Movement asserts that, in the lives of people with disabilities, "much of [the] medical presence is both unnecessary and counterproductive. . . [and] management of stabilized disabilities is primarily a personal matter and only secondarily a medical matter" (DeJong 1983, p. 15). They actively work to demedicalize disability, including reshaping its definition, and work to create environments and situations where people with disabilities can live independently and with minimal contact with medical care.

A most interesting example has emerged almost serendipitously. Winkler & Winkler (1991) suggest that single women who practice artificial insemination (AI) with "turkey basters" or other such materials, present a fundamental challenge to medicalization. This subterranean practice has been well-known in the women's health movement for sometime and apparently has proved quite successful. Because this practice requires no medical intervention, it raises important questions about the necessity of medical expertise and control even for infertile couples. The authors contend that demedicalization is already underway and argue for the demedicalization of AI for those women without reproductive maladies of their own.

Given the stature and power of medicine, demedicalization is usually only achieved after some type of organized movement that challenges medical definitions and control. Other factors can affect demedicalization. Some types of technology can led to a degree of demedicalization: turkey basters and take-home pregnancy tests are but two examples. And the recent upsurge in self-care erodes medical control. Changes in public policy or in insurance reimbursement eligibility can also affect demedicalization, but we do not yet have studies on how this works. For example, while due to state policy changes the mentally ill in the 1980s were clearly less cared for by psychiatry; their problems remained defined as medical, even as their needs were neglected. It is possible to have medicalized problems that remain untreated and uncared about. The ultimate key remains how the problem is defined and what types of interventions are deemed appropriate.

While evidence suggests that medicalization has significantly outpaced demedicalization, it is important to see it as a bidirectional process.

CROSS-CULTURAL RESEARCH

Most studies of medicalization have been in the American context. Its not clear whether medicalization is simply more advanced in American society or whether other societies have yet to be adequately studied.

Few cross-cultural or comparative studies have explicitly focused on medicalization. A significant exception are Lock's reports that in Japan menopause is less medicalized than in North America (Lock 1986) but that aging itself is increasingly medicalized (Lock 1984, see also Lock 1987). From a different perspective, Kleinman (1988) describes how in China patients suffering from difficulties with sleep, low energy, joylessness, and sadness are diagnosed having neurasthenia; he suggests that most could be rediagnosed as having a major depressive disorder (1988:13). In China the patients receive a physiological diagnosis, in North America a psychiatric one. While diagnosis and treatment differ, it can be argued that chronic demoralization is medicalized in both societies.

Given the dominance of Western biomedicine in the world, it would not be surprising to see the diffusion of biomedical categories to non-Western societies. Some unsystematic evidence suggests that this may be occurring for certain problems; for example, the medicalization of childbirth is increasing in societies that make medical childbirth a priority or that can afford the necessary medical resources (e.g. Colfer & Gallagher 1992). The extent to which deviant behavior is medicalized is still unclear, however. For example, when I asked neurologists and psychiatrists in Indonesia whether they saw or treated patients with anorexia, the overwhelming response was that such a disorder did not exist in Indonesia and doctors did not treat it; Earls (1981) reports the same situation in China. Nearly two decades ago Maccoby (1974) reported finding no hyperactive children in the schoolrooms of the People's Republic of China; more recent reports suggest that it has become the most common child psychiatric disorder, and large numbers of Chinese children are being treated with stimulant medications for hyperactivity or attentional deficit disorder (Earls 1981). This raises questions about whether Western medicalized concepts are exported to nonwestern societies, about the degree to which and under what conditions they are adopted, and about the impact and meaning they have in other cultures. In another context, it is clear that infant-formula manufacturers were active in promoting the medicalization of infant feeding the the Third World (Van Esterik 1989). We do not yet have much knowledge about the role of drug manufacturers and medical entrepreneurs in promoting and exporting medical definitions and treatments.

More cross-cultural studies would expand our understanding of medicalization in new directions. For example, how are anorexia, hyperactivity, obesity, and PMS defined and treated in other cultures? What does it mean whether or not a nonwestern society medicalizes a particular problem? How does a problem's definition relate to the culture and medical belief system? When certain phenomenon are found or identified in only a few cultures, anthropologists typically conceptualize these as Western "culture-bound syndromes"(Ritenbaugh 1982, Littlewood & Lipsedge 1987, T. Johnson 1987). How does medicalization interplay with culture-boundedness? What types of cultural and structural factors in societies encourage or discourage the medicalization of life's problems?

In short, it would be most useful to expand medicalization studies cross-nationally and cross-culturally, to investigate the issues of (i) indigious definitions of problems currently medicalized in the West, and (ii) the diffusion and exportation of medicalized conceptions and treatments to other societies.

ISSUES IN THE FUTURE OF MEDICALIZATION

Throughout this essay I have touched on a number of issues in medicalization research. Here I want to point to several that are critical for expanding our understanding of medicalization and demedicalization.

Medicine in the United States is changing. Medical authority is declining (Starr 1982); increasingly physicians are now employees (McKinlay & Stoeckle 1988). Corporate structures have increased power in terms of third-parties and the "buyers" of health services, to name only the most major changes. These are fundamental changes in the organization of medicine. What impacts are they having on medicalization? Similarly, what is the impact of the dismantling of the welfare state (and subsequent cutbacks)? Will this engender a redefinition to "badness" rather than sickness?

What is the relationship between the economic infrastructure of health care—primarily insurance reimbursement—and medicalization? What is the effect of continuing rising health costs and subsequent policy concerns with cost containment? Does this fuel or constrain medicalization and how? What impact could universal health insurance have on medicalization? Comparative studies of other industrialized health systems would be useful here.

Few authors have yet examined the influence of the AIDS epidemic on medicalization. While it clearly has an impact on the definition and treatment of homosexuality, and probably on drug addiction as well, we know little about the impact. And since AIDS is affecting medicine and our society in many ways, how else is it affecting medicalization? For example, what does HIV testing mean for extending medical surveillance?

While cases like obesity and "chronic fatigue syndrome" are still only partly investigated, in general, I believe we need to go beyond the accumulation of cases to investigate more carefully the causes of medicalization. This includes unearthing previously undetected dimensions of medicalization and contributing to a more integrated theory.

A few specific issues call for attention. Even after nearly two decades of writing, we know rather little about the extent of medicalization. As noted above, for example, menopause is medicalized conceptually, but it is not clear that it is widely medicalized in practice. We need now also to attempt to quantify the extent of medicalization of different problems and to begin to analyze variations and comparisons. This includes more empirical comparisons of medical and other types of social control. Two recent publications (Waitzkin 1991, Dull & West 1991) have presented glimpses of practicing doctors' views of medicalization. Given that some studies have suggested less medicalization may occur on the doctor-patient level than might be predicted by the existence of medical conceptions, research on the medicalization of perceptions and practices in everyday medical practice could be illuminating .

In sum, medicalization continues to be a rich area of sociological research and analysis. It may now be the right moment to focus more directly on investigating the structural underpinnings of medicalization, especially given the enormous changes occurring in medical organization and knowledge, and to expand our lens to examine cross-cultural dimensions of medicalization.

ACKNOWLEDGMENTS

My thanks to Irving K. Zola and the reviewers for helpful comments on this chapter.

Literature Cited

Armstrong, D. 1983. *Political Anatomy of the Body*. New York: Cambridge. 176 pp.

Arney, W. R. 1982. *Power and the Profession of Obstetrics*. Chicago: Univ. Chicago. 290 pp.

Azzarto, J. 1986. Medicalization of problems of the elderly. *Health Soc. Work* 11:189–95

Bayer, R. 1981. *Homosexuality and American Psychiatry: The Politics of Diagnosis*. New York: Basic

Becker, M. 1986. The tyranny of health promotion. *Public Health Rev*. 14:15–25

Bell, S. E. 1987a. Premenstrual syndrome and the medicalization of menopause: a sociological perspective. In *Premenstrual Syndrome: Ethical and Legal Implications in a Biomedical Perspective,* ed. B. E. Ginsburg, B. F. Carter, pp. 151–71. New York: Plenum

Bell, S. E. 1987b. Changing ideas: the medicalization of menopause. *Soc. Sci. Med.* 24:535–42

Bell, S. E. 1990. Sociological perspectives on the medicalization of menopause. *Ann. New York* 592: 173–8

Billings, B. B., Urban, T. 1982. The sociomedical construction of transexualism: an interpretation and critique. *Soc. Probl.* 29: 266–82

Binney, E. A., Estes, C. L., Ingman, S. R. 1990. Medicalization, public policy and the elderly: social services in jeopardy? *Soc. Sci. Med.* 30:761–71

Bosk, C. L. 1985. Social control and physicians: the oscillation of cynicism and idealism in sociological theory. In *Social Controls and the Medical Profession,* ed. J. P. Swazey, S. R. Scher, pp. 31–48. Boston: Oelgeschlager, Gunn. 268 pp.

Brumberg, J. J., 1988. *Fasting Girls: The Emergence of Anorexia Nervosa as a Modern Disease*. Cambridge: Harvard Univ. Press. 366 pp.

Bull, M. 1990. Secularization and medicalization. *Br. J. Sociol.* 41:245–61

Bury, M. R. 1986. Social constructionism and the development of medical sociology. *Sociol. Health Illness* 8:137–69

Carrier, J. G. 1983. Masking the social in educational knowledge: the case of learning disability theory. *Am. J. Sociol.* 88:948–74

Clarke, J. N. 1984. Medicalization and secularization in selected English Canadian fiction. *Soc. Sci. Med.* 18: 205–10

Colfer, C. J., Gallagher, E. B. 1992. Home and hospital birthing in Oman: an observational study with recommendations for hospital practice. In *Health and Health Care in Developing Countries,* ed. P. Conrad, E. B. Gallagher. Philadelphia, Penn: Temple Univ. Press. Forthcoming

Conrad, P. 1975. The discovery of hyperkinesis: notes on the medicalization of deviant behavior. *Soc. Probl.* 23:12–21

Conrad, P. 1976. *Identifying Hyperactive Children: The Medicalization of Deviant Behavior*. Lexington, Mass: D. C. Heath. 122 pp.

Conrad, P. 1977. Medicalization, etiology and hyperactivity: a reply to Whalen and Henker. *Soc. Prob.* 24:596–98

Conrad, P. 1979. Types of medical social control. *Sociol. Health Illness* 1:1–11

Conrad, P. 1987. Wellness in the workplace: potentials and pitfalls of worksite health promotion. *Milbank Q.* 65:255–75

Conrad, P., Schneider,J. 1980a. *Deviance and Medicalization: From Badness to Sickness*. St. Louis: Mosby. 311 pp.

Conrad, P., Schneider, J. 1980b. Looking at levels of medicalization: a comment of Strong's critique of the thesis of medical imperialism. *Soc. Sci. Med.* 14A:75–79

Conrad, P., Walsh, D. C. 1992. The new corporate health ethic: lifestyle and the social control of work. *Int. J. Health Serv.* 22: 89–111

Cornwell, J. 1984. *Hard-Earned Lives: Accounts of Health and Illness in East London*. New York: Tavistock. 250 pp.

Crawford, R. 1980. Healthism and the medicalization of everyday life. *Int. J. Health Serv.* 10:365–88

DeJong, G. 1983. Defining and implementing the Independent Living concept. In *Living for Physically Disabled People,* ed. N. M. Crewe, I. K. Zola., pp. 4–27. San Francisco: Jossey-Bass. 429 pp.

Denzin, N. K. 1987. *The Recovering Alcoholic*. Newbury Park, Calif: Sage. 246 pp.

Dull, D., West C. 1991. Accounting for cosmetic surgery: the accomplishment of gender. *Soc. Probl.* 38:54–70

Durkheim, E. 1933. *The Division of Labor in Society*. New York: Free Press (Originally published, 1893). 350 pp.

Earls, F. 1981. *Child psychiatry in China: Summary of a three month visit*. Unpublished paper, Dep. Psychiatry, Harvard Medical School. 8 pp.

Engelhardt, H. T. 1974. The disease of masturbation: values and the concept of disease. *Bull. Hist. Med.* 48:234–48

Erchak, G. M., Rosenfeld, R. 1989. Learning disabilities, dyslexia, and the medicalization of the classroom. In *Images of Issues,* ed. J. Best, pp. 79–97. New York: Aldine de Gruyter. 257 pp.

Estes, C. L., Binney, E. A. 1989. The biomedicalization of aging: dangers and dilemmas. *The Gerontol.* 29: 587–96

Fingarette, H. 1988. *Heavy Drinking: The*

Myth of Alcoholism as a Disease. Berkeley: Univ. California. 195 pp.
Foucault, M. 1965. *Madness and Civilization*. New York: Random. 239 pp.
Foucault, M. 1973. *The Birth of the Clinic*. New York: Vintage. 215 pp.
Foucault, M. 1977. *Discipline and Punish*. New York: Random. 333 pp.
Fox, P. 1989. From senility to Alzheimer's Disease: the rise of the Alzheimer's Disease movement. *Milbank Q*. 67:58–101
Fox, R. C. 1977. The medicalization and demedicalization of American society. *Daedalus* 106:9–22
Freidson, E. 1970. *Profession of Medicine*. New York: Dodd, Mead
Gabe, J., Calnan, M. 1989. The limits of medicine: women's perception of medical technology. *Soc. Sci. Med*. 28:223–32
Gallagher, E. B., Ferrante B. 1987. Medicalization and social justice. *Soc. Justice Res*. 1:377–92
Galliher, J. F., Tyree, C. 1985. Edwin Southerland's research on the origins of sexual psychopath laws: an early case study of the medicalization of deviance. *Soc. Probl*. 33:100–13
Goodstein, R. K., Page, A. W. 1981. Battered wife syndrome: overview of dynamics and treatment. *Am. J. Psychiatry* 138:1036–44
Greenberg, D. F. 1988. *The Construction of Homosexuality*. Chicago: Univ. Chicago Press. 635 pp.
Greil, A. L. 1991. *Not Yet Pregnant: Infertile Couples in Contempory America*. New Brunswick, NJ: Rutgers Univ. Press. 243 pp.
Gubrium, J. F. 1986. Oldtimers and Alzheimers. Greenwich, Conn: JAI. 222 pp.
Gusfield, J. R. 1967. Moral passage: the symbolic process in the public designations of deviance. *Soc. Probl*. 15:175–88
Gusfield, J. R. 1981. *The Culture of Public Problems: Drinking-Driving and the Symbolic Order*. Chicago: Univ. Chicago Press. 248 pp.
Haines, H. 1989. Primum non nocere: chemical execution and the limits of medical social control. *Soc. Probl*. 36: 442–54
Halleck. S. L. 1971. *The Politics of Therapy*. New York: Science House. 283 pp.
Halpern, S. A. 1990. Medicalization as a professional process: postwar trends in pediatrics. *J. Health Soc. Behav*. 31:28–42
Halpert, B. P. 1983. Development of the term "senility" as a medical diagnosis. *Minn. Med*. :421–24
Hansen, B. 1989. American physicians' earliest writings about homosexuals, 1880–1900. *Milbank Q*. 67, Suppl 1:92–108
Horwitz, A. V. 1991. *The Logic of Social Control*. New York: Plenum. 290 pp.
Hubbard R., Henifin, M. S. 1985. Genetic screening of perspective parents and workers: scientific and social issues. *Int. J. Health Serv*. 15:231–44
Illich, I. 1976. *Medical Nemesis*. New York: Pantheon. 294 pp.
Johnson, J. M., Waletzko, L. 1991, Drugs and crime: a study in the medicalization of crime control. *Perspect. Soc. Probl*. 3:197–220
Johnson, T. M. 1987. Premenstrual syndrome as a Western culture-specific disorder. *Cult. Med. Psychiatry* 11:337–56
Johnson, T. M. 1988. Physician impairment: social origins of a medical concern. *Med. Anthro. Q*. 2:17–33
Kaufert, P. A., Gilbert, P. 1986. Women, menopause, and medicalization. *Cult. Med. Psychiatry* 10:7–21
King, D. 1987. Social constructionism and medical knowledge: the case of transexualism. *Sociol. Health Illness* 9:352–77
Kleinman, A. 1988. *Rethinking Psychiatry: From Cultural Category to Personal Experience*. New York: Free Press. 237 pp.
Kurz, D. 1987. Emergency department responses to battered women: resistance to medicalization. *Soc. Probl*. 34:69–81
Levine, H. G. 1978. The discovery of addiction: changing conceptions of habitual drunkenness in America. *J. Stud. Alcohol* 39:143–74
Levine, M. P., Troiden, R. R. 1988. The myth of sexual compulsivity. *J. Sex. Res*. 25:347–63
Lichtenstein, M. 1988. *Co-dependency: the construction of a new disease*. Pres. Annu. Meet. East. Sociol. Soc., Philadelphia, Penn.
Lifton, R. J. 1986. *Nazi Doctors: Medical Killing and the Psychology of Genocide*. New York: Basic. 561 pp.
Light, D. W. 1989. Social control and the American health care system. In *Handbook of Medical Sociology*,, ed. H. E. Freeman, S. Levine, pp. 456–74. 548 pp.
Littlewood, R. Lipsedge, M. 1987. The butterfly and the serpent: culture, psychopathology and biomedicine. *Cult. Med. Psychiatry* 11:289–335
Lock, M. 1984. Licorice in leviathan: the medicalization of the care of the Japanese elderly. *Cult. Med. Psychiatry* 8:121–39
Lock, M. 1986b. Ambiguities of aging: Japanese experience and acceptance of menopause. *Cult. Med. Psychiatry* 10:23–46
Lock, M. 1987. Protests of a good wife and wise mother: the medicalization of distress in Japan. In *Health, Illness and Medical Care in Japan,* ed. E. Norbeck, M. Lock, pp. 130–57. Honolulu: Univ. Hawaii Press. 202 pp.
Low, S. M. 1988. The medicalization of heal-

ing cults in Latin America. *Am. Ethnol.* 15:136–54

Lyman, K. A. 1989. Bringing the social back in: a critique of the medicalization of dementia. *The Gerontol.* 29:597–605

Maccaby E. E. 1974. Impressions of China. *Soc. Res. Child Dev. Newslett.* (Fall): 5

MacPherson, K. I. 1981. Menopause as a disease: the social construction of a metaphor. *Adv. Nurs. Sci.* 3:95–113

McCrea, F. B. 1983. The politics of menopause: the "discovery" of a deficiency disease. *Soc. Probl.* 31:111–23

McDonald, M. 1989. The medicalization of suicide in England: laymen, physicians, and cultural change, 1500–1870. *Milbank Q.* 67 (Suppl.) 1:69–91

McKinlay J. B., Stoeckle, J. 1988. Corporatization and the social transformation of doctoring. *Int. J. Health Serv.* 18: 191–205

Melick, M. E., Steadman, H. J., Cocozza, J. J. 1979. The medicalization of criminal behavior among mental patients. *J. Health Soc. Behav.* 20:228–37

Murray, S. O., Payne, K. W. 1985. *The Remedicalization of homophobia: scientific evidence and the San Francisco bath decision.* Pres. Annu. Meet. Soc. Study Soc. Probl. Washington, DC

Nicholson, M., McLaughlin, C. 1987. Social constructionism and medical sociology: a reply of M. R. Bury. *Sociol. Health Illness* 9:107–26

O'Neill, J. 1986. The medicalization of social control. *Can. Rev. Sociol. Anthropol.* 23: 350–64

Parsons, T. 1951. *The Social System.* New York: Free Press. 575 pp.

Pastor, P. A. 1978. Mobilization in public drunkenness control: a comparison of legal and medical approaches. *Soc. Probl.* 25: 373–84

Pawluch, D. 1983. Transitions in pediatrics: a segmental analysis. *Soc. Probl.* 30:449–65

Peele, S. 1989. *Diseasing of America: Addiction Treatment Out of Control.* Boston: Houghton Mifflin. 321 pp.

Peyrot, M. 1984. Cycles of social problem development. *Sociol. Q.* 25:83–96

Pfohl, S. J. 1977. The "discovery" of child abuse. *Soc. Probl.* 24:310–23

Pitts, J. 1968. Social control: the concept. In *International Encyclopedia of Social Sciences* (Vol. 14) ed. D. Sills. New York: Macmillan

Proctor, R. 1988. *Racial Hygiene: Medicine Under the Nazis.* Cambridge: Harvard Univ. Press. 313 pp.

Riessman, C. K. 1983. Women and medicalization: a new perspective. *Soc. Policy* 14(Summer):3–18

Ritenbaugh, C. 1982. Obesity as a culture-bound syndrome. *Cult. Med. Psychiat.* 6:347–61

Robbins, T. Anthony D. 1982. Deprogramming, brainwashing and the medicalization of deviant religious groups. *Soc. Probl.* 29: 266–82

Robertson, A. 1990. The politics of Alzheimer's Disease: a case study in apocalyptic demography. *Int. J. Health Serv.* 20:429–42

Roman, P. 1980a. Medicalization and social control in the workplace: prospects for the 1980s. *J. Appl. Behav. Sci.* 16:407–23

Roman, P. 1980b. Alternatives to the medicalization of deviant behavior. *Psychiatry* 43:168–74

Roman, P. 1988. The disease concept of alcoholism: sociocultural and organizational bases of support. *Drugs & Society* 2:5–32

Roman, P., Blum T. 1991. The medicalized conception of alcohol related problems: some social sources and some social consequences of murkiness and confusion. In *Society, Culture and Drinking Patterns Reexamined,* ed. D. Pittman, H. White, pp. 753–74. New Brunswick, NJ: Rutgers Univ. Press

Rosenberg, C. E. 1988. Disease and social order in America: perceptions and expectations. In *AIDS: The Burdens of History,* ed. E. Fee, D. M. Fox, pp. 12–32. Berkeley: Univ. California Press. 362 pp.

Rosencrance, J. 1985. Compulsive gambling and the medicalization of deviance. *Soc. Probl.* 3:275–85

Rothman B. K. 1989. *Recreating Motherhood: Ideology and Technology in a Patriarchal Society.* New York: Norton. 284 pp.

Rubinstein, R. A., Brown, R. T. 1984. An evaluation of the validity of the diagnostic category of Attention Deficit Disorder. *Am. J. Orthopsychiat.* 54:398–414

Safer, D. J., Krager, J. M. 1988. A survey of medication treatments for hyperactive/inattentive students. *J. Am. Med. Assoc.* 260:2256–59

Schneider, J. W. 1978. Deviant drinking as a disease: deviant drinking as a social accomplishment. *Soc. Probl.* 25:361–72

Schneider, J. W. 1985. Social problems theory: the constructionist view. *Annu. Rev. Sociol.* 11:209–29

Schneider, J. W., Conrad, P. 1980. The medical control of deviance: contests and consequences. In *Research in the Sociology of Health Care,* (Vol. 1), ed. I. A. Roth, pp. 1–53 Greenwich, Conn:JAI

Scott, W. J. 1990. PTSD in DSM-III: a case of the politics diagnosis and disease. *Soc. Probl.* 37:294–310

Scull, A. T. 1975. From madness to mental

illness: medical men as moral entrepreneurs. Eur. J. Sociol. 16:218–61

Snow, D. A., Baker, S. G., Anderson, L. et al. 1986. The myth of pervasive mental illness among the homeless. *Soc. Probl.* 33: 407–23

Sonnenstuhl, W. J. 1982. A comment on medicalization in the workplace. *J. Appl. Behav. Sci.* 18:123–25

Sonnenstuhl, W. J. 1986. *Inside an Emotional Health Program*. Ithaca, NY: ILR Press. 196 pp.

Spector, M., Kitsuse, J. I. 1977. *Constructing Social Problems*. Menlo Park, Calif: Cummings. 184 pp.

Starr, P. 1982. *The Social Transformation of American Medicine*. New York: Basic. 514 pp.

Stevens, P. E., Hall, J. M. 1991. A critical historical analysis of the medical construction of lesbianism. *Int. J. Health Serv.* 21: 291–308

Stimson, G. V. 1985. Recent developments in professional control: the impaired physician movement in the USA. *Sociol. Health Illness* 7:141–66

Strong, P. M. 1979. Sociological imperialism and the profession of medicine: a critical examination of the thesis of medical imperialism. *Soc. Sci. Med* 13A: 199–215

Szasz, T. 1963. *Law, Liberty and Psychiatry*. New York: Macmillan. 281 pp.

Tierney, K. J. 1982. The battered women movement and the creation of the wife abuse problem. *Soc. Probl.* 29:207–20

Teifer, L. 1986. In pursuit of the perfect penis: the medicalization of male sexuality. *Am. Behav. Sci.* 29:579–99

Trice, H. M., Beyer, i.M. 1984. Employee assistance programs: blending performance-oriented and humanitarian ideologies to assist emotionally disturbed employees. *Res. Commun. Mental Health* 4:245–97

Turner, B. S. 1984. *The Body and Society*. Oxford: Basil Blackwell. 280 pp.

Turner, B. S. 1987. *Medical Power and Social Knowledge*. Newbury Park, Calif: Sage. 254 pp.

Van Esterik P. 1989. *Beyond the Breast-Bottle Controversy*. New Brunswick, NJ: Rutgers Univ. Press. 242 pp.

Waitzkin, H. 1991. *The Politics of Medical Encounters: How Patients and Doctors Deal with Social Problems*. New Haven: Yale Univ. Press. 311 pp.

Walsh, D. C., Elinson, L. Gostin, L. 1992. Worksite drug testing. *Annu. Rev. Publ. Health* 13: In press

Weitz, R., Sullivan, D. 1985. Licensed lay midwifery and the medical model of childbirth. *Sociol. Health Illness* 7:36–55

Wender, P. 1987. *The Hyperactive Child, Adolescent and Adult*. New York: Oxford. 320 pp.

Wertz, R., Wertz D. 1989. *Lying In: A History of Childbirth in America.*. Expanded edition) New Haven: Yale Univ. Press. 323 pp. (Originally published, 1977)

Whalen, C. K., Henker, B. 1977. The pitfalls of politicization: a response to Conrad's "The discovery of hyperkinesis: notes on the medicalization of deviant behavior." *Soc. Probl.* 24:583–95

Wharton, C. S. 1987. Establishing shelters for battered women: local manifestations of a social movement. *Qual. Sociol.* 10:146–63

Winkler, D., Winkler, N. J. 1991. Turkey-baster babies: the demedicalization of artificial insemination. *Milbank Q*. 69:5–40

Woolgar, S., Pawluch, D. 1985. Ontological gerrymandering: the anatomy of social problems explanations. *Soc. Probl.* 32:214–27

Zola, I. K. 1972. Medicine as a institution of social control. *Sociol. Rev.* 20:487–504

Zola, I. K. 1983. *Socio-Medical Inquiries*. Philadelphia: Temple Univ. Press. 349 pp.

Zola, I. K. 1991. The medicalization of aging and disability. In *Advances in Medical Sociology*, pp. 299–315. Greenwich, Conn: JAI

Annu. Rev. Sociol. 1992. 18:233–51

THE CONCEPT OF FAMILY ADAPTIVE STRATEGIES

Phyllis Moen and Elaine Wethington

Life Course Institute, Cornell University, Ithaca, New York 14853

KEY WORDS: family decision making, families and social change, household economy. family transition, macro-micro linkages

---

Abstract

Is "family adaptive strategy" a useful concept? Does use of this concept link actions of individual families with macro-level social change? This chapter examines the concept of family adaptive strategies, noting that it is an intuitively appealing metaphor for family response to structural barriers and stressful events. It has been used principally as a sensitizing device, describing both macro-level and micro-level trends and patterns of behavior. But good examples of empirical investigations of family strategies are difficult to find. What we mean by a good example is one that uses the family adaptive strategy concept as an explanatory process. Three studies, by Elder (1974), Tilly & Scott (1978), and Hareven (1982b), do fruitfully draw on family strategies of adaptation using concrete measures of this hypothetical concept. We discuss various methodological issues related to this concept: the level of analysis, the unit of analysis, and problems of operationalization. In addition to these methodoological problems, there are also conceptual difficulties: what exactly is and is not a "strategy," whether families themselves view their actions as strategies or whether this label is based on researchers' analysis and interpretation, and whether strategies can be treated simultaneously as a cause and an effect. Several theoretical models serve to locate family strategies of

0360-0572/92/0815-0233$02.00

adaptation. A *structural approach* emphasizes the ways that larger social structural forces constrain the repertoire of available adaptations. A *rational choice* approach underscores the role of choice, within the confines of structural constraints, in an effort to maximize family well being. And a *life course* approach points to the importance of historical time, life stage, and context in delimiting both family problems and the possible strategies to deal with them.

INTRODUCTION

"Family adaptive strategy" is a construct with a certain intuitive appeal, bringing the family back in as an active participant in the larger society, an actor responding to, reworking, or reframing external constraints and opportunities. The metaphor of strategy invokes the role of families and households as flexible, decision-making units, actively choosing various patterns of behavior, rather than as merely compliant and submissive. It has been employed by social historians as a useful bridge between individual lives and collective behavior, a way of moving from impersonal social structures and forces to individual biographies (cf Bourdieu 1976, Tilly 1979, Hareven 1991). Sociologists have drawn on the notion of family strategies as a means of explaining the processes and consequences of social change and of depicting family and kinship as active ingredients in historical change (cf Thomas & Znaniecki 1974, Elder 1974). In addition, the "New Home Economists" have employed the concept in explaining the choices made to maximize the "family utility function" (cf Becker 1960, 1981, Schultz 1974).

Key considerations for scholars employing the concept of family strategies are the structural barriers limiting family options and behavior. Families are depicted as developing strategies precisely because there exist constraining economic, institutional, and social realities in the larger opportunity structure. Strategies, then, are the actions families devise for coping with, if not overcoming, the challenges of living, and for achieving their goals in the face of structural barriers. At a descriptive level, the metaphor of strategic action makes sense; families remain creative actors on a sometimes barren, sometimes hostile, stage.

But is the notion of family adaptive strategy more than a metaphor? How concretely can it be defined or operationalized? Can it be captured empirically? How useful is it in explaining family actions and inactions? While a potentially fruitful tool for locating family actions in their larger historical, cultural, social, and economic contexts, the family adaptive strategy construct presents both conceptual and methodological difficulties. We first describe some of the ways social historians, sociologists, and economists have employed the term, and then we discuss some of the analytical problems with the concept, as well as its theoretical underpinnings. Throughout the paper we suggest promising directions in the use of family adaptive strategies as a means of linking social change to individual and family change.

USES OF THE CONCEPT OF FAMILY STRATEGY

Tilly (1979) defined family adaptive strategy as a set of "implicit rules guiding the behavior" of family members, families, and households. These strategies have two functions: the first, a means of "familial rational calculation" to make economic and social decisions that affect the family as a whole; the second, "an application of preexistent perceptions and practices in dealing with everyday life," that is, a set of implicit decision rules for devising solutions to problems (Tilly 1987:124).

But few concepts in the family literature appear more frequently and with less specification in theory and operationalizations than the concept of family strategy. For example, strategies can be short-term tactics or long-term ventures; there is, as Smith (1987:118) points out, a difference between "planning for tomorrow and planning for the next generation." Moreover, the notion of strategy implies goals and objectives. To what ends do families maintain, adopt, or discard certain strategies?

A fruitful approach to identifying time frames and goals is in linking the concept of family strategy to that of the family as a household economy (Goode 1960, Kertzer & Hogan 1989, Smelser 1959, Tilly & Scott 1978). Both goals and means involve resource generation and allocation. Families most frequently plan short-term and long-term actions in order to consolidate or enhance their own economic situation and that of their children (Pitrou 1986, Zimmerman 1936). Families as collective entities send their members out to work, assign household tasks, share wages and resources, move from country to country or from city to city, buy farms, homes, televisions. Depicting families and households as role allocating, income pooling, and income spending units is both intuitively compelling and empirically valid (e.g. Davis 1976, Hareven 1978, Hill 1970, LePlay 1877–1879, Stack 1974).

At the micro level, what families do to achieve or maintain economic well-being or other objectives can be depicted as adaptive strategies. Thus the critical issue becomes discovering what leads to a change in strategy. A case in point is family response to shifting economic circumstance. In the face of economic upheavals families develop alternative strategies in an effort to lessen the gap between family needs and available resources. For example, the family breadwinner experiences unemployment and/or financial deprivation; other family members may then contribute to the family economy either by seeking paid work or by a more labor-intensive domestic activity (Elder 1974, Goldin 1981, Hareven 1982, Moen et al 1983, Tilly & Scott 1978).

Another example is when family consumption aspirations outstrip the breadwinner's wages. Modell (1978) draws on the concept of family income strategy to chart how Irish-born working-class families at the turn of the century in the northeastern United States sent their children to work and/or sought income from boarders and lodgers to increase the family's income and to maintain their families in the style of the relatively more affluent native-born working class. Other scholars have depicted variations in wives' and daughters' labor force and domestic activity as strategies in response to shifts in the demands of the family economy (Anderson 1971, Bennett & Elder 1979, Cross & Shergold 1986, Goldin 1981, Goldin & Sokoloff 1982, Hareven 1982b, Tilly & Scott 1978).

The employment of wives and daughters can be observed as a microlevel phenomenon as individual wives, mothers, and daughters decide (or are encouraged) to take paid jobs or, at the more macrolevel, as there are changes in the incidence, duration, rate, and timing of women's labor force participation within different populations. Most scholars draw on the notion of strategy in examining macrolevel social changes, for example, major shifts in family behavior in tandem with the transformation of Western society from an agrarian to an industrial economy, as well as in analyzing the protoindustrial phase of home-based manufacture (Hareven 1982b, Kriedte et al 1981, Modell & Hareven 1973, Tilly 1979, Tilly & Scott 1978).

Studies examining marriage and childbearing have typically taken such a macrolevel, demographic approach, viewing shifts in marital and fertility patterns as a family-level response to broader social and economic exigencies. For example, changes in childbearing are seen as a consequence of shifts in the costs and benefits, economic but also emotional, of children (Butz & Ward 1979, Easterlin 1961, 1980, Elder 1974, Engerman 1978, Espenshade 1979, Zelizer 1985). Often in these formulations, the active role of families and family members as decision-makers is implicit rather than explicit. The work by economist Richard Easterlin is a case in point. Easterlin assumes that cohorts have higher or lower fertility rates depending on their economic standing and prospects relative to that of earlier cohorts. But the actual **process** whereby men and women of particular cohorts weigh their aspirations and opportunities in formulating their "tastes" for children remains an assumption, reflected in the shifting patterns of fertility over time (e.g. Anderson 1986, Anderton & Bean 1985, Coale 1986, Coale & Watkins 1986, Hareven & Vinovskis 1978a,b, Vinovskis 1984).

Marriage "choices" are similarly inferred from behavior of individuals in particular historical, social, and economic contexts. We know little about the actual decision-making that leads to when and whether people marry; what we know is the fact and the timing of marriage (Modell 1980, Uhlenberg 1974).

The family adaptation strategy concept has also been invoked in describing the transitions into adulthood and old age, and the corresponding residential shifts involved in each. In the nineteenth and early twentieth century, in the absence of public "retirement" assistance, the family was responsible for the care of older relatives. The strategy by which this was frequently accomplished was the retention of one adult child within the parental household to help aging parents maintain a degree of economic independence (Chudacoff & Hareven 1979, Hareven 1982a).

The marshalling of kinship resources and obligations has also been depicted as a strategy employed by families. For example, the residential propinquity of newlyweds in the nineteenth century to at least one set of parents is described by Anderson (1971) as a conscious choice, with obvious benefits to the newlywed couple. The role of kin in caring for family members has been—and remains—an important research topic for scholars of the family (Hareven 1982a, Litwak & Szelenyi 1969, McCubbin & Patterson 1980, Mogey 1990, Shanas & Sussman 1977, Stack 1974).

The process of migration has also been analyzed as a family strategy facilitated through the kinship network (e.g. Glasco 1978, Kertzer & Hogan 1989). Hareven (1982b) has documented the importance of kin in chain migrations, wherein established residents assist in finding jobs for new immigrants. And in their recent study of Asian immigrants to the United States, Nee & Sanders (1991) document the importance of kinship ties for economic mobility.

Intergenerational transfers are important strategies as families shift economic, emotional, and human resources from one generation to the next in conjunction with shifts in the relative distribution of needs and responsibilities, abilities and assets (Hill 1970). Nee & Sanders describe the immigrant family as a "repository of cultural capital, accumulated both prior to immigration and during the process of incorporation" (1991:11). Various forms of human, social, and economic capital in the kinship network become strategic family assets that can be cultivated, tapped, and transmitted both within and across generations (Bott 1957, Coleman 1988, Glenn 1983, Hareven 1982b, Modell 1978, Nee & Sanders 1991).

Hareven (1991) has pointed out, however, that family strategies seem to be guided not exclusively by economic needs, but by the interaction of economic exigencies and cultural values. These cultural values arise from both family history and ethnic origins (e.g. Modell & Hareven 1973) and are sometimes in conflict with strategies that would seem more consistent with family economic need (e.g. Scott & Tilly 1975, Tilly & Scott 1978). Historical evidence as well as sociological research on family decision-making, allocation of family work and care, and the resolution of family conflict suggests that cultural factors regarding the maintenance of care, affection, and traditional role behaviors have an impact on the choice of family adaptive strategy

(Yans-McLaughlin 1971, Modell 1978, Pearlin et al 1990, Ross 1987, Stack 1974, Zelizer 1985).

Thus scholars draw on the family strategy construct as a sensitizing device to describe both macrolevel and microlevel processes: large-scale trends in fertility, labor force, migration, and marriage patterns are seen as indicators of strategies, as are family-level shifts in membership and role allocations within individual households. Family strategies, in both their macrolevel manifestations (as behavioral patterns and demographic trends) and their microlevel manifestations (as family and household decision-making processes) become ways of talking about social continuities and social change. But this raises the issue of level of analysis, discussed below.

METHODOLOGICAL ISSUES

We discuss in detail three methodological issues that are especially salient in the empirical investigation of family strategies: the level of analysis, the unit of analysis, and problems of operationalization.

Macro vs Micro Level of Analysis

As we have seen, family adaptive strategies may be considered at the level of individual families or at the collective level. In practice, social historians, economists, and sociologists have frequently operationalized family adaptive strategies as collective patterns of behavior, assumed to result from actions and decisions of individual families to improve their economic or social well-being (Moch 1987).

But generalizing from what is essentially descriptive trend data to the decision-making of actual families becomes then an inferential leap. Documenting collective trends and outcomes at the community or societal level does serve to establish the scope, incidence, and prevalence of different family strategies of adaptation; however, it does little to explicate the decision-making choices of ordinary families, or the mechanisms producing change in strategies over time. Consider, for example, the trends in wife/mother employment. Under what specific circumstances is having a wife seek paid employment seen as an alternative to the employment of children, moonlighting of the husband, and/or having a family take in boarders? How do individual families gauge the costs and benefits of such alternatives? Clearly, some options are constrained by the times in which families live, as well as the resources available to them. Thus, even when working at the macro level of population trends scholars need to consider how the repertoire of strategies of individual families both shapes and is modified by institutional, cultural, environmental, and interpersonal circumstances.

Unit of Analysis: Family Vs Household Vs Individual

Closely tied to the problem of the level of analysis is the choice of the appropriate unit of analysis in the study of family strategies. These choices boil down to studying households, studying family units, or studying individuals.

At an elementary level, researchers are aware that individuals, not families, make decisions (Thompson & Walker 1982). Yet family strategies represent more than just the sum of decisions of individual family members, reflecting instead at least tacit agreements among them. Particular strategies that emerge may or may not reflect the wishes of all family members (e.g. Hareven 1991, Saraceno 1989).

Power relations, frequently stratified by age and gender, obviously shape the decision-making process (Folbre 1987, Tilly 1987). A concrete example will clarify this point. Decision-making in families is known to be affected by the relative social positions of family members outside the family or household (Blood & Wolfe 1960, Huber & Spitze 1983, Safilios-Rothschild 1970, Scanzoni & Szinovacz 1980). Given traditional gender and age status systems in a society, it will typically be the husband's wishes that have the most impact on the family economic decision-making process, with consequent impact on the family's economic adaptation (Folbre 1987, Saraceno 1989, Tilly 1967). The husband's wishes have an impact not only on what type of decision will be made, but even on what weight the wishes of lower-status wife/mother and children are given. Thus a reliance on individual level data on decision-making and strategies may lead to a bias in data collection, depending on whose behavior and view of the decision-making process is being measured (Cornell 1987, Laslett & Brenner 1989, Saraceno 1989, Safilios-Rothschild 1969, Thompson & Walker 1982).

The unit of analysis is important as well when studying societies with more egalitarian gender and age status systems. Individuals may pursue their own distinctive strategies, sometimes even competitively or at cross-purposes with one another. The goals that individual family members are pursuing may or may not represent a family consensus. Exactly how conflicting strategies can coalesce into a "family" strategy—or even how family members with different goals achieve a consensus—is mostly uncharted territory (for a notable exception, see Hochschild 1989).

Problems of Operationalization

Measurement difficulties permeate studies of family strategies, because the concept of family adaptive strategy is more frequently invoked as a sensitizing device than as a tangible variable. As Watkins points out in her analysis of fertility trends, "the lack of fit between the stories told about the mechanics and the motivations behind the fall in marital fertility and the measures available to support or contradict these stories cautions against facile interpretations, comparison, and generalization of results" (1986:428–29). What are appropriate measures of family "mechanics and motivations"? Too often "strategies" represent a complex of concepts only poorly operationalized.

The level of analysis issue also becomes a measurement problem. Because scholars most often have access to collective outcomes (frequently in the form of broad patterns of behavior such as records of marriage, fertility, and co-residence) there has been a tendency to concentrate on these products of strategic decision-making, rather than the process itself. What is defined as "family strategy" is often a hypothetical construct, inferred from demographic and behavioral trends. But these trends, in turn, become reified as family strategies.

However, several scholars have in fact developed conceptual and operational models of family strategy. For example, Glen H. Elder, Jr. in his study, *Families of the Great Depression* (1974), defines three modes of adaptation as strategies of response to economic deprivation: changes in family needs (or claims), changes in consumption patterns, and changes in the source of economic resources. Families in the 1930s developed what were essentially two lines of adaptation: reducing expenditures, and/or generating alternative, supplementary sources of income. These were operationalized in terms of changes in the division of labor (such as the mother or adolescent child entering the labor force, or increases in household production) and family maintenance (in the form of public assistance or aid from kin). Elder hypothesizes that these adaptation strategies, along with concomitant changes in family relationships and social strains, serve as linking mechanisms between economic loss and developmental outcomes for children. Thus adaptation strategy is for Elder a sensitizing device for considering family response to loss; but he also incorporates it into his analysis through the use of concrete, measurable indicators. Elder's model assumes a mediating role for family strategies of adaptation.

Louise Tilly and Joan Scott in *Women, Work and Family* (1978) developed a process-oriented model of women's work as a family adaptation strategy in order to explain historical changes in women's participation in economic life. The underlying assumption of their model is that the labor of wives and daughters is a vital component of the family economy, underlying the survival of individual families. In the industrial and post-industrial eras, families have ensured their physical and economic survival by balancing the degree to which women engage in paid or unpaid labor, depending on overall economic opportunities and the family life cycle. Scott & Tilly operationalize these strategies using a combination of demographic data and surviving historical materials on individuals lives, to model the dynamic relationship between family strategies and social change, explaining why family roles are transformed over time. Tilly & Scott describe a process of family adaptation: Depending on the socioeconomic conditions, wives and daughters contribute to family economic well-being by performing unpaid labor, taking on paid work outside the home, and/or marrying in ways to preserve or enhance the family fortune.

Tamara Hareven in *Family Time and Industrial Time* (1982b) developed a process model of family adaptation as well in her study of the impact of industrialization on family structure and authority, community ties, and traditional culture. She operationalized family adaptation strategies using retrospective first-person accounts of individual family history and the family's migration to an industrial town, in tandem with more macrolevel information on economic and social conditions. Hareven linked socioeconomic circumstances to the structure and residence patterns of families. She examined as well the family adaptive responses to the demands of work environments that were alien to their cultural traditions, showing how the migration experience, combined with changing economic conditions, transformed family relations over succeeding generations.

Elder, Tilly, Scott, and Hareven all have developed concrete measures of the hypothetical construct, family strategies of adaptation. In doing so they are able to document the interactive relationship between social structural change, pre-existing cultural and social values in the family, and subsequent changes in the family over time.

CONCEPTUAL ISSUES

Just as there are methodological difficulties related to analyzing family adaptive strategies, so too there are potential conceptual pitfalls. One key conceptual issue concerns the delineation of precisely what family decisions and behavior fit under this broad rubric. As White points out concerning individual adaptation, in a sense all behavior can be seen as an "attempt at adaptation" (1974:49).

Also, it is open to question whether families themselves view as "strategies" the actions that researchers label as such after the fact or as what Bourdieu (1976:141) calls "implicit principles" by which households make decisions. For example, in discussing marital endogamy as a strategy in Kilmarnock, Scotland, Houston (1983) cautions that what is gleaned from the marriage registers is a record of marriage decrees, not the motivations behind them. Too few researchers have addressed this conceptual problem as explicitly as Houston. As Tilly (1967: 124) points out, there may well be both a family version of what constitutes family strategies and a scholarly version; one based on actual experience, the other on analysis and interpretation.

And finally, scholars need to avoid such conceptual pitfalls as "historicist functionalism" (Stinchcombe 1968), where the family adaptive strategy construct is simultaneously analyzed as a cause and as an effect. Strategies identified post hoc by researchers tend to be construed as having had a positive impact on families and the individuals within them, presumably because the family unit has survived. Stinchcombe (1968) has noted that it is an error to assume that the "best" adaptive strategy is necessarily the one selected most frequently. In the case of family adaptive strategies, even the "best" strategies impose personal and family costs. As Hareven (1991) and Saraceno (1989) have argued, "functionality" for one household member may be "dysfunctionality" for another. Moreover, at different points in historical time, family adaptive strategies may focus on concentrating the benefits for a select group of family members, rather than on maximizing benefits for family members equally. The practice of primogeniture is an obvious case in point: Eldest sons are a small minority of children.

The same family strategy may have many different, even contradictory antecedents—what Stinchcombe (1968) has defined as a case of equifinality. A current example of equifinality is the post hoc adaptive explanations that are given for interpreting wife employment as a family strategy. For instance, Wethington & Kessler (1989) report that the birth of first child leads to a higher probability of a wife staying home; but that the birth of additional children in other families leads to a higher probability for a homemaker going back to work. The former may be construed as emotionally adaptive for the social development of the child, while the latter may be construed as economically adaptive for the entire family unit. A strong argument can be made that wife employment is likely associated with low husband income (McLanahan & Glass 1985) but, equally plausibly, also is likely to be associated with high husband income (Pleck 1985), the latter because men and women of high educational attainment tend to marry and highly educated women are now more likely to be long-term participants in the labor force (Moen 1992). The former situation is generally interpreted as economically adaptive for the entire family whose survival may be threatened, but the latter could be construed as equally adaptive since it may arise from a desire to maximize family income by taking advantage of the wife's high earning potential and ability to pay for substitute household labor. Similarly, the disproportionate use of parental leaves and reduced work hours by Swedish mothers (compared to fathers) of young children may well be a consequence of strategic family decision-making to maximize family utility; but it also reflects the persistence of traditional gender norms promoting occupational segregation and the domestic division of labor (Moen 1989, Moen & Forest 1990). In sum, a "reasonable" adaptive scenario can be constructed—and empirically supported—for almost every family situation "causing" wife employment.

To better locate the family strategy construct and avoid such post hoc explanations, we consider several theoretical models, from structural theories to a perspective on choice making, and finally to an approach that links structures and actions over time, the life-course perspective.

Structural Responses to External Exigencies

A structural approach emphasizes the ways that larger social structural forces constrain, and to some extent determine, the repertoire of adaptations available to individual families in a given society. These social structural forces have impact not only on the adaptations that are possible, but also on which families—and which individuals within families—receive the most benefit from a given strategy (Saraceno 1989). Change in family adaptations over time, moreover, are assumed to be concomitant with social changes in these structural constraints (Hareven 1991). Four interlocking social structural systems are generally regarded as relevant: the economic opportunity structure; social status, caste, and educational stratification; gender relationships; and the age/generational hierarchy.

The economic organization of a society, and its social and political stratification systems, have an important impact on which families have access to resources for survival, achievement, and intergenerational mobility. According to this structural perspective, access to social and economic resources is the means by which social and economic differentiation between families is perpetuated. Family adaptive strategies are thus flexible only to the point that the social stratification system permits them to be (e.g. Bourdieu 1976).

Other social and cultural systems within a society (e.g. gender relationships, intergenerational hierarchy, religion, etc) also have an impact on family adaptive strategies. This is primarily a function of (although not exclusively limited to) social constraints regarding which individual family members have access to inheritance, education and other family economic investment, emotional sustenance, and even physical survival (e.g. Cornell 1987, Saraceno 1989).

Unfortunately, an exclusive focus on the power of these structural forces to mold family behavior over time results in misleading generalizations. Individual families tend to be depicted as at the mercy of forces beyond their control, their responses constrained to the point of total conformity to structural forces (Hareven 1991).

The recent "revolution" in historical research on the family, however, has tended to undermine the extreme version of the social structural perspective (Elder 1981, Hareven 1977). The new picture of family history, which is based on intense research activity in primary historical materials, contains three important components. First, families are depicted as having some power to control their immediate economic environment and chances for opportunity, primarily through planful strategic action (e.g. Hareven 1982b). Second, family structure and household composition, as well as relationships between members of individual families, are shown to be more complex and varied than the group and historical period norms predicted by social structural models (e.g. Elder 1981). Third, families are portrayed as having a "history" of their own which contributes to the perpetuation of their characteristics and structure over time, even in the face of structural and organizational forces predicted to destroy them (e.g. Gordon 1988, Gutman 1976).

In addition to the activity of social historians, the new feminist research on the family has also enriched understanding of the complex interaction of macrolevel social structure and individual family history. This research not only has awakened interest in studying the gender hierarchy as a powerful macrolevel social structure in its own right (Saraceno 1989), but also has uncovered the hidden history of women and children in families. From the new feminist perspective, women and children are depicted as having an impact on family structure and action, even if they are not the family's dominant members (e.g. Folbre 1987, Gordon 1988, Hochschild 1989).

Rational Choice

Structural rigidities inhibit the range of options, in the form of adaptive strategies, available to families and individuals. Still, the New Home Economists and some sociologists emphasize the role of choice, within the confines of structural constraints, and the interplay between historically delimited options and individual, or family, decision-making (Becker 1981, Berk 1980, Berk & Berk 1983, Coleman 1986, England & Farkas 1986, Schultz 1974). The fundamental basis of the New Home Economics is that the family acts so as to maximize its household utility, that is, the well-being of the family unit (Becker 1981). For example, from this viewpoint, decisions regarding employment and the domestic division of labor are made on the basis of economic and other pragmatic considerations. Men spend more hours in the paid labor force and fewer in domestic chores, from this perspective, simply because men have higher wage rates than do women and women are more "productive" in housework. The rational choice theoretical model would, therefore, posit changes in the adaptive strategies of families concomitant with changes in the relative economic rewards of men and women, in the costs and rewards of marriage, children, and divorce, and in the opportunity costs of decisions generally. How families embark upon a cost/benefit calculation, the role of altruism, the differential distribution of power within the family, and whether all family members have the same utility function remain open to speculation. Usually, moreover, in the application of this framework by economists, external structural constraints and the genesis of "tastes" are conspicuous in their omission. For example, why some couples choose to invest in themselves, remaining childless, while others scrimp to invest in their children's future education cannot be explained purely in terms of rational choice.

A Life-Course Approach

The notion of family adaptation strategies is closely linked to a life-course perspective on families and lives (Elder 1918, Elder & Caspi 1990, Hareven 1977). Life-course models combine aspects of structural and rational choice theories within a temporal framework to place family and individual strategies of adaptation in a larger historical, social, and cultural context of shifting opportunities and constraints, resources and demands, norms and expectations. These models are exemplified in the work of Thomas & Znaniecki (1974), Elder (1974), and Hareven (1978), all of whom have emphasized the importance of shifts in the configuration of demands and options or, similarly, resources and needs, as the impetus to a change in strategy. Transformations in the broader social, institutional, and economic environment produce fluctuations in family resources and needs (or aspirations); these, in turn, produce patterns of behavior designed to reduce the disparity between the two. The repertoire of family strategies may become transformed in light of demographic shifts in society at large. For example, increased longevity together with a decline in fertility has produced an extended "empty nest" phase, with parents (and especially mothers) now living for decades without children in the home (Riley & Riley 1989, Uhlenberg 1978). Thus historical change becomes an important ingredient in understanding the complexity of family adaptive strategies, and the notion of a gap between resources and needs serves to bridge the chasm between the micro and macro levels of analysis.

A life-course formulation also emphasizes the temporal nature of family strategies: their timing, duration, and sequence within the family cycle and the life course of the individual. Families are able to draw on various options across the life cycle, and are therefore differentially able to mobilize in response to external exigencies, contingent on the resources available and the subjective interpretations of family members. Families also pace the transitions of family members from one role to another to best fit the needs of the collectivity (Chudacoff & Hareven 1979, Hareven 1982a).

Additionally, the life-course emphasis on trajectories and timing also invokes the notion of cumulativeness, with conditions and choices in earlier times framing current options. There is, from this perspective, a sequence in phases of adaptation, from anticipatory plans, to definitions and redefinitions, to shifts in behavior, all of which are affected by available family resources and the broader opportunity structure (Moen et al 1983). Since lives in families are invariably interdependent, strategic actions may touch subsequent generations in quite unanticipated ways (Elder et al 1984, 1986, Furstenberg et al 1987).

Finally, a life-course approach to family adaptive strategies emphasizes the importance of context. Situational imperatives shape the repertoire of strategies available, as do previous experiences, subjective definitions, and the social, psychological, and material resources available (Elder & Caspi 1990, Liker & Elder 1983).

CONCLUSIONS

The concept of strategy calls forth the active (rather than the passive) role of the family unit and underscores the dynamic nature of family life; families mobilize and modify their plans and behavior as their circumstances change. As such, the concept of family strategy holds promise for specifying the processes that link individual lives with broad-scale social change. Individuals and families make choices in the face of the resources and constraints confronting them; their choices, in turn, themselves become a causal force shaping future resources and constraints, and thus contribute to trends and patterns of change in society at large. For example, the private decisions of individual husbands and wives regarding family size have direct implications for the fertility patterns of the community and society.

We have seen that the construct of family adaptive strategy remains somewhat imprecise, both in the development of testable theory and in the operationalization of variables. These conceptual ambiguities and measurement limitations necessitate greater specification for what has been thus far mostly a sensitizing device. Without a degree of consensus on strategy concepts and measurements we will be unable to study the range and distribution of the adaptive strategies of families. What is required are (i) greater specification of the various components of family strategies, (ii) recognition of family strategies as dynamic, social processes occurring in particular cultural, structural, and temporal contexts, and (iii) careful theoretical development and empirical documentation of the relationships between family strategies, broad societal shifts, and individual lives.

We suggest that a life-course perspective, with its focus on change over the family cycle and across historical time, might offer fruitful insights on alternative pathways of family strategic decision-making. Consider the concept of control cycles (Elder & Caspi 1990). Families move in and out of positions that make it possible to mobilize effectively in the face of external and internal threats. Their spheres of control, and their corresponding repertoire of strategies, shift over the life course, along with shifts in household composition, family needs, and family resources as well as external supports, demands, constraints, and opportunities.

Similarly, with the rise of individualism there have been broad historical reformations in what is seen as the family's purview and powers of control. For example, events related to the transition to adulthood—marriage, employment, independent living—were in nineteenth-century Europe and America typically tied to family adaptive strategies (Hareven 1991, Modell 1979). Today these are very much decisions of individuals qua individuals, not as family members (Bellah et al 1985). Today as well nuclear family households in advanced societies are seen and see themselves as autonomous, with fewer economic claims on the broader kin network than was true of families of the past (Stone 1979). Correspondingly, they have fewer strategic resources available to them (Rainwater 1974). Modell (1979) has also suggested that the extent of uncertainty and crisis facing American families has declined from the nineteenth through the twentieth centuries, with a concommitant reduction in the range of family adaptations.

In our view, family strategies have been too often depicted as dependent, rather than as intervening or independent variables. Yet we believe that the strength of this concept lies in its explanatory potential, as a way of understanding and bridging the gap between social structure, social change, and individual lives. As Tilly (1987:138) points out, focusing on family adaptive strategies "reintroduces a problematic, an intentionality and uncertainty in history, without abandoning systematic analysis."

Elder's (1974) work has shown, moreover, that family adaptive strategies mediate the transmission of orientations and behavior across the generations, providing what are frequently unintentional lessons to sons and daughters on positive as well as negative ways of coping with life's exigencies. The interplay between changing social circumstance and the individual, as mediated by family decision-making, is a fruitful area for future research.

At a more macro level, the question becomes how human societies cope with certain basic jobs—reproduction, sustenance, sexual control, socialization of children, nurturance, and protection. The notion of strategy is invoked implicitly if not explicitly to explain family behavior associated with these tasks. The range of possible "strategies" is surprisingly delimited, and in fact most human beings live within a small matrix of choices.

Assessing how the repertoire of family adaptive strategies is distributed and implemented across the social landscape, how strategies shift over the life course, how they touch the lives of all family members (even altering the subsequent life course of children), how they are transformed historically and culturally in the face of striking demographic and social changes, and how strategies of family adaptation serve to facilitate or hinder these changes are research issues that could provide a common frame of reference for the study of the family. Constructing alternative and testable models of family adaptive strategies offers a dynamic approach and rich research agenda to family scholars and to the growing number of scholars whose interests lie at the juncture between social and individual change.

Literature Cited

Anderson, B. A. 1986. Regional and cultural factors in the decline of marital fertility in western Europe. See Coale & Watkins 1986, pp. 293–313

Anderson, M. 1971. *Family Structure in Nineteenth Century Lancashire*. Cambridge, Eng: Cambridge Univ. Press

Anderton, D. L., Bean, L. L. 1985. Birth spacing and fertility limitation: a behavioral analysis of a nineteenth-century frontier population. *Demography*. 22:169–83

Becker, G. S. 1960. An economic analysis of fertility. In *Demographic and Economic Change in Developed Countries*, pp. 209–40. Natl. Bur. Committee Econ. Res., Special Conf. Ser., 11. Princeton, NJ: Princeton Univ. Press

Becker, G. S. 1981. *A Treatise on the Family*. Cambridge, Mass: Harvard Univ. Press

Bellah, R. N., Madsen, R., Sullivan, W. M., Swidler, A., Tipton, S. M. 1985. *Habits of the Heart: Individualism and Commitment in American Life*. New York: Harper & Row

Bennett, S., Elder, G. H. Jr. 1979. Women's work in the family economy: A study of depression hardship in women's lives. *J. Fam. Hist*. 4:153–76

Berk, R. A. 1980. The New Home Economics: An agenda for sociological research. In *Women and Household Labor,* ed. S. F. Berk, pp. 113–148. Beverly Hills, CA: Sage

Berk, S. F., Berk, R. A. 1983. Supply-side sociology of the family: The challenge of the New Home Economics. *Annu. Rev. Sociol*. 9:375–95

Blood, R. O., Wolfe, D. M. 1960. *Husbands and Wives: The Dynamics of Married Living*. New York: Free Press

Bott, E. 1957. *Family and Social Network: Roles, Norms, and External Relationships in Ordinary Urban Families*. London: Tavistock

Bourdieu, P. 1976. Marriage strategies as strategies of social reproduction. In *Family and Society. Selections from the Annales: Economies, Societes, Civilisations,* ed. R. Forster, 0. Ranum, pp. 117–44. Baltimore: Johns Hopkins Univ. Press

Butz, W. P., Ward, M. P. 1979. Will U.S. fertility remain low? A new economic interpretation. *Popul. Dev. Rev*. 5:663–88

Chudacoff, H. P., Hareven, T. K. 1979. From the empty nest to family dissolution: Life course transitions into old age. *J. Fam. Hist*. 4:69–83

Coale, A. J. 1986. The decline of fertility in Europe since the eighteenth century as a chapter in human demographic history. See Coale & Watkins 1986, pp. 31–181

Coale, A. J., Watkins, S. C. 1986. *The Decline of Fertility in Europe*. Princeton, NJ: Princeton Univ. Press

Coleman, J. S. 1986. Social theory, social research, and a theory of action. *Am. J. Sociol*. 91:1309–35

Coleman, J. S. 1988. Social capital in the creation of human capital. *Am. J. Sociol*. 94:S95-S120

Cornell, L. L. 1987. Where can family strategies exist? *Hist. Meth*. 20:120–23

Cross, G., Shergold, P. R. 1986. The family economy and the market: Wages and residence of Pennsylvania women in the 1890s. *J. Fam. Hist*. 11:245–65

Davis, H. L. 1976. Decision making within the household. *J. Consum. Res*. 2:241–60

Easterlin, R. A. 1961. The American baby boom in historical perspective. *Am. Econ. Rev*. 51:869–911

Easterlin, R. A. 1980. *Birth and Fortune*. New York: Basic

Elder, G. H. Jr. 1974. *Children of the Great Depression: Social Change in Life Experience*. Chicago: Univ. Chicago Press

Elder, G. H. Jr. 1978. Approaches to social change and the family. *Am. J. Sociol*. 84:SI–S38

Elder, G. H. Jr. 1981. History and the family: The discovery of complexity. *J. Marriage Fam*. 43:489–519

Elder, G. H. Jr., Liker, J. K., Cross, C. E. 1984. Parent- child behavior in the Great Depression: Life course and intergenerational influences. In *Life-span Development and Behavior,* v. 6., ed. P. B. Baltes, 0. G. Brim, Jr., pp. 111–59. New York: Academic Press

Elder, G. H. Jr., Caspi, A., Downey, G.

1986. Problem behavior and family relationships: Life course and intergenerational themes. In *Human Development and the Life Course: Multi-disciplinary Perspectives,* ed. A. Sorensen, F. Weinnert, L. Sherrod, pp. 293–340. Hillsdale, NJ: Lawrence Erlbaum

Elder, G. H. Jr., Caspi, A. 1990. Studying lives in a changing society: Sociological and personological explorations. In *Studying Persons and Lives,* ed. A. I. Rabin, R. A. Zucher, S. Frank, pp. 201–47. New York: Springer

Engerman, S. L. 1978. Changes in Black fertility, 1880–1940. See Hareven & Vinovskis 1978, pp. 126–53

England, P., Farkas, G. 1986. *Households, Employment, and Gender.* New York: Aldine

Espenshade, T. J. 1979. *The Value and Cost of Children.* Washington, DC: Popul. Ref. Bur.

Folbre, N. 1987. Family strategy, feminist strategy. *Hist. Meth.* 20:115–118

Furstenburg, F., Jr., Brooks-Gunn, J., Morgan, S. P. 1987. *Adolescent Mothers in Later Life.* New York: Cambridge Univ. Press

Glasco, L. 1978. Migration and adjustment in the nineteenth-century city: occupation, property, and household structure of native-born whites, Buffalo, New York, 1955. See Hareven & Vinovskis 1978, pp. 154–78

Glenn, E. N. 1983. Split household, small producer and wage earner: An analysis of Chinese-American family strategies. *J. Marriage Fam.* 45:35–46

Goldin, C. 1981. Family strategies and the family economy in the late nineteenth century: The role of secondary workers. In *Philadelphia: Work, Space, Family, and Group Experience in the 19th Century,* ed. T. Hershberg, pp. 277–310. New York: Oxford Univ. Press

Goldin, C., Sokoloff, K. 1982. Women, children, and industrialization in the early republic: evidence from the manufacturing censuses. *J. Econ. Hist.* 42:741–74

Goode, W. J. 1960. A theory of role strain. *Am. Sociol. Rev.* 25:483–96

Gordon, L. 1988. *Heroes of Their Own Lives: The Politics and History of Family Violence.* New York: Viking

Gutman, H. 1976. *The Black Family in Slavery and Freedom, 1750–1925.* New York: Pantheon

Hareven, T. K. 1977. Family time and historical time. *Daedalus* 106:57–70

Hareven, T. K., ed. 1978. *Transitions: The Family and the Life Course in Historical Perspective.* New York: Academic Press

Hareven, T. K. 1982a. The life course and aging in historical perspective. In *Aging and Life Course Transitions: An Interdisciplinary Perspective,* ed. T. K. Hareven, K. J. Adams, pp. 1–26. New York: Guilford

Hareven, T. K. 1982b. *Family Time and Industrial Time.* Cambridge, Eng: Cambridge Univ. Press

Hareven, T. K. 1991. The history of the family and the complexity of social change. *Am. Hist. Rev.* 96:95–124

Hareven, T. K., Vinovskis, M. A., eds. 1978a. *Family and Population in Nineteenth-Century America.* Princeton, NJ: Princeton Univ. Press

Hareven, T. K., Vinovskis, M. A. 1978b. Patterns of childbearing in late nineteenth-century America: The determinants of marital fertility in five Massachusetts towns in 1880. See Hareven & Vinovskis 1978a, pp. 85–125

Hill, R. 1970. *Family Development in Three Generations.* Cambridge, Eng: Schenkman

Hochschild, A. (with Machung, A.). 1989. *The Second Shift: Working Parents and the Revolution at Home.* New York: Viking

Houston, R. A. 1983. Marriage formation and domestic industry: Occupational endogamy in Kilmarnock, Ayrshire, 1697–1764. *J. Fam. Hist.* 8:215–29

Huber, J., Spitze, G. 1983. *Sex Stratification: Children, Housework, and Jobs.* New York: Academic Press

Kertzer, D. I., Hogan, D. P. 1989. *Family, Political Economy, and Demographic Change: The Transformation of Life in Casalecchio, Italy, 1861–1921.* Madison, Wisc: Univ. Wisc. Press

Kriedte, P., Medick, H.,Schlumbohm, J., eds. 1981. *Industrialization Before Industrialization.* Cambridge, Eng: Cambridge Univ. Press

Laslett, B., Brenner, J. 1989. Gender and social reproduction: Historical perspectives. *Annu. Rev. Sociol* 15:381–404

LePlay, F. 1877–79. *Les Ouvriers Europeans,* 2 ed. Tours: A. Mame et fils

Liker, J., Elder, G. H. Jr. 1983. Economic hardship and marital relations in the 1930s. *Am. Sociol. Rev.* 48:343–59

Litwak, E., Szelenyi, I. 1969. Primary group structures and functions: Kin, neighbors and friends. *Am. Sociol. Rev.* 34:465–81

McCubbin, H., Patterson, J. 1980. Family adaptation to crises. In *Family Stress, Coping and Social Support,* ed. H. McCubbin, A. E. Couble, J. Patterson, pp. 26–47. Illinois: Thomas

McLanahan, S., Glass, J. L. 1985. A note on the trend in sex differences in psychological distress. *J. Health Soc. Behav.* 26:328–35

Moch, L. P. 1987. Historians and family strategies. *Hist. Meth.* 20:113–15
Modell, J. 1978. Patterns of consumption, acculturation, and family income strategies in late nineteenth-century America. See Hareven & Vinovskis 1978, pp. 206–40
Modell, J. 1979. Changing risks, changing adaptations: American families in the nineteenth and twentieth centuries. In *Kin and Communities: Families in America*, ed. A. J. Lichtman, J. R. Challinor, pp. 119–44. Washington, DC: Smithsonian
Modell, J. 1980. Normative aspects of American marriage timing since World War II. *J. Fam. Hist.* 5:210–34
Modell, J., Hareven, T. K. 1973. Urbanization and the malleable household: An examination of boarding and lodging in American families. *J. Marriage Fam.* 35:467–79
Moen, P. 1989. *Working Parents: Transformations in Gender Roles and Public Policies in Sweden*. Madison, Wisc: Univ. Wisc. Press
Moen, P. 1992. *Women's Two Roles: A Contemporary Dilemma*. Westport: Greenwood
Moen, P., Forest, K. B. 1990. Working parents, workplace supports, and well-being: The Swedish Experience. *Soc. Psychol. Q.* 53:117–31
Moen, P., Kain, E. L., Elder, G. H. 1983. Economic conditions and family life: Contemporary and historical perspectives. In *American Families and the Economy: The High Costs of Living*, ed. J. Nelson, F. Skidmore, pp. 213–59. Washington, DC: Natl. Acad. Press
Mogey, J. 1990. *Aiding and Aging: The Coming Crisis in Support for the Elderly by Kin and State*. Westport: Greenwood
Nee, V., Sanders, J. 1991. *Family capital and social mobility: The incorporation of immigrants*. Unpublished draft
Pearlin, L. I., Mullan, J. T., Semple, S. J. Skaff, M. M. 1990. Caregiving and the stress process: An overview of concepts and their measurement. *The Gerontol.* 30:583–94
Pitrou, A. 1986. *Family policy and family strategy*. Symp. Univ. Konstanz, Germany, July
Pleck, J. H. 1985. *Working Wives/Working Husbands*. Beverly Hills, Calif: Sage
Rainwater, L. 1974. *What Money Buys: Inequality and the Social Meaning of Income*. New York: Basic
Riley, M. W., Riley, J. W., Jr. 1989. The lives of older people and changing social roles. *Ann. Am. Acad. Politic. Soc. Sci.* 503:14–28
Safilios-Rothschild, C. 1969. Family sociology or wives, family sociology? A cross-cultural examination of decision-making. *J. Marriage Fam.* 31:290–301
Safilios-Rothschild, C. 1970. Family power studies: A review, 1869–1969. *J. Marriage Fam.* 32:539–52
Saraceno, C. 1989. The concept of the family strategy and its application to the family-work complex: Some theoretical and methodological problems. *Marriage Fam. Rev.* 14:1–18
Scanzoni, J., Szinovacz, M. 1980. *Family Decision-Making: A Developmental Sex Role Model*. Beverly Hills, Calif: Sage
Schultz, T. W., ed. 1974. *Marriage, Family Human Capital, and Fertility. Suppl. to J. Polit. Econ.* Chicago: Univ. Chicago Press
Scott, J., Tilly, L. A. 1975. Women's work and family in nineteenth-century Europe. *Comp. Stud. Soc. Hist.* 17:319–23
Shanas, E., Sussman, M. B. 1977. *Family, Bureaucracy, and the Elderly*. Durham, NC: Duke Univ. Press
Smelser, N. J. 1959. *Social Change in the Industrial Revolution*. London: Routledge & Kegan Paul
Smith, D. S. 1987. Family strategy: More than a metaphor? *Hist. Meth.* 20:118–20
Stack, C. B. 1974. *All Our Kin: Strategies for Survival in a Black Community*. New York: Harper & Row
Stinchcombe, A. L. 1968. *Constructing Social Theories*. Chicago: Univ. Chicago Press
Stone, Lawrence. 1979. *The Family, Sex, and Marriage in England: 1500–1800*. New York: Harper Row
Thomas, W. I., Znaniecki, F. 1974 (orig. 1918). *The Polish Peasant in Europe and America,* Vols. I, II. New York: Octagon
Thompson, L., Walker, A. 1982. The dyad as a unit of analysis: Conceptual and methodological issues. *J. Marriage Fam.* 44:889–900
Tilly, L. A. 1979. Individual lives and family strategies in the French proletariat. *J. Fam. Hist.* 4:137–52
Tilly, L. A. 1987. Beyond family strategies, what? *Hist. Meth.* 20:123–26
Tilly, L. A., Scott, J. W. 1978. *Women, Work, and Family*. New York: Holt, Rinehart, Winston
Uhlenberg, P. 1974. Cohort variations in family life cycle experiences of U.S. females. *J. Marriage Fam.* 36:281–92
Uhlenberg, P. 1978. Changing configurations of the life course. In *Transitions: The Family and the Life Course in Historical Perspective,* ed. T. K. Hareven, pp. 65–98. New York: Academic Press
Vinovskis, M.A. 1984. Historical perspectives on rural development and human

fertility in nineteenth-century America. In *Rural Development and Human Fertility,* ed. W. A. Shutjer, C. S. Stokes, pp. 77–96. New York: Macmillan

Watkins, S. 1986 Conclusion. See Coole & Watkins 1986, pp. 420–49

Wethington, E., Kessler, R. C. 1989. Employment, parenting responsibility, and psychological distress: A longitudinal study of married women. *J. Fam. Issues*. 10:527–46

White, R. W. 1974. Strategies of adaptation: An attempt at systematic description. See Coelho et al 1974, pp. 47–68

Yans-McLaughlin, V. 1971. Patterns of work and family organization: Buffalo's Italians. *J. Interdisc. Hist*. 2:299–314

Zelizer, V. 1985. *Pricing the Priceless Child: The Changing Social Value of Children*. New York:Basic

Zimmerman, C. C. 1936. *Consumption and Standards of Living*. New York: Van Nostrand

Annu. Rev. Sociol. 1992. 18:253–80

CONCEPTS AND MEASUREMENT OF PRESTIGE

Bernd Wegener

Department of Sociology, University of Heidelberg, Heidelberg, Germany

KEY WORDS: social stratification, measurement of social status, social perception, theories of social inequality, psychophysical scaling

Abstract

Reviewing the major stratification theories that involve prestige as a concept, this chapter suggests that these theories differ in that they base prestige either on achievement, esteem, honor, or charisma. None of these theories is able to solve the problem of how theoretically to merge the idea of social closure with that of a hierarchy of positions. Empirically, research on prestige and prestige measurement has for some time been confronted with findings that demonstrate the inferior role of prestige in status attainment models. Dissensus in prestige judgments, regarding prestige of women in particular, is another recent concern. While the "dominant view" of prestige measurement, arguing for prestige consensus in society, is defended, emphasis is placed on studies that detect systematic interindividual variation of prestige judgments. The review concludes that empirically, prestige research has diversified and deals now with two different concept of prestige, one linked to the idea of a social hierarchy and the other to that of socially closed groups. A reconciliation of both views is wanting.

INTRODUCTION

In spite of the apparent success achieved in measuring prestige, several observers suggest that prestige is not a homogeneous phenomenon but that two types of prestige exist. For instance, Eisenstadt (1968:68) speaks of the "purely consummatory symbolic" side of prestige, as opposed to its structural

0360-0572/92/0815-0253$02.00

ramifications; Tumin & Feldman (1970:433) see prestige as a reward continuum set apart from its "moral worth"; and Udy (1980:159) describes two stratification systems, one shaped by prestige as a "system of beliefs" and the other by a "system of activities." I believe, the continual problem of how prestige can be "structural" accounts for these divergent interpretations. Even if we are convinced that prestige is veridical, as a variable sociologists have little use for it so long as they are unable to demonstrate that this variable matters: either the social structure of inequality is a source for determining prestige judgments, or prestige judgments determine social structure. Neither of these has yet been demonstrated satisfactorily.

Since the late 1970s, the situation has become especially acute. Social mobility research has shifted away from the status attainment paradigm, which had dominated the field since Blau & Duncan (1967); this shift resulted in a restoration of the concept of class as an analytical tool (Wright 1985, Goldthorpe 1987). Unfortunately, however, prestige is not particularly relevant to class theory. What is more, even within the traditional status attainment domain, the position of prestige seems to have been eroded, a point illustrated by Featherman et al (1975, Featherman & Hauser 1976). In a series of studies they demonstrated convincingly that mobility transmits socioeconomic status rather than prestige. At the same time, the most central assumption justifying the use of prestige as a scale, namely, that it does not vary according to individual judgment, has been challenged by increasing numbers of studies demonstrating systematic prestige dissensus rather than consensus. An important source of differential prestige judgments seems to be gender. Gender differences in mobility have gained attention, calling for new theories of prestige and social inequality (Acker 1980). However, despite these new developments, much energy continues to go into conventional prestige assessments (e.g. Nakao & Treas 1990). Not all prestige researchers are impressed by the new results, which concentrate on the inferior role of prestige in status attainment models, the evident dissensus of prestige judgments, and the gender issue.

In this review, I concentrate on two problems. One is the relationship of theories of prestige and the use of prestige in mobility research. The other centers on whether this use is justified given the new approaches and results. I begin by outlining major prestige theories, then briefly sketch the dominant view of empirical prestige research, turning next to new methods and results. I conclude that, entering the 1990s, prestige research has diversified and deals now with two different concepts of prestige.

FOUR TYPES OF THEORIES OF PRESTIGE

While most theories of social stratification involve some notion of prestige, the theories differ in how prestige is conceptualized. One important distinction is between the prestige of a social position and the prestige of a social aggregate (as, for instance, a *Stand*). By and large, stratification theories that emphasize order in society (e.g. functionalist theories) conceive prestige as an attribute of individuals or of individual social positions that form a hierarchy. Stratification theories that emphasize conflict (e.g. Weber) think of prestige as designating social aggregates, or individuals within social aggregates, influenced by social closure processes.

Another distinction is that between the subjective and the objective: Is prestige the product of *subjective* evaluations or is it an *objective* and structural reality? As I try to show below, this difference constitutes a dilemma: prestige can be neither one in isolation. However, to construe prestige as both subjective and objective confronts us with Hobbes's utilitarian dilemma or, in Parsons' generalization, with the problem of action and order (Parsons 1937). In Parsons' metatheoretical framework, this problem is resolved by distinguishing between two categorically different types of orientations of social actions: normative and rational.

Inasmuch as it deals with social prestige, Parsons' theory is elaborated below. At this point, I use his conceptual distinctions to develop a scheme for evaluating different theories of prestige. This scheme emerges by cross-tabulating the two types of stratification theories with the two types of orientations of social actions these theories primarily consider. We then have *rational-order* theories of prestige, *rational-conflict* theories, *normative-conflict* theories, and *normative-order* theories. Table 1 lists basic examples of these four types of theories. I portray the theories by discussing some of their main defenders, in turn arguing that the theories have different foundations: they are based either on achievement, esteem, honor, or charisma.[1]

Rational-order theories of prestige assume that the individual is guided by the rational motive of maximizing returns, but that society is based on functional prerequisites that determine what rewards are appropriate for the fulfillment of certain essential duties. In their formulation of the functionalist theory of stratification, Davis & Moore (1945) straightforwardly claim that prestige is what we get for achievements that are in line with societal needs, and that prestige differences constitute the system of social inequality. Parsons' early statements on stratification theory (Parsons 1940, 1953) differ from this account only in that Parsons emphasizes the need for an integrated system of values in a society, thus making the extent to which individuals act

[1] Apart from these different meanings of prestige, a terminological problem persists. Some writers use "prestige" interchangeably with "status"; others are careful to distinguish prestige as a symbolic entity from objective descriptions of rank, as in socioeconomic status scales. To make the confusion complete, "prestige status" is also used. In this review, I try to maintain the distinction between prestige and status by reserving the status for objective differences in assets, while prestige involves a valuative element.

Table 1 Types of theories of prestige and selected examples.

Sources of stratification	Orientations of social action: Normative (subjective)	Rational (objective)
Order (hierarchy)	Foundation of prestige: charisma Shils 1968, 1975 Eisenstadt 1968	Foundation of prestige: achievement Davis & Moore 1945 Parsons 1940, 1953
Conflict (social closure)	Foundation of prestige: honor Weber 1972 Kluth 1957	Foundation of prestige: esteem Homans 1961 Blau 1964

in accordance with values the basis for prestige. Because in Parsons' view, the occupational system provides the paramount value system, prestige has the quality of an achievement variable,[2] much as in Davis & Moore's theory.

Rational-conflict theories are based on exchange theories (Homans 1961). In these theories, prestige is conceived as a commodity that can be exchanged in transactions like money (Coleman 1990:129–31). However, prestige is "produced" through processes of asymmetrical exchange, that is, whenever benefits received cannot be reciprocated (Blau 1964). There is, however, a difficulty: Within the exchange framework, what distinguishes prestige from power? As Wrong (1979:237–57) notes, power is tied to a zero-sum condition such that if A, who has a power position, loses that position to B, B gains what A has lost. Thus, the quantity of power is fixed (for an opposing view, see Parsons 1967). In contrast, it seems that prestige, to the extent that it is the product of exchange processes, is available in ample supply (Goode 1978:72–75). But this is only true inasmuch as prestige is based on individuals' appreciation and praise, or, as Davis (1946) has made the distinction, on esteem. From the writings of Homans (1961:1 26–29) in particular, it becomes clear that, from the social exchange perspective, prestige is a function of esteem, and that it is within groups that this form of prestige is a commodity to be exchanged.

Max Weber's conception of prestige is the prototype of normative-conflict theories. For Weber, prestige is an attribute of *Stände* (Weber 1972:534), what Parsons translated as *status groups* (Weber 1947). This choice of translation is unfortunate because "status" seems to imply gradation (Ossowski 1963). Weber nowhere indicates that prestige or social honor is an

[2]Rational-order theories have an important empirical ramification in that they predict only little interrater variation in prestige judgments—the system of rewards will only work if there is prestige consensus in a society.

entity that can vary in degree. Rather, in Weber's thinking, prestige is a quality shared by members of one and the same status group (to use Parsons' term nonetheless) in identifying with that status group. It is a concept more similar to Geiger's (1932) notion of mentalities associated with certain strata than it is to the idea of a positional grading scheme. Weber states explicitly that the distribution of social honor determines the "social order" of a society (Weber 1972:531). However, the order Weber has in mind is an order of closure, not of hierarchy. Prestige is not based on achievement, money, occupation, productive assets, or authority. As Kluth (1957:46) puts it, "the property from which prestige flows is, in its core, not comprehensible by others." Only those who exhibit specific consummatory attributes can understand what it means to be congenial with other members of a status group who are thus equipped with equal social honor (Weber 1972:538, Kluth 1957:45–48).

Shils' (1968) and Eisenstadt's (1968) theories are examples of *normative-order theories of prestige*. In contrast to Weber's conception, which defines prestige as an attribute pertaining to social aggregates, Shils tries to distinguish individuals by their prestige but, like Weber's and unlike the functionalists' view, on normative if not transcendent grounds. In Shils' eyes, the basis of prestige is the exhibition of charisma. By the *charisma* of an individual Shils means that "what is thought to be his connection with. . . some very central feature of man's existence and the cosmos in which he lives" (Shils 1975:258). At the same time, charisma is embodied in occupational roles, giving the greatest charisma to those occupations that are "in their functions closest to the centers" (Shils 1968:107). Based on this quality, individuals possess authority and are entitled to deference.[3] The rank order of charisma in a society is well-defined in Shils' view, whereas the actual distribution of positions of deference may well be obscured and not in line with the order of charisma. Deference positions are correlated with privileges that are not evaluated consensually within a society (pp. 121–23). This is why Shils calls the use of popular evaluations of prestige for deriving prestige scales "patently unsatisfactory" (p. 120).

The question then is, how can charisma have structural consequences? Shils' center/periphery metaphor is not particularly helpful. Eisenstadt here is more explicit. Eisenstadt distinguishes between symbolic and structural aspects of prestige. To make the symbolic part structural, Eisenstadt focuses on the institutional bases of prestige, identifying three requirements: membership status, group authority, and charisma. So far as it is based on these three sources, prestige manifests itself in the recognition of the right to participate

[3] In a similar vein, Simmel speaks of an element of superiority (*Superioritätsnuance*) which prestige confers (Simmel 1923:103–04). Hodge (1981:413) explicitly parallels prestige with Weber's definition of charismatic authority.

in groups. The symbolic element is transformed into the structural through the right, awarded by prestige, to participate. Thus, Eisenstadt's theory takes up an important ingredient of Weber. It differs from Weber's idea of honor, however, as Eisenstadt sees individuals but not social aggregates as differentiated by prestige.

The Problem of Social Closure and Hierarchy

Since the different types of prestige theories find their foundation in either achievement, esteem, honor, or charisma, the problem of prestige seems to be how these different aspects can be brought together. In more abstract terms, and in view of the two factors that led to the classification in Table 1, the problem of prestige has two facets. One is how theoretically to merge the idea of social closure with that of hierarchy; the second, how to reconcile the subjective element of prestige with its objective component. Beginning with the second part, I demonstrate briefly that the two problems have a common core, despite their differences.

Apparently, interpreting prestige as a purely subjective phenomenon is of little sociological relevance. If judgments of prestige do not mirror objective social reality to some extent, we are left with only psychological effects—what Leopold (1916) termed *individual prestige*. Eliminating the subjective factor altogether, however, ruins the concept as well. Prestige must be conceptualized as a cognitive and valuative phenomenon if there is to be any point in distinguishing it from other stratification attributes like property or power. This Janus-headed quality of prestige finds a parallel in Parsons' (1937) analysis of the utilitarian dilemma. As Parsons writes:

> Either the active agency of the actor in the choice of ends is an independent factor in action, and the end element must be random; or the objectionable implication of the randomness of ends is denied, but then their independence disappears and they are assimilated to the conditions of the situation, that is to elements analyzable in terms of nonsubjective categories (p. 64).

Parsons' solution is to create the *unit act* in which the choice of ends is determined by norms. This line of reasoning is also illustrated in Parsons' stratification theory. In his early writings, Parsons assumes that the moral evaluation of social positions is guided by standards that reflect at the same time both "the actual system of effective superiority" and "the normative pattern of stratification" (Parsons 1940:843). But Parsons attributes some degree of "vagueness" to the way the coincidence of both aspects is met empirically. This vagueness results from the fact that an individual is evaluated morally along several dimensions: membership in a kinship unit, personal qualities, achievements, possessions, authority, and power. "The status of any given individual in the system of stratification in a society may be regarded as a resultant of the common valuations underlying the attribution of status to him in each of these six respects" (p. 48). In 1953, Parsons remodeled this idea in terms of his performance-sanction paradigm by matching the object of evaluation with its internalized image and roles with role expectations. The vagueness in the 1940 paper is now resolved by claiming that "the basic categories in terms of which we describe a system as a structure. . . are *the very same* as those in terms of which we describe the norms which regulate behavior or performance" (p. 393). Thus, value-standards "are classified in terms of the same dimensions or variables which differentiate units in the social system in a structural sense and which define the types of sanctioned performance of those units and hence the appropriate sanctions relative to those performances" (p. 398). From this vantage point, the only problem Parsons sees worth facing is how different functional evaluation standards—guided by problems of adaptation, goal attainment, integration, or pattern maintenance—are organized relative to each other in a given social system. In American society, he sees these standards ordered with the "adaptive" or "occupational" values forming the top of the hierarchy (p. 399). But underlying any such hierarchy is the theoretical decision to have the valuative and the structural side of the stratification system coincide in complete harmony. Thus in Parsons' stratification theory, the subjective and the objective are brought to match by fiat.

In his third major contribution to stratification theory, Parsons (1970) is more explicit in describing how the legitimation of the social order operates (Alexander 1983:231–76, Habermas 1981:420–44). By sketching his respective arguments, we can see how Parsons extends the arbitrary matching between the subjective and the objective sides of prestige into an equally arbitrary matching between the hierarchical and the social closure conceptions of prestige.

His main concern in 1970 is that "all societies institutionalize some balance between equality and inequality" (p. 19). Balancing means to make the factual rules of distribution compatible with the normative culture of a society. In modern societies, the normative culture places a premium on equality and egalitarian principles, but the distribution rules in different social subsystems are not generally aimed at generating equality. Therefore, compatibility of the empirical distribution rules with the normative culture is assured by institutions that make inequalities endurable to the individual. Prestige plays a role in this because "on the one hand, it asserts the basic importance of equality of membership status, but at the same time makes allowance for the inequalities which will result from achievement motives protected by equality of opportunity" (p. 68). Here, Parsons uses the concept of prestige as the institutional "code" of the generalized interchange medium of influence (Parsons 1967), corresponding to authority in the political context and property in the economic. The role of influence is to operate as a mechanism for integrating two levels: "that of collective solidarity. . . on the one hand and that of 'motivating' units, especially individuals," on the other (p. 48).

Where does prestige come from, and how is solidarity, rooted in equal membership status, compromised with "achievement motives?" The important point here is that Parsons bases prestige on consensus and that he locates the production of consensus in the communal and integrative subsystem of a society. However, consensus can only *justify* inequality; it cannot provide for its *legitimation*. Thus, the normative culture of a society results from a combination of two processes: The communal and integrational subsystem provides justification through consensus of individual beliefs; legitimation is provided by moral and fiduciary authority (Parsons & Platt 1973). The latter is given primacy by Parsons in that any result reached by consensus must be compatible with objective moral standards in order to be part of the normative culture. Thus, the order of social prestige justifies the stratification system through consensus because the principles of justification are legitimized by the "ultimate reality" on which moral authority rests.

The bottom line of these complex arguments is that Parsons, in his final contribution to stratification theory, wants to imply, first, that prestige serves a double function: Prestige is the expression of group solidarity, and it is a motivating agent for achievements. But both roles are in need of integration because group solidarity, based on equality of membership status, is not easily reconciled with the achievement motive's potential for inequality. The second implication of Parsons' theory, therefore, is that this integration is produced by a justifying consensus but that, due to its precarious nature, consensus is in need of backing from moral authority. "Only when this has worked out," Parsons writes, "can we speak of an acceptable *generalized* prestige status of a social unit" (Parsons 1970:68). But apart from coming close to having constructed a "holy" order of prestige (Wegener 1988:76), Parsons cannot but assure us that the blending of the two prestige components does indeed "work out."

Compared to the 1940 and 1953 versions, in his later writings, Parsons presupposes that the subjective and the objective sides of prestige coincide; he does not, however, provide the structural processes that create this convergence. Parsons' final analysis teaches us that the problem of merging the subjective and the objective is really just another side of the problem of social closure and hierarchy. While Parsons sees equality of membership status in a collectivity as required for prestige consensus, the resulting prestige hierarchy characterizes individuals and individual social positions (Parsons 1970:50). Thus, like Weber, Parsons distinguishes two different concepts of inequality. Using Weber's term, prestige as "social honor" applies to social collectivities. Based on "achievement motives," however, prestige applies to individuals.

Processes of social closure are associated with the former, and a hierarchy of positions with the latter.

From this analysis of the prestige problem (notwithstanding that it cannot be solved by any of several prestige theories), it is evident that prestige research should deal not with one but with two concepts of prestige: with prestige as a hierarchy of positions and prestige as an attribute of socially closed groups.

PRESTIGE AS A HIERARCHY OF POSITIONS: THE DOMINANT VIEW

Empirical prestige research is guided almost completely by the first understanding of prestige, by prestige as a hierarchy of positions. This research follows "Edwards' paradigm" (Edwards 1938) in that it assumes that occupational positions are visible and open to everyone, and that they are ordered along a single value dimension.[4] Whereas Edwards used education and income for classifying occupations according to prestige, in the reputational approach survey respondents are asked for their judgments. The study in which North & Hatt (1947) developed their National Opinion Research Center (NORC) scale was the model for many others. The data of this study were reanalyzed by e.g. Hatt (1950) and Reiss (1961). Based on the 1960 Census of Population, several new surveys were conducted in the 1960s (using nine response categories instead of the original five) to update the original scale (Hodge et al 1966a, Siegel 1971). The resulting prestige scores were also mapped into the 1980 occupational codes (Stevens & Hoisington 1987). Finally, the 1989 General Social Survey of NORC included a replicated prestige module from which scores for 740 occupational categories (1980 census codes) were computed (Nakao et al 1990, Nakao & Treas 1990). Compared to the previous NORC scales, the new feature of this scale is that it is based on a random assignment of occupational titles. An "overlapping" design was used such that not all respondents rated all titles. As Nakao et al (1990) write: "The methods employed in the U.S. studies remain the primary standard against which all other inquiries are evaluated" (p. 3).[5]

[4]This was also Sorokin's (1927) understanding of "interoccupational" prestige. However, Sorokin also identified the two most prominent sources of prestige: the contribution occupational work makes to "the functions of social organization and control" and "the degree of intelligence necessary for its successful performance" (p. 101). While the first of these attributes preshadows functionalist reasoning in stratification, the latter seems to reflect the enthusiasm for IQ measurement in the 1920s (Fryer 1922), something only a few would share today (Gould 1981).

[5] Although the applied methodologies differ, reputational prestige scales similar in impact to those in the United States were constructed (to cite only the most recent) in Great Britain (Goldthorpe & Hope 1974), Israel (Kraus 1976, Kraus et al 1978), Italy (de Lillo & Schizzerotto 1985), the Netherlands (Sixma & Ultee 1984), Germany (Wegener 1985), Finland (Alestalo & Uusitalo 1980), Canada (Pineo & Porter 1967), Australia (Quine 1986, Jones 1989).

The prestige projects that focus on reputation rest on the conviction that it is important to know how occupational positions are perceived and ranked by the population. Given that goal, the discussion circles around a small number of problems. Among these are whether prestige judgments arise from a consensus, whether the results exhibit cross-cultural and temporal stability, and how valid the scales are.

Consensus, Structural Identity, and Stability

At the center of prestige research on reputation stands the question of whether the prestige judgments are independent of personal characteristics of the judges or whether there is systematic interindividual variation. Since the study of North & Hatt, great care has been taken to establish empirically that there is little or no variation in judgment. Usually this has been demonstrated with aggregate level data. The arrays of mean judgment scores of subpopulations have been computed and then intercorrelated. By this method North & Hatt found no serious effects of education, occupation, sex, age, income, region, and city size on prestige judgments. In this and in many other studies using the same method, mean profile correlations of $0.5 < R < 0.7$ were found (Hodge et al 1966a, Siegel 1971, Goldthorpe & Hope 1974, Treiman 1977:59–78, Nakao & Treas 1990). From this it was concluded that, by and large, prestige judgments do not vary with personal attributes of judges.

While it is amazing that only correlations of means were used [since means are likely to reduce variation and subsequently increase covariation (Nosanchuk 1972)], it is also noteworthy that the reported numbers quite often contradict the conclusions drawn. To cite an early example: Reiss (1961:190) writes, "The size of these correlations amply demonstrate that the prestige status of occupations in American society is viewed in virtually the same way by major subgroups of the society." He also reports that only 36 of the 88 occupational titles in the original NORC study were given identical rating categories by more than 50% of the respondents, and only 6% of the 88 titles were placed into identical categories by more than 60% (pp. 162–63). The difficulty is, of course, when results should be interpreted as evidence of consensus and when not (Guppy & Goyder 1984:711–12). What is really at stake here is the theories on which we can draw for explaining judgment variations when we find them. Attempts made with this goal in mind are presented below.

Besides demonstrating consensus, aggregate prestige scales are widely thought to exhibit an extraordinary cross-cultural identity. Inkeles & Rossi (1956, Inkeles 1960) were among the first to show that occupational prestige scales of different countries are highly correlated. Comparing six industrialized societies they found a mean correlation of .91 (based on 7–30 common occupational titles). Inkeles & Rossi's conclusion was that societies are structurally similar, and that cultural differences have no effects on prestige judgments (also Tiryakian 1958, Thomas 1962, Haller et al 1972, Hansen & Converse 1976). This thesis was further supported by a study by Hodge et al (1966a) comparing 23 societies, which included industrially less developed countries. The mean correlation of prestige scales was reported as .83. Other cross-cultural studies leading to basically the same results are those by Haller & Lewis (1966), Armer (1969), Marsh (1971), and e. g. Yogev (1980).

The most comprehensive attempt to demonstrate intersocietal correlations of occupational prestige was ventured by Treiman (1977) who compared 55 countries. His study stands out because it is based on the *International Standard Classification of Occupations* (ISCO 1968). Supported by high intercorrelations among the national scales, he proposed a now widely used International Prestige Scale.[6] Building on Shils' prestige theory of charisma, Treiman justifies his scale thus: "Since occupations are differentiated with respect to power, they will in turn be differentiated with respect to privilege and prestige. Thus. . . these attributes of occupations will be highly correlated across societies" (Treiman 1976:289). Treiman also argues that prestige has similar characteristics across the borders of capitalist and socialist societies. (Inkeles & Rossi 1956 make a similar argument, as do Hodge et al 1966a and Marsh 1971). However, Hodge et al (1985) found differences for specific groups of occupations in eastern and western countries. Sawinski & Domanski (1991 a,b) document changes in the prestige of some occupations in Poland due to the ongoing process of political transformation in that country.

To assume the structural identity of societies means that prestige hierarchies should also be stable across historical periods and time. In spite of the methodological problems encountered in matching modern with historical occupational titles and in finding measures that are equivalent, some attempts have been made to confirm the temporal stability of occupational hierarchies. Hodge et al (1966b) report a correlation of .989 between the 1947 and 1963 NORC prestige scales. They also compare these scales to results of Smith (1943) and Counts (1925) and conclude that no substantial changes in occupational prestige in the United States have occurred since 1925. A similar conclusion is drawn by Plata (1975), who analyzed rank order prestige scales from five American studies over a period of 49 years. Fossum & Moore (1975) add to this comparison a 1968 prestige assessment with students as subjects. Tyree & Smith (1977) compared income data for 42 occupations over a period of 180 years, confirming a prediction by Duncan (1968) who

[6] Treiman's scale as well as other comparative scales based on the ISCO 1968 classification are presently faced with the problem that in 1988 the International Labour Office in Geneva issued a new classification.

inferred from short time comparisons that correlations over 180 years should not fall below .724. Treiman (1976) analyzed wealth and income data over six historical periods, beginning with fifteenth century Florence; and Burrage & Corry (1981) studied order of precedence records of the city of London from the fourteenth to the seventeenth century. They found basically little change.

What Do Prestige Scales Measure?

Attempts to establish the empirical validity of prestige scales have been made by using either subjective or objective approaches. In one of the subjective approaches to occupational rating, subjects are asked directly why they rated the occupations the way they did and what their primary focus was. Alternatively, subjects have to rate the occupations repeatedly on different dimensions, besides "social standing," e.g. "value to society," "power," "skill," "degree of autonomy." Generally, direct questioning did not elicit clearly dominant attributes that people associate with prestige. This convinced Goldthorpe & Hope (1974), for instance, that prestige evaluations do not really measure prestige but rather some overall "desirability" of occupations (p. 12; also Hauser & Featherman 1977:5). Similarly, the multiple rating studies found that most "material" aspects of occupations are highly correlated with prestige (Garbin & Bates 1966, Burschtyn 1968, Goldthorpe & Hope 1974, Coxon & Jones 1978, Wegener 1983). Of the individual capabilities perceived as required of occupational incumbents, "ability" and "effort" both correlate strongly (R = .95) with prestige rankings, according to Villimez (1974). Adler & Kraus (1985) find that "skills and knowledge" are the required capabilities that predict individual judgments of prestige best.

A third subjective, though indirect, method uses judgments of the similarity of occupations, applying multidimensional scaling and individual difference scaling procedures (Burschtyn 1968, Grasmick 1976, Kraus et al 1978, Seligson 1978, Beck et al 1979, Stewart et al 1980). Multidimensional scaling methods usually yield a general hierarchical dimension of occupations, but the approach has also been criticized for neglecting other meaningful occupational dimensions (Coxon 1971, Coxon & Jones 1978, Saltiel 1990). A somewhat related method, but one involving actual behavior, is to look at interaction matrices. The frequencies with which people interact in friendship relations or, for instance, in marital choice is in this case taken as an expression of similarities of status. Behind this idea stands the social-psychological theorizing on interpersonal attraction (Heider 1958). Examples are Laumann (1966), Pappi (1976), and Mayer (1977). In Mayer's work, the frequencies with which men of certain status levels marry women with fathers of certain status levels were put to a smallest space analysis; this process yielded basically a two-dimensional configuration. As in other studies of this type, the dimension capturing the largest proportion of variation is considered to represent "social status."

Another procedure involves the correlation of aggregate prestige scales with external attributes of occupations. The impressive results here are that standard prestige scores are closely associated with mean education and income levels of the occupations. Together they explain 83% of the variation of the NORC prestige scale, according to Duncan (1961). This has led Duncan to "predict" the prestige of occupations for which there were no direct prestige scores (or census codes) in the 1947 NORC scale from mean education and income levels. The result of Duncan's work was the often used socioeconomic index (SEI). This index has undergone several revisions since 1961. Hauser & Featherman (1977, Appendix B) tried to adapt Duncan's scale which had been based on the 1950 census classification, to the 1970 classifications without reestimating these scores. Stevens & Featherman (1981) provide that reestimation (based on Siegel's 1971 prestige scores). Featherman & Stevens (1982) revise these scores again, and Stevens & Cho (1985) adjust them to the 1980 census occupational classification scheme.

A final, objective validation method is to insert the prestige variable into status attainment models to test how well the scale measures the latent occupational constructs, compared to other measures, and whether inclusion of prestige increases the fit of such models. While it is clear that this approach can validate prestige only relative to social mobility processes, some controversy was created as to whether prestige or socioeconomic status is the superior measure in that context. Featherman et al (1975) argue forcefully that SEI scales are superior in terms of factor loadings and explanatory power. The amount of explained variance for the current occupation of US men, using education, first job, and origin as predictors, is $R^2 = .439$ when Duncan's SEI is used, but it is only .361 when Siegel's prestige scale is applied for the occupational variables, and .294 with Treiman's scale (Featherman & Hauser 1976). Similarly, when the three measures are compared directly in structural equation models, the socioeconomic status scale yields smaller error variances than do the prestige measures. In line with this, Treas & Tyree (1979) conclude from their study that "the socioeconomic index is superior to prestige scaling for the purpose of status attainment research" (p. 219). Featherman et al (1975, Hauser & Featherman 1977) demonstrate this fact also in comparing US with Australian mobility data. Moreover, in a recent paper using Blau & Duncan's (1967) data, Caston (1989) found that intergenerational mobility models cannot be improved by adding prestige and other occupational characteristics such as skill level, earnings, or work place autonomy to the models.

Featherman et al (1975:358) conclude that prestige is "a fallible index of occupational status" and that, with reference to occupational mobility, socioeconomic status is the more valid index. However, in a recent study, Kerckhoff et al (1989) have shown that in Britain prestige generates different results than it does in the United States. In comparing male occupational attainment in both countries, the authors used separate models in which occupational level is measured with common and indigenous prestige and socioeconomic status scales. Their major finding is that, measured by SEI scales, the models produce very similar results in both societies, but when measured by both common and indigenous prestige scales, a stronger relative effect of origin on occupation is detected in the Great Britain data. They conclude that each measure taps different aspects of the social mobility process, and that the societies differ in the transmission of prestige but not of socioeconomic status. Related results are also reported by Wegener (1985), showing with German data that the direct effects of education on mobility outcomes are significantly stronger in terms of prestige than in terms of socioeconomic status. While Kerckhoff et al (1989:1 73) venture "that the British intergenerational mobility process is more sensitive to public definitions of the general desirability of occupations," Wegener attributes the differences of the prestige and status effects to the educational system which, in Germany, puts more emphasis on conveying traditional values for occupational choice than on socioeconomic status gains. But educational credentialism, which is particularly strong in Germany (Müller et al 1990), may also play a role in this.

PRESTIGE AS SOCIAL CLOSURE: NEW METHODS AND RESULTS

Dissensus

An increasing number of studies analyze prestige judgments on an individual level, thus breaking with the research paradigm of the dominant view. Hyman (1953) was among the first to point to individual differences in "status awareness." Analyzing the original North & Hatt data, Hatt (1950) concluded that it was unjustified to speak of a unique prestige continuum, but that different subpopulations had different scales. Hatt tried to base this finding on *situs* categorizations of occupations, what Sorokin (1927:107–08) labeled "intraoccupational stratification" (Benoit-Smullyan 1944, Morris & Murphy 1959, Pavalko 1971, More & Suchner 1976, Villimez & Silver 1977). Also, it was early observed that judges tend to display "occupational egoism," giving more favorable prestige ratings to the occupations they themselves have or that are similar to their own (North & Hatt 1947, Blau 1957, Gerstl & Cohen 1964, Pavalko 1971, Goyder & Pineo 1977, Coxon & Jones 1978:53–55). Stehr (1974) demonstrated that prestige ratings of professional occupations judged by professionals differed depending on the position of the judges within that subpopulation. Beck et al (1979) illustrate the same effect for apprentice positions as judged by apprentices.

The discussion gained new life when Balkwell et al (1980, 1982, Bates et al

1986) tried to corroborate the consensus theses using 18 occupational titles to be rated and university students as judges. Their analysis is based on correlations among individual prestige scales, the average correlation being .745. From this the authors conclude that there is ample individual level consensus in prestige ratings. This finding is challenged by a series of papers by Guppy (1982, Guppy & Goyder 1984). Drawing on the findings of Kraus et al (1978), Goldthorpe & Hope (1974), and Jencks et al (1972), authors who have reported much lower mean interrater correlations (from .42 to .48), Guppy argues that prestige consensus is distributed unevenly in a society. Members of the upper strata have more firm and consistent views of the social world, making prestige consensus more likely in these groups than in lower strata. Data of three of the NORC prestige studies confirmed this assumption. Guppy & Goyder (1984) found decisive effects of education, occupation and race on the agreement on prestige judgments, and they conclude that "a social structural factor should be identified" for explaining variations in prestige ratings (p. 721). In a follow-up paper Guppy (1984) extends his finding to a comparison between Canada and the United States. However, Hodge et al (1982: 1194–95) argue that characteristics of judges never explain more than 25% of the variance in prestige ratings and that variability within status groups is substantial.

Another issue of systematic variation of prestige judgments centers on occupation and gender. The importance to mobility research is obvious. If no common prestige scale is appropriate for both men and women, then mobility research on women is flawed if it uses male measures for female prestige. A number of studies have sought to compare the mobility of men and women (Chase 1975, Treiman & Terrell 1975, McClendon 1976, Featherman & Hauser 1976, Wolf & Rosenfeld 1978, Treas & Tyree 1979, Rosenfeld 1979, Marini 1980, Sewell et al 1980, Roos 1981, Boyd & McRoberts 1982); most have concluded that the patterns of mobility of men and women do not greatly diverge. These studies were based on the assumption that all individuals in the same occupational position have the same social standing or prestige. Indeed, England (1979) found that the percentage of women in an occupation makes no significant difference in the prestige of occupations, and Bose & Rossi (1983) conclude from their study of college and household samples that occupation is the major determinant of prestige. The percent female and female incumbency do have a statistically significant effect on the prestige judgments, but this effect contributes only 1 to 2.5% to the variance in incumbent prestige scores (p. 329).

However, evidence is accumulating that judgments of prestige typically distinguish between positions and incumbents of positions, especially with regard to sex. Nilson (1976), for example, had the prestige of males and females rated in 17 occupations. The incumbents who violated the role expectation of an occupation with respect to sex were accorded lower social standing than those who conformed, especially men in female-typed occupations. Nilson also reports that male respondents were more likely to differentiate between the prestige of men and women in sex-typed occupations. Similarly, Guppy & Siltanen (1977) found that both men and women in sex-atypical occupations were accorded lower prestige than were the sex-typical incumbents. In a number of papers, Powell & Jacobs (1983, 1984a,b, Jacobs & Powell 1985) demonstrated, first, that there was less agreement regarding the prestige of female incumbents than of male incumbents, and second, that differences in the judgments of male and female incumbents depended on the sex compositions of the occupations. In particular, women received higher prestige ratings than men in traditionally female occupations; and men were judged higher than women if they were in occupations typically held by men. These effects seem to be less strong for women in high status positions (Hawkins & Pingree 1978, Crino et al 1983). Powell & Jacobs, however, conclude that the "sex penalty" is strong for both men and women in sex-atypical occupations, and that the occupational prestige hierarchy is really two hierarchies, each a sex-typical prestige hierarchy (Powell & Jacobs 1984b:187–88). Fox & Suschnigg (1989:358) take these results as evidence that prestige scales should be banned from stratification research comparing men and women and that income and power differences should be studied instead. Indeed, as McLaughlin (1978) demonstrates, the use of prestige may lead to misspecifications when the earnings of men and women are compared. These authors, however, fail to discuss the consequences of sex-typed prestige perceptions for occupational choice, accessibility of positions, and social closure. It is likely that sex-typed prestige perceptions keep men as well as women from entering sex-atypical occupations.

It seems that a reciprocal process applies to nonemployed women as housewives who, according to most studies, receive relatively high prestige scores (Bose 1973, Nilson 1978, Dworkin 1981, Schooler et al 1984), though judgments are dependent on the gender role norms held by the observers (Beeghley & Cochran 1988). An interesting interpretation of housewife prestige is proposed by Tyree & Hicks (1988). Looking at the differences in Bose's (1985) data in standard deviations of prestige given to male and female incumbents, these authors conclude that "women's ascribed sexual status acts as a sort of master status" (p. 1035) and, because fewer fixed stereotypes are attached to what women do, prestige judgments of female incumbents must be seen as "real nonattitudes" (p .1036; Converse 1964) that do not map prestige at all. Housewifery in particular, is a social position not possessing prestige but only "master status."

Psychophysical Scaling

In terms of measurement, one of the most exciting recent developments is the application of psychophysical scaling methods to prestige research. Except in experimental studies (Skvoretz et al 1974, Marshall & Gorman 1975, Grasmick 1976, Abbott & Kenkel 1988), the measurement problem is a much neglected issue in empirical prestige research. Modeled after the NORC procedures, most studies use conventional category rating methods with five or nine response categories, summing the weighted raw scores such that each rated occupation receives a value from 0 to 100. With nine categories supplied, the value of the *j*th occupation is

$$P_j = \sum_{i=1}^{9} (12.5)(i - 1) X_{ji}$$

where X_{ji} is the proportion of ratings received by the *j*th occupation with rating i. This transformation assumes that the measurement yields interval scale quality, an assumption hardly in line with anything we know from measurement research (see Gifi 1990:81–149 for the multivariate requirements necessary for this type of aggregation). Also, as is true of all category rating tasks, this method reduces interindividual variation to the number of categories respondents can choose from, so that extreme judgments cannot be assessed. These disadvantages have led to the use of magnitude estimation techniques, imported from psychophysics (Stevens 1975), for measuring prestige. Magnitude estimation differs from rating methods in that no response categories are provided for the respondent to select from. Instead, the subject is instructed to choose numbers for the stimuli of a series such that the ratios of the numbers correspond to the ratios of the subjective magnitude of the stimuli. Since magnitude estimations demand the mapping of subjective ratios into ratios of numbers, it seems natural to assume that magnitude estimation scales are ratio scales. The relevant measurement structures (Krantz 1972) in scaling of occupational prestige were tested by Orth (1982) and Wegener (1983, Orth & Wegener 1983). In addition, magnitude estimation with numbers can be supplemented by using other extensive modalities for responses, for instance, drawing lines of different lengths to represent ratios of stimulus intensities. Since the relations of both judgment modalities to a physical stimulus continuum are known to be power functions, the replicate measurement (indirect cross-modality matching or ICMM) should yield a power relation of the two series of responses. If for individual subjects,

$$A = k\, B_i^{\frac{\beta}{\alpha}}$$

results, with A_i and B_i responses for stimuli i in modalities A and B, and α and β known from sensory psychophysics, the individual judgments are consistent with the scale assumptions made (Lodge 1981, Wegener 1982).

Using numbers and lines as response modes, psychophysical scaling of prestige was applied in large scale surveys by Wegener (1985, 1988), examining ICMM consistency using only the consistent cases for further analyses. Coleman & Rainwater (1979) and Perman (1984) have applied only numerical magnitude estimation for prestige measurement. Wegener & Kirschner (1981) introduced a model for relating individual category ratings of prestige with magnitude prestige scales.

Psychophysical measurement of prestige does not confine judges to using only the response categories provided by a response scale. Forming ratios, individual relations of low to high prestige occupations of 1: 100 and more can easily be encountered in a magnitude task. An example is given in Figure 1 (adapted from Wegener 1990:74–75). Both panels of the figure refer to magnitude judgments of prestige (using numbers and lines) from roughly 4000 respondents surveyed in two cross-sectional probability samples representative for Germany. Fifty different occupational titles [from the *International Standard Classification of Occupations* (ISCO 1968)] were scaled. In the left panel, the mean magnitude prestige ranges (that is the ratios of the highest to the lowest prestige value given to any occupation by individuals) are plotted against the socioeconomic status of the judges. As can be seen, discrimination in terms of judgment range varies with status. Discrimination is low for low status judges and high for high status judges.

Based on these measurements, interindividual differences in prestige judgments can also be expressed in terms of the scale values themselves. If the mean magnitude prestige values for the 10 highest and for the 10 lowest judged occupations are plotted against the status of the judges, the right panel of Figure 1 results. As this panel shows, the higher status respondents tend to give higher prestige judgments to the 10 highest occupations and lower prestige judgments to the 10 lowest occupations, whereas low status respondents give higher judgments to the lowest and lower judgments to the highest occupations. This can be summarized simply: Low status observers tend to level the social grading continuum; high status observers tend to polarize it. Using conventional rating methods, Lewis (1964) and Alexander (1972) earlier found that lower status persons discriminate less than higher status persons.

Given the status dependency of prestige perceptions, it is easy to understand why other studies have found higher interrater prestige correlations for higher status respondents than for lower status respondents. The polarization of judgments in the higher strata is likely to increase correlations, whereas leveling the continuum will decrease correlations (when the respec-

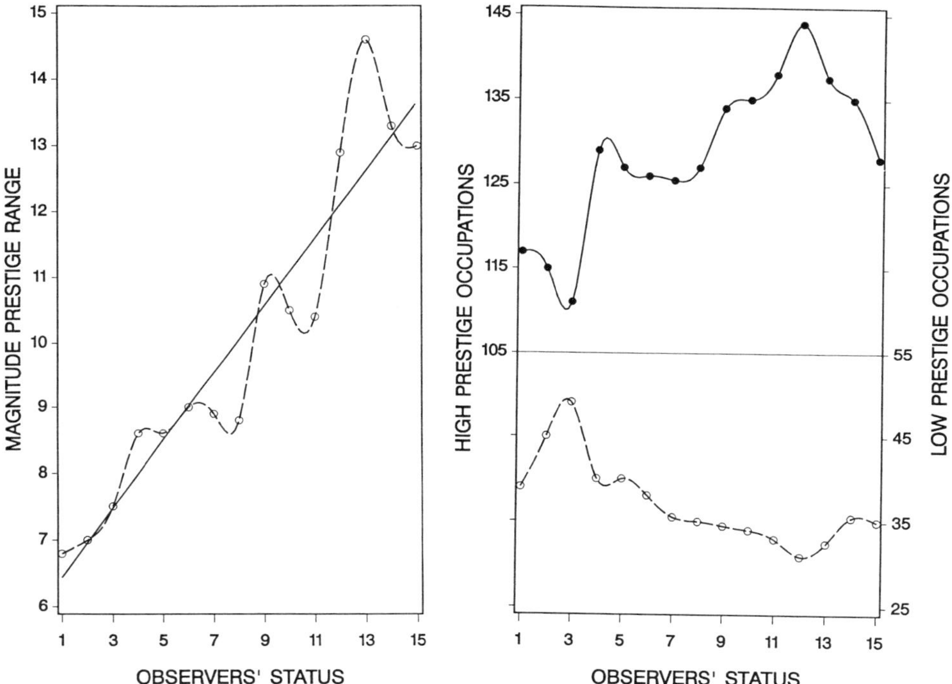

Figure 1 *Left panel:* Prestige discrimination range by observers' status. *Right panel:* Mean magnitude prestige scores for upper and lower 10 occupations by observers' status (solid: upper 10 occupations; dashed: lower 10). (Adapted from Wegener 1990:74–75).

tive coefficients of variation are not exceedingly different in both cases). This seems to be a less demanding explanation than the assumption that lower status group members lack knowledge and intelligence, as Hodge et al (1982:1195, Hodge & Rossi 1978) propose.

A Social Perception Theory of Dissensus

Perception theory can explain why judges on the upper end of the social ladder polarize the prestige continuum and why judges positioned toward the lower end level it. The perceptual processes relevant here are end-anchoring and directionality of ordering. End-anchoring describes the process by which, in making order judgments, subjects are guided by the end points of the order continuum. They anchor their judgments at the top and bottom end points

(Helson 1964). However, the top and the bottom anchors have asymmetrical effects depending on the direction in which stimuli are ordered by the judge. In this respect, the theory of end-anchoring makes the following assertions (De Soto & Albrecht 1968):

> (*a*) The bottom anchor in an ordering is more stable than the top anchor. In fact, the bottom anchor has the tendency to draw the top anchor down, thus shortening the range of judgments.
> (*b*) If the ordering is made along a dimension on which the individual is aware of being located, the position the individual has on that dimension affects the position of the two anchors. The position oneself is in tends to strengthen whichever anchor is closer to that position. Thus, judges in high status positions strengthen the top anchor in ordering. They will discriminate more than judges in low status positions who, by their low position, reinforce the bottom anchor. That is, high status respondents polarize social hierarchies, low status respondents level these hierarchies.
> (*c*) The direction of ordering, however, determines which end point operates as the top and which as the bottom anchor and, accordingly, which of the two anchors is stronger in affecting a person's judgment. It seems universally true that the direction of ordering runs from the preferred end point to the less preferred end point, that is we order from "good" to "bad" (De Soto & Bosley 1962, Lindenberg 1977). Therefore, *values* determine the direction of ordering and the strength of end anchors.

From this, a paradoxical conclusion must be drawn. Owing to end-anchoring and the directionality of ordering, the ability to discriminate social distributions is more pronounced for high-status respondents than for low-status respondents. The paradoxical finding is that these interindividual differences are not caused, as one might expect, by differences in value preferences in a society but rather by value consensus. Because high- and low-status individuals agree on what is to be preferred in a society, they agree on where to place the top and the bottom anchors. But because of the different locations of the judges in relation to the anchors, differential social perceptions result. This phenomenon has been labeled the value consensus paradox (Wegener 1987). With regard to prestige, what we see is that, according to end-anchoring theory, prestige consensus is possible only when high- and low-status groups in a society *differ* in their preferences for the anchor jobs. But it is difficult to imagine a society in which some prefer high status over low status and some prefer low status over high status. As De Swann (1989:262) recently observed: "Prestige distributions necessarily involve jealous relations." It must be concluded, therefore, that to the extent that discrimination differences with regard to social prestige exist, those of lower social status are disadvantaged. Their lack of discrimination excludes them from appreciating the strategic behavior typical of higher status positions and from acquiring information that would be relevant for gaining access to these higher positions. The value consensus paradox operates as a social closure mechanism that forcefully inhibits social mobility. While prestige is a "culturological construct" (Udy 1980:161), it also has structural consequences. These become visible, however, only if dissensus in prestige evaluations is taken seriously as a sociological problem.

CONCLUSION

According to the dominant view of prestige research, prestige is a variable representing a hierarchy of individual social positions. Following this conception, a considerable amount of knowledge has accumulated. First, as an aggregate scale, prestige reflects material advantages and thus may mirror the desirable features of positions. Accordingly, Sørensen (1991b:4) suggests that prestige is a multidimensional measure of welfare. Second, it is warranted to base prestige scales on individual prestige judgments even though interrater variation depends on rater characteristics to a certain extent. But following the argument of Hodge et al (1982), we can say that variation within groups is larger than variation between groups when conventional methods are used. Third, profile correlations of aggregation scales reveal that prestige exhibits high cross-cultural and temporal stability. These findings make it useful and mandatory to have updated aggregate prestige scales, like the new NORC scale, particularly because socioeconomic measures rely on such scales.[7]

Also, it would be misleading to identify this conception of prestige and its application with functionalism (as do Blaikie 1977, Horan 1978, Fox & Suschnigg 1989 and many others), since the notion of hierarchy need not be based on achievement and functional needs. It is compatible with Shils' idea of charisma and deference as the foundations of prestige (e.g. Treiman 1977, Hodge 1981); that is, rational as well as normative foundations of prestige are possible. The hierarchical conception seems to be restricted to societal processes characterized by "open" positions, that is, by the free supply of prestige based on whatever it takes to accumulate it. While prestige may be distributed in this way—being perhaps more common in some societies than in others—structural constraints may restrict the allocation of prestige and the

[7]This is not only true for Duncan's SEI but also for alternative measures like Sørensen's (1979) *Status Attainment Scale* which starts out from a rank order of occupational positions for which an aggregate prestige scale may be the appropriate choice (Wegener 1988: 168–74).

access to prestigious positions. Of special interest here are those instances in which prestige is itself of causal relevance for creating "closed" positions. Where this is the case, however, prestige applies not to individual positions within a hierarchy but to social aggregates. This is what Weber's social closure conception of prestige is about. In order for prestige to play this role, members of specific groups in a society must share homogeneous prestige perceptions. That is, they must see society in the same way. It seems that the long neglected study of judgment variation in prestige research is on its way to discovering instances of prestige closure. This review has covered two such instances: the mobility consequences of differential prestige discrimination due to the value consensus paradox and the sex-typing of occupational prestige perceptions by which men as well as women are kept from entering sex-atypical occupations. But other domains and mechanisms of prestige closure are bound to be uncovered as we learn more about the regularities of individuals' prestige perceptions.

In pursuing that course of research, it is important not to conceive the study of dissensus as opposed to the conventional hierarchical prestige paradigm. There is nothing wrong with studying two separate classes of phenomena. Theoretically, the hierarchical and the social closure conceptions of prestige are sociologically relevant. Considering both not only would bring prestige research more in line with the complexities of prestige theories, it would also reflect the present interest of mobility research in breaking away from an exclusive dedication to status attainment research.

Of course, there is still the problem of social closure and hierarchy, meaning the problem of how prestige, in qualifying members of social aggregates, is then transformed into a hierarchy of individual positions. While it is true that the different prestige theories have not been able to deal with this problem adequately (unless one is willing to follow Parsons in combining both levels by fiat), class theory has not found a solution either. Class theory is confronted with the same type of problem, though it is primarily interested not in the distribution of prestige but the distribution of income. Following Sørensen (1991 a,b), the decision to abandon the classic value theory of labor by current class theories, based either on Marxian (Wright 1985) or Weberian (Goldthorpe 1987) ideas, has led to identifying classes with groups of homogenous members without providing a theory of how income inequality and separate class interests are generated. Parallel to this, prestige theory is still lacking the structural mechanisms which transform differences in social honor into a prestige hierarchy. I argue here that until we find these mechanisms, prestige research is well advised to study the two phenomena in separation and not to confine itself to the dominant view. Entering the 1990s, prestige research seems on its way to doing just that.

Literature Cited

Abbott, W., Kenkel, W. F. 1988. The use of paired comparisons in the prestige ranking of occupations. *Humboldt J. Soc. Relat.* 15:105–17

Acker, J. 1980. Women and stratification: A review of recent literature. *Contemp. Sociol.* 9:25–39

Adler, I., Kraus, V. 1985. Components of occupational prestige evaluations. *Work Occup.* 12:23–39

Alestalo, M., Uusitalo, H. 1980. Prestige and stratification. A comparative study on occupational prestige and its determinants. *Commentationes Scientiarium Socialium* No. 15

Alexander, C. N. 1972. Status perceptions. *Am. Sociol. Rev.* 37:767–73

Alexander, J. C. 1983. *The Modern Reconstruction of Classical Thought: Talcott Parsons. Theoretical Logic of Sociology,* Vol. 4. Berkeley, Calif: Univ. Chicago Press

Armer, M. J. 1969. Intersociety and intrasociety correlations of occupational prestige. *Am. J. Sociol.* 74:28–36

Balkwell, J. W., Bates, F. L., Garbick, A. P. 1980. On the intersubjectivity of occupational status evaluations: A test of a key assumption underlying the "Wisconsin Model" of status attainment. *Soc. Forc.* 58:865–81

Balkwell, J. W., Bates, F. L., Garbick, A. P. 1982. Does the degree of consensus on occupational status evaluations differ by socioeconomic stratum? Response to Guppy. *Soc. Forc.* 60:1183–9

Bates, F. L., Garbick, A. P., Balkwell, J. W. 1986. Occupational prestige hierarchy: Methodological artifact or cultural category system. *Sociol. Spectrum* 6:321–43

Beck, U., Brater, M., Wegener, B. 1979. *Berufswahl und Berufszuweisung. Zur sozialen Verwandtschaft von Ausbildungsberufen.* Frankfurt/M.: Campus

Beeghley, L., Cochran, J. 1988. Class identification and gender role norms among employed married women. *J. Marriage Family* 50:719–29

Bendix, R., Lipset, S. M. eds. 1966. *Class, Status, and Power.* New York: Free Press. 2nd ed.

Benoit-Smullyan, E. 1944. Status types and status interrelations. *Am. Rev. Sociol.* 9: 151–61

Blaikie, N. W. 1977. The meaning and measurement of occupational prestige. *Aust. N. Zeal. J. Sociol.* 13:102–15

Blau, P. M. 1957. Occupational bias and mobility. *Am. Sociol. Rev.* 22:392–9

Blau, P. M. 1964. *Exchange and Power in Social Life.* New York: Wiley

Blau, P. M., Duncan, O. D. 1967. *The American Occupational Structure.* New York: Wiley

Bose, C. E. 1973. *Jobs and Gender: Sex and Occupational Prestige.* Baltimore, Md: John Hopkins Univ. Press

Bose, C. E. 1985. *Jobs and Gender: A Study of Occupational Prestige.* New York: Praeger

Bose, C. E., Rossi, P. H. 1983. Gender and jobs: Prestige standings of occupations as affected by gender. *Am. Sociol. Rev.* 48:316–30

Boyd, W., McRoberts, H. A. 1982. Women, men and socioeconomic indices: An assessment. In *Measures of Socioeconomic Status: Current Issues,* ed. M. G. Powers, pp. 129–59. Boulder, Colo: Westview

Burrage, M. C., Corry, D. 1981. At sixes and sevens: Occupational status in the city of London from the fourteenth to the seventeenth century. *Am. Sociol. Rev.* 46:375–93

Burschtyn, H. A. 1968. A factor-analytic study of occupational prestige. *Can. Rev. Sociol. Anthropol.* 5:156–80

Caston, R. J. 1989. Dimensions of occupational inequality and Duncan's socioeconomic index. *Sociol. Forum* 4:329–48

Chase, 1. 1975. A comparison of men's and women's intergenerational mobility in the United States. *Am. Sociol. Rev.* 40:483–505

Coleman, J. S. 1990. *Foundations of Social Theory.* Cambridge, Mass: Harvard Univ. Press

Coleman, R. P., Rainwater, L. 1979. *Social Standing in America.* London: Routledge & Kegan Paul

Converse, P. E. 1964. The nature of belief systems in mass public. In *Ideology and Discontent,* ed. D. E. Apter, pp. 206–61. New York: Free Press

Counts, G. S. 1925. The social status of occupation. A problem in vocational guidance. *School Rev.* 33:16–27

Coxon, A. P. 1971. Occupational attributes: Constructs and structure. *Sociol. Rev.* 5:335–54

Coxon, A. P., Jones, C. L. 1978. *The Images of Occupational Prestige.* London: Macmillian

Crino, M. D., White, M. C., DeSanctis, G. L. 1983. Female participation rates and the occupational prestige of the professions: Are they inversely related? *J. Vocat. Behav.* 22:243–55

Davis, K. 1946 *Human Society.* New York: Macmillan

Davis, K., Moore, W. E. 1945. Some principles of stratification. *Am. Sociol. Rev.* 10:242–49

De Lillo, A., Schizzerotto, A. 1985. *La valutazione social delle occupazioni per l'Italia conteporanea*. Bologna, Italy: Societa editrice il Mulino

De Soto, C. B., Bosley, J. J. 1962. The cognitive structure of social structure. *J. Abnormal Soc. Psych.* 64:303–07

De Soto, C. B., Albrecht, F. 1968. Cognition and social ordering. In *Theories of Cognitive Consistency,* ed. R. Abelson, E. Aronson, pp. 531–38. Chicago: Rand McNally

De Swann, A. 1989. Jealousy as a class phenomenon: The petite bourgeoise and social security. *Int. Sociol.* 4:259–71

Duncan, O. D. 1961. A socioeconomic index for all occupations. In *Occupations and Social Status,* ed. A. J. Reiss, pp. 109–38. New York: Free Press

Duncan, O. D. 1968. Social stratification and mobility: Problems in the measurement of trends. In *Indicators of Social Change,* ed. E. B. Sheldon, W. E. Moore, pp. 675–720. New York: Russell Sage Found.

Dworkin, R. 1981. Prestige ranking of the housewife occupation. *Sex Roles* 7:59–63

Edwards, A. M. 1938. *A Social-Economic Grouping of the Gainful Workers of the United States*. Washington DC: US Dep. Labor

Eisenstadt, S. N. 1968. Prestige, participation and strata formation. In *Social Stratification,* ed. J. A. Jackson, pp. 62–103. Cambridge, Mass: Harvard Univ. Press

England, P. 1979. Women and occupational prestige: A case of vacuous sex equality. *Signs* 5:252–65

Featherman, D. L., Jones, F. L., Hauser, R. M. 1975. Assumptions of social mobility research in the U.S.: The case of occupational status. *Soc. Sci. Res.* 4:329–60

Featherman, D. L., Hauser, R. M. 1976. Prestige or socioeconomic scales in the study of occupational achievement? *Sociol. Meth. Res.* 4:402–22

Featherman, D. L., Stevens, G. 1982. A revised socioeconomic index of occupational status: Application in analysis of sex differences in attainment. In *Measures of Socioeconomic Status: Current Issues,* ed. M. G. Powers, pp. 83–129. Boulder, Colo: Westview

Fossum, J. A., Moore, M. L. 1975. The stability of longitudinal and cross-sectional prestige rankings. *J. Vocat. Behav.* 7:305–11

Fox, J., Suschnigg, C. 1989. A note on gender and the prestige of occupations. *Can. J. Sociol.* 14:353–60

Fryer, D. 1922. Occupational-intelligence standards. *School Soc.* 1 6:273–77

Garbin, A. P., Bates, F. L. 1966. Occupational prestige and its correlates. A reexamination. *Soc.Forc.* 44:295–302

Geiger, T. 1932. *Die soziale Schichtung des deutschen Volkes*. Stuttgart: Enke

Gerstl, J. E., Cohen, L. K. 1964. Dissensus, situs, and egocentrism in occupational ranking. *Br. J. Sociol.* 15:254–61

Gifi, A. 1990. *Nonlinear Multivariate Analysis*. New York: Wiley

Goldthorpe, J. H. 1987. *Social Mobility and Class Structure in Great Britain*. Oxford: Clarendon. 2nd ed.

Goldthorpe, J. H., Hope, K. 1974. *The Social Grading of Occupations. A New Scale and Approach*. Oxford: Clarendon

Goode, W. J. 1978. *The Celebration of Heroes. Prestige as a Control System*. Berkeley, Calif: Univ. Calif. Press

Gould, S. J. 1981. *The Mismeasure of Man*. New York: Norton

Goyder, J. C., Pineo, P. C. 1977. The accuracy of self-assessments of social status. *Can. Rev. Sociol. Anthropol.* 14:235–46

Grasmick, H. G. 1976. The occupational prestige structure: A multidimensional scaling approach. *Sociol. Q.* 17:90–108

Guppy, L. N. 1982. On intersubjectivity and collective conscience in occupational prestige research: A comment on Balkwell-Bates-Garbin and Kraus-Schild-Hodge. *Soc. Forc.* 60:1178–82

Guppy, L. N. 1984. Dissensus or consensus: A cross-national comparison of occupational prestige scales. *Can. J. Sociol.* 9:69–83

Guppy, L. N., Siltanen, J. L. 1977. A comparison of the allocation of male and female occupational prestige. *Can. Rev. Sociol. Anthropol.* 14:320–30

Guppy, L. N., Goyder, J. C. 1984. Consensus on occupational prestige: A reassessment of the evidence. *Soc. Forc.* 62:709–25

Habermas, J. 1981. *Theorie des kommunikativen Handelns*. Vol. 2. Frankfurt/M.: Suhrkamp

Haller, A. O., Lewis, D. 1966. The hypothesis of international similarity in occupational prestige hierarchies. *Am. J. Sociol.* 72:210–16

Haller, A. O., Holsinger, D. B., Saraiva, H. U. 1972. Variations in occupational prestige hierarchies: Brazilian data. *Am. J. Sociol.* 77:941–56

Hansen, D. O., Converse, J. W. 1976. Cultural milieu and isolation as sources of intrasocietal variation in occupational prestige hierarchies: Recent Brazilian data. *Rural Sociol.* 41:371–81

Hatt, P. K. 1950. Occupation and social stratification. *Am. J. Sociol.* 55:533–43

Hauser, R. M., Featherman, D. L. 1977. *The Process of Stratification. Trends and Analyses*. New York: Academic Press

Hawkins, R. P., Pingree, S. 1978. Effects of changing proportions of the sexes on ratings of occupational prestige. *Psychol. Women Q*. 2:465–77

Heider, F. 1958. *The Psychology of Interpersonal Relations*. New York: Wiley

Helson, H. 1964. *Adaptation-Level Theory*. New York: Harper & Row

Hodge, R. W. 1981. The measurement of occupational status. *Soc. Sci. Res*. 10:396–415

Hodge, R. W., Treiman, D. J., Rossi, P. H. 1966a. A comparative study of occupational prestige. See Bendix & Lipset 1966, pp. 309–21

Hodge, R. W., Siegel, P. M., Rossi, P. H. 1966b. Occupational prestige in the United States: 1925–1963. See Bendix & Lipset 1966, pp. 322–34

Hodge, R. W., Rossi, P. H. 1978. Intergroup consensus in occupational prestige ratings: A case of serendipity lost and gained. *Sozialwissenschaftliche Annalen* 2:B59–B73

Hodge, R. W., Kraus, V., Schild, E. 0. 1982. Consensus in occupational prestige ratings: Response to Guppy. *Soc.Forc*. 60:1190–96

Hodge, R. W., Kraus, V., Meyer, G. S. 1985. Politische ldeologie und Berufsprestige: Eine vergleichende Analyse. In *Die Analyse sozialer Ungleichheit,* ed. H. Strasser, J. H. Goldthorpe, pp. 70–97. Opladen: Westdeutscher Verlag

Homans, G. C. 1961. *Social Behavior: Its Elementary Forms*. New York: Harcourt Brace Jovanovich

Horan, P. M. 1978. Is status attainment atheoretical? *Am. Sociol. Rev*. 43:534–41

Hyman, H. H. 1953. The relation of the reference group to judgments of status. In *Class, Status and Power,* ed. R. Bendix, S. M. Lipset, pp. 263–70. New York: Free Press

Inkeles, A. 1960. Industrial Man: The relation of status to experience, perception and value. *Am. J. Sociol*. 66:1–31

Inkeles, A., Rossi, P. H. 1956. National comparison of occupational prestige. *Am. J. Sociol*. 61:329–39

International Standard Classification of Occupations. 1968. *lnternationale Standardklassifikation der Berufe,* ed. by Statistisches Bundesamt Wiesbaden. Stuttgart

Jacobs, J. A., Powell, B. 1985. Occupational prestige: A sex-neutral concept? *Sex Roles* 12:1061–71

Jencks, C. M., Acland, H., Bane, M. J., Cohen, D., Gintis, H., Heyns, B., Michelson, S. 1972. *Inequality: A Reassessment of the Effect of Family and Schooling in America*. New York: Basic Books

Jones, F. L. 1989. Occupational prestige in Australia: A new scale. *Aust. N. Zeal. J. Sociol*. 25:187–99

Kerckhoff, A. C., Campbell, R. T., Trott, J. M., Kraus, V. 1989. The transmission of socioeconomic status and prestige in Great Britain and the United States. *Sociol. Forum* 4:155–77

Kluth, H. 1957. *Sozialprestige und sozialer Status*. Stuttgart: Enke

Krantz, D. H. 1972. Magnitude estimation and cross-modality matching. *J. Math. Psychol*. 9: 168–99

Kraus, V. 1976. *Social grading of occupations*. PhD thesis. Dep. Sociol., Hebrew Univ. Jerusalem

Kraus, V., Schild, E. O., Hodge, R. W. 1978. Occupational prestige in the collective conscience. *Soc. Forc*. 56:900–18

Laumann, E. O. 1966. *Prestige and Association in an Urban Community*. Indianapolis: Bobbs-Merrill

Leopold, L. 1916. *Prestige. Ein gesellschaftspsychologischer Versuch*. Berlin: DeGruyter

Lewis, L. S. 1964. Class and the perception of class. *Soc. Forc*. 42:336–40

Lindenberg, S. 1977. The direction of ordering and its relation to social phenomena. *Zeitschr. Soziol*. 2:223–21

Lodge, M. 1981. *Magnitude Scaling*. Beverly Hills, Calif: Sage

Marini, M. M. 1980. Sex differences in the process of occupational attainment: A closer look. *Soc. Sci. Res*. 9:307–61

Marsh, R. D. 1971. The explanation of occupational prestige. *Soc. Forc*. 50:214–22

Marshall, K. P., Gorman, B. J. 1975. Occupational prestige from preference orientations via the Markov chain alternative to response ranking techniques. *Soc. Sci. Res*. 4:41–64

Mayer, K. U. 1977. Statushierarchie und Heiratsmarkt - Empirische Analysen zur Struktur des Schichtungssystems in der Bundesrepublik und zur Ableitung einer Skala des sozialen Satus. In *Klassenlagen und Sozialstruktur,* ed. J. Handl, K. U. Mayer, W. Müller, pp. 155–232. Frankfurt/M.: Campus

McClendon, M. 1976. The occupational status attainment process of males and females. *Am. Sociol. Rev*. 41:52–64

McLaughlin, S. D. 1978. Occupational sex identification and the assessment of male and female earnings inequality. *Am. Sociol. Rev*. 43:909–21

More, D. M., Suchner, R. W. 1976. Occupational situs, prestige, and stereotypes. *Sociol. Work Occup*. 3:169–86

Morris, R. T., Murphy, R. J. 1959. The situs dimension in occupational structure. *Am. Sociol. Rev.* 24:231–39

Müller, W., Lüttinger, P., König, W., Karle, W. 1990. Class and education in industrial nations. In *Class Structure in Europe. New Findings from East-West Comparisons of Social Structure and Mobility,* ed. M. Haller, pp. 61–91. New York: Sharpe

Nakao, K., Hodge, R. W., Treas, J. 1990. *On Revising Prestige Scores for all Occupations. General Social Survey Methodological Report No. 69*

Nakao, K., Treas, J. 1990. *Computing 1989 Occupational Prestige Scores. General Social Survey Methodological Report No. 70*

Nilson, L. B. 1976. The occupational and sex related components of social standing. *Sociol. Soc. Res.* 60:328–36

Nilson, L. B. 1978. *Sex in Society: Perspectives on Stratification.* Belmont, Calif: Wadsworth

North, C. C., Hatt, P. K. 1947. Jobs and occupations. *Opinion News* 9:3–13. (Reprinted 1953 in *Class, Status and Power,* ed. R. Bendix and S. M. Lipset, pp. 411–26. New York: Free Press)

Nosanchuk, T. A. 1972. A note on the use of the correlation coefficient for assessing the similarity of occupation rankings. *Can. Rev. Sociol. Anthropol.* 9:357–65

Orth, B. 1982. A theoretical and empirical study of scale properties of magnitude estimation and category rating scales. See Wegener 1982, pp. 351–78

Orth, B., Wegener, B. 1983. Scaling occupational prestige by magnitude estimation and category-rating methods. A comparison with the sensory domain. *Eur. J. Soc. Psychol.* 13:417–31

Ossowski, S. 1963. *Class Structure in the Social Consciousness.* New York: Free Press

Pappi, F. U. 1976. Soziale Schichten als Interaktionsgruppen. Zur Messung eines "deskriptiven" Schichtungsbegriffes. In *Zwischenbilanz der Soziologie,* ed. M. R. Lepsius, pp. 223–42. Stuttgart: Enke

Parsons, T. 1937. *The Structure of Social Action.* New York: McGraw-Hill

Parsons, T. 1940. An analytical approach to the theory of social stratification. *Am. J. Sociol.* 45:841–62

Parsons, T. 1953. A revised analytical approach to the theory of social stratification. In *Class, Status, and Power,* ed. R. Bendix, S. M. Lipset, pp. 92–128. New York: Free Press. (Reprint 1954 in *Essays in Sociological Theory,* pp. 386–439. New York: Free Press)

Parsons, T. 1967. On the concept of influence. In *Sociological Theory and Modern Society,* ed. T. Parsons, pp. 355–82. New York: Free Press

Parsons, T. 1970. Equality and inequality in modern society, or social stratification revisited. In *Social Stratification: Research and Theory for the 1970s,* ed. E. O. Laumann, pp. 13–72. Indianapolis, Ind: Bobbs-Merrill

Parsons, T., Platt, G. 1973. *The American University.* Cambridge: Harvard Univ. Press

Pavalko, R. M. 1971. *Sociology of Occupations and Professions.* ltasca, Ill: Peacock

Perman, L. 1984. *Other than money: The nonmonetary characteristics of jobs.* PhD thesis. Dep. Sociol., Harvard Univ., Cambridge, Mass.

Pineo, P. C., Porter, J. 1967. Occupational prestige in Canada. *Can. Rev. Sociol. Anthropol.* 4:24–40

Plata, M. 1975. Stability and change in the prestige rankings of occupations over 49 years. *J. Vocat. Behav.* 6:95–99

Powell, B., Jacobs, J. A. 1983. Sex and consensus in occupational prestige ratings. *Sociol. Soc. Res.* 67:392–404

Powell, B., Jacobs, J. A. 1984a. Gender differences in the evaluation of prestige. *Sociol. Q.* 25:173–90

Powell, B., Jacobs, J. A. 1984b. The prestige gap: Differential evaluations of male and female workers. *Work Occup.* 11:283–308

Quine, S. 1986. Comparisons of Australian occupational prestige scales. *Aust. N. Zeal. J. Sociol.* 22:339–410

Reiss, A. J. 1961. *Occupations and Social Status.* New York: Free Press

Roos, P. 1981. Sex-stratification in the work place: Male-female differences in economic returns to occupation. *Soc. Sci. Res.* 10: 195–224

Rosenfeld, R. 1979. Race and sex differences in career dynamics. *Am. Sociol. Rev.* 45:583–609

Saltiel, J. 1990. Occupational prestige and sex typing in the collective conscience. *Qual. Quant.* 24:283–96

Sawinski, Z., Domanski, H. 1991a. Stability of prestige hierarchies in the face of social changes: Poland, 1958–1987. *lnt. Sociol.* 6:227–41

Sawinski, Z., Domanski, H. 1991b. Dissensus in assessment of occupational prestige: The case of Poland. *Eur. Sociol. Rev.* 7:253–65

Schooler, C., Miller, J., Miller, K. A., Richtand, C. N. 1984. Work for the household: Its nature and consequences for husbands and wives. *Am. J. Sociol.*90:97–124

Seligson, M. A. 1978. Prestige among peasants: A multidimensional analysis of preference data. *Am. J. Sociol.* 83:632–52

Sewell, W. H., Hauser, R. M., Wolf, W. C.

1980. Sex, schooling and occupational status. *Am. J. Sociol.* 83:551–83

Shils, E. A. 1968. Deference. In *Social Stratification,* ed. J. A. Jackson, pp. 104–32. Cambridge, Mass: Harvard Univ. Press

Shils, E. A. 1975. *Center and Periphery: Essays in Macrosociology. Selected Papers of Edward Shils.* Vol. 11. Chicago, Ill: Univ. Chicago Press

Siegel, P. M. 1971. *Prestige in the American occupational structure.* PhD thesis. Dep. Sociol., Univ. Chicago

Simmel, G. 1923. *Soziologie. Untersuchungen über die Formen der Vergesellschaftung.* Leipzig: Duncker & Humblot. 3rd ed.

Sixma, H., Ultee, W. C. 1984. An occupational prestige scale for the Netherlands in the eighties. In *Social Stratification and Mobility in the Netherlands,* ed. B. F. M. Bakker, pp. 29–40. Amsterdam: SISWO

Skvoretz, J., Windell, P., Fararo, T. J. 1974. Luce's axiom and occupational prestige: Test of a measurement model. *J. Math. Sociol.* 3:147–62

Smith, N. 1943. An empirical scale of prestige status of occupations. *Am. Sociol. Rev.* 8:185–92

Sorokin, P. A. 1927. *Social Mobility.* New York: Harper. (Reprint 1959 as part of *Social and Cultural Mobility.* Glencoe, Ill: Free Press)

Sørensen, A. B. 1979. A model and a metric for the intragenerational status attainment process. *Am. J. Sociol.* 85:361–84

Sørensen, A. B. 1991a. On the usefulness of class analysis in research on social mobility and socioeconomic inequality. *Acta Sociologica* 34:71–87

Sørensen, A. B. 1991b. *Employment relations and class structure.* Presented Conf. Impact of Industrial Transformations on Job Trajectories. Eur. Univ. Inst., Florence

Stehr, N. 1974. Consensus and dissensus in occupational prestige. *Br. J. Sociol.* 25: 410–27

Stevens, G., Featherman, D. L. 1981. A revised socioeconomic index of occupational status. *Soc. Sci. Res.* 10:364–95

Stevens, G., Cho, J. H. 1985. Socioeconomic indexes and the new 1980 census occupational classification scheme. *Soc. Sci. Res.* 14:142–68

Stevens, G., Hoisington, E. 1987. Occupational prestige and the 1980 U.S. labor force. *Soc. Sci. Res.* 16:74–105

Stevens, S. S. 1975. *Psychophysics: Introduction to its Perceptual, Neural and Social Prospects.* New York: Wiley

Stewart, A., Prandy, K., Blackburn, R. M. 1980. *Social Stratification and Occupations.* London: Macmillian

Thomas, R. M. 1962. Reinspecting a structural position on occupational prestige. *Am. J. Sociol.* 67:561–65

Tiryakian, E. 1958. The prestige evaluation of occupations in an underdeveloped country: The Philippines. *Am. J. Sociol.* 63:390–99

Treas, J., Tyree, A. 1979. Prestige versus socioeconomic status in the attainment process of American men and women. *Soc. Sci. Res.* 8:201–21

Treiman, D. J. 1976. A standard occupational prestige scale for use with historical data. *J. Interdisc. Hist.* 7:283–304

Treiman, D. J. 1977. *Occupational Prestige in Comparative Perspective.* New York: Academic Press

Treiman, D. J., Terrell, K. 1975. Women, work and wages: Trends in the female occupation structure. In *Social Indicator Models,* ed. K. Land, S. Spillerman, pp. 157–99. New York: Russell Sage

Tumin, M. M., Feldmann, A. 1970. Dissonance and dissensus in evaluation. In *Readings on Social Stratification,* ed. M. M. Tumin, pp. 428–35. Prentice Hall: Engelwood

Tyree, A., Smith, B. G. 1977. Occupational hierarchy in the US 1789–1969. *Soc. Forc.* 56:881–99

Tyree, A., Hicks, R. 1988. Sex and the second moment of prestige distributions. *Soc. For.* 66:1028–37

Udy, S. H. 1980. The configuration of occupational structure. In *Sociological Theory and Research,* ed. H. M. Blalock, pp. 156–65. New York: Free Press

Villimez, W. J. 1974. Ability vs. effort: Ideological correlates of occupational grading. *Soc. Forc.* 53:45–52

Villimez, W. J., Silver, B. B. 1977. Occupational situs as horizontal social position: A reconsideration. *Sociol. Soc. Res.* 61:320–36

Weber, M. 1947. *The Theory of Social and Economic Organization.* Trans. by A. M. Henderson and T. Parsons. New York: Oxford Univ. Press

Weber, M. 1972. *Wirtschaft und Gesellschaft.* Tübingen: Mohr-Siebeck. 5th ed.

Wegener, B. ed. 1982. *Social Attitudes and Psychophysical Measurement.* Hillsdale, NJ: Erlbaum

Wegener, B. 1983. Category-rating and magnitude estimation scaling techniques: An empirical comparison. *Sociol. Meth. Res.* 12:31–75

Wegener, B. 1985. Gibt es Sozialprestige? *Zeitschr. Soziol.* 14:209–35 (French transl. 1991. Le prestige social existe-t-il? In *Perspectives des sciences sociales en Allemagne aujourd'hui,* ed. E. K. Scheuch, pp.

264–312. Paris: Editions de la Maison des Sciences de L'homme)

Wegener, B. 1987. The illusion of distributive justice. *Eur. Sociol. Rev.* 3:1–13

Wegener, B. 1988. *Kritik des Prestiges.* Opladen: Westdeutscher Verlag

Wegener, B. 1990. Equity, relative deprivation, and the value consensus paradox. *Soc. Justice Res.* 4:66–86

Wegener, B., Kirschner, H. 1981. A note on estimating inter-scale relations in "direct" psychophysical scaling. *Br. J. Math. Statist. Psychol.* 34:194–204

Wolf, W. C., Rosenfeld, R. 1978. Sex structure of occupations and job mobility. *Soc. Forc.* 56:823–44

Wright, E. 0. 1985. *Classes.* London: New Left Books

Wrong, D. H. 1979. *Power: Its Forms, Bases and Uses.* New York: Harper & Row

Yogev, A. 1980. Validating the applicability of the standard international occupational prestige scale: Illustrations from Costa Rica and Israel. *Int. Rev. Modern Sociol.* 10:15–35

Annu. Rev. Sociol. 1992. 18:281–302

COMMITMENT TO WORK AND FAMILY

D. D. Bielby

Department of Sociology, University of California, Santa Barbara, California 93106

KEY WORDS: work/family interface, identity, meaning

Abstract

Demographic change and behavioral shifts in employment and household arrangements have caused scholars and social critics to question the nature of individuals' involvement with work and family. Interpreting the cultural meaning of those behavioral changes requires the study of individual commitment per se. This chapter reviews research on commitment to work and family by examining issues of definition, measurement, and specification of the concept of commitment, by assessing theoretical developments in the study of linkages between work and family, and by reviewing research that examines the relationship of work and family to gender, the life course, social origin, and race. The interrelationship between work and family commitment is examined, and issues to be resolved in future research are discussed.

INTRODUCTION

Combining paid work with family responsibilities, for years typical of many women from low-income, farm, and minority backgrounds, became by the close of the 1970s a viable life-style for the majority of women in the United States (Komarovsky 1982, Myrdal & Klein 1956, US Department of Labor 1979). Moreover, among all families, the proportion of dual-earner couples has nearly doubled since 1960—to about 55%. Meanwhile, the traditional

0360-0572/92/0815-0281$02.00

family form of a married couple with children and with the wife not in the paid labor force has declined to just 15% (Merrick & Tordella 1988). Over the same period, women's continuous participation in the paid labor force has risen, particularly among mothers of young children; gender differences in levels of education have declined; and the sex role attitudes of both men and women have become more egalitarian. Further, delay of age at first marriage, postponed onset of childbearing, lower fertility, and increases in divorce and single-parent households suggest that change has occurred in the organization and integration of work and family (Gerstel & Gross 1987, Thornton 1989). Thus, by the 1980s, men as well as women were confronted with the "balancing act" that follows changing involvements with the dual roles of paid work and family (Baruch et al 1983, Regan & Roland 1982).

Why Study Commitment to Work and Family?

Behavioral shifts in employment and household arrangements have generated considerable debate about their social significance. Both progressive and conservative commentators lament change in commitment to the family and to long-term love relationships and other forms of intimate bonds, and they question whether individuals still seek significant involvement with the institution of the family (Bellah et al 1985, Ehrenreich 1983, Lasch 1977). Others challenge the presumption that increasing variety in family and household arrangements indicates a declining commitment to the family (Aldous 1982, 1991, Bane 1976, Bernard 1982, Cancian 1987, Gerstel & Gross 1987, Thornton & Freedman 1983). While inferences about declines in commitment to work are often drawn from trends in employment behaviors such as absenteeism, job quits, overtime, and part-time work, there is little research on the link between these behavioral changes and subjective attachment to work (Hedges 1983). In short, in research on both work and family, scholars are often inclined to make attributions about commitment from knowledge of changes in behavior rather than to examine explicitly the relationship between the two (see Bielby & Bielby 1988, Gerson 1985).

In prevailing sociological research, an individual is committed to a behavior, role, value, or institution to the extent that it is a source of meaning or identity (Burke & Reitzes 1991). Individuals define themselves in relation to both sociocultural change and continuity through their commitments, revealing the cultural forms they defend, advocate, and enact in their personal lives (Wuthnow 1987, p. 338). Thus, aggregate change in work and family arrangements is culturally significant to the extent that it is reflected in the commitments of individual women and men. It is those commitments that concern us here. Moreover, understanding meaning in individuals' lives is of fundamental sociological interest, apart from the efficacy of commitment in predicting or understanding behavior. From this perspective, commitments are more than just behaviorally revealed preferences that underlie individual choices; they are ties that link individuals to social structure through the roles, organizations, individuals, and values with which they affiliate.

Examining commitment as it applies to work and family brings an original perspective to research on the work/family interface and overcomes limitations of other perspectives on the topic. For example, much of that research focuses on work-family role conflict (e.g. Voydanoff 1987) or work "stressors" (e.g. Bolger et al 1990) and shares an imagery of the intersection of work and family as a social "problem" (Greenhaus 1989). By treating work and family as mutually constraining, these conceptualizations overlook how work and family are integrated in ways that contribute meaning to the everyday lives of individuals. Work and family are more than just complications, they are sources of meaning and identity to which men and women balance commitment (Almquist et al 1980, Angrist & Almquist 1975, Bielby & Bielby 1984, Coombs 1979, Kessler & McRae 1982, Pleck 1983, Staines et al 1985). An adequate understanding of the work/family interface requires attending to the process by which those commitments are built and sustained.

This chapter reviews research on commitment to work and family by drawing upon the theoretical legacy of the concept of commitment. The first part of the chapter reviews issues in definition, measurement, and specification of commitment generally.[1] Next, theoretical developments in the study of linkages between work and family are summarized. That discussion is followed by a review of research that examines the relationship of work and family commitment to gender, age and the life course, social origin, and race. Finally, research on the interrelationship between work and family commitment is presented, followed by a conclusion in which issues pertaining to future research in the field are discussed.

DEFINITIONS OF COMMITMENT

Commitments are associated with sustained lines of activity across situations. Commitment is typically conceptualized in one of two ways, one emphasizing behavior and the other emphasizing identity as the locus of individual action (Burke & Reitzes 1991, Mowday et al 1979). Indeed, these differences appear in some of the earliest work on commitment. For example, Selznick (1949),

[1]In the study of commitment, it is also important to differentiate sex-role attitudes from commitment to work and family. The former represent an individual's judgment about appropriate roles for men and women in general, not the extent to which an individual's involvement in those roles is a source of meaning or identity (see Thornton et al 1983). Moreover, sex-role attitudes do not necessarily reflect an individual's intentions, aspirations, expectations, and subjective attachments regarding work and family. Research that explicitly differentiates commitment to work and family from both sex-role behavior and sex-role attitudes is relatively recent.

in his study of the TVA, regarded commitment in social action as an enforced line of activity, dictated by the force of circumstances. In contrast, Foote (1951) argued that identity was essential for understanding the motive or incentive for the enactment of role involvement.

According to the behavioral approach, commitment is conceptualized with respect to situational determinants that sustain a line of activity. Johnson (1973, p. 397), for example, defines "behavioral commitment" as "consequences of the initial pursuit of a line of action that constrain the actor to continue that line of action." In this view, commitment is located in the process of retrospection that binds an individual to behavioral acts (Becker 1960, Kiesler 1971, Salancik 1977). To the extent that an individual's prior association with a line of activity has been explicit, irrevocable, public, and volitional (Salancik 1977), subsequent behavior will be more stable (Becker 1956). Becoming committed entails increasing obligations to act such that abandonment of the line of activity becomes personally costly. Thus, recognition of "sunk" costs, foregone alternatives, and one's own role in creating the situation retrospectively construct commitment (Angle & Perry 1983). This view of commitment is used widely in the study of organizational commitment (e.g. Pfeffer & Lawler 1980, O'Reilly & Caldwell 1981) and is equally applicable to paid work and family roles.

According to the identity approach, commitment is conceptualized with respect to personal meaning. In Johnson's (1973, p. 395) terms, "personal commitment" is "a strong personal dedication to a decision to carry out a line of action." Most recent scholarship on commitment to work and family adopts this definition of the concept. That is, commitment is seen as an attachment that is initiated and sustained by the extent to which an individual's identification with a role, behavior, value, or institution is considered to be central among alternatives as a source of identity (e.g. Almquist & Angrist 1971, Becker 1956, Bielby & Bielby 1984, Morrow 1983, Rosenfeld & Spenner 1988, Safilios-Rothchild 1971). Centrality of identity implies that it is particularly significant, meaningful, or salient within an individual's personal hierarchy of identities or self-meanings (Burke 1980, Burke & Reitzes 1991. As such, the identity is more likely to be enacted and thus has consequences for behavioral consistency in lines of activity (Stryker 1981). Research on work (or family) commitment typically emphasizes the measurement of identity by assessing an individual's "involvement" (Lodahl & Kejner 1965, Yogev & Brett 1985), "central interest" (Dubin 1956, Mannheim 1983), or "orientation" (Bailyn 1970) with respect to a given activity or role.

So, for example, Haller & Rosenmayr (1971 p. 501) define female work commitment as "feelings about work or the 'meaning' it has for her." Almquist & Angrist (1971 p. 263) speak of career salience as "a central feature of adult life." Masih (1967, pp. 653–54) defines the same term as "(a) the degree to which a person is career motivated, (b) the degree to which an occupation is important as a source of satisfaction, and (c) the degree of priority ascribed to occupation among other sources of satisfaction." Less often, work and family commitment is defined as plans, intentions, preferences, or aspirations (Ajzen & Fishbein 1980) for particular combinations of work and family roles (Gersen 1985).

Both definitions are consistent with a view of commitment as a process through which subjective attachments guide moment to moment behavior. Their differences lie in the relative emphasis they give to self-motivation and self-meaning as the locus of committing actions. As Burke & Reitzes (1991, p. 241) note, differing formulations of commitment are not contradictory, but they also are not cumulative or mutually reinforcing; thus the task of reconciling their differences is left to future research. Several additional issues related to operationalization, measurement, and conceptualization also remain unresolved in work in this area. First, in choosing a definition, analysts do not always attend to a definition's operational consequences for the enactment of subjective attachments. So, for example, in operationalizing the behavioral definition, measurement of commitment is often confounded with those behaviors that simultaneously generate it. In operationalizing the identity definition, analysts typically assume individuals are fully cognizant of what is meaningful to them, are unencumbered by situational constraints or opportunities, and have the latitude to behave in a manner that corresponds with their identity.

Second, choices regarding the definition and operationalization of commitment often implicitly embody assumptions about the cognitive process through which commitment is developed and sustained. These assumptions have direct consequences for the specification of determinants of commitment (see Bielby & Bielby 1988). According to the behavioral definition, as individuals find themselves engaged in a particular pattern of employment and family responsibilities, subjective attachments are changed to be consistent with those engagements. Thus, commitments to work and family are functions of one's past and current experiences, responsibilities, and statuses. In this view, commitments are not determined by rational calculation based on expected costs and benefits of current and future activities. Individual differences in commitments to work and family reflect variability in the cumulative impact of prior committing behaviors, not differences in the current balance of their costs and benefits.

According to the identity definition, commitment is determined in one of two ways, either by rational choice or by noncognitive response. In the former, an individual commits to a line of behavior so long as it provides resources for meeting personal needs and values. Specifically, commitment to an activity is a function of the net rewards from the activity, the costs of leaving the activity, and the net rewards available for alternative activities (England & Farkas 1986, Farrell & Rusbult 1981, March & Simon 1958, Mowday et al 1982). Accordingly, individuals adjust their commitment to paid work and family solely on the basis of their current assessment of the net costs and benefits of performance in those roles and the costs of changing the distribution of their efforts at home and at work. Thus, in this view, commitment is a process that stabilizes behavior only to the extent that the balance of net costs and benefits is stable over time.

Noncognitive responses to committing situations emphasize the degree to which subjective orientation and intentions are habitual, rulelike, or taken for granted (Pfeffer 1982). Some social behaviors are "scripted" sequences of activities triggered by cues in the environment—not by rational or irrational decisions of individuals (Abelson 1976, Laws & Schwartz 1977, Schank & Abelson 1977). Thus, certain family and work activities would be viewed as habitual rather than intentional. Those activities are neither recognized as binding, nor evaluated with respect to the net benefit to be derived from them. Instead, an emotional or affective basis for the persistence of a particular mix of work and family roles is taken for granted (Collins 1981). Actions can take on rulelike status in guiding thought and action (Meyer & Rowan 1977, Zucker 1981), and if widely shared norms exist concerning appropriate orientations toward work and family, individuals may conform to those expectations without reflection upon other options available to them and may shape their commitments accordingly.

Clearly, whether an analyst subscribes to a definition of commitment that emphasizes the constraining impact of prior behaviors, the rational calculation of net future benefits, or the noncognitive habitual response affects how one models the determinants and consequences of commitment to work and family. However, analysts are seldom explicit about the assumptions of their approach to definition and measurement (Randall & Cote 1991) or about the implications of these for specification of models of work and family commitment.

Even among those sharing the same conceptual approach to commitment, there is often little concern about appropriate measures. Seemingly face valid measures are often assumed to be perfectly reliable although studies that empirically assess the quality of measurement find reliability across measures to be generally low and variable (Bielby & Bielby 1984). Relying on multiple indicators and explicitly modeling the relationship between observable indicators and the underlying construct of commitment is one way to avoid significant bias due to unreliability of measurement (e.g. Bielby & Bielby 1989, Lorence & Mortimer 1985).

Despite differences in approach to conceptualization, definition, and measurement, most analysts recognize gender, age, social origin, work context, and family factors as important determinants of work and family commitment. Before discussing research that focuses specifically on commitment, more general approaches to the work/family interface are discussed.

WORK-FAMILY INTERFACE: BEHAVIORAL AND SOCIAL PSYCHOLOGICAL LINKAGES

Contemporary research on connections between work and family has been influenced by functionalist scholarship from the 1950s. Scholarship dominating that era argued that separation of labor in the household and workplace was both necessary and appropriate in order to minimize competition between the sexes, thereby sustaining family cohesion and minimizing imbalance in the traditional locus of family power (Blood & Wolfe 1960, Parsons & Bales 1955). Theorizing about the institution of work and analyses of worker attachment omitted consideration of connections with the family that might compete with work as a central life interest (Dubin 1956).

Changes during the 1960s in familial and labor force arrangements, sex-role beliefs, and life-style patterns focused attention on variation in family and work behavior. In early analyses of difference (such as class differences in marital arrangements) and change (such as the rise in labor force participation among mothers of young children), scholars were constrained by prevailing theoretical assumptions that both sustained separateness between work and family and overlooked interaction between those domains. Thus, for example, women's paid labor was conceptualized as a role subordinated to their primary responsibilities for household labor. Their employment was nonetheless regarded as a social problem with negative consequences for the well-being of children and for the marital relationship (Hoffman 1963 1974, Rapaport & Rapoport 1971, Safilios-Rothchild 1970).

Through the next two decades, the convergence of several cumulatively distinct lines of research on the family, work, and the economy predisposed scholars to question underlying theoretical assumptions about the separation between the spheres of work and family and to consider broad connections between them. That scholarship includes research by family historians on industrialization and household and family structure (see Cherlin 1983), by Marxists on household production and reproduction and its relation to the economy (Hartmann 1981), by feminists on gender relations within the family (Chodorow 1978), by economists on the family and the "new home economics" (Becker 1981), and by proponents of the life-course perspective on the overlap between individual and family life cycles (Elder 1974). Research into the two-person career (Papanek 1973), the dual-career couple (Poloma 1972, Rapoport & Rapoport 1971), and the two-job family (Hood 1983) focused attention on the integration of work and family at the individual level.

Kanter's (1977) monograph about the "myth" of the separate worlds of work and family challenged the arbitrary separation of those institutions and argued for the importance of examining the processual nature of work and family dynamics. By considering connections, intersections, and transactions between workplaces and families, the reciprocal, microlevel dynamics between those spheres could be identified, including the impact of work and family behavior and of subjective attachments upon the individual over time. Kanter's "research frontier" included examining the relative absorptiveness of (including commitment to) an occupation, the effect of work hours and scheduling on family interaction, the effect of occupational rewards and resources upon the quality of family life, occupations as socializers of values, and the effects of the social psychological dimensions of work on the individual. Family influences on the work sphere include the effect of cultural traditions on workers, the role of family connections in occupational placement, and the effect of the family's emotional climate and demands upon worker orientations, motivations, abilities, emotional energy, and personal needs brought to the workplace.

Scholars now widely recognize the mutual influences between the spheres of work and family (Gutek et al 1981; for reviews see Aldous 1982, Ferree 1990, Menaghan & Parcel 1990, Piotrkowski et al 1987, Voydanoff 1987, Walker & Thompson 1989), and a considerable amount of empirical research has been published about the microlevel linkages between work and family behavior (see Voydanoff 1989). However, scholars tend to study unidirectional effects and concentrate on the impact of work on family. Findings can be organized into two areas: (a) the effects of spouses' socioeconomic resources upon family life (Booth et al 1984, Komarovsky 1964, Mortimer et al 1978, Mortimer & London 1984, Oppenheimer 1977, Simpson & England 1982); and (b) the organization and coordination of market labor with household and family responsibilities, especially the division of labor between spouses within and across the two spheres (Erickson et al 1979, Hartmann 1981, Scanzoni 1982, Stafford 1980, Walker & Woods 1976).

Another line of research investigates the microlevel linkages between features of work and the social psychological well-being of family members. These studies examine the effects of job structure, job satisfaction, and employment conditions on family members (Eckenrode & Gore 1990, Kohn & Schooler 1983, Miller et al 1979, Staines et al 1978, Staines et al 1985, Voydanoff 1983). Far fewer studies examine the impact of family on work; some examples are Hareven's study of the laborers of Manchester, New Hampshire (1975) and Crosby's study of relative deprivation and working women (1982).

Efforts to specify the dynamics of the work/family system come closer to acknowledging the importance of subjective attachments to work and family.

The work by Coser & Coser (1974) on careers as "greedy institutions" recognized the effect of high emotional involvement with organizations and occupations as they spill over onto family. Young & Willmott (1973, p. 31) identified the "symmetrical family" wherein the members of a dual-earner couple minimize differences of temperament, function, and skills as their family and paid labor responsibilities are executed. Pleck's (1977) research on the "work/family role system" identified the "asymmetrically permeable boundaries between work and family roles for both men and women" (p. 423), thereby recognizing that normative differences exist for men and women in the relative intrusion of family demands on work and work on family (see also Pleck & Staines 1985). Specifically, women allow (and are permitted to allow) family tasks and responsibilities to intrude on their paid work, but men are less inclined to do so. Men, in contrast, allow (and are permitted to allow) work to intrude on family time. Moen (1983) posits the work-family connection as a system of exchange of personal resources including commitment, skills, and energies, in return for economic security, status, and a sense of purpose and identity. The nature of the exchange varies by structure of the family and stage of the family life cycle.

Finally, some empirical work has investigated the ways in which work intrudes on the family and how family life affects experiences on the job (Piotrkowski 1978, Rapoport & Rapoport 1978). According to Piotrkowski et al (1987), the linkages between work and family spheres are complex and multiple. In their view, research that theorizes those linkages as contextually determined roles or behaviors neglects questions about individual-level processes that connect the systems. Thus, they argue, the fact that empirical research on the work/family linkages is not guided by a "single unifying framework" has slowed the pace of understanding their interaction. There is a clear need for further conceptual and empirical work that not only specifies work/family linkages, but particularly focuses upon the nexus of subjective attachments to them. The research on commitment is an important contribution to that frontier.

COMMITMENT TO WORK AND FAMILY

Empirical research typically focuses on either commitment to work or to family and less often on the interrelationship between the two. Moreover, most empirical research over the last three decades has focused on work commitment, as if commitment to family, in contrast, was a natural and unproblematic outcome of household arrangements. The findings discussed in the following sections are organized topically by gender, age, social origin, and race. Where appropriate, limitations of existing research and suggestions for future work are noted.

Gender

Overall, men and women in the paid labor force differ somewhat in their level of commitment to work (Agassi 1982, Andrisani 1978, Mannheim 1983) and to family (Bielby & Bielby 1989). For example, Sekaran (1983) found no gender differences in perceptions, absorption, or prioritizing in the salience of work and family roles among dual-career couples; she did, however, find that wives perceived themselves to be less job involved than their husbands. When identity is measured in both spheres, women are found to be slightly more identified with family than with paid employment; the reverse is true for men. However, sex differences in relative identification with work disappear when women have work statuses and experiences similar to men's and have the opportunity to identify as strongly with the work role as do men (Bielby & Bielby 1989). These findings for national samples have been replicated for women and men in blue collar jobs (Loscocco 1990a) and for a sample of Air Force personnel (Pittman & Orthner 1989). Furthermore, overall sex differences in commitment to work are disappearing as women's commitment catches up with men's; the commitment of men has remained relatively stable over the last three decades. Women's increased educational attainment and the expansion of job opportunities and rewards are associated with their increased attachment to the work sphere (Lorence 1987a).

Theoretical explanations for gender differences and change in relative subjective attachment to work usually emphasize either: (i) the consequences of gender socialization, or (ii) the effect of structural constraints in the labor market and in features of the job. The "gender socialization" explanation emphasizes the consequences of engaging in prescribed gender-based roles and attitudes (Moen & Smith 1986). This perspective is relevant to the allocation of commitments across the work/family interface, particularly when that allocation is associated with a normatively prescribed division of labor in household and in child-rearing responsibilities (Bielby & Bielby 1989, Moen 1983). The "structural" explanation attributes gender differences in work commitment to differences in workplace constraints and opportunities (Kanter 1976, Lorence 1987b, Loscocco 1989a 1990a 1990b, Pittman & Orthner 1989, Rosenfeld & Spenner 1988). This research consistently shows that work conditions and opportunities are the strongest determinants of work commitment, and that marital and family status have little if any impact. Thus, these studies suggest that most of the difference between men and women in work commitment is due to their differential placement in work and opportunity structures.

There is less research on family commitment, and it is less conclusive. However, some evidence suggests that a comparable "structural" explanation applies to family commitments. That is, differences between men and women in family commitment appear to be attributable to differences in family responsibilities and constraints. For example, Bielby & Bielby (1989) found that when men have household responsibilities similar to those of women, they are also as strongly committed to the family role as are women. Overall, more research is needed on the determinants of gender differences in family commitment and on how structural location in the work sphere affects family commitment and vice versa.

Age and the Life Course

The life-course perspective examines effects of the accumulation, timing, and sequence of experience on behavior (Elder 1985). Among relevant experiences are transitions from school to employment to retirement and from family of origin to establishing one's own household (Hogan 1980, Hill & Mattessich 1979). Since there is a behavioral component to work and family commitments, understanding those commitments calls for a life-course analysis. Little research seeks explanations beyond age-related patterns in work and family commitments, and most of that research examines involvement with the work sphere.

In a longitudinal study of the work commitment of female college graduates in early adulthood, Bielby & Bielby (1984) found the women's subjective attachment to their jobs was relatively stable in the early stages of their careers, despite family contingencies associated with household and family formation. Subjective disinvestments in attachment to work occurred at the time of marriage, but job commitments were reinvested by the time of childbearing and rearing. In a national sample of employed women, Moen (1986) found no decline in the preferences of married women working part-time for continuing to work in the absence of a financial need to do so. However, employed wives with children and full-time jobs exhibited lower preferences to continue employment.

In one of the first life-course assessments of age differences in work involvement, Lorence & Mortimer (1985) found that involvement changes over the life course as individuals move through the work cycle. Analyzing panel data on working men and women, they discovered that the stability of job involvement was low in the initial and later phases of the career, while individuals in early middle age exhibited the greatest stability in job involvement, due in large part to increasingly stable work experiences and rewards. Lorence & Mortimer compared the relative utility of the "aging stability hypothesis," which assumes that job involvement, like other attitudes, becomes more stable with age, against the "work career stage framework," which assumes that job involvement fluctuates over time in the face of changes in work characteristics associated with job seniority or experience, Lorence & Mortimer concluded that the aging stability hypothesis received greater support. Although extrinsic job rewards were associated with job involvement in the early stages of the career and the intrinsic reward of job involvement influenced the job involvement of all age groups, their effects were outweighed by the overall stabilization of job involvement that comes with age.

Subsequent work has sought to clarify the association between age and psychological attachment to the work role. The association between age and work commitment is neither linear nor invariant by gender (see Mannheim 1983, Safilios-Rothchild 1970). According to Lorence (1987c), among males, intrinsic job rewards attenuate the relationship between age and job involvement. In contrast, among women, age is associated with job involvement, even after controlling for work rewards, family characteristics, and other personal traits. Such net effects of age are presumably proxies for age-graded practices (Lodahl & Kejner 1965, McKelvey & Sekaran 1977) and values (Loscocco 1989b) associated with specific stages of the work and family life cycles. Research on work attitudes more generally suggests that relevant age-graded traits might include the characteristics of work such as promotion opportunities (Loscocco 1990b), substantive complexity (Kohn & Schooler 1983), job satisfaction (Mortimer & Lorence 1989), and family traits such as marriage (Mannheim 1983, Orthner & Pittman 1986) and spousal support (Mortimer et al 1986).

The relationship between age and work commitment also extends to the study of criminal activity, deviance, and illegitimate activity as work. Applying Becker's approach to commitment, Hirschi (1969) developed a theory of social control to explain criminality and deviance as due to tenuous or broken ties to society. The major argument of Hirschi's theory is that individuals who have personal investments in themselves in the form of education, career, and personal relationships are less likely to engage in deviant behavior because they are able to rationally anticipate the risk of losing their investments in conventional behavior. In a life-course assessment of stability and change in criminal activity, Sampson & Laub (1990) found that both job stability and marital attachment were significant deterrents to adult criminal activity, outweighing prior and concurrent levels of personal investments in educational, work, and economic goals. The social control perspective that motivates this research has been criticized for its emphasis on rational choice in investment behavior while neglecting the process by which individuals derive meaning and identity from deviant social roles (Heimer & Matsueda 1991). Nevertheless, the findings of Sampson & Laub (1990) highlight how subjective attachments to other individuals and the strength of personal bonds to social institutions lead to age-related change in criminal activity. Other recent responses to social control theory including Hagan's (1991) work on the residual effects of subculture identification and Matsueda's (1992) work on the influence of appraisals of the self as a rule violator indicate the importance of subjective attachments and meaning in continuing involvement in the sphere of illegitimate work. The extent to which sources of those attachments and meanings are age-graded is in only the earliest stage of exploration and should prove a productive line of investigation in the future (Hagan & Polloni 1988).

Even less is known about the association between age and family commitment and the age-graded traits responsible for that association (Aldous 1990, Hood 1983, Scanzoni & Arnett 1987, Scanzoni et al 1989). While there are few life-course studies on commitment to family per se, Huber & Spitze (1980) have examined commitment to marriage by analyzing spouses' response to the question: "has the thought of getting a divorce from your husband/wife ever crossed your mind?" Among both men and women they found that thoughts of divorce were more likely if the wife had recent labor force experience and if the marriage was of shorter duration. Among wives, thoughts of divorce were more likely if the spouse did not participate equally in a number of household tasks and if the wife held egalitarian beliefs about the division of labor. Among men, thoughts of divorce were more likely if there was little difference in age between spouses, and if the wife had never been divorced. These sex differences are consistent with England's (England & Kilbourne 1990) argument about women's greater relationship specific investments in marriage.

Although the Huber & Spitze study did not examine commitment directly, its findings are relevant for two reasons. First, it disaggregates time- and age-dependent behavioral and attitudinal factors associated with subjective attachment to the family. Second, it provides insight into the relative importance of the subjective meanings that husbands and wives attach to personal behavior, household labor, and market resources in their consideration of divorce. Analyses like this that focus more directly on commitment to family should generate further insight into the life-course determinants of subjective attachments work and family. A life-course approach to analyzing involvement with the family sphere should include the timing and length of marriage, timing, number, and ages of children, timing of critical life events, men's and women's educational and labor force options, and options for alternative close relationships.

Social Origin and Race

Despite a considerable amount of research studying effects of social origin on work and family behavior (see Mortimer & London 1984, Piotrkowski 1978), still social origin and race are often cursorily treated as "background" variables in this research (cf Beneria & Stimpson 1987). Rarely is their association with subjective attachments like commitment to work and family examined substantively.

Panel surveys of college cohorts from the 1960s show parents' socioeconomic origin to be positively related to the importance of a career among male college seniors (Mortimer et al 1986) and negatively related to the career commitment of female college graduates early in their careers (Bielby & Bielby 1984). Spenner & Rosenfeld (1990) found a similar negative effect for a cohort of women who were juniors and seniors in 1966 (see also Pittman & Orthner 1989). In that era, men from affluent families appeared to anticipate careers much like those of their fathers, whereas women from such families did not. There is no research assessing whether the sex differences in social background have changed in recent decades, although it would be reasonable to hypothesize that those differences have attenuated since then. There is little research on the impact of social origin on work commitment later in the career cycle. Given that the impact of proximate work conditions on work commitment is substantially stronger than that of personal traits and that the stability of work commitment increases with age, it seems unlikely that there are substantial effects of social origins net of schooling and early career experiences. However, future research should consider examining the direct effects of social origins and, perhaps more importantly, the indirect effects mediated by schooling and early work experiences.

Research on the relationship of socioeconomic origin to family commitment is quite sketchy. Overall, Pleck & Lang (1978) report that 50% of employed men and 73% of employed women rate their families higher in personal importance than work, but others (e.g. Young & Willmott 1973) find that lower-middle class men report primary satisfaction from family over work and thus are more family-centered than upper-middle class men. The extent of family commitment among the urban poor has generated considerable debate. Although commitment has not been studied directly, Stack's (1974) research points to adaptive household arrangements and kinship relations that enhance the well-being of children in the face of erratic or chronically low incomes (also see Kelly 1989, Taylor 1990).

In a study of commitment to social fatherhood that includes race as well as social origin, adolescent males' plans for living arrangements following a hypothetical unplanned pregnancy were analyzed (Marsiglio 1988). Black and white males had similar intentions to assume parental responsibilities by living with their child and the child's mother. Moreover, their decisions did not differ in the weight they gave to personal preferences and responsiveness to the subjective norms espoused by their own fathers. Regardless of race, males whose fathers had achieved higher levels of education were more likely to also weigh their father's advice with their own personal attitudes in forming a decision.

Race is routinely included in research on work commitment but is rarely a central substantive concern. It is often the case that race is treated dichotomously, with all nonwhites aggregated into a single category. In at least one instance (Lorence 1987c), race is included in the statistical model but its coding is not reported, precluding interpretation of the effect. In other instances racial differences are reported as statistically non- significant (Moen 1986), but the substantive implications of similarities between whites and nonwhites is not discussed. Moreover, the numbers of minorities included in representative samples is often too small to detect differences by race, should they exist. Not surprisingly, the findings that do exist are mixed, some showing minorities to be more committed to work (Loscocco 1989a, Pittman & Orthner 1988), others showing those groups to be less committed (Andrisani 1978, Lorence 1987b, 1987c), and many showing no significant effect of race. Overall, research is needed that theorizes social origin and race in models of work and family commitment and designs samples that include sufficient minority respondents to obtain reliable results.

The Interrelationship between Work and Family Commitment

How do work and family commitments interrelate? Pittman & Orthner (1988, 1989, Orthner & Pittman 1986) confirm the importance of including aspects of family support as well as job and economic factors to explain commitment to work. In a path analysis of job commitment among Air Force personnel, Orthner & Pittman (1986, Pittman & Orthner 1989) found that job commitment was best explained by the "fit" between the organization and self/family. Degree of "fit" was indicated by life satisfaction, perception of organizational responsiveness to families and the quality of the organizational environment as a child rearing milieu, and spousal support for one's career. Their results suggest that an organization that accommodates the familial concerns and constraints of its employees is able to sustain a higher level of work commitment among its labor force.

In a study directly examining the reciprocal relationship between work and family commitment, Bielby & Bielby (1989) found no significant relationship among the two for men and a negative relationship for the effect of family commitment on work commitment among women. Thus, their data from the late 1970s suggests that married working women give precedence to family in balancing work and family identities. In contrast, married men may have the discretion to build a commitment to both spheres without trading one off against the other. They speculate that among couples subscribing to traditional gender role norms, a husband strongly committed to work is perceived as simultaneously fulfilling his "provider" role within the family. Bielby & Bielby (1992) provide support for this interpretation in research showing that traditional beliefs about a husband's provider role account for wives' greater reluctance to relocate for personal job advancement. Finally, Ladewig & McGee (1986), analyzing dual earner couples in a southern city, found that high levels of wives' work commitment contributed to perceptions of lower levels of marital adjustment among both spouses, while husbands' work commitment had no such effect. Again, subscription to traditional gender role beliefs and norms may account for the gender asymmetry in the link between involvement in the spheres of work and family. Moreover, shifts toward more progressive beliefs on the part of both husbands and wives should contribute to attenuation of those asymetries.

Some recent research suggests new accommodations between work and family may be emerging. For example, Tiedje et al (1990) report that women juggling multiple activities balance role enhancement against role conflict when combining work and family responsibilities. Findings on stress and coping indicate that dual-career couples who achieve a cognitive balance between parenthood and demanding jobs do not necessarily experience high levels of distress (Guelzow et al 1991, see also Verbrugge 1987). Others observe that changes in conflict and stress at the work/family interface are associated with increased integration of work and family roles, not declines in involvement. Changes like these suggest that recent adaptations to balancing multiple roles and responsibilities may be redefining normative expectations about the interdependence of work and family life (see Hochschild 1989), and thus the personal meanings assigned and identities derived from them.

CONCLUSION

Research on commitment to work and family has focused on how these two spheres are incorporated as important sources of identity in the lives of individuals. Over the past three decades, a cumulative line of research has emerged that links work and family commitment to work context, family context, gender, age, and to a lesser extent, social origin and race. As the field has matured, scholars have increasingly exploited longitudinal data and models, examined reciprocal relationships between work and family, and recently, considered cross-national comparisons (e.g. Lincoln & Kalleberg 1985, Loscocco & Kalleberg 1988). Despite these markers of a maturing field, conceptual and methodological issues stand in the way of genuine cumulative advancement.

One issue is the treatment of levels of analysis. For example, in the study of commitment to work, analysts do not always attend to conceptual distinctions among commitment to work, to an organization, and to a job, and to their implications for measurement (Randall & Cote 1991). Similarly, in the study of family commitment, distinctions between family, marriage, and relationships are often blurred. Further, treatment of "class" differences in commitment to work and family range from gross distinctions between blue collar and professional milieux on the one hand, to individuals' location in detailed organizational and job hierarchies on the other. In sum, there needs to be greater attention to the objects of individual commitments, e.g. work, organizations, jobs, families, marriages, and relationships, and to which aspects of social structural location are consequential for those commitments, e.g. job settings, organizational context, or class conceived more broadly in terms of economic locations and interests or cultural and community context.

A second issue concerns commitment as outcome versus process. In principle, most scholars recognize commitment as a process that evolves over time. However, in practice, empirical work almost always models commitment as an outcome at one point in time, to be explained by proximate work and family conditions, subjective dispositions, and (in longitudinal studies) commitment at a prior point in time. Rarely are analysts' decisions about causal ordering, recursive versus nonrecursive effects, and discrete versus continuous time dynamics grounded in explicit conceptualizations of the commitment process. Whether the process is viewed as one of retrospective commitment to prior behaviors, rational calculation of costs and benefits of a future line of activity, or taken-for-granted conformity to internalized norms has clear implications for how the process should be modeled over time. Until these issues are addressed, the findings of existing quantitative studies should be considered descriptive "reduced forms" of more complex explanatory causal models.

With some exceptions, the study of commitment is a field in which scholars have had little to say about policy issues regarding the balancing of commitment to work and family. For example, research on gender and work commitment indicates that gender differences disappear when men and women face similar career opportunities. While this would seem to belie employers' rationalizations that job segregation is the result of women's lower work commitment, the issue is rarely addressed in the empirical literature (but see Desai & Waite 1991). Similarly, employers are just beginning to address men's and women's demands for new workplace policies that accommodate family involvement (Friedman 1987). However, one organizational response, the implementation of a "mommy track" or "daddy track," presumes that those wishing to accommodate family demands are incapable of sustaining a high level of work commitment. This presumption is inconsistent with much of the empirical research, but the issue has not as yet been addressed by those who study work and family commitment.

In sum, the research reviewed in this chapter goes beyond analysis of demographic change in workforce behavior and household arrangements, to examine how work and family provide meaning and identity in the lives of individuals. As such, it bridges classical sociological concerns with social structure, microlevel processes, and cultural meanings. The conceptual and methodological issues noted above will no doubt continue to challenge scholars seeking to understand the interrelationships of commitment to work and family. While there are formidable challenges to continued progress in this field, the important sociological issues are never the easy ones to pursue.

ACKNOWLEDGMENTS

I would like to thank William T. Bielby, John Hagan, and Ross Matsueda for comments on earlier versions of this chapter.

Literature Cited

Abelson, R. 1976. Script processing in attitude formation and decision making. In *Cognition and Social Behavior,* ed. J. Carroll, J. Payne, pp. 33–45. Hillsdale, NJ: Erlbaum

Agassi, J. 1982. *Comparing the Work Attitudes of Women and Men*. Lexington, Mass: Heath

Ajzen, I., Fishbein, M. 1980. *Understanding Attitudes and Predicting Social Behavior*. Englewood Cliffs, NJ: Prentice

Aldous, J. 1982. From dual-earner to dual-career families and back again. In *Two Paychecks: Life in Dual Earner Families,* ed. J. Aldous, pp. 11–26. Beverly Hills: Sage

Aldous, J. 1990. Family development and the life course: Two perspectives on family change. *J. Marriage Fam*. 52:71–83

Aldous, J. 1991. In the families' ways. *Contemp. Soc*. 20:60–62

Almquist, E., Angrist, S. 1971. Role model influences on college women's career aspirations. *Merrill-Palmer Q*. 17:63–79

Almquist, E., Angrist, S., Mickelsen, R. 1980. Women's career aspirations and achievements: College and seven years after. *Sociol. Work Occup*. 7:67–84

Andrisani, P. 1978. Work attitudes and labor market experience: Other findings. In *Work Attitudes and Labor Market Experiences,* ed. P. Andrisani, E. Applebaum, R. Koppel, R. Miljus, pp. 135–74. New York: Praeger

Angle, H., Perry, J. 1983. Organizational commitment: individual and organizational influences. *Sociol. Work Occup*. 10:23–46

Angrist, S., Almquist, E. 1975. *Careers and Contingencies: How College Women Juggle with Gender*. New York: Dunellen

Bailyn, L. 1970. Career and family orientations of husbands and wives in relation to marital happiness. *Hum. Relat*. 23:7–113

Bane, M. J. 1976. *Here to Stay*. New York: Basic

Baruch, C., Barnett, R., Rivers, C. 1983. *Lifeprints*. New York: McGraw-Hill

Becker, G. 1981. *A Treatise on the Family*. Cambridge: Harvard Univ. Press

Becker, H. 1956. Careers, personality, and adult socialization. *Am. J. Sociol*. 62:53–63

Becker, H. 1960. Notes on the concept of commitment. *Am. J. Sociol*. 66:2–40

Bellah, R. N., Madsen, R., Sullivan, W. M., Swidler, A., Tipton, S. M. 1985. *Habits of the Heart*. Berkeley: Univ. Calif. Press

Beneria, L., Stimpson, C. 1987. *Women, Households, and the Economy*. New Brunswick: Rutgers

Bernard, J. 1982. *The Future of Marriage*. New Haven: Yale

Bielby, D., Bielby, W. 1984. Work commitment, sex-role attitudes, and women's employment. *Am. Sociol. Rev*. 49:34–47

Bielby, D., Bielby, W. 1988. Women's and men's commitment to paid work and family. In *Women and Work,* ed. B. Gutek, A. Stromnberg, L. Larwood, 3:49–63. Beverly Hills: Sage

Bielby, W., Bielby, D. 1989. Family ties: Balancing commitments to work and family in dual earner households. *Am. Sociol. Rev*. 54:76–89

Bielby, W., Bielby, D. 1992. I will follow him: Family ties, gender-role beliefs, and reluctance to relocate for a better job. *Am. J. Sociol*. 97:1241–67

Blood, R., Wolfe, D. 1960. *Husbands and Wives*. Glencoe: Free Press

Bolger, N., DeLongis, A., Kessler, R., Wethington, E. 1990. The microstructure of daily role-related stress in married couples. In *Stress Between Work and Family,* ed. J. Eckenrode, S. Gore, pp. 95–115. New York: Plenum

Booth, A., Johnson, D., White, L. 1984. Women, outside employment, and marital instability. *Am. J. Sociol*. 90:76–83

Burke, P. 1980. The self: Measurement requirements from an interactionist perspective. *Soc. Psychol. Q*. 43:8–29

Burke, P., Reitzes, D. 1991. An identity theory approach to commitment. *Soc. Psychol. Q*.54:39–51

Cancian, F. 1987. *Love in America*. Cambridge: Cambridge Univ. Press

Cherlin, A. 1983. Changing family and household. *Annu. Rev. Sociol*. 9:1–56

Chodorow, N. 1978 *The Reproduction of Mothering*. Berkeley: Univ. Calif. Press
Collins, R. 1981. On the microfoundations of macrosociology. *Am. J. Sociol*. 86:84–1014
Coombs, L. 1979. Measures of commitment to work. *J. Popul*. 2:03–23
Coser, L., Coser, R. 1974. *Greedy Institutions*. New York: Free
Crosby, F. 1982. *Relative Deprivation and Working Women*. New York: Oxford Univ. Press
Desai, S., Waite, L. 1991. Women's employment during pregnancy and after the first birth: Occupational characteristics and work commitment. *Am. Sociol. Rev*. 56:51–66
Dubin, R. 1956. Industrial workers worlds: A study of the central life interests of industrial workers. *Soc. Prob*. 3:31–42
Eckenrode, J., Gore, S. 1990. *Stress between Work and Family*. New York: Plenum
Ehrenreich, B. 1983. *The Hearts of Men*. Garden City: Anchor
Elder, C. 1974. *Children of the Great Depression*. Chicago: Univ. Chicago Press
Elder, G. 1985. *Life Course Dynamics*. Ithaca: Cornell Univ. Press
England, P., Farkas, G. 1986. *Households, Employment, and Gender*. New York: Aldine
England, P., Kilbourne, B. 1990. Markets, marriages, and other mates: The problem of power. In *Beyond the Marketplace: Rethinking Economy and Society*, ed. R. F. Friedland, A. F. Robertson, pp. 163–88. New York: Aldine de Gruyter
Ericksen, J., Yancey, W. Ericksen, E. 1979. The division of family roles. *J. Marriage Fam*. 41:01–13
Farrell, D. Rusbult, C. 1981 Exchange variables as predictors of job satisfaction, job commitment and turnover. *Organ. Behav. Hum. Perf*. 28:8–95
Ferree, M. 1990. Beyond separate spheres. *J. Marriage Fam*. 52:66–84
Foote, N. 1951. Identification as the basis for a theory of motivation. *Am. Sociol. Rev*. 26:4–21
Friedman, D. 1987. Family-supportive policies: The corporate decision-making process. *Conf. Board* 897:–47
Gerson, K. 1985. *Hard Choices*. Berkeley: Univ. Calif. Press
Gerstel, N., Gross, H. E. 1987. *Families and Work*. Philadelphia, Penn: Temple Univ. Press
Greenhaus, J. 1989. The intersection of work and family roles. In *Work and Family*, ed. E. Goldsmith, pp. 23–44. Newbury Park, Calif: Sage
Guelzow, M., Bird, G., Koball, E. 1991. An exploratory path analysis of the stress process for dual-career men and women. *J. Marriage Fam*. 53:51–64
Gutek, B., Nakamura, C., Nieva. V. 1981. The interdependence of work and family roles. *J. Occup. Behav*. 2:–16
Hagan, J. 1991. Destiny and drift: Subcultural preferences, status attainments, and the risks and rewards of youth. *Am. Sociol. Rev*. 56:67–82
Hagan, J., Polloni, A. 1988. Crimes as social events in the life course: Reconceiving a criminological controversy. *Criminology* 26:7–100
Haller, M., Rosenmayr, L. 1971. The pluridimensionality of work commitment. *Hum. Relat*. 24:01–18
Hareven, T. 1975. Family time and industrial time: Family and work in a planned corporation town, 1900–24. *J. Urban Hist*. 1:65–89
Hartmann, H. 1981. The family as the locus of gender, class, and political struggle: The example of housework. *Signs* 6:65–94
Hedges, J. N. 1983. Job commitment in America: is it waxing or waning? *Monthly Labor Rev*. 106:7–24
Heimer, K., Matsueda, R. 1991. *Role-taking, social cognition, and delinquency: A theory of differential social control*. Pres. Annu. Meet. Am. Sociol. Assoc., Cincinnati
Hill, R., Mattessich, P. 1979. Family development theory and life-span development. In *Life-Span Developmental Behavior*, ed. P. B. Baltes, O. G Brim, 2:61–204. New York: Academic
Hirschi, T. 1969. *Causes of Delinquency*. Berkeley: Univ. Calif. Press
Hochschild, A. 1989. *The Second Shift*. New York: Viking
Hoffman, L. 1963. Mother's enjoyment of work and effect on the child. In *Employed Mother in America*, ed. I. Nye, L. Hoffman, pp. 142–64. Chicago: Rand McNally
Hoffman, L. 1974. Effects of maternal employment on the child: A review of the research. *Dev. Psychol*. 10:04–28
Hogan, D. P. 1980. The transition to adulthood as a career contingency. *Am. Sociol. Rev*. 45:61–76
Hood, J. 1983. *Becoming a Two-Job Family*. New York: Praeger
Huber, J., Spitze, G. 1980. Considering divorce: An expansion of Becker's theory of marital instability. *Am. J. Sociol*. 86:5–89
Johnson, M. 1973. Commitment: A conceptual structure and empirical application. *Sociol. Q*. 14:95–406
Kanter, R. 1976. The impact of hierarchical structures on the work behavior of women and men. *Soc. Prob*. 23:15–30
Kanter, R. 1977. *Work and Family in the United States*. New York: Sage
Kelly, R. 1989. The urban underclass and the future of work-family relations research. In *Work and Family*, ed. E. Goldsmith, pp. 45–54. Newbury Park, Calif: Sage

Kessler, R., McRae, J. 1982. The effect of wives' employment on the mental health of married men and women. *Am. Sociol. Rev.* 7:16–27

Kiesler, C. 1971. *The Psychology of Commitment*. New York: Academic

Kohn, M., Schooler, K. 1983. *Work and Personality*. Norwood, NJ: Ablex

Komarovsky, M. 1964. *Blue Collar Marriages*. New York: Random

Komarovsky, M. 1982. Female freshmen view their future: Career salience and its correlates. *Sex Roles* 8:99–314

Ladewig, B., McGee, G. 1986. Occupational commitment, a supportive family environment, and marital adjustment: Development and estimation of a model. *J. Marriage Fam.* 48:21–9

Lasch, C. 1977. *Haven in a Heartless World*. New York: Basic

Laws, J., Schwartz, P. 1977. *Sexual Scripts*. New York: Dryden

Lincoln, J., Kalleberg, A. 1985. Work organization and workforce commitment: A study of plants and employees in the U. S. and Japan. *Am. Sociol. Rev.* 50:38–60

Lodahl, T. M., Kejner, M. 1965. The definition and measurement of job involvement. *J. Appl. Psychol.* 49:4–33

Lorence, J. 1987a. Subjective labor force commitment of U.S. men and women, 1973–1985. *Soc. Sci. Q.* 68:45–60

Lorence, J. 1987b. A test of the "gender" and "job" models of sex differences in job involvement. *Soc. Forc.* 66:21–42

Lorence, J. 1987c. Age differences in work involvement. *Work Occup.* 14:33–57

Lorence, J., Mortimer, J. 1985. Job involvement through the life course: A panel study of three age groups. *Am. Sociol. Rev.* 50:18–38

Loscocco, K. 1989a. The interplay of personal and job characteristics in determining work commitment. *Soc. Sci. Res.* 18:70–94

Loscocco, K. 1989b. The instrumentally oriented factory worker: Myth or reality? *Work Occup.* 16:–25

Loscocco, K. 1990a. Reactions to blue-collar work. *Work Occup.* 17:52–77

Loscocco, K. 1990b. Career structures and employee commitment. *Soc. Sci. Q.* 71:3–68

Loscocco, K., Kalleberg, A. 1988. Age and the meaning of work in the United States and Japan. *Soc. Forc.* 67:37–56

Mannheim, D. 1963. Male and female industrial workers: Job role centrality, and work place preference. *Sociol. Work Occup.* 10:13–436

March, J., Simon, H. 1958. *Organizations*. New York: Wiley

Marsiglio, W. 1988. Commitment to social fatherhood: Predicting adolescent males' intentions to live with their child and partner. *J. Marriage Fam.* 50:27–41

Masih, L. 1967. Career saliency and its relation to certain needs, interests, and job values. *Pers. Guidance J.* 45:53–58

Matsueda, R. 1992. Reflected appraisals, parental labeling, and delinquency: Specifying a symbolic interactionist theory. *Am. J. Sociol.* 97: Forthcoming

McKelvey, W., Sekaran, U. 1977. Toward a career-based theory of job involvement: A study of scientists and engineers. *Admin. Sci. Q.* 2:81–305

Menaghan, E., Parcel, T. 1990. Parental employment and family life: Research in the 1980s. *J. Marriage Fam.* 52:079–98

Merrick, T. W., Tordella, S. J. 1988. Demographics: people and markets. *Popul. Bull.* 43:–48

Meyer, J., Rowan, B. 1977. Institutionalized organizations: Formal structure as myth and ceremony. *Am. J. Sociol.* 83:40:3

Miller, J., Schooler, C. Kohn, M., Miller, K. 1979. Women and work: The psychological effects of occupational conditions. *Am. J. Sociol.* 85:6–94

Moen, P. 1983. The two-provider family. In *Family Studies Review Yearbook*, ed. D. Olson, B. Miller, 1:97–427. Beverly Hills: Sage

Moen, P. 1986. Women at work: Commitment and behavior over the life course. *Sociol. Forum* 1:50–75

Moen, P., Smith, K. 1986. Women at work: Commitment and behavior over the life course. *Sociol. Forum* 1:24–38

Morrow, P. 1983. Concept redundancy in organization research: The case of work commitment. *Acad. Manage. Rev.* 8:86–500

Mortimer, J., Hall, R., Hill, R. 1978. Husbands' occupational attributes as constraints on wives' employment. *Sociol. Work Occup.* 7:85–313

Mortimer, J., London, J. 1984. The varying linkages of work and family. In *Work and Family: Changing Roles of Men and Women*, ed. P. Voydanoff, pp. 20–35. Palo Alto: Mayfield

Mortimer, J., Lorence, J., Kumka, D. 1986. *Work, Family, and Personality*. Norwood NJ: Ablex

Mortimer, J., Lorence, J. 1989. Satisfaction and involvement: Disentangling a deceptively simple relationship. *Soc. Psychol. Q.* 52:49–65

Mowday, R., Porter, L., Steers, R. 1982. *Employee-Organization Linkages*. New York: Academic

Mowday, R., Steers, R., Porter, L. 1979. The measurement of organizational commitment. *J. Voc. Behav.* 14:24–47

Myrdal, A., Klein, V. 1956. *Women's Two*

Roles: Home and Work. London: Routledge

Oppenheimer, V. 1977. The sociology of women's economic role in the family. *Am. Sociol. Rev.* 42:87–405

O'Reilly, C., Caldwell, D. 1981. The commitment and tenure of new employees: Some evidence of postdecisional justification. *Admin. Sci. Q.* 26:97–616

Orthner, D., Pittman, J. 1986. Family contributions to work commitment. *J. Marriage Fam.* 48:73–81

Papanek, H. 1973. Men, women, and work: Reflections on the two person-career. *Am. J. Sociol.* 78:52–72

Parsons, T., Bales, R. 1955. *Family, Socialization and Interaction Process.* Glencoe Ill: Free

Pfeffer, J. 1982. *Organizations and Organization Theory.* Boston: Pitman

Pfeffer, J., Lawler, J. 1980. Effects of job alternatives, extrinsic rewards, and behavioral commitment on attitude toward the organization: A field test of the insufficient justification paradigm. *Admin. Sci. Q.* 25:8–56

Piotrkowski, C. 1978. *Work and the Family System.* New York: Free

Piotrkowski, C., Rapoport, R., Rapoport, R. 1987. Families and work. In *Handbook of Marriage and the Family,* ed. M. Sussman, S. Steinmetz, pp. 251–83. New York: Plenum

Pittman, J., Orthner, D. 1988. Predictors of spousal support for the work commitments of husbands. *J. Marriage Fam.* 50:35–48

Pittman, J., Orthner, D. 1989. Gender differences in the prediction of job commitment. In *Work and Family: Theory, Research, and Applications,* ed. E. Goldsmith, pp. 227–47. Newbury Park, Calif: Sage

Pleck, J. 1977. The work-family role system. *Soc. Prob.* 24:17–27

Pleck, J. 1983. Husbands' paid work and family roles: Current research issues. In *Research on the Interweave Social Roles,* ed. H. Lopata, J. Pleck, 3:51–333. Greenwich, Conn: Jai

Pleck, J., Lang, L. 1978. *Men's family role: Its nature and consequences.* Working Paper. Wellesley, Mass: Wellesley Coll. Ctr. Res. on Women

Pleck, J., Staines, G. 1985. Work schedules and family life in two-earner couples. *J. Fam. Issues* 6:1–82

Poloma, M. 1972. Role conflict and the married professional woman. In *Toward a Sociology of Women,* ed. C. Safilios-Rothchild, pp. 187–98. Lexington, Mass: Xerox

Randall, D., Cote, J. 1991. Interrelationships of work commitment constructs. *Work Occup.* 18:94–211

Rapoport, R., Rapoport, R. 1971. *Dual-Career Families.* Baltimore: Penguin

Rapoport, R., Rapoport, R. 1978. *Working Couples.* New York: Harper

Regan, M. C., Roland, H. E. 1982. University students: A change in expectations and aspirations over the decade. *Sociol. Educ.* 55:23–8

Rosenfeld, R., Spenner, K. 1988. Women's work and women's careers. In *Social Structures and Human Lives,* ed. M. Riley. Vol. 1: *Social Change in the Life Course,* pp. 285–305. Newbury Park, Calif: Sage

Safilios-Rothchild, C. 1970. The influence of the wife's degree of work commitment upon some aspects of family organization and dynamics. *J. Marriage Fam.* Nov:81–91

Safilios-Rothchild, C. 1971. Towards the conceptualization and measurement of work commitment. *Hum. Relat.* 42:89–93

Salancik, G. 1977. Commitment and the control of organizational behavior and belief. In *New Directions in Organizational Behavior,* ed. B. Staw, G. Salancik, pp. 1–54. Chicago: St.Clair

Sampson, R., Laub, J. 1990. Crime and deviance over the life course: The salience of adult social bonds. *Am. Sociol. Rev.* 55:09–27

Scanzoni, J. 1982. *Sexual Bargaining.* Chicago: Univ. Chicago

Scanzoni, J., Arnett, C. 1987. Enlarging the understanding of marital commitment via religious devoutness, gender role preferences and locus of marital control. *J. Fam. Issues* 8:36–56

Scanzoni, J., Polonko, K., Teachman, J., Thompson, L. 1989. *The Sexual Bond.* Newbury Park, Calif, Calif: Sage

Schank, R., Abelson, R. 1977. *Scripts, Plans, Goals, and Understanding.* Hillside, NJ: Erlbaum

Sekaran, U. 1983. How husbands and wives in dual-career families perceive their family and work roles. *J. Voc. Behav.* 22:88–302

Selznick, P. 1949. *TVA and the Grass Roots.* Los Angeles: Univ. Calif. Press

Simpson, I., England, P. 1982. Conjugal work roles and marital solidarity. In *Two Paychecks: Life in Dual Earner Families,* ed. J. Aldous, pp. 147–171. Beverly Hills: Sage

Spenner, K., Rosenfeld, R. 1990. Women, work, and identities. *Soc. Sci. Res.* 19:66–99

Stack, C. 1974. *All Our Kin.* New York: Harper

Stafford, F. 1980. Women's use of time converging with men's. *Monthly Labor Rev.* 103:7–9

Staines, C., Pleck, J., Shepard, L., O'Connor, P. 1978. Wives' employment status and marital adjustment: Yet another look. *Psychol. Women Q.* 3:0–120

Staines, G., Pottick, K., Fudge, D. 1985. The effects of wives' employment on husbands' job and life satisfaction. *Psychol. Women Q.* 9:19–24

Stryker, S. 1981. Symbolic interactionism. In *Social Psychology,* ed. M. Rosenberg, R. Turner, pp. 3–29. New York: Basic

Taylor, R. 1990. Need for support and family involvement among black americans. *J. Marriage Fam.* 52:84–90

Thornton, A. 1989. Changing attitudes toward family issues in the United States. *J. Marriage Fam.* 51:73–93

Thornton, A., Alwin, D., Camburn, D. 1983. Causes and consequences of sex-role attitudes and attitude change. *Am Sociol. Rev.* 48:211–27

Thornton, A., Freedman, D. 1983. The changing American family. *Popul. Bull.* 38:–44

Tiedje, L., Wortman, C., Downey, G., Emmons, C. Biernat, M. Lang, E. 1990. Women with multiple roles: Role-compatibility perceptions, satisfaction, and mental health. *J. Marriage Fam.* 52:63–72

US Department of Labor. 1979. *1979 Employment and Training Report of the President.* Washington, DC: US Govt Printing Off.

Verbrugge, L. 1987. Role responsibilities, role burdens, and physical health. In *Spouse, Parent, Worker,* ed. J. Crosby, pp. 154–66. New Haven: Yale

Voydanoff, P. 1983. Unemployment and family stress. In *Research on the Interweave of Social Roles,*. ed. J. Lopata, J. Pleck, 3:39–50. Greenwich, Conn: Jai

Voydanoff, P. 1987. *Work and Family Life.* Newbury Park, Calif: Sage

Voydanoff, P. 1989. Work and family: A review and expanded conceptualization. In *Work and Family,* ed. E. Goldsmith, pp. 1–22: Newbury Park, Calif: Sage

Walker, K., Woods, M. 1976. *Time use: A measure of household production of family goods and services.* Washington, DC: Am. Home Econ. Assoc.

Walker, L., Thompson, A. 1989. Gender in families: Women and men in marriage, work, and parenthood. *J. Marriage Fam.* 51:45–87

Wuthnow, R. 1987. *Meaning and Moral Order.* Berkeley: Univ. Calif. Press

Yogev, S., Brett, J. 1985. Patterns of work and family involvement among single and dual-earner couples. *J. Appl. Psych.* 70:54–68

Young, M., Willmott, P. 1973. *The Symmetrical Family.* New York: Pantheon

Zucker, L. 1981. Organizations as institutions. In *Perpectives in Organization Sociology: Theory and Research,* ed. S. Bacharach, pp. 1–48. Greenwich: Jai

Annu. Rev. Sociol. 1992 18:303–26

THE SELF-CONCEPT OVER TIME: Research Issues and Directions

David H. Demo

Department of Human Development and Family Studies, University of Missouri-Columbia, Columbia, Missouri 65211

KEY WORDS: self-evaluation, life course, situational variability

---

Abstract

Although theoretical attention has been devoted to the situational variability of the self-concept, empirical investigations continue to rely on one-shot methodologies. Such efforts assume that data obtained through these methods can be generalized to other situations in the person's life, even to subsequent years or stages in the life course. Self-concept is a structural product of reflexive activity, but it is also susceptible to change as the individual encounters new roles, situations, and life transitions. The data reviewed in this paper suggest that: (i) self-evaluation generally becomes more favorable through the life-span; (ii) self-evaluation is represented by a "moving baseline" from which situational fluctuations emerge; (iii) self-concept is characterized by both stability and change over the life course; and (iv) environmental stability plays an important role in self-concept stability. Several avenues of research are recommended to develop an accurate, meaningful, and testable theory of the self-concept over time.

INTRODUCTION

Most researchers view self-concept as a set of structured self-attitudes that is relatively stable and "characteristic" of an individual. While numerous studies

0360-0572/92/0815-0000$02.00

have examined structural dimensions of self-concept, very few have focused on temporal aspects of self-concept, i.e. changes in self-concept from one situation to another, from one relationship to another, or from one year or stage in the life course to the next. As a result, little is known about the social conditions responsible for change and stability in self-concept.

This review demonstrates that the dominant structural conceptualization of self-concept and the concomitant failure to study the dynamic, changing, emerging qualities of self-concept, are the products of three related and widespread methodological practices in self-concept research: (i) a preoccupation with one-shot measures of self-esteem, (ii) an overreliance on samples of adolescents and college students, and (iii) the tendency to measure self-esteem in detached classroom and experimental situations.

The objective of this paper is to integrate social psychological, sociological, and developmental research on self-concept. I argue that to understand self-concept we must conceptualize it as a moving baseline with fluctuations across situations (Demo 1985, Savin-Williams & Demo 1983) and life stages. This involves recognizing that the self-concept is simultaneously a complex structure and a process, that it is stable, but that it is also dynamic. I also argue that to capture the dynamic qualities of self-concept it is necessary to obtain repeated measurements and to include naturalistic observations. I move now to a brief review of the evidence that self-concept has both structural and processual qualities, recognizing that this evidence corresponds to two general models used by self-concept researchers and that different points of view exist within each model.

THE STRUCTURAL MODEL

Many researchers and theorists view self-concept as a multifaceted structure of thoughts, attitudes, images, schemas, or theories regarding the self as an object (e.g. Carver & Scheier 1981, Cheek & Hogan 1983, Epstein 1980, Greenwald & Pratkanis 1984, Hoelter 1985, Kihlstrom & Cantor 1984, Markus 1983, McGuire & McGuire 1981, Rosenberg 1979). Typically, it is also assumed that self-concept is a configuration of personality characteristics that is relatively stable and generalizable from one situation to the next. This view corresponds to the trait model, widely espoused in personality research and in social psychology, which posits that personality characteristics are stable over time and account for consistencies in behavior across different situations.

The exemplar of contemporary sociological research on the self, Morris Rosenberg (1979) summarizes two decades of research by outlining an elaborate and insightful description of the structure of human self-concept. He specifies "regions" of the self-concept (extant, desired, and presenting selves), each with several specific components. The extant self, for example, is comprised of social identity elements, role-sets, and dispositions, while the desired self consists of an idealized image (fantasies), a committed image (actual goals), and a moral image (what we feel we "should be") or superego. Rosenberg's detailed description provides an excellent understanding of the structure of self-reflection, but it is also a static view on the self that is fixed at one point in time.

Many other investigators have used rigorous factor-analytic procedures to study the cognitive structure of self-concept. As might be expected, psychologists and sociologists conceptualize the structure of self-concept somewhat differently, with psychologists typically describing a system of traits and sociologists describing a structure of roles or identities. Recent advances have led researchers to describe self-concept as a system of schemas or generalizations about the self based on personal experiences and characteristics (Markus & Sentis 1982); as an associative memory network storing traits (Bower & Gilligan 1979); as a hierarchical category structure consisting of traits and values (Carver & Scheier 1981, Kihlstrom & Cantor 1984); as an identity salience hierarchy (Serpe 1987, Stryker 1980); or as a multidimensional meaning space (Greenwald & Pratkanis 1984, Hoelter 1985). There is also considerable evidence that the cognitive content and organization of the self varies across individuals (Greenwald & Pratkanis 1984).

THE PROCESSUAL MODEL

Even casual observers of human behavior recognize the situational shifts and fluctuations, the mild surges and the dramatic plunges, that are typical of an individual's feelings about and attitudes toward oneself. Turner (1968:94) distinguishes between "self-image," which refers to the individual's self-picture at a given moment, and "self-conception," which refers to one's relatively enduring and stable "sense of 'the real me'." Burke (1980:20) suggests viewing the self-image as "the 'current working copy' of the identity. As a 'working' copy, it is subject to constant change, revision, editing, and updating as a function of variations in situation and situational demands." This conceptualization is helpful in that it enables us simultaneously to consider the situationally variable aspects of self-concept (here termed the self-image) and the more lasting, relatively stable and durable self-conception that one carries across relationships, situations, and contexts. Likewise, Markus & her associates (1986, 1987) characterize self-concept as a relatively stable universe of different self-conceptions, and they describe the working self-concept as a temporary subset of situationally relevant self-conceptions, including core self-conceptions (Gergen 1968) or self-schemas. Markus & Wurf (1987:306) assert that "the working self-concept, or the self-concept of the moment, is best viewed as a continually active, shifting array of accessible self-knowledge." The problem, however, is that few have attempted to integrate these two views or to study the structure of self-concept as both stable over time and situationally variable.

Research on self-verification processes (Swann 1983, Swann & Hill 1982) suggests an explanation for the seemingly paradoxical findings that self-concept is both stable over long periods of time (e.g. Block 1981, Costa & McCrae 1980) and yet susceptible to change. Swann & Hill (1982) designed an experiment in which individuals who described themselves as either dominant or submissive received feedback from a confederate that either confirmed or refuted their self-conceptions. Subsequent to the feedback, some of the individuals were given an opportunity to interact with the confederate, while others were not. Interestingly, individuals who received discrepant feedback and who had an opportunity to interact with the source of this information, actively fought the challenge to their self-descriptions. In contrast, individuals receiving discrepant feedback but deprived of further interaction with the confederate experienced considerable change in their self-descriptions.

These and other studies indicate that people monitor their feedback from others (Snyder & Gangested 1982) and pursue different strategies to verify and sustain their perceptions of themselves. For example, there is evidence that people selectively interact with others who see them as they see themselves (Backman & Secord 1962), actively choose roles (Backman & Secord 1968) and social environments (Pervin 1967) that are consistent with their self-conceptions, selectively attend to self-confirmatory feedback (Swann & Read 1980), and reinterpret, devalue, or dismiss discrepant feedback (Kulik et al 1986, Rosenberg 1979, Swann 1983, Tesser & Campbell 1983). As a result, the self protects itself against change, with even laboratory-induced changes disappearing within a few days (Swann & Hill 1982). Thus, seemingly paradoxical findings may be reconciled in that generalized self-concept is stable over extended periods of time while situation-specific self-images, or working self-concepts, are malleable.

An important task, then, is for researchers to devote greater attention to integrating structural and dynamic perspectives. Traditional theories (reflected appraisals, social comparisons, self-perception) suggest that self-attitudes change, fluctuate, stabilize, revert to an earlier level, and change again. Our lives are lived in constantly changing roles and situations embedded in the course of human development and social change. But as the following section demonstrates, the limitations of prevailing research methodologies have prevented the processual perspective from being systematically applied in empirical research, and consequently little is known about the emergent, dynamic, changing qualities of human self-images.

THE PRESUMED STABILITY OF SELF-CONCEPT

It is important to note that self-concept stability and change, as used here, are distinct from what Rosenberg (1979:57) and others define as self-consistency: "the motive to act in accordance with the self-concept and to maintain it intact in the face of potentially challenging evidence." It seems clear that such a motive exists and that individuals need a fairly consistent picture of who they are in order to know how to act in different situations, but attention is being focused here on another dimension of self-concept. We are interested in the nature and degree of change, the modifications and revisions in self-attitudes, the shifting self-evaluations, peaks and valleys in feelings of self-worth, that occur despite the proclivity to see oneself as the same person everyday.

Cheek & Hogan's (1983:256) review indicates "overwhelming empirical evidence for the stability of self-concepts." Unfortunately, three normative methodological practices eliminate sources of variation in self-concept, leading researchers to overstate true stability in self-concept: (i) most studies are cross-sectional and rely on a single measurement; (iii) 90% of studies on the self are studies of a single dimension—self-esteem (McGuire et al 1978)—which may be more stable than other dimensions; and (iii) developmental studies typically assess short-term stability (e.g. one year to the next) among two age groups (adolescents and college students), ignoring long-term patterns across the life course.

A few studies, most designed by developmental psychologists, have followed individuals through adolescence, and others have examined self-concept during the transition from adolescence into early adulthood. Curiously, only indirect attention has been devoted to self-concept at more mature points in the life cycle, e.g. mid-life or old age, and Rossan (1987) proposes that theories of identity development may have only limited relevance for adult identity. Further, studies that have employed a temporal perspective have examined self-concept in a social vacuum, ignoring linkages between changes in the life course and changes in self-concept. The following section reviews the available evidence on self-concept over the life course and presents strategies for studying the self over time, strategies that recognize the structural and processual properties of self-concept and direct attention to the self's ongoing stability and malleability.

SELF-CONCEPT THROUGH THE LIFE COURSE

Self-concept, like other dimensions of personality, is a function of interacting biological, developmental, and social processes across the life course. It is acquired through patterns of interaction with others and is modified as children and adults develop new cognitive and intellectual capabilities and confront new social demands and processes.

Infancy

Infants appear to develop a sense of self as subject or causal agent ("I") prior to developing a sense of self as object ("Me") (Harter 1983). Once they acquire the ability to recognize the consequences of their own behavior, to act intentionally, and to distinguish themselves from others in their environment (around 12–15 months), the ongoing relationships they have with parents and significant others are increasingly influential in shaping a preliminary and rudimentary self-schema. The self-schema that emerges between 15 and 24 months is dominated by internal images of one's own physical characteristics (Lewis & Brooks-Gunn 1979), an important advance in establishing a sense of self that is stable and consistent across situations and over time, and an apparent prerequisite for self-evaluative emotions and self-regulation (Lewis et al 1989, Stipek et al 1990).

One limitation to understanding early self-development is reliance on mirror studies of visual self-recognition (Harter 1983). As a result, our knowledge is limited to ontogenetic trends in self-recognition, and we know little about early cognitive-developmental and social processes involved in generating other thoughts and feelings about the self. Many other dimensions of personality (e.g. aggressiveness, submissiveness, shyness) are measured using behavioral observations, but self-concept studies rarely make use of this methodology (Savin-Williams & Jaquish 1981), which seems well-suited for studying the influence of social interaction on early self-development. Theories of the self (psychoanalytic, social learning, symbolic interactionist) emphasize the influence of early parent-child relations, suggesting that greater attention should be devoted to naturalistic studies of parent-child evaluative interactions (Shrauger & Schoeneman 1979).

Studies of child-caretaker relations are also needed as the social context of childhood changes and increasing percentages of young children spend significant amounts of time in day-care settings. A number of studies (mostly of preschoolers) report that quality interactions between caretakers and children are associated with children being positive, intelligent, and sociable (MacKinnon & King 1988). But we do not know how self-concept development varies as a function of day-care variables such as frequency of attendance and quality of interactions, nor do we know how these processes may vary for children of different family and socioeconomic circumstances.

Childhood

Between ages 2 and 4, children's rapidly expanding cognitive abilities enable them to think in symbolic terms, to understand object constancy, and to view themselves as objects. Piaget (1962) labeled this stage preoperational egocentrism, in which children assume that others recognize their inner thoughts and feelings, but they lack the role-taking abilities necessary to distinguish their own thoughts and feelings from those of others. Consequently, the preschooler's emerging sense of self does not include a stable set of self-feelings or self-attitudes, but is limited to one's name, aspects of gender identity, age, body image, possessions, personal characteristics, and favorite activities (Keller et al 1978). These categorical self-descriptions are not constant, however, changing in form and content from one situation to the next. Gender identity, for example, is a process characterized by several stages. Two year olds understand and respond to the label boy or girl in referring to themselves (Lewis & Brooks-Gunn 1979); four year olds use these labels correctly in classifying others and show preferences for gender-appropriate toys and activities; but it is not until age 5 or 6 that children understand that gender is fixed and constant (Marcus & Overton 1978). Thus, the content and structure of self-concept change with each stage of self-development, and within each stage there is evidence of both stability and malleability from one context to another.

What we lack, however, is an understanding of how this developmental progression occurs, of how social and cognitive-developmental processes influence children's developing self-theories in the preoperational years. Understanding these processes should be a high priority, given that lifelong patterns of self-reflection likely are being formed during these years. The instrumental action of toddlers and preschoolers is structured by only a few clearly understood social roles and, like those of infants, their emerging self-concepts are strongly influenced by interactions with a restricted set of significant others. The limited social environment in which they live, combined with their egocentric point of view, precludes the use of social comparisons (Suls & Mullen 1982). Thus, research should be designed to examine: (i) temporal comparison processes, by observing how children respond to and judge their own actions, accomplishments, and failures, and (ii) reflected appraisals, by observing how influential socializing agents react to children's behavior.

By age 5 or 6, as children enter concrete operations, they regularly judge their positive and negative qualities and possess a fairly coherent, hierarchically organized, core or "baseline" self-concept. Increased cognitive sophistication and improved role-taking abilities enable children to consider the perceived judgments and reactions of numerous others in their expanding social environment, and formal interaction with teachers and peers in age-graded educational settings facilitates social comparisons (Entwisle et al 1987, Suls & Mullen 1982). Suls & Mullen describe social comparisons during middle childhood as indiscriminate because children are generally unable to distinguish between similar others (classmates) and dissimilar others (parents) for purposes of comparison. Further complicating matters is the reality that others are similar and dissimilar on numerous dimensions. Parents, for example, tend to be dissimilar in terms of cognitive abilities and certain physical characteristics (height and weight), but are likely to be similar on social structural characteristics (socioeconomic status and race) and other physical features (skin color). Limited cognitive abilities during middle childhood preclude children from understanding these distinctions, thereby restricting use of reflected appraisals and social comparisons, at least until age 7 or 8 (Ruble et al 1980).

Children are able to judge their own actions, however, and to compare recent performances, abilities, qualities, and physical characteristics with earlier ones (Suls & Mullen 1982). It is likely, therefore, that at this stage self-evaluations and self-attributions of autonomous, efficacious activity, and experiences facilitating the sense of self as an active, causal agent in one's environment, are the most important processes for children's developing self-theories (Entwisle et al 1987, Gecas & Schwalbe 1983). Unfortunately, research and theory have generally ignored self-concept during the transition to full-time schooling (Entwisle et al 1987), and thus we know little about the social processes influencing early self-images.

Later in childhood (ages 9 to 11), advanced inductive reasoning and improved classification abilities enable children to understand multiple causes for behavior. These cognitive advances, combined with the challenges of schoolwork, generate reorganized ways of thinking and refined abilities to compare one's own performances with those of children who are similar on evaluated dimensions. Self-evaluation becomes a salient, lifelong concern during this period, and limited evidence (discussed in the next section) suggests that children's thoughts and feelings about themselves are generally positive as they begin elementary school but are more negative, self-critical, and self-doubting in later childhood.

There are several processes that may explain decreasing self-acceptance during later childhood. First, self-concept is characterized by a social exterior at this stage, meaning that children attach importance to, and judge themselves on, abilities and achievements (Damon & Hart 1982, Rosenberg 1986). Academic performances are of particular concern at this age, and Entwisle et al (1987) argue that negative feedback is prevalent, if not normative, among elementary school teachers. Children's reference groups also change during this period as identification with peers increases and parental influence wanes. Greater reliance on perceived, often negative, evaluations of peers challenges self-concept and stirs self-doubts. It is reasonable, therefore, that self-esteem generally decreases from middle to late childhood.

Adolescence

Researchers generally regard adolescence as a period characterized by considerable biological, social, psychological, and developmental change.

Although it is widely understood that these changes occur in broader social, historical, cultural, and institutional contexts (Dornbusch 1989), there is some debate concerning the proportion of adolescents who are troubled by these changes and the proportion who go through this stage without tumult (e.g. see Montemayor 1983, Offer et al 1981, Simmons & Blyth 1987). Cognitively, early adolescence (12–15) marks the development of formal operational thought, sophisticated deductive reasoning, and more efficient, diversified information processing. The acquisition of these skills enables adolescents to efficiently test hypotheses about themselves at a time when they are extremely introspective and self-conscious. The structure of self-concept during this developmental period is dominated by a psychological interior of inner thoughts, feelings, attitudes, desires, beliefs, fears, and expectations (Damon & Hart 1982, Rosenberg 1979, 1986).

Disruptions to the ways in which early adolescents view themselves are precipitated by physical and physiological changes that are both dramatic and self-evident (accelerating hormonal production, growth spurts, voice changes, acne). Socially, the transition to junior high school presents a number of challenges, including the adjustments associated with having several teachers, making new friends, and perhaps learning a foreign language (Hirsch & Rapkin 1987, Rosenberg 1979, Simmons et al 1979). Furthermore, early adolescents gradually emancipate from parents, parent-adolescent conflict heightens (Montemayor 1983), peer involvement intensifies, and concerns turn to dating and sexual activity. The coterminous and ongoing nature of these processes strikes at the core of self-concept and may generate greater disturbances to self-concept at ages 12 and 13 than at any other point in the life cycle (Simmons et al 1979, Rosenberg 1979:230).

However, with continuing maturation and adjustments to new social roles, physical characteristics, and cognitive abilities, adolescents redefine their self-theories. Issues of ego-identity (Erikson 1959) are resolved in late adolescence, even if only temporarily, as thoughts about the self involve less frequent references to childhood and more frequent references to adulthood. Self-cognitions are reorganized and reintegrated, self-consciousness wanes, stability of self is restored, and levels of self-esteem rise steadily as individuals move through this developmental period (Bachman et al 1978, Demo & Savin-Williams 1983, Dusek & Flaherty 1981, McCarthy & Hoge 1982, Offer et al 1981, O'Malley & Bachman 1983, Savin-Williams & Demo 1984; Simmons & Blyth 1987). Table 1 documents the consistency of the finding that global self-esteem increases through the adolescent years.

McCarthy & Hoge (1982) offer several reasonable explanations for growing self-acceptance during this period: (i) the self-esteem motive may strengthen during this period; (ii) greater self-understanding and more efficient role-taking may facilitate adolescents' abilities to understand and fulfill the

Table 1 Studies examining developmental trends in self-evaluation across the life-course

Study	Sample Description	Scale	Age Group	N	Mean	SD	Major Findings
Demo and Savin-Williams (1983)	60% black, 40% white sample of male and female, lower, lower-middle, and middle class students enrolled in grades 5–8 in parochial schools	Coopersmith (54 items)	10 11 12 13	157 180 232 239	33.75[1] 32.67 31.67 31.15	3.55 3.84 4.10 4.07	Self-esteem increases consistently from fifth to eighth grade.
Simmons and Blyth (1987)	Stratified, random sample of Milwaukee public school children in grades 6–10	Rosenberg-Simmons Self-Esteem Scale (6 items)	10 11 13 14	621 552 361 314	3.38 3.41 3.86 3.96	N/A	Self-esteem and self-stability improve significantly from late childhood to early adolescence.
Rosenberg (1979)	Stratified, random sample of Baltimore public school children in grades 3–12	Rosenberg-Simmons Self-Esteem Scale (6 items)	8–11 12–14 15–18	819 649 516	4.0[2] 3.8 4.4	N/A	Global feelings of self-esteem decline slightly in early adolescence and then rise significantly in later adolescence.
McCarthy & Hoge (1982)	Roughly half white and half black students in public and parochial schools, ranging from working class to upper-middle class	Rosenberg (10 items)	12 13 14 15 16 17	546 775 478 	2.91 3.03 3.07 3.12 3.11 3.22	.41 .43 .42 .47 .45 .44	Self-esteem increased significantly over the 1-year period for all 3 cohorts, and the across-cohort pattern suggests systematic developmental growth in self-esteem

Bachman, O'Malley, & Johnston (1978)	Nationally representative sample of males (Youth in Transition Project)	Rosenberg (revised; 10 items)	15	1,622	3.74	.52	Self-esteem levels rose gradually throughout high school and early adult years, increasing one full standard deviation over the eight-year period.
			17	1,501	3.83	.49	
			18	1,492	3.88	.50	
			19	1,408	3.90	.49	
			23	1,594	4.22	.48	
National Longitudinal Surveys (Center for Human Resource Research, 1981)	Nationally representative sample of males and females (NORC cohort of youth)	Rosenberg (10 items)	16	1,539[3]	3.14	.39	Self-esteem was significantly higher among cohorts of young adults than among adolescents.
			17	1,508	3.22	.40	
			18	1,468	3.25	.40	
			19	1,546	3.29	.41	
			20	1,602	3.28	.42	
			21	1,584	3.32	.41	
			22	1,566	3.33	.41	
O'Malley & Bachman (1983)	Nationally representative sample of males and females (Monitoring the future project)[4]	Rosenberg (4 items)	17 (1976)	113	4.13	.69	Self-esteem rises gradually but significantly during adolescence and during the transition into early adulthood.
			20 (1979)	(wtd.)	4.32	.65	
			17 (1976)	129	4.18	.64	
			21 (1980)	(wtd.)	4.30	.74	
			17 (1977)	134	4.18	.63	
			20 (1980)	(wtd.)	4.39	.56	
Kanouse et al. (1980)	National sample of males and females, with low-income and minority students oversampled (National Longitudinal Survey-class of 1972)	Rosenberg (4 items)	18	16,582	3.92	.65	Developmental increase in self-esteem during transition to adulthood, scores increasing one-half standard deviation over four-year period.
			19	20,100	4.12	.55	
			20	19,418	4.19	.59	
			22	19,324	4.26	.58	

Table 1 Studies examining developmental trends in self-evaluation across the life-course

Study	Sample Description	Scale	Age Group	N	Mean	SD	Major Findings
Helson & Moane (1987)	Representative sample of senior class of private women's college	Adjective Check List	27	78	48.64	10.74	Measures of self-regarding attitudes showed impressive stability and more favorable self-regard over time.
			43	78	52.04	10.40	
Morganti et al. (1988)	White, lower-middle and middle class	Monge semantic differential (29 items)	14–16	60	151.90	22.52	General developmental pattern of increasing self-evaluation; two oldest groups had significantly higher self-evaluation than two youngest groups.
			25–34	60	152.01	23.03	
			45–54	60	153.69	22.47	
			60–69	90	159.72	22.51	
			70–79	90	161.63	22.59	
			80+	90	160.63	22.61	
Jaquish & Ripple (1981)	White, highly educated, primarily middle class	Coopersmith (54 items)	18–25	70	34.1	6.7	Linear progression in self-esteem until late adulthood; adults aged 26–60 had higher self-esteem than the elderly
			26–39	58	36.5	6.9	
			40–60	51	38.2	5.7	
			61–84	39	31.5	7.1	

Gove, Ortega, & Style (1989)	Stratified probability sample of adults aged 18 and older in the U.S.	Rosenberg (8 items)	18–25	408	6.48[5]		No significant zero-order relationship between age and self-esteem, but after adjusting for income, education, sex, and race, self-esteem is highest among persons aged 75+, lower among those 55–74, followed by those 26–54, and lowest among those 18–25.
			26–34	397	6.56		
			35–44	392	6.66		
			45–54	355	6.61		
			55–64	275	6.80		
			65–74	253	6.78		
			75+	106	7.08		
Nehrke, Hulicka, & Morganti (1980)	Male veterans living in a V.A. Domiciliary	Monge semantic differential (29 items)	50–59	33	151.33[6]	30.75	Self-evaluation scores increased with age, with the oldest group reporting significantly more favorable self-evaluation than the youngest group
			60–69	33	152.51	34.47	
			70+	33	166.76	21.34	

NOTE: Studies examining short-term change and stability in self-evaluation within one developmental period (e.g., adolescence) and studies examining dimensions other than self-evaluation are not included. I would like to thank Ravenna Helson, Frank Mott, and Milton Nehrke for providing additional data from their studies.

[1]In this study, the Coopersmith scale was coded so that lower scores indicated higher self-esteem.

[2]The average scores reported for these three age groups are median scores; means and standard deviations were not available.

[3]The Ns reported here correspond to the total number of respondents in each age group, so actual Ns for Rosenberg Self-Esteem Scale (not available) are slightly lower.

[4]A cohort-sequential design was used, involving seven different groups of high school students studied during their senior year and followed up one to four years later. The three groups reported here were included because at least three years separated base-year and follow-up measurements.

[5]These are adjusted means; Gove et al. (1989) also present unadjusted means.

[6]Standard deviations for adjusted scores were not available, so unadjusted means and standard deviations are presented here.

expectations of others; (iii) increased personal autonomy affords adolescents greater latitude to select activities in which they are interested and to delete roles in which their performance is less satisfactory; and (iv) self-esteem may solidify during adolescence and become less susceptible to evaluations by others. In support of the latter explanation, Ellis et al (1980) found that roughly midway through adolescence (10th grade, or about age 16) individuals shifted from evaluating themselves primarily on external standards of achievement to rating themselves primarily on internal standards of personal happiness.

Adulthood

The transition into adulthood coincides with the emergence of dialectical reasoning, enhanced problem-solving, peak intellectual abilities (Horn & Donaldson 1980, Schaie 1983), and optimal memory (Evans et al 1984). These new skills and abilities enable a broader, more complex self-definition and stronger feelings of self-worth. Although social comparisons with similar others remain the primary mechanism for self-assessment (Suls & Mullen 1982), these comparisons are not as consequential as during adolescence. The central task at this stage is forging adult identity. Role-identities of student and son or daughter become peripheral as socialization unfolds into new role-identities (spouse, parent, worker) (Gecas & Mortimer 1987).

As Table 1 indicates, the available studies offer compelling evidence that self-evaluation (usually measured as global self-esteem) increases from early adolescence on through the remainder of the life course. Although considerably less research has been conducted on the adult portion of the life course than on earlier periods, a number of studies report increasing self-regard during the important transitions into early adulthood (Bachman et al 1978, Kanouse et al 1980, Offer & Offer 1975, O'Malley & Bachman 1983) and parenthood (Ruble et al 1990).

Only minimal changes in intelligence and memory occur during middle adulthood, or ages 40 to 65 (Baltes et al 1980, Schaie 1983), and problem-solving in real-life situations is optimal (Denney & Palmer 1981). Thus, the cognitive processes shaping self-concept during this period are quite similar to those of young adulthood. A number of social and personal events that typically occur during mid-life elevate consciousness (Helson & Moane 1987, Neugarten 1968) and trigger a major self-reassessment. Among these events are realization of one's own mortality, relations with adolescent children (Demo et al 1987) and aging parents, deaths of parents and/or close friends, divorce, remarriage, and stepfamily relations.

Again, few studies have examined the influence of these social and developmental processes on self-concept. Research illustrates that job involvement and job satisfaction are highest between ages 40 and 65 (Bray & Howard

1983), and we know that performance in the work setting, occupational conditions, and socioeconomic attainment are tied to personal efficacy and self-esteem (Hughes & Demo 1989, Kohn & Schooler 1983, Rosenberg 1979, Schwalbe 1985). Herzog et al (1982) document that age-related improvements in a number of life domains (housing, community, work) are important in explaining increasing levels of subjective well-being with age. Other studies report increasing self-confidence (Haan 1981), competence (Clausen 1991), and self-esteem (see Table 1) through the middle adult years. But we know more about levels than about processes of self-development during mid-life. Analysts need to study the timing and sequencing of life events (e.g. promotion, divorce, remarriage), the social conditions (e.g. marital and family relations, social support), and developmental processes (e.g. maturation, generativity) that shape self-theories during middle adulthood.

Although social comparisons with similar others remain important during middle age, Suls & Mullen (1982) argue that comparisons with dissimilar others, especially younger coworkers, become increasingly salient and influential. This occurs for two reasons: (i) dissimilar comparisons satisfy the need to feel unique, worthwhile, and special during mid-life reassessment; and (ii) competition in the workplace fosters comparisons with coworkers who may be younger, stronger, quicker, or better educated. In addition, Helson & Moane (1987) observe that coping skills and self-discipline improve during middle age, and Gove et al (1989) report that, compared to younger adults, older adults are better adjusted and more at ease socially. All of these processes should enhance feelings of self-worth.

By late adulthood (around age 65) there is some loss of verbal or fluid intelligence (Schaie 1983), slowing of memory processes (Evans et al 1984), and decline in problem-solving (Denney & Palmer 1981), but these changes tend to be gradual. More dramatic is the shift in social interaction patterns that occurs as social networks change due to retirement and deaths of friends. Old friends are lost, new friends are made, time spent in leisure activities and volunteer work increases, and sense of autonomy increases (Palmore et al 1984).

Theory and research on self-concept among the elderly are inadequate and, as a result, it is difficult to explain self-development in the later years. Suls & Mullen (1982) present evidence that social comparisons are less important at this stage due to simple loss of comparison others. Consequently, temporal comparisons predominate, most notably reminiscing or life review (Butler 1963). Reminiscing about past experiences, roles, and selves leads to a reorganized self-concept and may facilitate favorable self-evaluations. Limited evidence (summarized in Table 1) suggests that self-esteem peaks in the late adult years (roughly 65–75), until physical and cognitive deterioration associated with failing health, less flexibility, limited social interaction and role-identities (Britton & Britton 1972), precipitates negative thoughts and feelings about the self.

This section has concentrated on self-development across the life course as one perspective for researching the self over time. As the next section illustrates, a second perspective views self-evaluation as a "moving baseline" that varies from one social context to the next.

SELF-EVALUATION AS A "MOVING BASELINE" THROUGH THE LIFE COURSE

Several recent studies provide evidence that self-evaluation is characterized by a "baseline" view of oneself from which situational variations emerge. Most people view themselves in a fairly consistent manner over extended periods of time but occasionally feel better or worse about themselves than is typically the case. Savin-Williams & Demo (1983) measured "snapshots" of adolescents' self-feelings from one naturalistic situation to the next. Individuals were paged randomly (by a "beeper") wherever they happened to be (school, home, restaurant) for one week. Each time they were signaled they completed a short self-report inventory of their self-feelings (confident, powerful, weak, ashamed) at that moment. Their scores for the entire week were then regressed on one another using time series analyses.

The results indicated that less than one third of the sample could be characterized as having "stable," enduring self-feelings, i.e. positive (or negative) self-descriptions at one moment were followed by positive (or negative) self-descriptions at subsequent measurements. An even smaller group comprising 11% of the sample had "oscillating" self-feelings, that is, a patterned instability in which one self-feeling level would be high, the following one low, the next high, and so forth. This group represents approximately the same percentage of "storm and stress" adolescents reported in other studies (Adelson 1979, Hill 1980, Offer & Offer 1975). The third and largest group (60% of the sample) had self-feelings that fluctuated mildly; they were neither predictably stable nor predictably unstable from one situation to the next. This suggests that for most individuals self-feelings can be represented by a "baseline" or standard self-picture from which situational variations emanate.

Following their panel of adolescents from seventh through tenth grade, Savin-Williams & Demo (1984) found that both "experienced" self-esteem (measured by self-report) and "presented" self-esteem (measured by peers and participant observers) were stable components of self-concept during the supposedly "turbulent" adolescent years. These analyses suggest that while self-concept may exhibit fluctuations from a baseline over short periods of time (e.g. one situation to the next), the basic core structure of self-concept remains fairly stable over longer periods of time.

Recent work in life-span developmental psychology and structural symbolic interactionism supports this conceptualization. A study by Mortimer et al (1982) is particularly informative because several dimensions of self-concept were measured at three points in time: freshman year in college, senior year, and ten years after graduation. Factor analyses of a semantic differential scale identified four dimensions (well-being, sociability, competence, and unconventionality) which exhibited a substantial degree of normative stability over the measurement period; that is, the ordering of individuals on each self-concept dimension remained essentially the same over 14 years spanning college and early adulthood. Further analyses substantiated the four-factor structure at each point in time and revealed a relatively invariant pattern of intercorrelations among the factors at each measurement. They also examined ipsative stability (intraindividual changes in the ordering or salience of particular dimensions) and found that the organization of self-image components was remarkably stable over time. In a similar analysis examining other dimensions of self-concept, Serpe (1987) observes an impressive pattern of stability across five identities relevant to college students: academic roles, athletic/recreational roles, extracurricular roles, friendship roles, and dating roles.

The studies described above, involving naturalistic observation and longitudinal surveys, support the conclusion that self-concept is both stable over long periods of time and situationally variable. I now examine the contextual and environmental changes that seem to generate fluctuations from a baseline or standard self-concept.

THE ROLE OF ENVIRONMENTAL STABILITY IN SELF-CONCEPT STABILITY

Throughout the life course individuals experience multiple role changes, life transitions, and turning points that are embedded in the course of human development, socialization, and social change. The argument presented here is that applying life-span and life-course perspectives to the study of self-concept will enable researchers to examine the social pathways and life trajectories that facilitate a stable self-concept and the life events and experiences that seem to disrupt self-concept.

The work of Mortimer and her colleagues (1982) supports the conclusion of many investigators that self-concept is stable throughout life, with points of "disturbance" along the way. Cheek & Hogan's (1983:253) review yields a representative conclusion: "rather than being situationally constituted it [self-concept] is the result of a *developmental* process that begins in childhood and culminates in an internalized character structure that is relatively stable throughout adulthood. . . ." (*original emphasis*). But evidence of stability, continuity, and the important role played by developmental processes should not distract researchers (especially social psychologists) from elucidating the social processes that prompt changes and disruptions in self-concept. Aging and maturation are accompanied by social timetables and by age-graded norms and life events. Age or life stage alone does not account for much variation in self-concept, as Erdwins & Mellinger (1984:394) report in a study of women aged 29–55, but "significant variation does occur among women who have assumed different life roles."

In an important paper on adult development and social theory, Dannefer (1984:107) reminds us of the "uniquely 'open' or 'unfinished' character of the human organism in relation to its environment" and of the identifiable "plasticity [of] characteristics previously assumed to be stable throughout the life course." Dannefer argues that constancy and change in personality are too often assumed to be the results of ontogenetic developmental patterns (e.g. adolescent "turmoil," early adult "growth," and mid-life "crisis") and that such accounts ignore the social organization of development, obscuring the influence of complex social environments.

The research conducted by Mortimer and her collaborators is provocative in this regard. They contend that the stability they observed in self-attitudes from late adolescence into early adulthood is particularly impressive because of the many changes (in marital status, employment, and parenthood) that their panel members experienced over that period. It is plausible, however, that certain environmental changes, particularly normative changes or ones involving success or prestige, may actually facilitate crystallization and stability of self-concept. Early adulthood is a period in the life course when several socially prescribed events occur, many of which involve the acquisition of new roles and statuses (employee, spouse, parent) that may stabilize and socially anchor one's self-concept and enhance feelings of self-worth (Clausen 1991, Ruble et al 1990). During this period a number of self-doubts may be erased, questions about oneself may be answered, and new goals and directions established, resulting in a relatively secure, developmentally mature self-concept. The empirical evidence is sparse, however, suggesting that an important avenue for future research is to explore the hypothesis that "maturation," growth, and stability may be generated by specific and socially prescribed changes in social roles and relationships.

Further, environmental stability may be a function of the life course, with fewer role changes and disruptions in social relationships occurring after early adulthood. Glenn (1980:603) explains that the important role changes that occur during young adulthood cause an intense period of resocialization and restructuring of values and attitudes, after which both geographic and social mobility decline and significant life events are spaced further apart. It is plausible, therefore, that self-concept is more malleable in early adulthood than in subsequent years, owing both to a relatively stable environment in the latter period and to a reliance on established patterns and processes of self-reflection. This view is consistent with Epstein's (1973) assertion that some aspects of personality may solidify over time and become resistant to change (also see Finn 1986, Moss & Susman 1980), but further analyses of self-concept during middle and later adulthood will be required to test this hypothesis. It is also reasonable to expect unpleasurable and stigmatizing events (divorce, losing a job) to be destabilizing (Baltes et al 1980), shattering one's confidence, disrupting social relationships and routines, and presenting the challenge of further adjustments. This notion is consistent with the literature on socialization processes over the life course (see Bush & Simmons 1981), which indicates that periods of stability and continuity are typically followed by turning points and discontinuity.

The life-course perspective in sociology (Elder 1985, 1991, Hagestad 1990) derives from a separate tradition and has not been applied to the study of self-concept, but the value of this approach is its view of the organism and the situation within an interacting dynamic over the life span. Because the life course and its developmental paths are linked to social change, successive birth cohorts experience the same historical events (war, migration, prosperity) at different ages, resulting in different life trajectories. As one illustration, American children born between 1950–1955 grew up in a prosperous period, encountered an adolescence scarred by the Vietnam War, and entered young adulthood during the "me-decade" of the 1970s. But the birth cohort of 1956–1960 experienced the turbulent Vietnam years as young children, missed the draft, and went to high school and college during the recessionary but self-centered 1970s. These two cohorts experienced the same slice of history but from developmentally different vantage points that may have resulted in significantly different experiences, values, attitudes, and self-concepts. By comparing across cohorts it is possible to trace linkages between age and historical location, between life history and social surroundings.

Elder (1991) argues that an adequate conceptualization of the life course involves recognition of three distinct meanings of age: (i) developmental age, one's stage in the aging process from birth to death; (ii) social age, the social meanings of age expressed in the timetables, expectations, and turning points of the life course; and (iii) historical age, or time in the course of social change. By calling attention to comparisons within and across age-linked cohorts, a life-course perspective provides important directions for the study of self-concept over time: Within cohorts, how does the timing and arrangement of life events affect self-attitudes? For example, it would be reasonable to expect the self-feelings of a teenage mother to be considerably less stable than those of a parent just a few years older. How do the effects on self-concept of various life transitions (widowhood, divorce, remarriage, work transitions) vary as a function of their timing in the life course and their intersection with other role trajectories? For example, how does the salience and ordering of role identities change when a trajectory of job advancement coincides with marital dissolution and diminished parental involvement? How are life-course patterns and variations in self-concept experienced by members of different races, genders, religions, and other social groups? Gecas & Mortimer (1987) argue that the early adult transition (principally the transition from school to work) may be more detrimental to the self-concept of lower class individuals, compared to individuals in the middle and upper class, because of social class differences in occupational conditions, such as job complexity and opportunities for self-direction. Across cohorts, how do age-stratified historical experiences influence self-concept processes? For example, were there generational differences in the effects of the "me-decade," in viewing the self as "institutional" versus "impulsive" (Turner 1976), or in perceiving self in terms of what one *does* versus what one *is* (McGuire & McGuire 1986)?

In sum, life-span and life-course frameworks provide two complementary perspectives for viewing self-concept in relation to interacting processes (biological, developmental, and social) over the life course.

CONCLUSIONS: TOWARD A RECONCEPTUALIZATION OF SELF-CONCEPT

It has been argued that researchers need to pursue new avenues of investigation to understand the changing properties of self-concept over time. In many cases the theoretical groundwork has been laid, but researchers have not yet capitalized on these insights. Most studies of self-concept continue to rely on one measure of one dimension, usually global self-esteem, measured at one point in time, producing "an unduly constricted view of self-process and the way behavior is shaped in situations" (Turner & Schutte 1981:3).

We must measure self-concept as both a structure and a process, i.e. a dynamic structure that responds to situational stimuli, incorporates new elements, rearranges, adjusts, and stabilizes temporarily before encountering new stimuli and undergoing further revisions. Some of the preliminary research examining cross-situational stability in self-feelings supports the view that self-feelings may be represented by a moving baseline. This theory balances the structural and processual views by recognizing the persistent core of self-identity but it also directs attention to the features of social interaction that generate changing levels and configurations of self-image.

One high priority in this area of research is to move beyond classroom administration of our favorite questionnaires and to accept the challenge of measuring self-feelings in the wide range of contexts in which they are felt, e.g. family, school, peer group, and work settings. The position taken here is that many elements of self-concept are lost in sterile classroom and experimental conditions. Triangulation may be achieved through qualitative approaches, open-ended free descriptions of self (McGuire & McGuire 1986,

McGuire et al 1986, Turner & Schutte 1981), in-depth interviewing, case histories, and extended observation periods, providing rich data to complement the sophisticated quantitative data that are commonly examined.

A second promising area for investigation is continuity and change over the life course. The research to date is extremely lopsided, with 12 and 13 year olds forming the floor and 18 to 22 year olds representing the ceiling of our convenience samples. A number of studies portray early adolescence as a period of self-concept disturbance, but without considerable research on self-concept stability at other stages in life there is no reference point against which to judge early adolescence, thereby making it difficult to justify declarations that this is a "crisis" period.

Self-concept is a structure but it is also a process. It is stable but it also changes. It may be described by a moving baseline, or a process of structural change. These conclusions should be subjected to systematic analysis, however, requiring researchers to examine this interesting and complex phenomenon as it actually exists: over time.

ACKNOWLEDGMENTS

I wish to thank the following people for their critical comments and very helpful suggestions: Rosemary Blieszner, Glen H. Elder, Jr., David D. Franks, Viktor Gecas, James W. Michaels, Ritch C. Savin-Williams, Michael L. Schwalbe, Roberta G. Simmons, and Mark L. Wardell.

Literature Cited

Adelson, J. 1979. Adolescence and the generalization gap. *Psychol. Today* 12(9): 33–37

Bachman, J. G., O'Malley, P. M., Johnston, J. J. 1978. *Youth in Transition*. Vol. 6. *Adolescence to Adulthood: A Study of Change and Stability in the Lives of Young Men*. Ann Arbor, Mich: Inst. Soc. Res.

Backman, C. W., Secord, P. F. 1962. Liking, selective interaction, and misperception in congruent interpersonal relations. *Sociometry* 25:321–35

Backman, C. W., Secord, P. F. 1968. The self and role selection. See Gordon & Gergen 1968, pp. 289–96

Baltes, P. B., Reese, H. W., Lipsitt, L. P. 1980. Life-span developmental psychology. *Annu. Rev. Psychol*. 31:65–110

Block, J. 1981. Some enduring and consequential structures of personality. In *Further Explorations in Personality*, ed. A. L. Rubin, J. Aronoff, A. M. Barclay, R. A. Zucker. New York: Wiley

Bower, G. H., Gilligan, S. G. 1979. Remembering information related to one's self. *J. Res. Pers*. 13:420–32

Bray, D. W., Howard, A. 1983. The AT&T longitudinal studies of managers. See Schaie 1983, pp. 266–312

Brim, O. G. Jr., Kagan, J., eds. 1980. *Constancy and Change in Human Development*. Cambridge, Mass: Harvard Univ. Press

Britton, J. H., Britton, J. 0. 1972. *Personality Changes in Aging. A Longitudinal Study of Community Residents*. New York: Springer

Burke, P. J. 1980. The self. Measurement requirements from an interactionist perspective. *Soc. Psychol. Q*. 43:18–29

Bush, D. M., Simmons, R. G. 1981. Socialization processes over the life course. In *Social Psychology: Sociological Perspectives*, ed. M. Rosenberg, R. H. Turner, pp. 133–64. New York: Basic Books

Butler, R. N. 1963. The life review: An interpretation of reminiscence in the aged. *Psychiatry* 26:65–76

Carver, C. S., Scheier, M. F. 1981. *Attention and Self-Regulation: A Control Theory Approach to Human behavior*. New York: Springer-Verlag

Center for Human Resource Research. 1981. *The National Longitudinal Surveys Handbook*. Columbus: Ohio State Univ. Press

Cheek, J. M., Hogan, R. 1983. Self-concepts,

self-presentations, and moral judgments. See Suls & Greenwald 1983, pp. 249–73

Clausen, J. S. 1991. Adolescent competence and the shaping of the life course. *Am. J. Sociol.* 96:805–42

Costa, P. T. Jr., McCrae, R. R. 1980. Still stable after all these years: Personality as a key to some issues in adulthood and old age. In *Life Span Development and Behavior,* ed. P. B. Baltes, 0. G. Brim Jr., 3:65–102. New York: Academic

Damon, W., Hart, D. 1982. The development of self-understanding from infancy through adolescence. *Child Dev.* 53:841–64

Dannefer, D. 1984. Adult development and social theory: A paradigmatic reappraisal. *Am. Sociol. Rev.* 49:100–16

Demo, D. H. 1985. The measurement of self-esteem: Refining our methods. *J. Pers. Soc. Psychol.* 48:1490–1502

Demo, D. H., Savin-Williams, R. C. 1983. Early adolescent self-esteem as a function of social class: Rosenberg and Pearlin revisited. *Am. J. Sociol.* 88:763–74

Demo, D. H., Small, S. A., Savin-Williams, R. C. 1987. Family relations and the self-esteem of adolescents and their parents. *J. Marriage Fam.* 49:705–15

Denney, N. W., Palmer, A. M. 1981. Adult age differences on traditional and practical problem-solving measures. *J. Gerontol.* 36:323–28

Dornbusch, S. M. 1989. The sociology of adolescence. *Annu. Rev. Sociol.* 15:233–59

Dusek, J. B., Flaherty, J. F. 1981. The development of the self-concept during the adolescent years.*Monogr. Soc. Res. Child Dev.* 46:(4, Ser. 191). 67 pp.

Elder, G. H. Jr. 1985. *Life Course Dynamics: Trajectories and Transitions, 1968–1980.* Ithaca, NY: Cornell Univ. Press

Elder, G. H. Jr. 1991. The life course. In *The Encyclopedia of Sociology.* ed. E. F. Borgotta, M. L. Borgotta. New York: Macmillan. In press

Ellis, D. W., Gehman, W. S., Katzenmeyer, W. G. 1980. The boundary organization of self-concept across the 13 through 18 year age span. *Educ. Psychol. Meas.* 40:9–17

Entwisle, D. R., Alexander, K. L., Pallas, A. M., Cadigan, D. 1987. The emergent academic self-image of first graders: Its response to social structure. *Child Dev.* 58:1190–1206

Epstein, S. 1973. The self-concept revisited: Or a theory of a theory. *Am. Psychol.* 28:404–16

Epstein, S. 1980. The self-concept: A review and the proposal of an integrated theory of personality. In *Personality: Basic Issues and Current Research,* ed. E. Staub, pp. 82–132. Englewood Cliffs, NJ: Prentice-Hall

Erdwins, C. J., Mellinger, J. C. 1984. Mid-life women: Relation of age and role to personality. *J. Pers. Soc. Psychol.* 47:390–95

Erikson, E. H. 1959. The problem of ego-identity. *Psychol. Issues* 1:101–64

Evans, G. W., Brennan, P. L., Skorpanich, M. A., Held, D. 1984. Cognitive mapping and elderly adults: Verbal and location memory for urban landmarks. *J. Gerontol.* 39:452–57

Finn, S. E. 1986. Stability of personality self-ratings over 30 years: Evidence for an age/cohort interaction. *J. Pers. Soc. Psychol.* 50:813–18

Gecas, V., Schwalbe, M. L. 1983. Beyond the looking-glass self. Social structure and efficacy-based self-esteem. *Soc. Psychol. Q.* 46:77–88

Gecas, V., Mortimer, J. T. 1987. Stability and change in the self-concept from adolescence to adulthood. In *Self and Identity: Perspectives Across the Lifespan,* ed. T. Honess, K. Yardley, pp. 265–86. London: Routledge & Kegan Paul

Gergen, K. J. 1968. Personal consistency and the presentation of self. See Gordon & Gergen 1968, pp. 299–308

Glenn, N. D. 1980. Values, attitudes, and beliefs. See Brim & Kagan 1980, pp. 596–640

Gordon, C., Gergen, K. J., eds. 1968. *The Self in Social Interaction,* Vol. 1. New York: Wiley

Gove, W. R., Ortega, S. T., Style, C. B. 1989. The maturational and role perspectives on aging and self through the adult years: An empirical evaluation. *Am. J. Sociol.* 94:1117–45

Greenwald, A. G., Pratkanis, A. R. 1984. The self. In *Handbook of Social Cognition,* ed. R. S. Wyer, T. K. Srull, 3:129–78. Hillsdale, NJ: Erlbaum

Haan, N. 1981. Common dimensions of personality development: Early adolescence to middle life. In *Present and Past in Middle Life,* ed. D. H. Eichorn, J. A. Clausen, N. Haan, M. P. Honzik, P. H. Mussen, pp. 117–51. New York: Academic Press

Hagestad, G. O. 1990. Social perspectives on the life course. In *Handbook of Aging and the Social Sciences,* ed. R. H. Binstock, L. K. George. New York: Academic Press. 3rd ed.

Harter, S. 1983. Developmental perspectives on the self-system. In *Handbook of Child Psychology,* ed. E. M. Hetherington, 4:275–385. New York: Wiley

Helson, R., Moane, G. 1987. Personality change in women from college to midlife. *J. Pers. Soc. Psychol.* 53:176–86

Herzog, A. R., Rodgers, W. L., Woodworth, J. 1982. *Subjective Well-Being among Dif-*

ferent Age Groups. Ann Arbor, Mich: Inst. Soc. Res.

Hill, J. P. 1980. Growing up too fast? The social ecology of adolescence and the early assumption of "adult"' behaviors. *Coll. Hum. Ecol. Ecologue* 5–6:15–19. Lansing, Mich: Mich. State Univ.

Hirsch, B. J., Rapkin, B. D. 1987. The transition to junior high school: A longitudinal study of self-esteem, psychological symptomatology, school life, and social support. *Child Dev*. 58:1235–43

Hoelter, J. 1985. The structure of self-conception: Conceptualization and measurement. *J. Pers. Soc. Psychol*. 40:138–46

Horn, J. L., Donaldson, G. 1980. Cognitive development in adulthood. See Brim & Kagan 1980, pp. 445–529

Hughes, M., Demo, D. H. 1989. Self-perceptions of Black Americans: Self-esteem and personal efficacy. *Am. J. Sociol*. 95:132–59

Jaquish, G. A., Ripple, R. E. 1981. Cognitive creative abilities and self-esteem across the adult life-span. *Hum. Dev*. 24:110–19

Kanouse, D. E., Haggstrom, G. W., Blaschke, T. J., Kahen, J. P., et al. 1980. *Effects of Postsecondary Experiences on Aspirations, Attitudes, and Self-conceptions*. Santa Monica, Calif: Rand

Keller, A., Ford, L. H., Meacham, J. A. 1978. Dimensions of self-concept in preschool children. *Dev. Psychol*. 14:483–99

Kihlstrom, J. F., Cantor, N. 1984. Mental representations of the self. *Adv. Exp. Soc. Psychol*. 17:1–47

Kohn, M. L., Schooler, C. 1983. *Work and Personality: An Inquiry into the Impact of Social Stratification*. Norwood, NJ: Ablex

Kulik, J. A., Sledge, P., Mahler, H. I. M. 1986. Self-confirmatory attribution, egocentrism, and the perpetuation of self-beliefs. *J. Pers. Soc. Psychol*. 37:499–514

Lewis, M., Brooks-Gunn, J. 1979. *Social Cognition and the Acquisition of Self*. New York: Plenum

Lewis, M., Sullivan, M., Stanger, C., Weiss, M. 1989. Self development and self-conscious emotions. *Child Dev*. 60:146–56

MacKinnon, C. E., King, D. 1988. Day care: A review of literature, implications for policy, and critique of resources. *Fam. Relat*. 37:229–36

Marcus, D. E., Overton, W. F. 1978. The development of cognitive gender constancy and sex role preferences. *Child Dev*. 49:434–44

Markus, H., Sentis, K. 1982. The self in social information processing. See Suls 1982, pp. 41–70

Markus, H. 1983. Self-knowledge: An expanded view. *J. Pers*. 51:543–65

Markus, H., Kunda, Z. 1986. Stability and malleability of the self-concept. *J. Pers. Soc. Psychol*. 51:858–66

Markus, H., Wurf, E. 1987. The dynamic self-concept: A social psychological perspective. *Annu. Rev. Psychol*. 38:299–337

McCarthy, J. D., Hoge, D. R. 1982. Analysis of age effects in longitudinal studies of adolescent self-esteem. *Dev. Psychol*. 18:372–79

McGuire, W. J., McGuire, C. V., Child, P., Fujioka, T. 1978. Salience of ethnicity in the spontaneous self-concept as a function of one's ethnic distinction in the social environment. *J. Pers. Soc. Psychol*. 36:511–20

McGuire, W. J., McGuire, C. V. 1981. The spontaneous self-concept as affected by personal distinctiveness. In *Self-Concept: Advances in Theory & Research*, ed. M. D. Lynch, A. A. Norem-Hebeisen, K. J. Gergen, pp. 147–71. Cambridge, Mass: Ballinger

McGuire, W. J., McGuire, C. V. 1986. Differences in conceptualizing self versus conceptualizing other people as manifested in contrasting verb types used in natural speech. *J. Pers. Soc. Psychol*. 51:1135–43

McGuire, W. J., McGuire, C. V., Cheever, J. 1986. The self in society: Effects of social contexts on the sense of self. *Br. J. Soc. Psychol*. 25:259–70

Montemayor, R. 1983. Parents and adolescents in conflict: All families some of the time and some families most of the time. *J. Early Adolesc*. 3:83–103

Morganti, J. B., Nehrke, M. F., Hulicka, I. M., Cataldo, J. F. 1988. Life-span differences in life satisfaction, self-concept, and locus of control. *Int. J. Aging Hum. Dev*. 26:45–56

Mortimer, J. T., Finch, M. D., Kumka, D. 1982. Persistence and change in development: The multidimensional self-concept. In *Life-Span Development and Behavior*, ed. P. B. Baltes, O. G. Brim Jr., 4:263–313. New York: Academic Press

Moss, H. A., Susman, E. J. 1980. Constancy and change in personality development. See Brim & Kagan 1980, pp. 530–95

Nehrke, M. F., Hulicka, I. M., Morganti, J. B. 1980. Age differences in life satisfaction, locus of control, and self-concept. *Int. J. Aging Hum. Dev*. 11:25–33

Neugarten, B. L. 1968. The awareness of middle age. In *Middle Age and Aging*, ed. B. L. Neugarten, pp. 43–98. Chicago: Univ. Chicago Press

Offer, D., Offer, J. B. 1975. *From Teenage To Young Manhood: A Psychological Study*. New York: Basic

Offer, D., Ostrov, E., Howard, K. I. 1981. *The Adolescent: A Psychological Self-Portrait*. New York: Basic Books

O'Malley, P. M., Bachman, J. G. 1983. Self-esteem: Change and stability between ages 13 and 23. *Dev. Psychol.* 19:257–68

Palmore, E. B., Fillenbaum, G. G., George, L. K. 1984. Consequences of retirement. *J. Gerontol.* 39:109–16

Piaget, J. 1962.*Play, Dreams, and Imitation in Childhood.* New York: Norton

Pervin, L. A. 1967. Satisfaction and perceived self-environment similarity: A semantic differential study of college-student interactions. *J. Pers.* 35:623–34

Rosenberg, M. 1979. *Conceiving the Self.* New York: Basic Books

Rosenberg, M. 1986. Self-concept from middle childhood through adolescence. In *Psychological Perspectives on the Self,* ed. J. Suls, A. G. Greenwald, 3:107–36. Hillsdale, NJ: Erlbaum

Rossan, S. 1987. Identity and its development in adulthood. In *Self and Identity: Perspectives Across the Lifespan,* ed. T. Honess, K. Yardley, pp. 304–19. London: Routledge & Kegan Paul

Ruble, D. N., Boggiano, A. K., Feldman, N. S., Loebl, J. H. 1980. A developmental analysis of the role of social comparison in self-evaluation. *Dev. Psychol.* 16:105–15

Ruble, D. N., Fleming, A. S., Stangor, C., Brooks-Gunn, J., Fitzmaurice, G., Deutsch, F. 1990. Transition to motherhood and the self. Measurement, stability, and change. *J. Pers. Soc. Psychol.* 58:450–63

Savin-Williams, R. C., Jaquish, G. A. 1981. The assessment of adolescent self-esteem: A comparison of methods. *J. Pers.* 49:324–36

Savin-Williams, R. C., Demo, D. H. 1983. Situational and transituational determinants of adolescent self-feelings. *J. Pers. Soc. Psychol.* 44:824–33

Savin-Williams, R. C., Demo, D. H. 1984. Developmental change and stability in adolescent self-concept. *Dev. Psychol.* 20:1100–10

Schaie, K. W. 1983. The Seattle longitudinal study: A 21-year exploration of psychometric intelligence in adulthood. In *Longitudinal Studies of Adult Psychological Development,* ed. K. W. Schaie, pp. 64–135. New York: Guilford

Schwalbe, M. L. 1985. Autonomy in work and self-esteem. *Sociol. Q.* 26:519–35

Serpe, R. T. 1987. Stability and change in self. A structural symbolic interactionist explanation. *Soc. Psychol. Q.* 46:77–88

Shrauger, J. S., Schoeneman, T. J. 1979. Symbolic interactionist view of self-concept: Through the looking glass darkly. *Psychol. Bull.* 86:549–73

Simmons, R. G., Blyth, D. A., Van Cleave, E. F., Bush, D. M. 1979. Entry into early adolescence: The impact of school structure, puberty, and early dating on self-esteem. *Am. Sociol. Rev.* 44:948–67

Simmons, R. G., Blyth, D. A. 1987. *Moving into Adolescence: The Impact of Pubertal Change and School Context.* New York: de Gruyter

Snyder, M., Gangested, S. 1982. Choosing social situations: Two investigations of self-monitoring processes. *J. Pers. Soc. Psychol.* 43:123–35

Stipek, D. J., Gralinski, J. H., Kopp, C. B. 1990. Self-concept development in the toddler years. *Dev. Psychol.* 26:972–77

Stryker, S. 1980. *Symbolic Interactionism.* Menlo Park, Calif: Benjamin/Cummings

Suls, J., ed. 1982. *Psychological Perspectives on the Self,* Vol. 1. Hillsdale, NJ: Erlbaum

Suls, J., Mullen, B. 1982. From the cradle to the grave: Comparison and self-evaluation across the life-span. See Suls 1982, pp. 97–125

Suls, J., Greenwald, A. G., eds. 1983. *Psychological Perspectives on the Self,* Vol. 2. Hillsdale, NJ: Erlbaum

Swann, W. B. Jr. 1983. Self-verification: Bringing social reality into harmony with the self. See Suls & Greenwald 1983, pp. 33–66

Swann, W. B. Jr., Read, S. J. 1981. Self-verification processes: How we sustain our self-conceptions. *J. Exp. Soc. Psychol.* 17:351–72

Swann, W. B. Jr., Hill, C. A. 1982. When our identities are mistaken: Reaffirming self-conceptions through social interaction. *J. Pers. Soc. Psychol.* 43:59–66

Tesser, A., Campbell, J. 1983. Self-definition and self-evaluation maintenance. See Suls & Greenwald 1983, pp. 1–31

Turner, R. H. 1968. The self-conception in social interaction. See Gordon & Gergen 1968, pp. 93–106

Turner, R. H. 1976. The real self. From institution to impulse. *Am. J. Sociol.* 81:989–1016

Turner, R. H., Schutte, J. 1981. The true self method for studying the self-conception. *Symb. Interact.* 4:1–20

Annu. Rev. Sociol. 1992. 18:327–50

MODELS FOR SAMPLE SELECTION BIAS

Christopher Winship

Department of Sociology, Northwestern University, 1810 Chicago Avenue, Evanston, Illinois 60201

Robert D. Mare

Department of Sociology, University of Wisconsin, 1180 Observatory Drive, Madison, Wisconsin 53706

KEY WORDS: sampling, selection bias, methodology, statistics

Abstract

When observations in social research are selected so that they are not independent of the outcome variables in a study, sample selection leads to biased inferences about social processes. Nonrandom selection is both a source of bias in empirical research and a fundamental aspect of many social processes. This chapter reviews models that attempt to take account of sample selection and their applications in research on labor markets, schooling, legal processes, social mobility, and social networks. Variants of these models apply to outcome variables that are censored or truncated—whether explicitly or incidentally—and include the tobit model, the standard selection model, models for treatment effects in quasi-experimental designs, and endogenous switching models. Heckman's two-stage estimator is the most widely used approach to selection bias, but its results may be sensitive to violations of its assumptions about the way that selection occurs. Recent econometric research has developed a wide variety of promising approaches to selection bias that rely on considerably weaker assumptions. These include a number of semi- and nonparametric approaches to estimating selection models, the use of

0732-0582/92/0410-0327$02.00

panel data, and the analyses of bounds of estimates. The large number of available methods and the difficulty of modelling selection indicate that researchers should be explicit about the assumptions behind their methods and should present results that derive from a variety of methods.

INTRODUCTION

Sample selection is a generic problem in social research that arises when an investigator does not observe a random sample of a population of interest. Specifically, when observations are selected so that they are not independent of the outcome variables in the study, this sample selection leads to biased inferences about social processes. A wide variety—perhaps the majority—of research traditions in sociology rely on designs that are vulnerable to sample selection biases. To rely exclusively on observational schemes that are free from selection bias is to rule out a vast portion of fruitful social research. Indeed, to understand how social positions affect the behaviors of their incumbents, one often must study the processes through which individuals are selected into such positions. Selectivity is not only a source of bias in research, but also the subject of substantive research.

An intuitive appreciation of the ways that selection bias affects inference has always been part of sound research practice. In recent decades, however, many social scientists have formalized the ways that selectivity can affect inferences about social processes through the use of *models* for sample selection bias. These models demonstrate formally how and why bias comes about, and they also show the common formal structure of an array of substantive investigations affected by sample selection bias.

In a linear regression model, selection occurs when data on the dependent variable are missing nonrandomly conditional on the independent variables. Elementary statistical methods in this situation generally yield biased and inconsistent estimates of the effects of the independent variables. For example, if a researcher uses ordinary least squares (OLS) to estimate a regression model where large values of the dependent variable are underrepresented in a sample, the estimates of slope coefficients may be biased.

Sociologists increasingly use models to take account of sample selection bias. A growing methodological literature has also focused on the general issue of the contaminating influence of nonrandom selection on causal inference (Berk 1988, Lieberson 1985). Outside of sociology, especially in economics, applied and theoretical research on selection has been much more extensive, yielding many hundreds of articles. The recent literature on models for sample selection bias develops three major themes: (*a*) Selection is pervasive and results naturally from human behavior (e.g. Roy 1951, Gronau 1974, Heckman 1974, Lewis 1974, Willis & Rosen 1979, Heckman &

Sedlacek 1985, 1990, Heckman & Honore 1990); (*b*) models for sample selection share a close affinity with models for assessing program treatment and other types of effects in experimental and nonexperimental contexts (e.g. Ashenfelter 1978, Barnow et al 1980, Lalonde 1986, Heckman & Robb 1985, 1986a,b, Heckman & Hotz 1989); (*c*) models for selection bias are only as good as their assumptions about the way that selection occurs, and estimation strategies are needed that are robust under a variety of assumptions (Arabmazar & Schmidt 1982, Goldberger 1983, Lee 1982, Wainer 1986, Barnett et al 1991).

This article reviews the significance of selection bias in social research, the problem of modeling selection, and technical issues that arise in correcting for selection bias; we emphasize recent econometric research. We focus on the problem of estimating a linear regression model in the presence of selection. Because Heckman's (1979) estimator has been used extensively in the recent social science literature, we emphasize its problems and extensions. In this review we: (*a*) show why selection on the dependent variable leads to biased and inconsistent estimates of parameters in a regression model; (*b*) review contexts in which selection arises in sociological research and consider some of the models that have been proposed; (*c*) provide a simple classification of alternative selection models; (*d*) discuss Heckman's estimator and its limitations; (*e*) describe semiparametric and nonparametric generalizations of Heckman's estimator; and (*f*) discuss other approaches to selection, including Manski's bound approach and methods that rely on panel data.

An exhaustive review of the literature on issues related to selectivity is impossible within the available space. We emphasize material that is unfamiliar to most sociologists at the neglect of other topics. Berk (1983) and Berk & Ray (1982) introduce selection models to sociologists, and Maddala (1983) and Amemiya (1985) summarize the literature developed during the 1970s that is concerned with estimators other than Heckman's. We do not discuss the statistics literature on missing data (Little & Rubin 1987), and we touch only briefly on causal inference in nonexperimental research and the closely related issue of social program evaluation. These issues have spawned a substantial recent literature (e.g. Lieberson 1985, Holland 1986, Wainer 1986, Berk 1988, Marini & Singer 1988, Manski & Garfinkel 1992).

THE STRUCTURE OF SELECTION

We illustrate selection bias for a single regression equation. The ideas presented here extend easily to more complex models, including those with discrete and other limited-dependent variables and those with multiple dependent variables in the regression model. Selection bias results from a correlation between the error and the independent variables. Consider an example, first used by Hausman & Wise (1977) in their discussion of selection bias. In the 1970s the US government supported several income maintenance experiments, which were based on samples of families with incomes below a specified level. The experiments were designed to reveal whether income supplements for poor persons affect their willingness to work, but the data from the experiments have proved useful for other investigations as well (e.g. Hannan et al 1977, 1978). In the following discussion, we ignore the original purpose of the experiments and focus on problems created when the control subjects of the experiments are used to answer other research questions.

Truncated Samples—Explicit Selection

Consider the problem of estimating the effect of education on income from a sample of persons with incomes below $15,000. This is shown in Figure 1, where individuals are sampled at three education levels: low (L), medium (M), and high (H). When observations with values of the dependent variable that are beyond a certain bound are excluded, the resulting sample is *truncated*. This is also termed explicit selection inasmuch as whether an observation enters the sample is an exact function of the dependent variable (Goldberger 1981). In Figure 1, sample truncation leads to an estimate of the effect of schooling that is biased downward from the true regression line, a result of the $15,000 ceiling on the dependent variable. Under certain conditions—that is, if there is only a single regressor, if the distribution of the independent variables is multivariate normal, or if the independent variables follow a specific class of stable distributions—then all the regression coefficients are biased downwards (Goldberger 1981, Ruud 1986). In general, however, selection may bias estimated effects in either direction.

A sample that is restricted on the dependent variable is effectively selected on the error of the regression equation; at any value of the independent variables, observations with sufficiently large positive errors are eliminated from the sample. As shown in Figure 1, as the independent variable increases, the expected value of the error becomes increasingly negative, making them negatively correlated. Because this contradicts the standard assumption of OLS that the error and the independent variables are uncorrelated, OLS estimates are biased.

Censored Samples—Explicit Selection

A different type of explicit selection occurs when the sample *includes* persons with incomes of $15,000 or more, but all that is known about such persons is their educational attainment and that their incomes are $15,000 or greater. When the dependent variable is outside of a known bound but the exact value of the variable is unknown, the sample is *censored*. If these persons' incomes

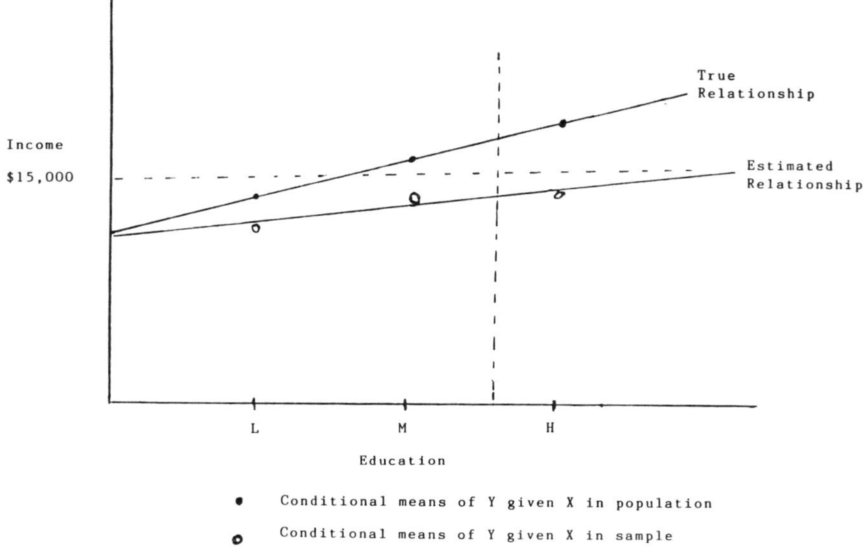

Figure 1 Estimating the effect of education on income from a sample of persons with incomes below \$15,000. Samples are at three education levels: low (L), medium (M), and high (H).

are coded as \$15,000, OLS estimates are biased and inconsistent for the same reasons as in the truncated sample. Since true incomes are unknown, the expected value of the error at any level of education is negative and becomes increasingly negative as education increases, in contradiction to the OLS assumption that the expected value of the error is zero.

Censored and Truncated Samples—Incidental Selection

A third type of selection occurs when censoring or truncation is a stochastic function of the dependent variable. In the example, the *probability* that income is unobserved is a function of income or, equivalently, a function of education and the error. This is termed incidental selection (Goldberger 1981). As we show below, biases in OLS estimates similar to those for explicit selection are the result.

Selection on Measured Independent Variables

Yet another type of selection occurs when the dependent variable is missing solely as a function of the measured independent variable(s); for example, the sample is selected on educational attainment alone. If persons with high levels of schooling are omitted from the model, an OLS estimate of the effect on income for persons with lower levels of education is unbiased if schooling has a constant linear effect throughout its range. Because the conditional expectation of the dependent variable at each level of the independent variable is unaffected by a sample restriction on the independent variable, when a model is properly specified OLS estimates are unbiased and consistent (DuMouchel & Duncan 1983).

SOCIAL SCIENCE EXAMPLES OF SELECTION BIAS

In this section we review examples drawn from the sociology literature of the effects of sample selection bias and of approaches designed to take selectivity into account. Many of these examples illustrate where it has been fruitful both to correct for selection bias and to incorporate the selection process into the substantive investigation. In econometrics, where much basic research on selection bias has been done, many of the applications have been to labor economics. Many studies by sociologists that deal with selection problems have been in the cognate area of social stratification. Problems of selection bias, however, pervade sociology, and attempts to grapple with them appear in the sociology of education, family sociology, criminology, the sociology of law, social networks, and other areas. We select examples where analysts have used models for selection bias, but one could name many other cases where selection biases exist but have thus far been neglected.

Trends in Employment of Out-of-School Youths

Mare & Winship (1984) investigate employment trends from the 1960s to the 1980s for young black and white men who are out of school. Many factors affect these trends, but a key problem in interpreting the trends is that they are influenced by the selectivity characteristic of the out-of-school population. Over time, the selectivity changes because the proportion of the population that is out of school decreases, especially among blacks. Because persons who stay in school longer have better average employment prospects than do persons who drop out, the employment rates of nonstudents are lower than they would be if employment and school enrollment were independent (Mare et al 1984). Observed employment patterns are biased because the probabilities of employment and leaving school are dependent. *Ceteris paribus,* as enrollment increases, employment rates for out-of-school young persons decrease. To understand the employment trends of out-of-school persons, therefore, one must analyze jointly the trends in employment and school enrollment. The increasing propensity of young blacks to remain in school explains some of the growing gap in the employment rates between blacks and whites (Mare & Winship 1984). In this case selectivity is a key part of the substantive interpretation.

Selection Bias and the Disposition of Criminal Cases

A central focus in the analysis of crime and punishment are the determinants of differences in the treatment of persons in contact with the criminal justice system; for example, the differential severity of punishment of blacks and whites (Peterson & Hagan 1984). A sample of persons who are convicted of crimes is highly selective. Of those who commit crimes only a portion are arrested; of those arrested, only a portion are prosecuted; of those prosecuted, only a portion are convicted; of those convicted, only a portion are sent to prison. Common unobserved factors may affect continuation from one stage of this process to the next. Indeed, the stages may be jointly determined inasmuch as legal officials may process cases mindful of the likely outcomes later in the process. The chances that a person will be punished if arrested, for example, may affect the eagerness of police to arrest suspects. Analyses of the severity of sentencing that focus on persons already convicted of crimes may be subject to selection bias and should take account of the process through which persons are convicted (Hagan & Parker 1985, Peterson & Hagan 1984, Zatz & Hagan 1985).

Scholastic Aptitude Tests and College Success

Manski & Wise (1983) investigate the determinants of graduation from college, including the capacity of Scholastic Aptitude Test (SAT) scores to predict individuals' probabilities of graduation. Studies based on samples of students within colleges find that SAT scores have little predictive power. Yet these studies may be biased because of the selective stages between taking the SAT and attending college. Some students who take the SAT do not apply to college; some apply but are not admitted; some are admitted but do not attend; and those who attend are sorted among the colleges to which they have been admitted. Each stage of selection is nonrandom and is affected by characteristics of students and schools that are unknown to the analyst. When one jointly considers the stages of selection in the college attendance decision, along with the probability that a student graduates from college, one finds that the SAT score is a strong predictor of college graduation.

Women's Socioeconomic Achievement

Analyses of the earnings and other socioeconomic achievements of women are potentially affected by nonrandom selection of women into the labor market. The rewards that women expect from working affect their propensities to enter the labor force. Outcomes such as earnings or occupational status, therefore, are jointly determined with labor force participation, and analyses that ignore the process of labor force participation are potentially subject to selection bias. Many studies in economics (e.g. Gronau 1974, Heckman 1974, 1979) and sociology (Fligstein & Wolf 1978, Hagan 1990, England et al 1988) use models that represent simultaneously women's labor force participation and the market rewards that they receive.

Analysis of Occupational Mobility from Nineteenth Century Censuses

Nineteenth Century Decennial Census data for cities provide a means of comparing nineteenth and twentieth century regimes of occupational mobility in the United States (Grusky 1986, Hardy 1989). Although one can analyze mobility by linking the records of successive censuses, linkage is only possible for persons who remain in the same city and keep the same name over the decade. Persons who die, emigrate, or change their names are excluded. Because mortality and migration covary with socioeconomic success, the process of mobility and the way that observations are selected for the analysis are jointly determined. Analyses that jointly model mobility and sample selection offer the possibility of avoiding selection bias (Hardy 1989).

Bias in Network Analysis

One concern of social network studies is to examine the consequences of social network structure for individuals; for example, Marsden & Hurlbert (1987) examine the effects of network density—that is, the strength of ties that a person has with others with whom they discuss important matters—on personal happiness. Network density is observable only for persons with enough contacts for density measures to be computed; isolates have no network at all. Because isolation is both a cause and a consequence of one's happiness, analyses that exclude isolates are subject to selection bias. Number of contacts and the outcomes of network structure can be analyzed jointly to take the potential selection bias into account.

MODELS OF SELECTION

We now provide a brief classification of selection models at varying levels of complexity. We start by discussing the censored regression or tobit model. Due to limited space we forego discussion of the very closely related truncated regression model (see Hausman & Wise 1976, 1977). For more detailed classifications, see Amemiya (1985) and Heckman (1987).

Tobit Model

The censored regression or tobit model is appropriate when the dependent variable is censored at some upper or lower bound as an artifact of how the data are collected (Tobin 1958, Maddala 1983). For censoring at a lower bound, the model is:

$$Y^*_{1i} = X_i\beta + \epsilon_i \quad 1.$$

$$Y_{1i} = Y^*_{1i} \text{ if } Y^*_{1i} > 0 \quad 2.$$

$$Y_{1i} = 0 \text{ if } Y^*_{1i} \leq 0, \quad 3.$$

where, for the ith observation, Y^*_{1i} is an unobserved continuous latent variable, Y_{1i} is the observed variable, X_i is a vector of values on the independent variables, ϵ_i is the error, and β is a vector of coefficients. We assume that ϵ_i is uncorrelated with X_i and is independently and identically distributed. The model can be generalized by replacing the threshold zero in Equations 2 and 3 with a known nonzero constant. The censoring point may also vary across observations, leading to a model that is formally equivalent to models for survival analysis (Kalbfleisch & Prentice 1980, Lancaster 1990).

OLS estimates of Equation 1 are subject to selection bias. For observations for which $Y_{1i} > 0$, the model implies

$$\begin{aligned} Y_{1i} &= X_i\beta + E[\epsilon_i \mid Y^*_{1i} > 0] + \eta_i \\ &= X_i\beta + E[\epsilon_i \mid \epsilon_i > -X_i\beta] + \eta_i \end{aligned} \quad 4.$$

where η_i is the difference between ϵ_i and $E[\epsilon_i \mid Y^*_{1i} > 0]$ and is uncorrelated with both terms. Selection bias results because $E[\epsilon_i \mid \epsilon_i > -X_i\beta]$ in Equation 4 is a function of $-X_i\beta$. The less $-X_i\beta$, that is, the less the rate of censoring, the greater is the conditional expected value of ϵ_i. The negative correlation between $-X_i\beta$ and ϵ_i implies that OLS estimates of the regression of Y_i on X_i are biased and inconsistent. An equation analogous to Equation 4 can be constructed for observations for which $Y_{1i} = 0$, producing a parallel analysis. Thus, inclusion of observations for which $Y_{1i} = 0$ leads to similar problems. Equation 4 also shows how selectivity bias may be interpreted as an omitted variable bias (Heckman 1979). The term $E[\epsilon_i \mid Y^*_{1i} > 0]$ can be thought of as an omitted variable that is correlated with X_i and affects Y_1. Its omission leads to biased and inconsistent OLS estimates of β.

Mare & Chen (1986) use the tobit model to examine the effects of parents' socioeconomic characteristics on years of graded schooling completed by their offspring, a variable that is censored for persons with more than 12 years of school. Seltzer & Garfinkel (1990) and Seltzer (1991) use tobit models to analyze the determinants of property and child support awards to mothers and amounts paid by noncustodial fathers after divorce, which are zero for substantial proportions of mothers. In studying how families finance college educations, Steelman & Powell (1989) construct tobit models of the sources of college funding, including parents' contributions, loans, savings, and scholarships, each of which has a logical floor of zero. Hoffman (1984) uses a tobit model to examine the determinants of pious bequests in rural Lyonnais and Beaujolais between 1521 and 1737.

Standard Sample Selection Model

A generalization of the tobit model is to specify that a second variable Y^*_{2i} affects whether Y_{1i} is observed or not. That is, retain the basic model Equation 1, but replace 2 and 3 with:

$$Y_{1i} = Y^*_{1i} \text{ if } Y^*_{2i} > 0 \quad 5.$$

$$Y_{1i} = 0 \text{ if } Y^*_{2i} \leq 0 \quad 6.$$

Variants of this model depend on how Y_{2i} is specified. Commonly Y^*_{2i} is determined by a binary regression model:

$$Y^*_{2i} = Z_i\alpha + v_i \quad 7.$$

$$Y_{2i} = 1 \text{ if } Y^*_{2i} > 0 \quad 8.$$

$$Y_{2i} = 0 \text{ if } Y^*_{2i} \leq 0, \quad 9.$$

where Y^*_{2i} is a latent continuous variable. A classic example is a model for the wages and employment of women, where Y_{1i} is the observed wage, Y_{2i} is a dummy variable indicating whether a women works, and Y^*_{2i} indexes a woman's propensity to work (Gronau 1974). In a variant of this model, Y_{2i} is hours of work and Equations 7–9 are a tobit model (Heckman 1974). In both variants, Y^*_{1i} is only observed for women with positive hours of work. One can modify the model by assuming, for example, that Y_{1i} is dichotomous. If ϵ_i and v_i follow a bivariate normal distribution, this leads to a bivariate probit selection model. Maddala (1983) and Lee (1983) discuss these and other variants of the model.

The bias in an OLS regression of Y_{1i} on X_i in the general selection case is similar to that in the tobit model. When $Y^*_{2i} > 0$,

$$\begin{aligned} Y_{1i} &= X_i\beta + E[\epsilon_i \mid Y^*_{2i} > 0] + \eta_i \\ &= X_i\beta + E[\epsilon_i \mid v_i - Z_i\alpha > 0] + \eta_i \end{aligned} \quad 10.$$

The OLS regression of Y_{1i} on X_i is biased and inconsistent if ϵ_i is correlated with $v_i - Z_i\alpha$, which occurs if ϵ_i is correlated with either v_i or the Z_i. If the variables in Z_i are included in X_i, ϵ_i and Z_i are uncorrelated by assumption. If, however, Z_i contains additional variables, then ϵ_i and Z_i may be correlated.

When $\sigma_{\epsilon\upsilon} = 0$ selection depends only on the observed variables in Z_i not in X_i. In this case, propensity score methods (Rosenbaum & Rubin 1983) are appropriate for correcting for selectivity (Heckman & Robb 1985, 1986a,b).

Treatment Effects

The problem of selection is closely related to the problem of estimating treatment effects in the presence of nonrandom assignment. Consider the following model for the effect of a dichotomous variable Y_2 on a continuous variable Y_I:

$$Y_{Ii} = X_i\beta + Y_{2i}\gamma + \epsilon_i, \qquad 11.$$

where γ is the treatment effect to be estimated and all other notation is defined as above. We can estimate Equation 11 consistently by OLS if X_i and Y_{2i} are uncorrelated with the error ϵ_i, a condition that is met if assignment to the two treatment levels is random, or random conditional upon the X_i. In the latter case OLS corrects for the correlation between Y_{2i} and X_i in estimating γ. When assignment to Y_{2i} is a function of the error, Y_{2i} is determined endogenously. In this case, methods used to correct for selection can also be used to correct for the endogeneity of Y_{2i} (Heckman, 1976b, 1978). Alternatively, instrumental variable methods can be used if instruments for Y_{2i} are available.

The relationship between the treatment and the selection models can be understood by first considering Rubin & Holland's structure for measuring causal effects (Holland 1986, Rubin 1978). Assume that associated with each observation there are two variables, Y^0_{Ii}, which is the outcome on variable Y_1 for observation i when it is assigned to treatment level $Y_{2i} = 0$, and Y^1_{Ii} which is the outcome on variable Y_1 for observation i when it is assigned to treatment level $Y_{2i} = 1$. Rubin & Holland then define the causal effect of the treatment for the ith observation as the difference: $Y^1_{Ii} - Y^0_{Ii}$. The average causal effect, γ, is then the average of this difference across observations. In almost all situations we only observe either Y^0_{Ii} or Y^1_{Ii} for any given observation. As a result the observation-level and the average treatment effect cannot be directly estimated.

This framework can be generalized to the regression case by rewriting Equation 11 as two equations, one for each value of Y_{2i}:

$$Y^0_{Ii} = X_i\beta + \epsilon_{Ii} \qquad Y_{2i} = 0 \qquad 12.$$

$$Y^1_{Ii} = X_i\beta + \gamma + \epsilon_{2i} \qquad Y_{2i} = 1 \qquad 13.$$

In Equation 13 γ denotes how the intercept differs between when $Y_{2i} = 0$ and when $Y_{2i} = 1$ and is equal to the average treatment effect. By itself Equation

12 is subject to selection bias in that data are "missing" on Y^0_{1i} when $Y_{2i} = 1$. Likewise Equation 13 is subject to selection bias in that data are "missing" on Y^1_{1i} when $Y_{2i} = 0$. Unless Y_{2i} is determined randomly (given X_i), OLS estimates, whether taken separately from Equations 12 and 13 or jointly from 11, are subject to selection bias.

The problem of estimating treatment effects is an example of the general problem of causal analysis with nonexperimental data. The assessment of a treatment effect is a "missing data" problem in that, for each case, we observe the dependent variable under only one condition, and the effect of treatment is the difference for the case between the dependent variable under that condition and the alternative condition (Holland 1986, Rubin 1978). Thus, any type of causal analysis is potentially a problem in selection.

Endogenous Switching Regressions

The treatment model can be generalized to the endogenous switching model, which allows the effects of the independent variable to vary across treatments (Maddala 1983, Mare & Winship 1988). Then the model becomes:

$$Y^0_{1i} = X_i\beta_1 + \epsilon_{1i} \qquad (Y_{2i} = 0) \tag{14.}$$

$$Y^1_{1i} = X_i\beta_2 + \epsilon_{2i} \qquad (Y_{2i} = 1), \tag{15.}$$

where γ becomes part of the intercept in β_2 and Y_2 is determined by Equations 7–9. This model is suitable for assessing the effects of a social classification Y_2 on a consequence of membership in this classification Y_1—such as the effect of academic track placement on achievement or the effect of labor market sector on earnings—and how the effects of exogenous characteristics vary across levels of Y_2. By itself Equation 14 is subject to selection bias in that data are "missing" on Y^0_{1i} when $Y_{2i} = 1$. Likewise Equation 15 is subject to bias in that data are "missing" on Y^1_{1i} when $Y_{2i} = 0$. Only if, conditional on the X_i, observations enter levels of Y_{2i} at random, are OLS estimates of Equations 14 or 15 unbiased.

The covariances of the disturbances in this model provide information about the nature of selectivity into each group. Denote the covariances of Equations 7 and 14 and of 7 and 15 as $\sigma_{\epsilon 1 \upsilon}$ and $\sigma_{\epsilon 2 \upsilon}$ respectively. Their signs reveal whether, given that the X_i, observations are positively or negatively selected into levels of Y_2. If $\sigma_{\epsilon 2 \upsilon} > 0$, then observations are positively selected into the condition $Y_2 = 1$, and if $\sigma_{\epsilon 1 \upsilon} < 0$, then observations are positively selected into the condition $Y_2 = 0$. The covariances reveal whether the *regime* of sorting observations into classes follows the principle of, for example, comparative advantage (which holds if observations are positively selected into both groups) or some other principal.

Gamoran & Mare (1989) use endogenous switching models to examine the effects of academic tracking on the achievement of high school students when they are nonrandomly assigned to tracks. In these models Equations 14 and 15 predict the academic achievement levels of students in non-college and college bound tracks, respectively. The independent variables include the students' prior levels of achievement and social backgrounds. Each student is viewed as having two possible achievement outcomes, namely, achievement were he or she assigned to the college track Y^1_{1i}, and achievement were he or she assigned to the noncollege track Y^0_{1i}. In fact, however, each student is observed in only one track, and her or his (expected) achievement in the other track is censored. Equation 7 represents the process by which students are assigned to the college or non-college tracks. Gamoran & Mare consider two forms of Equation 7, a structural form and a reduced form. In the structural form, the independent variables include not only the social background and prior achievement levels of students but also their expected levels of achievement in the two tracks. This represents the idea that track assignment decisions, whether made by parents, school officials, or the students themselves, may be affected by expectations of how well a student will perform in alternative tracks. In practice, expected levels of achievement are only partially observed and it is necessary to solve for the reduced form of Equation 7, which includes not only the exogenous predictors of track assignment but also, subject to some constraints, the determinants of expected achievement, as represented in 14 and 15. Equations 14, 15, and the reduced form of 7 are estimated jointly. By modelling track assignment, one can take account of the selection bias that may occur if Equations 14 or 15 were estimated alone. Conversely, the model allows one also to explore how expected achievement may affect track assignment. By placing restrictions on the models, one can test alternative ideas about the ways that schools and families make tracking decisions (Gamoran & Mare 1989, Mare & Winship 1988).

In other applications of endogenous switching models, Sakamoto & Chen (1991) assess the effects of labor market sector on earnings taking into account the nonrandom allocation of workers to sectors; Willis & Rosen (1979) examine the effects of college attendance on earnings in a model for the self-selection of students with varying abilities to alternative levels of schooling; and Manski et al (1992) estimate the effects of being raised in a female-headed family on high school graduation, using a variant of the treatment model to take account of self-selection of individuals into family statuses.

ESTIMATORS

A large number of estimators have been proposed for selection models. Until recently, all of these estimators made strong assumptions about the distribution of errors. Two general classes of methods, maximum likelihood and nonlinear least squares, typically assume bivariate normality of ϵ_i and v_i. The most popular method is that of Heckman (1976a, 1979), which only assumes that v_i in equation (7) is normally distributed and $E[\epsilon_i \mid v_i]$ is linear. Computer software packages such as *LIMDEP* (Greene 1990) implement a number of estimation strategies and selection models, including cases where the selection equation is a tobit model, a multinomial logit, or multiple criteria model, and the structural equation is a linear, probit, or tobit model.

Recently researchers have been concerned with the sensitivity of the Heckman estimator to the normality and linearity assumptions. Because maximum likelihood and nonlinear least squares make even stronger assumptions, they are typically more efficient (Nelson 1984) but even less robust to violations of distributional assumptions. This lack of robustness is also a property of Olson's (1980) linear probability estimator which assumes that errors are uniformly as opposed to normally distributed. The main concern of the recent literature is the search for alternatives to the Heckman estimator that do not depend on normality and linearity assumptions. Thus we do not review the estimators that make stronger assumptions (Maddala 1983, Amemiya 1985). Instead we first describe the Heckman estimator, discuss the concerns with its sensitivity, and review alternatives that have been proposed.

Heckman's Estimator

The Heckman estimator involves (*a*) estimating the selection model (equations 7–9); (*b*) calculating the expected error, $\hat{v}_i = \mathrm{E}[v_i \mid v_i > -Z_i\alpha]$, for each observation using the estimated α; and (*c*) using the estimated error as a regressor in 1. We can rewrite Equation 10 as:

$$Y_{1i} = X_i\beta + \mathrm{E}(\epsilon_i \mid v_i > -Z_i\alpha) + \eta_i. \qquad 16.$$

If ϵ_i and v_i are bivariate normal and $\mathrm{Var}(v_i) = 1$ then $\mathrm{E}(\epsilon_i \mid v_i) = \sigma_{\epsilon v} v_i$ and

$$\mathrm{E}(\epsilon_i \mid v_i > -Z_i\alpha) = \sigma_{\epsilon v}\ \phi(-Z_i\alpha)/[1\text{-}\Phi(-Z_i\alpha)] = \sigma_{\epsilon v}\ \lambda(-Z_i\alpha) \qquad 17.$$

where ϕ and Φ are the standardized normal density and distribution functions respectively. The ratio $\lambda(-Z_i\alpha)$ is the inverse Mills' ratio. Substituting Equation 17 into 16 we get:

$$Y_{1i} = X_i\beta + \sigma_{\epsilon v}\ \lambda(-Z_i\alpha) + \eta_i \qquad 18.$$

where η_i is uncorrelated with both X_i and $\lambda(-Z_i\alpha)$. The assumption that ϵ_i and v_i follow a bivariate normal distribution is needed: (*a*) to obtain a linear relationship between ϵ_i and v_i and (*b*) to obtain a marginally normal error v_i which produces the Mills ratio formula. No other properties of the bivariate normal are used in arriving at equation 18. In particular, no assumptions are needed about the marginal distribution of ϵ_i or its higher moments. This contrasts with the method of maximum likelihood (e.g. Amemiya 1985), which makes stronger assumptions.

The steps in Heckman's estimator are: (*a*) estimate α in 7 using a probit model; (*b*) use the estimated $Z_i\hat{\alpha}$ to calculate $\hat{\lambda}(Z_i\hat{\alpha}) = E[v_i \mid v_i > -Z_i\hat{\alpha}] = \phi(-Z_i\alpha)/[1 - \Phi(-Z_i\alpha)]$; and (*c*) estimate β and $\sigma_{\epsilon v}$ in (18) by replacing $E[v_i \mid v_i > -Z_i\alpha]$ with $\lambda(-Z_i\alpha)$. Estimation of Equation 18 by OLS gives consistent parameter estimates, but special formulas are needed to get correct standard errors because the errors, η_i, are heteroskedastic and correlated (Heckman 1979, Maddala 1983).

The precision of the estimates in Equation 18 is sensitive to the variance of λ and collinearity between X and λ. The variance of λ is determined by how effectively the probit equation at the first stage predicts which observations are selected into the sample. The better the prediction, the greater the variance of λ, and the more precise estimates will be. Collinearity will be determined in part by the overlap in variables between X and Z. If X and Z are identical, then the model is only identified because λ is nonlinear. Since it is seldom possible to justify the form of λ on substantive grounds, successful use of the method usually requires that at least one variable in Z not be included in X. Even in this case X and $\lambda(-Z\alpha)$ may be highly collinear leading to imprecise estimates.

Robustness of Heckman's Estimator

Because of the sensitivity of Heckman's estimator to model specification, researchers have focussed on the robustness of the estimator to violations of its several assumptions. Estimation of 7–9 as a probit model assumes that the errors v_i are homoskedastic. When this assumption is violated, the Heckman procedure yields inconsistent estimates (Arabmazar & Schmidt 1981), though procedures are available to correct for heteroskedasticity (Hurd 1979).

The assumed bivariate normality of v_i and ϵ_i in the selection model is needed in two places. First, normality of v_i is needed for consistent estimation of α in the probit model. Second, the normality assumption implies a particular nonlinear relationship for the effect of $Z_i\alpha$ on Y_{2i} through λ. If the expectation of ϵ_i conditional on v_i is not linear and/or v_i is not normal, λ misspecifies the relationship between $Z_i\alpha$ and Y_{2i} and the model may yield biased results.

Several studies have analytically investigated the bias in the single equation (tobit) model when the error is not normally distributed. In a model with only an intercept–that is, a model for the mean of a censored distribution—when errors are not normally distributed, the normality assumption leads to substantial bias. This result holds even when the true distribution is close to the normal (for example, the logistic) (Goldberger 1983). When the normality assumption is wrong, moreover, maximum likelihood estimates may be worse than simply using the observed sample mean. For samples that are 75% complete, bias from the normality assumption is minimal; in samples that are 50% complete, the bias is substantial in the truncated case, but not the censored; and in samples that are less than 50% complete, it is substantial in almost all cases (Arabmazar & Schmidt 1982).

That estimation of the mean is sensitive to distributional misspecification suggests that the Heckman estimator may not be robust and raises the question of how commonly such problems arise in practice. In addition, even when normality holds, the Heckman estimator may not improve the mean square error of OLS estimates of slope coefficients in small samples (50) (Stolzenberg & Relles 1990). This appears to parallel the standard result that when the effect of a variable is measured imprecisely, inclusion of the variable may enlarge the mean square error of the other parameters in the model (Leamer 1983).

No empirical work that we know of directly examines the sensitivity of Heckman's method for a standard selection model. However, several recent studies (Lalonde 1986, Lalonde & Maynard 1987) evaluate the closely related methods for assessing the impact treatment effects in nonexperimental settings. The models are made up of two equations, one predicting whether an individual participates in, for example, a job training program, and the other providing the effects of the program and other regressors on the individual's wages. This work compares the estimates of the effects of programs on wages from applying OLS and variants of Heckman's methods to nonexperimental data to estimates from data where individuals are randomly assigned to treatment conditions. Compared to OLS, Heckman's estimates yield program effects that are closer to the experimental results. The Heckman estimates, however, often differ substantially from the experimental estimates and tend to fluctuate depending on which variables are included in the selection equation. The various estimates reported by Lalonde have large standard errors, mainly because of small samples; hence they are not a definitive appraisal of the Heckman methods. But this research strongly suggests that Heckman's method is no panacea for selection problems and, when its assumption are not met, may yield misleading results.

Extensions of the Heckman Estimator

There are two main issues in estimating Equation 18. First, is the equation that predicts selection into the sample consistently estimated? That is, are estimates of α, which derive from the selection equation, consistent? This depends on the assumptions that (*a*) the independent variables in that equation (Z_i) have linear effects, and (*b*) the errors in the selection equation are normally distributed. Assumption (*a*) depends on the same considerations as any linear model as to whether interactions or other nonlinear transformations of the regressors should be included. Unfortunately, a strong substantive rationale for the regressors included in the selection equation is often unavailable. Likewise, assumption (*b*) in practice seldom rests on a firm substantive basis.

Second, what nonlinear function should be chosen for λ, which dictates how the predicted probabilities of sample selection affect the dependent variable in Equation 18? When bivariate normality of errors holds, λ is the inverse Mills ratio. When this assumption does not hold, inconsistent estimates may result. Moreover, since the regressors in the main and sample selection equations (X_i and Z_i) are often highly collinear, estimates of β in (18) may be sensitive to misspecification of λ.

Much of the recent research on models for selection has focussed on developing estimators that do not rely on these distributional and functional form assumptions. Most work thus far is theoretical, although some applications of these new methods have been carried out. Many of the new estimators relax the assumptions of Heckman's two-step approach. The approach of many of the new models is as follows. First, the selection model, Equations 7–9, is estimated using a nonparametric method for binary regression models. These methods include Manski's maximum score method (1975, 1985), which is implemented in *LIMDEP*, nonparametric maximum likelihood estimation (Cosslett 1983), weighted average derivatives (Stoker 1986, Powell et al 1989), and kernel estimation (Bierens 1990, Ichimura 1988, Klein & Spady 1987). Spline methods and series approximations (Hardle 1990) are also available but are, as far as we are aware, an unexplored approach. Two bases for evaluating these methods are (*a*) the trade-off that they make between efficiency and the strength of their prior assumptions, and (*b*) their asymptotic distribution. Chamberlain (1986) establishes a theoretical upper bound for the efficiency of nonparametric methods under particular assumptions. Kernel methods (Ichimura 1988, Klein & Spady 1987) and variants of the weighted average derivatives (Stoker 1991) reach this bound, but other methods that make weaker assumptions, such as the method of scoring (Manski 1975), do not. For still others, the efficiency is unknown (Cosslett 1983). We discuss some of the assumptions made in alternative semiparametric and nonparametric approaches below. Asymptotic normality has been established for all these estimators except those of Manski and Cosslett.

Kernel Estimation

As far as we are aware, kernel estimation is the only nonparametric approach that has been used for the first stage of selection models in empirical applications. This approach is as follows. Asssume that we have multiple observations of Y_2 for each possible value of the vector Z_i. Let $g(Z)$ be the function for the conditional mean of Y_2 on Z. Then a nonparametric estimator of the conditional mean functions is:

$$\hat{g}(Z) = \Sigma_i Y_{2i} \qquad \text{for all } Z_i = Z.$$

For example, if we were predicting whether individuals were employed or not (Y_{2i}) from their level of educational attainment (Z_i), our nonparametric estimate would simply be the proportion of persons who are employed at each level of educational attainment. This estimator makes no assumption about how Z enters g, (for example, that it is linear, making the model semiparametric), or about the distribution for the error υ (which would make the model parametric). If data are grouped so that multiple values of Y_{2i} are known for each value of Z_i, this procedure is straightforward. If, however, Z_i varies continuously, so that there is at most one observation of Y_{2i} at each value of Z_i, kernel estimation is required.

The kernel method uses observations (Y_{2j}, Z_j) where Z_j is close to Z_i to estimate the mean of Y_{2i}. We assume that g_i is continuous and calculate a weighted average of the Y_{2i} to estimate g_i, where observations with Z_j that are close to Z_i are weighted more heavily than observations that are further away; that is, $\hat{g}_i = \Sigma_j K_{i\,j} Y_{2j} / \Sigma_j \mathrm{K}_{ij}$, where $K_{ij} = K[(Z_i - Z_j)/h]$. K is assumed to have a maximum at zero and to decrease as the absolute size of $Z_i - Z_j$ increases. Although many functions are possible for K, the choice of function does not usually affect the estimates. The researcher selects h, known as the bandwidth of K, to control the smoothness of the estimator (Hardle 1990). As the sample increases, h should gradually approach zero, which guarantees a consistent estimate of g_i.

As in Heckman's method, the second stage is to estimate Equation 18, using the estimates of α or g_i from the first stage. Several approaches are available to estimate 18 without parametrically specifying λ. One approach is to approximate λ through a series expansion (Newey 1990) such as Edgeworth series (Lee 1982), or by step functions (Cosslett 1991), with the number of terms gradually increasing with sample size. A second possibility is to use kernel methods to estimate λ (Robinson 1988, Powell 1987, Ahn & Powell 1990). By one interpretation, this is a generalized difference estimator (Powell 1987). In this approach one differences out the nuisance function $\lambda(g_i)$ by estimating Equation 18 across differences between pairs of observations:

$$Y_{1i} - Y_{1j} = (X_i - X_j)\beta + [\lambda(g_i) - \lambda(g_j)] + \epsilon_i - \epsilon_j. \qquad 19.$$

If one only uses pairs for which the probability of selection is equal ($g_i = g_j$), then the terms in λ simply drop out of Equation 19 and OLS can be used. If λ

is continuous, for pairs i, j for which $g_i \cong g_j$, $\lambda(g_i) \cong \lambda(g_j)$, and the $[\lambda(g_i) - \lambda(g_j)]$ will be near zero. Powell's procedure uses all pairs and weights more heavily pairs for which the difference $g_i - g_j$ is less. As the sample increases, more weight is placed on pairs for which $g_i \cong g_j$, thus guaranteeing consistency of the estimator. Powell's approach will only identify the effects of Xs that vary across individuals with the similar g. As a result, it is not possible to identify the intercept using his approach. Estimates of intercepts may be important in both the treatment and endogenous switching models.

Empirical Applications

All three of these methods have been compared to Heckman's normal estimator using a common model on a single set of data. Several investigators have used Mroz's (1987) model on the labor force participation of married women. In this model, the dependent variable is annual hours worked; a selection equation models whether or not a woman worked more than zero hours. Mroz uses Heckman's two-stage method for estimating the model. Newey et al (1990) and Ahn & Powell (1990) use semi- and nonparametric methods. These studies provide a common context for comparing (*a*) Heckman's method, (*b*) weighted kernel estimation of the hours equation and probit estimates of the selection equation, (*c*) series expansion estimation of λ with probit estimates of the selection equation, and (*d*) weighted kernel estimation of both the hours and the selection equations. Methods (*b*) and (*c*) are semiparametric; method (*d*) is nonparametric.

The weighted kernel and series expansion results are generally similar to those from Heckman's method although their standard errors are typically slightly larger. When kernel methods are used for both the hours and selection equations, some coefficients differ markedly from the other methods, and the standard errors are much larger than for the other methods. Nonparametric estimates for the selection equation are very imprecise. At least in this example, moreover, results are sensitive to alternative estimation approaches. The nonparametric procedures make the weakest assumptions, but their standard errors are so large as to imply that the data are consistent with a very wide range of results.

Manski's Bound Approach

Although semi- and nonparametric methods are conservative, they are not free of assumptions. For example, in Ahn & Powell's model, λ is assumed to be a function of a single index, g_i, and to enter Equation 18 additively. Without such assumptions it is often impossible even to put a bound on the conditional mean of Y_1 given X, the usual quantity estimated in regression analysis, much less obtain a consistent point estimate. In an important set of papers Manski (1989, 1990, 1991) shows that, without prior assumptions about the selection process, it is impossible to obtain point estimates of the true regression model when selection occurs. Under some conditions, however, it is possible to place bounds on the estimated regression coefficients in the absence of assumptions about the selection process. A regression model can be written as:

$$E(Y_1 \mid X) = E(Y_1 \mid X,Y_2 = 1)P(Y_2 = 1) + E(Y_1 \mid X,Y_2 = 0)P(Y_2 = 0), \quad 20.$$

where all of the notation is as defined above. All of the components in Equation 20 can be estimated from observed data except $E(Y_1 \mid X,Y_2 = 0)$, the regression of Y_1 on X for cases that are not in the selected sample. Unless one can put bounds on this value, sample data provide no information about the true regression of Y_1 on X. Manski derives bounds for $E(Y_1 \mid X,Y_2 = 0)$ when Y_1 is dichotomous and for conditional *medians* when Y_1 is continuous (Manski 1989, 1990, 1991). In general the tightness of the bound varies inversely with the proportion of cases in the sample that are censored. Somewhat surprisingly, Manski shows that it is easier to obtain bounds for regression estimates when the dependent variables are dichotomies or medians than when they are continuous. Manski has written a computer program for doing this type of analysis. Although researchers are in the habit of seeking a point estimate for parameters of interest, this usually comes at the price of making questionable identifying assumptions. Manski shows that these assumptions can be relaxed if one is willing to settle for an informative range of possible parameter values.

Methods Based on Panel Data

Panel data are useful for estimating treatment effects when subjects are nonrandomly assigned to conditions, and also enable one to take account of some kinds of nonrandom sample selection (Heckman & Robb 1985, 1986a,b; Heckman & Hotz 1989). If selection is only on the observed independent variables, then selection bias is not a problem. Panel data enable one to control some unobserved as well as observed variables and may in some cases alleviate selection bias. We consider models with fixed, observation-specific effects, although the approach can be generalized to models with random effects and, in some cases, with time-varying effects. The model is:

$$Y_{1it} = X_{it}\beta + v_i + \epsilon_{it} \quad 21.$$

where t indexes time and v_i is an unobserved component that is unique to each cross-sectional observation but is invariant over time. The selection equation is:

$$Y_{2it} = Z_{it}\alpha + \gamma v_i + \eta_{it}, \qquad 22.$$

where the selection rule is given by Equations 5 and 6 above. If ϵ_{it} and η_{it} are uncorrelated, and we can take account of v_i, then selection is on the observed independent variables alone and Equation 21 is estimable by OLS. A method of taking account of v_i is to take deviations of the variables in 21 from their observation-specific means. One can estimate:

$$Y_{1it} - \overline{Y}_{1i} = (X_{1it} - \overline{X}_{1i})\beta + (\epsilon_{it} - \epsilon_i), \qquad 23.$$

which yields estimates of β in 21 because v_i is invariant over time. This eliminates v_i and thus the selection problem. The key assumption is that the unobserved determinants of selection are time invariant characteristics of the observations. If the unobserved determinants of selection depend on time, then a more complex model is required.

CONCLUSION

Infallible models for sample selection bias do not exist. Methods are rapidly evolving and, at present, different methods may yield different results. We do not know definitively the robustness of Heckman's estimator and its generalizations across different empirical contexts. We do know that, in some contexts, methods that make weaker assumptions give different results from Heckman's estimator, but the weaker assumptions may come at the cost of greatly reduced precision. When selection is an issue, therefore, empirical results are likely to remain ambiguous (Manski 1989). What should the researcher do? Because one's results may depend on the method used, researchers should be explicit about the assumptions behind their methods and should present estimates using a variety of methods. Manski et al (1992) exemplify this approach in their analysis of the effects of family structure on the likelihood dropping out of high school, which includes parametric and nonparametric models, and an analysis of bounds.

ACKNOWLEDGMENT

The research was supported by grants from the National Institute of Child Health and Human Development and the National Science Foundation. The authors are grateful to Charles Manski, Peter Marsden, John Hagan, and Tom Cook for helpful discussions and comments on an earlier draft. The authors also appreciate the bibliographic assistance of Ruth Sandor and Carol Sleeva and the assistance of Barbara Corry and Nancy Bennett in preparing the manuscript.

Literature Cited

Ahn, H., Powell, J. J. 1990. Semiparametric estimation of censored selection models with a nonparametric selection mechanism. Madison, Wisc: Dep. Econ., Univ. Wisc.

Amemiya, T. 1985. *Advanced Econometrics*. Cambridge, Mass: Harvard Univ. Press

Arabmazar, A., Schmidt, P. 1981. Further evidence of robustness of the tobit estimator to heteroscedasticity. *J. Economet*. 17:253–58

Arabmazar, A., Schmidt, P. 1982. An investigation of the robustness of the Tobit estimator to non-normality. *Econometrica* 50:1055–63

Ashenfelter, 0. 1978. Estimating the effect of programs on earnings. *Rev. Econ. Stat*. 60:47–57

Barnett, W. A., Powell, J., Tauchen, G. 1991. *Nonparametric and Semiparametric Methods in Econometrics and Statistics*. Cambridge: Cambridge Univ. Press

Barnow, B. S., Cain, G. G., Goldberger, A. S. 1980. Issues in the analysis of selectivity bias. In *Eval. Stud. Rev.*, 5:43–59, ed. E. W. Stromsdorfer, G. Farkas. Beverly Hills, Calif: Sage

Berk, R. A. 1983. An introduction to sample selection bias in sociological data. *Am. Sociol. Rev*. 48:386–98

Berk, R. A. 1988. Causal inference for sociological data. In *The Handbook of Sociology*,, ed. N. J. Smelser, pp. 155–72. Newbury Park, Calif: Sage

Berk, R. A., Ray, S. C. 1982. Selection biases in sociological data. *Soc. Sci. Res*. 11:352–98

Bierens, H. 1990. Kernel estimators of regression functions. In *Advances in Econometrics 1990,* ed. T. Bewley, pp. 99–144. Cambridge, UK: Cambridge Univ. Press

Chamberlain, G. 1986. Asymptotic efficiency in semi-parametric models with censoring. *J. Economet*. 32:189–218

Cosslett, S. R. 1983. Distribution-free maximum likelihood estimator of the binary choice model. *Econometrica* 51:765–81

Cosslett, S. R. 1991. Semiparametric estimation of a regression model with sampling selectivity. In *Nonparametric and Semiparametric Methods in Econometrics and Statistics*,, ed. W. A. Barnett, J. Powell, G. Tauchen, pp. 175–98. Cambridge: Cam bridge Univ. Press

DuMouchel, W. H., Duncan, G. J. 1983. Using sample survey weights in multiple regression analyses of stratified samples. *J. Am. Stat. Assoc*. 78:535–43

England, P., Farkas, G., Kilbourne, B., Dou, T. 1988. Explaining occupational sex segregation and wages: findings from a model with fixed effects. *Am. Sociol. Rev*. 53:544–58

Fligstein, N. D., Wolf, W. 1978. Sex similarities in occupational status attainment: are the results due to the restriction of the sample to employed women? *Soc. Sci. Res*. 7:197–212

Gamoran, A., Mare, R. D. 1989. Secondary school tracking and stratification: compensation, reinforcement, or neutrality? *Am. J. Sociol*. 94:1146–83

Goldberger, A. S. 1981. Linear regression after selection.*J. Economet*. 15:357–66

Goldberger, A. S. 1983. Abnormal selection bias. In *Studies in Econometrics Time Series, and Multivariate Statistics*, ed. S. Karlin, T. Amemiya, L. A. Goodman, pp. 67–84. New York: Academic Press

Greene, W. H. 1990. *LIMDEP*. New York: Econometric Software

Gronau, R. 1974. Wage comparisons—selectivity bias. *J. Polit. Econ*. 82:1119–43

Grusky, D. B. 1986. *American Social Mobility in the 19th and 20th Centuries. CDE Working Paper 86–28*. Madison: Cent. Demogr. Ecol., Univ. Wisc.-Madison

Hagan, J. 1990. The gender stratification of income inequality among lawyers. Soc Forces 68:835–55

Hagan, J., Parker, P. 1985. White-collar crime and punishment. *Am. Sociol. Rev*. 50:302–16

Hannan, M. T., Tuma, N. B., Groeneveld, L. P. 1977. Income and marital events: evidence from an income-maintenance experiment. *Am. J. Sociol*. 82:1186–211

Hannan, M. T., Tuma, N. B., Groeneveld, L. P. 1978. Income and independence effects on marital dissolution: results from the Seattle and Denver income- maintenance experiments. *Am. J. Sociol*. 84:611–34

Hardle, W. 1990. *Applied Nonparametric Regression*. New York: Cambridge Univ. Press

Hardy, M. A. 1989. Estimating selection effects in occupational mobility in a 19th-century city. *Am. Sociol. Rev*. 54:834–43

Hausman, J. A., Wise, D. A. 1976. The evaluation of results from truncated samples: The New Jersey income maintenance experiment, *Ann. Econ. Soc. Measurement* 5/4:421–45

Hausman, J. A., Wise, D. A. 1977. Social experimentation, truncated distributions, and efficient estimation. *Econometrica* 45: 919–38

Heckman, J. J. 1974. Shadow prices, market wages and labor supply. *Econometrica* 42: 679–94

Heckman, J. J. 1976a. The common structure of statistical models of truncation, sample selection and limited dependent variables and a simple estimator for such models. *Ann. Econ. Soc. Measurement*. 5:475–92

Heckman, J. J. 1976b. Simultaneous equation models with continuous and discrete endogenous variables and structural shifts. In *Studies in Nonlinear Estimation,* ed. S. Goldfeld, R. Quandt, pp. 235–72. Cambridge, Mass: Ballinger

Heckman, J. J. 1978. Dummy endogenous variables in a simultaneous equation system. *Econometrica* 46:931–59

Heckman, J. J. 1979. Sample selection bias as a specification error. *Econometrica* 47:153–61

Heckman, J. J. 1987. Selection bias and self-selection. In *The New Palgrave,* ed. J. Eatwell, M. Milgate, P. Newmann, pp. 287–97. New York: Stockton

Heckman, J. J., Robb, R. 1985. Alternative methods for evaluating the impact of interventions. In *Longitudinal Analysis of Labor Market Data,* ed. J. J. Heckman, B. Singer, pp. 156–245. Cambridge: Cambridge Univ. Press

Heckman, J. J., Sedlacek, G. 1985. Heterogeneity, aggregation, and market wage functions: an empirical model of self-selection in the labor market. *J. Polit. Econ.* 93:1077–25

Heckman, J. J., Robb, R. 1986a. Alternative methods for solving the problem of selection bias in evaluating the impact of treatments on outcomes. In *Drawing Inferences from Self-Selected Samples,* ed. H. Wainer, pp. 63–107. New York: Springer- Verlag

Heckman, J. J., Robb, R. 1986b. Alternative identifying assumptions in econometric models of selection bias. Adv. Econ. 5:243–87

Heckman, J. J., Hotz, V. J. 1989. Choosing among alternative nonexperimental methods for estimating the impact of social programs: the case of manpower training. *J. Am. Stat. Assoc.* 84:862–74

Heckman, J. J., Honore, B. E. 1990. The empirical content of the Roy model. *Econometrica* 58:1121–50

Heckman, J. J., Sedlacek, G. 1990. Self-selection and the distribution of hourly wages. *J. Labor Econ.* 8:S329–63

Hoffman, P. T. 1984. Wills and statistics: tobit analysis and the counter reformation in Lyon. J. *Interdis. Hist.* 14:813–34

Holland, P. W. 1986. Statistics and causal inference. *J. Am. Stat. Assoc.* 81:945–70

Hurd, M. 1979. Estimation in truncated samples. *J. Economet.* 11:247–58

Ichimura, H. 1988. *Semiparametric Least Squares Estimation of Single Index Models. Technical Report*. Minneapolis: Dept. Econ., Univ. Minn., Minneapolis

Kalbfleisch, J. D., Prentice, R. L. 1980. *The Statistical Analysis of Failure Time Data.* New York: Wiley

Klein, R. W., Spady, R. S. 1987. An efficient semiparametric estimator of the binary response model. Morristown, NJ: Bell Commun. Res.

Lalonde, R. J. 1986. Evaluating the econometric evaluations of training programs with experimental data. *Am. Econ. Rev.* 76:604–20

Lalonde, R., Maynard, R. 1987. How precise are evaluations of employment and training programs: evidence from a field experiment. *Eval. Rev.* 11:428–51

Lancaster, T. 1990. *The Econometric Analysis of Transition Data.* Cambridge: Cambridge Univ. Press

Learmer, E. E. 1983. Model choice and specification analysis. In *Handbook of Econometrics,* Vol. 1, ed. Z. Griliches, M. D. Intriligator, pp. 284–327. Amsterdam: North-Holland

Lee, L. F. 1982. Some approaches to the correction of selectivity bias. *Rev. Econ. Stud.* 49:355–72

Lee, L. F. 1983. Generalized econometric models with selectivity. *Econometrica* 51: 507–12

Lewis, H. G. 1974. Comments on selectivity biases in wage comparisons. *J. Polit. Econ.* 82:1145–56

Lieberson, S. 1985. *Making it Count: The Improvement of Social Research and Theory*. Los Angeles: Univ. Calif. Press

Little, R. J. A., Rubin, D. B. 1987. *Statistical Analysis with Missing Data.* New York: Wiley

Maddala, G. S. 1983. *Limited-Dependent and Qualitative Variables in Econometrics.* Cambridge: Cambridge Univ. Press

Manski, C. F. 1975. Maximum score estimation of the stochastic utility model of choice. *J. Economet.* 3:205–28

Manksi, C. F. 1985. Semiparametric analysis of discrete response: asymptotic properties of the maximum score estimator. *J. Economet.* 27:313–33

Manski, C. F. 1989. Anatomy of the selection problem. *J. Hum. Resources* 24:343–60

Manski, C. F. 1990. Nonparametric bounds on treatment effects. *Am. Econ. Rev.* 80: 319–23

Manski, C. F. 1991. The selection problem. In *Advances in Econometrics 1990,* ed. C. Simms. New York: Cambridge Univ. Press

Manski, C. F., Wise, D. A. 1983. *College Choice in America.* Cambridge, Mass: Harvard Univ. Press

Manski, C. F., Garfinkel, I., eds. 1992. *Evaluating Welfare and Training Pro-*

grams. Cambridge, Mass: Harvard Univ. Press

Manski, C. F., McLanahan, S. S., Powers, D., Sandefur, G. D. 1992. Alternative estimates of the effects of family structure during adolescence on high school graduation. *J. Am. Stat. Assoc*. 54:25–37

Mare, R. D., Winship, C. 1984. The paradox of lessening racial inequality and joblessness among black youth: enrollment, enlistment, and employment, 1964–1981. *Am. Sociol. Rev*. 49:39–55

Mare, R. D., Winship, C., Kubitschek, W. N. 1984. The transition from youth to adult: understanding the age pattern of employment. *Am. J. Sociol*.. 89:326–58

Mare, R. D., Chen, M. D. 1986. Further evidence on number of siblings and educational stratification. *Am. Sociol. Rev*. 51:403–12

Mare, R. D., Winship, C. 1988. Endogenous switching regression models for the causes and effects of discrete variables. In *Common Problems/Proper Solutions: Avoiding Error in Quantitative Research,* ed. J. S. Long, pp. 132–60. Newbury Park, Ca lif: Sage

Marini, M. M., Singer, B. 1988. Causality in the social sciences. In *Sociological Methodology,* ed. C. C. Clogg, pp. 347–411. San Francisco: Jossey-Bass

Marsden, P. V., Hurlbert, J. S. 1987. Small networks and selectivity bias in the analysis of survey network data. *Soc. Networks* 9:333–49

Mroz, T. A. 1987. The sensitivity of an empirical model of married women's hours of work to economic and statistical assumptions. *Econometrica* 55:765–99

Nelson, F. D. 1984. Efficiency of the two-step estimator for models with endogenous sample selection. *J. Economet*. 24:181–96

Newey, W. K. 1990. *Two-step series estimation of sample selection models*. Pap. presented 1988 European Meet. Econometrica Soc.

Newey, W. K., Powell, J. L., Walker, J. R. 1990. Semiparametric estimation of selection models: some empirical results. *Am. Econ. Rev*. 80:324–28

Olson, R. J. 1980. A least squares correction for selectivity bias. *Econometrica* 48:1815–20

Peterson, R., Hagan, J. 1984. Changing conceptions of race: towards an account of anomalous findings of sentencing research. *Am. Sociol. Rev*. 49:56–70

Powell, J. L. 1987. *Semiparametric Estimation of Bivariate Latent Variable Models. Working Paper No. 8704*. Madison, Wisc: Soc. Systems Res. Inst., Univ. Wisc.

Powell, J. L., Stock, J. H., Stoker, T. M. 1989. Semiparametric estimation of index coefficients. *Econometrica* 57:1403–30

Robinson, P. M. 1988. Root-N-Consistent semiparametric regression. *Econometrica* 56:931–54

Rosenbaum, P., Rubin, D. B. 1983. The central role of the propensity score in observational studies for causal effects. *Biometrika* 70:41–55

Roy, A. D. 1951. Some thoughts on the distribution of earnings. *Oxford Econ. Pap*. 3:135–46

Rubin, D. B. 1978. Bayesian inference for causal effects: the role of randomization. *Ann. Statist*. 6:34–58

Ruud, P. 1986. Consistent estimation of limited dependent variable models despite misspecifications of distribution. *J. Economet*. 32:157–87

Sakamoto, A., Chen, M. D. 1991. Inequality and attainment in the dual labor market *Am. Sociol. Rev*. 56:295–308

Seltzer, J. A. 1991. Legal custody arrangements and children's economic welfare. *Am. J. Sociol*. 96:895–929

Seltzer, J. A., Garfinkel, I. 1990. Inequality in divorce settlements: an investigation of property settlements and child support awards. *Soc. Sci. Res*. 19:82–111

Steelman, L. C., Powell, B. 1989. Acquiring capital for college: the constraints of family configuration. *Am. Sociol. Rev*. 54:844–55

Stoker, T. M. 1986. Consistent estimates of scaled coefficients. *Econometrica* 54:1461-81

Stoker, T. M. 1991. Equivalence of direct, indirect, and slope estimators of average derivatives. In *Nonparametric and Semiparametric Methods in Econometricas and Statistics,* ed. W. A. Barnett, J. Powell, G. Tauchen, pp. 99–118. Cambridge: Cambridge Univ. Press

Stolzenberg, R. M., Relles, D. A. 1990. Theory testing in a world of constrained research design: the significance of Heckman's censored sampling bias correction for nonexperimental research. *Sociol. Meth. Res*. 18:395–415

Tobin, J. 1958. Estimation of relationships for limited dependent variables. *Econometrica* 26:24–36

Wainer, H., ed. 1986. *Drawing Inferences from Self-Selected Samples*. New York: Springer-Verlag

Willis, R- J., Rosen, S. 1979. Education and self-selection. *J. Polit. Econ*. 87:S507–36

Zatz, M. S., Hagan, J. 1985. Crime, time, and punishment: an exploration of selection bias in sentencing research. *J. Quant. Criminol*. 1:103–26

Annu. Rev. Sociol. 1992. 18:351–71

SOCIOLOGICAL PERSPECTIVES ON AMERICAN INDIANS

C. Matthew Snipp

340 Agriculture Hall, Department of Rural Sociology, University of Wisconsin-Madison, Madison, Wisconsin

KEY WORDS: American Indians, race and ethnicity, stratification, urbanization, demography

Abstract

The sociology of American Indians incorporates perspectives from across the social sciences. Recently, sociologists have taken a greater interest in American Indians, perhaps because American Indians have become increasingly visible in the diverse ethnic mosaic of American society. This review focuses on the position of American Indians in the US socioeconomic hierarchy: their numbers, where they live, and their social and economic well-being. The collapse and revitalization of the Indian population has been a central issue within American Indian demography. The recent growth in the population has been accompanied by increasing urbanization. These developments have significant implications for the socioeconomic well-being of American Indians in contemporary society.

INTRODUCTION

In the mosaic of American society, few groups are as embedded in the history, culture, and political system as American Indians.[1] American Indians are, of course, descendants of the first inhabitants of this land; many of this

[1]The terms Native American, American Indian, and Indian are used interchangeably in this discussion.

0360–0572/92/0815–0351$02.00

nation's most prominent geological features bear Indian names; Indians have an abiding presence in the national folklore; American Indians are the only ethnic group specifically recognized in the Constitution, and they continue to have a separate legal status different from that of other Americans. To highlight the unique social position of American Indians, this essay focuses on their numbers, where they reside, and the socioeconomic conditions in which they live.

A review is necessarily selective. The topics chosen are meant to provide readers with a basic understanding of the position of American Indians in the US socioeconomic hierarchy—a fundamental sociological concern. This discussion begins with the demography of American Indians which describes the near extinction and then resurgence of an Indian population that has, in turn, become increasingly urbanized. These processes are closely tied to the current socioeconomic status of American Indians, the final subject of this chapter.

Until recently, sociologists paid little attention to American Indians. The reasons for this neglect are not entirely clear. In contrast, historians, anthropologists, educators, and others have written extensively about American Indians. Thus, the literature relevant to the sociology of American Indians is disparate, spread widely across the disciplines of history and the social sciences.

One reason sociologists have written so little about American Indians may be that much of the discipline is oriented toward urban behavior and social organization. Among rural sociologists, agriculture and agricultural communities have been a central concern. Until recently, American Indians have lived in isolated rural enclaves, distant from the mainstream of urban American society. With a few exceptions, American Indians have not been heavily involved in farming, nor are reservations typically regarded as important agricultural regions. American Indians have remained outside ordinary sociological inquiry.

Until recently, data for American Indians have been sparse, and Indians have been largely invisible in national recordkeeping systems. Furthermore, American Indians are too few in number to permit reliable estimates from most surveys or public opinion polls. Data for American Indians are difficult to obtain. Studies of American Indians are frequently restricted to qualitative fieldwork, or case studies with small-scale surveys—research strategies deployed by individual scholars with limited resources. Large-scale surveys such as the General Social Survey or the Census Bureau's Current Population Survey lose sight of American Indians. Or, American Indians are overlooked in the first place. Topics that lend themselves to case studies or field observation such as patterns of drinking behavior or tribal politics are better researched.

Given the problems, the sparse sociological literature on American Indians is hardly surprising. However, as American Indians have increased in numbers and become more urbanized and more politically visible, they have received more attention from sociologists. Sociological interest is spurred by growing awareness that the recent large increases in the American Indian population are part of the increasing diversity of American society, with numbers of non-European ethnic minorities also growing. In this respect, the demography of American Indians is an exceedingly important subject.

THE DEMOGRAPHY OF AMERICAN INDIANS

The 1990 US census enumerated 2.0 million American Indians and Alaska Natives. This number is remarkable because the Indian population has not been this large for several centuries. From about 1500 to 1890, the American Indian population collapsed and seemed destined for extinction. American Indians may have numbered as many as ten million before European contact, but at the close of the nineteenth century, less than a quarter million survived (Thornton 1987, Dobyns 1983). The American Indian population has rebounded throughout this century, and particularly since 1950, there has been extraordinary growth.

Historical Demography: 1492 to 1890

POPULATION ESTIMATES Estimating the American Indian population circa 1500 has preoccupied an interdisciplinary group of scholars (Roberts 1989). Precontact population estimates have potentially important implications for assessments of the organizational complexity of indigenous American societies and the probable impact of European settlement. Large populations ostensibly require a high degree of political complexity to sustain social order; they are more likely to produce economic surpluses that make trade and trading networks possible; and large populations may be more likely to develop a complex symbolic culture. A large pre-Columbian population also means that the arrival of Europeans was an epic disaster for indigenous societies.

The precontact North American Indian population was once believed to be small, with a primitive level of social organization that was virtually unaffected by the arrival of Europeans. The first systematic estimates of the precontact population were published by Smithsonian anthropologist James Mooney in 1910 and later reevaluated by the eminent anthropologist, Alfred Kroeber (Swanton 1928, Kroeber 1939). By their reckoning, 900,000 to 1.15 million American Indians inhabited North America (above Mexico) around 1600.

The Mooney-Kroeber estimates became authoritative. They were not seriously challenged in scientific writing for nearly 30 years. Significantly, these estimates implied that precontact indigenous societies were rudimentary with very little cultural content.

In 1966, Dobyns argued that the Mooney-Kroeber estimates were seriously flawed because they depended on ethnohistorical sources such as diaries and mission records. Not only was such evidence inaccurate, it also failed to account for the massive mortality from European-borne diseases such as smallpox. Epidemics devastated Indian communities decades before extensive contact with Europeans. Dobyns used estimates of depopulation from disease and other causes to suggest that the precontact population was perhaps as large as ten to twelve million (Dobyns 1966).

Dobyns' research launched an intense debate that still goes on.[2] Early criticisms of Dobyns' analysis focused on flaws in his methodology (Driver 1969, Thornton & Marsh-Thornton 1981). Nonetheless, revisions of Dobyns' estimates yielded numbers significantly larger than the Mooney-Kroeber figures (cf Thornton & Marsh-Thornton 1981). Ubelaker (1976a,b) reconstructed Mooney's estimates from his original notes and concluded that Mooney's estimate should have been near 2.2 million instead of the published estimate of 1.15 million.

There are many other estimates of the precontact American Indian population (Johansson 1982). For example, Denevan (1976) proposed a 1492 population of 4.4 million. Dobyns (1983) reestimated that the population north of Mesoamerica might have been 18 million. There are at least 18 different estimates of the pre-Columbian North American population that range from 900,000 to 18 million (Thornton 1987, p. 26).

Consensus exists only on three points. The first is that the Mooney-Kroeber estimates are too low—but how much too low is unclear. Second, larger populations imply that American Indian societies were more complex than once believed. Third, the arrival of Europeans nearly eradicated the American Indian population.

CAUSES OF DECLINE The American Indian population collapse had three main causes: epidemic disease, warfare, and genocide. Epidemic disease was the deadliest factor. European-borne diseases sparked "virgin soil" epidemics that spread quickly throughout the Americas (Crosby 1972, 1976, Dobyns 1983, Thornton 1987, MacNeill 1976). Diseases common in Europe and Africa—smallpox, cholera, typhus, diphtheria, and influenza for instance—were unknown in the western hemisphere (McNeill 1976).

American Indians had no acquired immunity to these diseases, and this made epidemics especially nightmarish. For example, an epidemic in the high

[2]Dobyns' work is part of a large body of research dealing with the aboriginal population of the western hemisphere; see for example Cook & Borah (1960, 1971, 1974), and Denevan (1976).

plains decimated two Mandan villages, reducing their number from about 2000 to perhaps less than 40 in a few weeks (McNeill 1976, p. 205). The Pilgrims benefitted from a series of epidemics that annihilated eleven Massachusetts Indian towns along the coast bearing their name, leaving the land open for settlement (Ubelaker 1976b). The English colonists viewed epidemics as evidence of God's favor, making their settlements preordained by a higher power (Thornton 1987).

Smallpox often killed its victims within a few hours (McNeill 1976). The first smallpox epidemic occurred within a few years of Columbus's arrival. Some speculate that in 1520–1524, the first outbreak of smallpox spread across the Americas with mortality perhaps exceeding 50% (Dobyns 1983, p. 13).[3] The virulence of epidemic disease caused one missionary in 1699 to write that "the Indians die so easily that the bane look and smell of a Spaniard causes them to give up the ghost" (quoted in Crosby 1972, p. 58).

Warfare with Euro-Americans and with other tribes also took a toll on American Indian lives, though mortality from wars was less than from disease. The federal government has assumed responsibility for at least 30,000 war-related Indian deaths and acknowledged that this estimate was probably too low (Thornton 1987, p. 49). Furthermore, deaths in wars before 1776 should be added to this number, along with deaths in conflicts with other Indians and in individual skirmishes with non-Indians at the frontier. In reality, it is impossible to determine precisely how many American Indians lost their lives in warfare. The number of casualties may have been as low as 150,000, or as high as 500,000 (Thornton 1987, p. 49).

The impact of genocide is even more difficult to assess. Incidents involving the premeditated extermination of Indian populations have been documented for the eastern seaboard, Texas, and California (Jennings 1975, Thornton 1987). The California Indian population declined from over 250,000 to less than 20,000 within 100 years. Mooney ascribed this collapse mainly to the predations of the Spanish missions and "to the cruelties and wholesale massacres perpetrated by the miners and early settlers" (quoted in Thornton 1987, p. 49).

One of the difficulties in assessing the impact of genocide is definitional. If genocide includes the lives lost from the destruction of tribal culture, then its impact can be seen as much greater. In the first half of the nineteenth century, tens of thousands of Indians were removed forcibly from their homes east of the Mississippi and moved west. The most infamous of these removals was the so-called "Trail of Tears" in which the Cherokee lost nearly half of their 20,000 population (Thornton 1984, 1990). Removals of other tribes were also devastating though less well-known (Foreman 1932). In addition to the eastern removals, the destruction of the great buffalo herds in the west

[3]Dobyns (1983) provides a useful chronology of known epidemics in North America.

undermined the plains tribal cultures. The forced settlement of these nomadic tribes on reservations led to deadly outbreaks of famine, disease, and violence (Thornton 1987).

Contemporary Perspectives: 1890–1990

POPULATION GROWTH Modern American Indian demography coincides with the final major Indian-military skirmish at Wounded Knee, South Dakota (1894), the closing of the frontier, and the spread of large-scale industrial capitalism. With American Indians removed from the east and settled on reservations in the west, hostile public opinion toward Indians diminished. In fact, the steady decline of the Indian population coincided with public policies to hasten the anticipated extinction of American Indians by encouraging cultural assimilation (Hoxie 1984). Measures were adopted to pressure Indians into farming (Carlson 1981), and boarding schools tried to eradicate all traces of tribal culture from Indian children (Szasz 1977).

The results of these efforts, in retrospect, might not have been what reformers of the time hoped. Despite a long and deliberate campaign to extinguish tribal culture, often with oppressive measures (Hoxie 1984, Prucha 1984), the wholesale assimilation of American Indians failed to materialize. In fact, the American Indian population has grown steadily throughout this century: somewhat slowly from 1900 to 1950, but rapidly since then (Snipp 1989), and tribal culture is flourishing.

Since 1950, the Indian population has grown dramatically. High birthrates and increased longevity have had an obvious role, but there are also other reasons (Thornton et al 1991, Snipp 1989). Until recently the Census Bureau miscounted American Indians, especially in cities. In a special report for the 1950 Census, the Census Bureau concluded that urban Indians are "substantially misclassified" (US Bureau of the Census 1953, p. 3–5B). In 1960, the Census Bureau changed its procedures and implemented racial self-identification. This improved the coverage of persons not easily identified by enumerators as American Indian, resulting in an increase of about 47%. Another large increase also was documented for 1970, and an even larger increase of 73% was recorded in the 1980 census. Changes in racial self-identification account for much of this growth—though how much is uncertain (Passell 1976, Passell & Berman 1986, Snipp 1989).

Little attention has been paid to American Indian self-identification. It is clear that the boundaries of the American Indian population are fluid. American Indians have had exceedingly high rates of intermarriage with non-Indians (Thornton et al 1991). Recent data indicate that American Indians continue to be highly exogamous, especially in diverse urban marriage markets (Sandefur & McKinnell 1986, Snipp 1989).

The high rates of intermarriage among American Indians have implications for understanding the large increases in the American Indian population since 1960. Historically high rates of intermarriage obviously have meant that there are large numbers of persons with mixed ancestry—empirical evidence attests to this fact (Snipp 1989). In the past, many American Indians may have chosen to identify themselves as "white." Until recently, identifying oneself as an ethnic minority was tantamount to acknowledging a social stigma, and it exposed oneself to discrimination in housing and employment, among other problems.

Furthermore, for most of this century, the federal government has attempted to destroy all vestiges of tribal culture (Hoxie 1984). Especially insidious were efforts to indoctrinate Indian children with the notion that tribal culture was a stigma to be remedied by emulating the ideals of Euro-American society (Szasz 1977). Hence, powerful incentives prompted persons of mixed ancestry to discard, conceal, or omit their American Indian background, regardless of their cultural upbringing. However, this situation changed dramatically after 1960.

The 1960s and 1970s have been described as "a propitious time for ethnicity" (Roosens 1989, p. 17), and certainly it was a time for a reawakening or resurgence in American Indian ethnic identification. Events in this period included large scale political mobilization, articulation of a pan-Indian ideology, efforts to promote the renewal of tribal culture, and a resurgence of personal pride in American Indian ancestry (Hertzberg 1971, Nagel 1986, Cornell 1988, Roosens 1989, Weibel-Orlando 1991). These developments made American Indian ethnic identification more acceptable.

URBANIZATION OF AMERICAN INDIANS

American Indian Rural-Urban Migration

In modern history, American Indians have never been an urban population.[4] In 1980, about half of the Indian population resided in rural areas (Snipp 1989). As recently as 1930, barely 10% of American Indians lived in urban areas while over half of all other Americans were city dwellers.

Price (1968) observed distinct generations of urban Indian immigrants to Los Angeles. The first generation, composed mainly of Oklahoma Indians, arrived during the 1930s, and then later in the 1940s and early 1950s. Many of these Indians were fleeing the hardships of dustbowl Oklahoma, and then later, were taking advantage of the massive economic growth in post-war California (Price 1968).

[4]There is, however, ample evidence that some pre-Columbian societies lived in large, complex settlements, especially in the southwest and Mississippi river valley (see Thornton et al 1982). The Cahokia settlement near what is now St. Louis, Missouri may have had a population as large as 40,000 (Peregrine 1991).

The second wave of immigrants identified by Price (1968) were the result of "Termination" era programs implemented by the federal government in the early 1950s (Fixico 1986). These programs were designed to abolish the special status of Indian lands and encourage reservation Indians to move to preselected urban areas. Termination policies and relocation efforts fell out of favor in the late 1960s and were repudiated by new legislation in 1975 (Sorkin 1978, Fixico 1986, O'Brien 1989, Gross 1989).

The effects of the urban relocation programs have not received much attention, but they appear to have had far-reaching impacts. Between 1952 and 1972, over 100,000 American Indians were assisted in moving to urban residences (Margon 1976, Sorkin 1978, p. 25). Of course, many of these relocatees did not stay in urban areas, and high program drop-outs rates were cited by critics of relocation (Fixico 1986, O'Brien 1989). Yet, most of the cities that were once served as relocation centers still have large Indian populations (Snipp 1989).

The economic benefits of urban relocation are questionable. Some evidence suggests that urban relocation improved the economic circumstances of participants (Clinton et al 1975, Sorkin 1978), while other studies are less sanguine (Gundlach & Roberts 1978, Snipp & Sandefur 1988, O'Brien 1989).

Of course, the federal government's attempts to relocate reservation Indians were not the only factors involved in the urbanization of American Indians. Census data indicate that Indians participate in the same migration streams as other US residents, and except for a brief hiatus in the 1970s, these streams have taken population away from rural areas (Long 1988, Snipp 1989). Furthermore, about 25,000 American Indians participated in World War II (Hagan 1979, p. 158), and this experience also encouraged urban settlement (Hagan 1979, Fixico 1986).

Not surprisingly, the factors affecting American Indian rural-urban migration are complex. Perceived opportunities in urban labor markets, the chance to escape reservation poverty, and inducements such as those offered in the relocation programs were obviously important (Hackenberg & Wilson 1972). However, offsetting the usual economic reasons for leaving the reservation were ceremonial obligations, extended family ties, language barriers, and a distaste for urban life—all powerful sources of residential inertia (Hodge 1971).

Adaptation to Urban Environments

The large influx of American Indians to urban areas prompted numerous studies in the 1960s and early 1970s (Thornton et al 1982). This work often focused on how American Indians coped with the alien culture and lifestyle they found in cities. Cultural assimilation was a central theme in this literature.

Ablon (1964, 1965, 1971) focused on the experiences of Indians who arrived in the San Francisco Bay Area via the Bureau of Indian Affairs' (BIA's) relocation programs. She observed that newly urbanized American Indians often did not adjust easily to city life. Urban relocatees typically lacked the skills needed to compete successfully in urban labor markets, and the BIA often failed to address the needs of relocated Indians (Ablon 1964, 1971). Ablon observed that urban Indians did not readily surrender their culture for the sake of joining the urban mainstream; instead, they steadfastly resisted assimilation.

The experience of urban American Indians contradicted assimilationist expectations. Unlike other urban immigrants, American Indians did not readily adopt Euro-American culture. Racial discrimination may have posed barriers that denied entry into the dominant culture (Bahr & Chadwick 1972). Studies of urban Indian populations also documented the persistence of tribal culture and ethnic identity (Chadwick & Stauss 1975, Guillemin 1975, Chadwick & White 1973, Roy 1962, Stauss & Chadwick 1979, Waddell & Watson 1971).

American Indian resistance to assimilating Euro-American ways has caused social scientists to rethink expectations for this group. Attention has shifted from the anticipated dissolution of Indian culture toward explanations for the apparent persistence and vitality of cultural traditions in urban environments (Vogt 1957).

One explanation for the persistence of tribal culture among urban American Indians can be found in the ways they are able to transform ordinary urban landscapes to make them suitable for cultural expression (Guillemin 1975). For example, the dangers and physical demands of high steel construction work allowed Mohawk men opportunities to exhibit the bravery and risk-taking traditionally expected of them (Blumenfeld 1965).

Four institutions that are particularly important arenas of social interaction and cultural expression are bars, pow-wows, Indian Centers, and churches (Weibel-Orlando 1991). Pow-wows are community events imported from reservation traditions to urban venues. On reservations, pow-wows are held in ceremonial locations while in urban areas they are most often sponsored by informal groups or pan-Indian organizations and held in gyms or public auditoriums. Similarly, urban Indian churches resemble reservation missions (Weibel-Orlando 1991), and bars and Indian Centers provide urban analogues to the off-reservation bars and tribal headquarters of reservation life (Weibel-Orlando 1991).

Another important factor in the persistence of urban Indian ethnicity has been the emergence of pan-Indianism. This is a supra-tribal ideology that unites the interests of American Indians by virtue of their common heritage, independent of the social and political agendas of particular tribes (Thomas 1965). Pan-Indianism is particularly important as a unifying force because urban Indian populations are tribally heterogeneous.

Although pan-Indianism has flourished with the recent growth of urban Indian populations (Cornell 1988), its roots are relatively old. Around 1807, the Shawnee war chief Tehcumseh organized a pan-Indian revolt against encroaching western settlers (Prucha 1984). Later in the century, the Ghost Dance movement spread among numerous tribes in the west (Thornton 1986). However, modern pan-Indianism has its origins in Indian organizations that were formed in the early twentieth century (Hertzberg 1971).

In the late nineteenth century, responding to the federal government's systematic campaign to destroy all traces of traditional tribal culture (Hoxie 1984), Indian advocacy groups and organizations formed to preserve it (Hagan 1985). These groups resembled benevolent societies and were often organized by mixed-ancestry Indians who had moved to the city, working with the non-Indian supporters (Hertzberg 1971).

The spread of pan-Indianism has been extremely important since 1950 as an organizational basis for urban Indian social life (Cornell 1988). With a few exceptions, community events and social gatherings for urban Indians are typically pan-Indian affairs—all tribes are welcome. Furthermore, the ideology of pan-Indianism has been important for political mobilization (Nagel 1986). This ideology has been the basis for mobilizing political action for local controversies (Weibel-Orlando 1991) as well as for building support for Indian issues across the nation (Cornell 1988).

Alcohol Consumption, Crime, and Mental Health

Alcohol abuse and related health problems are a leading killer of American Indians on reservations and in cities alike (Snipp 1989). Some evidence suggests that the sociological etiology of problem drinking varies for urban and reservation Indians (May 1977).

The transition to urban life may be one factor responsible for problem drinking among urban Indians. The move to an urban area is for some, if not many, American Indians an intensely alienating and anomic experience (Graves 1971). It removes them from the tightly bonded social milieu of reservation life and places them in foreign, disorienting city environments.

The loss of traditional social ties and family bonds is anomic and promotes heavy drinking and related problems such as incidents with police (Ablon 1965, Ferguson 1968, Graves 1971, Dozier 1966, Littman 1970). Problem drinking may also be exacerbated because Indian communities, urban or reservation, have neither acknowledged the problems of alcoholism nor discouraged excessive alcohol consumption, suggest Littman (1970) and Locklear (1977). However, other authors are skeptical about this explanation (Lemert 1982). Recent evidence clearly shows that American Indian communities are aware of the problems caused by excessive alcohol consumption and that they have taken measures to prevent it (Weibel-Orlando 1990).

Urban Indian drinking may also differ from that of reservation Indians because of the importance of urban "Indian bars" as social institutions (Ablon 1965, Weibel-Orlando 1990). Indian bars are a venue for affirming ethnic identity within the community. Furthermore, in urban areas where substantial status differences exist within the Indian community, shared drinking experiences in a recognized Indian bar may be an important "leveling" mechanism for building ethnic solidarity. Shared drinking experiences among urban Indians may be "a way for one successful in the larger society to demonstrate to fellow Indians that he is still 'Indian'" (Thornton et al 1982, p. 43). In one study, local Indian leaders reported that drinking in the local Indian bar was important for staying in touch with their constituents (Weibel-Orlando 1990).

It should hardly be surprising that excessive alcohol consumption leads to encounters with police. American Indian arrest rates are considerably higher than for blacks or whites. However, a very large number of these arrests are for alcohol related offenses (Jensen et al 1977, May 1982). One study found that 71% of the Indian arrests appearing in Uniform Crime Report data were connected with alcohol (Stewart 1964, quoted in May 1982). This study also found that American Indians are disproportionately represented in prison populations. Other studies report that once arrested, American Indians receive harsher treatment in the judicial system, and that they do not effectively utilize resources such as legal assistance (Hall & Simkus 1975, Hagan 1976, May 1982).

While alcohol related offenses appear to make up the bulk of American Indian arrests, American Indians are not more predisposed to other kinds of criminal activity than other groups (May 1982). For instance, homicide is about as common on the Navajo reservation as it is in the population at large (May 1982). Likewise, property crimes are not reported at excessively high rates for American Indians (May 1982).

One explanation for American Indian criminality focuses on the alienation of urban life, the disorganizing influence of relocation, and the absence of traditional institutions for restraining individual behavior (Graves 1971, Garbarino 1971). Another perspective emphasizes discrimination, oversurveillance by police, and differential sentencing (Hagan 1976, Hall & Simkus 1975, Chadwick et al 1976). May (1982) also points out that the existing literature has failed to address some potentially unique characteristics of American Indian criminal behavior. One is that American Indians, at least those living on reservations, are subject to a special criminal code; there is a differential use of police force on reservations; and the Indian population is extremely young, and hence at risk for delinquent behavior (May 1982, p. 235).

The mental health of urban Indians has not received much attention in the sociological literature. Some studies have focused on the emotional adjustment of urban American Indians. Urban relocation is a predictably stressful event with consequences for other spheres of daily life such as marital stability (Garbarino 1971). Likewise, Olson (1971) argues that the development of a distinctive ethnic identity by urban Indians is a response to the loss of other elements of their cultural environment.

Mental health professionals have written extensively about the unique psychological needs of American Indians (cf May & Dizmang 1974). Some writers stress that there are profound differences in the needs of American Indians compared with other groups (Foster 1988). Other specialists tend to downplay these differences (Fuchs & Havighurst 1972, Chapter 6). In any event, the sociological literature on this subject is sparse and one to which sociologists could make valuable contributions.

STRATIFICATION AND DEVELOPMENT

Poverty

Historically, American Indians have been one of the poorest segments of American society. The economic standing of American Indians lagged behind that of African-Americans until 1980. Small gains for Indians in the 1970s and declining conditions for blacks have resulted recently in economic parity between these groups (Snipp 1989).

The dire economic circumstances of American Indians were not systematically documented until the 1920s when a commission under the leadership of Lewis Meriam undertook an extensive study of American Indians and federal policies affecting them[5] (Institute for Government Research 1928, Prucha 1984). The so-called *Meriam Report* found American Indians living in extreme economic hardship; the report harshly criticized the federal government. Not only was this study an early benchmark, it also served as the blueprint for economic reforms enacted by the Roosevelt Administration as part of the "Indian New Deal" (Prucha 1984).

Despite the promises of the Indian New Deal, American Indians did not participate in the general economic recovery that accompanied World War II. In the aftermath of World War II, little attention was paid to the economic

[5]This research was sponsored by the Institute for Government Research, a forerunner of the Brookings Institution.

problems of Indian country. Indeed, throughout the 1950s, federal policymakers implemented the notorious Termination legislation to abolish Indian lands (Fixico 1986).

In the 1960s, the rediscovery of poverty also meant a new recognition of American Indian hardships. The problem of poverty among American Indians was documented in a number of reports published in this period (Brophy & Aberle 1966, Sorkin 1971, Levitan & Hetrick 1971, Levitan & Johnston 1975). These publications described the poor living conditions and limited economic opportunities for American Indians.

In the late 1960s, near the peak of the so-called War on Poverty, American Indians were one of the most disadvantaged groups in American society: the poorest, least educated, most unemployed, and unhealthiest (Levitan & Hetrick 1971). In 1969, one third of all American Indian families had incomes below the official poverty threshold, and this number was higher for reservation families (Snipp 1989). Similarly, in 1970, less than half of all reservation adults were in the labor force, and reservation unemployment rates frequently exceeded 20% (Snipp 1989).

The descriptive work of the late 1960s and early 1970s was followed by a number of methodologically sophisticated studies aimed at finding the causes of poverty and unemployment among American Indians. This work attempted to construct multivariate models with data from large-scale surveys (Gundlach & Roberts 1978, Gwartney & Long 1978, Trosper 1980, Sandefur & Scott 1983, Snipp & Sandefur 1988). The findings from these studies were not surprising in showing that human capital—education and experience—were essential for competing successfully in the job market. American Indians typically had few of the resources necessary to compete in the labor market.

Labor market discrimination may also contribute to the disadvantages of American Indian workers. To the extent that discrimination can be estimated in multivariate models, some evidence suggests that it exists (Gwartney & Long 1978, Trosper 1980). However, Sandefur & Scott (1983) discount the impact of discrimination. Whether discrimination is a serious problem for American Indian workers is unclear. However, unlike women and African-Americans, there is little research showing that American Indians are systematically segregated into lower status, lesser paid occupations.

Of course, American Indian women are certainly not immune from gender discrimination. They are systematically paid less than their male counterparts in similar circumstances (Snipp 1990, Snipp & Aytac 1990). Yet we know very little about the special circumstances of American Indian women.

Persistently high poverty rates have led some researchers to suggest that some reservations are ripe for the development of an "underclass" (Sandefur 1989). However, there is little or no research about reservation "underclasses," and disagreements about the meaning of the concept limit work on this subject (Sandefur 1989). Informal economies also are known to thrive on reservations, but little has been written about them (Sherman 1988).

Education

The persistent finding that American Indians lack the skills and especially the education to successfully compete in the job market underscores a pressing problem. In 1970, only 22% of American Indian adults had completed high school, while 55% of white adults had done so (Snipp 1989). Ten years later, 56% of American Indians reported 12 or more years of schooling (69% for white adults), but such gains are somewhat misleading because GEDs among American Indians are widespread (Snipp 1989). Perhaps a more telling statistic is that in 1980, 26% of Indian youths aged 16 to 19 had withdrawn from school without a diploma (US Bureau of the Census 1983).

The lack of education among American Indians does not result from a lack of exposure to educational institutions. American Indians have a long history of experience with western education under the auspices of missionaries and federal authorities (Szasz 1977, 1988, Fuchs & Havighurst 1972). Until recently, these schools have been far more concerned with "civilizing" American Indians, that is, detribalizing and acculturating them, than with educating them (Fuchs & Havighurst 1972, Szasz 1977, Hoxie 1984).

Changes in federal policy since the mid-1970s facilitated the participation of American Indians in educational systems (Szasz 1977, Gross 1989). Indian school board members and tribally controlled school systems are considerably more common than in the past. Perhaps most significant is that 24 tribally controlled colleges have formed in the past 25 years (Carnegie Foundation 1989). Most of these fledgling institutions are two-year community colleges though a few offer baccalaureate and master's degrees. These institutions are especially significant because of the dearth of American Indians with advanced education.

The sharp rise in numbers of high school graduates has not translated into an equal rise in college attendance. In fact, some evidence suggests that American Indian college entrants have diminished since the 1960s (Snipp 1989). Of American Indians who attend college, approximately 88% typically enroll in public institutions (Fries 1987).

Furthermore, from 1975 to 1981, the number of American Indian baccalaureate degree recipients stayed nearly constant—about 3500—despite an increase in the "college age" population (Fries 1987). Over half of these degrees were in the social sciences, education, and the humanities. Barely 20% were in the physical or biological sciences. A small increase in American Indian doctorates occurred, but the numbers are exceedingly small: rising from 93 in 1975–1976 to 130 in 1980–1981 (Fries 1987).

Reservation Development

Most discussions of reservation development focus on the social and economic structure of reservations and their position in the regional, national, or even international economy (Stanley 1978, Vinje 1982). The literature on international development, especially for Third World countries has been especially influential. Concepts such as dependency, internal colonialism, and incorporation into the world economy frequently have been used to explain the economic position of American Indian tribes.

Economic dependency describes the lack of economic power that American Indians possess in relation to non-Indians. The unequal distribution of power in the market skews bargaining relationships in favor of non-Indians and facilitates the exploitation of Indians (White 1983). Furthermore, this unequal balance of power is sustained by the political and military dominance of the federal government (Jorgensen 1978).

The origins and reproduction of economic dependency among Indians typically is explained in terms of contact with Europeans and their capitalistic economic systems (White 1983). The colonial fur trade was particularly instrumental in bringing American Indians into the world economy (Wolf 1982). The international spread of capitalism meant that American Indians acquired production technologies—guns, steel traps, and knives—that made them more efficient hunters (Kandulias 1990).

European mercantilists enjoyed a monopoly over manufactured goods, but the decentralized organization of many American Indian societies made a similar monopoly over furs much more difficult to achieve (White 1983). While some groups such as the Iroquois were relatively effective in organizing trade relations with Europeans (Bradley 1987), many other tribes were considerably less successful. American Indian dependency on manufactured goods and European control over the supply of these goods gave European traders a powerful lever in negotiations (Hall 1989).

In the twentieth century, Euro-American control over product markets for resources such as coal and agriculture has been blamed for reproducing economic dependency, in a manner not unlike the fur trade (Jorgensen 1978, Ruffing 1978). American Indians are highly dependent on Euro-American business interests for access to the capital and technology they need to develop their reservations (Gilbreath 1973, Snipp 1988b, White 1990). This dependency has often resulted in gross exploitation if not outright fraud (Richardson & Farrell 1983, Ambler 1990).

The process by which American Indians have been brought into the world economy and made economically dependent has been described as "incorporation" (Wolf 1982, Hall 1989, Chase-Dunn & Hall 1991). This concept describes the process governing contacts between pre-capitalist and capitalist societies—a subject that Hall (1989) argues is overlooked in the world systems literature. Compared with assimilationist perspectives that predict cultural change or absorption as a result of contact, incorporation implies that precapitalist societies become encapsulated and deliberately isolated for the purpose of economic exploitation.

The incorporation of American Indian societies is consistent with perspectives of reservations as "internal colonies." Internal colonialism is another term borrowed from the development literature (see Hechter 1975) that has been widely influential in describing the isolated, dependent conditions among American Indians (Hagen & Schaw 1960, Anders 1979, 1980, 1981, Bee & Gingerich 1971, Watkins 1977, Ortiz 1980, Snipp 1986).

In many respects, internal colonialism appears to be a particularly apt description for many Indian reservations. They are often located in isolated areas, highly dependent on external sources for goods and services, and their quasi-sovereign political status further isolates them from Euro-American society. The neo-colonial analogy is perhaps most striking for those reservations with significant natural resources. Reservation resources most often at stake include agricultural lands (Levitan & Johnston 1975, Carlson 1981), water (McCool 1987), timber (AIPRC 1977), and energy resources (Jorgensen et al 1978, Ortiz 1979, 1980, Ambler 1990). Notably, while reservation resources have been sought by Euro-American interests, American Indian labor has seldom been the object of capitalist expansion (Miner 1976, Jacobsen 1984).

Proponents of internal colonialism models argue that as in other colonial relations, natural resources are extracted from reservations as raw materials for processing elsewhere. These resources are returned to the reservation as manufactured goods sold for premium prices. The dependency and attendant exploitation inherent in this relationship is manifest in several ways. One is that reservations seldom have control over resource development (Ortiz 1979, Jorgensen et al 1978). Only recently have Indian tribes organized for the purpose of sharing bargaining resources and gaining control over reservation development (Ambler 1990). Perhaps most revealing is that members of tribes with significant energy resources do not have a higher standard of living than members of less well-endowed tribes (Snipp 1988b).

Although natural resource development is perhaps most highly visible, other types of development also have been taking place. By virtue of their location and a multitude of other factors, reservations face many obstacles to economic growth (Gilbreath 1973, Cornell & Kalt 1990, Snipp & Summers 1991a,b). However, some reservations have been especially successful pursuing a market strategy tagged as "the legal road to economic development" (Olson 1988).

Ethnic enterprises are often successful because they find a vacant niche in the market (Waldinger et al 1990). The "legal road to economic development" is a type of ethnic entrepreneurship built around the unique legal and political status of American Indians. This status gives them access to market niches not available to other potential competitors. For example, the Boldt decision provided tribes living around the Puget Sound of Washington State with fishing rights to 50% of the salmon harvest. This enabled them to develop a vigorous fishing and aquaculture industry. Other tribes have used money from treaty rights settlements for investment purposes (White 1990). Tribes also have used this strategy to develop gambling and duty-free stores exempt from state taxes and regulation. Others have entertained proposals for hazardous waste sites, circumventing state and local regulations.

CONCLUSION

The certainty that American Indians will disappear from society no longer exists. On the contrary, on the eve of the Columbian quincentennary, American Indians are more numerous than they have been for several centuries. Perhaps this bodes well for the rest of the nation. As the noted jurist Felix Cohen wrote "Like the miner's canary, the Indian marks the shift from fresh air to poison gas in our political atmosphere; and our treatment of Indians, even more than our treatment of other minorities, reflects the rise and fall in our democratic faith" (quoted in Fey & McNickle 1959, p. vi).

The growth in numbers of American Indians has been accompanied by increasing diversity. This has meant large changes in the ways that Indians earn their livelihood, practice their culture, and conceive of their identity. Yet American Indians have successfully maintained their distinctive position in a large and complex society.

Like the people to which it is devoted, the sociology of American Indians is a small but growing literature. It includes many issues that could not be covered in the space of this article. But heeding Cohen's words, there can be little doubt that this literature will continue to offer important insights about American Indians and the larger society in which they live.

Acknowledgments

I would like to thank Joane Nagel and two anonymous reviewers for helpful comments on an earlier draft of this manuscript.

Literature Cited

Ablon, J. 1964. Relocated American Indians in the San Francisco bay area: social interactions and Indian identity. *Hum. Organ.* 23:296–304

Ablon, J. 1965. American Indian relocation: problems of dependency and management in the city. *Phylon* 26:362–71

Ablon, J. 1971. Retention of cultural values and differential urban adaptation: Samoans and American Indians in a west coast city. *Soc. Forc.* 49:385–93

Ambler, M. 1990. *Breaking the Iron Bonds.* Lawrence, Kans: Univ. Press Kans.

American Indian Policy Review Commission (AIPRC). 1977. *Final Report of the American Indian Policy Review Commission.* Washington, DC: US Govt. Printing Off. (USGPO)

Anders, G. 1979. The internal colonization of Cherokee Native Americans. *Dev. Change* 10:41–55

Anders, G. 1980. Theories of underdevelopment and the American Indian. *J. Econ. Issues* 40:681–701

Anders, G. 1981. The reduction of a self-sufficient people to poverty and welfare dependence: an analysis of the causes of Cherokee Indian underdevelopment. *Am. J. Econ. Sociol.* 40:225–37

Bahr, H. M., Chadwick, B. A. 1972. Contemporary perspectives on American Indians: a review essay. *Soc. Sci. Q.* 53:606–18

Bee, R. L., R. Gingerich. 1971. Colonialism, classes, and ethnic identity: Native Americans and the national political economy. *Stud. Comp. Natl. Dev.* 12:70–93

Blumenfield, R. 1965. Mohawks: round trip to the high steel. *Transaction* 3:19–22

Bradley, J. W. 1987. *Evolution of the Onondaga Iroquois.* Syracuse, NY: Syracuse Univ. Press

Brophy, W. A., Aberle, S. D. 1966. *The Indian: America's Unfinished Business.* Norman, Okla: Univ. Okla. Press

Carlson, L. A. 1981. *Indians, Land, and Bureaucrats.* Westport, Conn: Greenwood

Carnegie Foundation for the Advancement of Teaching. 1989. *Tribal Colleges: Shaping the Future of Native Americans.* Princeton, NJ: Princeton Univ. Press

Chadwick, B. A., White, L. C. 1973. Correlates of length of urban residence among Spokane Indians. *Hum. Organ.* 32:9–16

Chadwick, B. A., Stauss, J. 1975. The assimilation of American Indians into urban society: the Seattle case. *Hum. Organ.* 34:359–69

Chadwick, B. A., Stauss, J., Bahr, H. M., Halverson, L. K. 1976. Confrontation with the law: the case of American Indians in Seattle. *Phylon* 37:163–71

Chase-Dunn, C., Hall, T. D., eds. 1991a. *Core/Periphery Relations in Precapitalist Worlds.* Boulder, Colo: Westview

Chase-Dunn, C., Hall, T. D. 1991b. Conceptualizing core/periphery hierarchies for comparative study. See Chase-Dunn & Hall 1991, pp. 5–44

Christenson, J. A., Flora, C. B. eds. 1991. *Rural Policy in the 1990s.* Boulder, Colo: Westview. In press

Clinton, L., Chadwick, B. A., Bahr, H. M. 1975. Urban relocation reconsidered: antecedents of employment among Indian males. *Rur. Sociol.* 40:117–33

Cook, S. F., Borah, W. 1960. *The Indian Population of Central Mexico, 1531–1610. Ibero-Americana, No. 4.* Berkeley, Calif: Univ. Calif. Press

Cook, S. F., Borah, W. 1971–1974. *Essays in Population History: Mexico and the Caribbean.* Vols. 1–2. Berkeley, Calif: Univ. Calif. Press

Cornell, S. 1988. *The Return of the Native.* New York: Oxford Univ. Press

Cornell, S., Kalt, J. P. 1990. Pathways from poverty: economic development and institution-building on American Indian reservations. *Am. Indian Cult. Res. J.* 14:89–125

Crosby, A. W. Jr. 1972. *The Columbian Exchange: Biological and Cultural Consequences of 1492.* Westport, Conn: Greenwood

Crosby, A. W. Jr. 1976. Virgin soil epidemics as a factor in the aboriginal depopulation in America. *Wm. Mary Q.* 33:289–99

Denevan, W. M. 1976. *The Native Population of the Americas in 1492.* Madison, Wisc: Univ. Wisc. Press

Dobyns, H. F. 1966. Estimating aboriginal American population: an appraisal of techniques with a new hemispheric estimate. *Curr. Anthro.* 7:395–416

Dobyns, H. F. 1983. *Their Number Become Thinned.* Knoxville, Tenn: Univ. Tenn. Press

Dozier, E. P. 1966. Problem drinking among American Indians: the role of socio-cultural deprivation. *Q. J. Stud. Alcohol.* 27:72–87

Driver, H. E. 1969. *Indians of North America.* Chicago: Univ. Chicago. 2nd ed. rev.

Duncan, C. M. ed. 1991. *Rural Poverty in America.* Westport, Conn: Greenwood

Ferguson, F. N. 1968. Navajo drinking: some tentative hypotheses. *Hum. Organ.* 27:159–67

Fey, H. E., McNickle, D. 1959. *Indians and Other Americans.* New York: Harper & Row

Fixico, D. L. 1986. *Termination and Relocation.* Albuquerque, NM: Univ. New Mexico

Foreman, G. 1932. *Indian Removal*. Norman, Okla: Univ. Okla.

Foster, D. V. 1988. Consideration of treatment issues with American Indians detained in the Federal Bureau of Prisons. *Psychiatr. Ann*. 18:698–701

Fries, J. E. 1987. *The American Indian in Higher Education 1975–76 to 1984–85*. Washington, DC: Cent. Educ. Statist., US Dep. Educ.

Fuchs, E., Havighurst, R. J. 1972. *To Live on this Earth*. Albuquerque, NM: Univ. New Mexico

Garbarino, M. S. 1971. Life in the city: Chicago. See Waddell & Watson 1971, pp. 168–205

Gilbreath, K. 1973. *Red Capitalism*. Norman, Okla: Univ. Okla.

Gomberg, E. L., White, H. R., Carpenter, J. A. eds. 1982. *Alcohol, Science, and Society Revisited*. Ann Arbor, Mich: Univ. Mich.

Graves, T. D. 1971. Drinking and drunkenness among urban Indians. See Waddell & Watson 1971, pp. 274–311

Gross, E. R. 1989. *Contemporary Federal Policy Toward American Indians*. Westport, Conn: Greenwood

Guillemin, J. 1975. *Urban Renegades: The Cultural Strategy of American Indians*. New York: Columbia Univ.

Gundlach, J. H., Roberts, A. E. 1978. Native American Indian migration and relocation: success or failure. *Pac. Sociol. Rev*. 12: 117–28

Gwartney, J. D., Long, J. E. 1978. The relative earnings of blacks and other minorities. *Indust. Lab. Relat. Rev*. 31:336–46

Hackenberg, R. A., Wilson, C. R. 1972. Reluctant emigrants: The role of migration in Papago Indian adaptation. *Hum. Organ*. 31:171–86

Hagan, J. 1976. Locking up the Indians: a case for law reform. *Can. Forum* 55:16–18

Hagan, W. T. 1979. *American Indians*. Chicago: Univ. Chicago. Rev. ed.

Hagan, W. T. 1985. *The Indian Rights Association*. Tucson, Ariz: Univ. Arizona

Hagen, E. E., Schaw, L. B. 1960. *The Sioux on the Reservation: An American Colonial Problem*. Cambridge, Mass: Cent. Int. Stud.

Hall, E. L., Simkus, A. A. 1975. Inequality in the types of sentences received by Native Americans and whites. *Criminology* 13: 199–222

Hall, T. D. 1989. *Social Change in the Southwest, 1350–1880*. Lawrence, Kans: Univ. Press Kans.

Hechter, M. 1975. *Internal Colonialism*. Berkeley, Calif: Univ. Calif.

Hertzberg, H. W. 1971. *The Search for an American Indian Identity*. Syracuse, NY: Syracuse Univ.

Hodge, W. H. 1971. Navajo urban migration: an analysis from the perspective of the family. See Waddell & Watson, pp. 346–91

Hoxie, F. E. 1984. *A Final Promise: the Campaign to Assimilate the Indians, 1880–1920*. Lincoln, Nebr: Univ. Nebr.

Institute for Government Research. 1928. *The Problem of Indian Administration [The Meriam Report]*. Baltimore, Md: Johns Hopkins Univ.

Jacobsen, C. K. 1984. Internal colonialism and Native Americans: Indian labor in the United States from 1871 to World War II. *Soc. Sci. Q*. 65:158–71

Jennings, F. 1975. *The Invasion of America*. New York: Norton

Jensen, G. F., Stauss, J. H., Harris, V. H. 1977. Crime, delinquency, and the American Indian. *Hum. Organ*. 36:252–57

Johannson, S. R. 1982. The demographic history of the native peoples of North America: a selective bibliography. *Yearbk. Phys. Anthropol*. 25:133–52

Jorgensen, J. C. 1978. A century of political economic effects on American Indian society, 1880–1980. *J. Ethnic Stud*. 6:1–82

Jorgensen, J. G., Clemmer, R. O., Little, R. L., Owens, J. J., Robbins, L. A. 1978. *Native Americans and Energy Development*. Cambridge, Mass: Anthropol. Resource Cent.

Kardulias, P. N. 1990. Fur production as a specialized activity in a world system: Indians in North American fur trade. *Am. Indian Cult. Res. J*. 14:25–60

Kroeber, A. L. 1939. *Cultural and Natural Areas of Native North America. Am. Archaeol. Ethnol. No. 38*. Berkeley, Calif: Univ. Calif.

Lemert, E. M. 1982. Drinking among American Indians. See Gomberg et al 1982, pp. 80–95

Levitan, S. A., Hetrick, B. 1971. *Big Brother's Indian Programs: with Reservations*. New York: McGraw-Hill

Levitan, S. A., Johnston, W. B. 1975. *Indian Giving: Federal Programs for Native Americans*. Baltimore, Md: Johns Hopkins Univ.

Littman, G. 1970. Alcoholism, illness, and social pathology among American Indians in transition. *Am. J. Pub. Health* 60:1769–87

Locklear, H. 1977. American Indian alcoholism: program for treatment. *Sociol. Work* 22:202–07

Long, L. 1988. *Migration and Residential Mobility in the United States*. New York: Russell Sage

Margon, A. 1976. Indians and immigrants: a comparison of groups new to the city. *J. Ethnic Stud*. 4:17–28

May, P. A. 1977. Explanations of Native

American drinking: a literature review. *Plains Anthropol.* 22:217–28
May, P. A. 1982. Contemporary crime and the American Indian: a survey and analysis of the literature. *Plains Anthropol.* 27:225–38
May, P. A., Dizmang, L. H. 1974. Suicide and the American Indian. *Psychiatr. Ann.* 4:22–38
McCool, D. 1987. *Command of the Waters: Iron Triangles, the Federal Water Development Program, and Indian Water.* Berkeley, Calif: Univ. Calif.
McNeill, W. H. 1976. *Plagues and Peoples.* Garden City, NY: Doubleday
Miner, H. C. 1976. *The Corporation and the Indian.* Columbia, Mo: Univ. Missouri
Nagel, J. 1986. The political construction of ethnicity. See Olzak & Nagel 1986, pp. 93–112
O'Brien, S. 1989. *American Indian Tribal Governments.* Norman, Okla: Univ. Okla.
Olson, J. W. 1971. Epilogue: the urban Indian as viewed by an Indian caseworker. See Waddell & Watson 1971, pp. 399–408
Olson, M. 1988. The legal road to economic development: fishing rights in western Washington. See Snipp 1988, pp. 77–112
Olzak, S., Nagel, J., eds. 1986. *Competitive Ethnic Relations.* Orlando, Fla: Academic
Ortiz, R. D., ed. 1979. *Economic Development in American Indian Reservations, Dev. Ser. No. 1.* Albuquerque, New Mex: Inst. Native Am. Dev., Univ. New Mex.,
Ortiz, R. D., ed. 1980. *American Indian Energy Resources and Development, Dev. Ser. No. 2.* Albuquerque, New Mex: Inst. Native Am. Dev., Univ. New Mex.
Passel, J. S. 1976. Provisional evaluation of the 1970 census count of American Indians. *Demography* 13:397–409
Passel, J. S., Berman, P. A. 1986. Quality of 1980 census data for American Indians. *Soc. Biol.* 33:163–82
Peregrine, P. 1991. Prehistoric chiefdoms on the American midcontinent: a world system based on prestige goods. See Chase-Dunn & Hall 1991, pp. 193–211
Price, J. A. 1968. The migration and adaptation of American Indians to Los Angeles. *Hum. Organ.* 27:168–75
Prucha, F. P. 1984. *The Great Father.* Vols. I, II. Lincoln, Nebr: Univ. Nebr.
Richardson, J., Farrell, J. A. 1983. The new Indian Wars. *Denver Post.* Special reprint, November 20–27, Denver, Colo.
Rix, S. E. ed. 1990. *The American Woman, 1990–91.* New York: Norton
Roberts, Leslie. 1989. Disease and death in the New World. *Science* 246:1245–47
Roosens. E.E. 1989. *Creating Ethnicity: The Process of Ethnogenesis.* Newbury Park, Calif: Sage
Roy, P. 1962. The measurement of assimilation: the Spokane Indians. *Am. J. Sociol.* 67:541–51
Ruffing, L. T. 1978. Navajo economic development: a dual perspective. See Stanley 1978, pp. 15–86
Sandefur, G. D. 1989. American Indian reservations: the first underclass areas? *Focus* 12:37–41
Sandefur, G. D., Scott, W. J. 1983. Minority group status and the wages of Indian and black males. *Soc. Sci. Res.* 12:44–68
Sandefur, G. D., McKinnell, T. 1986. American Indian intermarriage. *Soc. Sci. Res.* 15:347–71
Sherman, R. T. 1988. *A Study of Traditional and Informal Sector Micro-Enterprise Activity and its Impact on the Pine Ridge Indian Reservation Economy.* Washington, DC: Aspen Inst. Humanities Stud.
Snipp, C. M. 1986. The changing political and economic status of the American Indians: from captive nations to internal colonies. *Am. J. Econ. Sociol.* 45:145–58
Snipp, C. M., ed. 1988a. *Public Policy Impacts on American Indian Economic Development. Dev. Ser. No. 4.* Albuquerque, NM:Inst. Native Am. Dev., Univ. New Mex.
Snipp, C. M. 1988b. Public policy impacts and American Indian economic development. See Snipp 1988, pp. 1–22
Snipp, C. M. 1989. *American Indians: The First of This Land.* New York: Russell Sage
Snipp, C. M. 1990. A portrait of American Indian women and their labor force experiences. See Rix 1990, pp. 265–72
Snipp, C. M., Sandefur, G. D. 1988. Earnings of American Indians and Alaska Natives: the effects of residence and migration. *Soc. Forc.* 66:994–1008
Snipp, C. M., Aytac, I. 1990. The labor force participation of American Indian women. *Res. Hum. Capital Dev.* 6:189–211
Snipp, C. M., Summers, G. F. 1991a. American Indians and economic poverty. See Duncan 1991
Snipp, C. M., Summers, G. F. 1991b. American Indian development policies. See Christenson & Flora 1991
Sorkin, A. L. 1971. *American Indians and Federal Aid.* Washington, DC: Brookings Inst.
Sorkin, A. L. 1978. *Urban American Indians.* Lexington, Mass: Heath
Stanley, S. ed. 1978. *American Indian Economic Development.* The Hague: Mouton
Stauss, J. H., Chadwick, B. A. 1979. Urban Indian adjustment. *Am. Indian Cult. Res. J.* 3:23–38

Swanton, J. R. ed. 1928. Smithsonian Miscellaneous Collections, Vol. 80. Washington, DC: Smithsonian Inst.

Szasz, M. C. 1977. *Education and the American Indian*. Albuquerque, NM: Univ. New Mex.

Szasz, M. C. 1988. *Indian Education in the American Colonies, 1607–1783*. Albuquerque, NM: Univ. New Mex.

Thomas, R. K. 1965. Pan-Indianism. *Midcontinent Am. Stud. J.* 6:75–83

Thornton, R. 1984. Cherokee population losses during the "Trail of Tears": a new perspective and a new estimate. *Ethnohistory* 31:289–300

Thornton, R. 1986. *We Shall Live Again*. New York: Cambridge Univ. Press

Thornton, R. 1987. *American Indian Holocaust and Survival*. Norman, Okla: Univ. Okla.

Thornton, R. 1990. *The Cherokees*. Lincoln, Nebr: Univ. Nebr.

Thornton, R., Marsh-Thornton, J. 1981. Estimating prehistoric American Indian population size for United States area: implications of the nineteenth century population decline and nadir. *Am. J. Phys. Anthropol.* 55:47–53

Thornton, R., Sandefur, G. D., Grasmick, H. G. 1982. *The Urbanization of American Indians*. Bloomington, Ind: Ind. Univ.

Thornton, R., Sandefur, G. D., Snipp, C. M. 1991. American Indian fertility in 1910, and 1940 to 1980. *Am. Indian Q.* 15: 359–67

Trosper, R. L. 1980. *Earnings and Labor Supply: A Microeconomic Comparison of American Indians and Alaskan Natives to American Whites and Blacks, Publication* No. 55. Boston, Mass: Soc. Welfare Res. Inst., Boston Coll.

US Bureau of the Census. 1983. *1980 Census of Population, General Social and Economic Characteristics, United States Summary, PC8O- 1-Cl.* Washington, DC: USGPO

US Bureau of the Census. 1953. *Special Reports: Nonwhite Population by Race*. Washington, DC: USGPO

Ubelaker, D. H. 1976a. Prehistoric new world population size: historical review and current appraisal of North American estimates. *Am. J, Phys. Anthro.* 45:661–66

Ubelaker, D. H. 1976b. The sources and methodology for Mooney's estimates of North American Indian populations. See Denevan 1976, pp. 243–88

Vinje, D. C. 1982. Cultural values and economic development: U.S. Indian reservations. *Soc. Sci. J.* 19:87–99

Vogt, E. Z. 1957. The acculturation of American Indians. *Annals* 311:137–46

Waddell, J. O., Watson, 0. M. eds. 1971. *The American Indian in Urban Society*. Boston: Little, Brown

Waldinger, R., Aldrich, H., Wand, R., et al. 1990. *Ethnic Entreprenuers*. Newbury Park, Calif: SAGE

Watkins, M. ed. 1977. *Dene Nation: The Colony Within*. Toronto: Univ. Toronto Press

Weibel-Orlando, J. 1991. *Indian Country, L.A.* Urbana, Ill: Univ. Ill.

White, R. 1983. *The Roots of Dependency*. Lincoln, Nebr: Univ. Nebr.

White, R. H. 1990. *Tribal Assets*. New York: Henry Holt

Wolf, E. R. 1982. *Europe and the People Without History*. Berkeley, Calif: Univ. Calif.

Annu. Rev. Sociol. 1992. 18:373–93

MEDIA IMAGES AND THE SOCIAL CONSTRUCTION OF REALITY

William A. Gamson, David Croteau, William Hoynes, and Theodore Sasson

Boston College, Chestnut Hill, Massachusetts 02167

KEY WORDS: discourse, framing, images, television, hegemony

"Big Brother is you, watching."

Mark Crispin Miller (1988)

Abstract

Ideally, a media system suitable for a democracy ought to provide its readers with some coherent sense of the broader social forces that affect the conditions of their everyday lives. It is difficult to find anyone who would claim that media discourse in the United States even remotely approaches this ideal. The overwhelming conclusion is that the media generally operate in ways that promote apathy, cynicism, and quiescence, rather than active citizenship and participation. Furthermore, all the trends seem to be in the wrong direction—toward more and more messages, from fewer and bigger producers, saying less and less. That's the bad news.

The good news is that the messages provide a many-voiced, open text that can and often is read oppositionally, at least in part. Television imagery is a site of struggle where the powers that be are often forced to compete and defend what they would prefer to have taken for granted. The underdetermined nature of media discourse allows plenty of room for challengers such as social movements to offer competing constructions of reality and to find support for them from readers whose daily lives may lead them to construct meaning in ways that go beyond media imagery.

0360-0572/92/0815-0373$02.00

INTRODUCTION

By now the story is familiar. We walk around with media-generated images of the world, using them to construct meaning about political and social issues. The lens through which we receive these images is not neutral but evinces the power and point of view of the political and economic elites who operate and focus it. And the special genius of this system is to make the whole process seem so normal and natural that the very art of social construction is invisible.

This chapter is about this story. For the most part, we accept its general argument, using it to raise questions and draw out implications for which there are—or might be—empirical evidence. Sometimes we think important qualifications and reservations are in order. The story we tell has more tension and contest in the process. It is less determined than the original and leaves more room for challengers and ordinary citizens to enter as active agents in constructing meaning (cf Ryan 1991).

We emphasize the production of images rather than facts or information because this more subtle form of meaning construction is at the heart of the issue. But the distinction between conveying images and conveying information and facts is not very useful. Facts, as much as images, take on their meaning by being embedded in some larger system of meaning or frame. The term "images" is useful in reminding us of the importance of the visual, of attention to verbal imagery, and other modes of conveying a broader frame—through music, for example.

A focus on images also allows us to connect our discussion with postmodernist writers who play off the two meanings of the word. Images are, on the one hand, reproductions, but they have a second meaning as well: a mental picture of something not real or present. Baudrillard (1988) argues that dramatic changes in the technology of reproduction have led to the implosion of representation and reality. Increasingly, the former becomes dominant as "simulacra" are substituted for a reality that has no foundation in experience.

Conscious design to persuade is largely irrelevant for our purposes. We assume that a wide variety of media messages can act as teachers of values, ideologies, and beliefs and that they can provide images for interpreting the world whether or not the designers are conscious of this intent. An advertisement, for example, may be intended merely to sell cigarettes to women, but incidentally it may encode a message about gender relations and what it means to be a "woman."

In talking about those who decode such messages, we use the term "reader" rather than "audience." As Fiske (1987) suggests, the latter term "implies that television reaches a homogeneous mass of people who are all essentially identical, who receive the same messages, meanings, and ideologies from the same programs and who are essentially passive." By readers, we mean those who "read" or decode sights and sounds as well as printed text. Reading media imagery is an active process in which context, social location, and prior experience can lead to quite different decodings. Furthermore, it is frequently interactive, taking place in conversation with other readers who may see different meanings.

The first section below deals with the organization of imagery production. The economics and technology of "the consciousness industry" (Enzensberger 1974) have been changing rapidly. We examine arguments concerning the increasing concentration of ownership and control in this industry and whether or not it makes any difference in the content of the images it produces. The emergence of media conglomerates with a global market has led to an unprecedented integration of multiple media which can simultaneously market the same message in multiple forms through a dazzling array of new technologies. We examine the implications of such changes for political consciousness among media readers.

The next section examines the messages in the imagery, focusing on the implications for understanding the operation of power in American society and world politics. We find it useful to distinguish two realms of content—one "naturalized" and taken for granted, the other contested terrain with collective actors offering competing interpretations. The failure to make this distinction allows writers to talk past each other, each addressing a different realm.

We then turn to arguments concerning the readers of media imagery and the role they play in negotiating meaning. Some writers on media content ignore the decoding process, assuming an undifferentiated audience in which the dominant meaning will be passively accepted by everybody. Those who examine how people actually use the media in constructing meaning invariably challenge such assumptions and find various kinds of oppositional and negotiated readings of cultural texts.

The consequences of the media role for democratic politics seem largely negative, promoting apathy, cynicism, and quiescence at the expense of political participation. We conclude, no doubt predictably, that things are pretty bad but not hopeless. It isn't just Big Brother in our heads, but a whole bunch of unruly siblings, including a few black sheep with whom we may identify if we choose.

THE POLITICAL ECONOMY OF IMAGE PRODUCTION

Researchers have long been interested in the social and economic organization of the mass media. In the 1970s, a series of organizational studies examined how the news is produced. Tuchman (1978) suggested that the organization of news into "beats" had a great influence on what was and was not considered newsworthy. Sigal (1973) examined the relationship between journalists and their sources and found that journalists rely to a great degree on official sources and routine channels. While such standard newsgathering techniques may be essential for journalists to do their work, the consequence, Sigal suggests, is that journalists "are exploited by their sources either to insert information into the news or to propagandize."

Gans (1979) further explored the relationship between reporters and sources. He argues that the power of official sources, combined with the need for journalistic efficiency, ultimately structures how news organizations decide what's news. Gans suggests that "efficiency and source power are parts of the same equation, since it is efficient for journalists to respect the power of official sources." And Epstein's (1973) analysis of network television news found that "the pictures of society that are shown on television as national news are largely—though not entirely—performed and shaped by organizational considerations." In particular, he argues that the economic and organizational logic of network television structures the scope and form of network news.

Ownership and the Market

More recently, researchers and critics have looked beyond the internal demands of media organizations to understand the context in which media images are produced. Ownership of media organizations has been a particular concern. Bagdikian (1990) articulates the most well-known argument about the problems of media monopoly. He argues that a "private ministry of information" has emerged in the past 25 years, as ownership of major media has become increasingly concentrated.

The third edition of his book (1990) reports that in the United States "twenty-three corporations control most of the business in daily newspapers, magazines, television, books and motion pictures"—down from 46 in 1983. This, he argues, has grave consequences for democracy: concentrated ownership of media inevitably narrows the range of information and imagery that is disseminated. In short, "contrary to the diversity that comes with a large number of small, diverse, media competitors under true free enterprise, dominant giant firms that command the nature of the business produce an increasingly similar output" (Bagdikian 1990).

Bagdikian raises a central question about the relationship between competition and diversity. While his argument is complex, an underlying premise is that competition is more likely to encourage a wide-ranging, diverse media. Responding in large part to Bagdikian, Entman (1989) argues that the connection between newspaper competition and quality news is not at all clear. He suggests that competition has "negligible effects" on newspaper quality and that there are sound theoretical reasons for suspecting that this would be the case.

Entman is quick to point out that local newspaper monopoly, one of Bagdikian's central concerns, is "a product of the very same economic market forces that putatively nourish free press ideals." Because it is the free market system that has produced local newspaper monopolies, Entman is skeptical about the claim that we should look to competition for a solution. He makes an important distinction between the economic market and the marketplace of ideas, arguing that ensuring diversity in the latter should be the principal focus for those concerned about democracy. If publishers in a competitive market follow free enterprise norms of profit maximization, it is likely, Entman argues, that newspapers will provide a least common denominator product that attracts a mass audience and pleases advertisers. In short, "success in the economic market seems to contradict service to the idea market."

Entman tested the relationship between competition and four measures of quality, using data from 91 newspapers facing varying degrees of competition. His regression analysis demonstrated very little relationship between newspaper competition and his measures of quality news. McCombs's (1988) content analysis of Canadian newspapers arrived at similar results.

So what are we to make of the argument that competition encourages higher quality, more diverse media content? The data seem compelling, and there are strong theoretical reasons for expecting that newspapers in competition will not compete by increasing quality or diversity. At the same time, Entman's discussion of local newspaper monopolies does not adequately deal with several larger issues raised by Bagdikian and others who have written about the media monopoly. First, Entman does not deal clearly with the issue of advertising. Second, he does not discuss the horizontal integration of the new media empires. Third, he does not address the larger implications of corporate control of media imagery.

Advertising

Imagery production in the United States is overwhelmingly a for-profit enterprise, heavily dependent upon advertising. Media organizations use news and other programming as a commodity to attract an audience which they can then sell to advertisers. Beyond its size, these advertisers are concerned with the "quality" of their audience (defined in terms of purchasing power) and the company which their advertisements keep. Bagdikian (1978) offers the example of a *Detroit News* editor who instructed his staff to aim its reporting at people in their thirties with hefty salaries. The story choices, he explained in a memo, "should be obvious: they won't have a damn thing to do with Detroit and its internal problems." The editor calls for more stories about "the horrors that are discussed at suburban cocktail parties."

The need to attract advertisers induces programmers and editors to produce content that is likely to create a "buying mood." Herman & Chomsky (1988) point out that large corporate advertisers will have little interest in sponsoring media content that targets audiences with little buying power or that produces images critical of corporations. More generally, advertisers shy away from sponsoring material that is disturbing—since such material interferes with the buying mood they wish to maintain.

Steinem (1990) describes the continual problems that *Ms.* had with advertisers before the magazine decided to abandon advertising altogether. Especially in women's magazines, advertisers demanded a "supportive editorial atmosphere" or "complementary copy." She describes the "insertion orders" given to advertising salespeople from various manufacturers. S.C. Johnson & Son, makers of Johnson wax and numerous other products, ordered that its ads "should not be opposite extremely controversial features or material antithetical to the nature/copy of the advertised product." Procter & Gamble, a powerful and diversified advertiser, ordered that "its products were not to be placed in *any* issue that included *any* material on gun control, abortion, the occult, cults, or the disparagement of religion. Caution was also demanded in any issue covering sex or drugs, even for educational purposes" (italics in original).

Advertising, then, is a force toward the homogenization of imagery, but not merely because such imagery is inoffensive. Advertising inevitably competes for attention with non-advertising content. Dull and predictable stories or programs make ads all the more interesting, their freshness and visual innovativeness standing out in contrast. Program content should not only create the proper buying mood but should avoid upstaging the advertising content that pays the bill. As we discuss below, the flood of upbeat images has an implicit political message.

Global Media Ownership

Bagdikian is not merely concerned with local newspaper monopolies. He points out that a few large multinational corporations are now global media empires, owning large portfolios of newspapers, magazines, television stations, movie studios and publishing houses. This kind of ownership concentration opens up new possibilities for these empires in the production of imagery.

Media giants can beam the same images and ideas at a national and global audience in different forms via different media. The different components of the media empire are used to promote and reinforce each other and to sell affiliated products. When corporations own both the production houses and distributors of media images, they can guarantee themselves a captive audience for their product.

Bagdikian paints a vivid picture of how corporations are taking advantage of their wide ranging media properties. He suggests the fondest scenario for media giants is:

> [A] magazine owned by the company selects or commissions an article that is suitable for later transformation into a television series on a network owned by the company; then it becomes a screenplay for a movie studio owned by the company, with movie sound track sung by a vocalist made popular by feature articles in the company-owned magazines and by constant playing of the sound track by company-owned radio stations, after which the songs become popular in a record label owned by the company and so on, with reruns on company cable systems and rentals of its videocassettes all over the world. (Bagdikian 1990)

New technologies, which were once seen as democratizing forces, only accentuate this trend toward both horizontal and vertical monopoly. Neuman (1991) argues that there is an enormous potential in the new communications technologies for a diverse pluralism and increased participation in public life but concludes that it is unlikely to be realized: "When new technologies conducive to increasingly diverse and smaller scale mass communication emerge, commercial market forces and deeply ingrained media habits pull back hard in the other direction." The result is an increase in volume but not a corresponding increase in diversity, a "pattern of common-denominator and politically centrist political communication. The new media will not change this in the main."

Corporate Ownership

Finally, Bagdikian is concerned that the few corporations who own most of the media have strikingly similar interests. Media empires are not simply a result of the market system; they also serve as cheerleaders for it. Bottom-line pressure to turn a profit plus the need to protect the image of corporations as good citizens will continue to put pressure on journalists to create media content that is politically safe.

Take the case of General Electric, owner of NBC. Putnam (1991), editor of *National Boycott News,* describes how he was called by NBC's *Today* show in June, 1990 about a story on consumer boycotts. He was asked about "the biggest boycott going on right now." After some research, he called his interlocutor to tell her that "The biggest boycott in the country is against General Electric." "We can't do that one," she responded immediately. "Well, we could do that one, but we won't." The boycott against General Electric, stimulated by its leading role in the production of nuclear weapons, was supported by an estimated one percent of US consumers and had reportedly cost GE $60 million in sales, largely from hospitals refusing to buy their medical equipment. The eventual story on NBC described boycotts against Philip Morris, Hormel, Nike, and several other corporations but had no mention of the boycott of GE products.

Herman & Chomsky (1988) suggest that deregulation in the 1980s increased profit-making pressures and led to an increase in corporate takeovers and takeover threats. As a result, media organizations "have lost some of their limited autonomy to bankers, institutional investors, and large individual investors whom they have had to solicit as potential 'white knights'."

The argument, however, goes beyond the direct defense or promotion of corporate interests to include broader, indirect cultural effects. Like Bagdikian, H. Schiller (1989) suggests that commercial concerns dictate important elements of media content, prompting a privatization of culture. In his argument, the media are the central component of an "organic process by which the corporate 'voice' is generalized across the entire range of cultural expression." Barthes (1973) suggests the whole bourgeois culture is made to appear "normal" and "universal" in the cultural mythologies conveyed in media programming and advertising. The promise offered is access to such a culture through the purchase of consumer goods.

New information technologies only increase this advantage since their high cost limits access. Private wire services, electronic press kits, private video and computer networks provide corporate America with new ways to communicate with journalists and the public. D. Schiller (1986) concludes that these new technologies give corporations the ability "to restrict access to strategic information about their activities while at the same time gaining unparalleled control over the flow of positive images to the public at large."

In sum, Entman's suggestion that it is simplistic to champion competition among multiple media organizations to provide a wider marketplace of ideas is useful. Global media empires need to be understood as a new phenomenon. New technologies appear to enhance and reinforce the same general ownership pattern and increase the range and power of the production of imagery by large corporations with many shared ideological and cultural interests. The net result is a homogenization of imagery that celebrates existing power relationships and makes them seem a normal and acceptable part of the natural order.

MESSAGES

If all we have learned is that reality construction takes place in a commercialized space that promotes a generalized "feel good about capitalism," this does not take us very far. It leaves open a bewildering array of messages that are produced in many voices and many modes and that can be read in many different ways. Whatever we can learn from reality construction by examining the production process, it leaves a great deal open and undetermined.

The media images produced by the process can be treated as texts that take many forms—visual imagery, sound, and language. The difficulties of tracking the messages in these texts are compounded by the problem of layers of meaning. Some part of the meaning is "naturalized"—that is, it comes to us in the form of taken-for-granted assumptions. One cannot take texts at face-value since they contain subtexts; a whole set of texts may have an even more invisible metamessage.

Many different disciplines take on this daunting task of decoding media texts. Typically, researchers carve out some particular domain of discourse on which to focus their attention—for example, race, class, or gender relations, or policy domains such as health, housing, energy, and the like. The research is some form of text or discourse analysis with different disciplines emphasizing different techniques. No short review could hope to do justice to the thousands of insightful analyses of media imagery.

We confine our attention to three issues with particular relevance for political consciousness: (*a*) issues raised by the concept of hegemony, (*b*) framing and frame transformation, and (*c*) the fragmentation effect.

Hegemony

Perhaps the word is better left at home but one cannot dismiss the issues it raises. Gramsci's (1971) enduring contribution was to focus our attention beyond explicit beliefs and ideology to see how the routine, taken-for-granted structures of everyday thinking contribute to a structure of dominance. Gramsci urged us to expand our notion of ideology to include the world of common sense.

In usage, however, the term has lost its more specific reference to this world of common sense and seems to mean no more in most cases than the dominant message in some domain of discourse—in particular, the message of powerful state and corporate actors. But what kind of hegemony is it when one can frequently observe instances in which elites have been forced to defend supposedly hegemonic ideas, sometimes even unsuccessfully, against the attacks of challengers? The very act of having to defend one's premises and assumptions, even if the challengers are a minority lacking significant political power, would seem to belie the existence of hegemony.

The existence of contests over meaning has led some media critics to propose making the concept of hegemony more flexible (Hallin 1987, Kellner 1990, Rapping 1987). Kellner makes the argument most succinctly:

> The hegemony model of culture and the media reveals dominant ideological formations and discourses as a shifting terrain of consensus, struggle, and compromise rather than as an instrument of a monolithic, unidimensional ideology that is forced on the underlying population from above by a unified ruling class. . . . The hegemony approach analyzes television as part of a process of economic, political, social, and cultural struggle. According to this approach, different classes, sectors of capital, and social groups compete for social dominance and attempt to impose their visions, interests, and agendas on society as a whole. Hegemony is thus a shifting, complex, and open phenomenon, always subject to contestation and upheaval.

We have no quarrel with the approach—in fact, we actively adopt it in this chapter. But using the term "hegemony" to describe it salvages a jargon-laden word while losing much of the original Gramscian meaning. We would do better to abandon the term while saving an important distinction between two separate realms of media discourse.

One realm is uncontested. The social constructions here rarely appear as such to the reader and may be largely unconscious on the part of the image producer as well. They appear as transparent descriptions of reality, not as interpretations, and are apparently devoid of political content. Journalists feel no need to get different points of view for balance when they deal with images in this realm. When they conflate democracy with capitalism or matter-of-factly state that the United States is attempting to nurture and spread democracy abroad, they express images from this realm.

It is worth noting that even on hotly contested issues, there may be subtle messages about what is "normal." Hoynes & Croteau (1989) examined the guest list for ABC's *Nightline* for 865 programs over a 40-month period in the middle to late 1980s. They make the point that *Nightline* does not merely reflect who the serious players are on a policy issue; it is an influence in defining them for other journalists. *Nightline* is itself an important player in creating spokespersons.

They commend the show for giving a voice to foreign guests, even those from countries in serious conflict with the United States—something comparatively rare on American television. But criticism of US foreign policy comes almost exclusively from these foreign sources. On Central American policy, for example, Nicaraguan foreign minister, Alejandro Bendaña made some 11 separate appearances. Elliott Abrams was *Nightline*'s most frequent spokesman of choice to articulate and defend American policy. In 40 months, only "two guests (out of 68) were anti-intervention spokespersons." So while conflicting frames were presented, suggesting open debate and contention, the metamessage was that Abrams' highly controversial frame was *the* American frame, one that largely excluded domestic critics. At the same time, by relying so heavily on foreign spokespersons to critique US policy, *Nightline* made dissenting views "foreign by definition (and often 'anti-American' by implication)" (Hoynes & Croteau 1989).

Much of media discourse, however, does involve struggles over meaning. That actors differ in their resources and access and that some have enormous power advantages in such contests does not make it part of the natural or hegemonic realm. Even an uneven contest on a tilted playing field is a contest. Moreover, great success in getting one's preferred meanings featured prominently in media discourse does not ensure dominance in the meaning constructed by readers.

This distinction between realms has the additional advantage of focusing attention on movement between them. Gamson & Modigliani (1989) studied the shifting media discourse on nuclear power from the beginning of the nuclear age in 1945 through the accident at Chernobyl in 1986. Until the early 1970s, there was no anti-nuclear power discourse in the mass media. Nuclear power was a naturalized symbol of technological progress, part of the long story of human mastery of nature. Even the partial melt-down at the Fermi nuclear reactor near Detroit in 1966 failed to produce any media discourse on the merits and demerits of nuclear power.

It moved into the contested realm during the 1970s. Gamson (1988) traces the role of the environmental and anti-nuclear power movements in this evolution, showing the complex interaction among movement and more institutionalized actors in the process. On this issue, at least, far from aiding the maintenance of hegemony, challengers were helped by the media. The meanings preferred by powerful corporate and political actors proved vulnerable and media norms and practices worked to some extent against their preferred interpretation.

Even on US intervention in Central America, there were significant breaks in hegemony. Hallin (1987) examined media coverage of Central America in the early 1980s and found important differences from coverage of Vietnam in the 1960s. He suggests that issues that had been uncontested in media coverage of Vietnam were contested in the Central American coverage. For example, "questions about the American stance toward revolution not publicly aired in the United States since the onset of the Cold War [broke] into the arena of mass political communication" in coverage of Central America. And media discourse questioned both the suitability of a Cold War interpretation of the conflict and the credibility of American officials. Still, Hallin emphasizes that powerful constraints limit the impact of such challenges.

The anti-intervention movement contributed to the shifting discourse on US policy. Ryan (1991) studied the impact of a local anti-intervention group on media coverage of Central America in the mid-1980s. She found that the group, against long odds, "succeeded in presenting an alternative to government and other dominant frames once reported without contest in their local media." While the discourse did not fundamentally change, the group temporarily opened the local media to a different interpretation of the situation in Central America. Like Hallin, Ryan warns against exaggerating this success, noting that "to sustain themselves as a permanent alternative news source would have required more resources than [the group] commanded."

Public controversies also die. That which was once contested becomes naturalized. By studying symbolic contests historically, examining media discourse over time, one can trace movement between realms in either direction. What is uncontested now may be difficult or impossible to detect without contrast with a discourse in which such matters were once denaturalized and matters of contested meaning.

Contemporary discourse on affirmative action provides a clear example. Even those with a coded racist message do not challenge the idea of equal opportunity. "I support equal rights for all, special privileges for none," claimed erstwhile Klansman David Duke in the 1991 Lousiana governor's campaign (*Time Magazine,* Nov. 4, 1991:32). All sides take equality of opportunity for granted as the only legitimate goal even as they argue over whether affirmative action programs help to achieve it or instead make "some more equal than others" (cf Gamson 1992). Contrast this uncontested idea with the words of University of Virginia Professor Paul Barringer in 1900 (quoted in Woodward 1966):

> The negro race is essentially a race of peasant farmers and laborers. . . . As a source of cheap labor for a warm climate, he is beyond competition; everywhere else he is a foreordained failure, and as he knows this he despises his own color. . . . Let us go back to the old rule of the South and be done forever with the frauds of an educational suffrage.

Framing and Frame Transformation

Media sociologists have come to rely increasingly on the concept of frame (Tuchman 1978, Gitlin 1980, Lang & Lang 1983, Gamson & Modigliani 1989). As a concept, it seems both indispensable and elusive. Frame plays the same role in analyzing media discourse that schema does in cognitive psychology—a central organizing principle that holds together and gives coherence and meaning to a diverse array of symbols. "Media frames," Gitlin (1980) writes, "largely unspoken and unacknowledged, organize the world both for journalists who report it and, in some important degree, for us who rely on their reports."

As used by Goffman (1974), the concept of frame maintains a useful tension or balance between structure and agency. On the one hand, events and experiences are framed; on the other hand, we frame events and experiences. Goffman warns us that "organizational premises are involved, and those are something cognition arrives at, not something cognition creates or generates." At the same time, he calls attention to the fragility of frames in use and their vulnerability to tampering. This underlines the usefulness of framing as a bridging concept between cognition and culture. A cultural level analysis tells us that our political world is framed, that reported events are pre-organized and do not come to us in raw form. But we are active processors and however encoded our received reality, we may decode it in different ways. The very vulnerability of the framing process makes it a locus of potential struggle, not a leaden reality to which we all inevitably must yield.

While this antinomy in the framing concept is a virtue, there are unnecessary ambiguities and problems that contribute to its elusiveness. First, there is an inherent ambiguity in the use of a word that has two somewhat different meanings in English—frame as in picture frame and frame as in the frame of a building. Most researchers who use the concept seem to emphasize the latter sense of frame as a latent structure. But the meaning of frame as boundary sometimes slips in as well, especially in Goffman (1974).

There is a more fundamental ambiguity in the level of abstraction implied by the concept and what it is that is being framed. First, it is possible to talk about the framing of particular events or stories—for example, the accident at Three Mile Island (TMI). Or, one can speak of issue-frames—for example, nuclear power—in which events such as the TMI accident, appear in an ongoing strip, requiring continuing interpretation. Or, one can speak of larger frames that transcend a single issue, such as a cost-benefit frame for analyzing many issues. In specifying issue-frames, one can aggregate or disaggregate subframes, and researchers to date have provided few guidelines or consensus about what is the appropriate level of abstraction.

The concept of frame also may be too static to do justice to its intended use—to study a process of constructing meaning. The action for most observers is in change over time, in what Snow and his colleagues call "frame transformation" (Snow & Benford 1988, Snow et al 1986). Especially where there is contest, one focuses on changes and how they occur, including changes in what is taken for granted.

With this conception, a frame is more like a storyline or unfolding narrative about an issue. Bennett (1975) uses the term "scenario" to express this more dynamic conception of framing. Stories frame events as they occur over time. "Narratives are organizations of experience," writes Manoff (1987). "They bring order to events by making them something that can be told about; they have power because they make the world make sense."

An interest in processes of frame transformation focuses attention on the contested sector where social actors compete in sponsoring their preferred frames. This approach shifts attention to media discourse as an outcome or dependent variable. Because of their presumed influence, the media become, to quote Gurevitch & Levy (1985), "a site on which various social groups, institutions, and ideologies struggle over the definition and construction of social reality." The media, in this view, provide a series of arenas in which symbolic contests are carried out among competing sponsors of meaning (cf Kellner 1990).

Participants in symbolic contests read their success or failure by how well their preferred meanings and interpretation are doing in various media arenas. Prominence in these arenas is taken as an outcome measure in its own right, independent of evidence on the degree to which the messages are being read by the public. Essentially, sponsors of different frames monitor media discourse to see how well it tells the story they want told, and they measure their success or failure accordingly.

Gamson & Stuart (1992), for example, studied the symbolic contest over issues of nuclear war and Soviet-American relations by examining more than 700 editorial cartoons over a 40-year period. They acknowledge that most readers either ignore editorial cartoons entirely or rarely grasp the meaning intended by the cartoonist. The relevant readers of the messages here are not the general public but the sponsors of different frames, using the cartoonists as a peanut gallery, providing feedback on how they are doing.

Fragmentation

Many media analysts focus on broader cultural effects that go beyond what the concept of frame seems able to capture. The most prominent example is the proposition that the total media experience leads to a fragmentation of meaning. One version of this argument is developed by a diverse group of writers who are generally collected under the rubric of postmodernism.

The new global networks of information and communication, in this argument, have compressed time and space. More of the world is accessible to more people, making the globe a smaller place. Viewers are able to sit in their own living rooms and "access" the world via satellite. Live television coverage of Scud missile attacks in progress or of students demonstrating in Tiananmen Square provide viewers with "real-time" access to events on the other side of the globe.

The compression of time leads to a preoccupation with the immediacy of surface meaning and the absence of depth. News comes in quotations with ever shorter sound bites. The spectacle of seeing journalists donning gas masks during the Persian Gulf War overshadows the reality that there was no chemical attack. The information may be correct or misleading, but the immediacy of the experience remains in the images one retains.

The preoccupation with immediacy results in a proliferation of fleeting, ephemeral images which have no ability to sustain any coherent organizing frame to provide meaning over time. Advertising is the vanguard of the fleeting image, but news programs lag only slightly behind. The "action news" formula adopted by many local news programs packs 30 to 40 short, fast items to fill a twenty-two and one-half minute newshole. "One minute-thirty for World War III," as one critic described it (Diamond, 1975). The result is a fragmented sense of reality (see Harvey 1989, Lyotard 1984).

For some postmodernists (Huyssens 1984), the fragmentation of reality has a positive side, bringing with it a promise of flourishing diversity and cultural pluralism. But applied to the experience of the media, fragmentation has few celebrators. Taylor (1987) argues that television is "the first cultural medium in the whole of history" to present the past as a "stitched-together collage of equi-important and simultaneously existing phenomena largely divorced from geography and material history and transported to the living rooms and studies of the West in a more or less uninterrupted flow." Because there is no contextual constraint for the reception of images, the media spectacle is experienced with "heightened intensity, bearing a mysterious charge of affect" (Jameson 1984).

In postmodernist argument, it is not simply the fleeting imagery in different issue domains but the long-term effects of the electronic media that produce fragmentation. It was McLuhan (1964) who first brought attention to the medium itself rather than the content, an insight pursued by postmodernists such as Baudrillard (1983, 1988). Distinctions between entertainment and news are artificial because they are all part of the same media spectacle, interspersed with the same advertisements in a seamless, everpresent montage.

The primary effect, regardless of content, is to substitute hyperreal representations ("simulacra") for the "real" world. Baudrillard contends that such mediated simulations have come to conceal the absence of reality. Unlike a map which has referents in the real world, "Simulation is no longer that of a territory, a referential being or a substance. It is the generation by models of a real without origin or reality: a hyperreal" (1988). In the "photo opportunity," for example, an event is created for the specific purpose of being represented in a media image, to be consumed by viewers as reality.

Following McLuhan, Baudrillard (1983, 1988) argues that in the postmodern condition the boundary between representation and reality implodes. As a result, the experience and foundation of the real disappears. "Disneyland is presented as imaginary," he writes, "in order to make us believe that the rest is real, when in fact all of Los Angeles and the America surrounding it are no longer real but of the order of the hyperreal and of simulation." Advertisers tout the "naturalness" of synthetic foods. Nostalgia creates demand for imaginary styles of the past. Watergate, says Baudrillard, was a "scandal", which helped to cover up the routinely scandalous nature of politics. The moral and political principles reaffirmed through the Watergate investigation helped to conceal their ultimate absence in the real political world.

It does not require a postmodernist perspective to come to the conclusion that news media provide a fragmented and confusing view of the world. Bennett (1988) analyses the news product as a result of journalistic practices that combine to produce such an effect. "The fragmentation of information begins," he argues, "by emphasizing individual actors over the political contexts in which they operate. Fragmentation is then heightened by the use of dramatic formats that turn events into self-contained, isolated happenings."

The result is news that comes to us in "sketchy dramatic capsules that make it difficult to see the connections across issues or even to follow the development of a particular issue over time." The structure and operation of societal power relations remain obscure and invisible. The implication of this line of argument is that if people simply relied on the media, it would be difficult to find any coherent frame and they would feel confused about many if not most issues.

READERS

Many people undoubtedly are confused by some issues—and some by most issues —but they are able to draw on their own experiential knowledge and popular wisdom along with media fragments to make sense of most of them. Hall (1982) reminds us that people are not "cultural dopes," passively reading texts as the producers intend. Texts in general and media imagery in particular can be read in different ways—to use the jargon, they are polysemic. Texts may have a preferred meaning and point of view which the reader is invited to accept. But many readers decline the invitation, either entering into some negotiation with the dominant meaning or rejecting it outright with an oppositional reading.

Eco (1979) calls texts "open" when they do not attempt to close off alternative meanings and narrow their focus to one, easily attainable meaning, but rather when they are open to a richness and complexity of readings. Much of television discourse seems especially open in this sense. The news, Fiske (1987) argues, is "a montage of voices, many of them contradictory, and its narrative structure is not powerful enough to dictate always which voice we should pay most attention to, or which voice should be used as a framework by which to understand the rest."

Certain symbolic devices increase the openness of a text. Fiske (1987) discusses five—irony, metaphor, jokes, contradiction, and hyperbole—showing how each depends on the simultaneous presence of different meanings. Irony, for example, is a statement that appears to say one thing while actually meaning another. Metaphors describe one thing in terms of something else and frequently have unspecified entailments. "The collision of discourses in irony and metaphor," Fiske writes, "produces an explosion of meaning that can never be totally controlled by the text and forced into a unified sense. . . . The contradictions are always left reverberating enough for sub-cultures to negotiate their own inflections of meaning." While there is a tension with forces of closure that attempt to close down potential meanings in favor of preferred ones, television imagery—including the news spectacle—is heavily infused with all of these devices that keep it open.

Viewers' Work

There was once a strong tendency in cultural studies to make assumptions about how people understand media imagery without actually taking the trouble to find out. In the last ten years, influenced by Morley's (1980, 1986) pioneering work, this tendency has been counter-acted by ethnographic studies of how real viewers make sense of various television texts. Hobson (1980, 1982) went into people's homes and observed and talked to them about the meaning of television in their lives. Palmer (1986) observed children watching television in their homes and interviewed them as well. Liebes & Katz (1990) had groups of couples from five different cultures watch *Dallas* and discuss it, recording their comments during the program and afterwards. Livingstone (1990) examined how viewers made sense of popular British and American soap operas.

These ethnographic studies all emphasize what Katz (1990) calls "viewers' work"—viewers who are wide awake and draw on their wisdom and experience in making sense of what they see on television. Of course, some work a lot harder than others. Liebes's (1991) study of the interaction in 50 Jewish and 20 Arab families during and after watching Israeli television news suggests the systematic nature of the interaction between the frames that viewers start with and their characteristic reading of what they see. In hardline Jewish nationalist families, the text was accepted at face value as a transparent representation of reality; they assumed what MacCabe (1981) calls the subject position of "dominant specularity" invited by the text. In hardline Arab nationalist families, the text was read oppositionally—in effect, inverting the identifications and point of view suggested by the text. "Jewish doves and Arab moderates, on the other hand, negotiate with the text, confronting it with their personal and collective experience," Liebes (1991) writes. The negotiators do the bona fide viewers' work.

Using Media Imagery

These ethnographic studies focus on specific texts and how they are interpreted by different readers but other studies compare media work and viewers' work on the same issue domain. The question here is not how the readers understand specific texts but what are the parallels and differences in the two discourses and what is the use that people make of media imagery as a resource.

Swidler (1986) invites us to think of culture "as a 'tool kit' of symbols, stories, rituals, and world-views, which people may use in varying configurations to solve different kinds of problems." If the problem is making sense of the world of public affairs, media imagery provides many of the essential tools. Of course, those tools that are developed, spotlighted, and made readily accessible have a higher probability of being used. Whether this is true for any given issue must rest on empirical evidence that shows which images are playing a central role in the construction of meaning.

Gamson (1992) examined a series of "peer group conversations" among American working people on four issues—affirmative action, nuclear power, troubled industry, and Arab—Israeli conflict. He shows how some groups were able to construct shared frames for understanding these issues that integrated media discourse, popular wisdom, and experiential knowledge. The particular combination of resources and people's ability to integrate these multiple resources varied from issue to issue. On affirmative action, for example, media discourse entered in a more secondary and supportive role, but the media were more likely to be the primary resource for constructing meaning about nuclear power and Arab-Israeli conflict.

Graber (1988) did a series of intensive, open-ended interviews with a small panel of respondents, exploring what they paid attention to in the media and how they incorporated media materials into their understanding. Rather than having them interpret particular texts, she conducted a content analysis of the newspaper and television news program that they claimed as their major source of news. Media impact, she concludes, depends on the salience of specific issues to the individual. While people's attention is influenced by media cues about what is an important story, they "evaluate news in light of past learning and determine how well it squares with the reality that they have experienced directly or vicariously."

The most persuasive direct evidence that media frames really do make a difference in how readers understand issues comes from the experimental work of Iyengar & Kinder (1987, Iyengar 1991). Using actual news broadcasts on events, they carefully edited them and showed comparable but different versions to research subjects, randomly assigned to different experimental conditions. Iyengar & Kinder (1987) demonstrate that where the television news spotlight is focused helps to define the standards that viewers apply in evaluating presidential performance.

Using similar methods, Iyengar (1991) provides evidence on how the form of presentation in news reporting affects attributions of responsibility. He contrasts two forms —the "episodic" and the "thematic." The episodic form, by far the most common one, "takes the form of a case study or event-oriented report and depicts public issues in terms of concrete instances." In contrast, the much rarer thematic form emphasizes general outcomes, conditions, and statistical evidence.

By altering the format of television reports about several different political issues as presented to experimental and control groups, Iyengar shows how people's attributions of responsibility are affected. More specifically, he shows that exposure to the episodic format makes viewers less likely to hold public officials accountable for the existence of some problem and less likely to hold them responsible for alleviating it. They tend to attribute causal responsibility for problems to victims rather than to societal forces. These results provide additional evidence for the fragmentation effects described above and for its primary consequence of obscuring the operation of societal power relations.

Iyengar (1991) also found important individual differences, reflecting the use of cultural resources beyond media discourse on some issues and differences in political sophistication. Some people have learned to read critically and continue to draw on a broader public discourse than is reflected in general audience media. Experiential knowledge and popular wisdom also teach about societal power relations. Those who bring something to the media imagery they encounter, construct reality by negotiating it in complex ways that we are only beginning to understand. Furthermore, they often do it in interaction with friends and family, adding yet another layer of complexity to the decoding process.

CONCLUSION

Ideally, a media system suitable for a democracy ought to provide its readers with some coherent sense of the broader social forces that affect the conditions of their everyday lives. It is difficult to find anyone who would claim that media discourse in the United States even remotely approaches this ideal. Paletz & Entman (1981) describe the major consequences of media depictions as "frustration, misdirected anger, and apathy, not insight and political activism." Edelman (1988) observes that "News about 'public affairs' encourages the translation of personal concerns into beliefs about a public world people witness as spectators rather than participants." Bennett (1988) notes the main effects of mass media news in American politics as "Setting limits on the imaginable and the politically possible; arriving too late (and doing too little) to educate people and get them involved in policy making."

The overwhelming conclusion is that the media generally operate in ways that promote apathy, cynicism, and quiescence rather than active citizenship and participation. Furthermore, all the trends seem to be in the wrong direction—toward more and more messages, from fewer and bigger producers, saying less and less. That is the bad news.

The good news is that the messages provide a many-voiced, open text that can and often is read oppositionally, at least in part. Television imagery is a site of struggle where the powers that be are often forced to compete and defend what they would prefer to have taken for granted. The underdetermined nature of media discourse allows plenty of room for challengers such as social movements to offer competing constructions of reality and to find support for them from readers whose daily lives may lead them to construct meaning in ways that go beyond media imagery.

ACKNOWLEDGMENTS

We wish to thank Harvey Molotch, two anonymous reviewers, and the members of the Boston College Media Research and Action Project (MRAP) who served as a continuing resource for us at all stages of this project.

Literature Cited

Bagdikian, B. 1978. The best news money can buy. *Human Behav*. October:63–66

Bagdikian, B. 1990. *The Media Monopoly*. Boston: Beacon. 3rd ed.

Barthes, R. 1973. *Mythologies*. London: Paladin

Baudrillard, J. 1983. *In the Shadow of the Silent Majorities*. New York: Semiotext(e)

Baudrillard, J. 1988. *Selected Writings*, ed. Mark Poster. Stanford, Calif: Stanford Univ. Press

Bennett, W. L. 1975. *The Political Mind and the Political Environment*. Lexington, Mass: Heath

Bennett, W. L. 1988. *NEWS: The Politics of Illusion*. New York: Longman. 2nd ed.

Diamond, E. 1975. *The Tin Kazoo: Television, Politics, and the News*. Cambridge, Mass: MIT Press

Eco, U. 1979. *The Role of the Reader*. Bloomington: Ind. Univ. Press

Edelman, M. 1988. *Constructing the Political Spectacle*. Chicago: Univ. Chicago Press

Entman, R. 1989. *Democracy without Citizens*. New York: Oxford Univ. Press

Enzensberger, H. M. 1974. *The Consciousness Industry*. New York: Seabury

Epstein, E. J. 1973. *News from Nowhere*. New York: Random House

Fiske, J. 1987. *Television Culture*. London/New York: Routledge

Gamson, W. A. 1988. Political discourse and collective action. In *From Structure to Action: Comparing Social Movement Research across Cultures*, ed. B. Klandermans et al, pp. 219–44. Greenwich, Conn: JAI

Gamson, W. A. 1992. *Talking Politics*. New York: Cambridge Univ. Press

Gamson, W. A., Modigliani, A. 1989. Media discourse and public opinion on nuclear power. *Am. J. Sociol*. 95:1–37

Gamson, W. A., Stuart, D. 1992. Media discourse as a symbolic contest: The bomb in political cartoons. *Soc. Forum* 7:55–86

Gans, H. 1979. *Deciding What's News*. New York: Random House

Gitlin, T. 1980. *The Whole World Is Watching*. Berkeley: Univ. Calif. Press

Goffman, E. 1974. *Frame Analysis*. New York: Harper & Row

Graber, D. 1988. *Processing the News*. New York: Longmans. 2nd ed.

Gramsci, A. 1971. *Selections from the Prison Notebooks*. (Ed. Q. Hoare, G. N. Smith) New York: Int. Publ.

Gurevitch, M., Levy, M. R., eds. 1985. *Mass Communication Review Yearbook 5*. Beverly Hills, Calif: Sage

Hall, S. 1982. The rediscovery of ideology: The return of the repressed in media studies. In *Culture Society and Media*, ed. M. Gurevitch et al, pp. 56–90. London: Methuen

Hallin, D. 1987. Hegemony: The American news media from Vietnam to El Salvador. In *Political Communication Research*, ed. D. Paletz, pp. 3–25. Norwood, NJ: Ablex

Harvey, D. 1989. *The Condition of Postmodernity*. Cambridge, Mass: Basil Blackwell

Herman, E. S., Chomsky, N. 1988. *Manufacturing Consent*. New York: Pantheon

Hobson, D. 1980. Housewives and the mass media. In *Culture, Media, Language*, ed. S. Hall, D. Hobson, A. Lower, P. Willis, pp. 105–14. London: Hutchinson

Hobson, D. 1982. *Crossroads: The Drama of a Soap Opera*. London: Methuen

Hoynes, W., Croteau, D. 1989. Are you on the Nightline guest list? *Extra* 2(Jan/Feb):1–15

Huyssens, A. 1984. Mapping the postmodern. *New German Critique* 33:5–52

Iyengar, S. 1991. *Is Anyone Responsible?: How Television News Frames Political Issues*. Chicago: Univ. Chicago Press

Iyengar, S., Kinder, D. R. 1987. *News that Matters*. Chicago: Univ. Chicago Press

Jameson, F. 1984. Postmodernism, or the cultural logic of late capitalism. *New Left Rev*. 146:53–92

Katz, E. 1990. *Viewers' Work*. Wilbur Schram Memorial Lecture, Univ. Ill., Urbana

Kellner, D. 1990. *Television and the Crisis of Democracy*. Boulder, Colo: Westview

Lang, G. E., Lang, K. 1983. *The Battle for Public Opinion: The President, the Press, and the Polls During Watergate*. New York: Columbia Univ. Press

Liebes, T. 1991. *How Arab and Jewish families decode television news in Israel*. Pres. Sympos. on Media, Protest, and Political Violence, Jerusalem

Liebes, T., Katz, E. 1990. *The Export of Meaning: Cross-Cultural Readings of "Dallas"*. New York: Oxford Univ. Press

Livingstone, S. 1990. *Making Sense of Television*. London: Pergamon

Lyotard, J. 1984. *The Postmodern Condition*. Manchester: Manchester Univ. Press

MacCabe, C. 1981. Realism and film: Notes on Brechtian theses. In *Popular Television and Film*, ed. T. Bennett et al, pp. 216–35. London: Br. Film Inst.

Manoff, R. K. 1987. Writing the news (by telling the "story"). In *Reading the News*, ed. R. K. Manoff, M. Schudson, pp. 197–229. New York: Pantheon

McCombs, M. E. 1988. Concentration,

monopoly, and content. In *Press Concentration and Monopoly,* ed. R. G. Picard et al, pp. 129–37. Norwood, NJ: Ablex

McLuhan, M. 1964. *Understanding Media.* New York: Signet

Miller, M. C. 1988. *Boxed-In: The Culture of TV*. Evanston, Ill: Northwestern Univ. Press

Morley, D. 1980. *The "Nationwide" Audience: Structure and Decoding*. London: Br. Film Inst.

Morley, D. 1986. *Family Television*. London: Comedia

Neuman, R. 1991. *The Future of the Mass Audience*. New York: Cambridge Univ. Press

Paletz, D. L., Entman, R. M. 1981. *Media, Power, Politics*. New York: Free Press

Palmer, P. 1986. *The Lively Audience: A Study of Children around the TV Set*. Sydney: Allen & Unwin

Putman, T. 1991. The GE boycott: A story NBC wouldn't buy. *Extra* 4(Jan/Feb):4–5

Rapping, E. 1987. *The Looking Glass World of Non-Fiction TV*. Boston: South End Press

Ryan, C. 1991. *Prime Time Activism*. Boston: South End Press

Schiller, D. 1986. Transformations of news in the U.S. information market. In *Communicating Politics,* ed. P. Golding et al, pp. 19–36. New York: Holms & Meier

Schiller, H. 1989. *Culture, Inc*. New York: Oxford Univ. Press

Sigal, L. V. 1973. *Reporters and Officials*. Lexington, Mass: Heath

Snow, D., Benford, R. D. 1988. Ideology, frame resonance, and participant mobilization. In *From Structure to Action: Comparing Social Movement Research across Cultures,* ed. B. Klandermans et al, pp. 197–217. Greenwich, Conn: JAI

Snow, D., Rochford, E. B. Jr., Warden, S. K., Benford, R. D. 1986. Frame alignment processes, micromobilization, and movement participation. *Am. Sociol. Rev*. 51: 464–81

Steinem, G. 1990. Sex, lies, and advertising. *Ms*. July/August:18–28

Swidler, A. 1986. Culture in action: Symbols and strategies. *Am. Sociol. Rev*. 51:273–86

Taylor, B. 1987. *Modernism, Postmodernism, Realism*. Winchester, Eng: School of Art Press.

Tuchman, G. 1978. *Making News*. New York: Free Press

Woodward, C. V. 1966. *The Strange Career of Jim Crow*. New York: Oxford Univ. Press

Annu. Rev. Sociol. 1992. 18:395–417

THE SOCIOLOGY OF MEXICO: Stalking The Path Not Taken

D. E. Davis

Department of Sociology, New School for Social Research, New York, NY 10003

KEY WORDS: dependency, development, democracy, social movements, urbanization

Abstract

Why did dependency theory fail to take strong root among sociologists of Mexico over the sixties and seventies; and why, in contrast, did Mexico's sociologists tend to study social movements and the state instead? Using these questions as a starting point, this paper examines the divergent paths of research on Mexico taken by both North American and Mexican sociologists over the past several decades. In seeking the origins of these unique patterns, the paper assesses the nation's revolutionary history, the institutional training of Mexican and North American sociologists, the corporativist and collectivist structure of politics and society, the social and political activism of Mexican sociologists, and the ruling party's appropriation of dependency rhetorics for its own political purposes. These unique legacies, in combination with Mexico's history of rapid and concentrated urbanization, are then examined with respect to their impact on recent and forthcoming research. Among the highlighted studies are those that examine territorially based struggles in cities and regions and their reciprocal impact on identity, collective action, and political power.

INTRODUCTION

In the US sociological literature on Latin America, studies abound of industrial or exporting capitalists, multinational firms, the international economy, and the impact of each on macroeconomic development trajec-

0360-0572/92/0815-0395$02.00

tories. There are considerably fewer investigations of other social classes and their domestic practices. Especially lacking are inward-oriented studies that take local political problems and social conditions as their principal concern. Yet there does appear to be one striking exception to this unequal development of the literature: writing on Mexico.

A remarkable number of sociological works on Mexico are concerned with domestic social and class forces and their impact on internal political conditions. *The Poverty of Revolution: The State and the Urban Poor in Mexico* (Eckstein 1988), *Mexico: Class Formation, Capital Accumulation, and the State* (Cockcroft 1980), *The Limits to State Autonomy: Post-revolutionary Mexico* (Hamilton 1982), *Mexico's Dilemma: The Political Origins of Mexico's Crisis* (Newell & Rubio 1984), *Unions and Politics in Mexico: the Case of the Automobile Industry* (Roxborough 1984), and *Modern Mexico: State, Economy, and Social Conflict* (Hamilton & Harding 1986) are just a few of the more recent and best known examples.

The international context of development is of course an important backdrop in several of these books. But by and large, issues of external dependency or a preoccupation with multinational firms and the international economy do not dominate this sociological writing on Mexico, even when issues like the current economic crisis are discussed (Newell & Rubio 1984, Hamilton 1986). This suggests a paradox: scholars writing about the Latin American country perhaps most under the political, economic, and geographic sway of the capitalist core may be among those least likely to embrace the principal analytic concerns of world-system or dependency theory.

Consider this: in one of the first English language books on dependence and underdevelopment in Latin America (Cockcroft et al 1972), the two principal chapters on Mexico are titled "Control and Cooptation in Mexican Politics" and "Coercion and Ideology in Mexican Politics." Also consider that at about the same time that sociologists like Andre Gunder Frank and Fernando Enrique Cardoso formulated the dependency paradigm in the Brazilian and Chilean contexts, Mexico's most noted sociologist—Pablo González Casanova—was writing his nation's counterpart to *Dependence and Underdevelopment in Latin America*. Called *Democracy in Mexico* (1970), González Casanova's seminal book turned away from external dynamics and explored the relationships between civil society and domestic political practices, a theme that was to engage Mexican sociologists in debate for years to come. Within Mexico, in fact, the unstated consensus among sociologists is that dependency and world-system theories never took hold the way they did in other countries.

This is not to say that all sociological studies of Mexico shun the dependency and world system traditions and ignore international economic conditions or multinational capitalist enterprises. Works on Mexico by Alejandro Portes (1979), Portes & John Walton (1981), Gary Gereffi (1983), and Maria Patricia Fernandez-Kelly (1983) are just a few of the best that have made important progress in this regard. Nor is it to say that domestic political arrangements or internal class and social practices have been ignored by sociologists examining other Latin American countries. Several US-based sociologists, such as Maurice Zeitlin (1984), Carlos Waisman (1987), and Mauricio Font (1990), pursue this methodology; and surely they have added to an already sizeable body of internally oriented work on countries like Chile, Argentina, and Brazil produced by those nations' own resident sociologists. Moreover, even scholars employing the dependency or world-system perspective have been known to focus on internal social and political practices to a certain extent (Evans 1987, Corradi 1985, Cardoso & Faletto 1979, Evans 1979). Thus any purported general patterns of exceptionality in the scholarship on Mexico may be a matter of degree and nuance more than a sharp qualitative break.[1]

Nonetheless, a notable difference appears in the nature of sociological work on Mexico, at least to the extent that a surprisingly large number of sociologists of Mexico explicitly depart from the general disciplinary preoccupation with dependency and the world-system, and have done so almost from the moment these paradigms hit the scene.

This departure, moreover, masks an additional and equally compelling logic. For example, among those sociologists focusing on internal conditions in Mexico, we see more Mexicans than Americans. Among those US sociologists who do focus primarily on domestic concerns in Mexico, most appear to be political sociologists who draw heavily on assumptions developed in the American politics tradition. US sociologists, consequently, tend to be most preoccupied with the manipulative and authoritarian character of the Mexican state. Their Mexican counterparts, in contrast, focus on a broader range of domestic concerns, including social movements and urban-based political problems, although they frequently analyze these issues with respect to state power.

Given these unique patterns, the sociology of Mexico is worth examining in greater detail, not only on its own merits but also for what it has to say about the historical groundedness and dissemination of development ideas. It is of course impossible to review all the sociological writings on Mexico in the limited space available here. But we can use questions about the origins and extent of Mexico's departure from the dependency tradition, and about the differences between US and Mexican sociologists in this and other regards, to organize material and partially limit our focus of study.

We begin by presenting sociological writings in their institutional setting

[1]I wish to thank Alejandro Portes for this caveat.

and showing how this may have set Mexico's sociology on a slightly different analytic path than other Latin American countries. Then we analyze Mexico's unique historical experiences and the ways this also influenced the content of sociological study, both US and Mexican. We conclude with a discussion of recent developments in Mexican sociology and their possible direction over the next few years.

THE INSTITUTIONAL CONTEXT OF DEVELOPMENT THOUGHT

To understand the specific character of the sociological literature on Mexico, especially its turn away from dependency theory and world-systems approaches, a good place to start is the institutional context in which Mexico's sociologists were writing during the 1960s and 1970s. The training and intellectual community of sociologists in Mexico differed markedly from that in Brazil and Chile, where dependency theory took strongest root (Furtado 1964, Frank 1967, Dos Santos 1970, Cardoso & Faletto 1979, Evans 1979). In Brazil and Chile, for example, the Economic Commission on Latin America (ECLA) fostered strong institutional and personal linkages between economists and sociologists. This not only introduced sociologists from these countries to dependency theory early on, it also made them particularly open to their economic colleagues' initial ideas about dependence.

Mexican scholars, in contrast, were never as strongly identified with ECLA; and the linkages between sociologists and economists were never so well cemented in Mexico as they were in many countries of the southern cone. If anything, Mexican sociologists were institutionally linked with political scientists more than with economists. These networks were seen most especially at the UNAM, or National Autonomous University of Mexico, which also served as the launching pad for party activists, future politicians, and opposition movement leaders (Camp 1976, 1981, 1985).

Mexican sociologists, in short, were less likely to be institutionally exposed to dependency theory and its economic proponents in the initial years of its formulation; they were less likely to be involved in an intellectual community that directly concerned itself with economic policymaking; and they were probably much more likely to be confronted with government politics in their personal lives and social networks.

Mexico's premier sociologist, Pablo González Casanova, is a case in point, and a critical one at that (see Peréz Espino 1985). In the late 1950s and early 1960s, while teaching in the joint faculty of political and social science at the UNAM, González Casanova was preoccupied with national politics both in theory and in practice. In the preface to his best known work, *Democracy in Mexico*, González Casanova underscores his own activism and claims that his main goal was "the search for a political course that will peacefully and civilly resolve the major national problems" (1970:ix).

González Casanova like many Mexican sociologists at the time found elective affinity with political scientists, and he employed categories used by political scientists to study patterns of development in Mexico, even economic ones (1970:4). Accordingly, he focused more on state structures and state power than on class power and international economic forces and conditions, though the latter concerned him as well. This was evident in the elaborate three-tiered framework he used to examine relationships between society, party structures, and state power in *Democracy in Mexico*. It was also clear in his treatment of economic development, which González Casanova defined as a "moral and political problem" far broader than the "mere growth of the national product or the increase in the standard of living" (1970:3).

Cardoso & Faletto and other *dependistas*, in contrast, tended to use the same concepts and categories as their economist colleagues (1979: 5–6), and thus they focused primarily on the economic articulations between the national and the international economy. Of course, Cardoso & Faletto also paid some attention to domestic politics, especially populism. And both Mexican sociologists and their southern cone counterparts in the *dependista* school shared an originating concern with domestic inequalities, class power, international conditions, and the way they interacted with each other to limit the economic development of Latin America. Yet in the complex whole under study, *dependistas* of the southern cone emphasized international conditions and dominant class power in the economy, leaving other classes, politics, and the state relatively underexplored. Sociologists in Mexico, in contrast, developed a concern with politics and the state that paralled the work of southern cone political scientists, like Guillermo O'Donnell (1973), much more than that of fellow sociologists Cardoso & Faletto. As a result, the international concerns associated with dependency theory never made it to the forefront of debate in Mexican sociology.

Indicative of this is the fact that the first serious, book-length treatment of dependency theory by a Mexican sociologist did not appear in Mexico until 1979, close to eight years after Cardoso & Faletto's work was published in Brazil and the same year Peter Evans' *Dependent Development* was published in the United States. Unlike Evans' book on Brazil, however, this book by González-Casanova–trained sociologist Sergio Zermeño from the UNAM was openly critical of the dependency approach. Titled *Imperialismo y Desarrollo Capitalista Tardío: Una Crítica al Concepto de Dependencia* (1979), the book suggested that dependency theory was just a ruse to redirect attention away from real structures of state and class power internal to Mexico that could and should be challenged.

From the mid-1970s to date, moreover, only a handful of articles in the discipline's principal journal, the UNAM-based *Revista Mexicana de Sociología* (*RMS*), openly discussed the dependency paradigm and did so favorably. One of the few was a piece by US sociologists Evans and Gereffi (1980). The small number of Mexican sociologists who sought to make generalizations about economic development and its social and class manifestations in Mexico took a markedly different tack: They focused on the mode of production (de la Peña 1979, Pipitone 1979), on the internal dynamics of peripheral capitalism (Singlemann et al 1979), and, perhaps most frequently, on the balance of political power within and between classes and the state (Cinta 1980, Durand Ponte 1980, Labastida 1977, 1980).

WHERE DEVELOPMENT SOCIOLOGY MEETS HISTORY

If Mexican sociologists failed to embrace dependency theory as fully as their southern cone counterparts during the 1970s, what were they studying? Social movements were by far the most discussed subject. Their importance to the field was evidenced in a bibliography on the topic published in the *RMS* in 1985, which presented 372 articles or books published in Mexico on social movements between 1968 and 1984 alone (Koppen 1985).[2]

Much of the attention paid to this particular topic, rather than to dependency theory, for example, is due to the nation's own historical peculiarities. One key factor is absolutely critical: the Mexican Revolution. This experience altered both the reality and the perception of external dependency and at the same time produced a history of social movements and state-civil society tensions that became part of the nation's political culture and intellectual life. Mexico's revolutionary legacy was not merely an experiential background that somehow embedded itself in the collective consciousness of Mexican sociology. It was a source of sustained scholarship and willful political struggle in which many of Mexico's sociologists themselves played an active part, especially during the 1970s. To review Mexico's history, then, is to know Mexico's sociology and to know its preoccupation with social movements and their uniquely political character.

In the eyes of citizens and sociologists alike (Córdova 1972, 1980), Mexico's 1910 Revolution was a popular uprising against a strong state that had ceded substantial control of the domestic economy to foreign firms then in cahoots with an exporting bourgeoisie (see also Hart 1988). The Revolution's success in ousting this "triple alliance" not only demonstrated the real political possibilities of overturning external dependency. It also brought to power a

[2]Koppen's bibliography was part of a larger project directed by Pablo González Casanova at the UNAM's *Instituto de Investigaciones Sociales*. Koppen cites pieces in Spanish published (and occasionally presented at conferences) in Mexico between 1968 and 1984.

state that labeled itself as nationalist and that for several critical decades actively limited foreign investment and fostered the growth of a national bourgeoisie (Leal 1986, Hamilton 1982). Perhaps most important, Mexico's Revolution underscored the critical role played by grassroots movements in fighting foreign domination and the state (Warman 1980, Knight 1990). The lesson for sociologists was that collective struggles for national determination could be successful even when they challenged powerful external forces.

Decades after the 1910 Revolution made its mark, the national preoccupation with collective organization and social struggles remained. This was particularly the case with respect to peasants and workers, on whose back the Revolution had unfolded and who throughout the 1960s, 1970s, and 1980s continued to struggle for their rights (Harvey 1990, Pérez Arce 1990). Indeed, some of Mexico's most respected sociologists gained their stature through studies of peasants (Stavenhagen 1970, Bartra 1974, 1980, Gómez Tagle 1974) and workers' organizations (Basurto 1975, Trejo Delarbre 1986). The *RMS* bibliography of Mexico's social movement literature shows that close to one half (159) of all studies were devoted to peasant or worker movements (Koppen 1985).

The historical legacy of collective organization and social activism in Mexico went beyond peasants and workers, however, and the work of sociologists reflected this too. In Koppen's bibliographic account, there were a measurably large number of studies of urban social movements (65), municipal movements (41),[3] indigenous movements (28), and movements of university workers (27) or university students (22). Less frequent in practice, and thus less studied, were state workers movements (8) and religious movements (3). Most telling, perhaps, were 10 studies of so-called *movimientos patronales*. A literal translation of these would be employers' movements, but they are best understood as businessmen's organizations.

That such organizations were included in the *RMS* in a bibliography on social movements says as much about sociology in Mexico as it does about businessmen's organizations. Social movements were so embedded in the institutional politics and everyday practice of Mexican society that they became the conceptual point of departure for sociological studies of a remarkably broad range of phenomona, including the private sector. In the United States, studies of businessmen's associations might be classified under a sociology of organizations heading, and in other Latin American countries they might be considered studies of the class structure. Yet in Mexico, where business lobbies were juridically required to organize together in keeping with

[3]All categories cited here are based on Koppen's categories, except the state workers movements, a category I derived from her distinct listings of state workers and teachers movements. Municipal movements are those struggles around local politics and local elections.

corporatist practices (Luna 1985), these organizations were considered just one more example of the collective organization of distinct individuals to protect their interests and/or to promote their own ends: i.e. a social movement.

One reason social movements were so pervasive in Mexico over the 1970s—both as a conceptual tool for analyzing society and in everyday practice—was that the Revolution gave life to a political system that both legitimized and institutionalized collective organization and action. As sociologist Raúl Trejo Delarbre (1986) and others (Córdova 1972, Hamilton 1982) well explain, in the aftermath of the Revolution corporatism brought a wide variety of previously mobilized social classes directly into government and politics, where they participated institutionally on the basis of collective identities (labor, peasant, popular middle class) rather than as individuals. Mexican scholars not only argued that their nation's unique political history gave citizens a legitimate—at least a formally recognized—institutional basis for making collective political claims about social policy and economic development (Leal 1975). They also analyzed the impact of this history on citizens' experiences with popular power, even when institutional accommodation was not easily forthcoming. Studies by Neil Harvey (1990), Francisco Pérez Arce (1990), and Maria Lorena Cook (1990), in fact, show how corporatist structures give both organization and incentive for grassroots mobilization, even when changing those corporatist structures is the goal.

Compared to many other Latin American countries then, especially the more authoritarian nations in the southern cone, Mexico was exceptional in the extent to which popular sectors, grassroots organizations, and even national businesses were encouraged and able to participate politically, despite the absence of formal democracy. In Mexico's own history, as in its sociology, social struggles and the "self-organization of society," as Carlos Monsiváis (1987) calls it, clearly reigned as the nation's central problematic.

FROM SOCIAL MOVEMENTS TO THE STATE AND BACK AGAIN

Still, the rhetoric of popular participation frequently triumphed over reality; and as the Revolution institutionalized itself through the development of a large bureaucracy, the Mexican state became more skillful in coopting grassroots mobilization so as to undermine social movements and popular power. With these developments, the gap between the theory and practice of popular political participation became itself the object of academic study during the mid- and late-1970s. Mexican scholars like José Luis Reyna (1974) and Lorenzo Meyer (1977) explored the corporatist state's capacity for cooptation, echoing a concern that González Casanova had raised in *Democracy* in Mexico several years earlier. Although the nation's political scientists led the way in these studies, soon Mexican sociologists also analyzed the nation's political and economic development in terms of the Mexican state's control over popular organizations (Córdova 1979, Alonso 1982, 1985, Trejo Delarbre 1986).

Once Mexico's own scholars turned to the manipulative character of the Mexican state, and the ways this reduced the potential for democratic participation, their US counterparts found a ready subject for study as well. The United States sent several budding scholars to mine this new terrain, many of whom were schooled in the writings of Juan Linz, Samuel Huntington, and other modernization-oriented political scientists and political sociologists who had long focused on state power and its relationship to democracy. Among the most well-received products of those expeditions were Susan Eckstein's *The Poverty of Revolution* (1977, 1st ed.), Richard Fagen & William Touhy's *Politics and Privilege in a Mexican City* (1972), Wayne Cornelius's *Politics and the Migrant Poor* (1975), Susan Kaufman Purcell's *The Mexican Profitsharing Decision: Politics in an Authoritarian Regime* (1975), and Merillee Grindle's *Bureacrats, Politicians, and Peasants in Mexico* (1977). All of these explored the ways in which the state and ruling party wielded power over classes and mobilized groups in Mexico.

Yet the question still remains as to why neither US nor Mexican scholars succeeded in actively integrating their concern with the state, or its control over social movements, into a discussion of international forces and conditions. Why didn't they look at the state's role in dependent development, for example, as Peter Evans did in his classic 1979 work on Brazil? To do this in the Mexican context would have been perfectly logical, since by the late 1960s and early 1970s, multinational firms and foreign capital were starting to dominate the Mexican economy for the first time in years (Villareal 1977, Concheiro & Fragoso 1978). Or, why didn't Mexico's sociologists link the structure or nature of the state to the peculiarities of peripheral industrialization, a task undertaken by other southern cone scholars with a similar interest in domestic politics, like Guillermo O'Donnell (1973)?

Part of the answer may rest in the nature of training received by US scholars in Mexico, especially their institutional and intellectual ties to classic traditions in American political science.[4] Yet in order to answer these questions fully, we also need a closer view of political and economic conditions at this specific juncture in Mexico's history.

For one thing, the first signs of foreign economic dominance in the late 1960s and early 1970s were accompanied by a startling prosperity, coming on

[4]José Luis Reyna, one of the most well-known Mexican political scientists to turn to studies of the state's manipulative character, was also trained in the United States, at Cornell University.

the heels of the so-called "Mexican miracle." It was difficult to warm to notions like the development of underdevelopment when Mexico was experiencing its most stunning growth rates ever. Far more important, perhaps, was the series of political explosions that Mexico experienced starting in 1968, that linked the university to civil society and that challenged a previous calm. Precisely at the moment that dependency theory was taking off in other countries, then, Mexico and its sociological community were knee-deep in the most consequential domestic social struggles and internal political challenges since the consolidation of the Revolution 40 years earlier. These events generated a wave of protests against the state and started a new round of sociological studies on social movements and their relationship to the state.

The watershed events were a series of student protests that laid bare the state's repressive character, which was further demonstrated by the government's violent actions against hundreds of protesters in what came to be known as the *Tlatelolco* massacres. Because these 1968 protests owed their origins to conflicts in and over the university, especially at the UNAM, many of Mexico's sociologists were themselves active participants in the protests. Several of the best sociological works of the 1970s, like Sergio Zermeño's 1978 book, *México: Una Democracia Utópica: El Movimiento Estudiantil de 1968,* grew directly out of this *realpolitik* experience and led the way for more serious examination of civil society and its declining power vis-a-vis the state (Gilly 1971, Poniatowska 1971, Hellman 1978, Basañez 1981, Zermeño 1987). Given these internal dynamics and their larger meaning to Mexico's citizens, to focus analytically on external forces or conditions was to turn away from the momentous struggles within.

One additional factor rang the death knell for dependency theory and cemented the Mexican preoccupation with internal social and political conditions: the fact that over the 1970s Mexico's ruling leaders appropriated notions of external dependence for their own political purposes. This was clearly evidenced in the 1970–1976 administration of Luis Echeverría, perhaps the most studied period in Mexican sociology (Labastida 1977, Paoli Bolio 1979, Saldivar 1981, Newell & Rubio 1984). Sociologists wrote extensively about Echeverría's critiques of foreign capital and his support for *tercermundismo*, or "thirdworldism," which they saw as spearheading the ruling party's efforts to revive its faltering legitimacy after *Tlatelolco*. Given Echeverría's rhetoric, many Mexican sociologists found dependency arguments anything but enlightened or neutral social scientific theories about larger processes of change. Rather, these theories were indistinguishable from real political positions and policy strategies that found voice in the Mexican government during the 1970s. To accept arguments about dependency was to toe the government line, or at least to accept the ruling party's appropriation of the theory. For sociologists who had long cherished their role as independent social critics, and who after 1968 saw themselves as bearers of civil society's challenge to the coercive state, this was anathema.

WHAT'S OLD IS NEW

In many ways, distancing themselves from dependency theory and taking another analytic path has proven to be a wise though not necessarily calculated move for sociologists of Mexico. Although many of Mexico's sociologists remained out of the limelight for two decades when dependency theory had its day in the sun, now that social movements and democratization are starting to replace dependency theory as the frontier topics of sociological research in Latin America (see Touraine 1987, Slater 1985, Fals Borda 1986, 1990, Cardoso 1987, Lechner 1987, Baino 1988), they stand at the forefront of current debate.[5]

Although Mexico's unique political and institutional history will set bounds on the transferability of its literature, there are nonetheless several areas in which the body of sociological work on Mexico can lead future debate, even among sociologists of other countries. One clearly is in social movement research. After several decades of studying the origins, composition, and political impact of popular mobilizations, sociologists of Mexico have accumulated substantial insight in their studies of movements and their relationship to the state and political change (Zermeño 1978, Castells 1984, Carr & Anzaldua 1986, Davis 1988, Foweraker & Craig 1990).

Mexico's sociologists have taken social movement analysis in directions still relatively unexplored in other contexts by highlighting the ways that legal and juridical constraints structure popular identities and mobilization and thus determine movement outcomes (Azuela de la Cueva 1989, Craig 1990). In addition, much of the research coming from Mexico has challenged prevailing notions about what might be considered "new," as opposed to traditional, social movements, by highlighting their historical character and by linking culture and identity to class (Knight 1990). The Mexican literature also has challenged the so-called "autonomy" of social movements by showing how frequently they are embedded in the institutional structures of the state (Davis 1989), or how often autonomy is not a real state of affairs but rather something to aspire to (Foweraker 1990). With the rest of the world just now rediscovering social movements, at times calling them new, and also debating their autonomy, these findings suggest it may be time to give Mexican sociology its due.

[5]It may in fact be no accident that one of the first comprehensive treatments of Latin American social movements published in English is fellow Mexicanist's Susan Eckstein's new edited volume, *Power and Popular Protest: Latin American Social Movements* (1989).

The second area in which Mexico's historical legacies can help its sociology secure a place within larger disciplinary debates is, ironically, in the field of development. As dependency and world-system theory now face mounting challenge, perhaps best exemplified in the recent Stern-Wallerstein debates (Stern 1988a,b, Wallerstein 1988), even sociologists from the dependency tradition are turning to the historically specific, political and social dynamics of development and away from the past preoccupation with international economic forces and conditions (Evans & Stephens 1988). By having avoided dependency theory's preoccupation with external determinants, and seeking instead a better handle on the domestic social and political underpinnings of national development trajectories, Mexico's sociologists may be years ahead of others in charting this new terrain. Even if their accounts fail to transfer fully, given Mexico's revolutionary heritage or the unique state-class relations it produced, internally oriented sociological accounts of the country's development trajectories still serve as a pedagogically useful "national counterfactual" for further reflection and study.

That Mexico's sociology holds the potential to offer new ways of analyzing development trajectories is perhaps clearest in recent studies of the debt crisis. As the most visible—and perhaps consequential—manifestation of peripheral economic development in contemporary Latin America, the debt crisis has captured widespread attention from scores of development scholars, both here and in the region itself. Most accounts available in the United States have focused on the international forces and conditions, like the Eurocurrency crisis, overlending of US banks, and pressures brought to bear by multinational firms, that brought heavy indebtedness to Latin American countries; and works by sociologists number among them (Dewitt and Petras 1981). Yet few sociologists of Mexico have taken this angle.[6] Because their accounts tend to focus domestically (see González Casanova and Aguilar Camín), they are instructive.

One argument, presented by Roberto Newell & Luis Rubio (1984), is that the declining legitimacy of the one-party dominated state vis-à-vis civil society spurred it to introduce unsound economic policies (see also Loaeza & Segovia 1987, Paulson 1988). Another theory, articulated by Nora Hamilton (1986), underscores the domestic political constraints on the state's economic policy posed by finance and industrial capitalists. A third view examines the tensions between populism—or the popular participation of subordinate classes—and macroeconomic efficiency (González Casanova 1981, Carr 1986, Tamayo 1990, Zermeño 1987, 1990).

[6]One of the few sociologists that takes this perspective was trained with Wallerstein; and even she has tempered her discussion of the international banking system with a view to the Mexican state's autonomy (Glasberg 1987).

These three sets of scholars diverge with respect to which class or social groups the state's political relationship is most economically disastrous. However, all three head toward a similar conclusion: both political and economic development trajectories are determined by the fit—or lack thereof—between state and class structures on one hand, and between social mobilizations and political practices on the other. If the social and class bases for political participation are compatible with the state's economic policymaking patterns and objectives, both political stability and economic growth are likely. If the fit is uneasy, neither is likely (see Walton & Ragin 1989, Davis 1990, Zermeño 1990).

Theoretically speaking, one of the most striking propositions that emerges from these studies of Mexico's economic crisis is that some grassroots political participation may be a necessary condition of sustained economic development. This is an idea that challenges prevailing notions about the relationships between authoritarianism and economic development proposed by Latin American political scientists like Guillermo O'Donnell (1973). Yet this idea also challenges prevailing opinion that pluralist democracy is the best route to achieve either political or economic stability, at least in the Mexican case. Mexico's Zermeño has gone so far as to suggest that populism may be the only "'sane' form of [political] integration" for Latin American countries facing economic crisis (1990:173). Accordingly, the principal question that Mexican sociologists continue to pursue today is not whether democracy brings development, or vice versa, or even which political system or economic development objective should be used to structure the other, but rather, what the degree of fit is between certain forms of political participation and economic policymaking.

Given these findings, perhaps Mexico's sociology can offer some guiding light to practitioners and scholars in other countries facing economic hardship and political mobilization, including those of Eastern Europe and the formerly authoritarian southern cone. A reliance on Western European and American-centered models for study of East European and Latin American countries has frequently meant a failure to discuss alternative forms of political participation or to question the extent of "fittedness" between western-style liberalization strategies—both economic and political—and existing social structures and political practices. A view to the Mexican experience may offer a needed break from these old ways of seeing.

CAPTURING PAST STRENGTHS IN FUTURE STUDIES

As others increasingly turn to findings produced by sociologists of Mexico over the past two decades, where will Mexico's own scholarship be heading? One possible direction is the political and economic relationship between

Mexico and the United States. Now that our countries may be even more closely tied through the free trade agreement looming on the horizon, centers for US-Mexican Studies, like Wayne Cornelius's at the University of California, San Diego, capture bilateral funding and offer incentive and facilities to examine these transnational linkages and their impact. These new trade developments, in fact, may bring Mexico's sociologists more forcefully into a debate with other scholars attentive to international forces and conditions. If this occurs, an existing and rapidly growing body of sociological work on Mexican migration (Tienda 1980, Portes & Bach 1985, Browning & de la Garza 1986, Massey et al 1987), border economies (Messmacher 1983, Herzog 1990), *maquiladoras* (Seligson & Williams 1981, Fernandez-Kelly 1983, Shaiken 1990), international relations (Pastor & Castaneda 1988, Roett 1991), and various other dimensions of international capital and labor flows will surely capture much of the limelight (Portes & Walton 1981, Sassen 1988, Cornelius 1991).

Yet these particular topics still appear to generate most interest from US sociologists of Mexico, at least to date. Within the nation itself, signs point in a slightly different direction: to more focused study of urban problems and the ways that the state and social movements come together—or apart—in the urban domain. Indeed, as Mexico City claims its place as the world's largest and most polluted city, urban concerns are once again at the forefront of study and debate among many of the nation's resident sociologists. The concern with urban dynamics is not new. It has long captured the sociological imagination; and as a theme that dominates much of the literature on Mexico, urban problems stand right behind social movements and the state as a principal focus of attention in Mexico's sociology.

The focus on the urban domain, not unlike the focus on the state and social movements, is historically rooted in a longstanding disciplinary concern with the dynamics of political and economic development. As Mexico embarked on rapid urbanization-led industrial development over the 1950s, its capital city grew dramatically, through rural-urban migration and natural population increase. This state of affairs generated a wave of studies on the relationships between urbanization and economic development during the late 1960s and early 1970s, especially as mediated through the migration process. One seminal work conceived within this framework was Jorge Balan, Harley Browning, and Elizabeth Jelin's *Men in a Developing Society* (1973). Another critical work of the time, which focused on these themes and introduced the political dimension of urban economic development, was John Walton's *Elites and Economic Development* (1977). Even the works by Wayne Cornelius and Susan Eckstein on the cooptive character of the Mexican state, in *Politics and the Migrant Poor in Mexico City* and *The Poverty of Revolution*, both noted earlier, grew out of an original concern with urban-rural migration and urbanization patterns.

The relationships between migration, urbanization, and political or economic development captured widespread attention from both US and Mexican scholars in the field of sociology (see also Portes 1971, Walton & Sween 1973) and political science (see also Ames 1970, Reyna 1971). The salience of these research concerns was perhaps best seen in the 1970 foundation of the journal, *Latin American Urban Research* (*LAUR*), which hosted the works of many of these scholars during its eight short years of existence.

Much of the original preoccupation with the urban bases of social, political, and economic development on the part of US scholars can be attributed to their exposure to ideas about modernization and change, especially as seen in the work of urban sociologists and anthropologists of the Chicago School. That both Robert Redfield (1941, 1957) and Oscar Lewis (1963, 1965) conducted their seminal work on Mexico also may help explain why US scholars were so eager—and well prepared—to elaborate or criticize these fundamental ideas in the Mexican urban context. Yet the influence of these themes also was powerful among Mexican scholars themselves. One of Mexico's most esteemed anthropologists, Larissa Lomnitz, also focused on the internal social, political, and economic structure of an urban community (Lomnitz 1977). Her 1974 work on "The Social and Economic Organization of a Mexican Shantytown," published in *LAUR*, stands as a classic study, both here and in Mexico.

There were differences between US and Mexican urban scholarship, however. As a whole, Mexican urban scholars have been less concerned about general theory, or the macro relations between urbanization and political or economic "modernization," and more concerned with the empirical fact of overurbanization and the specific urban social and political problems this produced. This explains why, when the Mexican sociological literature in the mid-1970s turned to the state and its larger role in political and economic development, many US urban sociologists and political scientists followed the wave while Mexican urbanists generally continued to focus on specific urban problems. Mexican scholars' preoccupation with urban dynamics was evidenced by the foundation of various specialized departments and centers in Mexican universities devoted principally to urban studies. The Center for Studies of Demography and Urban Development (as it is now called) at the Colegio de México, run by Luis Unikel until his death in 1980, was one of the most renowned.

With institutional support, Mexico's urban sociologists produced a myriad of studies on the spatial development of Mexico City and on the populations that inhabit the city's ever-expanding borders (Unikel 1976, Connolly 1982,

Garza 1985, Rubalcava & Schteingart 1985, Schteingart 1989).[7] Yet as Mexico City expanded and became denser at unparalleled rates, urban conditions deteriorated and urban services and infrastructure were unable to accommodate population growth and demands. In the legacy of mobilization so familiar to Mexican citizens, many took to the streets or organized themselves to make urban claims on the state.

Taking a cue from the writings and extensive visits to Mexico by Manuel Castells during this critical period of the late 1970s, Mexico's own top urban sociologists began to work extensively on the origins and impact of these territorially bounded struggles over the provision and administration of services for particular neighborhoods or cities (Ramírez Saiz 1981, 1990, Perlo & Schteingart 1989, Ziccardi 1985). This new body of work fit nicely with the existent disciplinary preoccupation with social movements—and the state—evidenced by other Mexican sociologists at the time. By the early 1980s, studies of urban social movements had practically superseded studies of the state and class-based social movements as the principal subject of sociological study. This occurred because urban social movements were some of the few organized collectivities that worked relatively independently of the state and corporatist political structures. Although the Mexican state consistently tried to undermine their autonomous potential, their multi-class character, organization around single issues, and legitimacy in local communities gave these movements formidable disruptive power (Moctezuma & Navarro 1980, Castells 1984, Azuela de la Cueva 1989). It was the potential of these new movements to make demands on the state, as well as to elude cooptation, that spurred citizens and scholars alike to pay attention to their emergence and power in the domestic political scene.

OPENING NEW FRONTIERS: TERRITORIAL STRUGGLES IN POLITICAL AND ECONOMIC CHANGE

Through studies of urban movements, sociologists in Mexico have introduced a theme that stands on the cutting edge of study today: the territorial—or spatial—dynamics of political and economic change. By territorial dynamics we mean those social, political, or economic processes that occur within specific spatial or territorial boundaries, or that arise in response to specific spatial or territorial concentrations. In many ways, this brings Mexican sociology full circle in its ongoing dialogue with the nation's past legacies, since territorial dynamics were central in early historical periods. Studies of

[7]Mexico City captured most interest not only because of the enormity of its problems, but also because the nation's principal research universities, both the UNAM and the Colegio de México, were located there.

the uprisings that brought about the 1910 Revolution, for example, highlighted the regionally based, antimetropolitan sentiment of those who challenged Mexico City's political and economic dominance (Hart 1988, Meyer 1986); and the revolutionary leadership's successful efforts to wield political control over rebellious provincial populations was a key factor in consolidating one-party rule back in the 1920s and 1930s (Nugent 1989, Knight 1990).

In past periods the most consequential territorially based concerns were regional imbalances or regional struggles (Katz 1988). Today, urban-based territorial struggles stand as more central, although a resurgence of regionally based opposition movements may change matters. Susan Eckstein is among those who chart new frontiers in analyzing territorially bounded urban social movements and their impact on politics in Mexico. Both in an epilogue to the new edition of her earlier book on the state and the urban poor (1988), and in a separate treatment of neighborhood mobilization in Mexico City's historic central areas (1989), Eckstein presents a detailed analysis of this neighborhood's longstanding efforts to fight displacement, the state's opposition to its demands, and the way this led to a political crisis with national repercussions. Others, like Peter Ward (1981, 1986), have analyzed the ways in which different political administrations in Mexico have responded to urban mobilizations, and the implications both for the state's legitimacy and for the movements themselves (see also Gilbert & Ward 1985). Still others have followed this line of thinking in a slightly different direction, highlighting the ways that urban problems and the social movements they produce can divide the state and lead to state incapacity and political crisis (Davis 1990).

What makes this literature on urban social movements and their impact on politics in Mexico different from much of the previous literature on social movements—or on the cooptive state—is precisely the territorial boundedness of the demands and the unique problems they pose for established political structures. That is, it is with territorially based demands, be they urban or regional, that the uneasy fit between political structures and social demands is most laid bare. This has occurred because urbanization and urban social movements produce political dissatisfactions not easily addressed by Mexico's incorporated political system, which is structured primarily around appeasing the class-specific concerns of organized labor and industrial capital. It also has occurred because urbanization and urban social movements produce demands that frequently compete with national development objectives. Accordingly, Mexican state actors have frequently split over urban policies or priorities, depending on whether they are concerned most with the urban or the national domain and depending on whether their allegiances are to specific classes or class-based sectors within the incorporated political system (Davis 1990). Moreover, neighborhood and other spatially bounded forms of organization have given citizens a chance to control the daily conditions of survival in ways that dispute the need for a centralized state based on class identities and sectoral structures for doing politics (Esteva 1987, Massolo 1986).

These findings clearly challenge previous ways of seeing social movements and the capacity of the state to coopt or accommodate these movements. In earlier work, Mexico's sociologists saw class-specific movements as much more politically powerful; even though these class-specific movements were also seen as easily cooptable, owing to their homogeneity. From the vantage point of more contemporary urban sociologists, however, social movements are most powerful when they are cross-class, rather than class-based, and this has occurred most frequently in urban and other territorially based movements, including movements for greater regional decentralization (Torres 1986) and regional political autonomy (Martínez Assad & Ziccardi 1986). In these conditions, the corporatist state is least able to conduct "business as usual" through cooptation, owing to the multiclass character of these movements and the rhetorics of democratization that generally accompany demands for territorially based political structures of participation (Gil Villegas 1986, López Monjardín 1986). Accordingly, urban problems, resurgent regional identities, and the territorially based demands they generate may lay at the heart of fundamental transformations in the state and class-based politics in Mexico.

CONCLUSION

Mexico's recent experience with territorially based movements and the sociological accounts of their origins and political effects suggests that the sociology of Mexico stands once again at the forefront of future research trends, especially as territorial movements—albeit more regionally and ethnically based than urban—emerge as salient and matters of great contention in the Soviet Union and other high profile countries of the world. If the remainder of the discipline is ready to abandon its eurocentrism and look south rather than inward or eastward, perhaps Mexico's unique historical and disciplinary experience will provide an imaginative basis for developing new types of comparative research on this and other compelling subjects. One-party states, or nations with a history of social movements, strong states, or urban problems, may learn most from the Mexican experience.

This means we may want to depart from past practices of comparing Latin American countries with others in the same region or with others in the same state of economic dependency or development. Once we as sociologists acknowledge the problems inherent in past ways of differentiating the discipline, we may choose to analyze specific Latin American countries, like Mexico, according to their past and present experiences of state-society relations, not according to their regional location or position in the world system. Though this might challenge well-established subdisciplinary boundaries that sustain certain types of studies, it should open new doors for comparative research and help country specialists talk to each other and to the rest of the discipline. It really is time to stop ghettoizing studies of Latin American countries under the rubric of dependency and world-system debates, and to start securing a place for these studies in other thematic sections of our discipline.

This is not to say that regional comparisons or dependency and world-system concerns are either theoretically irrelevant or misguided. Despite Mexican sociology's turn away from these issues, in fact, there is no doubt that such ideas still explain important dimensions of the development process. Yet so do other aspects of the national experience. Why not take a cue from Mexico's sociology and make ourselves aware that in certain country contexts, some themes are more and some less relevant? In Mexico, historical legacies, the social activism of sociologists, and the peculiarities of domestic politics together brought one take on dependency that differentiated Mexico's sociologists from their peers in other Latin American countries. To recognize this is to understand the impact of intellectual choices, institutional allegiances, and national context on the formation of research ideas and the dissemination of development theory. This may be the most important sociological finding of all.

ACKNOWLEDGMENTS

I would like to thank Alejandro Portes for his critical review and helpful comments on earlier drafts of this paper. Additional thanks also go to Susan Eckstein, Andrew Arato, Jeffrey Goldfarb, Neale Ronning, and Adamantia Pollis.

Literature Cited

Alonso, J. 1982. *El Estado Mexicano*. Mexico: Nuevo Imagen

Alonso, J. 1985. *La Tendencia al Enmascaramiento de los Movimientos Políticos*. Mexico: CIESAS

Ames, B. 1970. Bases of support for Mexico's dominant party. *Am. Polit. Sci. Rev.* 3:153–67

Azuela de la Cueva, A. 1989. *La Ciudad, la Propiedad Privada, y el Derecho*. Mexico: El Colegio de Mexico

Baino, R. 1988. *Transición y Cultura Política en Chile*. Chile: FLACSO

Balan, J., Browning, H., Jelin, E. 1973. *Men in a Developing Society: Social and Geographical Mobility in Monterrey Mexico*. Austin: Univ. Texas Press

Bartra, R. 1982. *El Reto de la Izquierda*. Mexico: Grijalbo

Bartra, R. 1974. *Estructura Agraria y Clases Sociales en México*. Mexico: Era

Bartra, R. 1986. Capitalism and the peasantry in Mexico. See Hamilton & Harding 1986, pp. 286–300

Basañez, M. 1981. *La Lucha por la Hegemoniá en México: 1968–1980*. Mexico: Siglo XXI

Basurto, J. 1975. *El Desarrollo del Proletario Industrial*. Mexico: Inst. de Investigaciones Sociales, UNAM

Browning, H., de la Garza, R. 1986. *Mexican Immigrants and Mexican Americans*. Austin: Univ. Texas Mexican Monogr. Ser.

Camp, R. 1976. Education and political recruitment in México. *J. Interam. Stud. World Affairs* 18:295–323

Camp, R. 1981. *La Formación de un Gobernante: La Socialización de los Líderes*

Políticos en México Post-Revolucionario. Mexico: Fondo de Cultura Economica
Camp, R. 1985. *Intellectuals and the State in Twentieth Century Mexico*. Austin: Univ. Texas Press
Cardoso, F.E. 1987. Democracy in Latin America. *Polit. & Soc*. 15:23–43
Cardoso, F.E., Faletto, E. 1979. *Dependency and Underdevelopment in Latin America*. Berkeley: Univ. Calif. Press
Carr, B. 1986. The Mexican economic debacle and the labor movement: A new era or more of the same? See Hamilton & Harding 1986, pp. 205–33
Carr, B., Anzaldua Montoya, R., eds. 1986. *The Mexican Left, the Popular Movements, and the Politics of Austerity. Monogr. Ser. No. 18*. La Jolla: Ctr. US-Mexican Studies, Univ. Calif., San Diego
Castells, M. 1984. *The City and the Grassroots: A Cross-Cultural Theory of Urban Social Movements*. Berkeley: Univ. Calif. Press
Cinta, R. 1980. Burguesía nacional y desarrollo. In *El Perfil de México*,, pp. 165–209. Mexico: Siglo XXI
Cockcroft, J. 1980. *Mexico Class Formation, Capital Accumulation, and the State*. New York: *Monthly Rev*.
Cockcroft, J., Frank, A. G., Johnson, D. 1972. *Dependency and Underdevelopment: Latin America's Political Economy*. New York: Doubleday
Concheiro, E., Fragoso, J. M. 1978. *El Poder de la Gran Burguesía*. Mexico: Cultura Popular
Connolly, P. 1982. Uncontrolled settlements and self-build: What kind of solution? In *Self-Help Housing: A Critique*, ed. P. Ward, pp. 141–74. London: Mansell
Cook, M. L. 1990. Organizing opposition in the teacher's movement in Oaxaca. See Foweraker & Craig 1990, pp. 199–213
Córdova, A. 1972. *La Formación del Poder Político en México*. Mexico: Era
Córdova, A. 1979. *La Política de Masas y el Futuro de la Izquierda en México*. Mexico: Era
Córdova, A. 1980. *La Ideología de la Revolución Mexicana*. Mexico: Era
Cornelius, W. 1975. *Politics and the Migrant Poor in Mexico City*. Stanford: Stanford Univ. Press
Cornelius, W. 1991. *The Changing Role of Mexican Labor in the U.S. Economy*. San Diego, Calif: Ctr U.S.-Mexican Stud.
Corradi, J. 1985. *The Fitful Republic: Economy, Society, and Politics in Argentina*. Boulder: Westview
Craig, A. 1990. Legal constraints and mobilization strategies in the countryside. See Foweraker & Craig 1990, pp. 59–78
Davis, D. 1988. Protesta social y cambio político en México. *Rev. Mex. Sociol*. 50:89–125
Davis. D. 1989. Divided over democracy: the embeddedness of state and class conflicts in contemporary Mexico. *Polit. & Soc*. 17: 247–80
Davis, D. 1990. Urban social movements, intrastate conflicts over urban policy, and political change in Mexico. *Comp. Urban & Community Res*. 3:133–63
de la Peña, S. 1979. Acumulación capitalista y población. *Rev. Mex. de Sociol*. 41:1369–1421
Dewitt, P., Petras, J. 1981. The political economy of international debt. In *Class, State, and Power in the Third World*, ed. J. Petras, pp. 96–108. London: Zed
Dos Santos, T. 1970. The structure of dependence. *Am. Econ. Rev*. 60:235–46
Durand Ponte, V. M. 1980. México dependencia o independencia en 1980? In *El Perfil de México*, pp. 209–89. Mexico: Siglo XXI
Eckstein, S. 1988. [1977, 1st ed.] *The Poverty of Revolution: The State and the Urban Poor in México*. Princeton: Princeton Univ. Press. 2nd ed.
Exkstein, S. 1989. *Power and Popular Protest: Latin American Social Movements*. Berkeley: Univ. Calif. Press
Eckstein, S. 1990. Urbanization revisited: inner-city slum of hope and squatter settlement of despair. *World Devel*. 18:165–81
Esteva, G. 1987. Regenerating people's spaces. *Alternatives* 12:125–52
Evans, P. 1979. *Dependent Development: The Alliance of Multinational, State, and Local Capital in Brazil*. Princeton: Princeton Univ. Press
Evans, P. 1987. Three views of regime change and party organization in Brazil. *Polit. & Soc*. 15:1–23
Evans, P., Gereffi, G. 1980. Inversión extranjera y desarrollo dependiente: una comparacion entre Brasil y México. *Rev. Mex. de Sociol*. 42:9–71
Evans, P., Stephens, J. 1988. Development and the world economy. In *Handbook of Sociology*, ed. N. Smelser, pp. 739–73. Newbury Park: Sage
Fagen, R., Tuohy, W. 1972. *Politics and Privilege in a Mexican City*. Stanford: Stanford Univ. Press
Fals Borda, O. 1986. Conocimiento y Poder Popular: Lecciones con Campesinos de Nicaragua, México, y Colombia. Colombia: Punto de Lanza
Fals Borda, O. 1990. Social movements and political power: evolution in Latin America. *Int. Sociol*. 5: 115–127
Fernandez-Kelly, M. P. 1983. *For We are Sold, I and My People: Women and Industry*

in México's Frontier. Albany: State Univ. NY Press

Font, M. 1990. *Coffee, Contention, and Change in the Politics of Modern Brazil*. London: Basil Blackwell

Foweraker, J. 1990. Popular organization and institutional change. See Foweraker & Craig 1990, pp. 43–59

Foweraker, J., Craig, A. L. 1990. *Popular Movements and Political Change in México*. Boulder: Lynne Rienner

Frank, A. G. 1967. *Capitalism and Underdevelopment in Latin America: Historical Studies of Chile and Brazil*. New York: Monthly Rev.

Furtado, C. 1964. *Development and Underdevelopment: A Structural View of the Problems of Developed and Underdeveloped Countries*. New York: Columbia Univ. Press

Garza, G. 1985. *El Proceso de Industrialización en la ciudad de México*. Mexico: El Colegio de México

Gereffi, G. 1983. *The Pharmaceutical Industry and Dependency in the Third World*. Princeton: Princeton Univ. Press

Gilbert. A., Ward, P. 1985. *Housing, the State, and the Poor: Policy and Practice in Three Latin American Cities*. Cambridge: Cambridge Univ. Press

Gil Villegas, F. 1986. Descentralización y democracia: una perspectiva teórica. See Torres 1986, pp. 33–69

Gilly, A. 1971. *La Revolución Interrumpida*. México: El Caballito

Glasberg, D. S. 1987. International finance capital and the relative autonomy of the state: México's foreign debt crisis. *Res. Polit. Econ.* 10:83–108

Gómez Tagle, S. 1974. Organización de las sociedades de credito ejidál de la Laguna. Cuadernos del CES, no. 8. Mexico: El Colegio de México

González Casanova, P. 1970. *Democracy in México*. New York: Oxford Univ. Press

González Casanova, P. 1981. *El Estado y los Partidos Políticos en México*. Mexico: Era

González Casanova, P., Aguilar Camín, H. 1985. *México Ante la Crisis: El Impacto Social y Cultural*. Mexico: Siglo Veintiuno

Grindle, M. 1977. *Bureaucrats, Politicians, and Peasants in México*. Berkeley: Univ. Calif. Press

Hamilton, N. 1982. *The Limits to State Autonomy: Post-revolutionary México*. Princeton: Princeton Univ. Press

Hamilton, N. 1986. State-class alliances and conflicts: issues and actors in the Mexican economic crisis. See Hamilton & Harding 1986, pp. 148–77

Hamilton, N., Harding, T. 1986. *Modern Mexico: State, Economy, and Social Conflict*. Beverly Hills: Sage

Hart, J. M. 1988. *Revolutionary Mexico: The Coming and Process of the Mexican Revolution*. Austin: Univ. Texas Press

Harvey, N. 1990 Peasant strategies and corporatism in Mexico. See Foweraker & Craig 1990, pp. 183–99

Hellman, J. A. 1978. *Mexico in Crisis*. New York: Holmes & Meyer

Herzog, L. 1990. *When North Meets South: Cities, Space, and Politics on the U.S.-México Border*. Austin: Univ. Texas Press

Katz, F., ed. 1988. *Riot, Rebellion, and Revolution: Rural Social Conflict in México*. Princeton: Princeton Univ. Press

Knight, A. 1990. Historical continuities in social movements. See Foweraker & Craig 1990, pp. 78–105

Koppen, E. 1985. Bibliografía de movimientos sociales en México. *Rev. Mex. de Sociol.* 47:261–98

Labastida del Campo, J. 1977. Proceso político y dependencia en México (1970–1976). *Rev. Mex. de Sociol.* 39:193–227

Labastida del Campo, J. 1980. Los grupos dominantes frente a las alternativas de cambio. In *El Perfil de México*, pp. 99–164. Mexico: Siglo XXI

Leal, J. F. 1980. *México Estado, Burocracía y Sindicatos*. Mexico: El Caballito

Leal, J. F. 1986. *The Mexican state:1915–1973: a historical interpretation. See Hamilton & Harding 1986, pp. 21–43*

Lechner, N., ed. 1987. *Cultura Pólitica y Democratización*. Argentina: Consejo Latinoamericana de Ciencias Sociales

Lewis, O. 1963. *Life in a Mexican Village: Tepoztlan Restudied* . Urbana: Univ. Ill. Press

Lewis, O. 1965. Urbanization without breakdown: a case study. In *Contemporary Cultures and Societies in Latin America*, ed. D. Heath, R. Adams, pp. 424–37. New York: Random House

Loaeza, S., Segovia, R. 1987. *La Vida Política Mexicana en Crisis*. Mexico: El Colegio de México

Lomnitz, L. 1974. The social and economic organization of a Mexican shantytown. *Latin Am. Urban Res.* 4:135–55

Lomnitz, L. 1977. *Networks and Marginality: Life in a Mexican Shantytown*. New York: Academic

López Monjardín, A. 1986. *La Lucha por los Ayuntamientos: Una Utopia Viable*. Mexico: Siglo XXI

Luna, M. 1985. Transformaciones del corporativismo empresarial y tecnocratización de la política. *Rev. Mex. de Sociol.* 47:125–39

Martínez Assad, C., Ziccardi, A. 1986. El municipio libre entre la sociedad y el Estado. *Rev. Mex. de Sociol.* 48:7–51

Massey, D., Alarcon, R., Durand, J., González, H. 1987. *Return to Aztlan: The Social*

Process of International Migration from Western México. Berkeley: Univ. Calif. Press

Massolo, A. 1986. Que el gobierno entienda, lo primero es la vivienda! *Rev. Mex. de Sociol.* 48:195–239

Messmacher, M. 1983. *La Interdependencia en la Frontera Norte de México: Población, Industria, Comercio y Turismo en la Región de Piedras Negras, Coahuila*. Mexico: SEP

Meyer, L. 1977. Historical roots of the authoritarian state in Mexico. In *Authoritarianism in Mexico,* ed. J. L. Reyna, R. S. Weinert, pp. 3–23. Philadelphia, Penn: ISHI

Meyer, L. 1986. Un tema añejo siempre actual: el centro y las regiones en la historia mexicana. See Torres 1986, pp. 23–33

Moctezuma, P., Navarro, B. 1980. Las luchas urbanos populares la coyuntura actual. *Teoría y Política* 5:101–24

Monsivaís, C. 1987. *Entrada Libre (crónicas de una sociedad que se organiza)*. Mexico: Era

Newell, R., Rubio, L. 1984. *Mexico's Dilemma: The Political Origins of Economic Crisis*. Boulder: Westview

Nugent, D. 1989. *Rural Revolt in Mexico and U.S. Intervention*. San Diego, Calif: Ctr. U.S.-Mexican Stud.

O'Donnell, G. 1973. *Modernization and Bureaucratic-Authoritarianism: Studies in South American Politics*. Berkeley: Inst. Int. Stud., Univ. Calif.

Paoli Bolio, J. 1979. El cambio de presidente: elecciones Mexicanas de 1976. *Rev. Mex. de Sociol.* 41:325–52

Pastor, R., Castañeda, J. 1988. *Limits to Friendship: The U.S. and Mexico*. New York: Random House

Paulson, B. W. 1988. The Mexican debt crisis: a case study in public sector failure. *J. Soc., Pol., Econ. Stud.* 13:371–94

Pérez Arce, F. 1990. The enduring union struggle for legality and democracy. See Foweraker & Craig 1990, pp. 105–21

Pérez Espino, E. 1985. *Índice Cronológico de Obras de Pablo González Casanova. Rev. Mex. de Sociol.* 47:253–63

Perlo, M., Schteingart, M. 1984. Movimientos sociales urbanos en México. *Rev. Mex. de Sociol.* 46:105–27

Pipitone, U. 1979. Crisis, estancamiento, y´estructuración de la economía capitalista. *Rev. Mex. de Sociol.* 41:1470–1503

Poniatowska, E. 1971. *La Noche de Tlatelolco*. Mexico: Era

Portes, A. 1979. La inmigración y el sistema internacional: algunas características de los mexicanos recientemente emigrados a Estados Unidos. *Rev. Mex. de Sociol.* 41:1257–79

Portes, A. 1971. Urbanization and politics in Latin America. *Soc. Sci. Q.* 52:235–48

Portes, A., Bach, R. 1985. *Latin Journey*. Berkeley: Univ. Calif. Press

Portes, A., Walton, J. 1981. *Labor, Class, and the International System*. New York: Academic

Purcell, S. K. 1975. *Decisionmaking in an Authoritarian Regime*. Berkeley: Univ. Calif. Press

Ramírez Saiz, J. M. 1981. *El Movimiento Urbano Popular en México*. Mexico: Siglo XXI

Ramírez Saiz, J. M. 1990. Urban struggles and their political consequences. See Foweraker & Craig 1990, pp. 234–47

Redfield, R. 1941. *The Folk Culture of Yucatan*. Chicago: Univ. Chicago Press

Redfield, R. 1957. *The Primitive World and its Transformation*. Cornell: Cornell Univ. Press

Reyna, J. L. 1971. *An empirical analysis of political mobilization: the case of México. Latin Am. Stud. Prog. Dissertation Ser., No. 26*. Ithaca: Cornell Univ.

Reyna, J. L. 1974. Control político, estabilidad y desarrollo en México. In *Cuadernos del Centro de Estudios Sociologicos*. Mexico: El Colegio de México

Roett, R., ed. 1991. *México's External Relations in the 1990's*. Boulder: Westview

Roxborough, I. 1984. *Unions and Politics in Mexico: The Case of the Automobile Industry*. Cambridge: Cambridge Univ. Press

Rubalcava, R. M., Schteingart, M. 1985. Diferenciación socio-espacial intraurbana en la área metropolitana de la Ciudad de México. *Estudios Sociol.,* 3:9–19

Saldívar, A. 1981. *Ideología y Política del Estado Mexicano, 1970–1976*. Mexico: Siglo XXI

Sassen, S. 1988. *The Mobility of Labor and Capital*. Cambridge: Cambridge Univ. Press

Schteingart, M. 1989. *Los Productores del Espacio Habitable: Estado, Empresa, y Sociedad en la Ciudad de México*. Mexico: El Colegio de México

Seligson, M., Williams, E. J. 1981. *Maquiladoras and Migration: Workers in the Mexico–U.S. Border Industrialization Program*. Austin: Univ. Texas Mexico-U.S. Border Research Program

Shaiken, H. 1990. *Mexico in the Global Economy: High Technology and Work Organization in Export Industries*. San Diego, Calif: Ctr. U.S.-Mexican Stud.

Slater, D., ed. 1985. *New Social Movements and the State*. Holland: CEDLA

Singelmann, P., Quesada, S., Tapia, J. 1979. El desarrollo capitalista periférico y la transformación de las relaciones de clases en el campo. *Rev. Mex. de Sociol.* 41:1167–81

Stavenhagen, R., ed. 1970. *Agrarian Problems and Peasant Movements in Latin America.* New York: Doubleday

Stern, S. 1988a. Feudalism, capitalism, and the world-system in the perspective of Latin America and the Caribbean. *Am. Hist. Rev.* 93:829–72

Stern, S. 1988b. Ever more solitary. (Stern's reply to Wallerstein). *Am. Hist. Rev.* 93:886–97

Tamayo, J. 1990. Neoliberalism encounters neocardenismo. See Foweraker & Craig 1990, pp. 121–37

Tienda, M. 1980. Familism and structural assimilation of Mexican immigrants in the United States. *Int. Migration Rev.* 14:383–408

Torres, B., ed. 1986. *Descentralización y Democracia en México.* Mexico: El Colegio de México

Touraine, A. 1987. *Actores Sociales y Sistemas Políticos en América Latina.* Chile: PREALC/OIT

Trejo Delarbre, R. 1986. The Mexican labor movement: 1917–1975. See Hamilton & Harding 1986, pp. 177–205

Unikel, L. 1976. *El Desarrollo Urbano de México.* Mexico: El Colegio de México

Villareal, R. 1977. The policy of import-substituting industrialization. In *Authoritarianism in Mexico,*ed. J. L. Reyna, R. S. Weinert, pp. 67–109. Philadelphia, Penn: ISHA

Waisman, C. 1987. *Reversal of Development in Argentina.* Princeton: Princeton Univ. Press

Wallerstein, I. 1988. Comments on Stern's Critical Tests. *Am. Hist. Rev.* 93:873–85

Walton, J. 1977. *Elites and Economic Development:Comparative Studies in the Political Economy of Latin American Cities.* Austin: Univ. Texas Press

Walton, J., Sween, J. 1973. Urbanization, industrialization, and voting in Mexico a longitudinal analysis of official and opposition party support. *Soc. Sci. Q.* 52:743–59

Walton, J., Ragin, C. 1989. Austerity and dissent: social bases of popular struggle in Latin America. In *Lost Promises: Debt, Austerity, and Development,* ed. W. Canak. Boulder: Westview

Ward, P. 1981. Political pressure for urban services: the response of two Mexico city administrations. *Dev. Change* 12:379–407

Ward, P. 1986. *Welfare Politics in Mexico: Papering Over the Cracks.* Boston: Allen & Unwin

Warman, A. 1980. *We Come to Object: The Peasants of Morelos and the National State.* Baltimore: Johns Hopkins Univ. Press

Zeitlin, M. 1984. *The Civil Wars in Chile: Or, the Bourgeous Revolutions that Never Were.* Princeton: Princeton Univ. Press

Zermeño, S. 1987. La democracia como identidad restringida. *Rev. Mex. de Sociol.* 49:4–14

Zermeño, S. 1990. Crisis, neoliberalism, and disorder. See Foweraker & Craig 1990, pp. 160–183

Zermeño, S. 1979. *Imperialismo y Desarrollo Capitalista Tardío: Una Crítica al Concepto de Dependencia.* Mexico: UNAM Inst. de Investigaciones Sociales

Zermeño, S. 1978. *México Una Democracia Utopica. El Movimiento Estudiantil de 1968.* Mexico: Siglo XXI

Ziccardi, A. 1985. Problemas urbanos: proyectos y alternativas ante la crisis. See González Casanova & Aguilar Camín 1985, pp. 52–87

Annu. Rev. Sociol. 1992. 18:419–48

REGIONAL PATHS OF DEVELOPMENT

Gary Gereffi and Stephanie Fonda

Department of Sociology, Duke University, Durham, North Carolina 27706

KEY WORDS: East Asia, Latin America, South Asia, sub-Saharan Africa, paths of development, development theories

Abstract

Development is the key challenge facing human society. The essence of development is to improve the quality of life, yet the striking technological revolutions of recent years have not resulted in better living conditions for most of the world's population. These contrasts are not limited to comparisons between advanced industrial and developing societies; they are also reflected in starkly differing patterns of development within the third world.

Five broad theoretical perspectives frame much of the literature on regional paths of development: neoclassical economics, world-systems/dependency theories, the developmental state, institutional analysis, and marxism. While these approaches are general in nature, there are marked affinities between individual theories and the experience of particular regions in the third world.

Our review focuses on four third-world regions: Latin America, East Asia, South Asia, and sub-Saharan Africa. East Asia comes out on top according to almost all indicators of economic and social development, followed by Latin America, South Asia, and, at a considerable distance from the rest, Africa. The comparative analysis of the paths of development followed in these regions not only generates useful insights about concrete development processes; it also serves as a tool for refining development theory itself, and points to promising new areas of research.

0360-0572/92/0815-0419$02.00

INTRODUCTION

The twentieth century has seen breathtaking technological changes. Since the era of horse-drawn carriages and the introduction of the first telephones at the turn of the century, we have witnessed modern transportation and communications revolutions that now allow us to cross oceans in supersonic passenger aircraft in a matter of hours, send documents by facsimile machines anywhere in the world within minutes, and explore the outer reaches of the universe. Despite these staggering accomplishments, in 1991 "more than 1 billion people, one-fifth of the world's population, live on less than one dollar a day—a standard that Western Europe and the United States attained two hundred years ago" (World Bank 1991:1).

Why is there such a sharp contrast between technological development and social underdevelopment? Is the gap between rich and poor countries widening or narrowing? How have the different regions of the world been coping with the development challenge? These questions are difficult not only because of the immense diversity of human experiences around the globe, but also because the concept of development does not lend itself to easy definition or measurement.

The essence of development is to improve the quality of life. This generally calls for higher incomes, which are the result of gains in productivity and technological advances among nations. Economic progress, in turn, depends on a number of other development objectives: better education, improved health and nutrition, a cleaner environment, a reduction of poverty, more equality of opportunity, an enhancement of individual freedoms, and a richer cultural environment. The multidimensional nature of development, and the fact that these desired objectives do not necessarily occur together, help to account for some of the disparities in international living standards and the trade-offs in national development outcomes. But many of the contradictory aspects of global development still remain, sparking intense debates that vary according to the geographical regions and countries one is considering.

Focus of Our Review

The objective of this paper is to examine the current controversies and evidence on regional paths of development in the third world, and to draw out some of the theoretical implications of the comparative study of these regional trajectories. The review consists of three main parts. First, we outline five major theoretical perspectives that have been used to analyze third world development: neoclassical economics, world-systems/dependency theories, the developmental state, institutional analysis, and marxism. In practice, each of these perspectives has been applied selectively, thus illuminating certain processes of change while downplaying others. Second, we utilize statistical comparisons and a variety of case study materials to trace the development trajectories of four major third world regions in the 1980s: Latin America, East Asia, South Asia, and sub-Saharan Africa. From this comparison, it is apparent that regional paths of development reflect very different modes of integration into the world economy. Finally, we show that comparing these regional development experiences not only generates useful insights about concrete development processes, it also serves as a tool for refining broad theories of development and pointing to new areas of research.

A Note on Bibliographic Sources

Although there is a wealth of material on the development of the four regions we have selected, a count of all the articles that appeared in *American Sociological Review, American Journal of Sociology,* and *Social Forces* from 1980 to 1990 indicates that much of the literature addressing major third world topics does not appear in the major sociological journals. We also examined all the book reviews in *Contemporary Sociology* during the same time period in order to get an idea of the number of books that have been published recently on the third world.

Articles that looked at one or more third world countries were relevant for our purposes. The 11-year timeframe was divided into two blocks (1980–1985 and 1986–1990) to check for differences in the frequency of articles published on this topic.

We found that 4% to 6% of the total number of articles and book reviews published in the sociological journals included third world cases. These percentages were remarkably stable across all four journals and the two time periods as well. Asia was the most frequently studied region in the articles that appeared in the *American Sociological Review,* the *American Journal of Sociology,* and *Social Forces,* while the greatest number of third world books reviewed in *Contemporary Sociology* were concerned with Latin America. These regional preferences were consistent for both time periods. Although these statistics are admittedly crude, they indicate the need to look beyond mainstream sociological sources for relevant literature on our topic.

THEORETICAL PERSPECTIVES AND CONTROVERSIES

Theories of development have evolved rapidly during the past decade. In an effort to capture the major sources of controversy in the development field, this review highlights five broad theoretical perspectives that frame much of the literature on regional paths of development: neoclassical economics, world-systems/dependency theories, the developmental state, institutional analysis, and marxism. These theoretical approaches diverge in their assumptions, levels of analysis, empirical assessments, and prescriptions for change (see So 1990). However, the internal evolution of these theories in the 1980s, and their tendency to be selectively applied to the geographical areas they fit best, provide us with important benchmarks for assessing not only the development experiences of these regions but also their impact on development theory itself. (For a discussion of similar theoretical categories with regard to Africa, see Lubeck, this volume.)

The regional development literature in the 1980s reflects the main features of what has been called "the new comparative political economy" (see Evans & Stephens 1988). Development paths are viewed as historically contingent, and there is an emphasis on the role of external as well as institutional factors in shaping domestic development outcomes. Because of their concern with problems of conjunctural causation and multiple paths to the same point, researchers often prefer comparisons of small numbers of cases or the analysis of single cases set in a comparative framework (see Ellison & Gereffi 1990). Historical and comparative approaches thus serve as "orienting strategies" or directives in the establishment of theoretical research programs that evolve as they attempt to explain new patterns of development in a global setting (Wagner & Berger 1985).

NEOCLASSICAL ECONOMICS There has been a resurgence in the political impact of neoclassical economics in the third world during the 1980s. This perspective has been closely associated with the World Bank and its prominent sister institution, the International Monetary Fund (IMF), which often condition their lending decisions on the willingness of developing nations to conform to neoclassical economic policies and related institutional changes.

The neoclassical framework advocates laissez-faire trade policies (e.g. low tariffs, few import controls, and no export subsidies), a free labor market, stable real exchange rates, competitive market structures, wage restraint, and a limited, non-interventionist role for the government in the economy. Neoclassical economists also tend to defend traditional notions of comparative advantage in which resource-rich third world countries are encouraged to concentrate on exports of raw materials and labor-intensive manufactures, and to abandon attempts to promote advanced industrialization through industrial policies that seek to improve a country's position in the existing international division of labor.

The espousal of neoclassical economics by international financial organizations like the World Bank and the IMF is particularly significant because they have the policy networks to diffuse their message to a wide range of countries, and the economic resources to make their opinions matter. Frequently, the preferences of these institutions are framed in terms of explicit cross-regional comparisons. The World Bank's *World Development Report, 1987,* for instance, argues that the outward-oriented development strategies of East Asia are far superior in terms of exports, economic growth, and employment to the inward-oriented development strategies pursued in Latin America, South Asia, and elsewhere (World Bank 1987: Ch. 5; see also Balassa 1981: 1–26; Balassa et al 1986). The clear implication of the World Bank's argument is that the newly industrializing countries of East Asia (South Korea, Taiwan, Hong Kong, and Singapore) are a model to be emulated throughout the developing world.

The available cross-country evidence, however, suggests a more cautious assessment concerning the performance of outward-oriented and inward-oriented economies. For example, the former tend to do better when the world economy is expanding, while an inward-orientation is more successful when world demand grows slowly. Furthermore, serious doubts have been raised about a variety of other issues concerning the definitions, measurements, and causal mechanisms that underlie the generalizability of the neoclassical claims (see Wade 1990: 16–22 for a succinct overview of this debate).

WORLD-SYSTEMS/DEPENDENCY THEORIES World-systems theory, which drew heavily on earlier marxian ideas of imperialism and capitalist exploitation, has been closely associated with the work of Immanuel Wallerstein (1974, 1979, 1989). This theory postulates a hierarchy made up of core, semiperipheral, and peripheral nations in which upward or downward mobility is conditioned by the resources and obstacles affecting distinct sets of nations. According to this perspective, a country's mode of incorporation into the capitalist world-economy is the key variable that determines national development outcomes. Leaving one structural position implies taking on a new role in the prevailing division of labor, rather than escaping from the system. Thus the possibilities for autarchic paths of development are quite limited.

World-systems theory has given rise to a comprehensive sociology of development that cuts across all world regions. The periphery and semiperiphery are composed predominantly of countries from Africa, Asia, and Latin America, while the core nations are concentrated in Europe, North America, and most recently, Japan. Countries that fall within the semiperiphery, such as South Korea and Taiwan in East Asia, Mexico and Brazil in Latin America, India in South Asia, and Nigeria and South Africa in Africa, are particularly important to the theory because they promote the stability and legitimacy of the three-tiered world-system (Wallerstein 1974, Arrighi & Drangel 1986, Arrighi 1990). Nonetheless, the extreme diversity of the countries found in the core, semiperiphery, and periphery calls for a more disaggregated analysis of national development trajectories to understand why similarly situated countries respond differently to external economic challenges.

Dependency theory, which emerged in the 1960s in opposition to most of the claims of modernization theory, also emphasizes external linkages but with a more specific focus on third world nations. Whereas modernization studies tended to argue that the salvation of the periphery lay in closer investment and trade ties with the core nations, the dependency approach highlights the exploitative potential of these relationships for the periphery (Valenzuela & Valenzuela 1978). Evidence from a number of Latin American and African cases seemed to indicate that links to the center were the source of many of the third world's problems, rather than a solution.

Dependency theory qualified its initial claims with a new wave of case studies in the 1970s and 1980s that diverged sharply from earlier "stagnationist" views that claimed dependency could only lead to underdevelopment and revolution (see Gereffi 1983: Ch. 1 and Haggard 1989 for an overview of this debate). The notion of dependent development stresses the fact that structural dependency on foreign capital and external markets in the more advanced countries of the third world constrains and distorts, but is not incompatible with, capitalist economic development (Biersteker 1978, Evans 1979, Gold 1981, Lim 1985, Bradshaw 1988). Industry case studies adopted bargaining perspectives that looked at the interaction between the state, multinational corporations, and national business elites in shaping local development options in the relatively dynamic manufacturing sectors (Gereffi 1983, Bennett & Sharpe 1985, Newfarmer 1985). This bargaining framework sparked a vigorous debate about the limits of dependency analysis and the possibilities for dependency reversal (see Grieco 1984, Encarnation 1989).

THE DEVELOPMENTAL STATE Most development theories dealing with late industrialization, dependent development, or unequal exchange in the world-system give a great deal of attention to the state. Their main concern is to clarify the role of the state in exercising direct and indirect influence on the economic growth of industrial late-comers. The concept of a "developmental state" focuses on the political will, the ideological coherence, the bureaucratic instruments, and the repressive capacity needed to formulate and implement effective economic policies to promote high-speed capitalist growth.

The earliest versions of the developmental-state perspective examined the performance of peak economic agencies in postwar Japan (see Johnson 1982, 1987, Friedman 1988). This literature is now quite broad in scope, however, and it contributes to a comparative understanding of the politics of late industrialization in different regions of the world (see Wade & White 1984, Chu 1989, Wade 1990, and Collier 1979 for useful overviews of these issues).

Most third world nations have been characterized by authoritarian regimes, but the nature and evolution of these political systems and their ability to effectively implement national development strategies vary by region. In Latin America, attention has shifted from trying to explain the rise of bureaucratic-authoritarian regimes that emphasized advanced import-substituting industrialization in the 1960s and 1970s (Collier 1979), to accounting for "redemocratization"—i.e. the much heralded series of bloodless transitions from authoritarian to democratic rule that occurred in South America during the mid to late 1980s (O'Donnell et al 1986, Stepan 1988). It is too early to tell, however, whether democratic governments and their more export-oriented development strategies will fare better than their predecessors in alleviating the persistent problems of poverty and social marginalization, while continuing to try to attract foreign capital.

In East Asia, there have been attempts to reformulate the bureaucratic-authoritarian model to explain the greater coercive capacity and more exclusionary character of the developmental state in countries like South Korea and Taiwan, as well as the impact of the distinctive East Asian regional configuration resulting from the dual influence of US hegemony and the Japanese economy (Cumings 1984, 1989). Gradual political liberalizations within the region, together with the chilling effects of the Tiananmen Square crackdown on the prodemocracy movement in China, have occupied center stage in the last few years. This has left political analysts groping for compelling comparative explanations of how the timing and character of democratization and industrialization in East Asia as well as Latin America are related to domestic factors (such as economic policy, social structure, and political coalitions) and to the position of each region in the world-system.

In Africa, patrimonial political regimes are disproportionately influenced by small "presidential cliques" and the absence of relatively autonomous, development-oriented bureaucracies. This has rendered the state incapable of formulating and implementing the kinds of national economic strategies found in other third world regions (Evans 1989b, Lubeck, this volume).

INSTITUTIONAL ANALYSIS The study of institutions is undergoing a revival in the social sciences, although institutionalism has disparate meanings in different disciplines. In organization theory and sociology, the new institutionalism entails "a rejection of rational-actor models, an interest in institutions as independent variables, a turn toward cognitive and cultural explanations, and an interest in properties of supraindividual units of analysis that cannot be reduced to aggregations or direct consequences of individuals' attributes or motives" (DiMaggio & Powell 1991:8). Institutionalism has had a direct impact on the study of third world industrialization in two main areas: the social embeddedness of economic networks, and the role of culture.

Economic networks illustrate how formal and informal business arrangements are organized in different societies. Economic transactions are structured by different principles of social coordination that lie between the organizational extremes of "markets" (i.e. externalized transactions between independent firms) and "hierarchies" (i.e. a series of internalized transactions within the organizational structure of a single firm) (Williamson 1985). The concept of "networks" elaborates this typology by focusing on decentralized but repetitive and stable transactions between organizations that usually are knit together by social bonds of kinship, ethnicity, or trust (Granovetter 1985). Within the third world, economic networks have been a key to understanding the flexibility and dynamism embodied in various kinds of production structures, such as East Asian enterprise groups (Hamilton et al 1987, Hamilton & Biggart 1988, Orrú et al 1991), international subcontracting arrangements and regional divisions of labor in global industries (Henderson 1989, Doner 1991), and the burgeoning informal sectors of developing societies (Portes et al 1989).

The rapid growth of the East Asian newly industrializing countries also has refocused attention on the role of culture in national development (Ellison & Gereffi 1990:394–97, Gereffi 1989b). A number of writers argue that Confucianism confers certain advantages over other traditions in the quest for economic advancement. Because Confucian beliefs stress the importance of sobriety, education, achievement, and reciprocal social obligations, these characteristics are thought to have facilitated the national consensus around high-speed economic growth evident in Japan and the East Asian newly industrializing countries since the 1950s and 1960s (Johnson 1982, Berger & Hsiao 1988). In Latin America, a divergent set of cultural norms based upon an Ibero-Catholic or Hispanic heritage has been identified as impeding the economic progress of the region (see Valenzuela & Valenzuela 1978).

Sweeping arguments about the impact of culture on development in East Asia, Latin America, or other third world areas run into a variety of problems, however. First, regions are not culturally homogeneous; this is particularly true of East Asia with its mix of Confucianism, Taoism, and Buddhism as well as a significant Christian minority. More importantly, in terms of the timing of high-speed growth, both the Confucian and Ibero-Catholic traditions have existed for centuries. However, the dynamic shifts in economic performance in both regions, especially in East Asia, have occurred primarily in the past few decades. Furthermore, the same Confucian beliefs that now are said to facilitate rapid industrialization in East Asia were criticized by several generations of Western scholars for inhibiting economic development (see Hamilton & Kao 1987).

A more sophisticated cultural interpretation is needed. Cultural factors are historically situated and shaped by institutions. Symbols, stories, rituals, and world-views are continuously adapted and recombined to solve different kinds of problems (Swidler 1986). The construction of institutionalized, rationalized "myths" becomes a powerful tool in promoting structual changes among existing organizations and creating new organizational forms (Meyer & Rowan 1991). Culture probably is most important in constructing strategies of action and outlining an acceptable range of solutions to development problems, whether they are optimally efficient or not, rather than in explaining specific development outcomes.

MARXISM Finally, marxian perspectives focus on the exercise of power by dominant elites. They draw attention to patterns of inequality common to most large-scale societies and emphasize the role of the state in maintaining the system of private property that gives rise to class conflict. Marxism argues that under capitalism, economic growth is contingent upon profits accumulated through the exploitation of low-wage labor and the repression of subordinated classes.

Marxian arguments are prominent in several of the theoretical approaches discussed above, especially the world-systems (Wallerstein 1974, 1979, Arrighi 1990), dependency (Amin 1976, Evans 1979, Kim 1987), and some state-centered perspectives (Cumings 1989). Traditional marxism seems to have lost ground as a general theory of capitalist development and underdevelopment, however, due to the inability of third world revolutionary movements to institutionalize successful socialist development models and to the recent fragmentation of the Soviet Union and the socialist bloc in Eastern Europe.

With this backdrop, the remainder of our review highlights distinctive regional paths of development and indicates the implications of these patterns for refining general development theories.

THIRD WORLD REGIONS COMPARED: A STATISTICAL OVERVIEW

Sub-Saharan Africa, East Asia, South Asia, and Latin America have sharply contrasting development profiles, although they are frequently grouped together under the third world label. These differences are exemplified by various economic and social indicators of development (see Tables 1 and 2).

In terms of the level and rate of growth of GNP per capita, East Asia has outdistanced the other regions of the third world. Latin America had a regional GNP per capita of $1,950 in 1989, followed by East Asia ($540), sub-Saharan Africa ($340), and South Asia ($320) (Table 1). However, the perspective changes considerably if we separate China from the East Asian newly industrializing countries. China has a GNP per capita of $350, which is similar to that of sub-Saharan Africa and South Asia, but the East Asian entrepôt city-states of Hong Kong and Singapore rank among the World

Table 1 Economic and social indicators by country and region

Region/Country	Population (millions) mid-1989	Area (thousands of square miles)	Population Density (people per square miles)	GDP (US$ billions) 1980	GDP (US$ billions) 1989	GNP per ca Dolla 1980	
Sub-Saharan Africa[a]	480.4	23,066	20.8	NA	161.8	NA	
Nigeria	113.8	924	123.2	91.1	28.9	1,010	
Tanzania	23.8	945	25.2	4.4	2.5	280	
Kenya	23.5	580	40.5	6.0	7.1	420	
East Asia[b]	1,552.4	15,582	99.6	NA	895.2	NA	
People's Republic of China	1,113.9	9,561	116.5	252.2[f]	417.8	290	
South Korea	42.4	99	428.3	58.3	211.9	1,520	4
Taiwan	20.1	36	558.3	41.5	148.5	2,340	7
South Asia[c]	1,130.8	5,158	219.2	NA	317.2	NA	
India	832.5	3,288	253.2	142.0	235.2	240	
Latin America & Caribbean[d]	421.2	20,385	20.7	NA	809.2	NA	1
Brazil	147.3	8,512	17.3	210.7	319.2[f]	2,050	2
Mexico	84.6	1,958	43.2	166.7	200.7	2,090	2

Notes: [a] Sub-Saharan Africa refers to all countries south of the Sahara except South Africa.
[b] East Asia refers to all the low- and middle-income economies of East & Southeast Asia and the Pacific, east c including China and Thailand.
[c] South Asia consists of Bangladesh, Bhutan, India, Myanmar, Nepal, Pakistan, and Sri Lanka.
[d] Latin America and the Caribbean refers to all American and Caribbean economies south of the United S
[e] Because manufacturing is generally the most dynamic part of the industrial sector, its share of GDP is s separately.
[f] 1979
[g] 1988.
NA = Not available.

Sources: World Bank (1982: 110–111, 114–115; 1983: 152–153; 1991: 204–205, 208–209, 258–259); and the fi for Taiwan are from CEDP (1991: 3, 4, 23, 29, 41, 199) and DGBAS (1986: 232).

Bank's high-income countries with per capita GNPs of $10,350 and $10,450, respectively (World Bank 1991:205), while Taiwan ($7,510) and South Korea ($4,400) are ahead of all other third world nations in per capita income.[1]

These per-capita income figures reveal the dramatic reversals of fortune that have befallen some African and Latin America countries in the 1980s. Between 1980 and 1989, Nigeria, Tanzania, Kenya, and Mexico all had substantial drops in their GNP per capita. Nigeria's decline was the most precipitous, from slightly over $1,000 in 1980 to $250 in 1989, while Tanzania's per capita income dropped by more than 50% and Kenya's by almost 20%. Mexico's average income in 1989 also declined from its level ten

[1]The Middle East was not included in this discussion because it differs from Third World countries in significant ways.

Distribution of GDP (percent)						
Agriculture 1989	Industry 1989	Manu-facturing[e] 1989	Services etc 1989	Life expectancy at birth (years) 1989	Infant Mortality Rate (per 1,000 live births) 1989	Adult Illiteracy (percent) 1985
32	27	11	38	51	107	52
31	44	10	25	51	100	58
66[g]	7[g]	4[g]	27[g]	49	112	NA
31	20	12	49	59	68	41
24	44	33	34	68	35	29
32	48	34	20	70	30	31
10	44	26	46	70	23	NA
5	44	36	51	NA	NA	10
32	26	17	41	58	95	59
30	29	18	41	59	95	57
10[g]	39[g]	27[g]	52[g]	67	50	17
9[g]	43[g]	31[g]	48[g]	66	59	22
9	32	23	59	69	40	10

years earlier, while Brazil's increased by less than 25%. During the same period, the East Asian newly industrializing countries nearly tripled their per capita incomes (Table 1).

Regional divisions of labor in agriculture, industry, and services have emerged within the third world. The sub-Saharan African and South Asian economies place far more emphasis on agriculture and extractive industries, while manufacturing has been the cornerstone of development for the East Asian and Latin American newly industrializing countries. The manufacturing sector's share of GDP in the newly industrializing countries in 1989 ranged from 23% (Mexico) to 36% (Taiwan), which is well above the level of the United States, and, in several cases, it is even above Japan's manufacturing/GDP ratio of 30% (World Bank 1991:209).

By 1989, the East Asian countries had clearly established themselves as the third world's premier exporters, especially of manufactures. Taiwan and South Korea topped the list with $66.5 and $62.3 billion in exports, respectively, followed by China ($52.5 billion), Brazil ($34.4 billion), and Mexico ($23 billion) (see Table 2). Manufactured products constituted over 90% of total exports in the East Asian newly industrializing countries and around 70% of China's and India's exports. For the Latin American nations, manufactures are only about one half to one third of total exports, while in sub-Saharan Africa manufactures are just above 10% of the export total.

The maturity or sophistication of a country's industrial structure can be measured by the complexity of the products it exports. Here again, the East

Table 2 Exports and External Debt by Region and Country

Region/Country	Exports (US$ billions) 1980	Exports (US$ billions) 1989	Exports/GDP (percent) 1980	Exports/GDP (percent) 1989	Total External Debt (US$ billions) 1989	Percentage Share of Exports: Primary Commodities 1980	Primary Commodities 1989	Textiles & Clothing 1980	Textiles & Clothing 1989	Machinery & Transport Equipment 1980	Machinery & Transport Equipment 1989	Other Manufactures 1980	Other Manufactures 1989
Sub-Saharan Africa	NA	30.9	NA	19	NA	NA	89[c]	NA	2[c]	NA	1[c]	NA	8[c]
Nigeria	26.0	9.0	29	31	32.8	99[a]	99[c]	0	0[c]	0	0[c]	1[a]	1[c]
Tanzania	0.5	0.3	12	12	4.9	84	88[c]	8	6[c]	1	1[c]	7	5[c]
Kenya	1.3	1.1	22	15	5.7	84	87[c]	1	1[c]	3	1[c]	12	11[c]
East Asia	NA	195.3	NA	22	NA	NA	31[c]	NA	20[c]	NA	22[c]	NA	27[c]
People's Republic of China	18.3	52.5	8[b]	13	44.9	53	30	16	25	5	7	26	38
South Korea	17.5	62.3	30	29	33.1	10	7	29	23	20	38	41	32
Taiwan	19.8	66.3	48	45	NA	NA	8	NA	15	NA	36	NA	42
South Asia	NA	23.4	NA	7	NA	NA	30[c]	NA	33[c]	NA	5[c]	NA	32[c]
India	6.7	15.5	5	6	62.5	41[a]	27[c]	22[a]	23[c]	7[a]	7[c]	30[a]	43[c]
Latin America & Caribbean	NA	112.0	NA	14	NA	NA	66[c]	NA	3[c]	NA	12[c]	NA	21[c]
Brazil	20.1	34.4	10	11	111.3	61	48[c]	4	3[c]	17	20[c]	18	29[c]
Mexico	15.3	23.0	9	11	95.6	61[a]	55	3[a]	2	19[a]	24	17[a]	19

Notes: See Table 1.
[a] 1979.
[b] 1981.
[c] 1988.

Sources: World Bank (1982: 124–125, 138–139; 1983: 166–167, 178–179; 1991: 230–231, 234–235, 244–245). 1980 figures for Taiwan are from CEDP (1991: 23, 208).

Asian newly industrializing countries are the most advanced. Machinery and transport equipment, which utilize capital- and skill-intensive technology, account for well over one third of their overseas sales. In Mexico and Brazil, this sector represents one fifth to one fourth of total exports (Table 2).

Up to this point, the discussion has focused on economic indicators of change and development. But economic development does not automatically lead to improvements in the standard of living, nor does a lack of economic development mean that living conditions are not getting better.

Three social indicators of development are presented in Table 1: life expectancy at birth, the infant mortality rate, and adult illiteracy. These social indicators match closely the economic patterns already described. The regions of the third world that are worst off economically (sub-Saharan Africa and South Asia) are the same regions with the lowest life expectancy, the highest infant mortality, and the highest adult illiteracy. Conversely, East Asia and Latin America have longer life expectancies, substantially lower rates of infant mortality, and less adult illiteracy.

In summary, third world regions do not conform to a uniform developmental pattern. East Asia has moved well ahead of the other regions during the past decade. Latin America, which was on a par with East Asia ten years ago, has now fallen well behind. Sub-Saharan Africa and South Asia, however, continue to occupy the lowest rungs on the development ladder. In the remainder of this paper, we review selected studies that illustrate why and how this differentiation has occurred.

LATIN AMERICA

An intense comparative dialogue has emerged between Latin Americanists and East Asianists concerning the relevance of the theories that have been used to explain and interpret each region's development experience. Some of the East Asian specialists have used Latin American theories, especially the dependency and bureaucratic-authoritarian approaches, to frame the discussion of their cases and often to critique the applicability of these theoretical perspectives to East Asia (e.g. Amsden 1979, Barrett & Whyte 1982, Cumings 1984, Lim 1985, Gold 1986, Kim 1987, Deyo 1989, Haggard 1989). Scholars of Latin America, on the other hand, have been relying on the East Asian cases as an impetus to qualify and revise the theories that originally were developed in a Latin American context (e.g. Evans 1987, Fishlow 1989, Whitehead 1989, Gereffi 1989a,b, Gereffi & Wyman 1990, Fajnzylber 1990). In addition, the literature on East Asia, even when not explicitly comparative, has attempted recently to place the region's distinctive characteristics in the context of general development theory (e.g. Johnson 1987, Koo 1987, Lincoln & McBride 1987, Hamilton et al 1987, Hamilton & Biggart 1988, Amsden 1989, Westney 1989, Wade 1990, Orrú et al 1991).

Latin America is distinctive, however, in that it was the first third-world region to industrialize, and it followed a development trajectory that relied heavily on multinational corporations to establish its leading industries. Whereas foreign investors in Latin America traditionally concentrated on export-oriented projects in mining, oil, and agriculture, multinational corporations in the post-World War II era emphasized import-substituting investments in advanced manufacturing industries like automobiles, chemicals, machinery, and pharmaceuticals whose output was destined primarily for the relatively large domestic markets in Latin America (Evans 1979, Gereffi & Evans 1981, Gereffi 1983, Newfarmer 1985, Bennett & Sharpe 1985, Kaufman 1990). This continuing reliance on foreign direct investment in the development process in Latin America helps to explain why dependency has been a particularly thorny issue for the economies in the region (Stallings 1990).

In the 1970s and 1980s, Latin America's long-standing concerns about investment dependency gave way to a much more acute threat: the debt crisis. External indebtedness in Latin America rose tenfold between 1970 and 1980, from $23 billion to $223 billion. This debt burden was well beyond the region's absorptive capacity, and it contributed to inflationary pressures and balance of payments disequilibria of unprecedented magnitude (Urquidi 1991). Economic growth in the major Latin American economies came to a virtual standstill during the 1983–1990 period, as the high external debt burden required the allocation of 25% to 30% of foreign exchange proceeds merely to cover interest payments. One of Latin America's most prominent economists observed, "Most of the economies in the region were put in a position in which. . . they would be unable easily to resume growth, much less what until then was called 'development.' Zero GDP growth over a period of almost a decade, implying a decline of nearly 10% in per capita GDP, is an experience that few groups of countries in the world have had in the absence of a serious military defeat" (Urquidi 1991:5).

Even though the major international lenders agreed to implement measures like debt forgiveness and debt-for-equity swaps by the early 1990s in order to spur economic recovery in the region, irreparable damage had already been done. Sustained budget cuts in current expenditures on education and health, the rapid deterioration of basic infrastructure, the curtailment of technological innovation through reduced research and development spending, and the obsolescence of much of the region's industrial plants that had remained idle for nearly a decade led the United Nations Economic Commission on Latin America and the Caribbean to designate the 1980s as the "lost development decade" in Latin America (ECLAC 1990).

Pervasive poverty is a major problem throughout much of the region (Felix 1983). The contrast between the Latin American and East Asian newly industrializing countries in this regard could hardly be more striking. Data on household income show that the ratio between the wealthiest 20% and the poorest 20% of households is 33 to 1 in Brazil, 20 to 1 in Mexico, 8 to 1 in South Korea, 7.5 to 1 in the United States, 5 to 1 in Taiwan, and 4.3 to 1 in Japan (Gereffi 1990a:14–15). In Brazil, to take a dramatic example, the top 1% of the population in 1976 received a larger slice of national income than the entire bottom 50% (Hewlett 1982:321).

Latin America's biggest challenge in the 1990s is to attain higher levels of domestic productivity and international competitiveness while also striving to attain social equity. Fajnzylber (1990) points out that no Latin American country has managed to combine economic growth (defined as a 2.4% annual rate of increase in per capita GDP) with social equity (defined as a minimum ratio of 0.4 in group income shares of GDP between the bottom 40% and the top 10% of the population). Countries in other regions that have met both of these development objectives include: Spain, Portugal, Yugoslavia, Hungary, South Korea, Taiwan, China, and Thailand.

The continued high population growth rates have produced a steady expansion in Latin America's labor force, which has grown on the order of 3.5% annually. As real demand plunged during the recession of the 1980s, open unemployment led to a booming "underground economy" (Portes et al 1989, Benería & Roldan 1987). These frequently marginal activities produce no social security or productivity gains and therefore cannot be part of a long-term development strategy. If Latin American manufacturers are going to become internationally competitive, they will have to regard exports as a permanent preoccupation rather than an occasional line of business. In the meantime, multinational corporations probably will generate many of the export opportunities and markets for Latin America's economies. To paraphrase Albert Hirschman, Latin American manufacturers are "late late exporters" (Urquidi 1991). This reliance on multinational corporations, however, threatens to revive many of the long-standing concerns about investment dependence in the region (Gereffi 1989b, Stallings 1990).

EAST ASIA

Unlike Latin America, the East Asian economies have experienced rapid and sustained economic growth during the past three decades. In large part, this growth was predicated on an earlier turn to outward-oriented development. The decision by the East Asian newly industrializing countries to adopt a strategy of primary or labor-intensive export-oriented industrialization in the mid-1960s was neither inevitable nor easy, but it had a number of positive consequences for these countries. The economic gains in industrial competitiveness, full employment, and high sustained economic growth rates are among the most obvious, but equally important is the fact that export-oriented industrialization was spearheaded by local private firms, thus reducing the dependence of the East Asian newly industrializing countries on foreign capital (Haggard & Cheng 1987, Gereffi 1990b,c). The state in South Korea and Taiwan as well as in Japan has been more effective than its counterparts elsewhere in the developing world because of its ability to discipline big business (Johnson 1982, Amsden 1989, Wade 1990, Gereffi 1990b). This is far more difficult where multinational corporations are the dominant firms, as in Latin America.

From 1973 to 1979, Taiwan and South Korea shifted to secondary import-substituting industrialization in capital- and technology-intensive fields with an emphasis on defense-related and upstream industries such as steel, heavy machinery, shipbuilding, petrochemicals, computers, and automobiles (Cheng 1990, Haggard 1990, Gereffi & Wyman 1989). In both countries, advanced import-substitution was selective, and it was designed to sustain rather than supplant national exports as the basis for growth. This facilitated the push into secondary export-oriented industrialization in the 1980s, which was based on a more diversified array of technology- and capital-intensive, high-value-added exports. Secondary export-oriented industrialization allowed the East Asian newly industrializing countries to compete more effectively with the low-wage neighboring Asian countries such as the People's Republic of China, Indonesia, Malaysia, Thailand, and the Philippines, which were moving aggressively to capture the export markets for labor-intensive manufactures such as textiles, garments, and footwear (see Gereffi & Korzeniewicz 1990 on footwear).

In the East Asian newly industrializing countries, the authoritarian governments of South Korea and Taiwan adopted a highly successful "mercantilist" approach to global markets: overseas sales were equated at home with enhanced national security, profitability, and prestige. The favorable external conditions that made the East Asian newly industrializing countries' export success possible—such as rapid economic growth in key overseas markets (especially the United States), a nonprotectionist world trading atmosphere, and low relative wages—are fast disappearing, while the long-suppressed costs of high-speed growth are catching up with these economies.

The local difficulties associated with high-speed growth in East Asia are varied. Taiwan's rapid industrialization in the confines of a small island has created an "environmental nightmare" (Bello & Rosenfeld 1990:195–214), replete with a wide assortment of toxic wastes that are bespoiling air, water, and land alike. In addition, Taiwan is confronting a serious labor shortage and greater worker militance, which has led Taiwan's capitalists to accelerate their investments in the People's Republic of China and, following Singapore's example, to begin importing foreign workers (current estimates of the number of foreign workers in Taiwan range from 50,000 to 100,000). Finally, Taiwan also confronts a technological challenge as it tries to move from its conventional labor-intensive exports to heavier and high-tech industries like transportation equipment, electrical machinery, and computer components (Schive 1990).

South Korea has confronted serious insurrections from the working class, whose mobilization was facilitated by the highly concentrated industrial enterprises around which the national economy is built (Cumings 1989, Deyo 1989). The rapid growth of these massive industrial conglomerates (*chaebol*) in the 1970s and 1980s presents the South Korean state with a major challenge to its power in the economic realm, since the *chaebol* are trying to free themselves from state control of the financial system in order to chart their own course in global markets (Woo 1991). While the *chaebol* have been extremely effective in amassing capital and joining borrowed technology to large-scale manufacturing processes based on cheap labor, it remains to be seen whether they can provide an institutional context that encourages true innovation (Amsden 1989).

The key features of East Asia's success may lie less in the area of economic policy than in the region's dynamic institutional arrangements. The East Asian experience has been characterized by: (*a*) local ownership and control in their leading export and intermediate goods industries; (*b*) substantial backward and forward linkages within the domestic economy involving a wide variety of local business groups and subcontracting networks (Orrú et al 1991, Hamilton & Biggart 1988, Hamilton et al 1987); (*c*) a high level of endogenous technological development, although few of these countries (with the exception of Japan) have made true innovative technological breakthroughs; (*d*) industrialization by learning "best practice" management techniques from the shopfloor level to the state (Amsden 1989); and (*e*) state initiatives that "govern" the market, rather than substitute for it (Wade 1990).

SUB-SAHARAN AFRICA

Since independence, sub-Saharan Africa's development trajectory has been characterized by two main transitions: "from expansion to contraction in economic performance and from optimism to pessimism in political analysis" (Shaw 1991:5). These economic and political trends clearly pose special challenges. First, the sub-Saharan African economy is less stable than the other regions of the third world, a condition that is exacerbated by drought and global recession. Second, the cultures, geography, and political systems of sub-Saharan Africa's 51 countries and territories are exceptionally diverse, making it difficult to generalize about the problems of this region and the policies suitable to change them.

Nonetheless, there is strong consensus about one topic: African agriculture is suffering. Agricultural production is no longer able to keep pace with population growth, so an increasing number of Africans do not have access to adequate food resources (Berry 1984). Consequently, "the epidemic starvation for all but the very rich" typifying pre-colonial Africa has given way to "endemic undernutrition for the very poor" (Iliffe 1987:6).

The reasons for low agricultural productivity are interrelated. Poor soils, unstable climatic conditions, and inadequate farming techniques to deal with these conditions are a few of the obvious internal constraints on agricultural output (Richards 1983). However, these internal limitations do not receive the critical attention they require because of the greater priority given by public officials to foreign exchange controls, reduction of inflation, and import-substituting investments. In addition, attempts have been made by African governments to gain political control by usurping productive agricultural enterprises and farmer autonomy (Berry 1984, Bunker 1987). Thus actions by the government and its competing political factions have had the effect of discouraging productivity.

A number of external factors suggest that dependence on agriculture perpetuates sub-Saharan Africa's position in the lowest stratum of the third world. These include the continuation of relationships implemented during colonialism, worsening terms of trade, and changes in global demand for African agricultural products.

The argument addressing exploitative colonial relationships is not new, although there have been recent changes in this perspective. The first part of the argument is that colonialism instituted the reliance of African countries on the overseas sales of one or two primary agricultural products (Amin 1976). Consequently, African economies are now vulnerable to changes in the international terms of trade, global demand, and global pricing. This is as true for extractive commodities (minerals, fuels, and metals) as it is for agriculture (Leys 1982). Furthermore, economic ties of a colonial nature frequently result in the flow of surplus out of the third world. This depletion of resources results in the neglect of development and investment in these regions (Amin 1976, Berry 1984).

The majority of African industries use minimal technology. These include final-stage manufacturing (e.g. automobile assembly in Nigeria and Tanzania) as well as labor-intensive industries (e.g. textiles, apparel and leather). When more advanced technology is required, it is imported, thus further retarding African technological development (Leys 1982). This limits the creation of indigenous backward and forward linkages (Mytelka 1989) and increases the vulnerability of African industries to technological changes in competing regions (Biersteker 1987, Mihyo 1985, Mytelka 1985).

There is skepticism about whether the strategies pursued by African industrialists are capable of fostering economic growth at all (Beveridge & Oberschall 1979, Lubeck 1987). This skepticism represents a shift in focus from external to internal factors contributing to the African crisis (Lubeck 1987). After independence, the majority of capital was invested in agricultural and extractive export commodities (Ollawa 1983). Limited attempts at import-substituting industrialization were made, but this strategy was less successful in Africa than in East Asia or Latin America because the domestic demand for mass-produced commodities was too small, and the scarcity of indigenous sources of technology made it necessary to import most goods (Leys 1982).

Mytelka (1989) claims that import substitution was never actually pursued in Africa. Instead, "import reproduction" was the primary strategy. Import reproduction strategies are those that "ignore the extent to which products incorporate concepts of functionality, cost, quality, and aesthetics that correspond to the producer's principle market of sale" (Mytelka 1989:79). In other words, import reproduction fails to address the needs of the intended market, so that African industrialization was only superficially inward-oriented. As a result, import reproduction in Africa was exhausted by the mid-1970s, while import-substitution continued to bolster economies in other regions of the third world.

Industrialization in Africa has largely been funded by agricultural exports and foreign capital. Agricultural exports have not been sufficient to sustain industrialization owing to worsening terms of trade and declining productivity. This left foreign aid and direct investments by multinational corporations as the primary sources of development capital. Multinational corporations in particular have maintained control over industries through management, technological input, and investment, even after the 1967 period of indigenization in countries such as Nigeria, Kenya, Tanzania and Zaire (Mytelka 1989). Furthermore, the fact that the major economic agents of sub-Saharan African development were foreign capitalists and donors is an important reason why the African economy dramatically worsened in the 1970s and early 1980s with the decline of foreign aid and foreign direct investment.

The influence of foreign capital in parts of sub-Saharan Africa has fostered the emergence of "predatory" capitalism brokered by corrupt states, as exemplified by the cases of Zaire, Uganda, and Sudan (Evans 1989b, Callaghy 1984). According to Evans, "predatory" capitalism exists when "The preoccupation of the political class with rent seeking has turned the rest of society into prey" (Evans 1989b:570). Consequently, the development of a class capable of investing in long-term capitalist enterprises is inhibited.

Economic development in sub-Saharan Africa over the past 20 years has lagged behind that of other regions of the third world. Worsening social development has coincided with poor economic performance. Sub-Saharan

Africa has the lowest life expectancy, the highest rate of infant mortality, and the highest rate of illiteracy of the four regions examined here. This situation is perpetuated by the tendency of African governments to ignore primary education in favor of higher education. In addition, Africa's infrastructure has been neglected throughout the past 30 years, creating a disincentive for further investment by foreign capital. Rapid population growth and overcrowding in the cities place excess demands on agriculture and the underdeveloped industrial sector. Finally, the unequal distribution of wealth, disparate wages among African laborers, and Africa's long history of poverty (Iliffe 1987) are inimical to the growth of healthy domestic markets. It appears that sub-Saharan Africa is in a situation of long-term decline for which contemporary theories of development have few if any answers.

SOUTH ASIA

The South Asian economy is slightly better off than that of sub-Saharan Africa in terms of GNP per capita and GDP. However, South Asia accounts for approximately half of the world's poor, which means that it has a higher concentration of people living in poverty than sub-Saharan Africa or any other region of the third world (World Bank 1990:2). To offset the pervasive poverty, South Asian nations have pursued policies to improve access to social services and to encourage development. Sri Lanka, for example, has focused on providing social services, but it has been unable to increase the incomes of the poor due to slow economic growth (World Bank 1990:3). Similarly, a sluggish economy has inhibited the reduction of national poverty and unemployment in India, despite India's attempts at planned development over the past four decades (Bardhan 1984, Sinha 1988). Other countries in South Asia such as Pakistan have been more successful in reducing poverty, but social services have not yet improved (World Bank 1990:3). Consequently, the persistent problem of poverty lends a critical tone to the development trends in South Asia.

Like sub-Saharan Africa, the principal economic activity of the South Asian economies is agriculture. India, however, has periodically over the past 40 years eliminated its need for food imports, due in large part to the remarkable success of the Green Revolution in improving India's crop yields. Conversely, sub-Saharan Africa has not reaped the benefits of a successful Green Revolution and, therefore, continues to rely on imports to lessen the problem of food shortages.

The question of agricultural output in South Asia is often raised in the literature because agricultural trends are posited as an explanation for trends in industry. Ahluwalia (1985), for example, claims that because of the linkages between agriculture and industry, negligible growth in agriculture and in the income of agricultural laborers inhibits the demand for industrial products. Furthermore, Mathur claims that an increase in agricultural production is a necessary condition for strengthening industrialization, but it is not sufficient because it must occur in conjunction with a "build up in the capital goods producing capacity of the economy" and the provision of "adequate power, transport infrastructure and institutional finance" (Mathur 1990:275). As a result, the belief that a successful agricultural season is automatically followed by improvements in the industrial sector is incorrect.

The literature on industrial growth in South Asia, and particularly India, is characterized by a mix of pessimism and optimism. The pessimistic point of view highlights India's slowdown in industrial growth since the mid-1970s. This is attributed to India's adoption of the Mahalanobis model, which placed an excessively high priority on heavy industry and underemphasized the labor-intensive activities needed to employ India's massive work force (Sinha 1988). The slowdown in growth also has been explained in terms of the state's inefficient management of the "industrial policy framework," which sheltered industries regardless of costs or quality of production, failed to eliminate protection from competitive sectors, and closed off the economy so that there was little incentive for upgrading products (Ahluwalia 1985).

From the optimistic viewpoint, industrialization in India has progressed toward the desired objective of self-sufficiency because of India's tough stance vis-à-vis foreign capital, its strategy of import-substituting industrialization, and the improvement of indigenous technology (Chelliah 1988). Consequently, India's development has been driven by domestic forces, in contrast to sub-Saharan Africa's relatively greater reliance on foreign aid to generate economic growth.

The principal economic agents in India have been a triple alliance of multinational firms, domestic investors, and the state. Due to the assertive stance of the state in particular, India has demonstrated an ability to wrest segments of its economy from the control of multinational corporations. Grieco (1984), for example, shows how India was able to exploit opportunities provided by intense competition within the international computer industry during the 1970s and thereby increase the benefits for India despite the constraints that often hinder developing host countries in their relations with multinational firms. Grieco's primary argument is that the substantial, albeit incomplete, shift in power away from multinationals to the host country was mediated by the Indian state. Additional factors contributing to this transfer in power were India's large pool of low-wage, highly skilled labor, the overall increase in the number of international suppliers of small systems and inexpensive components, and the success of private indigenous firms that were able to make up for the relative stagnation of India's predominant public sector electronics firm, ECIL.

In a later study, Encarnation (1989) addresses India's success at actually "dislodging" multinational corporations from domestic markets. Encarnation examines the dynamic relationship between multinationals , the state, and indigenous firms, positing that changes in this relationship enabled India to "increase dramatically both the available range of plausible outcomes and the probability of securing their preferred outcome" (Encarnation 1989:4). For example, multinationals have maintained a bargaining advantage over the state, private indigenous firms, and state-owned firms because they had access to capital and technology necessary for Indian economic development. At the same time, however, the state and private domestic firms have cooperated to acquire control over the domestic market, dislodging multinational corporations through the growth of indigenous firms.

However, in the late 1980s and early 1990s, India changed economic strategies vis-à-vis multinational corporations and adopted "liberal" concessionary policies. Evans' (1989a) explanation of Brazil's comparable experience with the international computer industry provides insight into this recent shift in the balance of power between the Indian state and multinationals. Like India, Brazil pursued assertive policies in the computer industry in the early 1980s, whereby it relied on indigenous firms for its supply of small computers and discouraged imports and domestic production by the multinational companies. But by the late 1980s, Brazil's previously assertive position altered as it acceded to the demands of the multinationals. State-imposed barriers to foreign firms were lowered, resulting in the domination of the Brazilian market by giant foreign computer companies, such as IBM and Burroughs. Brazil's "pragmatic pursuit of foreign relations goals," Evans argues, "had won over principled defense of economic ideology" (Evans 1989a:231).

Brazil's massive foreign debt and its need to sustain economic growth led to a shift in the balance of power to the advantage of the multinational corporations. Similarly, India has also accrued a substantial foreign debt since the 1970s. India's total external debt was $7.8 billion in 1970, compared to $18 billion in 1981 and $62.5 billion in 1989 (World Bank 1983:178; World Bank 1991:244). As in the case of Brazil, India's increasing foreign debt burden and its need to generate economic growth have contributed to the liberalization of Indian economic policies in ways designed to attract foreign capital.

IMPLICATIONS FOR DEVELOPMENT THEORY

Important affinities exist between development theories and the paths of particular third world regions. Development theories are not created in a vacuum; they tend to reflect the experiences of certain countries, regions, and time periods that commanded attention when the theories were being elaborated. Consequently, problems may arise when attempts are made to generalize beyond these geographical and historical boundaries.

Development theories were gradually modified and expanded during the 1980s to provide a more integrated look at the manifold changes occurring in the world economy. Many of these transformations require a rethinking of the key suppositions of individual theories in order to capture similarities and contrasts in the experiences of different regions around the globe (Gereffi 1989b). This is an important indicator of the progress or growth of a theory (Wagner & Berger 1985). Thus, an explicit comparison of regional paths of development facilitates good theory-building. Some of the most significant recent shifts in development theory are highlighted below.

NEOCLASSICAL ECONOMICS East Asia comes closest to embodying the prescriptions of neoclassical economics, although the role of the state is far greater than strict neoclassical interpretations allow (see Wade & White 1984, Wade 1990). Despite the clear preference of neoclassical economics for export-oriented rather than import-substituting industrialization in the third world, both historical and comparative evidence points to several important lessons concerning national development strategies: (*a*) import-substituting industrialization and export-oriented industrialization are complementary and interactive sets of policies, rather than mutually exclusive alternatives (Gereffi 1989a, 1990a); (*b*) both inward-oriented and outward-oriented development strategies are susceptible to systematic constraints or vulnerabilities that prevent either from being a long-term economic panacea (Gereffi 1990c); (*c*) import substitution was not an unmitigated disaster for Latin America or India, nor was export-oriented industrialization a tribute to unbridled market forces in East Asia (see Bardhan 1984, Fishlow 1989, Whitehead 1989, Dore 1990, Haggard 1990); and (*d*) a substantial part of the East Asian economic success story seems to be predicated on deliberately "getting relative prices 'wrong'" through incentives and subsidies to local businesses that improve their position in the world-economy (Amsden 1989, Wade 1990).

Furthermore, the ordinarily staid international development banks recently have begun to give greater emphasis to the social investments needed to cope with the problems of persistent poverty and social marginality in the third world. In the two most recent *World Development Reports,* which focus on the themes of poverty (World Bank 1990) and development (World Bank 1991), the World Bank asserts that the productive use of "human capital" calls for policies that harness market incentives to furnish opportunities for the poor and that stress investment in health and education. Similarly, the Inter-American Development Bank's annual report for 1990 has a special section on "Working Women in Latin America." The region's 40 million working women suffer from a lack of training, barriers to credit and technology, and the double burdens of holding a job and running a household, despite their growing importance in the region's work force during the economic crisis of the 1980s (IADB 1990).

WORLD-SYSTEMS/DEPENDENCY THEORIES A growing number of studies have analyzed the dynamic patterns of competition and change in the world-economy over the past three decades. Instead of focusing on the categories of core, semiperipheral, and peripheral nations, new research is being done on the international divisions of labor that characterize global industries (Henderson 1989, Gereffi & Korzeniewicz 1990, Doner 1991). These studies show that the world-economy is indeed hierarchically organized, as world-systems theory postulates, but that the roles played by countries at different levels of development vary according to both the technological characteristics of the industries in question and the industrial strategies followed by nations that seek to move toward higher-value-added activities in global commodity chains (Gereffi & Korzeniewicz 1990). This approach links the macro-level issues concerning the structure of the world-economy with the meso-level characteristics of national development strategies and the micro-level emphasis on the social embeddedness of international and domestic subcontracting networks in local political and social contexts (Ellison & Gereffi 1990).

World-systems theory also helps us understand the recent dilemmas confronted by developing nations that try to alter their relationship to the capitalist world-economy. The socialist societies of Eastern Europe are testimony to the difficulties of exiting the world-system; they highlight the kinds of adjustments that will be required to adopt a new role in the global economy. Conversely, sub-Saharan Africa shows that non-incorporation in the world-system may bring the severest problems of all. Corrupt states, a weak national bourgeoisie, low levels of foreign investment, small domestic markets, and unstable export industries offer few resources from which to fashion viable development strategies.

The cross-regional comparisons of paths of development in the third world emphasize the need to broaden our views of dependent development (Gereffi & Wyman 1990, Haggard 1990). The concept of transnational economic linkages is useful in this regard. There are four main transnational economic linkages: foreign aid, foreign trade, foreign direct investment, and foreign debt. Different third world regions have distinct configurations of these external linkages which have led to varied patterns of development outcomes (Gereffi 1989b).

Many countries in Latin America and sub-Saharan Africa, for example, have relied heavily on foreign aid, investments by multinationals, and foreign debt at different stages of their economic trajectories, and these transnational linkages were shown to hinder or distort patterns of national development in various ways (Biersteker 1978, Evans 1979, Gereffi 1983, Newfarmer 1985). The East Asian newly industrializing countries, on the other hand, have enjoyed spectacular economic growth despite their dependency on foreign aid (in the 1950s) and foreign trade (since the 1960s), and the Indian state has had considerable success in bargaining with multinationals in the computer industry (Grieco 1984, Encarnation 1989). Dependency theory highlighted the structural constraints implied by transnational economic linkages in the Latin American and African contexts, but it failed to specify the institutional conditions that could lead to successful "dependency management" in the cases of East Asia and India.

A more comprehensive theory of dependency has to focus on the local as well as international conditions that allow domestic actors to use transnational linkages productively and selectively to serve national interests. A key to understanding the success of the East Asian newly industrializing countries and of India, for example, is the performance of diversified and technologically capable locally owned firms that aggressively sought out new export markets and backed the state in its tough bargaining with multinationals. Favorable international circumstances also helped, such as growing world markets for East Asian exports and new competitors in the global computer industry when India made its major gains. Dependency theory is not invalidated by a host country's able management of transnational economic linkages, but the scope of the theory must be expanded to identify the conditions under which "dependency management" can lead to positive development outcomes.

DEVELOPMENTAL STATE Developmental states promote "assertive industrialization," which refers to the use of state policy to force a country's position in the international division of labor to improve at an accelerated pace (Evans 1989a). The idea of assertive industrialization and the bureaucratic mechanisms that support it are found in a wide range of recent empirical studies of third world countries: Brazil (Evans 1979, 1989a, Adler 1987), Mexico (Gereffi 1983, Bennett & Sharpe 1985), South Korea (Amsden 1989, Woo 1991), Taiwan (Gold 1986, Wade 1990), India (Grieco 1984, Encarnation 1989), Nigeria (Biersteker 1987, Lubeck 1987), and Peru (Becker 1983), plus comparative volumes dealing with Latin America and East Asia (Newfarmer 1985, Deyo 1987, Fajnzylber 1990, Gereffi & Wyman 1990, Haggard 1990). All these works share what Evans (1989a) terms a post-dependency/bargaining perspective, which looks at the conflicts between the interests of transnational capital, domestic industrial coalitions, and third world states over local development priorities.

The developmental state approach has been further enhanced by comparative studies that disaggregate the institutional features of economic policy-making in specific regional settings. The research on East Asia, for example, highlights the ideological and organizational coherence of state economic bureaucracies, the policy networks that connect state bureaucracies to the private sector, and the social bases of these political regimes in order to explain variations in industrial adjustment policies within the region (Cheng & Haggard 1987, Chu 1989, Haggard 1990, Wade 1990).

INSTITUTIONAL ANALYSIS New applications for institutional analysis already have been mentioned in the preceding discussions of global commodity chains, transnational economic linkages, and the developmental state. In addition, the institutional perspective infuses research on third world business networks with a renewed appreciation of the importance of organizational culture and "industrialization by learning" at the micro-level of shop-floor practices.

In East Asia, it has been shown that the interfirm network structure of the major enterprise groups in South Korea, Taiwan, and Japan exhibits intrasocietal isomorphism and intersocietal variation, reflecting the different institutional principles that prevail in each of these three societies (Orrú et al 1991, Hamilton & Biggart 1988, Hamilton et al 1987). These interfirm linkages may be externalized in international subcontracting networks (Doner 1991), or they can form the basis for dynamic domestic subcontracting ties between large- and small-scale firms, many of which produce for export (Greenhalgh 1984, Amsden 1989). A growing number of studies on the informal economy within Latin America show how people in apparently marginal economic pursuits actually are joined in an integral way with the large firms and public institutions of the formal sector (Benería & Roldan 1987, Portes et al 1989).

MARXISM The current decline in the influence of marxian theories undoubtedly is bound up with the dizzying changes connected with "the end of the Cold War." Socialist societies are undergoing profound transformations around the world. The market reforms and ethnic conflicts in Eastern Europe, the disintegration of the Soviet Union, and China's procapitalist reforms and its sudden emergence as one of the world's leading exporters of manufactured goods raise fundamental questions about "remaking the economic institutions of socialism" (Nee & Stark 1989). The few remaining socialist societies in the third world—Cuba, Tanzania, and Vietnam—are increasingly isolated. However, Tanzania and Vietnam are now forging new ties with international investors, and even North Korea is moving closer to a rapprochement with its capitalist rival to the south.

Ultimately, development concerns quality of life. Our review shows that the regions in which agriculture remains dominant (sub-Saharan Africa and South Asia) have the poorest records of economic as well as social well-being. However, the experiences of Latin America and India, where poverty abounds despite relatively advanced levels of industrialization, indicate that industrialization per se is no guarantee of high living standards and more equitable patterns of income distribution. Higher levels of economic productivity in agriculture as well as industry, which give rise to improved social welfare, cannot be achieved without significant investments in the health, education, and training of the people who are expected to shoulder the burdens of economic development.

Literature Cited

Adler, E. 1987. *The Power of Ideology: The Quest for Technological Autonomy in Argentina and Brazil*. Berkeley: Univ. Calif. Press

Ahluwalia, I. J. 1985. *Industrial Growth in India*. Dehli: Oxford Univ. Press

Amin, S. 1976. *Unequal Development*. New York: Monthly Rev.

Amsden, A. H. 1979. Taiwan's economic history: A case of etatisme and a challenge to dependency theory. *Mod. China* 5:341–80

Amsden, A. H. 1989. *Asia's Next Giant: South Korea and Late Industrialization*. New York: Oxford Univ. Press

Arrighi, G. 1990. The developmentalist illusion: A reconceptualization of the semiperiphery. See Martin 1990, pp. 11–42

Arrighi, G., Drangel, J. 1986. The stratification of the world-economy: An exploration of the semiperipheral zone. *Review* 10:9–74

Balassa, B. 1981. *The Newly Industrializing Countries in the World Economy*. New York: Pergamon

Balassa, B., Bueno, G. M., Kuczynski, P. P., Simonsen, M. H. 1986. *Toward Renewed Economic Growth in Latin America*. Washington, DC: Inst. Int. Econ.

Bardhan, P. 1984. *The Political Economy of Development in India*. New York: Basil Blackwell

Barrett, R. E., Whyte, M. K. 1982. Dependency theory and Taiwan: Analysis of a deviant case. *Am. J. Sociol*. 87(5):1064–89

Becker, D. 1983. *The New Bourgeoisie and the Limits of Dependency: Mining, Class and Power in 'Revolutionary' Peru*. Princeton, NJ: Princeton Univ. Press

Bello, W., Rosenfeld, S. 1990. *Dragons in Distress: Asia's Miracle Economies in Crisis*. San Francisco: Inst. Food Dev. Policy

Benería, L., Roldan, M. 1987. *The Crossroads of Class and Gender: Industrial Homework, Subcontracting, and Household Dynamics in Mexico City*. Chicago: Univ. Chicago Press

Bennett, D. C., Sharpe, K. E. 1985. *Transnational Corporations Versus the State: The Political Economy of the Mexican Auto Industry*. Princeton, NJ: Princeton Univ. Press

Berger, P. L., Hsiao, H-H. M., eds. 1988. *In Search of an East Asian Development Model*. New Brunswick, NJ: Transaction

Berry, S. 1984. The food crisis and agrarian change in Africa: A review essay. *African Stud. Rev*. 27(2):59–112

Beveridge, A., Oberschall, A. 1979. *African Businessmen and Development in Zambia*. Princeton, NJ: Princeton Univ. Press

Biersteker, T. J. 1978. *Distortion or Development? Contending Perspectives on the Multinational Corporation*. Cambridge, MA: MIT Press

Biersteker, T. J. 1987. *Multinationals, the State, and Control of the Nigerian Economy*. Princeton, NJ: Princeton Univ. Press

Bradshaw, Y. W. 1988. Reassessing economic dependency and uneven development: The Kenyan experience. *Am. Sociol. Rev*. 53(5):693–708

Bunker, S. G. 1987. *Peasants Against the State: The Politics of Market Control in Bugisu, Uganda, 1900–1983*. Chicago: Univ. Chicago Press

Callaghy, T. 1984. *The State-Society Struggle: Zaire in Comparative Historical Perspective*. New York: Columbia Univ. Press

Chelliah, R. K. 1988. Reflections on Indian political economy and development. See Sinha 1988, pp. 9–28

Cheng, T.-J. 1990. Political regimes and development strategies: South Korea and Taiwan. See Gereffi & Wyman 1990, pp. 139–78

Cheng, T.-J., Haggard, S. 1987. *Newly Industrializing Asia in Transition: Policy Re-*

form and American Response. Berkeley: Inst. Int. Stud., Univ. Calif.
Chu, Y.-H. 1989. State structure and economic adjustment of the East Asian newly industrializing countries. *Int. Organ.* 43 (4):647–72
Collier, D. ed. 1979. *The New Authoritarianism in Latin America*. Princeton, NJ: Princeton Univ. Press
Council for Economic Planning and Development (CEPD). 1991. *Taiwan Statistical Data Book, 1991*. Taipei, Taiwan: CEPD
Cumings, B. 1984. The origins and development of the Northeast Asian political economy: Industrial sectors, product cycles, and political consequences. *Int. Organ.* 38(1):1–40
Cumings, B. 1989. The abortive abertura: South Korea in the light of Latin American experiences. *New Left Rev.* 173:5–32
Deyo, F., ed. 1987. *The Political Economy of the New Asian Industrialism*. Ithaca, NY: Cornell Univ. Press
Deyo, F. 1989. *Beneath the Miracle: Labor Subordination in the New Asian Industrialism*. Berkeley: Univ. Calif. Press
DiMaggio, P. J., Powell, W. W. 1991. Introduction. See Powell & DiMaggio 1991, pp. 1–38
Directorate-General of Budget, Accounting & Statistics (DGBAS). 1986. *Statistical Yearbook of the Republic of China*. Taipei, Taiwan: Executive Yuan
Doner, R. F. 1991. *Driving a Bargain: Automobile Industrialization and Japanese Firms in Southeast Asia*. Berkeley: Univ. Calif. Press
Dore, R. 1990. Reflections on culture and social change. See Gereffi & Wyman 1990, pp. 353–67
Economic Commission for Latin America and the Caribbean (ECLAC), United Nations. 1990. *Changing Production Patterns with Social Equity*. Santiago, Chile: ECLAC
Ellison, C., Gereffi, G. 1990. Explaining strategies and patterns of industrial development. See Gereffi & Wyman 1990, pp. 368–403
Encarnation, D. 1989. *Dislodging Multinationals: India's Strategy in Comparative Perspective*. Ithaca, NY: Cornell Univ. Press
Evans, P. B. 1979. *Dependent Development: The Alliance of Multinationals, State and Local Capital in Brazil*. Princeton, NJ: Princeton Univ. Press
Evans, P. B. 1987. Class, state, and dependence in East Asia: Some lessons for Latin Americanists. See Deyo 1987, pp. 203–6
Evans, P. B. 1989a. Declining hegemony and assertive industrialization: U.S.-Brazil conflicts in the computer industry. *Int. Organ.* 43(2):207–38
Evans, P. B. 1989b. Predatory, developmental, and other apparatuses: A comparative political economy perspective on the Third World state. *Sociol. Forum* 4: 561–87
Evans, P. B., Stephens, J. D. 1988. Development and the world economy. In *Handbook of Sociology,* ed. N. J. Smelser, pp. 739–73. Newbury Park, Calif: Sage
Fajnzylber, F. 1990. *Unavoidable Industrial Restructuring in Latin America*. Durham, NC: Duke Univ. Press
Felix, D. 1983. Income distribution and the quality of life in Latin America: Patterns, trends, and policy implications. *Latin Am. Res. Rev.* 18:3–34
Fishlow, A. 1989. Latin American failure against the backdrop of Asian success. See Gourevitch 1989, pp. 117–128
Friedman, D. 1988. *The Misunderstood Miracle: Industrial Development and Political Change in Japan*. Ithaca, NY: Cornell Univ. Press
Gereffi, G. 1983. *The Pharmaceutical Industry and Dependency in the Third World*. Princeton, NJ: Princeton Univ. Press
Gereffi, G. 1989a. Development strategies and the global factory. See Gourevitch 1989, pp. 92–104
Gereffi, G. 1989b. Rethinking development theory: Insights from East Asia and Latin America. *Sociol. Forum* 4:505–33
Gereffi, G. 1990a. Paths of industrialization: An overview. See Gereffi & Wyman 1990, pp. 3–31
Gereffi, G. 1990b. Big business and the state. See Gereffi & Wyman 1990, pp. 90–109
Gereffi, G. 1990c. International economics and domestic policies. In *Economy and Society: Overviews in Economic Sociology*, ed. A. Martinelli, N. Smelser, pp. 231–58. Newbury Park, Calif: Sage
Gereffi, G., Evans, P. 1981. Transnational corporations, dependent development, and state policy in the semiperiphery: A comparison of Brazil and Mexico. *Latin Am. Res. Rev.* 16(3):31–64
Gereffi, G., Wyman, D. 1989. Determinants of development strategies in Latin America and East Asia. In *Pacific Dynamics: The International Politics of Industrial Change*, ed. S. Haggard, C. Moon, pp. 23–52. Boulder, Colo: Westview
Gereffi, G., Korzeniewicz, M. 1990. Commodity chains and footwear exports in the semiperiphery. See Martin 1990, pp. 45–68
Gereffi, G., Wyman, D., eds. 1990. *Manufacturing Miracles: Paths of Industrialization in Latin America and East Asia*. Princeton, NJ: Princeton Univ. Press
Gold, T. B. 1981. *Dependent development in Taiwan*. PhD thesis, Harvard Univ. Cambridge, Mass.

Gold, T. B. 1986. *State and Society in the Taiwan Miracle*. Armonk, NY: Sharpe

Gourevitch, P. A. ed. 1989. The Pacific Region: Challenges to policy and theory. Special issue of the *Ann. Am. Acad. Polit. Soc. Sci. 505*.

Granovetter, M. 1985. Economic action and social structure: The problem of embeddedness. *Am. J. Sociol.* 91(3):481–510

Greenhalgh, S. 1984. Networks and their nodes: Urban society on Taiwan. *China Q.* 99:529–52

Grieco, J. 1984. *Between Dependency and Autonomy: India's Experience with the International Computer Industry*. Berkeley: Univ. Calif. Press

Haggard, S. 1989. The political economy of foreign direct investment in Latin America. *Latin Am. Res. Rev.* 24(1):184–208

Haggard, S. 1990. *Pathways from the Periphery: The Politics of Growth in the Newly Industrializing Countries*. Ithaca, NY: Cornell Univ. Press

Haggard, S., Cheng, T.-J. 1987. State and foreign capital in the East Asian NICs. See Deyo 1987, pp. 84–135

Hamilton, G. G., Kao, C-S. 1987. Max Weber and the analysis of East Asian industrialization. *Int. Sociol.* 2:289–300

Hamilton, G. G., Orrú, M., Biggart, N. W. 1987. Enterprise groups in East Asia: An organizational analysis. *Finan. Econ. Rev.* (Tokyo, Japan) 161:78–106

Hamilton, G. G., Biggart, N. W. 1988. Market, culture, and authority: A comparative analysis of management and organization in the Far East. *Am. J. Sociol.* 94 (Suppl.): S52-S94

Henderson, J. 1989. *The Globalisation of High Technology Production: Society, Space and Semiconductors in the Restructuring of the Modern World*. London: Routledge

Hewlett, S. A. 1982. Poverty and inequality in Brazil. In *Brazil and Mexico: Patterns in Late Development,* ed. S. A. Hewlett, R. B. Weinert, pp. 317–38. Philadelphia, Penn: Inst. Study Hum. Issues

Iliffe, J. 1987. *The African Poor*. Cambridge: Cambridge Univ. Press

Inter-American Development Bank (IADB). 1990. *Economic and Social Progress in Latin America:1990 Report*. Baltimore, Md: Johns Hopkins Univ. Press

Johnson, C. 1982. *MITI and the Japanese Miracle*. Stanford, Calif: Stanford Univ. Press

Johnson, C. 1987. Political institutions and economic performance: The government-business relationship in Japan, South Korea, and Taiwan. See Deyo 1987, pp. 134–64

Kaufman, R. 1990. How societies change development models or keep them: Reflections on the Latin American Experience in the 1930s and the postwar world. See Gereffi & Wyman 1990, pp. 110–138

Kim, K.-D., ed. 1987. *Dependency Issues in Korean Development*. Seoul, Korea: Seoul Natl. Univ. Press

Koo, H. 1987. The interplay of state, social class, and world system in East Asian Development: The cases of South Korea and Taiwan. See Deyo 1987, pp. 165–81

Leys, C. 1982. African economic development in theory and practice. *Daedalus* 3:99–124

Lim, H.-C. 1985. *Dependent Development in Korea, 1963–1979*. Seoul, Korea: Seoul National Univ. Press

Lincoln, J., McBride, K. 1987. Japanese industrial organization in comparative perspective. *Annu. Rev. Sociol.* 13:289–312

Lubeck, P., ed. 1987. *The African Bourgeoisie: Capitalist Development in Nigeria, Kenya and the Ivory Coast*. Boulder, Colo: Lynne Rienner

Martin, W., ed. 1990. *Semiperipheral States in the World-Economy*. Westport, Conn: Greenwood

Mathur, A. 1990. The interface of agricultural and industrial growth in the development process: Some facets of the Indian experience. *Dev. Change* 22:247–80

Meyer, J. W., Rowan, B. 1991. Institutionalized organizations: Formal structure as myth and ceremony. See Powell & DiMaggio 1991, pp. 41–62

Mihyo, P. 1985. *Bargaining for technology in Tanzania's public enterprises: Some policy issues*. Study prepared for the IDRC, Ottawa

Mytelka, L. K. 1985. Stimulating effective technology transfer: The case of textiles in Africa. In *International Technology Transfer: Concepts, Measures & Comparisons,* ed. N. Rosenberg, C. Frischtak, pp. 77–125. New York: Praeger

Mytelka, L. K. 1989. The unfulfilled promise of African industrialization. *African Stud. Rev.* 32(3):77–137

Nee, V., Stark, D., eds. 1989. *Remaking the Economic Institutions of Socialism: China and Eastern Europe*. Stanford, Calif: Stanford Univ. Press

Newfarmer, R., ed. 1985. *Profits, Progress and Poverty: Case Studies of International Industries in Latin America*. Notre Dame, Ind: Univ. Notre Dame Press

O'Donnell, G., Schmitter, P., Whitehead, L., eds. 1986. *Transitions from Authoritarian Rule*. Baltimore, Md: Johns Hopkins Univ. Press

Ollawa, P. 1983. The political economy of development: A theoretical reconsideration of some unresolved issues. *African Stud. Rev*. 26(1):125–55

Orrú, M., Biggart, N. W., Hamilton, G. G. 1991. Organizational isomorphism in East Asia. See Powell & DiMaggio 1991, pp. 361–89

Portes, A., Castells, M., Benton, L. A., eds. 1989. *The Informal Economy: Studies in Advanced and Less Developed Countries*. Baltimore, Md: Johns Hopkins Univ. Press

Powell, W. W., DiMaggio, P. J., eds. 1991. *The New Institutionalism in Organizational Analysis*. Chicago, Ill: Univ. Chicago Press

Richards, P. 1983. Farming systems and agrarian change in West Africa. *Prog. Hum. Geogr*. 7(1):1–39

Schive, C. 1990. The next stage of industrialization in Taiwan and South Korea. See Gereffi & Wyman 1990, pp. 267–91

Shaw, T. M. 1991. *Reformism and revisionism in African political economy in the 1990s*. Pres. Int. Stud. Assoc. Annu. Meet., Vancouver, Canada

Sinha, R. K., ed. 1988. *Economic Policy and Development in India*. New Delhi: Deep & Deep

So, A. Y. 1990. *Social Change and Development: Modernization, Dependency, and World-System Theories*. Newbury Park, Calif: Sage

Stallings, B. 1990. The role of foreign capital in economic development. See Gereffi & Wyman 1990, pp. 55–89

Stepan, A. 1988. *Rethinking Military Politics: Brazil and the Southern Cone*. Princeton, NJ: Princeton Univ. Press

Swidler, A. 1986. Culture in action: Symbols and strategies. *Am. Sociol. Rev*. 51(2):273–86

Urquidi, V. L. 1991. The prospects for economic transformation in Latin America: Opportunities and resistances. *LASA Forum* 22(3):1–9

Valenzuela, J. S., Valenzuela, A. 1978. Modernization and dependency: Alternative perspectives in the study of Latin American underdevelopment. *Comp. Polit*. 10:535–57

Wade, R. 1990. *Governing the Market: Economic Theory and the Role of Government in East Asian Industrialization*. Princeton, NJ: Princeton Univ. Press

Wade, R., White, G., eds. 1984. Developmental states in East Asia: Capitalist and socialist. *Inst. Dev. Stud. Bull*. 15:1–70

Wagner, D. G., Berger, J. 1985. Do sociological theories grow? *Am. J. Sociol*. 90(4):697–728

Wallerstein, I. 1974. *The Modern World-System, I: Capitalist Agriculture and the Origins of the European World-Economy in the Sixteenth Century*. New York: Academic

Wallerstein, I. 1979. *The Capitalist World-Economy*. New York: Cambridge

Wallerstein, I. 1989. *The Modern World-System, III: The Second Era of Great Expansion of the Capitalist World-Economy, 1730s–1840s*. New York: Academic

Westney, D. E. 1989. Sociological approaches to the Pacific region. See Gourevitch 1989, pp. 24–33

Whitehead, L. 1989. Tigers in Latin America? See Gourevitch 1989, pp. 142–51

Williamson, O. E. 1985. *The Economic Institutions of Capitalism*. New York: Free Press

Woo, J. 1991. *Race to the Swift: State and Finance in Korean Industrialization*. New York: Columbia Univ. Press

World Bank. 1982. *World Development Report 1982*. New York: Oxford Univ. Press

World Bank. 1983. *World Development Report 1983*. New York: Oxford Univ. Press

World Bank. 1987. *World Development Report 1987*. New York: Oxford Univ. Press

World Bank. 1990. *World Development Report 1990*. New York: Oxford Univ. Press

World Bank. 1991. *World Development Report 1991*. New York: Oxford Univ. Press

Annu. Rev. Sociol. 1992. 18:449–74

POPULATION AGING AND SOCIAL POLICY

*Peter Uhlenberg**

Department of Sociology and Carolina Population Center, University of North Carolina, Chapel Hill, North Carolina 27599

KEY WORDS: life course, generations, dependency, elderly, roles

Abstract

As the life course currently is structured, old age is socially defined as a stage of life beginning in the early sixties, in which retirement from work and many other social responsibilities is expected. Few incentives exist for older persons to make productive contributions to the society, and obstacles to their engagement in productive activities exist. Consequently, large transfers from the working population to the retired are required, and potential contributions of the elderly to societal well-being are lost. Further, adult children often face a long period of being responsible for their aging dependent parents. Changes occurring in the older population challenge this existing arrangement. Not only is the ratio of the older to younger adults increasing, but also an increasing proportion of adults entering old age have the ability to make significant contributions (i.e. they are well educated, healthy, economically secure, and politically astute). Concern over this growing mismatch between older people's abilities and the roles they are expected to fill leads to a discussion of social policy. How might social policy increase the productivity of the elderly and/or reduce the burden of supporting a growing dependent older population. Three major categories of policies responsive to this question are considered. The outcome of these policy debates will significantly shape the future of aging in the United States.

0360-0572/92/0815-0449$02.00

INTRODUCTION

Aging of populations is a pervasive phenomenon across all developed countries in the late twentieth century and is expected to continue into the twenty-first century. The proportion of people who are old in populations of developed countries, currently at an unprecedentedly high level, is projected to grow even larger in the future. Reasons for population aging, from a demographic perspective, are not particularly complicated. The age structure of a population is completely determined by past fertility, mortality, and migration patterns. The social, economic, and political implications of population aging, on the other hand, are both complex and subject to debate. This chapter reviews changes occurring in the size and composition of the older population and the social policy debates being generated by these changes.

This review is divided into three parts. First is an overview of how and why the older population is changing in size and composition relative to the non-old population. The changes noted in the first section, produced by past social changes, challenge the existing social structure. Several of these challenges are considered in the second section. Finally, three categories of social policies responsive to challenges of population aging are identified and a variety of policies within these categories discussed.

THE SOCIAL DEMOGRAPHY OF AGING

Significant population aging in the first half of the twentieth century occurred only in Europe, North America, and Oceania—the regions of the world where sustained fertility decline began. By 1950, in Sweden, where population aging had advanced the furthest, 10% of the population was over age 65. Between 1950 and 1990, the populations of developed countries continued to grow older, so that by the latter date, more than 12% of the population in Europe and North America was classified as old (Table 1). Other regions of the world, except Africa where fertility was not declining, began to experience population aging during this time interval. Looking ahead, population aging is expected over the next several decades in all regions of the world. United Nations (1988) projections show that the elderly will comprise more than a fifth of the population in countries that have the lowest fertility and mortality rates (e.g. Japan and Sweden), a proportion unprecedented in world history. The transformation of age structures now occurring throughout the world is linked closely to this demographic transition.

Demographic Causes of Population Aging

Stable population theory is a useful analytic tool for demonstrating effects of fertility and mortality rates upon the age structure of a population. Classic

Table 1 Proportion over age 65 and percent change in proportion old in populations of selected areas of the world: 1950–2025. Source: UN 1988)

	Percentage Over 65			Percentage Change in Old	
	1950	1990	2025	1950–90	1900–2025
World	5.1	6.2	9.7	22	56
More developed countries	7.6	11.7	17.4	54	49
Less developed countries	3.9	4.5	8.2	15	82
Africa	3.6	3.0	3.9	−16	30
Latin America	3.3	4.7	8.3	42	77
North America	8.1	12.1	17.4	49	44
Asia	4.1	5.0	10.0	22	100
Europe	8.7	13.1	18.4	51	40
Oceania	7.5	9.0	13.1	20	46
USSR	6.1	9.4	14.8	54	57
Japan	4.9	11.4	20.3	133	78
Sweden	10.3	17.7	22.2	72	25
USA	8.1	12.2	17.2	51	41

articles by Lotka (1922) and Dublin & Lotka (1925) show that any population, closed to migration and experiencing unchanging age-specific fertility and mortality rates over time, eventually achieves a fixed age distribution and a constant rate of growth. A population with unchanging vital rates and a fixed age distribution is called a stable population. By comparing several stable populations with differing fertility and mortality schedules, one can see how the age structure of a population changes as it moves from one equilibrium state to another (Coale 1972). The results of this exercise are revealing and provide a starting place for discussing the demographic determinants of population aging.

The proportions over age 65 in stable populations with various combinations of gross reproduction rates[1] (GRR) and life expectancies $\mathring{e}_o$ are shown in Table 2. In a high fertility (GRR = 4) and high mortality $\mathring{e}_o$ = 30) stable population, less than 2% of the population is elderly. In contrast, a low fertility (GRR = 0.8) and low mortality $\mathring{e}_o$ = 80) population has 26% over age 65. Reading across any row of Table 2 shows the effects of decreasing mortality on population aging when fertility is held constant, while reading down any column shows the effects of decreasing fertility when mortality is

[1]The gross reproduction rate may be interpreted as the average number of daughters that a cohort of females would have over its reproductive life if it experienced a given age-specific fertility schedule and no mortality.

Table 2 Percent over age 65 in stable populations with various combinations of fertility and mortality. (Source: Coale and Demeny 1983)

Gross Reproduction Rate	Expectation of Life (in years)					
	30	40	50	60	70	80
4.0	1.8	1.8	1.7	1.7	1.7	2.1
3.0	3.1	3.0	3.0	2.9	3.0	3.6
2.0	5.8	5.9	5.9	5.9	6.1	7.5
1.0	14.5	14.9	15.5	15.7	16.5	20.2
0.8	17.8	18.9	19.7	20.1	21.2	25.9

held constant. Several general principles regarding population aging are illustrated by data in this table. (i) Decreasing fertility always leads to population aging. (ii) Decreasing mortality from high to moderate levels leads to population "younging" when fertility is high. (iii) Decreasing mortality from moderate to low levels produces population aging. (iv) Fertility change has a much greater impact than mortality change upon an age structure. These conclusions help, in a crude way, to explain the pattern observed in Table 1. Populations with high fertility rates in recent years (e.g. those in Africa) have relatively few older persons, while those with a long history of low fertility (e.g. countries in Europe) have relatively large proportions of the old. Further, countries that have had generally declining fertility over the twentieth century (all developed countries) have experienced considerable population aging.

The Future of US Population Aging

Barring unexpected major demographic changes in the future, the US population will age slowly between 1990 and 2010 and then rapidly during the two decades following 2010. This is anticipated, of course, because the cohorts entering old age over this time interval vary in size. Up until 2010, the relatively small Depression-era birth cohorts will be reaching age 65. After 2010, the large post–World War II baby-boom cohorts will enter old age. The middle-level population projections made by the US Bureau of the Census (1989) predict that the proportion of the population over age 65 would grow from 12.6% to 13.9% between 1990 and 2010 and then balloon to 21.8% by 2030. The assertion that 22% of the US population will be old by the time the baby boom has entered old age is based upon this projection, and it understandably generates a good deal of interest. This figure is nearly twice the proportion currently old in the United States and significantly exceeds the experience of any part of the country heretofore. The state with the oldest population, Florida, had only 18% over age 65 in 1990.

Although those who will reach old age through the middle of the twenty-first century have already been born, the future path of population aging is not as clear as it might seem. To assert confidently that 22% will be old in 2030 indicates a failure to appreciate the inexactness of population forecasting. In 1971, the Census Bureau's middle-level projection for the proportion over age 65 in 2020 was 10.8%; in 1988 (just 17 years later), the projection was 17.7%. Both projections are mathematically correct, but they arrive at remarkably different conclusions because of changes in the conventional wisdom about future fertility and mortality trends. By 1988, it seemed reasonable to assume much lower fertility and much greater decline of mortality in the future than was assumed in 1971. The poor track record of population forecasting should undermine confidence that the expectations of demographers around 1990 will be realized over the next 40 years.

In addition to a projection based upon the middle assumptions, the 1988 Census Bureau population projections include a range of alternative scenarios. Each alternative scenario is based on a different combination of plausible assumptions regarding the future course of fertility, mortality, and migration. As noted above, assuming a middle value for each demographic variable produces the widely quoted projection that 21.8% of the population will be over age 65 in 2030. But if the lowest value on each variable should occur, 28.7% will be old. On the other hand, the highest value on each variable produces a population with 17.4% old. Looking at the results of these alternative plausible scenarios of future population aging leads to three observations. First, each projection indicates a substantial increase in proportion old in the future. Second, the range of plausible outcomes is wide—the high figure is 65% greater than the low figures. The social, economic, and political implications of 17.4% versus 28.7% are surely quite different. Third, we cannot be confident that the actual proportion of elderly in the population will fall within this wide range. This last observation needs further elaboration.

What happens if the age of mortality among the elderly rises more rapidly than the most optimistic assumption made in the Census Bureau projections? Siegel & Taeuber (1986) show that continued rapid declines in age-specific death rates, in conjunction with low fertility and low immigration, could produce a population in the year 2050 with 36% over age 65. At the other extreme, if mortality declines are modest and fertility returns to its mid-1960s level, as few as 13% of the population would be old (Uhlenberg 1988a). Admittedly, the extremes of 13% and 36% are both unlikely future outcomes. Yet substantial uncertainty regarding the actual age distribution in 2030 does exist.

Composition of the Older Population

Population aging no doubt has important implications for social change, but standing alone it fails to capture the full dynamic of the aging process. Not only does the size of the older population relative to the non-old population change over time, the individuals comprising the older population also change. The cohort life-course framework provides a simple and general organizing schema for studying change in the composition of the elderly. The seminal work in using cohort analysis to study social change is Ryder's (1964; 1965), and significant contributions that add a life-course perspective come from Elder (1975) and Riley et al (1988). Crucial concepts in this framework for studying changes in the older population deal with "cohort flow" and "cohort succession".

As a birth cohort ages through historical time, it flows across the various phases of the life-course. By the time a cohort arrives at the threshold of old age, it has been distinctively marked by experiences occurring over its earlier life. It has lost some members due to death and out-migration, and has gained new members by in-migration. Further, it has been shaped by the social structure and historical events that its members encountered as they occupied earlier phases of the life-course. Thus, the older population continuously changes as newcomers arrive with backgrounds that differ from those who arrived earlier. Change also occurs because of the selective loss of previous members of the older population due to death. The rate of turnover in the older population tends to be quite high because mortality rates at the older ages are high. In 1990, for example, 58% of the 32 million older people in the United States had entered old age within the past 10 years. When there is significant intercohort differentiation, as there has been in recent history, this process of cohort succession leads to rapid changes in the composition of the older population.

The range of characteristics (social, economic, psychological) that are potentially interesting and significant for understanding how the older population is changing over time is vast. Unfortunately, adequate empirical data to allow tracing historical change and projecting future change are limited. Several variables for which data exist are examined below, but clearly these are not the only areas in which change is occurring. In discussing these changes, attention is given to the past social changes that produced intercohort differentiation.

FERTILITY Significant fertility declines over the twentieth century are, as noted above, the primary cause of the aging of the American population. And the expected persistence of low fertility in the future is the basic reason for anticipating a continual aging of the population through the first third of the twenty-first century. There are, however, several other aspects of fertility patterns that affect the composition of the older population. Differential fertility across racial and ethnic groups and changes in the parity distribution of women merit special attention.

Black and Hispanic women in the United States have significantly higher birth rates than white women. In 1988, for example, the black fertility rate exceeded the white rate by 37%, while the Hispanic fertility rate exceeded the white rate by 53% (NCHS 1990). Reflecting these longstanding fertility differentials, the black and Hispanic populations are younger than the non-Hispanic white population. Thus non-Hispanic whites comprise a larger proportion of the older population than of the non-old population. In 1988, non-Hispanic whites made up 88% of the elderly, but only 72% of the population under age 18. Projections to 2030 show the proportion of elderly who are non-Hispanic white declining to 76%, but by that date only 59% of the children in the United States are expected to be non-Hispanic white (Uhlenberg 1988a). The higher concentration of racial and ethnic minorities in the younger ages than in the older ages will persist as long as non-Hispanic whites have lower fertility rates.

Since adult children frequently are viewed as the primary caregivers of the dependent elderly, it is surprising that little attention has been given to the number of surviving children that older persons have (Uhlenberg & Cooney 1990). The distribution of older persons by number of living children is determined by their past parity distributions and by survival rates of their children. Preston (forthcoming) has made projections for several cohorts for the time period at which they will be aged 85–89, i.e. at a stage of life when dependency is quite likely. Among women aged 85–89 in 1990, 25% had no surviving child and 26% had just one. In 2015, however, the situation will be quite different as the mothers of the baby boom occupy the oldest-old category. In that year, it is expected that 13% will have no child and 18% will have only one. The proportion of older women with two or more living children will decline in the more distant future, however, as women bearing children in the 1970s and 1980s enter the latest years of life.

MORTALITY The large mortality declines occurring in the first half of the twentieth century were concentrated in the younger ages, resulting in a younger population age distribution than there would have been in the absence of a mortality decline. More recently, however, the greatest relative growth in life expectancy has occurred at the oldest ages (McGill 1988). This decline of death rates at the older ages, along with a decline in the relative size of successive cohorts entering old age, is producing an aging of the older population. That is, the proportion of the older population that is over age 80 or 85 is increasing (Myers 1990). For example, between 1930 and 1990 the proportion of the elderly who were over age 85 increased from 4.1% to 10.3%. The relative growth of the oldest-old category will continue until it reaches 15.5% in 2010, after which it will decline as the large baby boom cohorts begin to enter old age. Twenty years later the oldest-old category will again grow rapidly as the baby boom advances into the terminal age category.

Neugarten (1974) was the first to call attention to the significance of the age heterogeneity of the older population. More recently, largely in response to a research funding initiative by the National Institute on Aging, the oldest-old have received considerable attention (Suzman & Riley 1985, Suzman & Willis—forthcoming, Rosenwaike & Logue 1985, Rosenwaike & Dolinsky 1987, Longino 1988).

A second important aspect of mortality patterns affecting the composition of the older population is the gender differential. The sex ratio (males per 100 females) is about 105 at birth, but this ratio then declines continuously as a cohort ages owing to higher mortality rates for males at every age. Among cohorts occupying the early stage of old age (65–69) the sex ratio currently is 80, while among those over age 85 it is only 44. Despite continuing research on causes of gender differences in mortality (Ory & Riley 1989), it is unclear what future trends will be. The survival advantage of females over males increased over most of this century but has declined slightly in more recent years. The future sex composition of the older population will be determined by the relative size of the various cohorts in old age (an aging of the older population implies a greater proportion of females) and the size of the gender differential in mortality (a convergence of rates would lead to a more balanced sex ratio).

A third factor related to declining mortality concerns the prevalence of disease and disability among the elderly. The relationship between declining mortality and health status of the elderly is debated, and adequate data to assess changes over the recent past do not exist. Health status might be improving if declining mortality reflects medical and lifestyle changes which reduce the prevalence of disease or lessen the disabling effects of chronic disease (Ycas 1987, Manton 1989a, 1990). But if lives are prolonged among those who are disabled and chronically ill, then the proportion of the elderly experiencing active and independent living may decrease (Crimmins & Pramaggiore 1988, Gruenberg 1977, Verbrugge 1984). It is clear, of course, that rates of disability increase rapidly as cohorts move into the later stages of old age. While 15% of those aged 65–69 need help with activities of daily living, about half of those over age 85 need assistance (Soldo & Agree 1988). Unless significant progress is made in reducing disabilities associated with arthritis, skeletal problems, visual disorders, Alzheimer's disease, diabetes, and other slow degenerative diseases, the increase of the oldest-old implies a growing proportion of the elderly with disabling medical conditions.

MIGRATION The variable flow of immigrants to the United States over the twentieth century has differentiated the nativity status distribution of cohorts entering old age. Because of the large waves of immigrants around the turn of the century, over 25% of those entering old age in the 1930s were foreign-born (Uhlenberg 1977). By 1980, reflecting the low level of immigration in the 1930s and 1940s, only 6% of those reaching age 65 were foreign-born. Increases in immigration in more recent decades will produce future growth in the proportion of foreign-born among the elderly, but not up to the levels occurring in the first half of this century. The significance of nativity status in later life has not been examined carefully. Nevertheless, one might speculate that the foreign-born approaching old age tend to be disadvantaged in relating to the complex bureaucratic structures of a modern society.

EDUCATION Over the first half of the twentieth century, the public educational system was expanding, and each successive cohort moving through the system surpassed all preceding cohorts in years of schooling completed. As a result, the educational gap between the old and the young in American society grew quite large. In 1970, for example, 79% of the population aged 20–24 had graduated from high school, compared to only 24% of those over age 65. Since about 1970, however, the educational attainment of successive cohorts entering young adulthood has stopped increasing. Consequently, the educational disadvantage of the elderly is declining, and by 2020 those entering old age are likely to have as much formal education as the younger adults in the population.

WORK Two significant changes in the organization of work have consequences for the elderly: the growth of retirement, and the increase in female labor force participation. A voluminous literature treats reasons for and implications of the institutionalization of retirement (Graebner 1980, Quinn & Burkhauser 1990). While there is debate about how large the change in labor force participation of older males was in the early twentieth century (Ransom & Sutch 1989, Moen 1987), a rapid increase in retirement rates after 1940 is well-documented (Tuma & Sandefur 1988). Among women, increasing retirement of the elderly in recent decades essentially has canceled the effect of increasing female labor force participation generally, so there has been little change in the proportion of older women who are working. By 1990, participation in the labor force was an important activity for relatively few men or women after age 65, and retirement was an integral part of the social definition of old age.

The past work experience of currently older women differs markedly from that older men. Older women are more likely either not to have participated in the labor force, or to have erratic and noncontinuous work histories. Further, those with work histories are more likely to have held low-paying jobs with few fringe benefits (O'Rand 1988). This gender difference in labor force experiences is an important reason for the lower economic status of women than men in later life. But work experiences of women and men are growing more similar as cohorts of women reaching young adulthood since 1970 have increasingly pursued work careers. When these cohorts enter old age in the future, the gender gap in economic status may diminish.

WELFARE STATE Despite decreasing labor force participation rates, the economic status of the elderly improved greatly between 1950 and the late 1980s (Ross et al 1987, Smeeding 1990). Between 1959 and 1987, the image of the elderly as an economically disadvantaged segment of the population increasingly became obsolete as the proportion of the elderly with incomes below the poverty line dropped from 35% to 12%. As Duncan & Smith write, "there appears to be little doubt that the economic status of the typical elderly person, when measured in a fairly comprehensive way, probably meets or exceeds that of the typical non-elderly person in the 1980s." (1989:264) Behind this dramatic improvement in the economic status of the elderly has been the expansion of the welfare state. The introduction of Medicare in 1965 and changes in the Social Security Programs since 1950 especially have been significant. Coverage under Social Security expanded to include most of the labor force, and benefits increased to a level that provides considerable income security in later life (Myles 1988). The economic status of the elderly could change in the future, but there is general consensus that cohorts entering old age over the next several decades should fare well (McGill 1988, Duncan & Smith 1989, Smeeding 1990).

WARS AND DEPRESSIONS Various cohorts of American men and women have been differentially affected by the wars and depressions occurring in the twentieth century. Each cohort occupies a unique life-course position at the time of a major historical event, and its future is shaped to some extent by this experience. Elder (1974, 1988) has elucidated some lingering consequences for specific cohorts that encountered the Great Depression and World War II during particular phases of their life courses. Vinovskis (1986) has studied Civil War veterans, while Laufer & Gallops (1985) have traced effects of the Vietnam War upon combatants. In addition to any psychological and social effects of military service (especially combat), the status of veterans also provides special entitlements for pensions and health care in old age. The proportion of men serving in the armed forces grew from 27% of the 1910 cohort (which reached age 65 in 1975) to 78% of the 1927 cohort, the cohort most affected by World War II mobilization (Winsborough 1978). Veterans of the Korean, Vietnam, and Persian Gulf conflicts will arrive at old age in the future. One can also trace out the variable impact of the Great Depression upon cohorts born before 1940.

MARRIAGE AND DIVORCE The marital status of cohorts entering old age is determined by marital formation and dissolution experiences which occurred earlier in the life course. Over this century, the proportion of men and women who never marry has not fluctuated widely, averaging about 6% among those who survive to old age. However, the other relevant variables determining marital status in old age have changed dramatically. As a consequence of decreasing mortality rates and increasing divorce rates, a smaller proportion of each cohort arrives at old age having ever experienced widowhood, while an increasing proportion has experienced an earlier divorce. Throughout this century, a majority of individuals with disrupted marriages in the young adult years due to divorce or widowhood have remarried, although age-specific remarriage rates have changed over time. Up until about 1965, remarriage rates were increasing; since then they have declined rapidly. Remarriage rates in 1985 were only half as large as they were in 1965 (Uhlenberg et al 1990). These changes in mortality, divorce, and remarriage have combined to produce a remarkable change in the marital status characteristics of cohorts entering old age.

At the beginning of the twentieth century, among those aged 55–64, widowed men outnumbered divorced men by more than 20 to 1 (Uhlenberg 1990). The demographic changes described above resulted in the divorced surpassing the widowed in this age category in the 1970s, and by 2000 it is projected that the ratio of divorced to widowed will be 3.7 to 1. Because males experience higher death rates and higher remarriage rates than do females, the number of widows greatly exceeds the number of widowers at every age. Nevertheless, over time women have followed the same general pattern of sharply falling rates of widowhood and increasing rates of divorce. In 1900, there were about 67 widows for each divorcee in the age category 55–64; by 2000, it is expected that divorcees will substantially outnumber widows. If recent patterns persist, it will be cohorts born after 1960 that experience the full impact of high divorce rates and low remarriage rates over their entire adult life course. Thus a continuing increase in the prevalence of divorced persons among those reaching old age through the first several decades of the next century can be anticipated.

Summary: 12 Statements About the Aging Population

Social and demographic changes occurring over the twentieth century are producing rapid changes in the size and composition of the older population toward the end of this century. The preceding discussion leads to the following conclusions:

(i) The proportion old in the population, which tripled between 1900 and 1990, is expected to continue to increase until 2030 when about 22% of the US population is projected to be over age 65.

(ii) Minorities and ethnics will comprise an increasing proportion of the older population, but a much larger proportion of the young than the old population will continue to be black or Hispanic.

(iii) For some time, the proportion of the elderly who have zero or only one surviving adult child will decline, but this trend will be reversed when the baby boom enters old age.
(iv) The proportion of the older population classified as the "oldest-old" is growing and will continue to grow, except for a temporary reversal when the baby boom is entering old age.
(v) Females have increasingly outnumbered males in old age, especially within the oldest-old segment.
(vi) The foreign-born proportion of the elderly has fallen dramatically and, despite some future increase, is not expected to return to levels common in the early twentieth century.
(vii) The educational status of the elderly is increasing rapidly, and the gap in educational attainment between the old and young may disappear by the middle of the twenty-first century.
(viii) Retirement has become institutionalized, and relatively few men and women are significantly engaged in the labor force past age 65.
(ix) The sharp contrast in work histories of older men and women, common up to the present, will diminish in the twenty-first century.
(x) Poverty rates among the elderly have declined sharply since 1950 and are now similar to those of the total population.
(xi) The proportion of the elderly who are veterans fluctuates considerably over time, reflecting the irregular occurrence of wars.
(xii) The number of older divorced persons will continue to increase rapidly through the early portion of the twenty-first century.

CHALLENGES OF POPULATION AGING TO THE SOCIAL STRUCTURE

During any period of history, the position of the elderly in the larger society is shaped both by the composition of the older population and by the structure of the major social institutions (familial, economic, political, religious, etc). Thus far the focus has been on changes in the older population. But the social structure also changes over time. Over the twentieth century, two closely related structural changes in American society have been especially critical in transforming the meaning of old age. One change is the institutionalization of retirement; the other is the expansion of the welfare state. These two developments have been discussed at length by others (Graebner 1980, Kohli 1988, Myles 1988, Quadagno 1988) and are not addressed here. Rather, I note two outcomes of these changes that interact significantly with population aging to create new challenges to the society. First, increasingly, the elderly have become dependent upon the state for economic support. Second, the principal activity of old age has become identified as leisure.

The changing size and characteristics of the older population, in combination with the social definition of old age as a time for retirement and leisure, have stimulated a discussion about the future of aging. To what extent is there a lack of "fit" between the older population and the structure of old age? Four specific challenges created by a poor match between the aging population and the social definition of old age are noted briefly in this section. By identifying these concerns or perceived challenges, I do not suggest that each one is accurate. Rather, these concerns are noted because they are the linkage between population aging and debates over aging policy. Policy debates generated by these perceived challenges of population aging are considered in the following section.

Economic Commitment

With the spread of retirement and development of the welfare state, the role of the state in managing a transfer of income from younger (working age) adults to older (retired) adults expanded rapidly. Prior to 1940, the federal government was not involved in supporting the elderly via social security and Medicare. As recently as 1960, Medicare did not exist and outlays for the Old Age and Survivors Insurance (OASI) program comprised only 12.6% of the federal budget and 2.3% of the GNP. By 1990, however, Medicare and OASI expenditures captured 27.7% of the federal budget and 6.4% of the country's GNP (Office of Management and Budget, 1991). As the population continues to age, with the elderly politically entitled to relatively high levels of economic support from government programs, the unwelcome issue of how to meet the growing economic commitment of supporting the dependent older population cannot be avoided. While the entitlement of the elderly to support may be justified because of their past transfers to the cohorts of elderly who preceded them, it is also obvious that taxes on the working population to support the aged have increased sharply in recent decades. Support of the elderly is a political issue—to what extent and by what means will money be transferred from the working population to the retired elderly?

Generational Equity

As the American economy expanded after World War II, the economic status of all age groups in the population improved from 1940 through 1969 (Smolensky et al 1988). After 1969, the economic status of the elderly continued to improve, but the economic plight of American children deteriorated. In 1969, 25% of the elderly were living in households with incomes below the official poverty line, compared to 14% of the children (population under age 18). By 1984, the relative position of young and old was reversed, with 12% of the old and 21% of the children living in poverty (Committee on Ways and Means 1989). These divergent trends in the well-being of the young and old dependents in American society were sharply focused in an article by Preston in 1984, and subsequently a great deal has been written on the issue of generational equity (Asahi Shimbun Publishing 1988, Duncan & Smith 1989, Johnson et al 1989, Kingson et al 1986, Palmer & Sawhill 1988).

It clearly is too simplistic to argue that increasing poverty among children is caused by the improved economic position of the elderly. The deteriorating economic plight of children is most closely related to the increasing number of children who do not benefit from the contributions of a father. Nevertheless, the argument that adequate investment in American youth is impeded by the high cost of supporting the elderly has many supporters. They note that since OASI and Medicare are not means-tested programs, a large portion of the expenditures in these programs goes to affluent, politically powerful, older persons. No parallel income and health programs exist for children. While one may deplore encouraging competition between supporters of the young and supporters of the old for scarce resources, the issue of generational equity is a persistent topic of public debate.

Caregiving Burden

Demographic change over the twentieth century has interesting implications for relationships between adults and their elderly parents. In particular, the number of adult years one can expect to live while an aging parent is still alive has increased dramatically. Now a woman should anticipate spending more years as the child of an elderly parent than as the mother of children under age 18 (Watkins et al 1987). While the expanding welfare state has reduced the obligations of adult children to provide direct economic support for their aging parents, it has not freed children from caregiving obligations. Adult children continue to assume responsibility for caring for impaired older parents, keeping them outside of institutions as long as possible. This caregiving role frequently lasts a long time and has significant consequences for the caregiver. Thus, as Brody (1985) notes, we have arrived at a situation where parent care is becoming a "normative family stress." Reflecting this growing concern over the effects upon middle-aged women of caregiving for the elderly, a flurry of studies on the burden of caregiving have appeared in gerontology journals in recent years. As Linda George writes, "Not since the debate about disengagement versus activity theory has a single issue so intensely captured the attention of gerontology researchers." (1990:580). Further, concerns about the economic, social, and emotional costs of caregiving extend beyond the burden it places upon the children (particularly daughters) of the old. Issues involving long-term care in institutions also command increasing attention. How will the needs of a rapidly growing population of impaired and dependent old persons be met in the future?

Social Roles for the Elderly

A fourth challenge of the aging of the US population concerns the roles available to the elderly in society. Since those reaching old age are increasingly well-educated, healthy, and economically secure, one might expect that they would increasingly make productive contributions to the society. But this does not appear to be happening. Opportunities and incentives for older persons to engage in productive social activities have declined in recent decades. Research on the contributions of the elderly in such areas as work, politics, family, religion, and volunteer service organizations is deficient, but there is no evidence that norms encouraging continuing contributions in these areas have developed (Uhlenberg 1988b). Indeed, the growing emphasis upon leisure activities in old age (Cutler & Hendricks 1990) suggests that the old increasingly are excused from societal responsibilities. Some emphasize the growing potential this provides for older persons to find personal fulfillment in retirement after years of hard work. Others express concern about negative consequences of encouraging the old to build their lives around leisure activities. Riley & Riley, for example, point to the waste of potential contributions and the trivialization of later life associated with older persons retreating from productive activities. They write, "increasing numbers of competent older persons and diminishing role opportunities cannot long coexist" (Riley & Riley 1989:28).

One might argue about the accuracy and/or significance of the four challenges of population aging to the society that are discussed in this section. But each one is a salient issue. That is, these concerns about a growing lack of "fit" between the older population and the roles they fill are being discussed. And these discussions lead to debates over what direction aging policy should take.

POPULATION DEBATES RELATED TO POPULATION AGING

Social policy debates related to population aging can be divided into three major categories. First are a set of policies that would alter the aging of the population. The logic behind this approach is that any challenge associated with an increasingly old population could be ameliorated by reducing the future aging of the population. A second category of policies stresses possibilities for altering the role played by the elderly in society. Policy proposals with this thrust emphasize the social construction of aging and the possibilities for changing how people function in old age. Finally, a third category of proposals deals with issues related to the locus of responsibility for supporting the dependent elderly. The current mix of responsibilities between the state, the family, and the individual could be altered in several directions. Several specific policy issues within each of these broad categories are discussed in this section.

Policies to Alter the Aging of the Population

The observation that "demography is not destiny" surely is correct. The future of aging depends upon many factors other than the relative size and composition of the older population. Nevertheless, population characteristics are relevant for the types of social challenges discussed in the preceding section, and it may be possible to use social policy to alter demographic behavior. Any comprehensive examination of aging policies must consider the possibility of altering each of the demographic variables that directly influences the age structure (fertility, migration, mortality).

PRO-NATALISM Most developed countries, including the United States, have experienced below-replacement level fertility since the 1970s, and the anticipated future aging of these populations is based upon the assumption of continued low fertility. Since the age structure of a population is sensitive to changes in fertility, as noted earlier, increasing the birth rate would slow (or stop, or reverse) future population aging. Policy proposals related to this approach must deal both with the effectiveness of pro-natalist policies and with the desirability of increasing fertility even if it is possible.

A lively discussion of pro-natalist policies occurred in the 1930s (Glass 1940, Spengler 1938) but then faded away with the post-war baby boom. Recent concerns over population aging have stimulated a revival of interest in this topic (Wattenberg 1989, Teitelbaum & Winter 1985). Evaluations of deliberate government efforts to increase fertility in European countries concluded that propaganda campaigns and modest economic incentives for bearing children have little effect (Demeny 1986, McIntosh 1986). Policies that create obstacles to preventing birth (bans on abortion and/or contraception) may be effective in the short run (Teitelbaum & Winter 1985), but they raise significant ethical issues and may be ineffective in the long run as populations find ways to circumvent the restrictions. Whether or not effective pro-natalist policies for modern societies could be designed is, at present, an open question.

If effective pro-natalist policies could be developed, two arguments against implementing them must be faced. One objection concerns the selectivity of those most likely to respond to economic incentives for increasing childbearing. If it is the least educated and least skilled women who increase their fertility (since they experience lowest opportunity costs for bearing children), then an increasing proportion of children would grow up in families with fewest resources for equipping children to become productive members of society. If the cost of increasing the proportion of the population that is not old is a reduction in its productive capacity, it is not clear that anything is gained. A second objection to countering population aging with increased fertility concerns the consequences of population growth. To the extent that sustained population growth threatens environmental quality, this cure for population aging may be worse than the illness.

HIGH IMMIGRATION Encouragement of higher immigration as a strategy to reduce population aging has received little attention and merits little. Whatever the pros and cons of encouraging immigration, the effect of differing immigration rates upon the age distribution is minimal. While the immediate effect of increasing the number of young adult immigrants is an addition to the size of the labor force and to the number of births, in the long run the immigrants and their children enter old age. Projections of the population under varying assumptions of migration level show how small the consequences are for the age distribution of the population. For example, with a TFR of 1.8, the proportion of the US population over age 65 in 2100 would be .240 if there was no future immigration, compared to .226 if there was an annual net immigration 700,000 (Coale 1986). Further, the effects of immigrants' ages, within a plausible range, upon the age composition of the total population are relatively insignificant (Arthur & Espenshade 1988). While immigration policy will have little impact upon the proportion of old people in the future, it will, of course, affect the total size of the population and the racial/ethnic composition of the old and non-old population.

RATIONING HEALTH CARE TO THE OLD Like fertility and migration, mortality patterns may be affected by social policy. Policies to invest fewer resources in extending life at the oldest ages could reduce the growth of the oldest-old population. Indeed, such ideas are receiving serious consideration in the form of a debate over rationing health care to the elderly (Callahan 1987, Smeeding 1987, Strosberg et al 1989).

The combination of new medical technology and the expansion of public funding of health care since 1970 has both reduced mortality at the older ages and greatly increased health care expenditures on the elderly (Davis 1986, Callahan 1986). With the prospect of an aging population and continuing technical advances, Aaron observes that:

> All developed nations face a profound dilemma—to bear the rapidly increasing costs of providing care to aging populations or, alternatively, to ration care, and in so doing deny some potential benefits to some patients. (1986:24)

Callahan (1987) responds to this challenge by proposing a schema for rationing government-financed health care to those above about age 80 (his assessment of when a "natural life span" has been lived out). Past this age, death would not be resisted by use of life-extending technologies; medical care would be used only to relieve suffering. While such a policy which explicitly rations health care on the basis of chronological age meets with vehement opposition from some (Binstock & Kahana 1988), the issue is not likely to fade away as long as health care expenditures continue their upward spiral.

CHANGING THE AGE OF OLD AGE The final policy proposal to alter the aging of the population is the most direct—it would change the chronological age at which a person is recognized as old (Torrey 1982, Uhlenberg 1988a). For a variety of purposes, reaching age 65 in contemporary society entitles one to special benefits—full Social Security benefits, Medicare coverage, tax advantages, and senior citizen discounts for many purchases. Reflecting the semi-official status of age 65, statistics on the older population routinely use the category 65+. Equally significant, it is around this age that labor force participation ceases for most individuals. Thus, despite the heterogeneity within cohorts at age 65 (Dannefer & Sell 1988), age 65 has become the threshold marking entrance into old age.

With increasing longevity and changing characteristics of cohorts approaching later life, the logic of maintaining age 65 as a beginning of old age can be questioned. Changing the age for entitlement to old age benefits might not affect biological aging, but it could alter the future economic burden of supporting a growing dependent older population. Indeed, a 1983 change in the Social Security Act calls for gradually increasing the age for full Social Security benefits to 67 by 2027. If the age criterion were advanced further (e.g. to 72) and extended to the whole range of old age entitlement programs, the effects of future population aging could be reduced significantly. However, changing the age of old age, without concurrent changes in other aspects of the social structure, would increase the vulnerability of the near-old population (Uhlenberg 1988a).

Policies to Increase Productivity or Decrease Dependency of the Old

A number of authors have noted the tendency of modern societies to divide the life course into three major stages—education, work, leisure (Best 1980, Riley 1978). Kohli (1986, 1988) argues that the key to understanding this tripartition of the life course is work. Education prepares the young for work, work is the central activity of adults, and retirement removes the old from work. Meyer (1986) and Mayer & Schoepflin (1989) stress the role of the welfare state in creating this periodization of life. The outcome, in any case, is an older population that is removed from education and work and which has no clear productive role in the society. As the relative size of this dependent older population increases, there may be growing interest in policies that would increase the productivity of the old and/or decrease their dependency upon the working population.

RESTRUCTURING THE LIFE COURSE The division of the life course into the three boxes of education, work, and leisure emerged with the institutionalization of education and retirement. The age stratification associated with these developments may harm human development at all stages of life. Young people prepare for work without adequate exposure to the realities of work.

Middle-aged people are overburdened with work responsibilities. And the elderly become obsolete, unproductive, and marginal to the society. This organization of the life course also significantly creates the economic burden of supporting a dependent older population. From both humanistic (Moody 1988) and economic (Morrison 1986) perspectives, an argument is made in favor of social policies that would encourage a greater mix of leisure, education, and work throughout life. Along with other potential benefits, restructuring the life course could increase the productive contributions of the elderly to the society.

In an economic system where the knowledge industry plays a central role, the need for life-long education to prevent obsolescence of skills as one ages seems obvious. The popularity of Elderhostel and the increased number of older persons in universities indicates some movement toward a greater role for education in later life (Moody 1988). But these approaches to life-long education reach mostly the college educated and have little impact upon extending the worklife. Government sponsored job training programs designed to upgrade skills needed in the labor market (Comprehensive Employment and Training Act; Job Training Partnership Act) have attracted very few older persons (Sandell 1988). Federally funded training programs might serve more older persons by focusing upon their special needs and characteristics (Sandell 1988). Formal higher educational systems might reach more elderly by introducing innovative and nontraditional programs (Okun 1982). Even more important, however, are employee-sponsored training programs that allow workers to upgrade skills and adapt to changes in job requirements necessitated by technological innovation (Meier 1988, Sterns 1986). Through tax credits, training subsidies, and other incentive schemes, government policy could encourage and facilitate investment in human capital formation over the entire life course (Moody 1988).

While increasing the economic productivity of older persons requires greater investment in their education, it is equally important to provide employment opportunities. Existing obstacles to the employment of older workers include both age discriminatory personnel practices and inflexibility of work options. The Age Discrimination in Employment Act of 1967, amended in 1978 and 1986, was designed to protect the rights of older workers with respect to hiring, discharge, pay, promotion and fringe benefits. Nevertheless, widespread discrimination against older workers is still reported (Sandell 1988). Greater enforcement of existing policy is needed to reduce this obstacle to continued employment of older workers.

The paucity of alternative work options in later life reflects the rigidity of the linear career plan that has evolved. Expectations of increasing job status and remuneration with seniority in the labor force limit options for moving to less demanding jobs with corresponding downward adjustments in salary and fringe benefits. Under these conditions, it is economically rational for employers to replace older workers with younger ones who can perform the same job at a lower cost. Opening up alternative work options could benefit those nearing the end of their work life (as well as other potential workers who desire something other than full-time, fixed schedule work). Providing more alternatives could be encouraged by appropriate social policy (Morrison 1986; Meier 1988). One appealing, but not widely available, option is phased retirement, where work hours are gradually reduced with reduced salary and partial pension payment. Another possibility involves creating annuitant pools of a company's retirees for temporary, full, or part-time work assignments (Morrison 1986). A variety of other well-known possibilities (part-time, flex-time, job sharing) are also available to increase the likelihood of matching desires for continued work in later life with employment opportunities.

Promoting life-long education, reducing age discrimination, and increasing alternative work options would lead to greater productivity of older persons provided that they were motivated to fill work roles. But would persons continue working later in life (or forgo early retirement) if these changes occurred? Are people retiring voluntarily because pensions plans make it economically feasible? Or, involuntarily because of disabilities and labor market obstacles? There is substantial agreement that both economic and non-economic factors influence the retirement decision and that retirement patterns could be modified through policy measures (Quinn & Burkhauser 1990, Sickles & Taubman 1986, Parnes 1988). Whether these policies should emphasize disincentives for retiring early (e.g. reduced pension benefits) or incentives for working longer (improved opportunities), or some combination of the two is, not surprisingly, debated on both ethical and empirical grounds.

DECREASING DEPENDENCE Numerous cross-sectional studies document the obvious: age is correlated with functional capacity and disability status. Older persons are more likely than younger adults to experience decrements in physical and cognitive ability that restrict ability to function independently. Consequently, a major concern related to an aging population is the expected increase in prevalence of older persons dependent upon others for care (Manton 1989a, Soldo & Manton 1985, Aaron et al 1989, Callahan 1986). But is the existing relationship between age and disability inevitable? Or, might it be altered through appropriate intervention?

For some time it has been common to separate the effects of specific disease processes on functional capacity and disability from the effects of aging per se. "Normal aging" is then interpreted as changes occurring over time in a cohort from which the diseased population has been excluded. This perspective counters an ageist view that confounds effects of disease with effects of growing older. On the one hand, it argues that greater attention should be directed toward reducing disease and/or its consequences among the elderly. This should result in reducing the relatively high incidence of disability that exists. On the other hand, this perspective accepts the premise that normal aging involves biological decline and increasing likelihood of disability, since these are observed in the non-diseased elderly.

More recently, the concept of "normal aging" has been criticized. Rowe & Kahn write:

> The emphasis on "normal" aging focuses attention on learning what most older people do and do not do, what physiologic and psychologic states are typical. It tends to create a gerontology of the usual. (1987:143)

Rather than accepting the aging process as fixed and immutable, a range of interventions are proposed that could alter the level of dependency in later life (Riley & Riley 1989). Changing behaviors related to exercise, diet, use of alcohol and drugs, etc, could reduce disabilities considered as part of normal aging (Rowe & Kahn 1987, Manton 1989b). Specific interventions in the health, education, and work institutions could increase sense of control (Rodin 1989) and improve levels of cognitive functioning (Standinger et al 1989) in later life. New approaches to rehabilitation have the potential of reversing or minimizing the dependency of older persons who are now neglected (Ory & Williams 1989). Policies that concentrate on improving the quality of later life can have the positive side-effect of lessening the future burden of caring for dependent older persons by reducing the incidence and prevalence of disabilities (Riley & Riley 1989).

Policies Affecting Locus of Responsibility

The third category of policy debates related to support of an aging population concerns the relative responsibility of the state, the family, and the older individual. This issue is simply noted here without elaboration. The central topic in this controversy is the future of the Social Security Program, and the literature dealing with this is vast. Should the state maintain or expand its current level of support of older persons? If so, how should the funding of OASI and Medicare be dealt with as the ratio of retirees to workers changes? If not, can adult children be induced to assume greater responsibility for their aging parents? (Changes in the American family raise a host of questions related to future inter-generational relations.) Or, should more emphasis be placed upon the responsibility of individuals to prepare for their own old age? The arguments and proposals surrounding these issues require a separate review article and cannot be explored within the limits of this paper.

CONCLUSION

Demographic changes over the twentieth century have produced the progressive aging of the US population. At the beginning of the century, 4% of the population was over age 65; by the end of the century it will be 13%. But population aging has not yet run its course. A dramatic increase in the older population will occur as the baby boom cohorts reach old age in the two decades following 2010. The "best guess" of the US Census Bureau indicates that 22% of the population will be over age 65 by 2030. While the agedness of this projected population is unprecedented, the societal significance of continued population aging depends, to large extent, upon how old age is socially structured.

As the life course currently is organized, old age is a stage of life beginning in the early 60s in which retirement from work and most other responsibilities is expected. This arrangement encourages a prolonged period of economic dependence at the end of life. Further, it provides few incentives for older persons to make productive contributions to the society, and it creates obstacles to their engagement in many productive activities. Consequently, large transfers from the working population to the retired are required, and potential contributions of the elderly to societal well-being are lost. In addition, many adult children face a long period of being responsible for the care of their aging dependent parents. The changing ratio of the older to younger adults associated with population aging challenges this structure of old age. This challenge is further accentuated by changes occurring in the characteristics of cohorts entering old age. These cohorts contain increasing numbers of individuals who are well educated, economically secure, politically astute, and in relatively good health. In short, demographic and social changes over the twentieth century have created a growing mismatch between the abilities of older people to make significant contributions and the social role they are expected to fill.

A concern over this mismatch leads to the discussion of aging policy. How might social policies increase the productivity of the elderly and/or reduce the burden of supporting a growing dependent older population? Three broad categories of social policy responsive to the challenges of population aging are suggested in this paper. First are policies that attempt to alter the age structure—i.e. reduce the proportion old in the population. Efforts to alter the actual age structure do not offer real long-term solutions, since modern demographic regimes inevitably produce populations with more than 20% over age 65. More promising are policies that advance the chronological age at which individuals are entitled to old-age benefits. A second cluster of policies aim to restructure the meaning of old age. One thrust would increase the role of education and work in later life, while a complimentary thrust focuses on interventions to reduce the disabilities and frailties associated with old age. A third category of policies addresses the relative role that the state, the family, and the individual should have in supporting the elderly.

The dynamics of population change and social change are stimulating a lively debate on how social policy might shape the future of aging. In this debate, many voices are competing to be heard. Many of the views expressed lack insight into fundamental aspects of population aging and life course dynamics. Social scientists can contribute to this important discussion by elucidating how the process of cohort succession alters the character of the older population and how the social structure shapes the aging experience.

ACKNOWLEDGMENTS

Thanks to Judith Blake, Glen Elder, and Matilda Riley for their helpful comments on the first draft.

Literature Cited

Aaron, H. J. 1986. When is a burden not a burden? the elderly in America. *Brookings Rev.* 4:17–24

Aaron, H. J., Bosworth, B. P., Burtless, G. 1989. *Can America Afford to Grow Old? Paying for Social Security.* Washington, DC: Brookings Inst.

Arthur, W. B., Espenshade, T. J. 1988. Immigration policy and immigrants' ages. *Popul. Dev. Rev.* 14:315–26

Asahi Shimbun Publishing (ed.) 1988. *Reflections on Aging.* Tokyo: Soc. Insurance Organ. Japan

Best, F. 1980. *Flexible Life Scheduling.* New York: Praeger

Binstock, R. H., Kahana, J. 1988. Review of D. Callahan, *Setting Limits: Medical Goals in an Aging Society. Gerontologist* 28:424–6

Brody, E. M. 1985. Parent care as a normative family stress. *Gerontologist* 25:19–29

Callahan, D. 1986. Adequate health care and an aging society: are they morally compatible? *Daedalus* 115:247–67

Callahan, D. 1987. *Setting Limits: Medical Goals in an Aging Society.* New York: Simon & Schuster

Coale, A. J. 1972. *The Growth and Structure of Human Populations.* Princeton, NJ: Princeton Univ. Press

Coale, A. J. 1986. Demographic effects of below-replacement fertility and their social implications. *Popul. Dev. Rev.* 12 (Suppl.):203–16

Coale, A. J., Demeny, P. 1983. *Regional Model Life Tables and Stable Populations.*). New York: Academic Press. 2nd ed.

Committee on Ways and Means, US House of Representatives. 1989. *Background Material and Data on Programs Within the Jurisdiction of the Committee on Ways and Means.* Washington, DC: USGPO

Crimmins, E. M., Pramaggiore, M. T. 1988. Changing health of the older working-age population and retirement patterns over time. In *Issues in Contemporary Retirement,* ed. R. Ricardo-Campbell, E. P. Lazear, pp. 132–61. Stanford, Calif: Hoover Inst. Press

Cutler, S. J., Hendrick, J. 1990. Leisure and time use across the life course. In *Handbook of Aging and the Social Sciences,*, ed. R. H. Binstock, L. F. George, pp. 169–85. New York: Academic Press. 3rd ed.

Dannefer, D., Sell, R. R. 1988. Age structure, the life course and "aged heterogeneity": prospects for research and theory. *Comprehensive Gerontology* 2:1–10

Davis, K. 1986. Aging and the health-care system: economic and structural issues. *Daedalus* 115:227–46

Demeny, P. 1986. Pronatalist policies in low-fertility countries: patterns, performance, and prospects. *Popul. Dev. Rev.* 12 (Suppl.):318–34

Dublin, L., Lotka, A. J. 1925. On the true rate of natural increase. *J. Am. Statist. Assoc.* 20:305–39

Duncan, G. J., Smith, K. R. 1989. The rising affluence of the elderly: how far, how fair, and how frail? *Annu. Rev. Sociol.* 15:261–89

Elder, G. H. Jr. 1974. *Children of the Great Depression.* Chicago: Univ. Chicago Press

Elder, G. H. Jr. 1975. Age differentiation and the life course. *Annu. Rev. Sociol.* 1:165–90

Elder, G. H. Jr., Clipp, E. 1988. Wartime losses and social bonding: influence across 40 years in men's lives. *Psychiatry* 51:177–98

George, L. K. 1990. Caregiver stress studies—there really is more to learn. *Gerontologist* 30:580–1

Glass, D. V. 1940. *Population Policies and Movements in Europe*. London: Oxford Univ. Press

Graebner, W. 1980. *A History of Retirement*. New Haven, Conn: Yale Univ. Press

Gruenberg, E. M. 1977. The failure of success. *Milbank Memorial Fund Q*. 55:3–24

Johnson, P., Conrad, C., Thomson, D. eds. 1989. *Workers Versus Pensioners: Intergenerational Justice in an Ageing World*. Manchester: Manchester Univ. Press

Kingson, E. R., Hirshorn, B. A., Cornman, J. M. 1986. *Ties That Bind: The Interdependence of Generations*. Washington, DC: Seven Locks

Kohli, M. 1986. Social organization and subjective construction of the life course. In *Human Development and the Life Course: Multidisciplinary Perspectives,* ed. A. B. Sorensen, F. E. Weinert, L. R. Sherrod, pp. 271–92. Hillsdale, NJ: Erlbaum

Kohli, M. 1988. Ageing as a challenge for sociological theory. *Ageing Soc*. 8:367–94

Laufer, R., Gallops, M. S. 1985. Life-course effects of Vietnam combat and abusive violence: marital patterns. *J. Marriage Fam*. 47:839–53

Longino, Charles F. 1988. A population profile of very old men and women in the United States. *Sociol. Q*. 29:559–64

Lotka, A. J. 1922. The stability of normal age distributions. *Proc. Natl. Acad. Sci. USA* 8:339–45

Manton, K. G. 1989a. Epidemiological, demographic, and social correlates of disability among the elderly. *Milbank Memorial Fund Q*. 67(Suppl. 1):13–58

Manton, K. G. 1989b. Life-style risk factors. *The Annals* 503:72–88

Manton, K. G. 1990. Mortality and Morbidity. In *Handbook of Aging and the Social Sciences,,* ed. R. H. Binstock, L. K. George, 64–90. New York: Academic Press. 3rd ed.

Mayer, K. U., Schoepflin, U. 1989. The state and the life course. *Annu. Rev. Sociol*. 15:187–209

McGill, D. M. 1988. Economic and financial implications of the aging phenomenon. *Proc. Am. Philos. Soc*. 132:154–71

McIntosh, C. A. 1986. Recent pronatalist policies in Western Europe. *Popul. Dev. Rev*. 12(Suppl.):335–358

Meier, E. L. 1988. Managing an older work force. In *The Older Worker,* ed. M. E. Borus, H. S. Parnes, S. H. Sandell, B. Seidman, pp. 167–189. Madison, Wisc: Industrial Relat. Res. Assoc.

Meyer, J. W. 1986. The institutionalization of the life course and its effects on the self. In *Human Development and the Life Course: Multidisciplinary Perspectives,* ed. A. B. Sorensen, F. E. Weinert, L. R. Sherrod, pp. 199–216. Hillsdale, NJ: Erlbaum

Moen, J. 1987. The labor of older men: a comment. *J. Econ. Hist*. 47:761–7

Moody, H. R. 1988. *Abundance of Life: Human Development Policies for an Aging Society* . New York: Columbia Univ. Press

Morrison, M. H. 1986. Work and retirement in an aging society. *Daedalus* 115:269–93

Myers, G. C. 1990. Demography of aging. In *Handbook of Aging and the Social Sciences,,* ed. R. H. Binstock, L. K. George, pp. 19–44. New York: Academic Press. 3rd ed.

Myles, J. 1988. Postwar capitalism and the extension of social security into a retirement wage. In *The Politics of Social Policy in the United States,* ed. M. Weir, A. Orloff, T. Skopcol, pp. 265–91. Princeton, NJ: Princeton Univ. Press

National Center for Health Statistics 1990. Advanced report of final natality statistics, 1988. *Monthly Vital Statist. Rep*. 39[41] (Suppl.)

Neugarten, B. L. 1974. Age groups in Am. society and the rise of the young-old. *Ann. Am. Acad. Polit. Soc. Sci*. 415:187–98

Office of Management and Budget. 1991. *Budget of the United States Government, Fiscal Year 1992*. Washington, DC: USGPO

Okun, M. A., ed. 1982. *New Directions for Continuing Education: Programs for Older Adults, No. 14*. San Francisco: Jossey-Bass

O'Rand, A. M. 1988. Convergence, institutionalization, and bifurcation: gender and the pension acquisition process. *Annu. Rev. Gerontol. Geriatrics* 9:132–55

Ory, M., Riley, M. W. eds. 1989. *Gender, Health and Longevity*. Bethesda, Md: Natl. Inst. Aging

Ory, M., Williams, T. F. 1989. Rehabilitation: small goals, sustained interventions. *The Annals* 503:60–71

Palmer, J. L., Sawhill, I. V., eds. 1988. *The Vulnerable*. Washington, DC: Urban Inst. Press

Parnes, H. S. 1988. The retirement decision. In *The Older Worker,* ed. M. E. Borus, H. S. Parnes, S. H. Sandell, B. Seidman, pp. 115–50. Madison, Wisc: Industr. Relat. Res. Assoc.

Preston, S. H. 1984. Children and the elderly in the U. S. *Sci. Am*. 251:44–9

Preston, S. H. Forthcoming. Cohort succession and the future of the oldest old. In *The*

Oldest Old, ed. R. Suzman, D. Willis. New York: Oxford Univ. Press. In press
Quadagno, J. 1988. *The Transformation of Old Age Security.* Chicago: Univ. Chicago Press
Quinn, J. F., Burkhauser, R. V. 1990. Work and retirement. In *Handbook of Aging and the Social Sciences,*, ed. R. H. Binstock, L. K. George, pp. 307–27. New York: Academic Press. 3rd ed.
Ransom, R. L., Sutch, R. 1989. The trend in the rate of labor force participation of older men, 1870–1930: A reply to Moen. *J. Econ. Hist.* 49:170–83
Riley, M. W. 1978. Aging, social change, and the power of ideas. *Daedalus* 107:39–52
Riley, M. W., Riley, J. W. 1989. The lives of older people and changing social roles. *The Annals* 503:14–28
Riley, M. W., Foner, A., Waring, J. 1988. Sociology of age. In *Handbook of Sociology,* ed. N. J. Smelser, pp. 243–90. Beverly Hills, Calif: Sage
Rodin, J. 1989. Sense of control: potentials for intervention. *The Annals* 503:29–42
Rosenwaike, J., Logue, B. 1985. *The Extreme Aged in America: A Portrait of an Expanding Population.* Westport, Conn: Greenwood
Rosenwaike, J., Dolinsky, A. 1987. The changing demographic determinants of the growth of the extreme aged. *Gerontologist* 27:275–80
Ross, C. M., Danziger, S., Smolensky, E. 1987. Interpreting changes in the economic status of the elderly, 1949–1979. *Contemp. Policy Issues* 5:98–112
Rowe, J. W., Kahn, R. L. 1987. Human aging: usual and successful. *Science* 237:143–9
Ryder, N. B. 1965. The cohort as a concept in the study of social change. *Am. Sociol. Rev.* 30:843–61
Ryder, N. B. 1964. Notes on the concept of a population. *Am. J. Sociol.* 69:447–63
Sandell, S. H. 1988. Public policies and programs affecting older workers. In *The Older Worker,* ed. M. E. Borus, H. S. Parnes, S. H. Sandell, B. Seidman, pp. 207–28. Madison, Wisc: *Indust. Relat. Res. Assoc.*
Serow, W. J., Sly, D. F. 1988. Trends in the characteristics of the oldest-old: 1940–2020. *J. Aging Stud.* 2:145–56
Sickles, R. C., Taubman, P. 1986. An analysis of the health and retirement status of the elderly. *Econometrica* 54:1339–56
Siegel, J. S., Taeuber, C. M. 1986. Demographic perspectives on the long-lived population. *Daedalus* 115:77–117
Smeeding, T. M. 1990. Economic status of the elderly. In *Handbook of Aging and the Social Sciences,* , ed. R. H. Binstock, L. K. George, pp. 362–81. New York: Academic Press. 3rd ed.
Smeeding, T. M., ed. 1987. *Should Medical Care be Rationed by Age?* Totowa, NJ: Rowman & Littlefield
Smolensky, E., Danziger, S., Gottschalk, P. 1988. The declining significance of age in the United States: trends in the well-being of children and the elderly since 1939. In *The Vulnerable,* ed. J. L. Palmer, I. V. Sawhill, pp. 29–54. Washington, DC: Urban Inst. Press
Soldo, B. J., Manton, K. G. 1985. Health status and service needs of the oldest-old: current patterns and future trends. *Milbank Memorial Fund Q.* 62:286–319
Soldo, B. J., Agree, E. M. 1988. America's elderly. *Popul. Bull.* 43:1–51
Spengler, J. J. 1938. *France Faces Depopulation.* Durham, NC: Duke Univ. Press
Staudinger, U. M., Cornelius, S. W., Bales, P. B. 1989. The aging of intelligence: potentials and limits. *The Annals* 503:43–59
Sterns, H. L. 1986. Training and retraining adult and older adult workers. In *Age, Health, and Employment,* ed. J. E. Birren, P. K. Robinson, J. E. Livingston, pp. 93–113. Englewood Cliffs, NJ: Prentice-Hall
Strosberg, M. A., Fein, I. A., Carroll, J. D., eds. 1989. *Rationing of Medical Care for the Critically Ill.* Washington, DC: Brookings Inst.
Suzman, R., Riley, M. W. 1985. Introducing the "Oldest-Old". *Milbank Memorial Fund Q.* 63:177–86
Suzman, R., Willis, D., eds. Forthcoming. *The Oldest Old.* New York: Oxford Univ. Press
Teitelbaum, M. S., Winter, J. M. 1985. *The Fear of Population Decline.* New York: Academic Press
Torrey, B. B. 1982. The lengthening of retirement. In *Aging from Birth to Death,* Vol.2, ed. M. W. Riley, R. P. Abeles, and M. S. Teitelbaum. Boulder, Colo: Westview
Tuma, N. B., Sandefur, G. D. 1988. Trends in the labor force activity of the elderly in the United States, 1940–1980. In *Issues in Contemporary Retirement,* ed. R. Ricardo-Campbell, E. P. Lazear, pp. 38–75. Stanford, Calif: Hoover Inst. Press
Uhlenberg, P. 1990. *Implications of increasing divorce for the elderly.* Pres. UN Int. Conf. on Aging Populations in the Context of the Family. Kita Kyushu, Japan
Uhlenberg, P. 1988a. Population aging and the timing of old-age benefits. In *Issues in Contemporary Retirement,* ed. R. Ricardo-Campbell, E. P. Lazear, pp. 353–77. Stanford, Calif: Hoover Instit. Press
Uhlenberg, P. 1988b. Aging and the societal significance of cohorts. In *Emergent Theo-*

ries of Aging, ed. J. E. Birren, V. L. Bergston, pp. 405–25. New York: Springer

Uhlenberg, P. 1977. Changing structure of the older population of the USA during the twentieth century. *Gerontologist* 17:197–202

Uhlenberg, P., Cooney, T. 1990. Family size and mother-child relations in later life. *Gerontologist* 30:618–25

Uhlenberg, P., Cooney, T., Boyd, R. 1990. Divorce for women after midlife. *J. Gerontol.: Soc. Sci.* 45:S3–11

United Nations. 1988. *World Demographic Estimates and Projections, 1950–2025.* (ST/ESA/SER. R79) New York: United Nations

United States Bureau of the Census. 1989. Projections of the population of the United States by age, sex, and race: 1988 to 2080. *Curr. Popul. Rep. (Series P-25, No. 1018).* Washington, DC: US Govt. Printing Off.

Verbrugge, L. 1984. Longer life but worsening health? Trends in health and mortality of middle-aged and older persons. *Milbank Memorial Fund Q.* 62:475–519

Vinovskis, M. A. 1986. *Have social historians lost the civil war? Some preliminary demographic considerations.* Pres. Annu. Meet. Am. Sociol. Assoc., New York

Watkins, S. C., Menken, J. A., Bongaarts, J. 1987. Demographic foundations of family change. *Am. Sociol. Rev.* 52:346–58

Wattenberg, B. J. 1989. *The Birth Dearth: What Happens When People in Free Countries Don't Have Enough Babies?* New York: Pharos

Winsborough, H. 1978. The statistical histories of the life cycle of birth cohorts. In *Social Demography,* ed. K. E. Taeuber, L. L. Bumpass, J. A. Sweet, pp. 231–59. New York: Academic Press

Ycas, M. 1987. Recent trends in health near the age of retirement: new findings from the health interview survey. *Soc. Security Bull.* 50:5–30

Annu. Rev. Sociol. 1992. 18:475–94

SUBURBAN COMMUNITIES

Mark Baldassare

Program in Social Ecology, University of California, Irvine, California 92717

KEY WORDS: suburbia, suburbanization, urban change, urbanization

Abstract

Suburban communities have experienced a radical transformation in the past century, and now they are where most Americans live. This chapter summarizes the historical evolution of the modern suburb, presents the major suburban theories, and reviews the empirical evidence on the suburban form and social structure. We discuss the suburbanization process in the context of urban decline and change. Finally we review the suburban crisis that has developed after decades of rapid population growth and industrialization. The challenges facing today's suburbs include political fragmentation in regional governance, a growth revolt by local residents, a declining quality of community life, and a lack of affordable housing. The response to the suburban crisis by governments, business, and local residents will affect future suburban growth and suburban form.

INTRODUCTION

Suburban communities are now the home and the work destination for most Americans. In 1970, the suburbs of metropolitan areas surpassed the central cities and nonmetropolitan areas in population size. By 1980, decades of suburban industrialization resulted in suburb-to-suburb commutes becoming the modal pattern for travel to work (Pisarki 1987). By 1990, 48% of Americans lived in suburban places, according to the US Census (Schneider 1991).

0360-0572/92/0815-0475$02.00

Suburban communities are understudied in sociology, relative to their size and importance. They are also not well understood, subject to urban biases and cultural myths about suburban living. This chapter reviews knowledge about the suburbs from a sociological perspective. It analyzes suburban theories, suburbanization processes in the context of urban change, the suburban form and social structure that exist today, and the suburban crisis that evolved after decades of rapid growth and industrialization.

We offer the following broad definition of suburban communities. They are the municipalities and places in metropolitan areas outside of the political boundaries of the large central cities. Suburban communities differ from central cities in the presence of sprawling, low density land use, the absence of a central, downtown district, and the existence of a politically fragmented local government. They differ from rural areas in that the economic activities of suburban residents and businesses are primarily in manufacturing and services, rather than in agriculture.

This chapter examines suburban communities in the contemporary US setting. We do not attempt to review the voluminous literature on the early suburbs, which is well-documented elsewhere (see Abbott 1987, Binford 1985, Fishman 1987, Jackson 1985). Nor do we examine the cross-cultural literature on urban deconcentration and suburban growth, which has been reviewed by others (see Berry 1976).

In an analysis of contemporary US suburbs, their unique features should be considered before any comparisons are drawn with other historical eras and other cultural contexts. The obvious differences include suburban dominance, rapid growth, and suburban industrialization. Other important distinctions are the strong powers of local government, limited federal government intervention, the national decline in manufacturing, racial diversity in American metropolitan areas, and Americans' preferences for small communities, detached dwellings, and homeownership.

SUBURBAN ERAS

Suburban communities have undergone dramatic change since the nineteenth century. Four eras have important consequences for their current situation. A review of their evolution helps us understand both the realities they face today and the public's ideals about suburban living.

In the preindustrial era, suburban communities were few in number and sparsely populated. The nineteenth century suburbs were mostly small towns focused on agriculture and trade, with railroads and dirt roads providing the weak links between suburbs and the city. Only the landed gentry and transport workers traveled to the city on a frequent basis (see Binford 1985, Fishman 1987, Jackson 1985). Suburbanization was slow and suburban population small.

The early urban-industrial era led to the formation of a "zone of commuters" (Burgess 1967). In the early twentieth century, commuter rail and limited automobile use allowed for the development of bedroom communities far from the central business district and outside the city limits. Their social composition was predominantly white, family-oriented, and middle class. Most of the employed residents commuted to white collar jobs in the industrial city. These were mainly small, low density communities, mostly composed of detached homes in all-residential areas. Though the suburban population was small, and many of these suburbs were eventually annexed by the central city, this was a critical time in the suburb's evolution. The rate of suburbanization was fairly rapid. These early suburbs also captured the general public's imagination and were often spoken of in almost utopian terms by urban planners, politicians, and private developers. Their presumed benefits included urban decongestion, lower residential densities, greater separation from the city's business district and, importantly, home ownership. These early suburbs became the public's ideal for future suburban developments. They also were seen as desirable solutions to emerging urban problems.

In the late urban-industrial era, the suburbs grew dramatically. Mass automobile use and large highways freed Americans from living near work (Hawley 1971). In the 1950s and 1960s, many central city residents moved to the suburbs, bought homes in large housing tracts, and commuted back to central city jobs. In these two decades, the suburbs in the United States increased from 35 million to 84 million residents, for a growth rate of 144% (US Bureau of the Census 1987). Sociologists began to take serious notice of the magnitude and scope of the suburban migration. Some worried about its implications for American culture, while others were dubious of the effects of this new suburban life on residents (Berger 1960, 1961, Dobriner 1958, Gans 1962, 1967, Whyte 1956). Few predicted its future impact on the American city, the national economy, and national politics.

The metropolitan era is the one in which the suburbs dominate American society. Since the 1970s, residence and employment are increasingly located in suburban regions. In 1970, 37% of Americans or 84 million people lived in the suburbs. By 1980, 44% of Americans or 100 million people lived in the suburbs (US Bureau of the Census 1987). The 1990 Census indicates that 48% of Americans now live in the suburbs. By 1980, suburban employment had grown to 33 million jobs, from only 14 million two decades previously, for a growth rate of 136%. Travel from a suburban home to a suburban workplace reached 25 million trips, or 37% of all commutes. Thus, commuting to work within the suburbs became more common than either central city-to-central city trips or suburb-to-central city commutes (Pisarki 1987).

The dominance of the suburban population has had a major impact on American politics. In presidential politics, for instance, since 1970 only one Democratic has won, while there have been four Republican victories.

Democrats still win in urban areas, but that vote has shrunk to 29% of the total. Republicans have won big in the suburbs, where 48% of voters now live (Schneider 1991). The dominance of suburban voters has also greatly reduced the political constituency for rebuilding America's central cities. For both cities and suburbs, the profound effects of the metropolitan era are still being discovered (Berry & Kasarda, 1977, Long & De Are 1981, Masotti & Hadden 1973).

THEORETICAL PERSPECTIVES

While empirical studies have proliferated rapidly, reflecting the increasing importance of suburbs, theory has received much less attention. Many suburban theories, in fact, are derived from urban theories. This has fostered an urban bias in examining suburban communities. Some scholars of the suburbs follow the school of urban ecology, others the political economy perspective, while some have turned to theories outside of sociology. No one theoretical perspective dominates suburban studies today, and this reflects the trend now evident in urban sociology.

The study of suburban communities has been most influenced by urban ecology, with its focus on the social organization of metropolitan regions (Burgess 1967, Park 1967, McKenzie 1967). This would include the spatial distribution of population and industries, racial segregation, economic specialization, status persistence in suburban neighborhoods, suburb-central city relationships, and the effects of transportation on suburban growth. The influence of urban ecology is also evident in studies of the social psychology of suburban life (Wirth 1938). This includes the study of local activity patterns, involvement in local politics, neighboring, and residents' well-being.

Suburban studies also draw insights from the political economy perspective. This theory focuses on how government and industry determine the patterns of suburban growth and development, for the profit of elites. For instance, Molotch (1976) has examined how local governments and local businesses act together to create a pro-growth municipal agenda. Others examine small, affluent suburbs as entities to serve the elite's efforts to escape high taxes for city welfare services (Miller 1981, Peterson 1981). Some have studied how pro-business federal policies and the decisions of large corporations are determining the growth of the Sunbelt suburban region (Sawers & Tabb 1984).

Another influence on suburban studies has been public choice theory. Tiebout (1956) argues that residents move to areas whose local governments satisfy their preferences for public goods. In a suburban region, residents select among the multitude of municipalities the one which offers them the best services. For instance, the elderly select suburbs where services are geared toward older adults, rather than children. Thus, some examine local government expenditures as predictors of the spatial distribution of populations. In addition, wealthy suburbs may develop policies that exclude the poor, limiting them to living in central cities. Thus, other studies would analyze how suburban fiscal policies can result in racial segregation and economic inequality.

Other scholars have emphasized the effects of physical design. They find the traditional detached home, residential neighborhood, and sprawling land use to have profound impacts on residents' attitudes and well-being. While suburban designs may be congruent with the lifestyles and preferences of white American middle class families, other groups may find them less than satisfying (Michelson 1976, 1977). Some have examined how suburban physical designs have fostered isolation, while others say they reinforce gender inequality (for instance, Hayden 1984, Popenoe 1985). Many argue the need for suburban innovations, such as higher densities, mixed land uses, more pedestrian walkways and new housing forms. New designs would reflect suburban social diversity, promote greater equality, and foster a sense of community.

Finally, a major predictor of suburban trends is the gap between the "ideal" and the "real" suburb. While the small, residential suburb is still preferred, most American suburbs have been in transition to large, diverse places in sprawling and congested regions (Baldassare 1986). Thus, studies focus on residents' dissatisfaction with the quality of life, including housing, neighborhood, local government, and public services. Further studies examine preferences for local policies that promise a return to the suburban ideals. These include public support for small, local governments over regional governmental entities and favoring of slow-growth policies over pro-development positions.

SUBURBANIZATION AND URBAN CHANGE

The nation's suburbanization is best understood in the context of several trends in urbanization and urban change that have been underway for many decades. A review of urban events at several points in the suburb's history will help place suburban growth and industrialization in perspective.

In the early urban-industrial cities, urban ecologists stated that foreign immigration and rising income led to the suburban "zone of commuters" (Burgess 1967, Park 1967a). Suburban growth was driven by an "invasion and succession" process in older, inner city neighborhoods. City areas became the destination points for recent, poor, immigrant workers. New residents moved to these areas because of their inexpensive housing and proximity to work. As a result of the "invasion," many of the long-term residents of these inner city areas moved to suburban areas further away from the central business district. Of course, all of this occurs because long-term residents can afford the higher costs of housing and city-to-suburb commutes. Thus, suburbs developed in an urban context of population growth and rising incomes.

Later, suburban expansion was accelerated by urban technological changes. McKenzie (1967) in the 1920s stated that the demographic and ecological trend of city residents moving to suburban communities was a direct result of transportation innovations such as private automobiles and commuter rail. Hawley (1950) argued that a diminished "friction of space" made urban deconcentration possible. Commuting times from home to work were drastically reduced by improved roads and mass transit, allowing many more central city workers to live in suburban communities. Ultimately, the proliferation of telecommunications and private automobiles, at relatively low costs to consumers, meant that what once took place in a large, high density city could now spread out in a large, low density, sprawling metropolitan region (Kasarda 1978). Thus, suburbs expanded in size and functions as a result of modern technology.

The "urban crisis" of the 1960s had a dramatic influence on suburban growth and social composition. A massive migration of poor, southern blacks dramatically changed northern cities. Many of these urban newcomers found no work and, instead, faced discrimination and economic deprivation. Central cities experienced high crime rates, high unemployment, racial tensions, increasing welfare costs, and rising taxes. These events resulted in large migrations from central cities and, more specifically, the movement of white middle class families to suburbs (Frey 1979, 1980).

The suburbanization of the United States has also been directly aided by federal government policies. The funding for constructing the interstate highway system provided the infrastructure needed to drastically lower the time and cost for commuting from suburbs to central cities. Thus, people and industries could move to a large suburban region surrounding the central cities. Mortgage deductions for owning a home provided an income tax incentive for moving from rental apartments to owner-occupied dwellings. The federal government also subsidized the cost of owning a suburban home through the veterans home loan programs (Baldassare 1986). Thus, federal policies favoring the suburbs encouraged a massive move out of the central city.

Regional population shifts within the United States are important in explaining recent suburbanization trends. There has been a migration of population out of the northern states into the southern and western metropolitan regions (Sternlieb & Hughes 1975). This has been described as a migration that is following employment opportunities, lower living costs, and the nation's newer communities. This regional shift has resulted in the growth of southern and western central cities, at the expense of large cities in the north. However, regional shifts also mean that Sunbelt suburbs have grown very rapidly, as they experience both spillover growth from the sunbelt cities and migrations from the northern states (Abbott 1987, Long & De Are 1981).

Finally, suburbs expanded as central cities experienced a fundamental economic restructuring during the 1970s and 1980s (Sassen 1990). Some of the central city manufacturing jobs have been totally lost from the national economy, as domestic products are replaced by foreign made goods and as multinational corporations move their US operations to less expensive overseas locations (Feagin 1985, Shelton et al 1989). However, there has also been a trend of industrial deconcentration within the United States, in efforts to reduce rents, taxes, and labor costs. Many manufacturers have moved their central city plants to outer suburban areas of the same metropolis. Others have relocated part or all of their operations from northern central cities to southern and western suburban areas (Perry & Watkins, 1977, Sawers & Tabb 1984, Tabb & Sawers 1984). As a result, the suburban communities in recent decades are industrializing as well as growing rapidly in population.

THE SUBURBAN FORM

Suburban communities were initially formed during decades of a massive, one-way movement of residents from central cities to suburbs (Tucker 1984). The early migrants were predominantly white middle class families moving to residential suburbs. The suburban profile is thus distinct from the central city in race, social status, and familism (Farley 1976, Guest & Nelson 1978). This migration led to the extreme racial and economic segregation of the suburbs, when contrasted with the make-up of central city population.

In recent decades, suburban industrial growth increased economic inequalities between central cities and suburbs (Kasarda 1976, 1978, 1980). Central cities lost blue collar jobs while suburbs were gaining manufacturing plants, office buildings, and retail outlets. This has led to the current mismatch between employment and people in metropolitan America, with those in need of jobs remaining in the city, while the blue collar jobs were relocating or expanding in the suburbs. Suburban employment has also resulted in rapid growth and a more socially diverse suburban population.

Racial change is now underway in suburbia and is a subject of intense study. Blacks are moving from central cities to suburbs, and the black suburban population is growing at a rapid rate (Clark 1979, Lake 1981, Nelson 1980, Schnore et al 1976). Still, blacks today are a small fraction of the total suburban population (Baldassare 1986), and the black migration largely involves the black middle class (Roof & Spain 1977, Winsberg, 1989). Blacks have typically moved to inner suburbs, in larger suburban municipalities and in areas already populated by blacks (Galster 1991, Logan & Schneider 1984, Marshall & Stahura, 1979a 1979b, Spain & Long 1981,

Stahura 1986, 1988). Indeed, there is evidence that racial segregation of suburban communities and the spatial separation of whites from minority groups has continued, despite the large numbers of blacks and other minorities moving to suburbs (Massey & Denton 1987, 1988, 1989, Massey & Eggers 1990).

The fact that extreme racial segregation persists in the suburbs has led to examinations of the dual housing market, local government policies, local community politics, and other factors that may limit suburban racial integration (Logan & Stearns, 1981, Stearns & Logan 1986). There is, of course, much anecdotal evidence of racial exclusion through local zoning, covenants, and real estate industry practices.

Suburban communities are also becoming socially diverse. The suburbs have gained in nonfamily households, as young adults without children move to suburban communities for job opportunities (Long & Glick 1976). The suburbs increasingly include older residents without children, as early migrants are aging (Fitzpatrick & Logan 1985, Stahura 1980). The suburbs are also becoming increasingly diverse in income, education, and occupational status, because many blue collar and service workers are moving to suburban employment centers (Baldassare 1986). Still, suburban regions are distinct from central cities on almost all social dimensions. Suburban regions are segregated by family status, age, income, and occupational status. Suburban communities are specialized, catering to the unique needs of different subgroups of the suburban population (Muller 1981, Michelson 1976, 1977).

Suburban communities are evolving into new forms as the metropolitan area grows. The current pattern seems to be one of a broad-based urban deconcentration of manufacturing, administration, retailing, and services (Berry & Cohen 1973, Schneider & Fernandez 1989, Zimmer 1975). Suburban communities are increasingly mixed in land uses, rather than geographically specialized; residential and industrial developments now often occur side by side (Guest 1976, 1978a, Logan 1976). Central cities appear to have little role as the administrative agent or dominating force behind suburban economic development, despite ecological theories to the contrary (Marshall & Stahura 1986, Wilson 1978). However, central cities appear to be providing municipal services for many suburban residents, even as their tax base declines, probably reflecting an increase in income from suburban weekday commuters and weekend tourists (Kasarda 1972).

A current controversy debates whether the modern suburban form exemplifies status change or status persistence. The traditional ecological argument is that urban neighborhoods go through life cycles, rising and then declining in social status. Several studies have found stability in the status rankings of suburban communities (Denowitz 1986, Guest 1978b, Stahura 1979). However, other evidence suggests that status change occurs over time, with inner suburbs declining in status as their affluent residents move to the newer outer suburbs (Choldin et al 1980, Guest 1979, Listokin & Beaton, 1983, Schwirian et al 1990, Stahura 1984). Growth, ecology, social structure, local policies, and economic trends interact and make it difficult to predict suburban status change (see Collver & Semyonov 1979, Guest 1978b, Logan & Semyonov 1980, Stahura 1987). Most likely, status persistence occurs only in special circumstances such as in high income suburbs, while status change is possible in most other places.

The gap between poor and wealthy suburbs is increasing, and suburban regions are becoming more socially stratified (Logan & Schneider 1981). The local government structure allows affluent communities to channel their tax resources into improving local services, which then attract more high status migrants (Logan & Schneider 1982, Schneider 1980, Schneider & Logan 1981). Also, higher status suburbs are now trying to attract industries, thus adding to the financial woes of the less affluent suburbs (Logan & Golden 1986).

THE SUBURBAN CRISIS

After several decades of rapid population growth and industrialization, significant problems are evolving in suburban communities. The response to these challenges is uniquely suburban in nature: resident's ideals and expectations about suburban communities, and the structure of government that exists today, are at odds with the realities of the large, sprawling suburban regions. In this section, we examine four critical suburban challenges.

Political Fragmentation

The suburban regions of today's metropolises contain dozens of local municipal governments, county governments, and single-purpose agencies. Political fragmentation refers to the fact that numerous local governments and agencies are pursuing their own fiscal, service, and land use policies.

The political fragmentation of suburban communities has been blamed for many problems found today in metropolitan areas. These include chronic fiscal strain in central cities, traffic congestion in suburban regions, the lack of affordable housing in suburban communities, inefficient local service delivery, and racial and income segregation in metropolitan areas (Bollens, 1986, Burnell & Burnell 1989, Danielson 1976, Dolan 1990, Dowall 1984, Kasarda 1978, Logan & Schneider 1981, 1982, Neiman 1980, Schlay & Rossi 1981, Schneider & Logan 1981, 1982). Indeed, some contend that political fragmentation represents a system of local government favored by white, affluent suburban homeowners who use incorporation and local zoning to avoid higher tax burdens for welfare, schools, and social services for the poor living in larger cities (Miller, 1981, Peterson 1981).

Metropolitan areas have been slow to react to political fragmentation, largely because of political resistance from local elected officials and suburban residents. Voters frequently turn down regional government proposals at the ballot box, and this voting pattern is very typical of suburban residents (Campbell & Dollenmeyer 1975, Zimmer 1976). Suburban surveys have found strong opposition to intra-county regional government, inter-county regional governments, and single purpose regional agencies to address metropolitan-wide problems such as environmental pollution (Baldassare 1989, 1991a,c). Older, high income residents and homeowners are more opposed to regional government, indicating a possible desire to avoid higher taxes for redistributive services. However, there are widely held negative perceptions that regional governments are unnecessary, large bureaucracies, less effective structures than current local governments and authorities, and ones that threaten the system of local political power. These stereotypes are consistent with the suburban values that emphasize distrust of large, urban government bureaucracies, a preference for decentralized public services, and a strong desire for local rule (see Baldassare, 1986, Fischer 1984, Popenoe 1985).

There are also scholars who point out that the benefits of regional government may be overstated. They have offered the argument that a system of small municipal governments in metropolitan areas can offer a wider variety of public service choices and can produce a high level of local citizen satisfaction (Ostrom & Parks 197.3, Ostrom 1983, Stein 1990, Tiebout 1956). Regional governments are perceived as large government bureaucracies which may not be flexible enough to adequately meet the diverse service needs of specialized populations in the suburban metropolis.

Still, there are examples of regional governments that have worked effectively in the past 20 years (Babcock 1991, Danielson & Doig 1982, Dowall 1984, Grant 1972, Kirlin 1991). Several metropolitan areas are adopting regional governments as residents lose faith in the ability of local government to manage growth-related local problems, including traffic congestion, pollution, and housing supply (Baldassare 1986, Bollens 1990, DiMento & Graymer 1991).

The Growth Revolt

One important response to the suburban change under way is the "growth revolt." These are the recent attempts by suburban residents to limit new development. Residents in a wide range of suburban communities, from older, affluent suburbs to recently built places on the outer fringes, are placing political pressures on their local governments to control the pace, type, and extent of new development (Dowall 1980, Glickfeld et al 1987, Morrison

1977, Rosenbaum 1978). Some have portrayed the growth revolt as a struggle between citizens and their pro-growth leaders, while others point out that suburban municipalities often embrace slow growth policies in response to population pressures and unwanted community change (Logan 1976, 1978, Logan & Molotch 1987, Lyon et al 1981, Marando & Thomas 1977, Maurer & Christenson 1982, Molotch 1976).

A large proportion of suburban residents appear to support growth controls. National surveys find opposition to new development in growing suburbs (Baldassare 1981). Local elections and community surveys have found large majorities of suburban residents favoring local growth limitations (Baldassare 1986, 1990, 1991b, Glickfeld et al 1987). However, suburban residents are more interested in limiting growth in their own community than in the suburban region as a whole, giving meaning to the term "NIMBYism." They are also staunchly opposed to local no-growth policies (Baldassare 1990). Citizen preferences for local growth policies reflect a desire to limit new developments locally, while allowing the regional economy to grow, presenting political and practical problems for suburban policy makers.

There has been speculation that affluent homeowners support growth controls for reasons of self-interest and economic gain (Danielson 1976, Ellickson 1977, Frieden 1979). Past research has found little support for this belief. Women, younger adults, and residents with high educational status are somewhat more supportive of growth controls; however, the perceptions of rapid growth and a declining quality of community life are more significant predictors of citizen support for local growth controls (Baldassare 1986, 1990, 1991b, Bollens 1990, Gottdiener & Neiman 1981, Neiman & Loveridge 1981, see also Van Liere & Dunlap 1980). Perceived local problems usually surpass social class and politics as the predictors of slow growth support. Thus, a new political movement seems to be forming around citizens' preferences for suburban growth controls (see Clark 1976, Clark & Ferguson 1983).

Growth controls are now in place in many suburbs, ranging from growth moratoria, planning pauses, and limits on local services (Burrows 1977, Dowall 1980, Scott et al 1975). Those municipalities with growth controls often have higher concentrations of homeowners and white collar residents; however, local growth controls are found in many rapidly growing areas that are not high status suburbs (Baldassare & Protash 1982, Protash & Baldassare 1983).

Local growth controls are supposed to have dramatic effects on growth, housing supply, and community composition. However, the evidence suggests that growth controls have little or no impact on these factors and, importantly, they do not improve the perceived quality of life (Baldassare & Protash 1982, Logan & Zhou 1989). Nevertheless, suburban politics today largely revolve around local growth policies.

Community Quality

When asked about their ideal residence, most Americans would prefer to live in a small community within commuting distance of a large city (De Jong 1977, Fuguitt & Zuiches 1975, Zuiches 1981, Zuiches & Fuguitt 1972). Many Americans have expressed these preferences by moving to a suburban community. Today, suburban communities receive positive evaluations from most of their residents. However, rapid growth and industrialization in recent decades have diminished many aspects of the quality of community life.

Classic urban theory has stressed the detrimental social and psychological effects of individuals living in large, dense, and heterogeneous central cities (McKenzie 1967, Milgram 1970, Park 1967a,b, Park et al 1967, Simmel 1969, Wirth 1938). Early empirical research indicated a higher concentration of social deviance problems in the inner city areas than in the suburban zone of commuters (Faris & Dunham 1967, Shaw & McKay, 1969).

National surveys indicate that most suburban residents express a high level of satisfaction with their communities. Compared to city residents, suburbanites are more likely to have positive overall ratings of their communities and their specific local features such as schools, roads, police, and parks (Baldassare 1981, Campbell et al 1976, Dahmann 1985, Marans & Rodgers, 1975). Suburban residents show a slight but consistent preference for social activities in their local area. Suburbanites are more likely than central city residents to know neighbors and to have neighborhood friends. However, they are not more socially involved than others (Fischer et al 1977, Fischer 1982, 1984).

Some argue that the apparent advantages that suburbs have over large cities only reflect differences in social class, familism, and length of residence (Gans 1962, 1967, Hawley 1972, Kasarda & Janowitz 1974). Others point to the effects of self-selection, that is, that most of the people who live in the suburbs are seeking the social lifestyle offered by small, low density communities (Michelson 1976, 1977). However, the physical distance of the suburbs from large cities and the downtown do seem to have implications for social relations and local activity patterns (Fischer 1984, Fischer & Jackson 1976, Hummon 1986).

Most of the research on the effects of suburban growth and industrialization indicates a diminished quality of community life. A few early studies found social problems associated with population change (Ogburn 1935, Wechsler 1961). In the 1970s, industrializing suburban regions achieved special notice for having problems once associated with urban areas such as congestion, social conflict, crime, and political tensions (Bensman & Vidich 1975, Hawley & Rock 1975, Masotti & Hadden, 1973, 1974, Schwartz 1976).

National surveys indicate that residents in rapidly growing suburbs express lower community satisfaction than do other suburbanites. They tend to have poorer evaluations of roads, mass transit, the locale's convenience, neighborhood safety, and neighbors (Baldassare 1981). Suburbanites in rapidly growing areas, however, are still more satisfied than central city residents. More recently, community studies in rapidly growing suburbs indicate a decline in the quality of community life over time. The decline in resident satisfaction is related to population growth, suburban industrialization, mixed land use, sprawling land use, and negative perceptions of traffic and growth problems (Baldassare 1986, 1991d, Cervero 1986, Pisarki, 1987).

Affordable Housing

The preference for owning a single family home is an ideal held by most Americans (Henretta 1984, Logan & Collver 1983, Perin 1977, Tremblay & Dillman 1983). For decades, suburban communities made the "American Dream" come true for millions of average, middle income families. Today, owning a detached dwelling has become an unrealized goal for many of the recent suburban middle class residents, and the lack of affordable housing for lower socioeconomic groups has become a critical problem in most suburban regions.

In the classic ecological studies, the small, residential suburbs in the "zone of commuters" had high proportions of homeowners, single family dwellings, and family households (Burgess 1967). In the post–World War II era, many factors led to the affordable ownership of single family housing in the suburbs. Inexpensive land and mass produced housing tracts reduced building costs. Low interest loans, income growth, tax policies, and federal home loan programs were incentives for consumers (Baldassare 1986). Young urban families in search of homeownership, larger homes, increased privacy and outdoor space found suburban communities very accommodating to their housing needs (Michelson 1976, Morris & Winter 1978, Rossi 1955).

The rapid growth and industrialization of the suburbs for the past two decades, however, altered the dynamics of most suburban housing markets. Employment growth in the suburban regions increased the demand for suburban housing. Suburban industrialization heightened the competition for available land. Both of these factors, as well as rising home building costs and higher mortgage interest rates, have dramatically increased the average cost of owning a single family home in most suburban regions (Baldassare 1986).

As evidence of the decline in housing affordability, suburban regions experienced a decrease in residents moving into owner-occupied homes, and an increase in moving out of owner-occupied homes in the 1970s and 1980s (Morrow-Jones 1989). Community surveys in suburban regions indicate that homeownership rates among new residents are considerably lower than they are for residents who moved into the region a decade earlier. Average monthly mortgage payments can be as much as four times higher for recent residents than for long-term residents. As a result, only the most wealthy newcomers to suburbia can afford to purchase a single family home today, while recent residents are more likely to be renters and to live in dense, attached dwellings. While most suburban apartment renters would still prefer to own a single family home, many of them say they are unlikely to attain this goal in the near future (Baldassare 1986).

The shortage of affordable housing means that suburban residents must either lower their housing expectations or change their location. Today, many suburban residents are choosing the latter, commuting long distances from the inexpensive single family housing on the suburban fringes to suburban employment centers. Thus far, inclusionary zoning policies to increase the supply of affordable housing have had limited success (Schwartz & Johnston 1983).

The problems involving affordable housing in the suburban regions are by no means limited to middle income families who cannot afford to buy a home. Blacks and other minorities moving to suburban employment centers face housing discrimination (Logan & Stearns 1981, Stearns & Logan 1986). Apartments for entry level employees and immigrant laborers are in short supply. Homelessness is a growing problem in industrial suburbs because marginal workers cannot afford the housing costs in suburban regions.

SUMMARY

Suburban communities have experienced a radical transformation in the past century. Once remote towns on the city's outskirts, they later became the small communities where a few affluent commuters lived. After World War II, suburbs provided the new housing developments where the growing middle class settled. Recently, they have become the sites for both population growth and industrial development.

The evolution of suburban communities reflects many fundamental changes in urban society. Early suburban settlements were dependent upon societal trends such as urban industrialization, immigration, income growth, and transportation technology. Later, the severity of the urban crisis and the federal government policies that followed were to favor suburban housing developments at the expense of central city reinvestment. Today, rapid growth and suburban industrialization is in the context of a major national economic restructuring and the movement of large manufacturers to suburban areas and less developed regions.

Sociologists have been examining the suburbs from a variety of theoretical perspectives. These include urban ecology theory, the political economy perspective, and public choice theory. Others have emphasized the effects of the physical design, while some focus on the importance of the gap between suburban ideals and suburban reality.

The suburban form that currently exists reflects the combined effects of urban change and suburban political structure. The social composition of the suburban regions reflects the large exodus of white, middle class families moving from declining central cities. The increasing social diversity and land use heterogeneity indicate the massive movement of jobs and industries to suburban regions. The social segregation and economic inequality that exist between suburban places point to the influence that local governments do have on housing and land use patterns.

The challenges facing suburban communities include political fragmentation in regional governance, a growth revolt by residents, a declining quality of community life, and a lack of affordable housing. These problems reflect decades of rapid growth and industrialization. The response to the suburban crisis by local governments, regional agencies, federal officials, businesses, and local residents will affect future suburban migration and the suburban form.

Future studies should consider the community structures that are evolving in response to the suburban crisis. For instance, "disurbs" that is, the dense, industrialized suburban areas provide office buildings, manufacturing plants, housing and retail services in close proximity (see Baldassare & Katz 1987, Garreau 1991). There are also "suburbs of suburbs" on the outskirts of the industrial suburban region, offering inexpensive housing and long commutes to workers in the industrialized suburban areas. In addition, large, planned communities and exclusive suburbs allow affluent suburban residents to isolate themselves from traffic and growth problems in the metropolitan region. Finally, immigrant enclaves are now developing in older, declining suburban communities. These provide low-cost housing for low-skilled workers in proximity to the new, industrialized suburbs.

Future studies should collect more detailed information on municipal decision-making. Some researchers have found that local government fiscal policies do significantly affect community structure and metropolitan inequality. Others have indicated that zoning and land use regulations have little or no consequence for local growth rates and the housing market. Such studies are based on the premise that officials intentionally pursue certain policies and avoid others to shape community structure. This research would be improved by surveys of suburban officials, gathering information on their motivations in adopting local policies.

Finally, field studies of suburban communities have been largely absent in recent times. The early observational reports on suburbs were influential in developing theories about the effects of suburban living. They were critical in the rejection of several myths, including the lack of suburban diversity. They helped place into perspective the effects of suburban community structure on individuals, compared with other factors such as social class and life cycle. Today, sociological theory and empirical knowledge about the suburban industrialized region are limited by the lack of in-depth, qualitative community studies.

Literature Cited

Abbott, C. 1987. The suburban sunbelt. *J. Urban Hist.* 13:275–301

Babcock, R. 1991. Implementing metropolitan regional planning. See DiMento & Graymer 1991, pp. 79–88

Baldassare, M. 1981. *The Growth Dilemma: Resident's Views and Local Population Change in the United States.* Berkeley: Univ. Calif. Press. 175 pp.

Baldassare, M. 1986. *Trouble in Paradise: The Suburban Transformation in America.* New York: Columbia Univ. Press. 251 pp.

Baldassare, M. 1989. Citizen support for regional government in the new suburbia. *Urban Aff. Q.* 24:460–69

Baldassare, M. 1990. Suburban support for no-growth policies: Implications for the growth revolt. *J. Urban Aff.* 12:197–206

Baldassare, M. 1991a. Is there room for regionalism in the suburbs? *J. Architect. Plan. Res.* 8:222–34

Baldassare, M. 1991b. The growth revolt in the suburbs: A new political movement? *Res. Commun. Sociol.* 2:59–75

Baldassare, M. 1991c. Public attitudes towards regional structures and solutions. See DiMento & Graymer 1991, pp. 105–120

Baldassare, M. 1991d. Transportation attitudes in suburbia: Trends in attitudes, behaviors and policy preferences. *Transportation* 18:207–22

Baldassare, M., Protash, W. 1982. Growth controls, population growth and community satisfaction. *Am. Sociol. Rev.* 47:339–46

Baldassare, M., Katz, C. 1987. Disurbia emerges as the successor to suburbia. *Newsday* August 14:85

Bensman, J., Vidich, A., eds. 1975. *Metropolitan Communities.* New York: New Viewpoints. 296 pp.

Berger, B. 1960. *Working Class Suburb.* Berkeley: Univ. Calif. Press. 143 pp.

Berger, B. 1961. The myth of suburbia. *J. Soc. Issues* 17:38–49

Berry, B. J., ed. 1976. *Urbanization and Counterurbanization.* Beverly Hills: Sage. 334 pp.

Berry, B. J., Cohen, Y. S. 1973. Decentralization of commerce and industry: the restructuring of metropolitan America. See Masotti & Hadden 1973, pp. 431–56

Berry, B. J., Kasarda, J. D. 1977. *Contemporary Urban Ecology.* New York: MacMillan. 497 pp.

Binford, H. 1985. *The First Suburbs.* Chicago: Univ. Chicago Press. 304 pp.

Bollens, S. 1986. A political-ecological analysis of income inequality in the metropolitan area. *Urban Aff. Q.* 22:221–41

Bollens, S. 1990. Constituencies for limitation and regionalism: Approaches to growth management. *Urban Aff. Q.* 26:46–67

Burgess, E. 1967. The growth of the city. See Park et al 1967, pp. 47–62

Burnell, B., Burnell, J. 1989. Community interaction and suburban zoning policies. *Urban Aff. Q.* 24:470–82

Burrows, L. 1977. *Growth Management: Issues, Techniques and Policy Implications.* New Brunswick, NJ: Cent. Urban Policy Res. 141 pp.

Campbell, A., Dollenmeyer J. 1975. Governance in a metropolitan society. See Hawley & Rock 1975, pp. 355–96

Campbell, A., Converse, P. E., Rodgers, W. L. 1976. *The Quality of American Life.* New York: Russell Sage Found. 583 pp.

Cervero, R. 1986. *Suburban Gridlock.* New Brunswick, NJ: Cent. Urban Policy Res. 248 pp.

Choldin, H. M., Hanson, C., Bohrer, R. 1980. Suburban status instability. *Am. Sociol. Rev.* 45:972–83

Clark, T. N., ed. 1976. Citizen preferences and urban public policy. *Policy Polit.* Vol. 4, No. 4

Clark, T. A. 1979. *Blacks in Suburbs.* New Brunswick, NJ: Cent. Urban Policy Res. 127 pp.

Clark, T. N., Ferguson, L. 1983. *City Money.* New York: Columbia Univ. Press. 440 pp.

Collver, A., Semyonov, M. 1979. Suburban change and persistence. *Am. Sociol. Rev.* 44:480–86

Dahmann, D. 1985. Assessments of neighborhood quality in metropolitan America. *Urban Aff. Q.* 20:511–35

Danielson, M. 1976. *The Politics of Exclusion.* New York: Columbia Univ. Press. 443 pp.

Danielson, M., Doig, J. 1982. *New York: The Politics of Urban Regional Development.* Berkeley: Univ. Calif. Press. 376 pp.

De Jong, G. F. 1977. Residential preferences and migration. *Demography* 14:169–78

Denowitz, R. 1986. Status change and persistence in Chicago suburbs: Multiple patterns of causation. *Sociol. Q.* 27:205–15

DiMento, J., Graymer, L., eds. 1991. *Confronting Regional Challenges*. Cambridge, Mass: Lincoln Inst.

Dobriner, W. 1958. *The Suburban Community,* New York: G. Putnam. 416 pp.

Dolan, D. 1990. Local government fragmentation: does it drive up the cost of government? *Urban Aff. Q.* 26:28–45

Dowall, D. E. 1980. An examination of population growth-managing communities. *Policy Stud. J.* 9:414–27

Dowall, D. E. 1984. *The Suburban Squeeze*. Berkeley: Univ. Calif. Press. 248 pp.

Ellickson, R. 1977. Suburban growth controls: An economic and legal analysis. *Yale Law J.* 86:385–511

Faris, R. Dunham, M. 1967. *Mental Disorders in Urban Areas*. Chicago: Univ. Chicago Press. 270 pp. 2nd ed.

Farley, R. 1976. Components of suburban population growth. See Schwartz 1976, pp. 3–38

Feagin, J. 1985. The global context of metropolitan growth: Houston and the oil industry. *Am. J. Sociol.* 90:1204–30

Fischer, C. S. 1982. *To Dwell Among Friends*. Chicago: Univ. Chicago Press. 451 pp.

Fischer, C. S. 1984. *The Urban Experience*. New York: Harcourt, Brace, Jovanovich. 371 pp.

Fischer, C. S., Jackson, R. 1976. Suburbs, networks and attitudes. See Schwartz 1976, pp. 279–307

Fischer, C. S., Jackson, R., Stueve, A., Gerson, K., et al. 1977. *Networks and Places*. New York: Free Press. 229 pp.

Fishman, R. 1987. *Bourgeois Utopias: The Rise and Fall of Suburbia*. New York: Basic Books. 241 pp.

Fitzpatrick, K. M., Logan, J. R. 1985. The aging of the suburbs, 1960–1980. *Am. Sociol. Rev.* 50:106–17

Frey, W. 1979. Central-city white flight. *Am. Sociol. Rev.* 11:411–23

Frey, W. 1980. Black in-migration and white flight: economic effects. *Am. J. Sociol.* 85:1396–417

Frieden, B. 1979. *The Environmental Protection Hustle*. Cambridge, Mass.: MIT Press. 211 pp.

Fuguitt, G., Zuiches, J. 1975. Residential preferences and population distribution. *Demography* 12:491–504

Galster, G. 1991. Black suburbanization: Has it changed the relative location of races? *Urban Aff. Q.* 26:621–28

Gans, H. 1962. Urbanism and suburbanism as ways of life: a re-evaluation of definitions. In *Human Behavior and Social Processes,* ed. A. Rose, pp. 625–48. Boston: Houghton Mifflin

Gans, H. 1967. *The Levittowners*. New York: Pantheon. 474 pp.

Garreau, J. 1991. *Edge City*. New York: Doubleday. 546 pp.

Glickfeld, M., Graymer, L. Morrison. K. 1987. Trends in local growth control ballot measures in California. *UCLA J. Environ. Law* 6:111–58

Gottdiener, M., Neiman, M. 1981. Characteristics of support for local growth control. *Urban Aff. Q.* 17:55–73

Grant, D, 1972. The metropolitan governance approach. In *North American Suburbs,* ed. J. Kramer, pp. 276–83. Berkeley: Glendessary

Guest, A. M. 1976. Nighttime and daytime populations of large American suburbs. *Urban Aff. Q.* 12:57–82

Guest, A. M. 1978a. Suburban territorial differentiation. *Sociol. Soc. Res.* 62:523–36

Guest, A. M. 1978b. Suburban social status: Persistence or evolution? *Am. Sociol. Rev.* 43:251–64

Guest, A. M. 1979. Patterns of suburban population growth, 1970–1975. *Demography* 16:401–15

Guest, A. M., Nelson, G. 1978. Central city-suburban status differences: Fifty years of change. *Sociol. Q.* 19:7–23

Hawley, A. H. 1950. *Human Ecology*. New York: Ronald . 456 pp.

Hawley, A. H. 1971. *Urban Society*. New York: Ronald . 348 pp.

Hawley, A. H. 1972. Population density and the city. *Demography* 9:521–29

Hawley, A. H., Rock, V., eds. 1976. *Metropolitan America in Contemporary Perspective*. New York: Wiley. 504 pp.

Hayden, D. 1984. *Redesigning the American Dream*. New York: Norton. 270 pp.

Henretta, J. 1984. Parental status and child's homeownership. *Am. Sociol. Rev.* 49:131–40

Hummon, D. 1986. Urban views: Popular perspectives on city life. *Urban Life* 15:3–36

Jackson, J. 1985. *Crabgrass Frontier*. New York: Oxford Univ. Press. 396 pp.

Kasarda, J. D. 1972. The impact of suburban growth on central city service functions. *Am. J. Sociol.* 77:1111–24

Kasarda, J. D. 1976. The changing occupational structure of the American metropolis: Apropos the urban problem. See Schwartz 1976, pp. 113–36

Kasarda, J. D. 1978. Urbanization, community and the metropolitan problem. In *Handbook of Contemporary Urban Life,* ed. D. Street, pp. 27–57. San Francisco: Jossey Bass

Kasarda, J. D. 1980. The implications of con-

temporary distribution trends for national urban policy. *Soc. Sci. Q.* 61:373–400
Kasarda, J. D., Janowitz, M. 1974. Community attachment in mass society. *Am. Sociol. Rev.* 39:328–39
Kirlin, J. 1991. Creating the conditions for devising reasonable and regional solutions. See DiMento & Graymer 1991, pp. 121–32
Lake, W. 1981. *The New Suburbanites: Race and Housing in the Suburbs*. New Brunswick, NJ: Cent. Urban Policy Res. 303 pp.
Listokin, D., Beaton, W. 1983. *Revitalizing the Older Suburb*. New Brunswick, NJ: Cent. Urban Policy Res. 243 pp.
Logan, J. R. 1976. Industrialization and the stratification of cities in suburban regions. *Am. J. Sociol.* 82:333–48
Logan, J. R. 1978. Growth, politics and the stratification of places. *Am. J. Sociol.* 84:404–16
Logan, J. R., Semyonov, M. 1980. Growth and succession in suburban communities. *Sociol. Q.* 21:93–105
Logan, J. R., Schneider, M. 1981. The stratification of metropolitan suburbs: 1950 to 1970. *Am. Sociol. Rev.* 46:175–86
Logan, J. R., Stearns, L. B. 1981. Suburban racial segregation as a nonecological process. *Soc. Forces* 60:61–73
Logan, J. R., Schneider, M. 1982. Governmental organization and city-suburb income inequality, 1970–1980. *Urban Aff. Q.* 17:303–18
Logan, J. R., Collver, O. 1983. Residents' perceptions of suburban community differences. *Am. Sociol. Rev.* 48:428–33
Logan, J. R., Schneider, M. 1984. Racial segregation and racial change in American suburbs, 1970–1980. *Am. J. Sociol.* 89: 874–88
Logan, J. R., Golden, R. M. 1986. Suburbs and satellites: Two decades of change. *Am. Sociol. Rev.* 51:430–37
Logan, J. R., Molotch, H. 1987. *Urban Fortunes*. Berkeley: Univ. Calif. Press. 383 pp.
Logan, J. R., Zhou, M. 1989. Do suburban growth controls control growth? *Am. Sociol. Rev.* 54:461–71
Long, L. H., Glick, P. C. 1976. Family patterns in suburban areas: recent trends. See Schwartz 1976, pp.39–68
Long, L. H., De Are, D. 1981. *Population redistribution, 1960 to 1980*. Washington DC: US Bur. Census
Lyon, L., Felice, L. G., Perryman, M. R., Parker, E. S. 1981. Community power and population increase: An empirical test of the growth machine model. *Am. J. Sociol.* 86:1387–1400
Marando, V. L., Thomas, R. D. 1977. County commissioners attitudes toward growth: A two-state comparison. *Soc. Sci. Q.* 58:128–38
Marans, R. W., Rodgers, W. 1975. Toward an understanding of community satisfaction. See Hawley & Rock 1975, pp. 299–354
Marshall, H., Stahura, J. M. 1979a. *Black and white population growth in American suburbs: Transition or parallel development? Soc. Forces* 58:305–28
Marshall, H., Stahura, J. M. 1979b. Determinants of Black suburbanization: regional and suburban size category patterns. *Sociol. Q.* 20:237–53
Marshall, H., Stahura, J. M. 1986. The theory of ecological expansion: The relation between dominance and suburban differentiation. *Soc. Forces* 65:352–69
Masotti, L. H., Hadden, J. K., eds. 1973. *The Urbanization of the Suburbs*. Beverly Hills: Sage. 600 pp.
Masotti, L. H., Hadden, J. K., eds. 1974. *Suburbia in Transition*. New York: New Viewpoints. 345 pp.
Massey, D. S, Denton, N. A. 1987. Trends in residential segregation of Blacks, Hispanics and Asians: 1970–1980. *Am. Sociol. Rev.* 52:802–25
Massey, D. S., Denton, N. A. 1988. Suburbanization and segregation in U.S. metropolitan areas. *Am. J. Sociol.* 94:592–626
Massey, D. S., Denton, N. A. 1989. Hypersegregation in U.S. metropolitan areas: Black and Hispanic segregation along five dimensions. *Demography* 26: 373–91
Massey, D. S., Eggers, M. 1990. The ecology of inequality: Minorities and the concentration of poverty, 1970–1980. *Am. J. Sociol.* 95:1153–88
Maurer, R. C., Christenson, J. A. 1982. Growth and nongrowth orientations of urban, suburban and rural mayors: Reflections on the city as a growth machine. *Soc. Sci. Q.* 63:350–58
McKenzie, R. D. 1967. The ecological approach to the study of the human community. See Parket al 1967, pp. 63–69
Michelson, W. 1976. *Man and His Urban Environment*. Reading, Mass: Addison Wesley. 273 pp.
Michelson, W. 1977. *Environmental Choice, Human Behavior and Residential Satisfaction*. New York: Oxford Univ. Press. 403 pp.
Milgram, S. 1970. The experience of living in cities. *Science* 167:1461–68
Miller, G. J. 1981. *Cities by Contract*. Cambridge, Mass.: MIT Press. 242 pp.
Molotch, H. 1976. The city as a growth machine. *Am. J. Sociol.* 82:309–32
Morris, E. W., Winter, M. 1978. *Housing, Family and Society*. New York: Wiley Press. 378 pp.
Morrison, P. A. 1977. Migration and rights of

access: New public concerns of the 1970s. *Rand Series P-5785*. 17 pp.
Morrow-Jones, H. A. 1989. Housing tenure change in American suburbs. *Urban Geogr*. 10:316–35
Muller, P. 0. 1981. *Contemporary Suburban America*. Englewood Cliffs: Prentice-Hall. 218 pp.
Neiman, M. 1980. Zoning policy, income clustering and suburban change. *Soc. Sci. Q*. 61:666–75
Neiman, M., Loveridge, R. 1981. Environmentalism and local growth control: A probe into the class bias thesis. *Environ. Behav*. 13:759–72
Nelson, K. 1980. Recent suburbanization of Blacks: How much, who and where? *J. Am. Plan. Assoc*. 46:287–300
Ogburn, W. 1935. Factors in the variation of crime among cities. *J. Am. Stat. Assoc*. 30:12–34
Ostrom, E. 1983. The social stratification-government inequality thesis explored. *Urban Aff. Q*. 19:91–112
Ostrom, E., Parks, R. 1973. Suburban police departments: too many and too small? See Masotti & Hadden 1973, pp. 367–402
Park, R. E. 1967a. The city: Suggestions for the study of human behavior in the urban environment. See Park et al 1967, pp.1–46
Park, R. E. 1967b. The urban community as a spatial pattern and a moral order. In *R. E. Park on Social Control and Collective Behavior*, ed. R. Turner, pp. 55–68. Chicago: Univ. Chicago Press
Park, R. E., Burgess, E. W., McKenzie, R. D., ed. 1967. *The City*. Chicago: Univ. Chicago Press. 239 pp. 2nd ed.
Perin, C. 1977. *Everything in Its Place: Social Order and Land Use in America*. Princeton: Princeton Univ. Press. 291 pp.
Perry, D., Watkins, A. , ed. 1977. *The Rise of the Sunbelt Cities*. Beverly Hills, Calif: Sage. 309 pp.
Peterson, P. W. 1981. *City Limits*. Chicago: Univ. Chicago Press. 268 pp.
Pisarki, A. 1987. *Commuting in America: A National Report on Patterns and Trends*. Westport, Conn: Eno Found. 78 pp.
Popenoe, D. 1985. *Private Pleasure, Public Plight: American Metropolitan Community Life*. New Brunswick: Transaction Press. 162 pp.
Protash, W., Baldassare, M. 1983. Growth policies and community status. *Urban Aff. Q*. 18:397–412
Roof, W. C., Spain, D. 1977. A research note on city-suburban socioeconomic differences among American Blacks. *Soc. Forces* 56:15–20
Rosenbaum, N. 1978. Growth and its discontents: Origins of local population controls. In *The Policy Cycle*, ed. A Wildavsky & J. May, pp. 43–61. Beverly Hills: Sage
Rossi, P. 1955. *Why Families Move*. Glencoe, Ill: Free Press. 220 pp.
Sassen, S. 1990. Economic restructuring and the American city. *Annu. Rev. Sociol*. 16:465–90
Sawers, L., Tabb, W., eds. 1984. *Sunbelt, Snowbelt: Urban Development and Regional Restructuring*. New York: Oxford Univ. Press. 431 pp.
Schlay, A., Rossi, P. 1981. Putting policies into urban ecology: Estimating net effects of zoning. In *Urban Policy Analysis*, ed. T. N. Clark, L. Ferguson, pp. 257–86. Beverly Hills: Sage
Schneider, M. 1980. Resource reallocation, population movement and the fiscal condition of metropolitan communities. *Soc. Sci. Q*. 61:545–66
Schneider, M., Logan, J. R. 1981. Fiscal implications of class segregation: Inequalities in the distribution of public goods and services in suburban municipalities. *Urban Aff. Q*. 17:23–36
Schneider, M., Logan, J. R. 1982. The effects of local government finances on community growth rates: A test of the Tiebout Model. *Urban Aff. Q*. 18:91–105
Schneider, W. 1991. Rule suburbia: America in the 1990s. *National J*. 39:2335–36
Schneider, M., Fernandez, F. 1989. The emerging suburban service economy: Changing patterns of employment. *Urban Aff. Q*. 24:537–55
Schnore, L., Andre, C., Sharp, H. 1976. Black suburbanization: 1930–70. See Schwartz 1976, pp. 69–94
Schwartz, B., ed. 1976. *The Changing Face of the Suburbs*. Chicago: Univ. Chicago Press. 355 pp.
Schwartz, S., Johnston, R. 1983. Inclusionary housing programs. *J. Am. Plan. Assoc*. 49:3–21
Schwirian, K., Hankins, F., Ventresca, C. 1990. The residential decentralization of status groups in American metropolitan communities. *Soc. Forces* 68:1143–63
Scott, R., Brower, D., Miner, D., ed. 1975. *Management and Control of Growth, Volume 1*. Washington DC: Urban Land Inst. 589 pp.
Shaw, C. R., McKay, H. D. 1969. *Juvenile Delinquency and Urban Areas*. Chicago: Univ. Chicago Press. 394 pp. 2nd. ed.
Shelton, B., Rodriguez, N., Feagin, J., Bullard, R., Thomas, R. 1989. *Houston: Growth and Decline in a Sunbelt Boomtown*. Philadelphia: Temple Univ. Press. 155 pp.
Simmel, G. 1969. The metropolis and mental life. In *Classic Essays on the Culture of*

Cities, ed. R. Sennett, pp.47–60. New York: Appleton

Spain, D., Long, L. H. 1981. Black movers to the suburbs: Are they moving to predominantly white neighborhoods? *Special Demographic Analyses, December*. Washington, DC: US Govt Printing Off. 23 pp.

Stahura, J. M. 1979. Suburban status evolution-persistence: a structural model. *Am. Sociol. Rev*. 44:937–47

Stahura, J. M. 1980. Ecological determinants of the aging suburban populations. *Sociol. Q*. 21:107–18

Stahura, J. M. 1984. A research note on the metropolitan determinants of persistence. *Soc. Forces* 62:767–74

Stahura, J. M. 1986. Suburban development, Black suburbanization and the civil rights movement since World War II. *Am. Sociol. Rev*. 51:131–44

Stahura, J. M. 1987. Suburban socioeconomic status change: A comparison of models. *Am. Sociol. Rev*. 52:268–77

Stahura, J. M. 1988. Changing patterns of suburban racial composition: 1970–1980. *Urban Aff. Q*. 23:448–60

Stearns, L. B., Logan, J. R., 1986. The racial structuring of the housing market and segregation in suburban areas. *Soc. Forces* 65:28–42

Stein, R. M. 1990. *Urban Alternatives*. Pittsburgh: Univ. Pittsburgh Press. 250 pp.

Sternlieb, G., Hughes, J. 1975. *Post-Industrial America: Metropolitan Decline and Inter-Regional Job Shifts*. New Brunswick, NJ: Cent. Urban Policy Res. 267 pp.

Tabb, W., Sawers, L., eds. 1984. *Marxism and the Metropolis: New Perspectives in Urban Political Economy*. New York: Oxford Univ. Press. 390 pp.

Tiebout, C. M. 1956. A pure theory of local expenditures. *J. Polit. Econ*. 64:416–24

Tremblay, K., Dillman, D. 1983. *Beyond the American Housing Dream*. New York: Univ. Press America. 157 pp.

Tucker, C. J. 1984. City-suburban population redistribution: What data from the 1970s reveal. *Urban Aff. Q*. 19:539–49

US Bureau of the Census. 1987. Patterns of metropolitan area and county growth, 1980 to 1987. *Curr. Popul. Rep., Ser. p-25, No. 1039*. 137 pp.

Van Liere, K., Dunlap, R. 1980. The social bases of environmental concern. *Publ. Opin. Q*. 44:181–97

Wechsler, H. 1961. Community growth, depressive disorders and suicide. *Am. J. Sociol*. 67:9–16

Whyte, W. H. 1956. *The Organization Man*. New York: Doubleday. 431 pp.

Wilson, F. D. 1978. The organizational components of expanding metropolitan systems. In *Social Demography,* ed. K. Taeuber, L. Bumpass, J. Sweet, pp. 133–56. New York: Academic Press

Winsberg, M. D. 1989. Suburbanization of higher income Blacks in major metropolitan statistical areas. *Urban Geogr*. 10:172–77

Wirth, L. 1938. Urbanism as a way of life. *Am. J. Sociol*. 44:1–24

Zimmer, B. 1975. The urban centrifugal drift. See Hawley & Rock 1975, pp. 23–92

Zimmer, B. 1976. Suburbia and the changing political structure. See Schwartz 1976, pp. 165–202

Zuiches, J. 1981. Residential preferences and rural population growth. In *Toward an Understanding of Nonmetropolitan America, ed*. A. Hawley and S. Mazie, pp. 72–115. Chapel Hill: Univ. North Carolina Press

Zuiches, J., Fuguitt, G. 1972. Residential preferences: implications for population redistribution in nonmetropolitan America. In *Population, Distribution and Policy,* Vol. 5, ed. S. Mazie, pp. 617–30. Washington DC: US Govt. Printing Off.

Annu. Rev. Sociol. 1992. 18:495–517

HISTORICAL STUDIES OF LABOR MOVEMENTS IN THE UNITED STATES

Howard Kimeldorf

Department of Sociology, University of Michigan, Ann Arbor, Michigan 48109

Judith Stepan-Norris

Department of Sociology, University of California, Irvine, California 92717

KEY WORDS: class conflict, working class, trade unions, strikes, political sociology

---

Abstract

This article reviews recent historical research on the American labor movement. Emphasizing the primacy of economic and political struggles waged between and within classes, our discussion highlights the contested past of organized labor. We begin by exploring key aspects of organized labor's political history, including its alleged "exceptionalism," and its relationship to the state under the New Deal. Then, turning to the industrial arena, we review the determinants of unionism and critically consider arguments about the conservative impact of formal organization on worker insurgency. Next we survey recent contributions by labor historians, whose work challenges many of the received sociological understandings of organized labor's development. Finally, we review some promising areas of inquiry within sociology, pointing in particular to research on social movements, organizational environments, and workers' consciousness.

INTRODUCTION

Sociological and historical studies of the American labor movement are flourishing. Not since the 1930s, when the "labor problem" was omnipresent,

0360-0572/92/0815-0495$02.00

has unionism commanded as much attention by sociologists. Spurred not only by the enduring intellectual problems posed by labor movements but also by the current crisis confronting organized labor in the United States, this growing body of sociological research and historical scholarship has significantly transformed our understanding of American labor unionism.

This review of recent sociohistorical studies of the American labor movement is divided into four sections. First, we survey the political history of organized labor, highlighting its early rejection of socialism and its deepening politicization under the New Deal. Second, we explore organized labor in its industrial setting, focusing on the determinants of unionism and the consequences of formal organization on industrial relations. Third, we turn to the "new" labor historians and trace the organizational development of American labor, drawing out some implications for sociological research. Finally, we point to some important emerging areas of inquiry.

LABOR'S POLITICAL HISTORY

The received interpretation of the American labor movement's involvement in political life is that—like its long dominant organization, the American Federation of Labor (AFL)—it has tended to rely solely on "economic strength" to realize its demands. Contrary to this characterization, recent historical research has shown that organized labor in the United States has never fully lived up to its apolitical image. The doctrine of "voluntarism," which the AFL embraced early on as its official position, was never accepted by its main rivals on the left, particularly the Socialists; nor was it accepted by the men and women who organized industrial unions a generation later. Even the national AFL chose to ignore, when convenient, its own policy of voluntarism by forging temporary ties with the Democratic Party in order to pass various legislation. American labor, then, has a unique political history which, while still largely hidden, is as rich as those of most other industrial societies.

American Exceptionalism

In most advanced industrial countries (as classical marxian theory predicted) workers have emerged as an organized class, possessing not only national union federations, but also, critically, their own labor or socialist political parties. A glaring exception is the American labor movement. Scholars have pondered the reasons for this exceptional pattern for over 80 years. A host of explanations, often contradictory, have been advanced to account for this American "exceptionalism," that is, for the absence of a working class–based socialist movement in the United States. In these explanations, a variety of factors are emphasized, including America's birth as a "new nation" with an egalitarian ethos and no feudal past, and the consequent invisibility and later fluidity of class lines; the frontier as a safety valve for discontent; the pace and breadth of economic growth and a rising material standard of living (perhaps even declining inequality of income and wealth) that provided individual success and undermined the working-class community; racism and massive immigration, which hindered class solidarity and at the same time impelled the upward mobility of successive generations of workers; early manhood suffrage, which prevented the fusion of political and economic struggles among American workers; and the presidential and single-member congressional electoral system itself, which has compelled the formation of broad cross-class coalitions and undercut the durability of the working class–based socialist or labor parties that flourished from time to time, on both a regional and a national level in this country (see Laslett & Lipset 1974).

A number of recent works have reintroduced some of these earlier themes, emphasizing, in particular, the effects of ethnic rivalries and national politics. The conservatism of the AFL, for example, has been located in America's ethnically split labor market, which, as Mink (1986) argues, impelled organization on the basis of craft and caste rather than class. Privileged craft workers thus found assimilation into middle-class reform politics relatively easy, forming odd nativistic coalitions to exclude those who threatened their favored position. This cross-class coalition, Mink concludes, fractured the working-class along intersecting ethnic and occupational lines—pitting native-born craft workers, closely allied with middle-class reformers, against the mass of foreign-born non-craft workers (also see Wilentz 1984a).

But the form taken by American politics was itself a decisive spur to the emergence and dominance of "pure and simple trade unionism," both Bridges (1984, 1986) and Shefter (1986) argue. Workers not only formed a small, and urban, minority in early America, they were also the recipients of the "free gift of the ballot." Absent the struggle for the franchise, artisans here, unlike those in Western Europe, were not compelled to engage in or lead common class-based struggles for political citizenship. Instead of launching politicized work-place struggles, American workers were drawn into cross-class coalition politics, through urban political machines. When the AFL emerged, it found itself in a double political bind: workers were already loyal Democrats or Republicans, and employers were vehemently hostile to anything smacking of radicalism. AFL leaders solved this dilemma by opting for a nondivisive "pure and simple" unionism while maintaining an exclusionist labor organization that deepened the split between craft workers and the mass of the unskilled. While this particular hybrid of cross-class political coalitions and militant craft unionism bears a distinctly American mark, it does not fit easily or neatly into the received exceptionalist framework. Indeed, as students of American working-class formation have recently suggested, the exceptionalist perspective rests on a number of unexamined premises.

First, as Zolberg (1986) argues, it is highly misleading to juxtapose the American case against a distinct European pattern characterized by advanced capitalism complete with an organized and class-conscious proletariat. On the eve of World War I, the three main advanced European nations—the United Kingdom, Germany, and France—were as different from each other as they were alike. Only in Germany, for example, was a socialist party able to mobilize the vast majority of workers' votes. And the percent unionized in each country runs more like a continuum: United Kingdom: 30–40%; Germany: 25–30%; United States: 20%; France: 15%. Hence, rather than characterize the American case as one that deviated from a distinct European pattern, it is more accurate to suggest that it represents one point (toward one end) of a continuum. In this way, Zolberg concludes, there are as many exceptions as there are cases.

Second, although the American labor movement's failure to commit to socialism has been seen as reflecting a low level of class consciousness among the rank-and-file, the ultimate success or failure of left parties may be a poor barometer of workers' "consciousness" or even of explicit political sentiments. Genuine expressions of class consciousness are easily missed when measured against an expected teleological outcome. Early European labor movements, Wilentz (1984b:3) argues, were "infinitely more complex, bearing little of the pure proletarianism once ascribed to them as a matter of course," while the pre–World War I American workers movement may have been much more so (also see Foner 1984).

Third, contrary to the prevailing imagery of the early absence of labor radicalism in United States, syndicalists and socialists were widespread and highly influential within major unions from the late nineteenth century until World War I; and though the AFL never formally endorsed the Socialist Party, its influence on the AFL was substantial (Laslett 1970). Samuel Gompers, in particular, was a socialist in his early days as a trade unionist, and he even saw himself as an American ally of Marx and Engels. In frequent fights with the socialists, Gompers maintained that his organization, the AFL—by mobilizing workers at the point of production—was actually truer to marxism than the socialists, who encouraged reliance on the electoral arena. How and why the revolutionary vision of Gompers and his associates became transmuted into defensive craft unionism remains a critical empirical question.

New Deal Research

The birth of the Congress of Industrial Organizations (CIO), workers' insurgency, and New Deal politics were intimately connected. In particular, the pro-labor Wagner Act, passed in 1935 was perhaps the most radical piece of legislation enacted by Congress in this century (Casebeer 1989). It not only defended the right of workers to organize, but prohibited unfair labor practices by employers and required them to bargain in "good faith," thus opening up possibilities for deep changes in labor/capital relations. Among its six statutory goals, for instance, was "industrial democracy," which suggested an ambitious, possibly far-reaching challenge to traditional managerial prerogatives. (Klare 1978:284–85). Current debates about labor's role in the creation and passage of the Wagner Act and related New Deal legislation revolve partly around varying conceptions of the state (cf Cornfield 1991). From a sort of neo-Weberian perspective, the state apparatus is seen as the crucial actor. Denying the importance of class relations and of class struggle, neither the actions of organized labor nor those of organized capital are considered crucial in the passage of New Deal legislation.

Skocpol & Amenta (1985), for instance, focus on the potential autonomy of political officials, state structures, and preexisting governmental policies in later struggles and policy outcomes. Employing this state-centric perspective to contrast the successful passage and institutionalization of the Agricultural Adjustment Act (AAA) with the failure to institutionalize the National Industrial Recovery Act (NIRA), Skocpol & Finegold (1982) trace the differing political outcomes to the AAA's location within an existing and extremely strong federal department that had a clear public-service mission, whereas the NIRA's operations relied on the enormous influence of industrialists instead of state managers.

In contrast, recent class-centered analyses focus on the relevance of capitalist and working-class activities in passing New Deal legislation. Quadagno (1988), for example, argues that the AFL's commitment to craft autonomy prevented skilled workers from pushing for old age benefits for all workers; and at the same time, because the majority of unskilled workers were still unorganized, this precluded their widespread mobilization as an effective political force. Significantly, it was those isolated pockets of organization among unskilled workers—most notably the miners—who pressed for passage of old age legislation. Yet their efforts only bore fruit when they entered into cross-class coalitions with middle-class groups.

Passage of the Wagner Act, Domhoff (1990) argues, was made possible by the devastating impact of the Depression, a split between Southern and Northern capital, and the unprecedented unity and militance of the working class. Placing social networks and class segments at the center of his analysis, Domhoff emphasizes Roosevelt's alliance with the industrial working class, and the participation of CIO leaders John L. Lewis and Sidney Hillman in planning the Wagner Act's predecessor, the NIRA. Hillman, in particular, took credit for the language in Section 7a of the NIRA which gave employees the right to organize and bargain collectively. Workers' insurgency plays a more decisive role in Goldfield's (1989) account of the Wagner Act. Especially crucial, he argues, was the fact that this insurgency was highly organized and in many cases led by political radicals. Fear of widespread radicalization and the growing prominence of Communist working-class organizational leadership were both critical in forcing government concessions. Contrary to most other interpretations, Goldfield denies that the Act preceded workers insurgency. Rather, the labor insurgency of 1934 and the later sitdown strikes themselves created powerful social pressures from the bottom-up that contributed significantly to the Act's passage and final form.

The goal of industrial democracy that inspired the original Wagner Act was never realized. Subject to extensive judicial review and public scrutiny, the Supreme Court ended up embracing, in Klare's (1978:292–3) words, "those aims of the Act most consistent with the assumptions of liberal capitalism and foreclosng those potential paths of development most threatening to the established order." The National Labor Relations Board (NLRB) and the Courts progressively chipped away at labor's rights under the Wagner Act. In 1938, as McCammon (1990) shows, the Supreme Court circumvented the "right" to interrupt production—one of the principal advances of the Wagner Act—by allowing employers to hire permanent replacement workers for strikers. Despite such legal assaults, the Wagner Act represented a clear departure from the pattern of "judicial antipathy" toward unions that has characterized American labor law ever since (Tomlins 1985). Whereas the Wagner Act led to a massive upsurge in new organizing and a significant expansion of union membership, both trends were reversed by subsequent legislation. As Wallace et al (1988) demonstrate, the Taft-Hartley Act of 1947 not only put the brakes on new organizing and growth, it also channeled labor protest in a less radical, more economistic direction. Similarly, the Landrum-Griffin Act of 1959 reduced strike activity over economic issues. Wallace et al conclude, therefore, that labor's radicalization during the 1930s was as much a product of the Wagner Act as its deradicalization following World War II was a consequence of Taft-Hartley and Landrum-Griffin.

LABOR AND INDUSTRIAL CONFLICT

The industrial arena is of course the life-blood of labor organization. It is there that grievances first arise, protest emerges, and organization takes shape. As such, the dynamics of the work place remain central to understanding labor movement development.

Determinants of Unionism

The recent decline in unionism has spawned a growing literature on the determinants of deunionization. Advancing a structuralist explanation for union stagnation, Bluestone & Harrison (1982) focus on the changing geography of production, as capital migrates from the highly unionized Northeast and Great Lakes states to more hostile union environments in the south, both in this country and abroad. Certainly, accelerated capital mobility has contributed to labor's decline. But as Bernstein (1960) pointed out some time ago, unions grow not only by "mopping up" already organized jurisdictions, but especially by reaching into new areas. Organizing the unorganized has historically been the surest route to long-term union growth.

Structuralist arguments also emphasize the shift to a "post-industrial" society and the resulting decline in the number of blue-collar workers (the traditional target of unions) relative to white-collar service employees (Troy 1986). While this is a compelling thesis, it fails to account for the recent experience of Canada, France, Britain, and most other industrialized countries, where similar occupational shifts have occurred but without a substantial decline in union density (Goldfield 1987). Survey research indicates, moreover, that the growing numbers of white-collar workers are only slightly less supportive of unions than their blue-collar counterparts—a remarkable finding given the historic neglect, and occasional hostility, directed at such groups by some leaders of organized labor (Freeman & Medoff 1984).

While capital mobility and the growth of white-collar employment have no doubt contributed to the drop off in union membership, such structural obstacles appear less critical than labor's own failure of nerve, as represented by the sharp decline in new organizing efforts in the face of growing managerial opposition (Freeman & Medoff 1984, Goldfield 1987). Indeed, unions have been spending less, in real dollars, to organize new workers, with the rate of expenditures per non-union worker falling from over one dollar in 1953 to 71 cents by 1974 (Goldfield 1987:206). In addition, the modern efforts at organizing lack the aggressiveness and creativity that they once had. Perhaps part of the reason for this declining enthusiasm can be found in the shifting political composition of the CIO's leadership. As Lipset (1960) argues, it is union leaders "with a calling" who initially organize unions, because they are the only ones who possess the necessary skills and the willingness to take risks for minimal compensation. Communists and socialists filled these roles in the early CIO organizing drives, but with the CIO purge of Communists in 1949–1950, most such activists were eliminated from the mainstream labor movement. Goldfield, in fact, finds evidence that the two surviving remnants of Communist-led unions achieved higher NLRB victory rates than their more conservative rivals (also see Lembcke 1988). So this inattention to organizing seems to stem partly from a simple failure of nerve.

While unions have been spending less on organizing, employers have devoted more of their resources to preventing unionization. Under President Reagan, the "union-prevention" business was one of the few growth industries, with annual sales of $2 billion in 1982 (Goldfield 1987: 193). These modern day proponents of "positive labor relations," like their union-busting predecessors, conduct vigorous campaigns to convince workers that unions are not in their best interests. When polite persuasion fails, many employers have simply violated the law, which, given the small size of many fines, is often less costly than complying. As a last resort, employers have taken to firing union activists: in 1980, one in twenty workers who favored a union was summarily fired (Freeman & Medoff 1984:231–2).

Even when unions win elections, collective bargaining is instituted in only two thirds of the cases (because employers have the obligation to bargain, not to reach agreement) (Freeman & Medoff 1984). Fantasia (1988) provides detailed case studies of how capitalists use legally permissible delays (between filings and elections) along with a combination of paternalism and repression to render union organizing less effective and to preclude collective bargaining agreements even after NLRB union victories.

None of these repressive strategies is new. Prior to the New Deal, "countermobilization" by employers was critical in retarding labor's self-organization. In one of the few empirical studies of employer resistance, Griffin et al (1986) investigated the impact of the National Association of Manufacturers, an antiunion employer association active during the first quarter of the century, on unionization. They found that as the level of NAM activity increased (measured by its size and expenditures), union growth, density, and membership all declined. Theirs is a compelling argument for considering the actions of capital in any discussion of the labor movement.

Unions and Industrial Conflict

The impact of unions on industrial conflict is a matter of continuing controversy. Do unions foment or dampen industrial conflict, or perhaps do both? What conditions produce one outcome or the other, and what are the consequences for industrial relations and labor movement development?

The received view holds that unions, like all formal organizations, exercise a generally conservatizing effect. It is argued, for example, that unions limit and eventually eliminate most expressions of rank-and-file spontaneity and direct action (Piven & Cloward 1979, Brecher 1972). Pluralists regard this as the crowning achievement of a "mature" industrial society where the labor contract serves, in Bell's (1961:261) words, as a "buffer between management and rank and file resentment." Many marxists, while critical of such "collaboration," nevertheless agree that unions play an important role in reproducing class relations on the shop floor (Aronowitz 1973, Burawoy 1985). Despite their contrasting political perspectives, both pluralists and many neomarxists see the labor contract as a mechanism for containing shop-floor activism. Unions, in this view, become crucial partners in a system of class collaboration.

It follows that conflict will subside as unions progressively incorporate workers, channeling their discontent into routinized grievance and arbitration procedures. Aronowitz (1973), for example, argues that the modern labor contract is predicated on containing and regulating shop floor conflict. But there are certainly exceptions, most notably the West Coast longshoremen, whose first contract, signed in 1934, gave them effective control over the pace and organization of their work while allowing individual workers to quit work at any time (Mills & Wellman 1987). More generally, Stepan-Norris & Zeitlin (1991a:1193) found that the cession of workers' control in CIO agreements was in no way predetermined by what David Brody calls the "contractual logic itself"; it had more to do with the political orientation of union leaders. Together, these studies indicate that the modern labor contract may meet the needs of militant workers just as it may meet those of their employers.

The relationship between unions and strikes is more complex, in part because of the multiple sources and goals of strike activity. Strike rates are affected not only by economic conditions (Ashenfelter & Johnson 1969), but also by strategic location (Wallace et al 1989) and the larger political context (Shorter & Tilly 1974). When, for example, labor is represented politically by a powerful oppositional group (e.g. where a large Communist Party exists), strike activity tends to increase (Hibbs 1976). However, when a strong labor movement finds its interests represented by a ruling social democratic party, protest often shifts from the work place to parliament, producing a decline in strike rates (Korpi & Shalev 1980). Finally, in countries such as the United States, where labor lacks political clout, job actions remain an important weapon—indeed, the only weapon available for most workers.

Given the multiplicity of forces shaping strike activity, generalizations are risky. It is clear that union organization and strike activity are positively related, even if it is difficult to establish the direction of causality (Snyder 1977, Edwards 1981). Beyond that, the relationship between unionization and industrial conflict is highly contingent, a product both of history and of relative class capacities.

ORGANIZATIONAL HISTORY OF AMERICAN LABOR

The major organizational episodes that shaped the American working class have been extensively documented by labor historians. Recent research undertaken by the new labor historians has gone beyond viewing unions merely as institutions and has begun moving in a sociological direction that links unionization efforts to larger processes of class formation (see reviews by Brody 1979, Kimeldorf 1991). This growing body of scholarship, rooted in history but drawing increasingly on the work of historical sociologists, challenges many of the basic assumptions and reigning interpretations guiding research on the organizational trajectory of American labor.

Emergence of the Modern Labor Movement (1865–1890)

The first effective national labor organization in the United States was the National Labor Union (NLU), established in Baltimore in 1866. This was a labor federation, however, which, unlike its major successors, enrolled in its ranks not only wage laborers, but also a host of professionals. Caught up in the social reformism of its day, the NLU began looking at Greenbackism and producer cooperatives as panaceas for the plight of workers. So it attracted middle-class activists hoping to advance their own reform agendas—which quickly led to the diversion of the NLU's original objectives and its rapid demise in 1872 (Grob 1969, Boyer & Morais 1975).

The NLU was dead but its reformist agenda lived on through the Knights of Labor (KOL), founded in Philadelphia in 1869. Led by the crusading Terrence Powderly, the Knights sought to unite all wage earners (except Chinese immigrants) for the ultimate purpose of abolishing the wage system. Like the NLU, the Knights, particularly Powderly, believed in the power of "cooperation." And like its predecessor, the KOL was exceedingly vague on how to get from the present system of industrial capitalism to its future state of producers' cooperatives. Condemning strikes as injurious to labor's cause, Powderly placed his faith in the power of education and political action to usher in the new society. After reaching a peak membership of around 700,000 during the tumultuous summer of 1886, the KOL entered a period of rapid decline from which it never recovered (Grob 1969, Shefter 1986, Montgomery 1987a).

Standard accounts trace the Knights' demise to its antipathy toward strikes, which alienated many trade unionists, and to its preferred practice of organizing solidaristic "Local Assemblies" that included all wage earners in a community. By failing to recognize differences in skill and occupation, the Knights supposedly depleted the organizational resources of craft workers in a futile effort to organize the unskilled. In contrast, it is argued, the Knights' chief rival, the craft-based AFL, survived and later flourished precisely because it accepted the deeply ingrained sectionalism of American labor (Perlman 1928, Ulman 1966, Grob 1969). But this received interpretation of the Knights' defeat has been undermined by recent research. Based on a careful statistical analysis of the Knights' activities in New Jersey, Voss (1989) finds no evidence that the organization's failure resulted from a split between its skilled and less skilled members. The Knights' defeat, Voss argues, owed more to fierce employer opposition than to any lack of solidarity among the Knights' own ranks. Similarly, the author of what is now widely regarded as the definitive history of the Knights contends that its greatest source of strength lay precisely in its practice of labor solidarity. Rather than being a major weakness, Fink (1985) argues, this effectively linked the masses of unskilled and semiskilled workers on the organization's periphery to skilled workers at its core. Like Voss, Fink attributes the Knight's demise to "initiatives from without." He identifies resistance from employers and the government as decisive in the organization's defeat.

The AFL and Its Left-Wing Challengers (1890–1920)

Repression also figures prominently in explanations of the AFL's "conservatism." Rejecting a kind of psychological reductionism that attributes the Federation's success to the conservative predispositions of its members, Vanneman & Cannon (1987) instead emphasize the importance of structural factors—particularly the strength of opposing forces—in accounting for the failure of radical alternatives to the AFL. Repression by local police forces and state militia and massive employer opposition to such left-wing groups as the Industrial Workers of the World (IWW) and the Socialists meant that, in many cases, the AFL was the only game in town. Rank-and-file support for the more successful AFL thus did not reflect a primitive understanding of politics or a lack of class consciousness, but was an expression, under those circumstances, of "simple rationality." In short, repression eliminated the left as a viable option for American workers (Ostreicher 1988).

A more far-reaching challenge to AFL historiography can be seen in the work of some new labor historians, who have begun questioning the whole idea that the AFL was conservative. Consider, for example, the charge of class collaboration frequently directed at the AFL for its role in dampening labor protest during World War I. It is certainly true that AFL leaders collaborated with employers and the government during the war to contain industrial unrest: union officers endorsed the wartime prohibition against strikes, actively disciplined recalcitrant members for delaying production, and in some industries cooperated with employers and government officials to formulate plans for industrial peace (Brody 1980, Haydu 1991). But, Montgomery (1987b) argues, such collaboration appears to have been guided by many of the same objectives—industrial democracy, economic citizenship, and social justice—that led the more advanced workers' movements of Britain, Germany, and France into similarly corporatist arrangements.

This "rehabilitation of reformism" (as a friendly critic (Maier 1987) refers to Montgomery's view) is elaborated more fully in Kazin's (1987) work on the San Francisco building trades. Focusing on the earlier prewar period in the AFL's history, Kazin argues that the city's construction workers were not the apolitical, economic conservatives so often depicted in the literature. On the contrary, they were actively involved in local politics, regularly supporting candidates and issues that reached far beyond their own constituencies.

Perhaps, as Mink (1986) argues, the national AFL ultimately became a conservative prisoner of its own restrictionist, antiimmigrant logic. At the same time, however, local craft unionists in San Francisco, Chicago, New York, and other large cities were an important source of left politics until the 1920s (Wrigley 1982).

None of this is to deny that the AFL represented the right-wing of American labor. Compared to such labor giants as Eugene Debs of the Socialists and Big Bill Haywood of the Wobblies, Samuel Gompers, the AFL's perennial president, was more conservative. In the national political arena, Gompers regularly lined up on the right, whether it was in calling for restrictive immigration or supporting an expansionist foreign policy. Further, in the conduct of daily union life, AFL locals were generally more exclusionary in their membership, more racist in their policies, and more autocratic in their governance than IWW or socialist-led unions. But when it came to the core of unionism—fighting for better working conditions, job control, and higher wages—many craft unions were every bit as tough as their left-wing rivals, sometimes more so.

This interpretation of craft unionism as militant and effective has far-reaching implications. Consider, for example, the received view of the AFL and the IWW as occupying opposite ends of the political spectrum. The IWW, with its inflammatory declarations of working-class emancipation, is typically located far to the left of the AFL. But once their contrasting rhetoric of "revolution" and "Americanism" is discounted, both organizations appear remarkably alike in their actual union practices—from their common emphasis on direct action at the point of production to their shared preoccupation with job control. This particular trade union orientation, coupled with an avoidance of political entanglements, constituted what some historians have termed a vague syndicalist impulse—characterized by direct action, labor solidarity, and challenges to managerial authority—that attracted tens of thousands of American workers to both the AFL and the IWW (Monds 1976, Montgomery 1979). In this interpretation, the AFL and the IWW represented not only opposite ends of the political spectrum, but also complementary sides of the same syndicalist coin (Dubofsky 1988).

This notion of syndicalism in the writings of labor historians appears in sociological analyses under the rubric of "workers' control." Inspired by Braverman's (1974) evocative portrayal of labor's degradation under advanced capitalism, recent studies of the labor process have explored the dynamics of class contestation and accommodation in production (Burawoy 1979, Clawson 1980, Gordon et al 1982, Gartman 1986). Yet, with few exceptions (Mann 1977, Wallace 1989), sociologists have all but ignored the issue of control often lying at the heart of these struggles, despite the implications of such syndicalist impulses for understanding both the exceptional militancy and economism of American labor.

The CIO and Industrial Radicalism

The history of the CIO and its relationship to the political left has been significantly rewritten during the past decade (Brody 1984, Zieger 1985). This revisionism, initiated by labor historians, has considerable relevance for sociological research.

A growing controversy surrounds the working-class insurgency that gave rise to the CIO during the 1930s. Challenging both liberal and radical characterizations of the Depression as the decade of industrial turbulence, Dubofsky (1979) writes of the "not so turbulent" 1930s, when "trade union opportunism, corporate co-optation, [and] New Deal liberalism" conspired to thwart "the emergence of durable working-class radicalism." Beneath the episodic eruption of industrial conflict, Dubofsky finds a deep "social inertia" reflected in the fact that the massive strike wave of 1934–1937 failed to involve fully 93% of the nation's labor force.

But this provocative thesis is immediately undermined by Dubofsky's notion that the proper measure of working-class social inertia is the rate of strike participation for the entire (non-farm) labor force—fully half of whom in 1930 were self-employed, professionals, and white-collar "persons gainfully employed" in trade, public service, professional services, domestic and personal service, and clerical occupations (US Census 1933, Tables 2 and 3). The relevant figures would be the percentage of wage laborers or, more important historically, of industrial workers who went out on strike in this compressed period of labor insurgency.

Further, this was a period of massive unemployment, especially among industrial workers, and although the unemployed could not strike, millions of them were involved in huge, organized marches and rallies. Unemployed councils, led by Communists and other radicals, sprang up in major cities and small towns, resisting evictions and organizing protests and demands for public job programs (Piven & Cloward 1979). Broad-based electoral parties, statewide organizations, and hundreds of local labor chapters also won organized labor's political support. In sum, insurgency took many diverse forms; the labor movement of the 1930s was far broader and deeper than the strike wave of 1934–1937.

Nevertheless, working-class quiescence, even in the turbulent 1930s, remains a central theme in American historiography, with many new left historians portraying the CIO as a conservative bureaucratic monolith, bent on disarming and integrating an otherwise rebellious proletariat (Radosh 1966, Aronowitz 1973). Minus the latent radicalism of the rank and file, this portrayal bears some rather striking similarities to the portrait of the 1930s painted by social historians whose work focuses on the cultural integration and resulting depoliticization of ethnic working-class communities (Kraditor 1981, Bodnar 1982).

Other historical work suggests that left-wing, anticapitalist ideas coexisted during the 1930s with such integrative forces (Brinkley 1990). In his study of a Rhode Island textile community, Gerstle (1989) shows that workers were capable of holding both radical and patriotic beliefs. The ideology of "Americanism," which framed debates among Rhode Island's textile workers, was subject to multiple interpretations. Understandings that drew on themes of nativism and individualism dragged workers to the right, while those that focused more on values of equality, participation, and democracy pulled them with equal force to the left. The theme of working-class incorporation running through both new left and social history has also been challenged by recent research on the CIO, which underscores the insurgent character of the industrial union movement, pointing in particular to the significant role played by Communists and their supporters in various unions (Cochran 1977, Levenstein 1981, Milton 1982, Stepan-Norris & Zeitlin 1989, Goldfield 1989). Historians have shown that Communist support drew on deep founts of earlier radicalism in such industries as auto (Keeran 1980), electronics (Schatz 1983), maritime (Nelson 1988), and public transportation (Freeman 1989).

The role of Communists during the "Red decade" remains a matter of considerable controversy (Zeitlin & Kimeldorf 1984, Draper 1985). Conventional wisdom denied the efficacy and, in some cases, legitimacy of Communist-led unions (Barbash 1948, Kampelman 1957, Glazer 1961). In this view, first popularized by Cold War liberals and later reinvigorated by the new left, Communist-led unions functioned less as legitimate labor organizations than as instruments of political agitation, ultimately more responsible to Moscow than to their own rank and file (Howe & Coser 1957, Klehr 1984). But recent research by historians and sociologists casts substantial doubt on this received interpretation. The CIO unions led by Communists and allied radicals were among the most consistent and effective in promoting racial equality (Prickett 1975), and the contracts they won were far more likely than those won by rival CIO unions "to undermine the sway of capital within production" (Stepan-Norris & Zeitlin 1991a). Even the prevailing view that Communists relied on dictatorial means to govern their unions has been called into question by recent research (Keeran 1980, Lembcke & Tattam 1984, Kimeldorf 1988). Indeed as Stepan-Norris & Zeitlin show (1991b), the odds favoring constitutional democracy in CIO unions were far higher if they were led by Communists and allied radicals than if they were led by shifting coalitions or anti-Communists.

Contrary to conventional historiography, moreover, recent work suggests that the Communist-led unions expelled from the CIO in 1949–1950 were not victims of their own "class collaborationist" policies during World War II (Halpern 1988, Stepan-Norris & Zeitlin 1991a, Kimeldorf, in press). Nor did they fail to fight back against the Red Scare (Ginger & Christiano 1987).

This, if true, makes the defeat and eventual demise of the Communist unionists all the more puzzling. Indeed, recent research reveals that they were remarkably resilient in early Cold War America. When running for union office, Communist-supported candidates were often successful. They lost power to internal opponents only in such unions as the National Maritime Union and the Transport Workers Union, where incumbent and popular union leaders broke with the Communist Party and put themselves at the head of the anticommunist opposition (Prickett 1975). Unable to dislodge the left elsewhere, the national CIO, following perfunctory trials in 1949 and 1950, expelled 11 of its affiliates on charges of being "communist-dominated."

The expulsion and eventual defeat of the Communist-led left silenced the voice of progressive social unionism. As the CIO drifted unchecked to the right during the early 1950s, the labor movement abandoned its oppositional role. In 1955, the CIO merged with the AFL, thus consummating a marriage of convenience out of which arose the peculiarly American form of contemporary business unionism (Zieger 1986).

THE NEW SOCIOLOGY OF LABOR MOVEMENTS

Our historical understanding of the American labor movement has been greatly enriched by the growing number of sociologists whose work self-consciously connects research on labor with more established fields within the discipline. Some of the most promising synthetic work of this kind draws on insights and findings from literature dealing with social movements, organizational environments, and workers' consciousness.

Social Movements

Drawing extensively on the concepts of social movement research, recent work implicitly challenges the effort to distinguish "old" materialist struggles rooted in class—of which the labor movement is seen as the best example—from the "new" social movements organized around collective needs and group identities (Melucci 1989). Thinking of organized labor as a social movement, moreover, has been a needed corrective—emphasizing contingency and contestation—to earlier sociological analysis, which focused on trade unions as organizations and workers as individuals with varying political attitudes (or on the individual correlates of their political behavior).

The willingness to view organized labor through the conceptual lenses of social movement theories partly reflects the decline of those versions of new left historiography in which unions appeared as mere vehicles for incorporating and co-opting the working class. Freed from the determinism of this earlier work, contemporary scholarship is better positioned to see the many similarities between organizing workers into unions and the organization of other protest groups (Griffin et al 1986, Voss 1989).

This social movement perspective has shifted the analytical focus from processes of institution-building and unionization toward a closer look at the social dynamics of mass mobilization (Shalev & Korpi 1980). In turn, there is growing interest in how the distribution of resources and power influences the relative class capacities of employers and workers alike (Offe & Wiesenthal 1980). Therborn (1983), for example, attempts to understand why, as he puts it, "some classes are more successful than others." His answer is that it is not the ideas held by workers, but their readiness to act as a class that matters: he traces such readiness both to their "intrinsic strength" derived from "power resources" and their "hegemonic capacity" to deploy their strength against opposition. Similarly, Lembcke & Howe (1986) found in their study of CIO unions that the membership's willingness to act was the major determinant of democratic control and more aggressive organizing strategies. A critical, underresearched question is how differential organizational capacities are related to political culture and then utilized (or not) by social actors.

Organizational Environment

Institutional economists have argued that the organizational environment, by shaping market forces, exerts a powerful influence on the character of labor movements (Levinson 1966, Averitt 1968). Recent sociological research not only confirms this supposition, but also further specifies the impact of the organizational setting on union formation, structure, and behavior.

Findings from the field of organizational ecology suggest that the existing population of labor organizations influences the timing and structure of subsequent union formation. In their historical analysis of founding rates for American unions, Hannan & Freeman (1987) uncovered a curvilinear relationship between the degree of union density and the number of new "foundings." Focusing on processes of organizational imitation and competition, they argue that a sudden surge in union foundings may inspire additional attempts until, with the exhaustion of potential organizers and resources, a situation of diminishing returns sets in, which then discourages further organizing initiatives. Looking at similar processes within the steel industry around the turn of the century, Conell & Voss (1990) argue that pre-existing unionization of craft workers by the Knights of Labor facilitated the subsequent organization of unskilled workers but also simultaneously encouraged occupational sectionalism rather than more solidary modes of organization. In this way, earlier forms of unionization shaped both the number and kind of new unions.

The "new structuralism" in the field of stratification is also influencing sociological research on labor, particularly evident in recent studies documenting the impact of industry structure on the interests and organizational capacities of both labor and capital (Reitman 1991). Industry concentration may enhance the organizational capacities of employers, as Kimeldorf (1988) shows in comparing the responses of American shipowners to waterfront unionism on both coasts. He traces the greater intransigence of employers in the West to the presence of three major shipping firms whose dominance of the region's economy enabled them to organize coast-wide opposition to unionism. In contrast, East Coast employers, who were internally divided by the more fragmented structure of the maritime industry, were incapable of organizing unified opposition.

Industry structure also influences the interests and organizational capacities of labor, as recent studies of the connections between market power and union politics suggest. Comparing unionization in Britain, Germany, and the United States, Marks (1989) argues that unions with poorly defined jurisdictional boundaries but high market power, such as miners and longshoremen, tend to be the most radical, whereas unions with low market power—regardless of their jurisdictions—tend to assume a more accommodating stance.

Similarly, Haydu's (1988) comparative analysis of early twentieth-century factory politics in Britain and the United States focuses on the early development of a mass market in America, which led to greater firm specialization prior to World War I and the earlier introduction of "scientific" managerial practices. This not only deskilled and cheapened metal workers' labor in the United States, but also undermined their bargaining position as well.

Much of this work documenting the impact of industry on union formation has focused on the organizing efforts of white craftsmen. Much more research is needed on the ways in which ethnicity (Carsten 1988, Hirsch 1990), gender (Milkman 1987) and race (Cornfield 1989) mediate—if, in fact, they do (cf Burawoy 1979)—between industry structure and working-class capacities.

Working-Class Consciousness

Most recent sociological research on workers' consciousness focuses either on the class identification of workers (Jackman & Jackman 1983, Vanneman & Cannon 1987) or on the sources of their varying ideological orientations or union loyalty (Morawska 1985, Lash 1984, Zingraff & Schulman 1984). Its relevance to understanding the labor movement is so far limited to identifying, through surveys, the "correlates" of "union consciousness" (Heneman & Sandver 1983).

But the study of workers' consciousness is being drawn in a more ethnographic direction by what are essentially phenomenological questions concerning both the meaning and social construction of consciousness (Fantasia 1988). Following the lead of social history, sociologists have explored the intersection of popular culture and class consciousness, emphasizing that they are complementary rather than antithetical (Willis 1977, Matza & Wellman 1980, Billings 1990).

These works depict the mental world of workers as complex and contradictory. Abercrombie, Hill & Turner (1980) argue that the components of any ideology, including that of the dominant class, lack internal consistency. In their account, workers receive ideological "messages" from the top of the social pyramid very selectively. Observations of behavior—however deferential or radical in appearance—provide few clues as to what individual workers are actually thinking and why. In particular, so-called workers' quiescence may simply reflect a sober pragmatism without implying any corresponding ideological reorientation or conversion (Mann 1982, Scott 1985). So, this classic antinomy—the relationship between behavior and consciousness—should remain a central question in research on workers' politics.

CONCLUSION

Our view of recent sociohistorical research on the American labor movement raises a number of important implications for sociological scholarship in particular.

First, conventional approaches premised on the exceptionalism of American labor may be misleading, or worse. While it is true that organized labor in the United States is unique in certain respects, the contrast that is usually drawn between "class conscious" Europe and "business unionist" America has prevented us from seeing the very substantial organizational and political differences within European labor on the one hand, and the striking commonalities between American unionism and many of its democratic counterparts on the other. To its credit, the exceptionalist paradigm has generated a number of provocative arguments—unfortunately, often advanced as established facts—concerning the peculiar interests of American workers and the reasons for their alleged political "backwardness." But, given the paucity of systematic cross-national historical data on worker consciousness, such claims about the unique character of American workers must be viewed with a healthy dose of skepticism.

Second, the ebbs and flows of American unionism reflect a variety of social currents. In attempting to explain labor's post-war conservatism and subsequent decline, sociological analysts have instinctively turned to structural explanations which emphasize the constraining logic of contract unionism or sectoral shifts in the economy. Here, however, comparative analysis demonstrates the limitations of a purely structural explanation. Studies of individual unions as well as comparisons across unions suggest that the institution of contract unionism is highly flexible, having conformed historically to the needs of conservative business unionism and radical insurgency alike. Similarly, the sectoral shift from manufacturing to services that has swept most industrialized nations since the 1960s has had very different consequences for the size and shape of organized labor in each country. Sociologists would do well to follow the lead of more historically sensitive social scientists and labor historians whose recent work gives greater play to human agency in arguing that the trajectory of American labor was decisively shaped by past struggles waged between and within contending classes.

Third, the organizational history of American labor defies standard teleological accounts that locate the seeds of trade union conservatism either in the deepest structures of our nation's past or in the hidden recesses of workers' minds. Recent work by social scientists and labor historians on the demise of the Knights, the hidden syndicalism of the AFL, and the vitality of Communist leadership in the CIO underscores the need to reconsider many of our most cherished and long-standing assumptions concerning the anti-radicalism of American labor. At the same time, newer scholarship invites us to rethink the political meaning of the major organizational battles that were fought throughout the nineteenth and twentieth centuries for the allegiance of the American working class.

Finally, as we are drawn into a closer dialogue with labor historians, sociologists must remain conversant with developments in our field, particularly in the areas of social movements, organizational environments, and workers' consciousness. Constructing a sound historical sociology of labor movements is necessarily an inter-disciplinary project, synthesizing the interpretative possibilities offered by the new labor history with recent theoretical contributions drawn from sociology and other disciplines.

Literature Cited

Abercrombie, N., Hill, S., Turner, B. 1980. *The Dominant Ideology Thesis*. London: George Allen & Unwin

Aronowitz, S. 1973. *False Promises: The Shaping of American Working Class Consciousness*. New York: McGraw Hill

Ashenfelter, O., Johnson, G. 1969. Bargaining theory, trade unions, and industrial strike activity. *Am. Econ. Rev.* 59:35–49

Averitt, R. 1968. *The Dual Economy: The Dynamics of American Industry Structure*. New York: Norton

Barbash, J. 1948. *Labor Unions in Action*. New York: Harpers

Bell, D. 1961. *The End of Ideology: On the Exhaustion of Political Ideas in the Fifties*. New York: Collier

Bernstein, I. 1960. Union Growth and Structural Cycles. In *Labor and Trade Unionism*, ed. W. Galenson, S.M. Lipset, pp. 73–89. New York: Wiley

Billings, D. 1990. Religion as opposition: A Gramscian analysis. *Am. J. Sociol.* 1:1–31

Bluestone, B., Harrison, B. 1982. *The Deindustrialization of America: Plant Closings, Community Abandonment, and the Dismantling of Basic Industry*. New York: Basic Books

Bodnar, J. 1982. *Workers' World: Kinship, Community, and Protest in an Industrial Society*. Baltimore: Johns Hopkins Univ.

Boyer, R., Morais, H. 1975. *Labor's Untold Story*. New York: United Electrical, Radio & Machine Workers of America. 2nd ed.

Braverman, H. 1974. *Labor and Monopoly Capital: The Degradation of Work in the Twentieth Century*. New York: Monthly Rev.

Brecher, J. 1972. *Strike! San Francisco*. San Francisco: Straight Arrow Books
Bridges, A. 1984. *A City in the Republic: Antebellum New York and the Origins of Machine Politics*. Cambridge: Cambridge Univ. Press
Bridges, A. 1986. Becoming American: The working classes in the United States before the Civil War. In *Working Class Formation: 19th Century Patterns in West Europe and the United States,* ed. I. Katznelson, A. Zolberg, pp. 157–96. Princeton, NJ: Princeton Univ. Press
Brinkley, A. 1990. The best years of their lives. *New York Rev. Books* June:16–21
Brody, D. 1979. The old labor history and the new: In search of an American working class. *Labor Hist*. 20:111–26
Brody, D. 1980. *Workers in Industrial America: Essays on the Twentieth Century Struggle*. New York: Oxford Univ.
Brody, D. 1984. Radicalism and the American labor movement: From party history to social history. *Polit. Power Social Theory* 4:255–61
Burawoy, M. 1979. *Manufacturing Consent: Changes in the Labor Process under Monopoly Capitalism*. Chicago: Univ. Chicago
Burawoy, M. 1985. *The Politics of Production: Factory Regimes under Capitalism and Socialism*. New York/London: Verso
Carsten, O. 1988. Ethnic particularism and class solidarity: The experience of two Connecticut cities. *Theory Soc*. 17:431–50
Casebeer, K. 1989. Drafting Wagner's act: Leon Keyserling and the precommittee drafts of the labor disputes act and the National Labor Relations Act. *Indust. Relat. Law J*. 11:73–131
Clawson, D. 1980. *Bureaucracy and the Labor Process: The Transformation of U.S. Industry, 1860–1920*. New York: Monthly Rev.
Cochran, B. 1977. *Labor and Communism: The Conflict that Shaped American Unions*. Princeton: Princeton Univ. Press
Conell, C., Voss, K. 1990. Formal organization and the fate of social movements: craft association and class alliance in the Knights of Labor. *Am. Sociol. Rev*. 55:255–69
Cornfield, D. 1989. *Becoming A Mighty Voice: Conflict and Change in the United Furniture Workers of America*. New York: Russell Sage
Cornfield, D. 1991. The U.S. labor movement: its development and impact on social inequality and politics. *Annu. Rev. Sociol*. 17:27–49
Domhoff, G. W. 1990. *The Power Elite and the State: How Policy is Made in America*. New York: Aldine De Gruyter
Draper, T. 1985. American Communism revisited. *New York Rev. Books* May 9:32–37
Dubofsky, M. 1979. Not so "turbulent years": another look at the American 1930s. *Am. Stud*. 24:5–20
Dubofsky, M. 1988. *We Shall Be All: A History of the Industrial Workers of the World*. Urbana: Univ. Ill. Press. 2nd ed.
Edwards, P.K. 1981. *Strikes in the United States, 1881–1974*. Oxford: Blackwell
Fantasia, R. 1988. *Cultures of Solidarity: Consciousness, Action, and Contemporary American Workers*. Berkeley: Univ. Calif. Press
Fink, L. 1985. *Workingmen's Democracy: The Knights of Labor and American Politics*. Urbana: Univ. Ill. Press
Foner, E. 1984. Why is there no socialism in the United States? *Hist. J. Workshop* 17:57–80
Freeman, J. 1989. *In Transit: The Transport Workers Union in New York City, 1933–1966*. New York: Oxford Univ. Press
Freeman, R, Medoff, J. 1984. *What Do Unions Do?* New York: Basic Books
Gartman, D. 1986. *Auto Slavery: The Labor Process in the American Automobile Industry, 1897–1950*. New Brunswick: Rutgers Univ. Press
Gerstle, G. 1989. *Working-Class Americanism: The Politics of Labor in a Textile City, 1914–1960*. London: Cambridge Univ. Press
Ginger, A., Christiano, D., eds. 1987. *The Cold War Against Labor: An Anthology*. Berkeley, Calif: Meiklejohn Civil Liberties Inst.
Glazer, N. 1961. *The Social Basis of American Communism*. New York: Harcourt, Brace & World
Goldfield, M. 1987. *The Decline of Organized Labor in the United States*. Chicago: Univ. Chicago Press
Goldfield, M. 1989. Worker insurgency, radical organization, and New Deal labor legislation. *Am. Polit. Sci. Rev*. 83:1257–82
Gordon, D., Edwards, R., Reich, M. 1982. *Segmented Work, Divided Workers: The Historical Formation of Labor in the United States*. Cambridge: Cambridge Univ. Press
Griffin, L., Wallace, M., Rubin, B. 1986. Capitalist resistance to the organization of labor before the New Deal: Why? How? Success? *Am. Sociol. Rev*. 51:147–67
Grob, G. 1969. *Workers and Utopia: A Study of the Ideological Conflict in the American Labor Movement*. Chicago: Quadrangle
Halpern, M. 1988. *UAW Politics in the Cold War Era*. Albany: State Univ. New York Press
Hannan, M., Freeman, J. 1987. The ecology of organizational founding: American labor

unions, 1836–1985. *Am. J. Sociol.* 92:910–43
Haydu, J. 1988. *Between Craft and Class: Skilled Workers and Factory Politics in the United States and Britain, 1890–1922*. Berkeley: Univ. Calif. Press
Haydu, J. 1991. "No change in existing standards?" Production, employee representation, and government policy in the United States, 1917–1919. *J. Soc. Hist.* 25:45–64
Heneman, H., Sandver, M. 1983. Predicting the outcome of union certification elections: a review of the literature. *Indust. Labor Relat. Rev.* 36:537–59
Hibbs, D. 1976. Industrial conflict in advanced industrial societies. *Am. Polit. Sci. Rev.* 70:1033–58
Hirsch, E. 1990. *Urban Revolt: Ethnic Politics in the Nineteenth-Century Chicago Labor Movement*. Berkeley: Univ. Calif. Press
Howe, I., Coser, L. 1957. *The American Communist Party: A Critical History (1919–1957)*. Boston: Beacon
Jackman, M., Jackman, R. 1983. *Class Awareness in the United States*. Berkeley: Univ. Calif. Press
Kampelman, M. 1957. *The Communist Party vs. the CIO: A Study in Power Politics*. New York: Praeger
Kazin, M. 1987. *Barons of Labor: The San Francisco Building Trades and Union Power in the Progressive Era*. Urbana: Univ. Ill. Press
Keeran, R. 1980. *The Communist Party and the Auto Workers Union*. Bloomington: Indiana Univ. Press
Kimeldorf, H. 1988. *Reds or Rackets? The Making of Radical and Conservative Unions on the Waterfront*. Berkeley: Univ. Calif. Press
Kimeldorf, H. 1991. *Bringing Unions Back In (Or Why We Need a New Old Labor History). Labor Hist.* 32:91–103
Kimeldorf, H. 1992. World War II and the deradicalization of American labor: The ILWU as a deviant case. *Labor Hist.* In press
Klare, K. 1978. Judicial deradicalization of the Wagner Act and the origins of modern legal consciousness, 1937–1941. *Minn. Law Rev.* 62:265
Klehr, H. 1984. *The Heyday of American Communism: The Depression Decade*. New York: Basic
Korpi, W., Shalev, M. 1980. Strikes, power and politics in the western nations, 1900–1976. *Polit. Power Soc. Theory* 1:301–34
Kraditor, A. 1981. *The Radical Persuasion, 1890–1917: Aspects of the Intellectual History and the Historiography of Three American Radical Organizations*. Baton Rouge: Louisiana State Univ.
Lash, S. 1984. *The Militant Worker: Class and Radicalism in France and America*. London: Heinemann
Laslett, J.H.M. 1970. *Labor and the Left: A Study of Socialist and Radical Influences in the American Labor Movement*. New York: Basic Books
Laslett, J.H.M., Lipset, S. M., eds. 1974. *Failure of a Dream? Essays on the History of American Socialism*. Garden City, NY: Doubleday
Lembcke, J. 1988. *Capitalist Development and Class Capacities*. New York: Greenwood
Lembcke, J., Tattam, W. 1984. *One Union in Wood: A Political History of the International Woodworkers of America*. New York: Int. Publ.
Lembcke, J., Howe, C. 1986. Organizational structure and the logic of collective action in unions. *Curr. Perspect. Soc. Theory* 7:1–27
Levenstein, H. 1981. *Communism, Anti-Communism, and the CIO*. Westport: Greenwood
Levinson, H. 1966. *Determining Forces in Collective Bargaining*. New York: Wiley
Lipset, S.M. 1960. The Political Process in Trade Unions: A Theoretical Statement. In *Labor and Trade Unionism*, ed. W. Galenson, S. M. Lipset. New York /London: Wiley
Maier, C. 1987. The 1920s—consolation or warning?: a response to David Montgomery. *Int. Labor Working Class Hist.* 32:25–30
Mann, M. 1977. *Consciousness and Action Among the Western Working Class*. London: Macmillan
Mann, M. 1982. The social cohesion of liberal democracy. In *Classes, Power, and Conflict: Classical and Contemporary Debates*, ed. A. Giddens, D. Held, pp. 373–95. Berkeley: Univ. Calif. Press
Marks, G. 1989. *Unions in Politics: Britain, Germany, and the United States in the Nineteenth and Early Twentieth Centuries*. Princeton: Princeton Univ. Press
Matza, D., Wellman, D. 1980. The ordeal of consciousness. *Theory Soc.* 9:1–27
McCammon, H. 1990. Legal limits on labor militance: U.S. labor law and the right to strike since the New Deal. *Soc. Problems* 37:206–29
Melucci, A. 1989. *Nomads of the Present: Social Movements and Individual Needs in Contemporary Society*. Philadelphia: Temple Univ. Press
Milkman, R. 1987. *Gender at Work: The Dynamics of Job Segregation by Sex during World War II*. Urbana: Univ. Ill. Press

Mills, H., Wellman, D. 1987. Contractually sanctioned job action and workers' control: the case of San Francisco longshoremen. *Labor Hist*. 28:167–95

Milton, D. 1982. *The Politics of U.S. Labor: From the Great Depression to the New Deal*. New York: Monthly Rev.

Mink, G. 1986. *Old Labor and New Immigrants in American Political Development: Union, Party, and the State, 1875–1920*. Ithaca: Cornell Univ. Press

Monds, J. 1976. Workers' control and the historians: a new economism. *New Left Rev*. 97:81–104

Montgomery, D. 1979. *Workers' Control in America: Studies in the History of Work, Technology, and Labor Struggles*. Cambridge: Cambridge Univ. Press

Montgomery, D. 1987a. *Fall of the House of Labor: Essays in American Working Class and Social History*. Cambridge: Cambridge Univ. Press

Montgomery, D. 1987b. Thinking about American workers in the 1920s. *Int. Labor Working Class Hist*. 32:4–24

Morawska, E. 1985. East European labourers in an American mill town, 1890–1940: the deferential-proletarian-privatized workers? *Sociology* 19:364–83

Nelson, B. 1988. *Workers on the Waterfront: Seamen, Longshoremen, and Unionism in the 1930s*. Urbana: Univ. Ill. Press

Offe, C., Wiesenthal, H. 1980. Two logics of collective action: theoretical notes on social classes and organizational form. *Polit. Power Soc. Theory*. 1:67–115

Ostreicher, R. 1988. Urban working-class political behavior and theories of American electoral politics, 1870–1940. *J. Am. Hist*. 74:1257–86

Perlman, S. 1928. *A Theory of the Labor Movement*. New York: Augustus M. Kelley

Piven, F. F., Cloward, R. 1979. *Poor Peoples Movements: Why They Succeed, How They Fail*. New York: Vintage Books

Prickett, J. 1975. *Communists and the Communist issue in the American labor movement, 1920–1950*. PhD thesis. Univ. Calif. Los Angeles

Quadagno, J. 1988. *The Transformation of Old Age Security*. Chicago/London: Univ. Chicago Press

Radosh, R. 1966. The corporate ideology of American labor leaders from Gompers to Hillman. *Stud. Left* 6:66–88

Reitman, S. 1991. The politics of the western federation of miners and the United Mine Workers of America: uneven development, industry structure, and class struggle. In *Bringing Class Back In: Contemporary and Historical Perspectives*, ed. S. McNall, R. Levine, R. Fantasia, pp. 203–22. Boulder: Westview

Schatz, R. 1983. *The Electrical Workers: A History of Labor at General Electric and Westinghouse, 1923–1960*. Urbana: Univ. Ill. Press

Scott, J. 1985. *Weapons of the Weak: Everyday Forms of Peasant Resistance*. New Haven: Yale Univ. Press

Shalev, M., Korpi, W. 1980. Working class mobilization and American exceptionalism. *Econ. Indust. Democracy* 1:31–61

Shefter, M. 1986. Trade unions and political machines: the organization and disorganization of the American working class in the late nineteenth century. In *Working Class Formation: Nineteenth Century Patterns in Western Europe and the United States*, ed. I. Katznelson, A. Zolberg, pp. 197–276. Princeton: Princeton Univ. Press

Shorter, E., Tilly, C. 1974. *Strikes in France, 1830–1968*. Cambridge: Cambridge Univ. Press

Skocpol, T., Finegold, K. 1982. State capacity and economic intervention in the early New Deal. *Polit. Sci. Q*. 97:255–78

Skocpol, T., Amenta, E. 1985. Did capitalists shape social security? *Am. Sociol. Rev*. 50:572–5

Snyder, D. 1977. Early North American strikes: a reinterpretation. *Indust. Labor Relat. Rev*.30:325–41

Stepan-Norris, J., Zeitlin, M. 1989. "Who gets the bird?" or, How the Communists won power and trust in America's unions. *Am. Sociol. Rev*. 54:503–23

Stepan-Norris, J., Zeitlin, M. 1991a. "Red" unions and "bourgeois" contracts? The effects of political leadership on the "political regime of production." *Am. J. Sociol*. 96:1151–1200

Stepan-Norris, J., Zeitlin, M. 1991b. *Insurgency, radicalism, and democracy in America's industrial unions. Los Angeles: Inst. Industr. Relat., Univ. Calif Work. Pap. Ser. 215*

Therborn, G. 1983. Why some classes are more successful than others. *New Left Rev*. 138:37–55

Tomlins, C. 1985. *The State and the Unions: Labor Relations, Law and the Organized Labor Movement in America 1880–1960*. Cambridge & New York: Cambridge Univ. Press

Troy, L. 1986. The rise and fall of American trade unions: The labor movement from FDR to RR. In *Unions in Transition: Entering the Second Century*, ed. S. M. Lipset. San Francisco: Inst. Contemp. Stud.

Ulman, L. 1966. *The Rise of the National Trade Union: The Development and Significance of its Structure, Governing Institutions, and Economic Policies*. Cambridge: Harvard Univ. Press. 2nd ed.

US Department of Commerce, Bureau of the

Census. 1933. *Abstract of the 15th Census of the United States: 1930*. Washington: US Govt. Printing Off.

Vanneman, R., Cannon, L. 1987. *The American Perception of Class*. Philadelphia: Temple Univ. Press

Verba, S., Scholzman, K. 1977. Unemployment, class consciousness, and radical politics: what didn't happen in the Thirties. *J. Polit.* 39:291–323

Voss, K. 1989. *Disposition is not action: the rise and demise of the Knights of Labor. Inst. Industr. Relat. Work. Pap. No. 16*. Berkeley: Univ. Calif.

Wallace, M. 1989. Aggressive economism, defensive control: contours of American labor militancy, 1947–81. *Econ. Industr. Democracy* 10:7–34

Wallace, M., Griffin, L., Smith, B. 1989. The positional power of American labor, 1963–1977. *Am. Sociol. Rev.* 54:197–214

Wallace, M., Rubin, B., Smith, B. 1988. American labor law: its impact on working-class militancy, 1901–1980. *Soc. Sci. Hist.* 12:1–29

Wilentz, S. 1984a. *Chants Democratic: New York City and the Rise of the American Working Class, 1788–1850*. New York: Oxford Univ. Press

Wilentz, S. 1984b. Against exceptionalism: class consciousness and the American labor movement, 1790–1920. *Int. Labor Work. Class Hist.* 26:1–24

Willis, P. 1977. *Learning to Labor: How Working Class Kids Get Working Class Jobs*. New York: Columbia Univ. Press

Wrigley, J. 1982. *Class Politics and Public Schools: Chicago 1900–1950*. New Brunswick: Rutgers Univ. Press

Zeitlin, M., Kimeldorf, H., eds. 1984. *Political Power and Social Theory 4*

Zieger, R. 1985. Toward the history of the CIO: a bibliographical report. *Labor Hist.* 26:485–516

Zieger, R. 1986. *American Workers, American Unions, 1920–1985*. Baltimore: Johns Hopkins Univ. Press

Zingraff, R., Schulman, M. 1984. Social bases of class consciousness: a study of southern textile workers with a comparison by race. *Soc. Forc.* 63:98–116

Zolberg, A. 1986. How many exceptionalisms? In *Working-Class Formation: Nineteenth-Century Patterns in Western Europe and the United States*, ed. I. Katznelson, A. Zolberg, pp. 397–455. Princeton: Princeton Univ. Press

Annu. Rev. Sociol. 1992. 18:519–40

THE CRISIS OF AFRICAN DEVELOPMENT: Conflicting Interpretations and Resolutions

Paul M. Lubeck

Merrill College, University of California, Santa Cruz, California 95064

KEY WORDS: Africa, crisis, development, industry, agriculture

Abstract

The depth and duration of economic decline, coupled with ecological degradation, political paralysis, and institutional decay, has created an unprecedented crisis in sub-saharan Africa. Explanations for the multiple crises of African development focus on debates regarding the necessity of following market-oriented economic policies, the capacity of African states to manage either development or reform and the way in which African institutions reproduce societies that are resistant either to state-centered development or to market forces. After allowing for events that are beyond the control of policy, the three schools—neoliberal, structural-nationalist, and institutional—are used to evaluate the literature on peasant agriculture, industry, and state policy. The experience of Nigeria indicates that commercial agriculture is increasing, that structural reforms can have some positive benefits and that its hydrocarbon sector can form a basis for regional industrialization. Finally, the rise of popular democratic movements suggests how the crisis has unleashed elements of a formerly passive civil society which promise to reform authoritarianism and discipline rentier states.

INTRODUCTION: AFRICAN DEVELOPMENT AND SOCIAL STRUCTURE

If the complexity and diversity of the literature on African development were not challenging enough for any reviewer, the depth and protracted duration of

0360-0572/92/0815-0519$02.00

the economic and social crisis render a review a truly daunting endeavor.[1] Indeed, the crisis is so severe and so intractable that it has literally overdetermined the terms of reference for the discourse on African development. Accordingly, after providing the reader with an empirical profile describing the African predicament, this review turns to the debate over the structural origins and proposed resolutions of the crisis. Organizationally, the latter can be grouped into three "schools," each represented by a body of informed studies that usually recommend practical policy reforms for each sector. Following the "schools" of interpretation, the literature is then reviewed in each sector—agrarian, urban-industrial, and state—with an eye to understanding how state policies, market forces, and uniquely African institutions have interacted with the world economy. Returning to civil society, the review concludes by assessing the potential contribution of Africa's nascent democratic movements to the resolution of Africa's developmental crisis.

The Intertwined Nature of Africa's Multiple Crises

Crisis, a term used to excess in sociological analysis, barely captures the bleak future predicted for Africa during the remainder of this century. Neither Latin America, typically described as experiencing "a lost decade," nor South Asia, a region sharing Africa's overpopulation problems, communal diversity, and trade imbalances, even approaches the depth and intractability of Africa's developmental nightmare. Indeed, while the latter regions may have stagnated or suffered relative declines in the 1980s, Africa is the only world region registering *absolute* declines on virtually all indices of socioeconomic development. More alarming, and especially challenging for orthodox development theory, is the staggering fact that, despite nearly a decade of submission to structural adjustment programs (SAPs) administered by the World Bank and the International Monetary Fund (IMF), neither the promised "accelerated growth," nor market equilibrium, nor new foreign investment has been forthcoming. Similarly, the United Nations' Special Session agreement between African states and the international community, whereby the former agreed to drastic "reforms" during 1986–1990 in exchange for increased concessionary lending from the latter, has not altered the drift toward mounting external debt and deteriorating living standards.

Sadly, despite this truly unprecedented political agreement among African states to transform domestic economic policies, the secretary-general's report on the five year Recovery Program (1986–1990) confirms that continental Africa's GDP (gross domestic product) per capita actually declined by an annual average of .7%, that the ratio of gross domestic investment to GDP

[1]In this review, Africa refers to sub-saharan Africa, excluding South Africa.

declined from 23.9% (1980) to 17.6% (1989), that gross domestic saving declined from 24% (1980) to 16% (1989) and that real net resource flows to Africa "actually declined, from $24.6 billion in 1986 to $23.3 billion in 1990" (United Nations 1991:2). Hence, both the World Bank and the United Nations' programs, emphasizing markets and states, respectively, now openly admit their failure to stem the tide of rising human misery in the 1980s.

Any review of development and social structure must grapple with Africa's alarming statistical trends: (i) the world's highest annual population growth rate (3.2% average), which will raise Africa's absolute size from 451 million (1987) to 673 million by 2000; (ii) an absolute decline in the index of per capita food production (−5 since 1979), annually requiring $18 billion worth of food imports for food deficits and for the estimated 30 million facing starvation (World Bank 1989a); (iii) the world's highest ratios of external, mostly public, debt to GNP (115%) and debt to export earnings (350%); (iv) the world's lowest rate of industrialization (10.5% of GNP); (v) the highest infant mortality rate (more than 150/1000) and the lowest average life expectancy (51 years); (vi) more than half the world's HIV infections (6 million) (Becker 1990, Larson 1990); (vii) the largest number of refugees (4 million); and (viii), despite a 2.5% annual increase in export commodity volumes between 1986 and 1990, an annual decline in export earnings of 16% (World Bank 1989a, 1991, United Nations 1991).

Before moving to key debates, let us note where there is wide agreement among scholars. In structural terms, all agree that the crisis is rooted in colonial boundaries and export patterns, cyclical drought, shifting ecological practices that degrade the environment, a Hobbesian elite struggle for shrinking resources, appalling health conditions, indifferent administration, and almost total statistical uncertainty. Similarly, most agree that the crisis arose from the interaction of multiple and reinforcing factors, the origin of which lies in global and natural systems—as distinguished from internal African institutional weaknesses or state policy decisions alone. Global changes in the 1980s, such as high interest rates and declining credit, crashing commodity prices, and the neoliberal attack on state economic institutions simply were not predicted by donor agencies during the commodity boom and economic nationalism of the 1970s (Lancaster 1990) when external debt was contracted. War, too, has ravaged the continent, robbing affected regions of their productive capacity while burdening neighbors with approximately four million refugees. Although internally generated civil wars have erupted in Uganda, Liberia, and Somalia, the superpowers and their allies have funded proxy-wars in Angola, Mozambique, Chad, Namibia, and Ethiopia (Martin & Johnson 1986). Climatic changes, too, are beyond human intervention or state pricing policies.

Interpreting the Crisis: Neoliberalism

While classical economic theory was never absent, the World Bank's report (1981), *Accelerated Development in Sub-Saharan Africa: An Agenda for Action,* stands as the defining text not only for market-oriented approaches but also for the intellectual opposition. Variously interpreted as either "a secular variant of the Book of Revelations" or "a recipe for accelerated starvation," this report "has attracted more attention, discussion and diatribes than any other study on Africa" (Green & Allison 1986:61). Initially commissioned by African governors at the Bank and edited by neoliberal Elliot Berg, the report marks a break with the "Basic Needs" philosophy of Robert McNamara and the beginning of neoliberal economic policies: removing barriers to competition and real market prices, removing state subsidies and reducing state economic intervention in general, stimulating export production by relying on natural comparative advantages, reforming overvalued exchange rates that protect inefficient import substituting industries, and rationalizing the administrative, data gathering, planning and strategic functions performed by African governments. Above all, the *Berg Report* recommended prioritizing agriculture, both domestic and export-oriented, by allowing unmediated market mechanisms to operate, by funding rural infrastructure like roads, technical inputs, and small-scale irrigation technologies, and by eliminating the urban bias of large-scale government projects.

Understandably, this power shift stimulated a debate among social scientists over structural adjustment, denationalization of economies and societies, and effective, sustainable development, a debate that focused sharply on the power of the World Bank. Acting simultaneously as a technical expert, a lender of last resort, a monitor of structural adjustment plans, a manager of agricultural development projects (ADPs), and the primary statistical agency for the region, the Bank came to symbolize global capitalist rationalization and external intervention, albeit in alliance with local ruling groups. Indeed, because the Bank collects, assesses, and implements the evidence on structural adjustment, while also providing soft loans, only a sociologist of knowledge can evaluate the Bank's methodology for assessing the success or failure of the structural adjustment plans.

The return of classical economics in place of state-centered developmental economics affected not only economists and policy makers as discussed above, but also the social sciences in general. Bates's (1981) work was exceptionally influential, for it combined microeconomics, rational choice theory, and state policy in a meaningful historical narrative to show how agrarian producers were injured by urban-biased state policy. In a second, equally influential work on economic institutions in Kenya, Bates (1989) extends his approach to explain how state intervention into markets often generates conflicts over distributional gains, supports monopoly interests, and distorts market forces among small producers to such a degree that famine is increased. Finally, Bates critiques the apolitical assumptions of neoclassical economics, arguing instead for a theory of economic institutions, one that explains Kenya's relative economic success as derived from rural class interests which demand that state economic institutions "unleash" rather than undermine market forces. Elsewhere Lofchie (1975) and Laitin (1986) offer neoliberal analyses of hunger and ethnic mobilization, respectively.

Neoliberal theory's preference for market forces as the appropriate route to capital accumulation was bolstered by unconventional support from classical marxist analysis. The turnabout in Leys' (1978) work exemplifies the rejection of world systems–dependency approaches for explaining underdevelopment in Kenya (Leys 1975). Swainson (1980), Njonjo (1977), and Cowen (1976) are emphatic in their support for market-based accumulation. Using concepts of labor time, and the "straddling" of household and wage labor opportunities, Cowen's work proved to be a pathbreaking analysis of how capital accumulation occurred among Kenya's fledgling bourgeoisie. Sender & Smith (1986), following the lead of Warren (1980), reinterpreted the economic history of Africa to argue that productivity and living standards have improved since colonization, that Africa's class structure and the political elite's mismanagement of economic surplus rather than external "scapegoats" contributed to the crisis, and finally, that the relative weakness of indigenous capital vis-à-vis state elites is the major obstacle to capitalist development. While criticizing the *Berg Report* for its generalization from weak evidence and an apolitical interpretation of state bureaucratic incompetence, they also point out how the administrative difficulties associated with foreign exchange controls limit their effectiveness as an alternative to devaluation in weak states with inefficient bureaucracies. In the same vein, Kitching (1980, 1982, 1987) directly attacks populist-nationalist icons, forcefully arguing against self-sufficiency and for involvement in international trade, guided by a developmentalist state, so as to maximize the progressive consequences of market forces. Again, the severity of the crisis makes for strange bedfellows.

The Response of Structural-Nationalism

Whereas neoliberalism extends the neoclassical paradigm, the structural-nationalist school is driven by an eclectic blend of theory—world systems, underdevelopment, anti-imperialist marxism, and African nationalism. Ironically, they note that it was colonial governments and global financial regulatory institutions like the World Bank that introduced state intervention and public corporations into African development planning (Williams 1985:3). Marxist critics like Bernstein (1990) and Beckman (1988a) see the authors of the *Berg Report* and the Bank as political actors who inflated weak data in order to rationalize capitalist development in Africa. Beckman views reforms as a transnational capitalist project managed jointly by local ruling groups and external donors, for "the breeding of responsible and capitalist oriented local ruling classes has been a conscious policy since the decolonization period." (1988a:30).

Historically, for non-oil producers, structural adjustment followed the exhaustion of private credit needed to cover increased petroleum-import costs. "Twenty African governments implemented IMF stabilization programs between 1979 and 1983, and by 1988 a further 22 had adopted World Bank adjustment policies" (Watts 1991:132). Austerity, currency devaluation, price reform, market discipline, and privatization were the code words for an unprecedented transfer of effective power from formally sovereign states to IMF/World Bank bureaucracies. A nationalist reaction was inevitable. When, in March 1989, the World Bank published a report purporting to show that reforming (SAP) countries had higher agricultural growth, faster export growth, stronger GDP growth, and larger investment than non-reforming countries during the 1980s, a predictable avalanche of enraged criticism put the Bank on the defensive (World Bank 1989b).

Under Adebayo Adedeji's leadership, the United Nations' Economic Commission for Africa (ECA) attacked the Bank's self-justificatory report and produced different results running the same data but using different statistical weightings and years of comparison. Having undermined the credibility of the Bank's analysis, the ECA argued forcefully that the Bank's deflationary policies destroyed the productive basis for recovery, encouraged nonproductive speculation, undermined Africa's industrialization, and, ultimately, threatened the very social fabric of African societies (Lancaster 1990). The ECA then launched its own program, *African Alternative Framework* (1989) which, predictably, argued that Africa's problems were deeply structural and arose from colonial-origin commodity systems—problems resolvable not by short-term shock treatments but rather by democratic institutions and a revitalized though streamlined public sector. Smarting from widespread methodological and empirical criticism from the ECA and others (Colclough & Green 1988), the Bank in November of that year produced a new report emphasizing sustainability, investing in human resources, growth with equity, an enabling environment, regional solutions, self-reliance, and a coalition among donors, much of which was lifted from the ECA's program (1989, Parfitt & Riley 1989). Hence, while the Bank remains on a neoliberal tack, implementation of structural adjustment plans requires the nurturance of a domestic coalition within the African state to administer and legitimate a policy that devalues domestic savings and the incomes of the salaried and wage-earning classes. The ECA alternative argues for greater democracy, social participation, regional common market solutions, and debt relief.

Accordingly, given the scale of the crisis, Africa has no option but to rely on a reformed state to regulate economic activity. The state must not be dismantled; without alternatives, parastatals must continue to provide goods and infrastructure. Therefore, chaos, starvation, and neocolonial national disintegration will follow if neoliberalpolicies are strictly implemented. Green (1985a, 1985b) has critically reviewed the evidence employed by the IMF/World Bank and showed that without debt relief and concessionary grants, Africa's primary commodity exporters can never hope to pay off their external debts (i.e. 350% of GDP), no matter how many neoliberal reforms are instituted internally. Since this "disequilibrium" is readily apparent, the political question directed to the neoliberals making policy at the IMF and World Bank is: how low will African living standards be driven and by what authoritarian means before debt relief is announced? On the other hand, if the ECA defense of the role of the African state is to be credible, especially to donors and lending agencies, then the administrative capacity of the African states becomes a critical issue (Ravenhill 1986). Regarding the feasibility of regional economic groupings as a solution, (i.e. Economic Community of West African States (ECOWAS) and Southern African Development Coordination Conference (SADCC)), is it reasonable to expect regional government to function when the demonstrated capacity of the state is so weak or absent in a number of instances? Yet, the structural-nationalist school's insistence on a role for the state will prevail, if only because there is a dearth of options now that international firms find Africa unprofitable and indigenous capital is still too weak to offer alternatives. Killick (1989) cautions neoliberals in their moment of triumph against demanding rigid orthodoxy, while advising nationalists that policies that use markets will be more effective than those that contradict markets. The question of interest for structural-nationalism is: what form of the state will satisfy internal demands for democracy and human rights and, at the same time, meet the need for rational resource allocations and financial discipline required by private capital?

Institutional Analysis

The last school focuses on the economic and social behavior of African producers and attempts to understand their motives in terms of their own moral economies and group rationalities. Basing their views on careful fieldwork among peasants and informal sector producers in cities, institutionalists are skeptical about the assumptions of individual rationality and short-term profit maximization underlying neoliberal policy reforms. Because market forces, incentives, and price signals must be mediated through existing institutions and social structures, outcomes may diverge significantly from neoliberal expectations. Further, like the structural-nationalist school, institutionalists know how difficult it is to collect reliable data under existing social conditions, so few accept the reliability of quantitative evidence churned out by the World Bank to justify structural adjustment plans and sectoral reform proposals. Likewise, they are skeptical of marxism's tendency to overemphasize the significance of increasing poverty and differentiation among the peasantry (Clough 1981, 1985) or the attribution of class consciousness to rebellious urban populists in Africa's cities (Lloyd 1974, Peace 1979).

Institutional analysts attempt to understand the behavior of African producers in terms of their moral economies, group rationalities, and articulated co-existence between formally capitalist and precapitalist spheres. The power of their analyses flows from their ability to explain why the behavior of African producers is quite rational in economic well as cultural terms, given their constraints and resources. Since African producers face known risks, great uncertainty, and institutional constraints, their responses to material incentives and market forces often contradict the expectations of state planners and rational choice assumptions. Though recognized by policy makers, such outcomes are defined as corruption, inefficiency, or cultural backwardness. Institutionalists argue that producers often choose to allocate resources—land, labor, and credit—for the reproduction of groups (i.e. households, lineages, Islamic brotherhoods, or cultural associations) precisely because these diversified investments guard against environmental risk, market uncertainties, and the political instability associated with planning in a way that assures that they recover a small surplus at the very least. These behaviors reproduce an insurance-like network of moral obligation at the expense of greater surpluses earned by specialized, profit-maximizing strategies.

Deeply rooted in the anarchic and relativist tradition of economic anthropology, some like Richards (1983, 1986) celebrate the resistance and autonomy of independent producers, thereby opening themselves to the charge of romantic "populism" (Watts 1983); still others are grappling with the policy implications of African institutional strategies. In the urban sector, institutionalists analyze the informal sector, artisanal producers, and the black marketeers, who are shown to be very calculating traders and inventive producers of indispensible commodities (Hart 1973, Gerry 1978). MacGaffey's detailed and empirically rich analysis of indigenous capitalism in Zaire, arguably the most corrupt and disarticulated state in Africa, shows how significant the informal sector can become in a situation of institutional decay (MacGaffey 1987). Whereas elsewhere intermediate industries evolve from informal sector origins, there is little evidence of movement up the ladder of productivity and technical complexity in Africa's informal sector. Organizationally, the pattern is bimodal: large firms are often articulated with transnationals or state industries, and artisanal, family enterprises like motor mechanics are isolated from the latter. A few intermediate or smallscale firms link the two types.

As a trained economist and historian, and a sociological field worker in her own right, Sara Berry is the doyen of the institutionalist school, yet one who tries to link her institutional analysis to questions raised by neoliberal policy reformers who endeavor to transform the productivity and behavior of smallholding farmers (1989). Thus, she provides a valuable perspective on the agrarian crisis, one worth quoting: "Low income farmers have trouble coping with risk not because they are innately conservative, but because they are poor" (Berry 1991:1); "to cope with increasing economic instability and decline . . . people pursued influence and opportunity through shifting alliances or by contesting the boundaries or structure of the networks themselves" (1991:11).

Hence, for all these reasons: "Structural adjustment policies and other development programs predicated upon the notion that markets with low barriers to entry and a high degree of resource mobility promote productive patterns of resource use may not be appropriate for African social realities" (Berry 1991:22).

Guided by the assertions of these three schools, let us turn to the agrarian sector in order to assess their explanatory power.

The Agrarian Sector: A Crisis of Peasants and Productivity

More than 70% of Africans live in rural areas, engaged mostly in agriculture, crafts, herding, petty trading, and migrant labor. Hence, any solution to the crisis must begin in the countryside and confront the resistance of the African peasantry to subordination to either state power or market forces—a structural conflict that Bunker (1987) admirably documents in the case of Uganda. A peasantry emerged in colonial Africa where it had not already existed, i.e. in Ethiopia, northern Nigeria, and Uganda (Post 1972, Cooper 1981a,b). By subordinating rural producers to the colonial state, to international firms within the world market, or to European farmers, African peasantries consolidated themselves around socially constructed communal identities which, in turn, allocated them resources in land, livestock, and labor services. This sector is the site simultaneously of crisis and transformation as commercial farming erodes its autonomy, as state infrastructure bolsters the politically privileged, and as market forces exacerbate differentiation between rich and poor peasants.

Using different labels—peasants, farmers, independent commodity producers—all the aforementioned schools have produced a literature on rural producers (Berry 1984, Heyer et al 1981, Bates 1989, Isaacman 1990). Sociologists of the peasantry inquire about: (i) their use of resources and their collective social identities; (ii) their patterns of differentiation and, particularly, whether a kulak or agrarian bourgeoisie has appeared; (iii) their relationship to, and resistance against, state institutions and administrative policies; and (iv) their behavioral response to changes in state policy, especially changes in access to inputs, investments, and producer prices. Again, the absence of reliable statistics and the decay of state administrative capacity thwarts closure of these questions, but partial, local answers exist at a reasonable empirical standard.

Virtually all schools agree that parastatal agencies like marketing boards have overtaxed, inefficiently managed, and undermined peasant output so egregiously as to have forced many of them out of state-regulated markets (Lofchie 1975, Williams 1985). Classical marxists like Sender & Smith (1986), however, argue that extraction of surplus from the peasantry is a necessary precondition for investment, higher productivity, and industrialization, all of which must be led by a hegemonic state. Hence, it is the weakness of the state and the cohesion of the fledgling capitalist classes that is prolonging the crisis of the transition to capitalism. Rejecting the external explanations proposed by dependency theory, Bates's (1981) pathbreaking work argues that state intervention and economic policies such as overvalued foreign exchange ratios subsidize the inefficient who are linked to the bureaucrats and their rural allies. Bates further argues that the crisis arises from the powerlessness of the rural producers to influence government pricing and input decisions. Assessing the African socialist experiment in Tanzania, Hyden (1980) argues in line with the institutionalists that the resistance of the "uncaptured peasantry" to state policy is much deeper than neoliberal rational-choice theorists presume, for the peasantry operates in a precapitalist "economy of affection" governed by the norms of redistribution and reciprocity. Thus Hyden doubts whether Bates' price reforms will alter peasant behavior unless peasant solidarity is first dissolved.

Mindful of the statistical uncertainty, the literature nonetheless exhibits several contradictory arguments about the role of the peasantry in the agrarian crisis. The first interpretation, described by Watts (1983) as a moral economy of the Hausa peasantry, by Hyden as the economy of affection, and by Berry as a proliferation of identities and claims over resources, stresses the conservative and rather involuted tendency of the African peasantry to retain their household organization, their situational ethnic and communal identities, and their autonomy from subordination to state, capital, or foreign domination. Hill (1972) first argued the case for the Chayanovian model of cyclical growth of income and labor as a household passed through a life cycle (Chayanov 1966). Inequalities and adaptation to changing access to resources encourage the formation of new communal and ethnic identities (Vail 1989); new religions bring discipline to new commercial and cultural networks; and shifting fortunes create opportunities to gain from affective ties to the rentier state such as occurred during the petroleum boom in Nigeria (Berry 1985, Lubeck 1986).

By studying the relationship between state policies, local markets, and changing social identities, the institutionalist perspective argues that these essentially precapitalist groups which are organized into households continued to exert primary control over the means of production, labor services, and sexual reproduction as well as access to education, the link to the modern sector. Hence, change is expressed as modernized versions of reconstructed communal group identities and networks for rural Africans and many urban dwellers (Barnes 1986). Institutionalists and others argue that change occurs: commodity production for the market increases; rural wage labor and seasonal and longer term migration become institutionalized in male life cycles; competition for limited land and water resources appear as tensions in the countryside; and a kulak strata slowly emerges from the village. Because population growth is high and urban opportunity comparatively low, the agrarian sector is continually reproduced in myriads of transitional forms that combine custom and capitalism. Peasant communities, therefore, resist state attempts to rationalize them into ujamaa villages (Hyden 1980) or to subordinate them as tenant farmers on large-scale irrigation schemes (Beckman 1987, Jega 1985, Carney 1988), or to require them to sell crops to state marketing boards. Robertson's (1987) thorough study of sharecropping arrangements in four regions of Africa—Ghana, Lesotho, Sudan, and Senegambia—also supports this view.

Accordingly, neither state intervention nor market forces have transformed African agriculture into a Green Revolution miracle, nor have they forced proletarianization by blocking the reproduction of the African peasant household. No simple reproduction crisis of the peasant household has appeared as a generalized phenomena despite the depth and scale of the contemporary crisis, although Bernstein (1979) developed an excellent theory to the contrary. To be sure, withdrawal, social tension, malnutrition, famine, landlessness, and migration in all probability have significantly differentiated the peasantry into distinct strata; but no widespread structural transformation has changed Africa's rural producers into landlords and peasants, that is, into agrarian capitialism, comparable to other world regions. Hence, the institutionalist argument is generally true and cannot be refuted by existing studies, even though the direction of the unevenly distributed trend is toward commercialization of agriculture and rural capital accumulation.

At the same time, a second theme in the literature focusing on peasant differentiation in highly commercialized and demographically dense regions supports the neoliberal and classical marxist argument that productivity gains are possible through commercialization of agriculture. For, state infrastructural investments, access to markets or the Africanization of formerly white settler agriculture has generated genuine African capitalist enterprises, large-scale peasant-merchant households, as well as myriads of hybrid intermediate forms. Thus Cowen (1981), Njonjo (1977), Leys (1978), and Swainson (1987) describe how peasant differentiation, combined with access to state power and redistribution resulted in an agrarian capitalist class in Kenya, one that Bates approves because they "create a framework of public policies that provides an economic environment highly favorable to all farmers, whether small or large" (1981:94). Njonjo's (1977) research on Kenyan peasant holdings demonstrates increased land concentration and differentiation: the top 2% held 69% of the land, in his survey. By comparison, blessed by surplus land and cheap migrant labor from the impoverished Sahelian states, agriculture in the Ivory Coast has been highly commercialized and subsidized by the state since independence. An agrarian capitalist class of landowners, investors, and plantation producers intimately linked to political power exists side by side with a differentiated peasantry who produce food and export crops (Bassett 1988).

In Zimbabwe, the situation is similar to Kenya's in that dualism exists between mostly white settler commercial farms and peasant small holders living in the "reserves." The significance of the 4,700 commercial farms is enormous: they produce Z$664 million of Z$738 million (90%) of gross agricultural production in 1981, employing 273,000 workers and representing about 47% of exports (Gaidzanwa 1986:250). Since independence, African commercial farmers have emerged in Zimbabwe and, as in Kenya, access to government settlement schemes and distribution of inputs has hastened peasant differentiation while increasing the peasant sector's share of overall agricultural production (Cliffe 1988). Clearly, the crisis accelerates the transition to commercialized agriculture, even outside of white settler states.

Nowhere is the change greater than in Nigeria. Between a quarter and a fifth of Africa's population lives in Nigeria; about 35% are urban (40 million); and the agrarian relations of the major groups have been commercialized for centuries. The neoliberal solution confronts the institutionalist perspective. For, a World Bank–designed, managed, and administered structural adjustment plan has transformed Nigeria's agrarian sector: the currency (Naira) has been devalued to $.08 from a height of $1.80 so as to create incentives for agrarian capital investment; the monthly minimum wage has declined from $201 (1981) to $16 (1990); marketing boards have been dismantled and state investment has shifted from urban-biased manufacturing to agriculture. The alliance between the Bank and reform-minded politicians is building rural roads, rationalizing river basin authorities, distributing subsidized inputs and HYV seeds, organizing tractor services, building fertilizer plants from Nigeria's abundant natural gas supplies, and, in general, fostering modernized linkages between industry and Nigerian agriculture. To be sure, transformation is neither fair nor pretty; rather it is fraught with corruption, mismanagement, waste, unrealistic crops (wheat), environmental degradation, and social tension, but it is resolving the problem of weak linkages between industry and agriculture.

In ADPs managed by the World Bank, a distinct class of kulak farmers is differentiating itself unambiguously from the peasantry, especially in the middle and northern states. Beckman (1988b) summarizes these changes; he argues convincingly that the peasantry is neither "marginalized" as underdevelopment theorists argue, nor "uncaptured" by the the state and market as Hyden (1980) argues for Tanzania. Instead, differentiation means that the poorer and the unlucky will be expelled or become rural wage and service workers as land prices rise; a wealthy commercial farming strata with credit and political and commercial links to urban centers will become more powerful and prevalent; and the middle peasantry will continue clientage, customary practices, and household activities so as to reproduce the peasantry as a social category. Indeed, with 40 million urban consumers, an industrial sector starved for inputs, and many rural producers who purchase food prior to harvest, the Nigerian market achieves the dimensions of scale missing in most African economies, yet necessary for profitable linkages with agro-industrial inputs from the engineering, petrochemical, and energy sectors. This is not to suggest that the transition to capitalist agriculture via the many routes mentioned will be smooth. Land seizures, conflict over water and other resources, and the struggle over the price of labor (a critical resource often in short supply for kulaks and capitalists alike), promise to disrupt the agrarian sector and channel dispossessed recruits toward social movements inspired by both religious and secular discourses (Lubeck 1985, Jega 1985).

To conclude, Hyden's uncaptured peasantry notion is too static, perhaps because Tanzania lacked differentiation during the precolonial and colonial era and because the Tanzanian state regime is split between anticapitalist populists and capitalist roaders. The literature shows that peasant differentiation and agrarian capitalism are far more prominent because of the crisis and because of the solutions posed by the alliance of donors and state officials.

Bernstein (1990) interprets the debate over evidence between the ECA and the World Bank as part of a wider strategy by the Bank and their allies to transform a stagnant region in a general context of global restructuring along neoliberal lines. Hence, the West Africa food shortage data in the *Berg Report* are seen as fortuitiously exaggerated by Bernstein and others in order to reform agriculture and deepen dependence on imported inputs and capitalist rationality in general. In many ways, the crisis is a rupture in the relationship between Africa's political elites and their transnational capitalist mentors. Increased concessionary lending, therefore, is the carrot to smooth the transition to capitalist agriculture and to force Africa to march to the same step as other regions in the global economy.

The Urban-Industrial Sector: Restructuring and Linkages

By the onset of the crisis of the 1980s, industry and manufacturing in particular accounted for a small share of Africa's GDP, and it has not grown appreciably since the mid-1960s. Bearing in mind the weaknesses of national accounting which do not take account of small-scale industrial output (Kennedy 1988), Africa's industrial performance remains an "unfulfilled promise" (Mytelka 1989). Between 1965 and 1986 industry's share of GDP grew from 19% to 25%, mostly from petroleum expansion, while the more significant manufacturing sector grew only from 9% to 10% of GDP (Riddell 1990:4–5). If industrialization stagnated before the era of neoliberal restructuring due to foreign exchange constraints, low productivity, and ceilings on internal demand, structural adjustment plans crushed even these weak initiatives. True enough, nationalists charge that structural adjustment plans "deindustrialized" Africa further by deflating urban incomes, closing parastatal industries, and thus lowering per capita rates of industrialization, for currency devaluation made imported raw materials and inputs too expensive, liberalization of tariffs increased competition when demand from urban income groups was falling, and privatization policies eliminated state industries or raised the cost of subsidized inputs like petroleum or electricity (Nixson 1986, Ekuerhare 1989).

Reviews of Africa's industrialization stress the interlocking character of inefficient state intervention and nonproductive parastatals, linkage effects of foreign control, poor design and technology transfers for African conditions, and excessive protection of inefficient industries within small markets (Meier & Steel 1989, Bienefeld 1985, Mytelka 1989). Riddell argues that import substitution was never fully attempted or completed, because the import share of consumer goods remained high, and further that while prospects for an industrial recovery after 1995 appear promising if structural reforms are implemented and foreign capital encouraged, such reforms will not be sufficient for Africa to become internationally competitive in manufactured exports "unless and until changes are made to address the problems of comparative inefficiency at the enterprise level" (Riddell 1990:38). An organizational revolution, however, is unlikely. Industry is concentrated in a few countries. Seven countries—Nigeria, Ghana, Ivory Coast, Kenya, Cameroon, Zambia, and Zimbabwe—represent approximately two thirds of the industrial value added and 75% of the population in Africa (Riddell 1990:16). Lacking international competitiveness for export growth as well as internal income growth, Africa's only source of growth depends upon population growth and interregional trade.

Nigeria possesses the greatest potential for industrialization. Blessed with petroleum, natural gas, tropical and savanna agriculture, and a large internal market of 120 million, Nigeria is a regional power whose import substituting industries expanded rapidly during the 1970s, only to wither from lack of foreign exchange under structural adjustment in the 1980s. Gorged by oil revenues that peaked at $25.3 billion in 1980, only to fall to $6.3 billion in 1986, an economic interventionist state became central to industrial investment (Forrest 1982, 1987). Driven by the anarchic strain of economic nationalism and rentier distributive politics, the Nigerian state overextended its weak managerial capacities by intervening into irrigated agriculture, motor vehicle assembly, intermediate industries (steel, paper, and machine tools) and a bevy (circa 850) of irrationally chosen public enterprises, too numerous to enumerate (Wilson & Lewis 1990). Indigenization of industry decrees constrained foreign capital's freedom and encouraged local investors to purchase shares in multinationals but failed to create a dynamic, innovative, and productive indigenous industrial bourgeoisie. Indigenous capital did expand in finance, construction, commerce, and to some degree, into manufacturing protected by the decrees (Biersteker 1987). Unable to supply reliably even the most minimal inputs such as water and electricity to industry, state intervention became an obstacle to industrialization, precisely because it served as the instrument of private accumulation by rentier elites and state contractors who, having accumulated wealth, were reluctant to invest in an uncertain environment.

Nationalists complained when the World Bank refused to grant loans for the completion of the Ajaokuta iron and steel complex, a neo-Stalinist, Soviet-designed blast furnace that had a final cost of $7 billion and a foreign exchange expenditure of $200,000/year just to import coal. Yet, neoliberal analysis justly attacks this classic error of nationalist planning, in which steel will be produced at six times the world market price (EIU 3:1989). By the time of the collapse of the civilian government (1983) and the petroleum boom (1982), Nigerian industries were heavily concentrated in consumer and agro-processing, dependent on imported inputs and raw materials (60%–70%) and highly protected by tariffs and an overvalued Naira. Considering these foreign exchange guzzlers, it is difficult to avoid the conclusion that restructuring is positive for the structural articulation of linkages within Nigeria's industries.

After resisting the IMF, Nigeria accepted a World Bank–administered structural adjustment plan, one that devalued the Naira, banned many food imports (wheat and rice), forced industries to develop local suppliers, ended import licensing, and in general attempted to force backward linkages between agriculture and industry (Stevens 1990). Guided by neoliberal and structuralist policy, the alliance of the World Bank and the Babangida military government has initiated a profound restructuring of agro-industrial linkages by forcing manufacturers to use local cotton, maize, vegetable oils, rubber, beer ingredients, paper, and construction materials (Synge 1989). Forward linkages from the state hydrocarbon sector—petroleum products, natural gas, petrochemicals—have also accelerated so that natural gas is now collected for electricity generation and fertilizer; refinery capacity of 435,000 barrels per day enables Nigeria to export products to West African states; petrochemical plants are producing for domestic industry; and more advanced petrochemical and a LNG plant (1995) have been authorized (Synge 1989). The combination of local sourcing and World Bank "advisors" has curtailed state sector expansion and forced the hydrocarbon industry to work more closely with private capital, probably to the benefit of Nigeria's industrialization.

Moseley's (1992) assessment of industrial restructuring dismisses the charge of "deindustrialization" put forward by nationalists like Olukoshi (1989). Instead, outcomes vary by sector, with those linked to agriculture and petroleum/gas adjusting reasonably well, while import dependent industries like electronics and motor vehicle assembly are flagging due to foreign exchange constraints. Forrest (1990) provides fascinating evidence for the rise of an indigenous spare motor part industry, illustrating his view that necessity creates opportunity for innovation outside the confines of the rentier state. Overall, despite the hardships endured, restructuring of the petroleum-led industrial sector was inevitable; linkages are key to industrial deepening; and the rise of legal and illegal exports to the West African region promises to fulfill Nigerian ambitions to be a regional power, although hardly an Asian NIC (Robson 1983). Instead, Nigeria appears to lumber awkwardly toward a chaotic form of industrialization, one searching for a balance between appropriate state intervention and rationalization of potentially strong entrepreneurial energies. The nationalist school has their most promising candidate in Nigeria, but a rise in petroleum prices is needed to fund the foreign exchange cost of industrialization oriented toward the domestic and regional markets.

State, Society, and Democracy

Though differentially defining it as cause or effect, all schools concur that the organizational incapacity of the African state, combined with weak authority relations to civil society, is a major obstacle to resolution of the development crisis. Though authority has never been strong, the nationalist argument that structural adjustment plans have weakened the legitimate relationship between African states and the coalition of groups that they dominate is essentially correct. A number of studies (Sandbrook 1986, Joseph 1987, Jackson & Rosberg 1982a) view African states as clientelistic, patronage-distributing agencies that tend to perpetuate personal rule; Houphouet-Boigny of the Ivory Coast ranks as the most accomplished. From the neoliberal perspective, Lele (1988) argues that opposition to relinquishing state control over the economy is not necessarily antimarket; rather opposition arises because SAPs destabilize the existing ethnic balance within the state, as in the case of northern Nigeria's conservative elite, who relied on the distribution of import licenses to maintain cohesion. Jackson & Rosberg (1982b) point out that if it were not for the international system, internal conflicts within African states would have already generated an internal collapse as the Somali case illustrates. Lonsdale's (1981) excellent review of the state in Africa deftly analyzes the sources of state weakness: a state without a nation; an illegitimate colonial genealogy; a managerial bourgeoisie without a productive basis of accumulation; and a peasant citizenry which favors populist autonomy. Informed by an institutionalist perspective, Ekeh (1986) contrasts the dichotomy between the typical African's loyalty and discipline toward family and communal group and the distrust and abuse of state institutions; Ekeh concludes that a cultural basis of legitimate rule must be constructed as a prerequisite to resolution of the crisis. Contributors to Chazan & Rothchild's (1988) volume offer a summary of the positions taken on the decline of the African state, yet conclude that it will prevail, though incoherently and perhaps with redefined boundaries (Ravenhill 1988).

More positively, Beckman (1982) views Nigeria as a fragmented bourgeois state, where the bourgeoisie-in-formation uses the state to further its class interest. In contrast, Hyden (1983) pessimistically concludes that the state has failed to capture its peasantry, that it lacks structural roots in society, and that, because it lacks a bourgeoisie with a culture and a will to rationally accumulate, no significant change is possible for the African state. While generalizing across states as diverse as Nigeria and Tanzania is impossible, it is becoming obvious that the economic crisis and adjustment policies are undermining the political structures that maintained personal, authoritarian and/or one-party rule since independence. The economic crisis is becoming a political crisis. Is change possible?

Faced with ever-declining standards of living and without resources that formerly coopted oppositions and nurtured clients, African states increasingly have had to rely on coercion to implement structural adjustment plans (Herbst 1990). Doornbos (1990) views the crisis as constituting a benchmark in the history of the African state. Because structural adjustment plans are externally planned, organized, and monitored, they bypass, marginalize, and privatize the former powers of the state. Donors now seek decentralized units with some claim to represent a civil society at the grass roots. Writing on the Ivory Coast, Crook (1990) boldly states that the Bank wanted the president of the Ivory Coast to resign to pave the way for their candidate.

The crisis of the postcolonial state, therefore, is profound and threatens to redraw the existing system of states. SAPs have undermined what little legitimacy states possessed and have reduced patronage distribution to a trickle. These developments have brought an unexpected rise in demands for popular democratic rule, not only from liberals like Diamond et al (1988) but from virtually all points on the theoretical spectrum (Nyong'o 1987, 1988, Mamdani 1987, Joseph 1990, Oyugi et al 1988, Ake 1990, Bates 1990, Mazrui 1990, Mkandawire 1988). Finally, from the nationalist left, Zack-Williams breaks with national-populist thought by bluntly damning the "kleptocracy" which destroyed the "nucleus of democratic participation inherited from the departing colonialists" (1990:32).

Conclusion

Colin Legum, veteran observer of African development, recently termed the revival of popular democratic participation expressed in food riots, strikes by workers, and demands by professional and middle class for elections as "Africa's second independence," whereby "Africa stands poised for its second period of liberation" (Legum 1990). Indeed, an astonishing number of popular movements have arisen to demand political change in one-party states ranging from Madagascar, Ivory Coast, Togo, Benin, Zaire, Cameroon, Mali, Kenya, Zambia, and Zaire. While they are too recent to generate a literature for analysis in this essay, they unquestionably represent the emergence of a new generational force demanding democracy, human rights, and the resolution of the economic and social crisis. What structural factors can articulate positively with these movements so as to contribute to the resolution of the crisis?

Given the declining trend of economic indicators and the rise in population, per capita income levels cannot rise significantly without an unforeseen shift in Africa's terms of trade. Infrastructural development, however, is possible. Neoliberalism has won the debate regarding the primacy of agriculture and limited state intervention into marketing of commodities. Accelerated debt relief is imperative. Politically, the end of the cold war has already reduced external support for tyrants and dictators, thus increasing the potential for accountability and a more legitimate state administration of economy and society. Here the resolution of the crisis in South Africa in favor of the democratic forces promises to provide southern, eastern, and central Africa with an industrialized growth pole upon which economic recovery of the region can be constructed. With all its resources, and despite its undisciplined organizational structures, Nigeria offers some hope as a growth pole for the West African region. As always, much depends on demand for African exports in the world economy.

Neither neoliberal nor structural-nationalist solutions alone are sufficient. Rather, attention should center on the proper mix of market forces and political intervention; the latter must reflect the capacity of the state to construct rational economic institutions and not to reproduce rentier fiefs. To ascertain the proper mix, institutionalist-derived knowledge is an invaluable component in constructing a form of authentic authority relations which can, in turn, create legitimate and disciplined economic organizations. Unlike world commodity prices, the social basis of legitimacy underlying the African state is one of the few structural factors of which Africans are in control. Discovering a new, more democratic social basis for accumulation can only enhance the prospects for African recovery.

ACKNOWLEDGMENTS

I would like to thank Peter Evans, Brian Folk, Stephen Bunker, and Michael Watts for their helpful comments. This research was supported by the Social Sciences Division and the Academic Senate Committee on Research of the University of California, Santa Cruz.

Literature Cited

Ake, C. 1990. The case for democracy. See Carter Center 1990, pp. 2–6

Barnes, S. 1986. *Patrons and Power.* Bloomington, Ind: Ind. Univ. Press

Bassett, T. 1988. The World Bank in Ivory Coast. Review. *African Polit. Econ.* 41:45–60

Bates, R. 1981. *Markets and States in Tropical Africa.* Berkeley: Univ. Calif. Press

Bates, R. 1989. *Beyond the Miracle of the Market: The Political Economy of Agrarian Development in Kenya.* Cambridge: Cambridge Univ. Press

Bates, R. 1990. Socio-economic bases of democratization in Africa: some reflections. See Carter Center 1990, pp. 29–34

Becker, C. 1990. The demo-economic impact of the AIDS pandemic in SSA. *World Dev.* 18:1599–1619

Beckman, B. 1982. Whose state: state and capitalist development in Nigeria. *Rev. African Polit. Econ.* 23:37–51

Beckman, B. 1987. Public investment and agrarian transformation in northern Nigeria. See Watts 1987, pp. 110–37

Beckman, B. 1988a. The post-colonial state: crisis and reconstruction. *Inst. Dev. Stud. Bull.* 19:26–34

Beckman, B. 1988b. Peasants and democratic struggles in Nigeria. *Rev. African Polit. Econ.* 41:30–45

Bernstein, H. 1979. African peasantries: a theoretical framework. *J. Peasant Stud.* 6:420–43

Bernstein, H. 1990. Agricultural 'modernization' and the era of structural adjustment: observations on sub-Saharan Africa. *J. Peasant Stud.* 18:3–35

Berry, S. 1984. The food crisis and agrarian change in Africa. *African Stud. Rev.* 27:59–112

Berry, S. 1985. *Fathers Work for Their Sons.* Berkeley: Univ. Calif Press

Berry, S. 1989. Social institutions and access to resources. *Africa* 59:41–55

Berry, S. 1991. *Coping with confusion: African farmers' responses to economic instability in the 1970's and 1980's.* Unpubl. ms. Johns Hopkins Univ., Baltimore

Bienefeld, M. 1985. The lessons of Africa's industrial failure. *Inst. Dev. Stud. Bull.* 16:145–64

Biersteker, T. 1987. *Multinationals, The State and Control of the Nigerian Economy.* Princeton: Princeton Univ. Press

Bunker, S. 1987. *Peasants Against the State: The Politics of Market Control in Bugisu, Uganda, 1900–1983.* Urbana: Univ. Ill. Press

Carney, J. 1988. Struggles over crop rights and labor within contract farming households in a Gambian irrigated rice project. *J. Peasant Stud.* 15:334–49

Carter Center. 1990. *African governance in the 1990s: Work. Pap. Second Annu. Sem. African Governance Program. Atlanta: Carter Center, Emory Univ.*

Chayanov, A. 1966. *Theory of Peasant Economy.* Homewood, Ill: Irwin

Chazan, N., Rothchild, D., eds. 1988. *The Precarious Balance: State and Society in Africa.* Boulder: Westview

Cliffe, L. 1988. Zimbabwe's Agricultural Success and Food Security. *Rev. African Polit. Econ.* 43:4–26

Clough, P. 1981. Farmers and traders in Hausaland. *Dev. Change* 12:273–92

Clough, P. 1985. The social relations of grain marketing in Northern Nigeria. *Rev. African Polit. Econ.* 34:16–34

Colclough, C., Green, R., eds. 1988. Stabilization for growth or decay. *Inst. Dev. Stud. Bull.* 19:1–80

Cooper, F. 1981a. Peasants, capitalists and historians: a review article. *J. Southern African Stud.* 9:127–54

Cooper, F. 1981b. Africa and the world economy. *African Stud. Rev.* 24:1–86
Cowen, M. 1976. *Capital and peasant households*. Unpubl. ms. Dep. Econ. Univ. Nairobi
Cowen, M. 1981. *The British state, state enterprise and an indigenous bourgeoisie in Kenya after 1945*. Unpubl. ms. London Polytechnic
Crook, R. 1990. Politics, the cocoa crisis, and administration in the Ivory Coast. *J. Mod. African Stud.* 28:649–69
Diamond, L., Linz, J., Lipset, S.M., eds. 1988. *Democracy in Developing Countries: Africa*. Vol. 2. Boulder: Lynne Rienner
Doornbos, M. 1990. The African state in academic debate: retrospect and prospect. The *J. Modern African Stud.* 28:179–98
Economic Commission for Africa. 1989. *African Alternative Framework to Structural Adjustment Programmes for Socio-Economic (Recovery and Transformation.* (E/ECA/CM.15/6/Rev.3). Addis Ababa: UN Econ. Commission for Africa
Economist Intelligence Unit: Nigeria. No. 3. 1989. London: Business Int.
Ekeh, P. 1986. Development theory and the African predicament. *African Dev.* XI:1–39
Ekuerhare, B. 1989. Second tier foreign exchange market and structure of industrial growth in Nigeria. In *Structural Adjustment in Nigeria,* ed. R. Olaniyan, C. Nwoke, pp. 48–62. Lagos: Nigerian Inst. Int. Affairs
Forrest, T. 1982. Recent developments in Nigerian industrialization. See Fransman 1982, pp. 324–44
Forrest, T. 1987. State capital, capitalist development and class formation in Nigeria. See Lubeck 1987, pp. 307–42
Forrest, T. 1990. *The advance of African capital: the growth of Nigerian private enterprise. Queen Elizabeth House Work. Pap., No. 24*. Oxford Univ.
Fransman, M., ed. 1982. *Industry and Accumulation in Africa*. London: Heinemann
Gaidzanwa, R. 1986. Drought and the food crisis in Zimbabwe. See Lawrence 1986, pp. 249–58
Gerry, C. 1978. Petty production and capitalist production in Dakar. *World Dev.* 6:1147–60
Green, R. 1985a. Sub-Saharan Africa: towards oblivion or reconstruction. *J. Dev. Planning* 15:9–41
Green, R., Mureithi, L., Ndegwa, P. eds. 1985b. *Development Options for Africa in the 1980s and Beyond*. Nairobi: East Africa Publ. House
Green, R., Allison, C. 1986. The World Bank's agenda for accelerated development. See Ravenhill 1986, pp. 60–84
Hart, K. 1973. Informal income opportunities and urban employment in Ghana. *J. Modern African Stud.* 11:61–89
Herbst, J. 1990. The structural adjustment of politics in Africa. *World Dev.* 18:949–58
Heyer, J., Roberts, P., Williams, G. 1981. *Rural Development in Tropical Africa*. New York: St. Martins
Hill, P. 1972. *Rural Hausa*. Cambridge: Cambridge Univ. Press
Hyden, G. 1980. *Beyond Ujamaa in Tanzania: Underdevelopment and an Uncaptured Peasantry*. Berkeley: Univ. Calif. Press
Hyden, G. 1983. *No Shortcuts to Progress*. Berkeley: Univ. Calif. Press
Isaacman, A. 1990. Peasants and rural social protest in Africa. *African Stud. Rev.* 33:1–121
Jackson, R., Rosberg, C. 1982a. *Personal Rule in Black Africa*. Berkeley: Univ. Calif. Press
Jackson, R., Rosberg, C. 1982b. Why Africa's weak states persist. *World Polit.* 37:1–19
Jega, A. 1985. *The state, peasants and rural transformation in Nigeria*. PhD thesis. Northwestern Univ., Evanston, Ill.
Joseph, R. 1987. *Democracy and Prebendal Politics in Nigeria*. Cambridge: Cambridge Univ. Press
Joseph, R. 1990. The challenge of democratization in Africa: some reflections. See Carter Center 1990, pp. 17–21
Kennedy, P. 1988. *African Capitalism: The Struggle for Ascendancy*. Cambridge: Cambridge Univ. Press
Killick, T. 1989. *A Reaction Too Far*. London: Overseas Dev. Inst.
Kitching, G. 1980. *Class and Economic Change in Kenya*. New Haven: Yale Univ. Press
Kitching, G. 1982. *Development and Underdevelopment in Historical Perspective*. London: Methuen
Kitching, G. 1987. The role of a national bourgeoisie in the current phase of capitalist development. See Lubeck 1987, pp. 27–55
Lancaster, C. 1990. Economic reform in Africa: is it working? *Washington Q.* 13:115–28
Laitin, D. 1986. *Hegemony and Culture*. Chicago: Univ. Chicago Press
Larson, A. 1990. The social epidemiology of Africa's AIDS epidemic. *African Affairs* 89:5–25
Lawrence, P., ed. 1986. *World Recession and the Food Crisis in Africa*. London: Currey
Legum, C. 1990. The coming of Africa's second independence. *Washington Q.* 13:129–40
Lele, U. 1988. Comparative advantage and structural transformation. In *The State of Development Economics,* ed. G. Ranis, T. Schultz, pp. 156–72. Oxford: Blackwell

Leys, C. 1975. *Underdevelopment in Kenya*. Berkeley: Univ. Calif. Press

Leys, C. 1978. Capital accumulation, class formation and dependency: the significance of the Kenyan case. *Socialist Register*. London: Merlin

Lloyd, P. 1974. *Power and Independence: Urban Africans' Perception of Inequality*. London: Routledge & Kegan Paul

Lofchie, M. 1975. Political and economic origins of African hunger. *J. Mod. African Stud.* 13:451–75

Lonsdale, J. 1981. State and social processes in Africa. *African Stud. Rev.* 24:139–227

Lubeck, P. 1985. Islamic protest under semi-industrial capitalism. *Africa* 55:369–90

Lubeck, P. 1986. *Islam and Urban Labor in Northern Nigeria: The Making of a Muslim Working Class*. Cambridge: Cambridge Univ. Press

MacGaffey, J. 1987. *Entrepreneurs and Parasites*. Cambridge: Cambridge Univ. Press

Mamdani, M. 1987. Contradictory class perspectives on the question of democracy: the case of Uganda. See Nyong'o 1987, pp. 78–95

Martin, D., Johnson, P., eds. 1986. *Destructive Engagement: Southern Africa at War*. Harare: Zimbabwe Publ.

Mazrui, A. 1990. Planned governance: economic liberalization and political engineering in Africa. See Carter Center 1990, pp. 23–28

Meier, G., Steel, W., eds. 1989. *Industrial Adjustment in Africa*. New York: Oxford Univ./World Bank

Mkandawire, T. 1988. Comments on Democracy and Political Instability. *Africa Dev.* 13:77–82

Moseley, K. 1992. Seizing the chance: economic crisis and industrial restructuring in Nigeria. In *Africa in the Nineties*, ed. T. Shaw, J. Nyang'oro. Boulder: Westview

Mytelka, L. 1989. The unfulfilled promise of African industrialization. *African Stud. Rev.* 32:77–137

Nixson, F. 1986. The crisis of industrial accumulation in Africa. See Lawrence 1986, pp. 29–40

Njonjo, A. 1977. *The Africanization of the white highlands*. PhD thesis, Princeton Univ.

Nyong'o, P., ed. 1987. *Popular Struggles for Democracy in Africa*. London: Zed

Nyong'o, P. 1988. The possibilities and historical limitations of import substitution industrialization in Kenya. In *Industrialization in Kenya*, ed. P. Coughlin, G. Ikiara, pp. 39–57. London: Currey

Olukoshi, A. 1989. Impact of IMF-World Bank programmes on Nigeria. See Onimode 1989, pp. 219–34

Onimode, B. ed. 1989. *The IMF, the World Bank and the African Debt*. Vols. I, II. London: Zed

Oyugi, W., Odhiambo, E.S.A., Chege, M., Gitonga, A.K., eds. 1988. *Democratic Theory and Practice in Africa*. Portsmouth, NH: Heinemann / London: James Currey

Parfitt, T., Riley, S. 1989. *The African Debt Crisis*. London: Routledge

Peace, A. 1979. *Choice, Class and Conflict*. New Jersey: Humanities

Post, K. 1972. Peasantization and rural political movements in West Africa. *Archives Europeennes de Sociologie* 13:223–54

Ravenhill, J., ed. 1986. *Africa in Economic Crisis*. London: MacMillan

Ravenhill, J. 1988. Redrawing the map of Africa. See Chazan & Rothchild 1988, pp. 282–307

Richards, P. 1983. Ecological change and the politics of African land use. *African Stud. Rev.* 26:1–72

Richards, P. 1986. *Coping With Hunger*. London: Allen and Unwin

Riddell, R. 1990. *Manufacturing Africa*. Portsmouth, NH: Heinemann

Robertson, A. 1987. *The Dynamics of Productive Relationships: African Share Contracts in Comparative Perspective*. Cambridge: Cambridge Univ. Press

Robson, P. 1983. *Integration, Development and Equity*. London: Allen & Unwin

Sandbrook, R. 1986. The state and economic stagnation in tropical Africa. *World Dev.* 14(3):319–32

Sender, J., Smith, S. 1986. *The Development of Capitalism in Africa*. London: Methuen

Stevens, C. 1990. Nigeria. See Riddell 1990, pp. 256–96

Swainson, N. 1980. *The Development of Corporate Capitalism in Kenya*. London: Heinemann

Swainson, N. 1987. Indigenous capitalism in post-colonial Kenya. See Lubeck 1987, pp. 137–63

Synge, R. 1989. *Nigeria to 1993: Will Liberalization Work? Report No. 1134*. London: Economist Intelligence Unit

United Nations. 1991. *Economic Crisis in Africa, Report of the Secretary General, UN General Assembly*. New York:UN

Vail, L., ed. 1989. *The Creation of Tribalism in Southern Africa*. London: Currey / Berkeley: Univ. Calif. Press

Warren, B. 1980. *Imperialism: Pioneer of Capitalism*. London: New Left Books

Watts, M. 1983. Good try Mr. Paul: populism and the politics of African land-use. *African Stud. Rev.* 26:73–83

Watts, M., ed. 1987. *State, Oil and Agriculture in Nigeria*. Berkeley: Univ. Calif/Inst. Int. Stud.

Watts, M. 1991. Visions of excess: African

development in an age of market idolatry. *Transition* 51:124–41

Williams, G. 1985. Marketing boards in Nigeria. *Rev. African Polit. Econ.* 34:4–16

Wilson, E., Lewis, P. 1990. *Public-private sector relations under the transition*. Pres. Stanford Conf. Democratic Transition and Structural Adjustment in Nigeria, Stanford Univ., August

World Bank. 1981. *Accelerated Development in Sub-Saharan Africa*. Washington: World Bank

World Bank. 1989a. *Sub-Saharan Africa: From Crisis to Sustainable Growth*. Washington: World Bank

World Bank. 1989b. *Africa's Economic Adjustment and Growth in the 1980s*. Washington: World Bank

World Bank. 1991. *World Development Report*. Washington: World Bank/Oxford Univ. Press

Zack-Williams, A. 1990. Sierra Leone: crisis and despair. *Rev. African Polit. Econ.* 49:22–34

SUBJECT INDEX

CUMULATIVE INDEXES

CONTRIBUTING AUTHORS, VOLUMES 1–18

CHAPTER TITLES, VOLUMES 1–18

INSTITUTIONS AND CULTURE

SOCIOLOGY OF WORLD REGIONS

ANNUAL REVIEWS SERIES

Volumes not listed are no longer in print

		Prices, postpaid, per volume: Until 12-31-91 USA & Canada / elsewhere	After 1-1-92 USA / other countries (incl. Canada)	Regular Order Please send Volume(s):	Standing Order Begin with Volume:
Annual Review of BIOPHYSICS AND BIOMOLECULAR STRUCTURE					
Vols. 1-11	(1972-1982)..........................	$33.00/$38.00	$55.00/$60.00		
Vols. 12-18	(1983-1989)..........................	$51.00/$56.00			
Vols. 19-20	(1990-1991)..........................	$55.00/$60.00			
Vol. 21	(avail. June 1992)................	$59.00/$64.00	$59.00/$64.00	Vol(s).______	Vol.___
Annual Review of CELL BIOLOGY					
Vols. 1-3	(1985-1987)..........................	$33.00/$38.00	$41.00/$46.00		
Vols. 4-5	(1988-1989)..........................	$37.00/$42.00			
Vols. 6-7	(1990-1991)	$41.00/$46.00			
Vol. 8	(avail. Nov. 1992)..............	$46.00/$51.00	$46.00/$51.00	Vol(s).______	Vol.___
Annual Review of COMPUTER SCIENCE					
Vols. 1-2	(1986-1987)..........................	$41.00/$46.00	$41.00/$46.00		
Vols. 3-4	(1988, 1989-1990)..............	$47.00/$52.00	$47.00/$52.00	Vol(s).______	Vol.___

Series suspended until further notice. Volumes 1-4 are still available at the special promotional price of $100.00 USA /$115.00 other countries, when all 4 volumes are purchased at one time. Orders at the specia price must be prepaid.

Annual Review of EARTH AND PLANETARY SCIENCES					
Vols. 1-10	(1973-1982)..........................	$33.00/$38.00	$55.00/$60.00		
Vols. 11-17	(1983-1989)..........................	$51.00/$56.00			
Vols. 18-19	(1990-1991)..........................	$55.00/$60.00			
Vol. 20	(avail. May 1992)................	$59.00/$64.00	$59.00/$64.00	Vol(s).______	Vol.___
Annual Review of ECOLOGY AND SYSTEMATICS					
Vols. 2-18	(1971-1987)..........................	$33.00/$38.00	$40.00/$45.00		
Vols. 19-20	(1988-1989)..........................	$36.00/$41.00			
Vols. 21-22	(1990-1991)..........................	$40.00/$45.00			
Vol. 23	(avail. Nov. 1992)...............	$44.00/$49.00	$44.00/$49.00	Vol(s).______	Vol.___
Annual Review of ENERGY AND THE ENVIRONMENT					
Vols. 1-7	(1976-1982)..........................	$33.00/$38.00	$64.00/$69.00		
Vols. 8-14	(1983-1989)..........................	$60.00/$65.00			
Vols. 15-16	(1990-1991)..........................	$64.00/$69.00			
Vol. 17	(avail. Oct. 1992)................	$68.00/$73.00	$68.00/$73.00	Vol(s).______	Vol.___
Annual Review of ENTOMOLOGY					
Vols. 10-16, 18	(1965-1971, 1973)				
20-32	(1975-1987)..........................	$33.00/$38.00	$40.00/$45.00		
Vols. 33-34	(1988-1989)..........................	$36.00/$41.00			
Vols. 35-36	(1990-1991)..........................	$40.00/$45.00			
Vol. 37	(avail. Jan. 1992)	$44.00/$49.00	$44.00/$49.00	Vol(s).______	Vol.___
Annual Review of FLUID MECHANICS					
Vols. 2-4, 7	(1970-1972, 1975)				
9-19	(1977-1987)	$34.00/$39.00	$40.00/$45.00		
Vols. 20-21	(1988-1989)	$36.00/$41.00			
Vols. 22-23	(1990-1991)	$40.00/$45.00			
Vol. 24	(avail. Jan. 1992)	$44.00/$49.00	$44.00/$49.00	Vol(s).______	Vol.___
Annual Review of GENETICS					
Vols. 1-12, 14-21	(1967-1978, 1980-1987) ...	$33.00/$38.00	$40.00/$45.00		
Vols. 22-23	(1988-1989)	$36.00/$41.00			
Vols. 24-25	(1990-1991)	$40.00/$45.00			
Vol. 26	(avail. Dec. 1992)................	$44.00/$49.00	$44.00/$49.00	Vol(s).______	Vol.___
Annual Review of IMMUNOLOGY					
Vols. 1-5	(1983-1987)	$33.00/$38.00	$41.00/$46.00		
Vols. 6-7	(1988-1989)	$36.00/$41.00			
Vol. 8	(1990)	$40.00/$45.00			
Vol. 9	(1991)	$41.00/$46.00	$41.00/$46.00		
Vol. 10	(avail. April 1992)	$45.00/$50.00	$45.00/$50.00	Vol(s).______	Vol.___